Oscar Niemeyer

Styliane Philippou

Oscar Niemeyer

Curves of Irreverence

Yale University Press New Haven and London

Designed by Penny Soultani

Printed in Singapore

Library of Congress Cataloging-in-Publication Data

Philippou, Styliane, 1965–
  Oscar Niemeyer : curves of irreverence / Styliane Philippou.
      p. cm.
  Includes bibliographical references.
  ISBN 978-0-300-12038-7 (cl : alk. paper)
  1. Niemeyer, Oscar, 1907—-Criticism and interpretation.
  2. International style (Architecture)—Brazil. I. Title.
  NA859.N5P52 2008
  720.92—dc22
                                            2008019024

A catalogue record for this book is available from The British Library

Frontispiece: Mondadori Headquarters, Segrate, Italy,
1968–75: first scheme, 1968

Image Credits

Unless otherwise specified, all drawings and sketches
are by Oscar Niemeyer. Drawings, sketches, photographs of models, historical black-and-white photographs of Oscar Niemeyer's buildings and the colour
photographs on pages 327 and 369 are courtesy of
Oscar Niemeyer and the Fundação Oscar Niemeyer.

Unless otherwise specified, all contemporary colour
photographs are by the author. Old postcards and
prints are from the author's collection. The black-and-
white photographs on pages 172 and 215 are by the
author.

Other image credits:

The positions of images are abbreviated as follows:
l=left, r=right, c=centre, t=top, b=bottom.

© FLC/ADAGP, Paris and DACS, London 2007: pp. 18
and 45; Acervo Casa de Lúcio Costa: pp. 19, 29, 56, 57,
58rb, 74, 83, 85 and 179; Acervo COPAN: pp. 144, 148l
and 150r; Arquivo Público do Distrito Federal: pp. 221rt,
221lb, 223lt, 223b, 227, 229t, 237r, 240, 251, 254, 262t,
262b, 264rb, 273l, 282, 301, 304l, 308t and 313b;
Biblioteca da Faculdade de Arquitetura e Urbanismo,
Universidade de São Paulo: pp. 37, 38 and 39l;
Biblioteca do Instituto de Estudos Brasileiros, Univer-
sidade de São Paulo: p. 25; Biblioteca e Centro de
Documentação, Museu de Arte de São Paulo Assis
Chateaubriand: p. 24r; Brascan Cem Anos no Brasil,
Acervo Instituto Moreira Salles: p. 51b; Cinemateca
Brasileira, Ministerio da Cultura: p. 126; Collection
Arnoldo Mondadori Editore: pp. 345, 346, 348c and 352;
Collection Marcos Veremis, courtesy of Marianna and
Thanos Veremis: pp. 44 and 51t; courtesy of the Architectural Review: p. 61; drawing by Alberto José Gomes:
p. 219; Escritório Burle Marx: pp. 39rt, 40, 48t, 50lt, 64t
and 167rt; Fundação Getúlio Vargas, Centro de Pesquisa e Documentação da História Contemporânea do
Brasil: p. 53; Fundo Mário de Andrade, Arquivo do Instituto de Estudos Brasileiros, Universidade de São Paulo:
p. 24l; Instituto do Patrimônio Histórico e Artístico Nacional: pp. 58t and 68l; photograph by André, Secretaria
de Estado de Cultura do Distrito Federal: pp. 316rc and
316rb; Photograph by Carlos, Arquivo Público do Distrito Federal: p. 259; photographs by Franz Weis: pp. 41,
118b and 260l; photographs by Marcel Gautherot,
Acervo Instituto Moreira Salles: pp. 10, 49, 162b, 234,
241b, 244l and 306b; photographs by Mário Fontenelle,
Arquivo Público do Distrito Federal: pp. 223rt, 224, 237l
and 302; photographs by Nelson Kon: pp. 11, 52, 66lb,
67t, 70b, 73r, 174, 175, 176b, 177t, 178l, 207b, 236, 303,
360b, 361t, 365b, 382, 383b, 384l, 384rt and 385;
Secretaria de Estado de Cultura do Distrito Federal:
pp. 316lt, 316lb and 355t; Staden, 1928, p. 163: p. 23.

To Franz Weis

Contents

Acknowledgements

This book's bibliography and footnotes contain the names of a long list of people, to whose time and toil, intellectual insights and critical probing of the questions central to this book I am deeply indebted. They bear witness to my own conversion to the celebrated Brazilian practice of cultural cannibalism or 'Antropofagia'. This book is a record of an open dialogue with all the architects, artists, poets, critics, scholars and others whom I joined at the Antropofagist banquet. If I may be allowed to single out the fellow guests on whose imagination I fed most voraciously, I should like to mention Oswald de Andrade, Lúcio Costa, Roberto Burle Marx, Le Corbusier, Stamo Papadaki, Gilberto Freyre, Robert Stam, Norma Evenson, Laurent Vidal and Jorge Schwartz. Needless to say, I do not intend to leave this cornucopian dining table. With this book, I hope to amplify the open invitation to a never-ending feast of delights.

Good architecture, like a good musical score, offers endless possibilities for performance and unending pleasure. This book owes its existence to the genius of Oscar Niemeyer. Of course, for any failings of interpretation only I am to be held accountable. I am also grateful to Oscar Niemeyer for welcoming me warmly into his studio in Rio de Janeiro, and for offering me access to, and permission to publish, drawings, photographs and documents in the collection of the Oscar Niemeyer Foundation.

Franz Weis, who has visited, photographed and relished the beauty of more Niemeyer buildings than any architect I know, offered this project his complete support from beginning to end. It is no exaggeration to say that it would not have taken off without his commitment, and would not have been completed without his unfailing encouragement. I will never find words to thank him enough for his trust, the inspiring discussions, his genuine enthusiasm and forbearance and the piano accompaniment during the long evening hours of writing. I dedicate this book to him with everlasting gratitude.

I am grateful to Richard Weston for invaluable encouragement and sound advice during the early stages of this book, and for his example as an architectural historian committed to fresh and insightful readings of twentieth-century architecture. Over the years of research, I had the opportunity to test ideas and sharpen my arguments at conferences and lectures at the universities of Cardiff; Cambridge, UK; Oxford Brookes; Oporto; Richmond, Virginia; Duke, North Carolina; and at the BRASA VIII congress on Brazilian studies at Vanderbilt, Tennessee. I have benefited enormously from valuable and most enjoyable discussions with Brazilianist scholars Jan Hoffman French and John French. At Yale University Press I am indebted to my editor, Gillian Malpass.

During my field trips in Brazil, I profited from exchanges with many people. I should like to mention Ivete Farah, Hugo Segawa, Cláudio Queiroz, Ruth Verde Zein, Roberto Segre, Lauro Cavalcanti, Luiz Otávio Rodrigues, Paulo Henrique Paranhos, José Pessôa, Walter José Ferreira Galvão and Sue Chester. I have been warmly received in numerous buildings designed by Niemeyer. I am especially indebted to Brazil's first lady, Marisa Letícia Lula da Silva, for authorising my visit to the Palácio da Alvorada on a day when she and President Luíz Inácio Lula da Silva were in residence. Sincere thanks also to Cláudio Soares Rocha, Gilberto and Marta Strunck, Alberto Dalva Simão, Luciano Pereira Lopes, Antônio Padua, Rita Nascimento Fonseca Brant, Dulce Pedra, Chiara Cappuzi, Gerard Fournier, Elisabetta Beria, Dressa Giraldo, Franco Lafata, Ambra Enrico and Lydia Lucia. I thank also Julia Peyton-Jones for a discussion on her experience of working as a client with Oscar Niemeyer.

I owe a debt to Ana Lúcia Niemeyer de Medeiros and Maria Fernanda Martins at the Oscar Niemeyer Foundation. I am delighted that my own photographs will support their work of disseminating the legacy of Oscar Niemeyer and promoting further research. Warm thanks are also due to Haruyoshi Ono and Isabela de Carvalho Ono at the Escritório Burle Marx, Maria Elisa Costa and Julieta Sobral at the Casa de Lúcio Costa, Cristina Zappa at the Instituto Moreira Salles, Fernando de Andrade at Niemeyer's office in Brasília, Affonso Celso Prazeres de Oliveira at the COPAN, and Marcelo Gomes Durães and Flavia Barreto Cohen at the Arquivo Público do Distrito Federal.

Marianna Veremi and Thanos Veremis, Evangelia Athanassiou, Dimitri Gonticas, Maria Rita Kessler, Julie Coimbra, Patricia Morgado, Oceano Vieira, João Moreira Salles, Laura Mulvey, Mary Pearce and Rosa Weis have contributed to this project in various ways. For their warm hospitality in Curitiba, Brasília and São Paulo, I extend my gratitude to Alexandro Pundek Rocha and Maria Cristhina de Souza Rocha. The Brazilian photographer Nelson Kon granted me access to his archive, and contributed a splendid set of images to this book. Michael Klontzas has generously offered his unrivalled knowledge of multimedia technology. A very special thanks to my copy editor, Philippa Baker, and to Penny Soultani who designed this book.

I am grateful to the following hotels for sponsorship during my field trips in Brazil: Le Meridien in Rio de Janeiro, Augusta Park Residence in São Paulo, San Marco and Kubitschek Plaza in Brasília, Ouro Minas Palace in Belo Horizonte, and Pousada das Flores in Salvador. I also received sponsorship from car rental company Sixt.

My fondest hope is that this book will prove worthy of the generosity of all those I have mentioned.

'Much more than parrots and banana trees'

If Descartes did not know how to get through the labyrinth, it was because he sought its secret of continuity in rectilinear tracks, and the secret of liberty in a rectitude of the soul.
Gilles Deleuze, *The Fold: Leibniz and the Baroque*

In 1937 the Modernist poet and scholar Mário de Andrade (1893–1945), one of the principal thinkers of the Paulista vanguard of the 1920s, presented his assessment of a painting in a colonial church in São Paulo:

The detailed engraving of a watermelon opposite Christ, in the *Last Supper*, is a raw touch of delirious ingenuousness. One cannot help smiling when faced with this cornucopian national table. The copier must have been Brazilian, or perhaps Portuguese with an intimate acquaintance with our national exuberance . . . He could not restrain himself, he failed to understand the mystical frugality of Da Vinci's table, he filled empty plates with engravings of watermelons . . . It is perhaps more on account of the abundance of the laden table, than because of the engravings of a possibly native watermelon, that these paintings reveal Brazil.[1]

Not all depictions of the Last Supper from the Italian Renaissance were of chaste frugality. It suffices to recall Paolo Veronese's lavish *Feast in the House of Levi* (1573, Gallerie dell'Accademia, Venice), renamed after the tribunal of the Inquisition found evidence of irreverence and heresy in the exotic 'scurrilities' – including a parrot, a New World trophy signifying wealth – in his theatrical *Last Supper*, painted for the refectory of the SS Giovanni e Paolo monastery. In his testimony, Veronese invoked the licence given to 'poets, painters and madmen'. Mário de Andrade, by contrast, interpreted the excessive elements of the Brazilian painter's 'cornucopian national table' as a representation of Brazil's utopian world of pleasure and plenitude.

Recasting the colonial European chroniclers' and nativist Romantics' descriptions of Brazil as a land of natural excess was part of the 1920s Paulista Modernism's ambitious project to define a Brazilian hybrid identity and a national aesthetic in opposition to

Europe, without, however, severing intellectual and artistic ties with the European avant-garde. Motifs of tropical luxuriance, exuberance and languid sensuality were appropriated and identified in the local Baroque of the seventeenth and eighteenth centuries as well as in twentieth-century Brazil's popular black culture, in cuisine, music and dance, and in the most exuberant of all Brazilian festivals: carnival. Rather than a radical break with the past and with Europe Brazilian Modernists like Mário de Andrade proposed a radicalization of the past and of European images of the Other, with a view to subverting European hegemony through an emulation of their forebears, infecting Cartesian European paradigms with the delirious exuberance of the ludic tropical Other.

Brazil's Modernist myth of tropicality was not that of the 'noble savage' but that of the irreverent cannibal. Appropriating the Eurocentric trope of cannibalism, early twentieth-century Brazilian Modernists turned it into a potent anticolonialist and anticonformist metaphor. As Hélio Oiticica would write in 1968, 'the myth of "tropicality" is much more than parrots and banana trees [and watermelons]: it is the consciousness of not being conditioned by established structures, hence highly revolutionary in its entirety. Any conformity, be it intellectual, social, or existential, is contrary to its principal idea.'[2] Inspired by the alleged practices of the native Tupinambá Indians, the concept of cultural cannibalism, 'Antropofagia', was first articulated in the 1920s by the poet Oswald de Andrade (1890–1954), author of the two most important manifestoes of Brazilian Modernism.[3] Adopted by Brazilian artists across a large spectrum of media, it offered an instrument to devour imported cultural products of the past and of the present, while also guaranteeing Brazil's emancipation from European catechizing traditions. As is often the case, twentieth-century Brazilian architecture took longer than other artistic prac-

1 Document prepared for the Brazilian federal agency Serviço do Patrimônio Histórico e Artístico Nacional (Service for the Protection of the National Historic and Artistic Heritage, SPHAN), quoted in Resende, p. 213. 2 Oiticica, 2004, p. 179. Elsewhere, Oiticica explained: 'as a cultural urgency, it was of first importance to grab all Brazilian roots in image . . . all things that had been put aside by Brazilian bourgeois pride, anxious for European elegance: pineapples, plastic flowers, parrots, macaws, samba, embroidered stuff etc.' Oiticica, 2005b, p. 309. 3 Returning from Europe in 1912, Oswald de Andrade introduced Futurism to Brazil.

tices to develop a formal repertoire inflected by the decolonialist Modernist discourse. But it was through architecture, the most public form of cultural production, that Antropofagia shaped the twentieth-century physical image of urban Brazil.

Born in the hot tropical summer in Rio de Janeiro on 15 December 1907, designer of more than six hundred buildings and still in practice, Oscar Niemeyer is the central figure of Brazilian architectural Modernism and one of the most important architects of the twentieth century. On Niemeyer's ninetieth birthday in 1997, Eric Hobsbawm observed: 'It is impossible to imagine Brazil in the twentieth century without Oscar Niemeyer.'[4] It is also impossible to begin to understand Niemeyer's bold formal experiments and innovative strategies for articulating space and programme without engaging with the complex socio-political and cultural dynamics that governed the imagining of the Brazilian twentieth century. His tireless and hugely productive career spans more than seven decades. His architecture was both forged by and helped forge the modern image of Brazil. For this reason, it also tells us a great deal about modern Brazil and Brazilian cultural practice.[5] Finally, Niemeyer's fiercely independent architectural journey also tells a great deal about architectural Modernism and about architecture in general.

By the mid-twentieth century, Brazilian architectural Modernism had been recognized as the 'first *national* style of modern architecture' by Reyner Banham.[6] The international architectural periodicals of the 1940s and 1950s dedicated hundreds of dithyrambic pages to the 'chosen land of the most original and most audacious contemporary architecture'.[7] There followed monographs on individual architects like Oscar Niemeyer and Affonso Eduardo Reidy (1909–64), who 'succeeded in translating the European architecture on which their own was founded into a freer and more spectacular idiom'.[8] Published simultaneously in Portuguese, English, French and German, Henrique E. Mindlin's *Modern Architecture in Brazil* (1956) enjoyed tremendous success. From an early day, Niemeyer was internationally recognized as the protagonist of what Henry-Russell Hitchcock described as Brazil's 'creation of a new national idiom within the international language of modern architecture', even though the achievement was a collective effort enabled by enlightened state and private patronage.[9] Establishing a complex reflexive relationship with European and later North American Modernism, infecting imported paradigms with the Brazilian Dionysian spirit associated with the 'irrational' African element of Brazilian culture and all things tropical, Niemeyer's architecture has also emerged as a proleptic, radical critique of canonical Modernist aesthetic formulae and moralizing ideologies.

'Since the 1930's [sic]', commented William Holford in 1957, 'architecture in Brazil had once more become the Mistress Art. Designers achieved something like the glamour of poets in Elizabethan England, or musicians at Salzburg.'[10] In 1973, Norma Evenson reiterated: 'Brazil is the only modern nation in which architecture may be said to provide a major source of national pride.'[11] In 1939, the thirty-two-year-old Niemeyer assumed leadership of the design team that created the first state-sponsored Modernist skyscraper in the world, the Ministry of Education and Public Health (1936–44) in Rio de Janeiro. Put together by the patriarch of modern Brazilian architecture, Lúcio Costa (1902–98), the design team united Brazil's 'purist battalion' against conservative forces and included Le Corbusier (1887–1965) as a consultant.[12] Mário de Andrade was one of the consultants and collaborators of Gustavo Capanema, the powerful minister of education who commissioned Costa to design the headquarters of the ministry responsible for regulating and managing Brazilian culture and cultural heritage. In the catalogue of the 1943 exhibition *Brazil Builds* at the Museum of Modern Art in New York, it was acknowledged that 'While Federal classic in Washington, Royal Academy archaeology in London and Nazi classic in Munich are still triumphant, Brazil has had the courage to break away from the safe and easy path with the result that Rio can boast of the most beautiful government building in the Western hemisphere.'[13]

In 1947, *L'Architecture d'Aujourd'hui* hailed the completed Ministry of Education as the 'first integrated materialization of the full doctrine of Le Corbusier'.[14] The Lusophile Costa was instrumental in forging a connection between 'the New Architecture' of Le Corbusier and the Portuguese colonial heritage, revalorized and reinterpreted as proto-Antropofagist. Niemeyer referred to a 'Brazilian Architectural Movement' with a 'dashing creative spirit'.[15] He privileged invention and an Antropofagist transformation of the Corbusian vocabulary, exploiting the expressive potential of structural elements and devices of environmental control such as the celebrated adjustable *brises-soleil*, and striving for monumentality and 'splendour', a 'free-flowing style' and 'lightness' – all qualities in excess of the functionalist fulfilment of programmatic

4 Eric Hobsbawm, quoted in Niemeyer, 2002, n.p.   5 Latin American history in general and Brazilian history in particular have traditionally been defined by charismatic personalities with an enduring influence on the way Latin American nations have been imagined. Thomas Skidmore notes the 'common desire' in late twentieth-century Brazil post military rule 'to capture the past through some unique personality', a desire reflected in a long series of best-seller biographies and fictional portraits of leading figures in Brazilian history: Skidmore, 1999, p. 211. The history of Brazil, argues Laurent Vidal, 'is not made, like that of other countries, with social struggles, revolutions, political battles, and the like, but with debates and ideas brought forward by illustrious men (the heroes), or through the affirmation of principles which the masses adopt as their own'; Vidal, p. 292. Oscar Niemeyer is undoubtedly one of Brazil's modern heroes. His contribution to the shaping of the physical image of modern Brazil validates his central position in the history of the country.   6 Banham, p. 39, emphasis in the original. The *Architectural Review* also hailed Brazil's 'national variety of an international style': *Architectural Review* 93, no. 557, May 1943, p. 134.   7 Bloc, p. 2.   8 Richards, 1960, p. 22.   9 Hitchcock, 1955, p. 12. In 1952, the president of the Brazilian Institute of Architects, Milton Roberto, referred to a 'common conscience': Roberto, p. 28. Sigfried Giedion also stressed that 'Brazil is one of the very few countries where citing only a few names makes one feel one is committing an injustice'; Giedion, 1952, p. 3.   10 Holford, 1957, p. 395.   11 Evenson, 1973, p. 99.   12 Lúcio Costa, quoted in Deckker, p. 16.   13 Goodwin, p. 92.   14 'Ministère de l'Éducation et de la Santé Publique', *Architecture d'Aujourd'hui*, year 18, nos 13–14, September 1947, p. 14.   15 Niemeyer, 1958b, p. 4.

Opposite and above, Lúcio Costa, Carlos Leão, Affonso Eduardo Reidy, Jorge Moreira, Ernani Vasconcellos and Oscar Niemeyer with Le Corbusier as consultant, Ministry of Education and Public Health, Rio de Janeiro, 1936-44; opposite, view of north elevation shielded with adjustable brises-soleil, photograph of 1947; above, view of south elevation pans de verre from roof garden designed by Roberto Burle Marx

requirements.[16] The landscape architect Roberto Burle Marx (1909–94) and the artist Cândido Portinari (1903–62), both long-term collaborators with Niemeyer in the course of the following decades, were responsible for some of the most transgressive elements of Brazil's seminal modern monument: luxurious tropical gardens of pleasure, dominated by the sensuous curves of the Brazilian landscape, and ornamental murals that disfigured the austere forms of orthodox Modernism, heralding the rehabilitation of the criminalized and ostracized 'wasted capital' of Loosian doctrine.

Spectacle and luxury, pleasure, beauty and sensuality were emphatically affirmed as legitimate pursuits in Niemeyer's personal architectural manifesto: a group of buildings on the shores of an artificial lake at Pampulha, a new suburb of Belo Horizonte (1940–43). Niemeyer considers the architectural complex of Pampulha as the fountainhead of a 'new' and 'bolder architecture, in the dimensions of Brazil'.[17] Architecture, he declares, must be 'functional, beautiful, and shocking'.[18] Violating established norms, his work gave prominence to formal innovation from an early stage. Echoing Oswald de Andrade's radicalization of the ludic life of the indigenous Brazilian societies, he recognized in the marginalized area of the beautiful and the pleasurable the possibility for a new aesthetic as well as a new cultural and social order. Giving him the opportunity to experiment freely with a wide range of ideas and forms, the Pampulha project served Niemeyer as a laboratory to call into question received knowledge, destabilize the authority of hegemonic models and explore untrodden ways.

An admirer of Antoni Gaudí's delicious excess, he favoured reinforced concrete for its plasticity, which permitted him to shape it to optimum formal effect and structural efficiency. Conjugating architectural, structural and topographical events to achieve maximum fluidity, Niemeyer prioritized the sensual reality of the architectural experience. Concrete was also a material suited to the economic and technological reality of Brazil, allowing for the full exploitation of the potential of the local workforce. Taking advantage of Brazil's advanced reinforced-concrete technology and working closely with highly committed structural engineers, Niemeyer found in concrete a material that enabled him to put forward structural along with formal innovations, motivated by a post-colonial wish to undo the image of Brazil as backward. A wilfully rich palette of fine materials and techniques, purposefully employed detailing and applied ornament combined with Burle Marx's intensified images of tropical nature and fully integrated artworks to create a unique body of work, motivated by a vision for a modern architecture 'in the dimensions of Brazil', with a repertoire of voluptuous curves and tropical motifs imagined as eminently Brazilian and epitomizing sensuality, eroticism, irrationality.

In 1952, Lúcio Costa posited the rejection of the dualism between 'beaux-arts academicism' and '[École] polytechnique functionalism', and the reaffirmation of 'the legitimacy of plastic intention' – that which distinguishes architecture from mere construction – as Brazil's contribution to the development of contemporary architecture.[19] Niemeyer rejected the Modernist break with the past and claimed the whole of the architectural inheritance into which he was born; in 'the great works of the past' he searched for those 'eternal laws' of artistic creation that are not

16 Niemeyer, however, never referred explicitly to Antropofagia. 17 Niemeyer, 1993c, pp. 66–74. 18 Niemeyer, 1994a, p. 28. The 'architect must innovate', Niemeyer says, 'not merely at the formal level but also in terms of structure and programme'; Niemeyer, 1974, p. lxxxi. 19 Lúcio Costa, 1952, pp. 4–6.

Casa do Baile, dance hall and restaurant, Pampulha, Belo Horizonte, Minas Gerais, 1940-43

specific to any particular epoch.[20] He justified the intoxicating and transgressive Otherness of his version of Modernist architecture, 'free of all prejudices and "taboos"', in terms of its affinities with Brazil's Baroque monuments and its 'conformity with the Brazilian climate and . . . fantastic tropical nature'.[21] Appropriating ideas from the Baroque allowed him to take off from a contextualized base and launch his resistance against the Modernist practices he observed in the process of becoming too rigid and dogmatic.[22] Risking controversy, from an early day his spatial and formal experiments were embedded in a discourse of dissent. Deliberately suspending and subtly undermining the rules of Modernist composition, he was able to manipulate and extend its formal possibilities, liberating a much-repressed architectural imagination and demystifying the socialist, rationalist and functionalist rhetoric of doctrinaire Modernism. His architecture of 'liberated . . . sensual curve[s]' and decorated surfaces, privileging the senses over reason, was marshalled against the dominance of clean white walls,

straight lines and right angles, which, for Niemeyer, 'issued from a European ethical tradition'.[23]

If the Loosian figure of the English gentleman embodied 'the truly modern style' of Apollonian Europe, Niemeyer found in the eroticized figure of the Brazilian woman of African descent, the *mulata*, the incarnation of the Dionysian *espirito de brasilidade*. Embracing all things revalorized and radicalized by the Brazilian Antropofagists enabled Niemeyer to extend to the world of architecture their strategies of empowerment and creative resistance against domination, and construct an Afrodisiac vocabulary of Brazilian architecture that does not

20 Niemeyer, 1962a, p. 19.   21 Niemeyer, 1947b, p. 22; Niemeyer, 1997a, p. 10.   22 In 1950, the editor of the *Architectural Review*, J.M. Richards, wrote that functionalism had been 'a useful battle-cry' and 'invaluable as a discipline', but hastened to add: 'Literal functionalism in fact only exists in the minds of those who use it as a stick with which to castigate a modern architecture they do not understand': Richards, 1950, p. 166. 23 Niemeyer, 1993c, p. 66.

exclude the Other and demands a rethinking of its representation.[24]

In its special issue on Brazil in November 1947, the *Architectural Forum* posed the question: 'How does it happen that a "backward" country can suddenly produce so vibrant and up-to-date an architecture?' Agonizing over the puzzling 'sensation' that the architecture of 'backward' Brazil created in the United States and Europe, the magazine put forward the Brazilian architects' response: 'Their work is an expression of cultural maturity, not technological wealth.' Referring to the Paulista Antropofagists, the author gave credit for this maturity to 'those intellectuals – writers, poets, painters and musicians – who brought about a complete reorientation of Brazilian culture in the first years after World War I'.[25] In 1953 – the year that Niemeyer's newly completed house at Canoas was visited by 'the masters from Europe and North America', who failed to appreciate its polymetric architecture[26] – Sigfried Giedion (1888–1968), one of the early propagandists of the Modern Movement and secretary-general of CIAM (the Congrès Internationaux d'Architecture Moderne), wrote:

> In today's architecture, there are two countries with higher overall standards than all others: Finland and Brazil. It is a good sign for our civilization that it does not emanate always from the same centre. Creative achievements appear suddenly in the remotest, marginal regions, which had remained provincial in former times: Finland and Brazil. How is it possible that these two countries that have been lying on the periphery of culture demonstrate a higher architectural standard? . . . Brazilian architecture developed suddenly, like a tropical plant . . . There is something irrational in the rise of Brazilian architecture.[27]

From an early day and with remarkable consistency European and North American architectural historians and critics, whether unequivocally celebrating or scathingly criticizing Brazil's 'lyrical, hybrid strain of Modernism',[28] drew attention to the marginality of Brazil and its cultural practice, assuming as axiomatic a European centre of civilization, which, as the above quotation demonstrates, sometimes stigmatizes even its own peripheralized regions.[29] Despite the unprecedented prestige and laudatory coverage granted to Brazilian architecture in the international architectural press of the 1940s and 1950s, Latin American architecture in general and Brazilian architecture in particular were largely excluded from historical surveys of modern architecture. Echoing the centuries-old Euro-narcissist justification of colonialism, Alberto Sartoris went as far as to praise Niemeyer for 'the extraordinary undertaking of intelligently disseminating the message of the creator of Ronchamp', adding that, 'In transmitting this message, he has also transmitted the European spirit that characterized it.'[30]

Ironically, Niemeyer concurs with Nikolaus Pevsner that Le Corbusier's Notre-Dame-du-Haut at Ronchamp (1950–55) was a creation under the spell of the Brazilian innovations, delighting in a project that reversed the process of colonization and inverted the relationship between centre and periphery. This view was recently echoed by Christian de Portzamparc, who protested that Ronchamp is frequently granted landmark status by a historiography that keeps quiet about Pampulha, Niemeyer's act of patricide.[31] Paulo Herkenhoff notes: 'It has been the fate of artists in Latin America to have to prove incessantly that the countries on the fringes have their own traditions in art . . . These countries are constantly being pressured with the burden of proving that they are not mirrors but full individualities, perfectly capable of participating in the contemporary system of symbolic exchanges.'[32] Niemeyer's work sprang from a collective endeavour to challenge the stereotypical image of Brazil and its cultural production as peripheral and underdeveloped, and participate in the system of cultural exchange on the basis of a radical equality of people and cultures.

Historians and critics of Niemeyer's architecture have consistently interpreted his aesthetics of excess as a reflection of Brazil's tropical Otherness – a perspective also frequently applied to Brazil's Baroque heritage. In 1943, John Summerson thought Brazil's 'fantasy of functionalism succeeds quite naturally the fantasy of Baroque . . . reach[ing] that dangerous and thrilling pitch which is the essence not only of this kind of Baroque but also, in other terms, the Le Corbusier kind of functionalism'.[33] For Giedion, writing nine years later, Niemeyer's 'tropical exuberance' was full of

24 It should be noted here that Niemeyer does not question Brazilian constructions of race and racialization of cultural manifestations; he takes them for granted as defined within the nationalist project that he sees it as his duty to serve. 25 *Architectural Forum*, 1947, p. 66. 26 'Report on Brazil', 1954, p. 235. 27 Giedion, 1982, p. 94. The overt reference to the peripheral condition of Finland and Brazil did not appear in the earlier version of this text; Giedion, 1952, p. 3. It was, however, retained in the version that appeared in 1956; Giedion, 1956, pp. ix–x. Aline Saarinen, the *New York Times'* reviewer of the 1955 MoMA exhibition *Latin American Architecture Since 1945*, echoed Giedion: 'there is in Latin America the excitement of countries suddenly awakened, through arteries of airlines, to communication with the rest of the world and quickly thrust into the modern age'; quoted in Real, p. 105. In a similar vein, Edwin Heathcote introduced his 2004 article in the *Financial Times* on Brazilian Modernist architecture with the following: 'It is a curious anomaly that the world's most complete Modernist metropolis should have sprung up not in Germany, Switzerland, France or the US, the home of the 20th century's great radicals in art and architecture, but in the middle of a developing country in the southern hemisphere, seemingly far removed from the centre of the action'; Heathcote, 2004, p. W18. 28 Weston, 1996, p. 192. 29 Ella Shohat and Robert Stam define Eurocentrism as 'the procrustean forcing of cultural heterogeneity into a single paradigmatic perspective in which Europe is seen as the unique source of meaning [and culture], as the world's center of gravity, as ontological "reality" to the rest of the world's shadow . . . Eurocentrism, like Renaissance painting, envisions the world from a single privileged point.' The authors also point out that 'Eurocentrism first emerged as a discursive rationale for colonialism'; Shohat and Stam, pp. 1–2. 30 Sartoris, p. 12. Sartoris recognized that 'Oscar Niemeyer's new architecture . . . does not confine itself to the old familiar paths'; Sartoris, p. 10. 31 Christian de Portzamparc, quoted in 'Oscar Niemeyer: La ville radieuse', 2002, pp. 51–53. 32 Herkenhoff, 1993, p. 106. 33 Summerson, p. 135. Here, Summerson is reviewing the aforementioned 1943 *Brazil Builds* exhibition catalogue, which also proposed a derivation of Brazilian Modernism from the country's eighteenth-century colonial Baroque.

Church of São Francisco de Assis, Pampulha, Belo Horizonte, Minas Gerais, 1940–42

'bright ideas but not without risk of losing a sense of proportion and balance'.[34] And for Pevsner, Niemeyer's nonconformity exemplified a 'mid-century irresponsibility', and 'a revival of radical individualism'. Oblivious to the consummate synthesis of form and structure in the Pampulha Church of São Francisco de Assis, Pevsner pilloried its 'Loch Ness Monster' roof as a manifestation of Brazil's 'revolt from reason', in the 'tradition of the boldest, most irresponsible eighteenth-century Baroque'.[35]

Schooled in a long Eurocentric tradition of exoticism and primitivism, the editor of *Casabella*, Ernesto Rogers, did not hesitate to compare the irreverent architecture of 'this capricious artist' – Oscar Niemeyer – to 'seductive' Brazilian flowers and 'ostentatious' Brazilian women, 'over-perfumed, over-coloured, highly sensual'. Resorting to the colonialist association of Brazil with the violent tropical jungle and its destructive disorder, the Swiss artist Max Bill condemned Niemeyer's Dionysian Modernism as 'jungle growth in the worst sense'.[36] At the Royal Institute of British Architects in 1961 Pevsner defended Niemeyer's monumental

architecture for the new federal capital of Brasília, arguing that his 'are the earliest buildings which are emphatically no longer of the so-called International Style'. And he added: 'they are buildings that have force, that have power, that have a great deal of originality, but they are, emphatically, anti-rational'. Pevsner resented what he saw as 'a revolt against rationalism', and included Niemeyer with Jørn Utzon and Hans Scharoun among others in 'a strange, impressive, if disjointed, group', responsible for a 'new post-modern anti-rationalism'.[37]

With reference to the 'first monumental application of many of the characteristic Corbusian elements' at the Ministry of Education and Public Health, Kenneth Frampton commented on the Brazilian team's transformation of the European architect's 'Purist components into a highly sensuous native expression which echoed in its plastic exuberance the 18th-century Brazilian

34 Giedion, 1982, p. 96.   **35** Pevsner, 1972, pp. 425–27.   **36** Ernesto Rogers and Max Bill, in 'Report on Brazil', 1954, pp. 235–50. **37** Pevsner, 1961, p. 236.

Baroque'. He acknowledged Niemeyer as 'the most brilliant exponent of this rhetorical manner', and Roberto Burle Marx as the creator of '"paradise gardens" . . . with newly domesticated plants which he himself had taken from the jungle'. Displacing the achievements of the Brazilian designers and repressing the new, exuberant dimensions their counter-Modernism opened up, Frampton put forward the 'indigenous Brazilian vegetation' as the basis of Brazil's 'new national style'.[38] Celebrating native parrots and banana trees while ignoring their instrumentalization, he reduced the cultural to the natural, exoticizing and romanticizing a self-consciously nationalist and tropicalist architecture and glossing over its revolutionary critique and subversive spirit. Rather than recognizing Brazilian Modernism as a non-conformist project informed by an anticolonialist perspective, he interpreted it as complicit with the colonial project of the domestication and civilization of the jungle, transformed into a benign source of delight.

The architect and Greek CIAM delegate Stamo Papadaki (1906–92), author of the first three monographs on Oscar Niemeyer (1950, 1956 and 1960), closely followed the Brazilian architect's work up to the inauguration of Brasília. As editor of *Progressive Architecture*, Papadaki also spoke of 'lyrical exuberance', but without denying it its radical content: 'Lyrical exuberance', he argued, 'is not or does not appear to be necessarily humble; it could, on the contrary, as in the *Leaves of Grass*, become aggressively fiery.' Following the publication of the *Architectural Review*'s 1954 'Report on Brazil', which included contributions by Walter Gropius, Max Bill, Ernesto Rogers and others, Papadaki lamented the lack of 'serious evaluation of Brazilian buildings'. This he attributed to their flouting of convention, interpreted by their detractors as 'abuse [of] grammar without fully understanding its rules' and as ignorance of the 'social aspects of architecture'. He expressed the hope that 'such an attitude [may be] the result of a passing post-war fatigue'.[39]

Unabashed by growing criticism, Niemeyer vigorously defended his imaginative plastic speculations in reinforced concrete. He countered Brazilian architects who demanded 'an architecture based on the traditions and culture of our people' but interpreted these in a narrow sense. And he also countered foreign visitors who 'work with powerful industries that demand more simple solutions so as to take advantage of prefabricated assemblies and systems of standardization' but 'lack . . . knowledge of [Brazilian] conditions of work'. Anticipating Ernst Bloch, he responded to criticism concerning the lack of social content in his work with the following statement: 'we refuse to pretend that there exists a basis for "social architecture". To do the contrary would mean to accept an architectural poverty, to deprive our architecture of what it has that is fresh and creative or to instil in our buildings political demagoguery.'[40] But just as his dissent over the values of functionalism is not a negation of function, his dissent over the value of so-called social architecture is not a negation of the social function of architecture. Niemeyer's intoxicating designs aspire to bring together private pleasure and public happiness. They address, he maintains, the poor in the street, inviting them to participate in the 'theatre of his illusions' and experience a moment of happiness. Niemeyer wholeheartedly subscribes to Nietzsche's view:

> Formerly, all artworks were displayed on the great festival road of humanity, as commemorations and memorials of high and happy moments. Now one uses artworks to lure poor, exhausted, and sick human beings to the side of humanity's road of suffering for a short lascivious moment; one offers them a little intoxication and madness.[41]

Late twentieth-century critical appraisals of architectural Modernism widened pertinent debates, and the complexities of the subject have now become apparent. Yet although earlier illusions of conformity and stylistic coherence have been shattered, Brazil's iconoclastic Modernism continues to remain marginal to all historical accounts of the genesis, development and decline of architectural Modernism. In Brazil, Niemeyer's reputation has reached cult status and he has received the most prestigious international honours, including the Lenin Prize (1963), the Premio Benito Juárez (1964), the French Grand Prix International d'Architecture et d'Art (1981), the Gold Medal of the American Institute of Architecture (1970), the Pritzker Architecture Prize (1988), the Gold Medal of the Royal Institute of British Architects (1998) and Japan's Praemium Imperiale (2004). Nevertheless, his polemical attitude, formal and ideological nonconformity and peripheral position in relation to Eurocentric historiography, along with the international architectural community's largely negative reception of Brasília's monumentality, and Brazil's troubled history during the military dictatorship (1964–85) that followed the creation of Brasília have been responsible for the wholesale dismissal of Niemeyer's later works and the continued marginalization of the early ones. Giedion was not alone in his view of Brazil as a country at the periphery of civilization: '[Niemeyer] was marginal,' Frank Gehry says. 'He was far away. We didn't understand his context. We just heard about someplace being hacked out of the middle of some jungle to make a new city. The whole idea seemed so antisocial to liberal architects.' Zaha Hadid confirms: 'The post-60's [sic] generation was against Modern monumentality – all those wide streets for the army to drive through . . . That's how some

38 Frampton, 1992, pp. 254–55. **39** Papadaki, 1956, pp. 9–10. Niemeyer and Papadaki maintained long-term correspondence; see Stamo Papadaki Papers. **40** Niemeyer, 1956b, pp. 11–14. **41** Nietzsche, p. 89.

people thought about it. They didn't pay enough attention to see that Oscar represented a totally different ideology.'[42]

Despite the dissolution of moral imperatives in art and architecture, Niemeyer's architecture is still largely viewed as heretic and mannerist, socially irresponsible, exuberant but licentious. Prevailing attitudes reflect old prejudices; presentations of his work express deference to the myths or ignorance of the facts or both. Held in high esteem by contemporary architects like Zaha Hadid, Rem Koolhaas, Norman Foster, Future Systems, Christian de Portzamparc and Santiago Calatrava, still commissioned to design small and large projects in the Old World and lately enjoying a kind of fashion status, Niemeyer has, nevertheless, still not convinced the critics and otherwise sober historians, who disparage his works as 'spectacles of the absurd, euphoric fragments of nature crystallized . . . [or] scenograph[ic]' (Manfredo Tafuri and Francesco Dal Co). Brazil's new federal capital, inaugurated in 1960 in the country's semi-arid central plateau, is habitually discussed as a city in or 'beyond the jungle', still a Eurocentric synonym for Brazil.[43] Niemeyer's buildings for Brasília are persistently decried as 'formalistic and repressive . . . simplistic and monumental . . . Neo-Classical' (Kenneth Frampton); they are overtly dismissed as 'inflated, diagrammatic and lacking in symbolic or sculptural substance' (William Curtis); they are disdained as 'conceptually thin, formally lifeless and indifferent to climate' (Richard Weston); they are openly depreciated as 'gratuitous . . . a fine show . . . of superfluous velleities' (Tafuri and Dal Co again), and so on.[44] Prudes and puritans still wish they could affix a bronze fig leaf onto the luxuriating curves that emanate from Niemeyer's pen.

Brazil's most lauded, defiant architect is still interpreted by mainstream historiography as a disciple of Le Corbusier, the European master, or 'A Misbehaved Pupil of [European] Rationalism'.[45] Niemeyer himself speaks of his 'tropicalization' of all he learnt from Le Corbusier.[46] Noting that 'the initial exuberance of modern Brazilian architecture contained within itself the seeds of such decadent formalism', Frampton argues that Le Corbusier's 'development at Chandigarh' may also be at the root of Niemeyer's downfall.[47] Lúcio Costa was the first to promote the view that Niemeyer's work 'proceeds directly from that of Le Corbusier', although he also noted the influence of Ludwig Mies van der Rohe. 'Above all', however, Costa emphasized the 'national genius, which found expression through [Niemeyer], in the same way that it found expression, in the eighteenth century, under very similar circumstances, through [the architect and sculptor Aleijadinho]' – the 'little cripple', born Antônio Francisco Lisboa (1738–1814). At a time when the work of Aleijadinho was being reappraised as essentially anticolonialist, marking 'the emancipation of the New World from the Old',[48] Costa postulated that there are greater affinities between these two temporally distant artists – for example between Niemeyer's complex at

Pampulha and Aleijadinho's Church of São Francisco de Assis (begun 1766) in the colonial town of Ouro Prêto – than between Niemeyer and Gregori Warchavchik (1896–1972), the Paulista pioneer of the Modern Movement in Brazil, whose work remained close to European prototypes.[49] In this way, Costa dated the birth of an independent Brazilian artistic consciousness to the eighteenth century, and the birth of an independent modern Brazilian architecture to Pampulha.

The decentralizing influence of Brazilian Modernism on European architecture has also received scant attention. Not until 1985 did Bruno-Henri Vayssière recognize the Brazilian derivation of the 'anti-Havre' of Royan – the French coastal city virtually destroyed by Allied bombing in 1945 and reconstructed in the 1950s as an emblematic modern city by a team of eighty-two architects and urbanists under the leadership of Claude Ferret. Vayssière attributed the Bordeaux architects' turn towards the Brazil of 1942 – 'at the time the only producer of a liberated architecture' – to a desire to resist the étatisme of architectural production in post-war France and escape what would be termed the 'politique des grands ensembles'.[50]

The authors of a 2003 publication on 'the invention' of Royan demonstrated the enormous impact on the Bordeaux architects of Brazil's 'tropical school' of architecture, especially Niemeyer's complex at Pampulha, following the September 1947 special issue of L'Architecture d'Aujourd'hui on Brazil, regular reports on modern Brazilian architecture in subsequent issues sustaining the enthusiasm. One of these authors, Gilles Ragot, acknowledges the Pam-

42 Frank Gehry and Zaha Hadid, quoted in Kimmelman. In the early 1960s, Niemeyer's architecture for Brasília was widely published. L'Architecture d'Aujourd'hui dedicated a whole issue to it in June–July 1960 and several pages in its issue of September–October 1960. With the exception of Niemeyer's work, Brazilian architecture received no further attention until June 1987. The January–February 1974 issue of L'Architecture d'Aujourd'hui was dedicated to Niemeyer's work primarily outside Brazil. Niemeyer suggests that Brazil's iconoclastic works of architecture did not worry the international critics until they multiplied and became a 'school', which threatened to invade 'other architectures and other continents', as happened with Le Corbusier; Niemeyer, 1980b, p. 23.   **43** Tafuri and Dal Co, p. 354. Government-sponsored publicity material for Brazil's new capital also referred to 'The city in the jungle, urbs ubi silva fuit', Penna, n.d., n.p. Reporting on the effect of the burgeoning capital on public opinion in Europe, the United States and South America, J.O. de Meira Penna wrote in 1959: 'And for the Europeans it is a double surprise. Just imagine this country which, in their ill informed minds, they till recently thought of as a vast virgin forest, populated by poisonous snakes and naked Indians, this country, that many thought was sunk in the lackadaisical inertia of the tropics, builds a capital city in but three years right in the heart of the jungle, raising delicate concrete structures where the crocodile and the leopard used to roam; this nation hurls its mighty tractors through the densest virgin forest in the world, to carve our gigantic highways'. J.O. de Meira Penna, quoted in Evenson, 1973, p. 162.
Even Lúcio Costa made use of the metaphor of the jungle when he said: 'We have to finish Brasília in five years or the jungle will come back'; quoted in Evenson, 1975, p. 485.
Niemeyer's fashion status was confirmed in 2000, when the Italian fashion house Prada used the French Communist Party Headquarters (1967–80), designed by Niemeyer, to present its collection (12 October).   **44** Frampton, 1992, p. 256; Curtis, 1987, p. 307; Weston, 1996, p. 218; Tafuri and Dal Co, p. 354.   **45** Segawa, 1997, pp. 291–311.   **46** Niemeyer, 1993c, p. 66.   **47** Frampton, 1992, pp. 256–57. Recently Frampton referred to the Ministry of Education and Public Health as 'Neo-Corbusian'; Frampton, 2002, p. 12. Thilo Hilpert went as far as to suggest that Niemeyer's sketches for Brasília look like 'paraphrases of Le Corbusier projects'; Hilpert, p. 4.   **48** Bury, p. 209.   **49** Lúcio Costa, 'Depoimento' (1948), in Lúcio Costa, 1997, p. 199; also in Lúcio Costa, 1952, p. 7.   **50** Ragot, 2003a, pp. 14–16.

pulha Church of São Francisco de Assis as 'the most dissonant work in the relatively conservative panorama' of architectural production from the years 1940–45, which hugely inspired French architects from the pages of 'the bible of the [post-war] generation'. 'With this work', Ragot observes, 'the Brazilians broke with the castrating moralism of rationalism'. Yet he maintains that the emigration of European architects and critics was the reason for the 'shift of the centre of gravity of modern architecture' towards the Americas. He also stresses the European origins and education of a number of Brazilian architects and, like André Bloc before him, upholds with only slight hesitation the date of Le Corbusier's first talk in Rio de Janeiro, 8 December 1929, as the symbolic 'date of the foundation of modern architecture in Brazil'.[51] Niemeyer, on the other hand, considers Warchavchik's first house in São Paulo, dating from 1927–28, 'the first manifestation of modern architecture in Brazil', and insists that his work at Pampulha 'marked the point of departure of a new architecture in Brazil. I was freed from the influence of Le Corbusier', he affirms, 'to embark on a search for plastic freedom and architectural invention.'[52]

In reaction to the persistent treatment of Brazilian architecture as derivative of a modern European, primarily Corbusian language, the Brazilian critic Carlos Eduardo Dias Comas appears eager to demonstrate a more historical 'Western' lineage for Niemeyer's architecture, piling evidence of 'a classical inheritance' or 'French legacy', links to 'Pompey' or Palladian examples. Comas, too, appears to be motivated by a Eurocentric anxiety to prove Brazilian architecture's European ancestry in order to guarantee recognition for modern Brazilian architecture's contribution to 'Western culture'. 'The point is', he says, 'that Brazilians cannot escape being at the very least half-Western, whatever their race or ancestry, through genetics, transculturation and acculturation. Their mixed heritage justifies their claim to draw on the whole of Western culture [a claim that has never been challenged] as well as to contribute to it.' Comas defines the intentions of the Brazilian architects in accordance with his historiographic brief: 'Costa, Niemeyer and their circle were concerned with the representation of a modernity based on [Western] tradition and the affirmation of national identity within Western culture.'[53] Although this may be partly true as far as Costa, for example, is concerned, Niemeyer strove for emancipation from a Western tradition that values Brazilian artists only as disciples of Western masters, modern or ancient, seeking to forge and affirm a Brazilian architectural identity independent from prevailing Western orthodoxies and of equal if not greater value. By no means does this suggest that Niemeyer's work is not indebted to those who toiled before him, and he has often acknowledged his debts to a number of architects and artists, underlining the 'decisive' influence of Le Corbusier.[54] Antopofagist critical devouring itself 'implies a gesture of acknowledgement'.[55] At the same time,

Niemeyer's self-conscious shifts, distortions and inversions of the canonical forms of the so-called Western architectural tradition bear witness to his creative resistance to conversion, which at times takes the form of subversion.

In a dialectical relationship with European avant-gardes, Niemeyer's highly inventive design explorations aimed to assure his audience that he was 'never catechized. What [he] really made was Carnival,' to return once more to Oswald de Andrade.[56] His irreverent mastication and hybridization of orthodox Modernist imports stemming from Western centres of 'civilization', and his articulation of a dissident perspective enabled him to expand the formal and conceptual limits of Modern architecture. Through a revalorization and radicalization of the marginalized aesthetics of the Brazilian Other, Niemeyer's architecture transgressed normative aesthetic doctrine, subverting hegemonic cultural models and sustaining his long journey into unknown territories. His imaginative conceptual, formal and spatial investigations were informed by a nationalist and anticoloniaslist Brazilian stance but their value reaches beyond the limits of Brazil.

What follows is an attempt to do justice to an extraordinary body of ideas and forms, which are a great deal more complex than they are generally believed to be, and to lay the foundations for informed dialogue and further study. Historians advance with their heads turned back. But what they are after is the future, not the past. They are like Italo Calvino's Marco Polo, for whom the past 'was always something lying ahead, and even if it was a matter of the past it was a past that changed gradually as he advance on his journey, because the traveler's past changes according to the route he [or she] has followed'.[57] The same may be said of architects and artists in general and of Brazilian Modernists in particular. Turning their heads towards the past, seeking a new vision of the past, Niemeyer and the other Brazilian Modernists who embarked on a journey towards a second, Brazilian, discovery of Brazil sought to recover their future and to construct a new vision of the future. Theirs was an Antropofagist turn towards the past, implying tribute as well as irreverence. Unavoidably, they changed their past in order to build a Brazilian tradition as the basis for an independent Brazilian art. To trace the route Niemeyer has followed is not to attempt to reproduce his journey but to contextualize it historically and culturally, to think it anew. It is also, if possible, to attempt to go after Niemeyer, not in order to de-route his journey, but in order to move with and venture beyond it, suggesting possible readings and encounters and inviting fresh ones, recognizing the dialogical, open-ended character of all architectural and all historical journeys.

51 Ragot, 2003b, pp. 121–211; Bloc, p. 2. J.M. Richards only shifted the 'point of departure of this spectacular development' to Le Corbusier's second visit in 1936; Richards, 1960, p. 18. **52** Niemeyer, 1993c, pp. 73–74. **53** See, for example, Comas, 2002b, p. 78, and Comas, 2002a. **54** Niemeyer, 1947a, p. 12. **55** Vieira, p. 109. **56** Oswald de Andrade, 2000, p. 592. **57** Calvino, p. 28.

Chapter One

Modernism and National Identity in Brazil or
How to Brew a Brazilian Stew

In December 1929, the *sauvage* Josephine Baker sang and danced in the salon of the luxury ocean liner *Lutétia*, sailing from Rio de Janeiro to Bordeaux. Le Corbusier was among the passengers. The 'machine à danser'[1] and the advocate of the *machine à habiter* were both returning from Latin American tours. As the *Lutétia* crossed the Atlantic, the Swiss architect wrote down the ten lectures he had 'improvise[d]' before a Buenos Aires audience in the Argentine spring, together with a 'Brazilian Corollary' based on two talks he had delivered in Rio de Janeiro on 8 and 9 December, at the Associação dos Arquitetos. The collection was published a year later, under the title *Précisions sur un état présent de l'architecture et de l'urbanisme*. Le Corbusier, who saw in the jazz of 'the simple naïve black'[2] an expression of the new epoch, dedicated part of each day of the voyage to sketch-

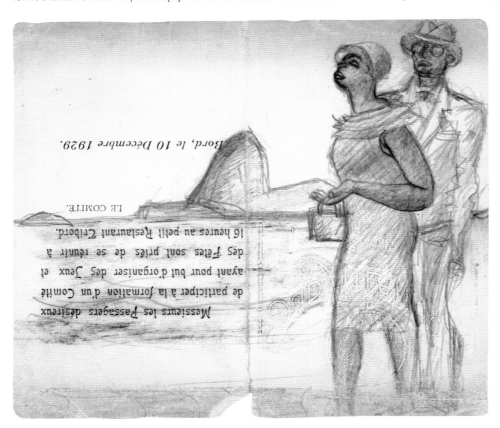

Le Corbusier, sketch of Le Corbusier and Josephine Baker in front of the Pão de Açúcar, Rio de Janeiro, pencil and pastel on an invitation card bearing the date 10 December 1929, 17 × 11 cm, Carnet B4, 239. The sketch must have been made aboard the ocean liner *Lutétia*.

1 Paul Morand, quoted in Haney, p. 69.   **2** Le Corbusier, 1991, p. 13. Le Corbusier first met Josephine Baker in September 1929 aboard the SS *Massília*, his 'floating home' for fourteen days, sailing from Europe to Buenos Aires. In November he attended her show in São Paulo, in December they walked around Rio's sights together, and Le Corbusier wrote a ballet for Baker; Cecília Rodrigues dos Santos et al., pp. 34, 43, 51; Le Corbusier, 1991, p. 12.

ing the African-American dancer *au naturel* in his cabin.[3] In the 'American Prologue' of *Précisions* he remembers how her *Baby* brought tears to his eyes in São Paulo.

'La Joséphine' had taken Paris by storm during *les années folles* (1919–29), when the Ville Lumière had fallen under the spell of black music and dance. From the beginning of the twentieth century, a number of avant-garde artists such as Paul Gauguin, Kasimir Malevich, Pablo Picasso, Fernand Léger, André Gide, Igor Stravinsky, Georges Bataille and others had 'discovered' and found inspiration in the art of Africa, Asia, America and Oceania. Without questioning its mythologization in Europe, they hoped that their own art would be liberated through contact with the 'primitive'.[4]

In Rio de Janeiro, Le Corbusier had shocked his hosts by following the painter Emiliano Augusto Cavalcanti de Albuquerque (1897–1976, known as Di Cavalcanti) – a Parisian acquaintance who had painted the architect's portrait in 1923 – to one of the poor neighbourhoods on the hills of the city. He praised both the functional architecture of the shanties and their black inhabitants:

> the black has his house almost always on the edge of the cliff, raised on *pilotis* in front, the door is at the back, toward the hillside; from up in the *favellas* one always has a view of the sea, the harbors, the ports, the islands, the oceans, the mountains, the estuaries; the black sees all that; the wind reigns, useful in the tropics.

To the 'civilized' Brazilian officials who found the black inhabitants of the hills to be 'extremely dangerous . . . savages', he replied that he

> found these blacks basically good: good-hearted. Then, beautiful, magnificent. Then, their carelessness, the limits they have learned to impose on their needs, their capacity for dreaming, their candidness resulted in their houses being always admirably sited, the windows opening astonishingly on magnificent spaces, the smallness of their rooms largely adequate.[5]

At the time of this, Le Corbusier's first visit to Rio, Lúcio Costa, the future author of the plan for Brasília, was still an adherent of the nationalist neocolonial style – a 'traditionalist' as he wrote to Le Corbusier later. The latter reported that his 1929 lectures 'provoked a particularly hostile reaction in Lúcio Costa'[6] – that 'charlatan' whom Le Corbusier spotted 'at the end of one of [his] lectures leaving with [his] books'.[7] The following year, Costa was trying his hand at 'contemporary' houses, fully converted to the ideas of the European master, having rejected the neocolonialist 'scenography, "style", archaeology'. Commissioned to design a house for Ernesto G. Fontes at Tijuca, Rio de Janeiro (1930), he proposed two alternative schemes: an 'eclectic-academic' one – his last project

in this vein and the one eventually constructed; and a 'contemporary' one – his first modern exploration. In an attempt to persuade his client to choose the second option, he furnished it with a mixture of colonial antiques and modern pieces. His change of direction, however, did not imply a rejection of colonial architecture, the study of which Costa considered 'indispensable' for Brazilian architects.[8] Although he spoke of the 'denationalization of architecture [as] a consequence of the internationalization of culture',[9] in the course of the following decades, Costa's work as well as the work of the other Brazilian Modernist architects reflected the new direction taken by Brazilian cultural nationalism or, following Benedict Anderson's formula, the new style in which the Brazilian nation was imagined.[10]

Lúcio Costa, Ernesto G. Fontes House at Tijuca, Rio de Janeiro, 1930: sketches for two alternative schemes – an 'eclectic-academic' and a 'contemporary' one

3 Haney, p. 157.   4 Picasso did, however, admit that African sculptures and masques stood in his studio more as 'witnesses than models'; quoted in Rubin (ed.), p. 17.   5 Le Corbusier, 1991, pp. 235, 9.   6 'It was the same Lúcio Costa', Le Corbusier added, 'who in 1936 led his team to my lectures'; in 'Petit historique du brise-soleil; extrait de l'œuvre de Le Corbusier', 1947.   7 Le Corbusier's note in the margin of his lecture notes, quoted in Tsiomis, 2006, p. 26. Costa returned the compliment in a letter to Le Corbusier in which he wrote that he entered halfway through one of his lectures and left five minutes later, 'scandalized, deeply convinced that [Le Corbusier was] a "charlatan"'; letter from Lúcio Costa to Le Corbusier, 26 June 1936, in Lissovsky and Moraes de Sá, p. 93.   8 Lúcio Costa, 'ENBA 1930–31: Situação do ensino na Escola de Belas Artes', 1930, in Lúcio Costa, 1997, p. 68.   9 Lúcio Costa, quoted in Calil, 2000, p. 571.   10 Benedict Anderson.

Probably unintentionally, Le Corbusier's admiration for the creativity of the black Cariocas helped advance the Brazilian nationalization of Modernist cosmopolitan artistic trends in general, soon to be followed by the Brazilianization of Corbusian architectural principles in particular. Le Corbusier's praise of popular architecture found him in agreement with the pioneer artists of Brazilian Modernism as well as with those young Brazilian intellectuals who were in the process of defining the identity of an imagined Brazilian national community. It should be remembered that it was a Brazilian painter that Le Corbusier had met in Paris who drew his attention to the slums on the *morro* – literally meaning hill but figuratively the squatter settlements built by the urban poor on the hillsides of Rio since the late nineteenth century. Perhaps Le Corbusier, like the French urbanist Donat-Alfred Agache (1875–1959) before him in 1927, climbed Morro da Favela, which subsequently gave its name to slum settlements throughout Brazil.[11]

Le Corbusier's approval of the architecture of the hillside shanties echoed the views of Gilberto de Mello Freyre (1900–1987), the sociologist who would become the most influential exponent of a unified Brazilian national culture and the leading figure in the redefinition of Brazilian racial identity. Freyre had heavily criticized the urban reforms initiated by Mayor Francisco Pereira Passos (1902–06), the 'Haussmann of the Tropics', during the first decade of the twentieth century, while Le Corbusier had praised these measures.[12] They included the opening of glamorous boulevards such as the 33-metre-wide Avenida Central lined with trees and electric lamp-posts, inaugurated on 15 November 1905 and renamed Avenida Rio Branco in 1912. Pereira Passos also oversaw the embellishment of the city with impressive squares and grand public buildings in the fashionable 'European style', like the Palácio Monroe (1904–06, demolished in 1976), the Teatro Municipal (Municipal Theatre, 1904–09), the Escola Nacional de Belas Artes (National School of Fine Arts, ENBA, 1906–08) and the Biblioteca Nacional (National Library, 1905–10).[13]

These 'civilizing' urban operations, which continued to transform central Rio through massive expropriation and demolition well into the 1940s, were responsible for the elimination of scores of unhygienic and overcrowded *cortiços* ('beehives' – overcrowded inner-city rented tenements) that restricted access to the port.

Avenida Central, Rio de Janeiro, inaugurated 15 November 1905, postcard, 1906

11 In contrast to Le Corbusier, for Agache the *favelas* represented a serious problem, and he recommended the resettlement of their inhabitants in new, specially constructed, hygienic social housing units; Valladares, pp. 17–18. **12** Deckker, p. 33. Le Corbusier admired both Pereira Passos's work and his methods. His 1936 Rio lectures were dedicated to him and in 1941, he wrote: 'In the early days the Prefect, who was considered a madman, used sometimes to go at night with a demolition squad to the house of some owner who refused to evacuate. He would raze it to the ground. Next morning the site was vacant; routine and selfish private interests had been vanquished. Methods pursued in the interests of the community must always be daring'; quoted in Evenson, 1973, p. 38, n. 8. **13** Paris would also serve as a model for the transformation of São Paulo into a European-style metropolis at the beginning of the twentieth century. In 1911, Mayor Antônio da Silva Prado (father of Paulo Prado) engaged the services of the French urbanist Joseph Antoine Bouvard (1840–1920), Director of Architecture at the city of Paris, where he had organized the Exposition Universelle of 1900, and author of a plan for Buenos Aires (1907–11). Bouvard's proposals for São Paulo, however, implemented during the administration of Mayor Raimundo da Silva Duprat (1911–14), were also indebted to Camillo Sitte's ideas.

PRAÇA MARECHAL FLORIANO, RIO DE JANEIRO

Francisco de Oliveira Passos, Teatro Municipal, Praça Marechal Floriano, Rio de Janeiro, 1904–09, postcard, 1910. *Opposite*, on Avenida Central, the Escola Nacional de Belas Artes (Adolfo Morales de los Rios, 1906–08) and, *in the foreground*, the Biblioteca Nacional (Hector Pépin, 1905–10). The engineer Francisco de Oliveira Passos, who won the competition for the design of the Teatro Municipal under the pseudonym Aquilla, was the son of Mayor Francisco Pereira Passos.

Their predominantly black evicted inhabitants fled to shanty towns up on the steep hills of Rio and in the suburbs of its *zona norte* (northern zone). Rio was 'becoming civilized' announced the newspapers of the time; it was shedding all 'exotic' elements and becoming Europeanized or 're-Europeanized' and, thus, modernized.[14] In the hillside neighbourhoods of the impoverished urban refugees, Freyre found 'a piece of old Rio' with its shady narrow streets. It was up there, he believed, that the 'true Brazilians' lived, the creators of samba, the theme of a 1925 painting by Di Cavalcanti.[15]

The discovery of African Brazilian culture and its virtues by Brazilians and foreign visitors should be considered in relation to the contemporaneous definition of Brazilian national identity, which, according to Freyre, whose theory proved extremely influential, is rooted in race mixing or *mestiçagem*. Not so long after the belated abolition of slavery in 1888, Brazil's definition of her unique, hybrid national identity went hand in hand with the reappraisal of the country's African heritage, which was found living on in twentieth-century Brazilian popular black culture. The country's smooth and virtually bloodless passage from colonial rule to independence was rapid, but the formation of its united national consciousness was a slower process. Before Freyre, it was a nineteenth-century Bavarian naturalist, Karl Friedrich Philipp von Martius (1769–1868), who first proposed, in 1844, a 'pragmatic

[Brazilian] historiography', based on the amalgamation of 'the three races, namely: the copper-colored or the American, the white or the Caucasian, and the black or the Ethiopian . . . a novel mixture'.[16]

The nineteenth-century Indigenismo movement, which received the royal patronage of Dom Pedro II, emperor of Brazil from 1831 to 1889, who distributed indigenous titles to his improvised nobility, had paved the way towards the replacement of imported European idols with tropical ones. A Romantic crusade for a national literature had been initiated by poets and historians like Francisco Adolfo de Varnhagen, who argued that, for 'Brazilian literature, the ancient language of our land [Tupí] is much more important than the study of Greek'.[17] Dom Pedro himself became conversant in the indigenous Tupí-Guarani language. Tupí themes

14 Freyre argued that 'The Portuguese colony of America had taken on qualities and conditions of life that were so exotic, from the European point of view, that the nineteenth century, during which Brazil's contacts with Europe were renewed – a different Europe now, industrial, commercial, mechanized, representing the triumph of the middle class – was in the nature of a re-Europeanization'; Freyre, 1986, p. 204.   15 Vianna, pp. 3–4. The opening of the Avenida Central resulted in the razing of the São Bento Hill, the partial razing of the Castelo Hill and the demolition of 641 structures. Echoing Le Corbusier, Freyre in 1936 judged 'the shanty . . . of the poor' – that is, the house built by the 'Negro or mestizo' in nineteenth-century Brazilian cities – as 'better adapted to the hot climate than many a rich dwelling'. The plan and materials of the shanties, Freyre postulated, 'combine to give better ventilation and lighting than those found in the patriarchal dwellings'; Freyre, 1986, p. 168.   16 Karl Friedrich Philipp von Martius, quoted in Burns, 1968, p. 42.   17 Fransisco Adolfo de Varnhagen, quoted in Burns, 1968, p. 45.

had featured in Brazilian literature long before the black cultural element received any serious appreciation. In the twentieth century, however, African culture was recognized not merely as an important constituent of Brazilian uniqueness, but as the pronounced part of the Brazilian mixture, strongly distinguishing it from Hispanic America.[18]

One hundred years after independence in 1822, the Brazilian intellectuals' and artists' second discovery of Brazil aimed to couple political independence with cultural emancipation and demanded the invention of an authentic hybrid Brazilian tradition on the basis of which to construct an autonomous Brazilian art. The quest for modernity was parallel to an intensified quest for *brasilidade* (Brazilianness), and the latter embraced all things that had remained relatively untouched by the intensive nineteenth- and early twentieth-century re-Europeanization of Brazilian society and culture, with its consequent economic and cultural dependency.

During the empire that had followed independence, lasting from 1822 to 1889, economic domination was British, and cultural domination French.[19] Literary figures like Antônio de Castro Alves (1847–71), the son of a slave and author of the great abolitionist poem 'Voices of Africa', or the subtle and subversive Joaquim Maria Machado de Assis (1839–1908), or the author of the scandal-breaking *O Mulato*, Aluísio Tancredo Gonzalves de Azevedo (1857–1913), constituted exceptions among the Brazilian literati, who, until the early twentieth century, had found intellectual nourishment predominantly in French literature. Paris represented the centre of civilization and navel of the art world. Generally, for the new urbanized social elite, things sophisticated were things European; they signified prosperity and progress. In 1909, the writer Elysio de Carvalho (1880–1925) described the best salon of Rio de Janeiro, presided over by Countess Sylvia Diniz, 'who can . . . evoke the mists of London, the landscapes, heights and snows of the Alps, the radiant beauty of the gardens and parks of Paris, the superb magic of Venice'.[20]

But by the beginning of the twentieth century, this Europeanizing modernization and urbanization was increasingly rejected by a nationalist movement that judged it 'a disintegrating force'.[21] They favoured instead a new modernity, capable of embracing truly Brazilian values and themes, stressing the importance of the Indian, the African and the rural heritage – that is, of those elements that differentiated Brazilian from European culture. Already in the 1910s, the erudite national composer Heitor Villa-Lobos (1881–1959) had composed *Três danças africanas* (1914–16).

While racial discrimination was real and pervasive, the 1920s witnessed a growing, active appreciation of things Indian and black by the dominant white and thoroughly Westernized Brazilian elite, influenced by Western ideologies and tastes that both encouraged their new attitude towards things exotic and determined the definition of the latter.[22] What lay at the periphery of Brazilian culture was acknowledged as being capable of enriching – but never challenging – the central core. Hans Staden's contested account of the anthropophagous practices of the savage Tupinambá Indians, written in 1557, was reprinted and became popular in 1925, with an English translation appearing in 1928, *Hans Staden: The True History of His Captivity*.[23] In 1921, the Pernambucano painter Vicente do Rêgo Monteiro (1899–1970) produced a drawing of the *Antropófago* (*Anthropophagite*), following a study of native Indians on the island of Marajó. Two years later, in Paris, he illustrated Pierre-Louis Duchartre's book *Légendes, croyances et talismans des Indiens de l'Amazone*, proposing a painting system based on motifs from ancient Amazonian ceramics from islands such as Maracá and Marajó. Parisian negrophilia of the 1920s and Francis Picabia's 'Manifeste cannibale dada' (1920) were not without their influence on Brazilian artists.

The Brazilians, however, were conscious of the fact that their turn towards the 'primitive' differentiated them from their European counterparts. At least, it was important for them to insist that it did not represent yet another slavish imitation of European models but, on the contrary, a turn away from these or, rather, an ingestion of the European rival, following the example of the

18 This view underestimated the importance of the African heritage of the island nations of the Caribbean, the eastern coast of Mexico, Argentina, Colombia and Venezuela. At independence there were majority black populations in Cuba (54 per cent), Venezuela (61 per cent) and Brazil (67 per cent); Gott, pp. 278–79.   19 In 1825 Portugal acknowledged the independence of Brazil (after the Court of St James had conferred recognition) in return for two million pounds sterling, part as Brazil's share of Portugal's debt to Great Britain. Emperor Pedro I also conceded to a series of commercial treaties favourable to Great Britain. In the course of the following decades, and despite occasional challenges from the Brazilians, British commercial and financial hegemony continued and Brazil's debts soared.   20 Elysio de Carvalho, quoted in Skidmore, 1993, pp. 95–96.   21 Mindlin, p. 2.   22 'With racism as the accepted and acceptable ideology of the republican elites, ex-slaves and African Brazilians generally faced heightened discrimination in the late nineteenth and early twentieth centuries. Perhaps the clearest evidence was the use of state funds to subsidize massive immigration of Europeans to take the slaves' place in field and factory . . . Not surprisingly, the labor movement in São Paulo was principally led by immigrants . . . The state itself began to see the immigrants as a threat, while the

Brazilian "national," that is, man of color, was now increasingly described as loyal and hardworking. Finally, in 1927, the program of subsidized immigration was suspended . . . In 1930 . . . Getúlio Vargas . . . decreed that two-thirds of all employees in the growing industrial establishments of the country should be Brazilians. While often evaded, this law greatly helped to open the way for blacks and mulattoes into the urban workforce. By the 1940s, . . . the urban proletariat fully included people of color'; Graham, pp. 49–50. On 3 July 1951, President Getúlio Vargas passed the Afonso Arinos Law (no. 1390) outlawing all forms of racial discrimination for the first time in Brazilian history, 'while sanctioning racist practices in public institutions ranging from schools and museums to government agencies'; Guzmán, p. 98.   23 The first English translation, by A. Tootal, appeared in 1874. It was issued by the Hakluyt Society to its members, with an introduction and notes by Sir Richard Burton. A literal translation of the original title reads: *The True History and Description of a Country of Savages, a Naked and Terrible People, Eaters of Men's Flesh, Who Dwell in the New World called America, Being Wholly Unknown in Hesse Both Before and After Christ's Birth Until Two Years Ago, When Hans Staden of Homberg in Hesse Took Personal Knowledge of Them and Now Presents His Story in Print*; 'Note to Introduction', Staden, p. 18.

'The Feast', 1557, woodcuts illustrating Hans Staden's Brazilian adventurelogue, with scenes representing the cannibal Tupinambá Indians and Hans Staden among the Tupinambá, identified as the man with the initials 'H S' above his head, beard, fig leaf and hands clasped in prayer

natives in Michel de Montaigne's essay 'Des Cannibales' (1580, translated into English in 1603). To the Brazilians, the 'primitive' was also autochthonous; the native was their legitimate heritage and contemporary reality. And their Antropofagist cultural and political programme moved well beyond the shock tactics of the French Surrealists.[24]

In 1926, Freyre published an article entitled 'On the Valorization of Things Black', which must be seen in the context of the contemporaneous Recife Regionalist Movement, of which he had formulated the manifesto. Freyre advocated cultural inde-

pendence; that is, liberation from nineteenth-century, primarily French models, and fostered a reappraisal of popular Brazilian traditions. The discovery and revalorization of the marginalized strong black presence in Brazilian culture by Brazilians and foreign visitors alike at the beginning of the twentieth century coincided with what the Peruvian poet César Vallejo called 'La conquista de París por los negros' (1925).[25] In 1931, the Afro-Cuban poet Nicolás Guillén (1902–89) put it in verse:

> It's great . . .
> now that Europe is stripping
> to toast itself in the sun
> and finds in Harlem and Havana
> the music of jazz and the 'son',
> you can be proud of being Negro, (while the boulevard
>   applauds),
> and, in the face of the White man's envy,
> you can talk real Negro too.[26]

But, in contrast to the Europeans who had to import the African Other, the Brazilians were able to claim as their own and export the Other craved by the Europeans. On 11 May 1923, Oswald de Andrade delivered a lecture at the Sorbonne stating that in Brazil 'black is a realist element'.[27] Alluding to Brazil's triple heritage, he spoke of the music of Villa-Lobos, that 'lives in the *urucungo* of the Black, in the rhythmic vivacity of the Indian, in the nostalgia of the Portuguese *fado*'.[28] The same year Tarsila do Amaral (1886–1973), daughter of wealthy landowners in São Paulo state, instructed by French-speaking tutors and trained in Paris, painted *A negra* (*The Black Woman*, Museu de Arte Contemporânea da Universidade de São Paulo) at the atelier of Fernand Léger. This turn towards Brazilian themes was concurrent with Tarsila do Amaral's experimentation with European Modernist aesthetic trends. When, in 1922, she had been the only woman to exhibit at the Salon Officiel des Artistes Français, she was still subscribing to an academic style. After her return to Brazil, the same year, she formed the Modernist 'Group of Five' with the pioneer Modernist painter of Brazil Anita Malfatti, Menotti del Picchia, Mário de Andrade and Oswald de Andrade. During her second Parisian sojourn (1922–24), she successfully combined Cubism with the emerging Brazilianism, which she was in a position to export.

24 See Oswald de Andrade, 2000.   **25** César Vallejo, 'La conquista de París por los negros', *Mundial*, Lima, 11 December 1925, cited in Franco, p. 320.   **26** Nicolás Guillén, 'Pequeña oda a un boxeador mulato', in *Sóngoro Consongo* (1931), cited in Franco, p. 132.   **27** Oswald de Andrade, quoted in Schwartz, p. 540. Brazil has the largest population of African descent outside Africa, the largest population of descendents of slavery, and the second largest black population in the world after Nigeria. Brazil's black population today remains at the bottom of the economic and social ladder.   **28** Oswald de Andrade, quoted in Herkenhoff, 2005, p. 23.

Pau-Brasil and Antropofagia

Beginning in 1915, Oswald de Andrade advocated a 'national' school of painting. In 1924, his Modernist 'Manifesto da Poesia Pau-Brasil' was published in *Correio da Manhã* in Rio de Janeiro. The following year, his poetry collection *Pau Brasil* was published in Paris, illustrated with a series of paintings by Tarsila do Amaral: among others, *A caipirinha* (*The Little Peasant Girl*), *Carnaval em Madureira* and *Morro da favela*.[29] The Brazilian Modernists of the 1920s identified the native and the black with Brazil's living popular tradition that the *belle époque* had repressed for its 'ignorance' and 'barbarity'. It was on this popular tradition that they drew, with the approval and encouragement of their European counterparts. In 1926, the year when his Futurist manifestoes were published in Rio de Janeiro, Filippo Tommaso Marinetti, too, posed for a photograph inside a *favela* at the centre of a group of bourgeois companions, framed by four black *favelados* and two policemen.

Filippo Tommaso Marinetti and his bourgeois companions, posing with four black *favelados* and two policemen in a *favela* of Rio de Janeiro, 1926

Tarsila do Amaral standing by her painting *Morro da favela*, at her first solo exhibition, Galérie Percier, Paris, June 1926

According to Mário de Andrade, in a lecture delivered in 1942, Brazil from 1922 to 1930 witnessed 'the most intellectual orgy that [her] artistic history had ever registered', concluded by the first carnival parade in 1930.[30] At the centenary of independence in 1922 the poet Menotti del Picchia announced the 'Brazilianization of Brazil', President Epitácio Pessoa authorized the creation of Brazil's first National Historical Museum, and the critic Ronald de Carvalho (1893–1935) called for a rejection of the European canon: 'Let us forget the marble of the Acropolis and the towers of the Gothic cathedrals.'[31] The 'fête' of the Semana de Arte Moderna, 11–17 February 1922, originally conceived by Le Corbusier's companion on the *morro*, Di Cavalcanti, and financed by coffee barons, celebrated the quest for a national modern art in Brazil's most dynamic economic centre, São Paulo.[32]

At the same time, it marked the end of what E. Bradford Burns calls 'the era of bucolic nationalism'.[33] Brazilian Modernist intellectuals sought independence from both Romantic nationalism and European artistic domination. Their programme may be seen as aiming at a critical appropriation of both the national and the cosmopolitan. Modernism was to function as a tool to keep nationalism in check, while nationalist ideals would harness any tendencies towards blind submission to European doctrines. In the São Paulo of the 1920s, Mário de Andrade asserted, 'the Modernist Movement was clearly aristocratic'. In the salons that emerged

29 Oswald de Andrade, 1989, pp. 310–11.   **30** Mário de Andrade, 2000, p. 595.   **31** Ronald de Carvalho, quoted in Burns, 1970, p. 274.   **32** See Aracy A. Amaral, 1998.   **33** Burns, 1968, p. 60.

after the festival of the Semana de Arte Moderna, the 'cult of tradition was strong but within the greatest [French] Modernism': Afro-Brazilian cuisine with Surrealism and champagne.[34]

Oswald de Andrade's 1924 Pau-Brasil manifesto, like the country itself, was named after the first product ever exported from Brazilian soil to Europe, furnished by Indians: brazilwood or pau-brasil – a tree that yields a red dye (brazilin).[35] The cover of his poetry collection *Pau Brasil*, designed by Tarsila do Amaral, paraphrased the national flag. At a time when Brazil 'imported everything, including coffins and toothpicks',[36] Oswald de Andrade proposed: 'Let us distinguish: Imported poetry. And Pau-Brasil Poetry, for export.' The revolution he called for could accommodate both nativist themes and European avant-gardes, 'medicine men and military airfields . . . Jungle and school'.[37] The rejection of regionalism and the affirmation of nationalism were seen as prerequisites for Brazil's participation in a universal culture. In 1924, Mário de Andrade wrote: 'We will only be civilized in relation to well-established civilizations the day we create the ideal, a Brazilian orientation. Then we will pass from imitation to creation. And then we will be universal, because we are national.'[38]

Tarsila do Amaral, cover for Oswald de Andrade's poetry collection *Pau Brasil*, 1925

Tarsila do Amaral contends that it was her *Abaporu* (literally 'man who eats [man]' in the Tupí-Guarani language, collection of Eduardo F. Costantini, Buenos Aires) of 1928 that inspired Oswald de Andrade, her husband, to conceive what has been proven as the most effective, most radical, most enduring and ingenious theoretical tool of Brazilian Modernism, ensuring at once ingestion of European avant-garde models and a national Brazilian modernity rooted in native traditions. Together with the poet and diplomat Raúl Bopp (1898–1984) and the writer Antônio de Alcântara Machado (1901–1935), Oswald de Andrade launched the Movimento Antropofágico: 'an artistic and literary movement rooted in the land of Brazil'.[39] Antropofagia appropriated the European and Eurocentric concept of cannibalism, associated with the natives of America and the Caribbean, radicalizing that which the Europeans most feared and hated and transforming it into a powerful instrument of ongoing artistic and cultural renovation.

The anthropologist William Arens has convincingly argued that the unsubstantiated European notion of cannibalism has been used 'as ideological justification for some very real forms of human exploitation'.[40] Modernist Antropofagia turned a myth that has served to sustain oppression of the primitive Other into an instrument of cultural emancipation. The two trends run parallel: a search for a firm rooting in Brazilian soil on the one hand and, on the other, a desire to devour the foreign models, taking over the enemies' attributes and destroying their Otherness in the process, in the manner of the imagined Indian anthropophagous ancestors. Oswald de Andrade's 'Manifesto Antropófago' synthesized insights from Michel de Montaigne, Friedrich Nietzsche, Karl Marx, Sigmund Freud and Hermann Keyserling and radicalized the barbarian metaphysics rejected by the writer Graça Aranha, 'the Negro's fetishism and the native's religious fear . . . that transformed the Brazilian imagination . . . into a veritable "jungle of myths".'[41] Published on 1 May 1928, in the *Revista de Antropo-*

34 Mário de Andrade, 2000, pp. 594–95. 35 In the Middle Ages in Europe, 'bresil' was a dye wood imported from the east: *Caesalpinia sappan*. The Portuguese adopted the name for trees with similar characteristics found in Brazil: *Caesalpinia echinata* and *Haematoxylum brasiletto*; Eliovson, p. 13. 36 Gomes, p. 605. The poster for the 1987–88 Parisian exhibition *Art brésilien du XX siècle* (*Brazilian Art of the Twentieth Century*) echoed the cover of Oswald de Andrade's poetry collection *Pau Brasil*, in a further paraphrase of the national flag. This time, 'Modernidade' ('Modernity') took the place of 'Ordem e Progresso' ('Order and Progress'), the slogan on the Brazilian flag. 37 Oswald de Andrade, 1989, p. 311. 38 Mário de Andrade, quoted in Oliven, p. 58. 39 Oswald de Andrade, quoted in Schwartz, p. 542. Tarsila do Amaral painted the *Abaporu* as a present for Oswald de Andrade's thirty-eighth birthday on 11 January 1928. 40 Arens, p. 184. The first image of American cannibals appeared on a map of 1502 (Staatsbibliothek, Munich), depicting a Brazilian cooking a human being. Amerigo Vespucci's *Mundus Novus*, first published in Paris in 1503, 'provided gruesomely circumstantial details' on cannibalism; Honour, pp. 8–10. 41 Nunes, p. 60. Graça Aranha (1868–1931), founder of the Brazilian Academy of Letters, gave the inaugural address at the Semana de Arte Moderna of 1922. One year earlier, in his *Estética da Vida* (*An Aesthetics of Life*), he had offered his interpretation of the three Brazilian races' contribution to the formation of the Brazilian 'soul'.

fagia, it was actually dated thus: 'In Piratininga, Year 374 of the Swallowing of Archbishop Pêro Fernandes Sardinha [sardine]', by the Caetés Indians. Illustrated with the woodcuts from Hans Staden's adventurelogue, it proposed this apparently historical, irreverent anthropophagous act of 1556 as the foundational act of resistance that marked the birth of a Brazilian (Antropofagist) consciousness.[42] The anniversary of the last day of 'free America' before Christopher Columbus's arrival, 11 October 1928, was chosen for the first World Conference of Antropofagia, which called for the 'de-Vespucciazation' and 'de-Columbusization' of the Americas and the 'de-Cabralization' of Brazil.

The most famous Indianist poem of Antônio Gonçalves Dias (1823–64), Brazil's greatest Romantic poet, had been entitled 'I-Juca-Pirama', that is, 'He who is worthy to be killed [and eaten]'. It presented the idea that only brave Indian warriors were considered fit to be eaten. In his 'Manifesto Antropófago', de Andrade recognized the inevitability and nutrient qualities of the European and offered an instrument to unite the native with the foreign, the savage with the civilized: 'Cannibalism alone unites us. Socially. Economically. Philosophically . . . Tupí, or not tupí, that is the question . . . I am only concerned with what is not mine. Law of Man. Law of the cannibal.'[43] His treatment of *Hamlet* with 'the cannibalistic vaccine' was meant to initiate the 'Carib Revolution' and proclaim the independence of Brazilian art and literature. The role of this vaccine was both aggressive and defensive: it aimed to contaminate the European with the tropical and, at the same time, to protect the native – no longer restricted to the Indian – against the viruses and catechisms of 'the dressed man'. Oswald de Andrade's Pau-Brasil poem 'Portuguese Error' had declared:

> The Portuguese arrived
> During a heavy rain
> And dressed up the Indian
> What a pity!
> Had it been a sunny morning
> The Indian would have undressed
> The Portuguese.[44]

At the Fourth Pan-American Congress of Architects in 1930 in Rio de Janeiro the 'anthropophagous delegate', engineer, architect and artist Flávio de Carvalho (1899–1973), presented his anticolonial urban utopia entitled 'The City of Naked Man' ('A Cidade do Homem Nu').

The manifesto Pau-Brasil had anticipated the powerful effect of the tropical vaccine: 'The Carnival in Rio is the religious outpouring of our race. Pau-Brasil. Wagner yields to the samba schools of Botafogo. Barbaric, but ours. Rich ethnic mix.'[45] And the 'Manifesto Antropófago' reiterated: 'We were never catechized. What we really made was Carnival.' Carnivalization and cannibalization became semantic equivalents, strategies of cultural

empowerment and methods of mixing diverse ingredients in order to obtain the essential hallmark of Brazilian identity: a novel mixture. European Modernism was not rejected, but the Brazilians were not converted either; they appropriated Modernism and transformed it, subverted it even, in the manner their forefathers had transformed Catholicism. They 'made Christ to be born in Bahia. Or in Belém do Pará.'[46] In effect, only the letter of cosmopolitan Modernism was rejected when Mário de Andrade, in 1924, declared: 'I am no longer modernist. But I am modern.'[47] The historian and film critic Paulo Emílio Salles Gomes provocatively announced: 'nothing is foreign'.[48] The Brazilians had consciously embarked on a process of creating a Brazilian modernity or a Luso-tropical modernity, as Freyre would eventually baptize it. The white cultural elite appropriated the local and the marginalized and nationalized it, thus universalizing it. At the same time, they appropriated universalist Modernism and nationalized it, thus particularizing and localizing it.

The Discovery and Redefinition of Brazil's Colonial Heritage

The São Paulo rebels' reconciliation with the popular element of Brazilian culture – urban and rural – was followed by the thesis that an authentic national Brazilian art should be based on an investigation of precisely this element. The Antropofagists travelled around Brazil in search of ethnographic material for examination and the roots of the popular culture they recognized as ancient. The contribution of the Swiss writer Blaise Cendrars, born Frédéric-Louis Sauser (1887–1961), to the discovery of Brazil's living tradition and its ancient pedigree has been widely acknowledged, perhaps even exaggerated, by the Paris-educated Brazilian elite. In 1917, Cendrars had written the plot for the black ballet *La création du monde*, with set designs by Léger and music by Darius Milhaud. And in 1921 he had published his *Anthologie nègre*, a collection of African creation myths and legends. He shared the place and year of his birth with Le Corbusier, introduced the Brazilians to *L'Esprit nouveau*, and organized his 'doctrinaire' compatriot's first visit to Brazil.[49] In Paris in the early 1920s the two had met the young Brazilian artists whom Cendrars was later to initiate to the primordial mysteries of their native land 'of inexpressible

42 It has been pointed out that Oswald de Andrade's Year 374 is the result of a miscalculation: it should have been Year 372 (1928 minus 1556). **43** Oswald de Andrade, 2000, p. 591. **44** Oswald de Andrade, 'Portuguese Error' (1925), trans. in Jackson, p. 102. **45** Oswald de Andrade, 1989, p. 310. **46** Oswald de Andrade, 2000, pp. 591–92. **47** Mário de Andrade, quoted in Schwartz, p. 544. **48** Paulo Emílio Salles Gomes, quoted in Calil, p. 564. **49** The Brazilian coffee baron and art Maecenas Paulo Prado, in close contact with Blaise Cendrars and Fernand Léger since 1911, financed Le Corbusier's 1929 visit to Brazil upon Cendrars's recommendation. To Prado's letter reporting that Le Corbusier's lectures went well, Cendrars replied: 'I'm happy for Jeanneret's success; he is a very nice boy, but a doctrinaire in his profession'; Tsiomis, 2006, p. 18.

grandeur, where civilization and savagery do not contrast but mingle, conjugate and marry, actively and disturbingly'.[50]

Cendrars 'discovered Brazil for Brazilians, in the words of Erdmute Wenzel White in *Les Années vingt au Brésil'* (1977).[51] He was fascinated by carnival, impressed by black samba dancers. It was he who introduced Gilberto Freyre to one of the bohemian *favelados*, Donga (Joaquim Maria dos Santos), who had the 'genius of popular music'. And Freyre acknowledged Cendrars as 'one of the two principle [sic] causes of "the movement for the valorization of things black" in Rio de Janeiro'.[52] It was Cendrars who brought Monsieur Level, director of the Parisian Galerie Percier, to the studio of Tarsila do Amaral, whose *A negra* featured on the cover of Cendrars's *Feuilles de Route* (1924). Oswald de Andrade had been introduced to Cendrars at the Montmartre atelier of Tarsila do Amaral, and dedicated to him his poetry collection *Pau Brasil* 'for the discovery of Brazil'.

During Holy Week 1924, Cendrars and the young Brazilian *futuristas* – the Modernists from industrialized São Paulo – travelled to the Baroque towns of Minas Gerais in an exploration of Brazil's golden age and carnivalized Catholicism.[53] Tarsila do Amaral declared that she found her *brasilidade* through that pilgrimage to the region, which gold mining had endowed with some of the finest examples of eighteenth-century sacred and secular art and architecture: 'Contact with a land steeped in tradition, the church paintings and the dwellings of those essentially Brazilian towns – Ouro Prêto, Sabará, São João del Rei, Tiradentes, Mariana and others – aroused a feeling of Brazilianness in me.'[54] Ouro Prêto, which on 12 July 1933 was designated Brazil's first national monument (and in 1980 Brazil's first UNESCO world heritage site), was the former Vila Rica, where national artistic and civic heritages met. It was the capital of the *capitania* of Minas Gerais with its rediscovered antiquities, as well as the stage of a 1789 plot for an inde-

Ouro Prêto, Minas Gerais

50 Blaise Cendrars, quoted in Calil, p. 568. 51 Bonet, p. 520. 52 Vianna, quoting Gilberto Freyre, pp. 73, 67. 53 The visit to Minas Gerais was actually led by Mário de Andrade, who had concluded his 1919 visit to the area with a text on Aleijadinho. 54 Tarsila do Amaral, quoted in Schwartz, p. 541. See also Eulalio.

pendent republic, known as the Inconfidência Mineira, and led by Tiradentes (Lieutenant Joaquim José da Silva Xavier, 1746–92), the eulogized 'protomartyr of independence', turned into the chief symbol of the republic following its proclamation in 1889.

Minas Gerais acquired a privileged position in the national memory and artistic imagination: it became the venerable birthplace of Luso-tropical civilization. The populist dictator Getúlio Dornelles Vargas (1883–1954) described Ouro Prêto as 'the Mecca of Tradition'.[55] Brazil's eighteenth-century 'Age of Gold' became an idealized Brazilian golden age, centred on the cities of Minas Gerais, the creation of Portuguese and African prospectors, the cradle of the national past, embodied in landmarks of Brazilianness in the local Baroque style – the Barocco Mineiro.[56]

The reappraisal of the Indian, the African and the popular did not overthrow the colonial. The artists and architects who embraced Modernism turned towards the colonial past in search of their cultural roots. What they did reject was contemporaneous conservative 'neocolonialismo', which, reacting against French academicism, resorted to an eclectic appropriation of elements from a variety of sources to create a picturesque mixture with little relation to Brazilian architectural history. For Lúcio Costa, too, it was a 1922 visit to the colonial town of Diamantina, in Minas Gerais, that marked a turning point in his understanding of Brazil's colonial heritage: 'I was immersed in the past, in its simplest, purest sense; a true past that I was unaware of, brand new to me,' he declared.[57] Although Costa continued to produce neocolonialist projects until 1930, he believed it was this moment of 'revelation' that led to his eventual rejection of neocolonialist 'scenography'.[58]

Appreciation was accompanied by a reappraisal of the colonial heritage, deemed necessary to counter the effect of nineteenth-century Europeanizing attitudes, which had been coupled with those anti-Lusitanian sentiments partly responsible for the abdication of Pedro I in 1831. One century later, thanks to the efforts of Gilberto Freyre, the colonial was redefined as a culturally mixed, hybrid culture and thus uniquely Brazilian. Highly roman-

Diamantina, Minas Gerais

55 Getúlio Dornelles Vargas, quoted in Williams, p. 254. **56** In the introduction to a 2006 exhibition on *Aleijadinho and His Time*, curator Fabio Magalhães wrote: 'By the end of the 17th century in Minas Gerais, region inhabited by warring anthropophagic natives known as 'Botocudos', abundant gold was found . . . The most surprising historical fact was the magnificent development that took place in a short time, less than a century . . . Minas Gerais moved from the Stone Age to become the avant-garde of civilization in the new world. In 80 years, Minas Gerais left behind the barbaric period and reached Enlightenment, in a giant step – from the 'Botocudos' tribes to the ideas that led to [the] Minas Conspiracy, based on the ideas of independence of the United States and the French Revolution'; 'Aleijadinho e seu tempo: Fé, engenho e arte', 2006. **57** Lúcio Costa, 'Diamantina' (n.d.), in Lúcio Costa, 1997, p. 27. Founded in 1713 as Arraial do Tijuco, the town prospered as a result of the large amounts of diamonds found in the region. In 1831, it was granted city rights and renamed Vila de Diamantina. It was designated a national monument in 1938, and a UNESCO world heritage site in 1999. **58** The Modernists' position towards the colonial heritage was radically new, considering that as late as 1943 in his monumental work on Brazilian culture, Fernando de Azevedo wrote: 'It is, however, with the installation of the Portuguese court in Brazil [1808] that, properly speaking, the history of our culture begins, for, until this time, one cannot find anything but sporadic manifestations of exceptional figures, educated in Portugal and under foreign influence'; Azevedo, p. 236.

Lúcio Costa, 1922, watercolour of one of Diamantina's most celebrated icons, the nineteenth-century *passadiço*, a covered footbridge linking the eighteenth-century Casa da Glória with the nineteenth-century house across Rua da Glória, constructed following their conversion to an orphanage of the order of São Vicente de Paulo

IGREJA DE SÃO FRANCISCO, (1741-1774) S. J. D' EL-REI

Aleijadinho (Antônio Francisco Lisboa) and Francisco de Lima Cerqueira, Church of São Francisco de Assis, São João del Rei, Minas Gerais, 1774

tures in Brazil made easier the identification of the mixed with the national. The Pau-Brasil manifesto had defined the Modernist project, too, in terms of a desired hybridity, aiming 'to reconcile native culture with a renovated intellectual culture . . . in a sort of hybrid plot to ratify the ethnic miscegenation of the Brazilian people'.[59] In her 1929 painting *Antropofagia* (José and Paulina Nemirovsky Foundation, São Paulo), Tarsila do Amaral interlocked a female body with the characteristics of her earlier *A negra*, with the body of her *Abaporu*.

Tarsila do Amaral, *Antropofagia*, 1929, ink and oil on canvas, 126 × 142 cm, José and Paulina Nemirovsky Foundation, São Paulo

ticized, it was recognized as the locus of Brazilian high-art heritage. The Baroque monuments were seen as the zenith of successful mixing, the point when the European became truly Brazilian. The Barroco Mineiro provided historical evidence of the continuity of racial mixing and hybridity – the defining characteristics of Brazilian national identity. It also offered concrete evidence of the achievements of the mixed, the 'real' Brazilians. And the absence of any significant pre-Columbian or, rather, pre-Cabralian struc-

The Myths and Symbols of *Brasilidade*

Through Freyre's romantic eyes, the Brazilian mixture was seen to be characterized by a 'reciprocity between the cultures, and not a domination of one by the other'.[60] Brazilian society and culture were 'Hybrid from the beginning'; hybridity was pronounced the primordial hallmark of the nation.[61] Cultural miscegenation was endemic to the Portuguese settlers, who were new neither to a life in the tropics nor to a mixing with the 'Moorish' element – Lisbon, after all, had been an Islamic city for four centuries. And miscegenation had been the distinguishing feature of Portuguese colonization due to a lack of Portuguese women.[62]

Freyre's first two books dealt with the formation of Brazilian society and shaped the myths of Brazilian identity, exploring the

59 Benedito Nunes, quoted in Vianna, p. 74.   **60** Freyre, 1986, p. 422.
61 Freyre, 1956, p. 81.   **62** As José Augusto Pádua has shown, José Bonifácio, the so-called 'patriarch of Brazilian independence', 'may have been the first Brazilian thinker to praise racial miscegenation'. Bonifácio also defined the Portuguese colonizers as 'mestizos of alanians and other Tartarian hordes, mixed with suevians and visigods, moors, negroes and jews, and with romans and iberians'; Pádua, p. 23.

development of the characteristics of this society on the basis of the metaphor of the house – the seat of the all-powerful families he firmly established at the centre of Brazilian society. The first book, *Casa grande e senzala* (*The Masters and the Slaves*) was published in 1933 and is literally translated as *The Big House and the Slave Quarters*. Focusing on the first three centuries of colonial Brazilian society, which was feudal, agrarian and aristocratic, it stressed the importance of Brazil's African cultural heritage while also romanticizing Brazilian slavery. According to the novelist Jorge Amado, 'Gilberto's book dazzled the country.'[63] Following the model introduced by Francisco Adolfo de Varnhagen's *História geral do Brasil* (1857), Freyre thought of Brazil as a whole. His *Casa grande e senzala* established both the official version of Brazil's colonial history and an attractive and highly exportable nationalist ideology.

Freyre's second book, *Sobrados e mucambos* (*The Mansions and the Shanties*),[64] published in 1936, extended the domestic metaphor in a description of the second epoch in the formation of Brazilian society and civilization: the transformation of a rural, slave-holding, polygamous and authoritarian patriarchate into an urban social and racial democracy. It focused on nineteenth-century Brazilian cities, apparently dominated by what Freyre calls 'the most dynamic element in . . . the formation [of the Brazilian people]: the mulatto'.[65] *The Mansions and the Shanties* covered the period from the arrival of the Portuguese monarch in Rio de Janeiro in 1808 to the overthrow of the Brazilian emperor in 1889. Freyre's epic trilogy was completed in 1959 with the publication of his more controversial *Order and Progress* – the motto adopted by the republic on its foundation. Freyre's dated ideas and view of Brazil as a 'racial democracy' where discrimination is based on social class rather than colour still have tremendous currency in Brazil today, in spite of historical and demographic realities.[66]

In the 1930s, *mestiço* nationalism replaced earlier nationalist ideologies centring upon the supremacy of white colonial culture, and transformed miscegenation from Brazil's disgrace to her defin-

ing feature.[67] By the end of the Old Republic (1889–1930) and the beginning of the authoritarian Vargas regime (1930–45), all Brazil recognized the emblems of her national identity. In 1934, Cândido Portinari painted *Mestiço* (Pinacoteca do Estado de São Paulo). *Samba de morro* or *favela samba* became the symbol par excellence of the emerging 'hopeful fiction that Brazil has transcended race prejudice'.[68] A series of national icons became firmly established. Carnival, 'replete with African and Ameridian orgiastic survivals', especially that of Rio de Janeiro, acquired the status of the ultimate national celebration.[69] The black-bean *feijoada* of the black slaves, which Tarsila do Amaral had offered her Parisian guests at rue Hégésippe Moreau in the 1920s, was adopted as the national dish. *Guaraná*, black coffee and Parati *cachaça* (sugarcane liquor) became the national drinks, and guava paste and cheese the national dessert. Previously illegal and traditionally politicized, *capoeira* was pronounced by Vargas the national sport in 1937. The African religion Candomblé was decriminalized in 1938, and the syncretic religion of Umbanda was institutionalized, with the first Umbanda Congress held in Rio de Janeiro in 1941. In 1943, Vargas decreed 19 April the 'Day of the Indian' – a national holiday honouring the nation's aboriginal population.

The emphasis was on the Brazilianization of things black and to a lesser extent things Indian to produce an exportable *mestiço* culture. Ary Barroso's *samba-exaltação* 'Aquarela do Brasil' (1939) glorified the beauties of the land, and Freyre was delighted samba dance was 'rounded into something more Bahian than African, danced by Carmen Miranda [a European dressed as a black Baiana] to the applause of sophisticated international audiences'.[70] The mestiza Nossa Senhora da Conceição Aparecida was chosen as the patron saint of Brazil. The Mineiro sculptor and architect Aleijadinho, the natural son of a Portuguese master builder and an Afro-Brazilian slave, was consecrated as the paradigmatic Brazilian artist. Freyre even detected subversive 'anti-European' qualities in the work of this Antropofagist *avant la lettre* – 'an expression of social revolt and of the Brazilian native and

63 Jorge Amado, quoted in Vianna, p. 53. It is worth noting that Freyre dedicated his book to the physician Nina Rodrigues, Brazil's controversial first ethnographer and first theoretical racist. As Lilia Moritz Schwarcz points out, 'If *Casa-Grande & Senzala* actually did represent a critique of racial and evolutionist analytical models, in that the author introduced cultural arguments, it is necessary to state that Freyre changes the terms and reveals new theoretical connections, but still orders the races hierarchically. The white man is always the civilizing example, closely followed by the native Indian with his habits of hygiene and feeding, and the black with the "lubricious religious fervor". The whole cultural interchange is presented in a harmonious environment'; Schwarcz, 2003, p. 13.   **64** Freyre points out that he chose the African name for 'the type of house diametrically opposed to the *noble house* . . . because the proletarian or laboring sector of our principal patriarchal cities . . . seemed to me predominantly African in its cultural traits, including its technique in home building'; Freyre, 1986, pp. xvi–xvii.   **65** Freyre, 1986, p. xxiv. Skidmore notes that 'The practical effect of [Freyre's] analysis was not, however, to promote . . . a racial egalitarianism. Rather, it served to reinforce the whitening ideal by showing graphically that the (primarily white) elite had gained valuable cultural traits from their intimate contact with the African (and Indian, to a lesser extent)'; Skidmore, 1993, p. 192. In an interview published in 1970, Freyre declared: 'a racial democracy is developing in Brazil. It exists today, but it is not yet perfect'; Freyre, 1974, p. 75.   **66** In Brazil, the existence of racism has consistently been denied. Racism was finally declared a crime punishable by imprisonment only in the constitution of 1988.   **67** It is important to note that, although *mestiçagem* or hybridity is undeniably at the basis of Brazilian national identity construction and central to artistic resistance to colonialism, attitudes towards biological and cultural miscegenation and syncretism have changed in recent times, at least among progressive Brazilian academics and black anti-racist militants. 'Cultural syncretism and biological miscegenation are no longer fashionable, and sometimes not even politically correct,' Matthias Röhrig Assunção notes. 'Praise of miscegenation has been historically associated, in Brazil, with the ideology of whitening promoted by Brazilian intellectuals in answer to European theories of "scientific" racism', and remains linked to 'the country's long indulgence in the myth of racial democracy.' Assunção also notes counter-reactions: for Hermano Viana, for example, 'the valorization of miscegenation is one of the most powerful weapons to be used in the anti-racist battle, in Brazil and outside Brazil'; Assunção, pp. 158–59. See also Sansone.   **68** John Charles Chasteen, quoted in Vianna, p. xiv.   **69** Freyre, 1970, p. xix.   **70** Gilberto Freyre, quoted in Vianna, p. 62.

mestizo wish for independence from white or European masters and exploiters of slave labor'.[71] The Modernist pilgrims to Minas Gerais had greatly admired the work of this prolific mulatto artist, especially his magnificent soapstone sculptures of the twelve lesser prophets (1795–1805) in the forecourt or *adro* of the Santuário do Bom Jesus de Matosinhos (1757–90), in Congonhas do Campo.

'Of Brazil one thing is certain,' stated Freyre, 'the regions or areas of greatest miscegenation are those that have been most

Aleijadinho (Antônio Francisco Lisboa), prophet Ezechiel, 1795–1805, soapstone, Santuário de Bom Jesus de Matosinhos, Congonhas do Campo, Minas Gerais

productive of great men.'[72] Today, many a Brazilian boasts of a real or imaginary mixed lineage. In contrast to Euclides da Cunha (1866–1909), whose celebrated 1902 national epic *Os Sertões* (*Rebellion in the Backlands*) regarded miscegenation with suspicion, for Freyre, miscegenation led to the formation of 'the Brazilian, the ideal type of modern man for the tropics', biologically, psychologically, sociologically or culturally *mestiço*.[73] Da Cunha's 'mestizo – a hyphen between the races . . . is almost always an unbalanced type . . . a degenerate one, lacking the physical energy of his savage ancestors and without the intellectual elevation of his ancestors on the other side'. Freyre dismissed the 'racial pessimism' and 'rigid biologic determinism'[74] of Da Cunha's book, which had been seen as 'the Bible of Brazilian nationality'. Echoing the other major figure in the shaping of Brazil's roots, Sérgio Buarque de Holanda (1902–82),[75] Freyre exalted the cordial, charming mulatto, 'loving black beans and pineapple', 'the Brazilian with a dash of African blood or some African trace in his formation; not the pure white or "European"'. Asserting the 'triumph of the mestizo and, principally, of the mulatto, of the half-breed', he argued that this figure's qualities are superior to those of 'the white or near white'.[76]

Freyre's foundational mythology embraced all aspects of life: bodily features and personal qualities, gestures and laughter, dance, music and musical instruments, festivals, food, sport, linguistic traits, eating and sleeping habits, superstitions, dress, pets, plants, colours, architectural elements, saints, national artistic heroes, medicaments and more – all viewed as products of the transculturation of African with European and native cultures. However, the African element, Freyre discovered, came to Brazil with the Portuguese invaders and even with the Jesuit fathers. He contemplated 'the possible African origin of the Jesuit system . . . it would appear that even the Spiritual Exercises were assimilated by Loyola from African sources'.[77]

Le Corbusier, too, had fallen under the spell of the beauty of mulatto women, sketching them assiduously during his first visit to Rio de Janeiro. In a spirit of euphoria, with an 'engine of light in his heart' aboard the *Lutétia*, he wrote to his Brazilian benefactor, the coffee baron Paulo Prado:

> I said my farewell to the continent in a hotel in Copacabana, with a whole afternoon of caresses with Jandyra, a mulatto girl, whose body, I swear, is beautiful, pure, delicate, perfect and adorably young . . . Behold the miracle. Corbu's imagination embodies the whole of America in the perfect, pure body of a cook.[78]

Throughout the Vargas era, sociologists and anthropologists furnished scientific evidence that helped construct the tradition the Modernist artists had discovered and devoured in the field. Anthropophagy was followed by anthropology. The emerging

71 Freyre, 1963, p. 210.   **72** Freyre, 1986, p. 430.   **73** Freyre, 1956, p. 68. Da Cunha himself was a mestizo of indigenous descent. **74** Cunha, pp. 84–85.   **75** Sérgio Buarque de Holanda published his *Raízes do Brasil* (*Roots of Brazil*) in 1936. According to him, the Brazilian 'cordial man' was not merely a man of gentle manners but also a man who tends to transfer the habits and attitudes of the private into the public sphere and vice versa.   **76** Freyre, 1986, pp. 412–31.   **77** Freyre, 1956, p. 76. Niemeyer also insisted on the importance of an appreciation of 'the influence of African, Arab and Asiatic cultures on the European continent'; Niemeyer, 1977b, p. 34.   **78** Le Corbusier, quoted in Calil, pp. 570–71.

anthropologist Claude Lévi-Strauss and his wife Dina ventured into studies of popular culture at first, followed by a journey to the state of Mato Grosso in 1935–36 to peer over its Indian tribes.[79] In 1934, Freyre organized the First Afro-Brazilian Congress, in Recife. And in 1936, the Sociedade de Etnografia e Folclore was created, directed by Mário de Andrade and Dina Lévi-Strauss.

The golden anniversary of the abolition of 'the infamous trade' in 1938 was widely celebrated with state-sponsored events. At the football World Cup of the same year, Brazil sent a national team that was no longer all white. The definition of *brasilidade* became an official concern of the Vargas state. From that era onwards the building of state, nation and culture became closely linked processes in modern Brazilian history. The three elements that the pioneers of Brazilian Modernism had discovered 'rooted in the land of Brazil' and resolved to use for the concoction of the 'cannibalistic vaccine' were now being sanctioned as the legitimate ingredients of *brasilidade*. These were the popular with its semantic equivalents: the African, the Oriental and the Amerindian; the Baroque, associated with the colonial and the Portuguese or Luso-Catholic (also Antropofagist *avant la lettre*); and, last but not least, tropical nature. Freyre's grand narrative of the development of Luso-tropical civilization offered an elaborate formula that served to explain the successful mixing of these elements, expected to function as levers of cultural emancipation. His scientifically packaged and optimistic ideology was, furthermore, much more exportable than Antropofagia.

Modernism and Cultural Nationalism:
'The permanent transformation of the Tabu into a totem'

State ideology embraced Modernism and Modernist artists embraced the state project of cultural nationalism, although not its totalitarian principles. The aestheticization of the popular was followed by the popularization of the aesthetic under the auspices of Vargas's dictatorial Estado Nôvo from 1937 to 1945. The Ministry of Education and Public Health was responsible for the creation of a national consciousness and for cultural *renovação*. Gustavo Capanema, its influential head from 1932 to 1945, turned to Mário de Andrade to draft a proposal for a new federal agency responsible for the protection of Brazil's cultural heritage, the Serviço do Patrimônio Histórico e Artístico Nacional (SPHAN), established by law in 1937.

Through the appropriation and inventive definition of the national past, European models were rendered harmless – both those of twentieth-century vanguards and those of remote golden ages and their renaissances. Modern Brazilians were emerging free of all foreign idols. With the upsurge of nationalism that followed the so-called revolution of 1930, the aestheticization of the

national had given way to the nationalization of the aesthetic. Modern Brazil was determined to build her own civilization, while at the same time preserving – and controlling – the memory of her colonial past. In 1936, the founding director of SPHAN, the Mineiro Rodrigo Melo Franco de Andrade, declared: 'The poetry of a Brazilian church of the colonial period is, for us, more moving than the Parthenon. And any statue that Aleijadinho carved into soapstone for the churchyard of Congonhas [do Campo] speaks to our imagination more loudly than Michelangelo's *Moses*.'[80] Six decades later, Niemeyer would confess: 'I am much more moved by an old colonial fazenda than a European medieval castle or a palace of the Renaissance.'[81]

The 1929 coffee crisis had obliged Tarsila do Amaral to leave her plantation and take a job as director of restoration at the São Paulo State Museum. Carnival was regulated. Black culture and what remained of the indigenous peoples were dealt with as ethnographic material. Colonialism was interpreted as a gift or, at least, as bearing ennobling gifts: language, religion, blood. The colonial historic and artistic heritage was catalogued, preserved, exhibited in the newly founded museums, decolonized, nationalized and thus transformed into an equally harmless ally in the creation of a national modern artistic expression. It all conformed to the principles of the 'Manifesto Antropófago': 'Cannibalism. The permanent transformation of the Tabu into a totem.'[82] In 1940, plaster casts of Aleijadinho's prophets were put on permanent display at the headquarters of SPHAN in the Modernist Ministry of Education and Public Health, and the first national park was founded in Itatiaia, the Atlantic Rain Forest near Rio de Janeiro. Cannibalization was directed towards the foreign as well as the local, the present as well as the past. The national artistic vanguard consumed all. They feasted on the European, the popular, the African, the Indian, the Brazilian Baroque and tropical nature. The Modernist Antropofagist banquet was Lucullian.

Between 1930 and 1945, Villa-Lobos composed *Bachianas Brasileiras*, a series of nine suites combining the music of Johann Sebastian Bach with Brazilian folk and popular music.[83] Mário de Andrade's proposal to catalogue and register works of popular culture together with those of high art was eventually dropped, but in 1937 the authoritarian Estado Nôvo extended state protection over 'open areas and locales especially blessed by Nature'.[84] Nature acquired the status of 'sacred heritage', fulfilling the wishes of the 'patriarch of independence' José Bonifácio de Andrade

79 See one of the testimonies of this expedition: Lévi-Strauss, 1965. 80 Rodrigo Melo Franco de Andrade, quoted in Williams, p. 105. 81 Niemeyer, 1993c, p. 75. 82 Oswald de Andrade, 2000, p. 591. 83 The term 'Bachianas' brought together Johann Sebastian Bach with the Baianas, African women of Bahia, some of whom made their way to Rio de Janeiro following the abolition of slavery and played a key role in the development of samba music and dance. 84 Estado Nôvo Constitution, quoted in Williams, p. 96.

e Silva (1763–1838, known as José Bonifácio),[85] and was officially included in the list of what Rodrigo Melo Franco de Andrade called 'the identity documents of the Brazilian nation'.[86] The term 'colonial' emerged free of negative connotations, most often signifying the 'traditional'. Things Portuguese or Luso-colonial had been redefined as Luso-Brazilian or Luso-tropical in the nationalist spirit.[87] Nature and the Luso-tropical cultural tradition, however imbued with the African or Indian Other, finally emerged as the privileged *loci* of *brasilidade*.

The 'drawing room and the jungle': Brazil's Tropical Modernism

The godfather of Luso-Brazilian or Luso-tropical culture, Gilberto Freyre, praised the Portuguese colonizers' 'predispositions of race, mesology, and culture', which helped them overcome 'those conditions of climate and soil that were unfavorable to the settlement of Europeans in the tropics,' stressing that Brazil was 'essentially tropical' or 'oriental', and in this sense different from Europe.[88] Freyre's *cultura luso-brasileira* may be described in Jonathan Friedman's words as 'a typical product of Western modernity that consists in transforming difference into essence'.[89] He celebrated the ecologically and culturally successful adaptation of the Portuguese colonists in the tropical environment, 'to be explained, to a large extent, in terms of a constant disposition on their part to adapt European values and European techniques to tropical conditions, going so far as to repudiate some of the European values and techniques and to adopt tropical ones instead'. A few years later, he observed emerging in Brazil a 'new synthesis of culture . . . at once European and tropical . . . European and Amerindian, boreal and tropical, and consequently really universalistic in its main designs and techniques . . . a combination of nature and culture'.[90]

The exaltation of tropical nature functioned also as a critique of the contemporaneous European exaltation of the machine and a demystification of industrial metropolitan civilization. The Antropofagists wished for a dialogue between the 'drawing room and the jungle', to use the words of their founding leader, rather than 'a match . . . of the "affirmation of mankind" against or with

the "presence of nature" ', like the one Le Corbusier dreamt of in the presence of Rio.[91] Oswald de Andrade's utopia, 'Pindorama matriarchy' envisaged a 'synthesis of a matriarchal production system centred on the life cycles of nature, on the body and on desire and, on the other hand, modern techno-scientific development'.[92] And, in the third book of his trilogy, Freyre emphasized the characteristically Brazilian 'blend of reason and emotion', of Apollonian and Dionysian elements.[93]

The sixteenth-century 'discovery' of the New World had also been chronicled as the discovery of a Garden of Eden, defined by orgiastic nature, free love and innocent nudity. The first chronicler of Brazil, Pêro Vaz de Caminha, scribe of the Portuguese fleet in the command of Pedro Álvares Cabral, marvelled to King Manuel of Portugal: 'Sire, the innocence of Adam himself was not greater than these people's.' In a letter, one enthusiastic early Jesuit missionary concluded: 'Anyone who elects to live in a terrestrial paradise must come to live in Brazil.' The glorification of the land and its abundant fertile beauty in nativist literature only increased in the course of the following centuries. In 1730, Sebastião da Rocha Pita's history of Brazil spoke of 'the earthly paradise regained', a country of 'all treasures . . . nectar and . . . ambrosia, the liquor and meat the cultured populace offered to its false gods'.[94]

Eighteenth-century Brazilian naturalists were keen collectors of indigenous plants, from the Amazon to Rio de Janeiro. Nineteenth-century European curiosity and enthusiasm for the exotic led to the organization of a number of scientific expeditions to the wilderness of imperial Brazil, triumphantly concluded with the collection of countless plants transplanted to the greenhouses of the Old World. The encounter of the European naturalists with the exuberant tropical nature of Brazil led to the reimagining of Brazilian geography and the reinvention of the land of exotic natural beauty – a seductive landscape offering the Europeans a wealth of images of the Other. Cultural and political Brazilian Romanticism glorified the 'virgin jungle' of Brazil, with the biggest river in the world and the most beautiful flora. Dom Pedro II's imperial mantle was embroidered with coffee and tobacco leaves, his mantelet made of toucan breast feathers, and a gilded serpent graced his sceptre.[95]

The twentieth-century Brazilian artists' rediscovery or reinvention of Brazil involved a rediscovery of a lost exotic paradise, which was also found threatened and in need of redemption. Otherness was found in the land as well as in its people, but, to repeat, the Brazilians turned their own Otherness into a special kind of talisman. Brazilian Otherness presented no danger; it had, after all, been identified by, and thus reduced to the categories of, the white cultured elite, which viewed the Brazilian Other from an unchallenged central position. Images of lush tropical nature were added to the Antropofagist totemic structure and served to further Brazilianize Brazilian Modernist art.

85 José Bonifácio, quoted in Pádua, p. 26.   **86** Rodrigo Melo Franco de Andrade, quoted in Williams, p. 90.   **87** Freyre's notion of Luso-tropicalism was fully developed by the 1950s. It is important to bear in mind that, for Freyre, Luso-tropical civilization is 'a particular form of accomplishment of the Portuguese in the world'; Freyre, 1963, p. 154, from a chapter entitled 'Brazil as a European Civilization in the Tropics'. Freyre defined what he considered to be the true expressions of the national culture of Brazil also as 'Classico-Baroque' or 'Euro-tropical'.   **88** Freyre, 1956, pp. 20–24.   **89** Friedman, p. 80.   **90** Freyre, 1963, p. 31.   **91** Oswald de Andrade, quoted in Subirats, p. 527; Le Corbusier, 1991, p. 236.   **92** Subirats, p. 527. Pindorama is the Tupi word for the land that became known as Brazil.   **93** Freyre, 1970, p. xxiii.   **94** Pêro Vaz de Caminha, Jesuit missionary; Sebastião da Rocha Pita, quoted in Burns, 1968, pp. 15, 13, 21.   **95** Schwarcz, 2004, p. 108. illustrations pp. 3, 61, 106.

In 1900, Afonso Celso de Assis Figueiredo Júnior (1860–1938), one of the founders of the Academia Brasileira de Letras (1897), had published his chauvinist paean *Porque me ufano do meu país* (*Why I Am Proud of My Country*), returning to the paradisiacal metaphor and introducing the notion of Brazil as the land of the future and the Brazilians as a chosen people: 'Let us have confidence in ourselves, let us have confidence in the future, and let us, above all, have confidence in God . . . If He has been especially magnanimous in his gifts to Brazil, it is because He has reserved for us an exalted destiny.'[96] Foreign visitors rhapsodized about the land of all fruits. Blaise Cendrars reported that, at the threshold of his first sojourn in his 'Utopialand', as the ship approached the coast, the passengers exclaimed: 'This is paradise on earth!' The Italian poet Giuseppe Ungaretti evoked images of abundance and innocent nudity: 'Amidst this new, delirious natural environment the Blacks [lived] apparently happily, deprived of nothing, with no need for clothing to cover themselves, able to obtain nourishment from the freely growing banana trees, always ready for dancing, religion, superstition, sorcery.'[97] The myth of a virgin land of unstained joy and boundless beauty was back with the promise for a radiant future. For the Austrian writer Stefan Zweig (1881–1942), Brazil was a powerful revelation; what had been to him a *terra incognita* was found to be 'destined undoubtedly to play one of the most important parts in the future development of our world'. In sharp contrast to brutal Nazi reality, he found in Brazil 'all these races – visibly distinct by their colour alone – liv[ing] in fullest harmony with one another'.[98] He subtitled his 1941 book on Brazil 'Land of the Future'.

Tarsila do Amaral, 'the most Brazilian of modern painters', included tropical flora and exotic creatures in her Pau-Brasil paintings (1923–27). In *Abaporu* the figure's only companion is 'a cactus bursting into absurd flower' and she spoke of this painting as 'a concentration of Brazil, the "green hell" '.[99] Lascivious Brazilian verdure signified a kind of infernal paradise; it promised tropical luxuriance, innocence and sensuality while also hiding danger, hostile savages, wild animals, insects and diseases. Tarsila do Amaral's exotic themes had enchanted her Parisian audience in the 1920s. Lush tropical nature promised excessive sensations. It was vigorous, bursting with energy. It was the abode of that distinctly Brazilian Dionysian spirit which, by 1970, Freyre recognized as having been successfully injected in all things imported from Europe, from Catholicism and democracy to *futebol*: 'the Dionysiac style

of football brilliantly exemplified by Pelé (in contrast to the originally Apollonian style of this sport imparted by the British)'.[100] In unison, national ideologists and Modernist artists – or Brazilian moderns, as they preferred to portray themselves – preached an Afro-Dionysian subversion of both their European ancestry and European rationalist catechism. To instil the Dionysian or the tropical became another form of Antropofagia or carnivalization. The spirit of Brazilian nature exoticized and thus Brazilianized imported alien bodies. Tropical Modernism was another name for the Antropofagist product.

'Tropicalism and discipline':
Towards a New Architecture, Brazilian and Modern

It was in the field of architecture that the idea of tropical nature as an essential part of the Brazilian mixture and an element with the power to Brazilianize foreign imports played a crucial role. In 1925, while still a fourth-year student in Rome, Rino Levi (1901–65) published in a São Paulo newspaper one of the earliest Brazilian texts advocating a new architecture for a new age. He also called for a new 'aesthetics of the city', which, he argued, in the case of Brazil, needs to be 'a city aesthetics of a Brazilian nature. In our climate, our natural setting and customs, our cities should have a different character from those of Europe.' He stressed the importance of the Brazilian natural environment as the basis on which to excel in the field of architecture and urban design: 'I believe that our flourishing vegetation and our incomparable natural beauties can and should suggest something original to our artists, giving our cities a charm of liveliness and colour unequalled in the world.'[101]

The same year, the Russian émigré Gregori Ilitch Warchavchik, trained in Odessa and Rome, published his article 'On Modern Architecture' in São Paulo and Rio de Janeiro, putting forward the most pure, orthodox principles of machine-age architecture, distinguished by reinforced concrete and forms based on logic, function and economy. For the pioneer of architectural Modernism in Brazil, modern 'machines for living in' needed only to be rational: the 'beauty of the façade must come from the rationality of the plan, just as the form of a machine is determined by the mechanism that is its heart'. In contrast to Walter Gropius, Warchavchik recommended the study of historical architecture, but urged that modern architects should 'not only stop copying

96 Afonso Celso, quoted in Skidmore, 1993, p. 100. **97** Blaise Cendrars and Giuseppe Ungaretti, quoted in Calil, pp. 564, 565. **98** Zweig, pp. 2, 7. In 1969, Norma Evenson explained that 'One of the peculiarities of Brazil is that in spite of the prevailing mythology of boundless resources and untapped wealth, Brazilians have yet to take possession of their land. The great spontaneous migration which populated the United States had no Brazilian counterpart, and today one might consider Brazil the world's oldest land of the futre [sic]'; Evenson, 1969, p. 19. **99** Tarsila do Amaral, p. 588. *Inferno Verde* (*Green Hell*) was the title of Alberto Rangel's Indianist short stories, published in 1907. The architect Flávio de

Carvalho wanted to install red lamps in the swimming pool of his Fazenda da Capuava (1938). 'So that when you dive in, you feel you are entering hell!'; quoted in Leite, p. 213. **100** Freyre, 1970, p. xxvi. In 1993, Pelé (Edson Arantes do Nascimento) became the first black Cabinet member in Brazil when President Fernando Henrique Cardoso appointed him minister of sport, a post he created for him. **101** Levi, p. 620. Levi undertook a number of study trips, together with Roberto Burle Marx, examining and collecting indigenous Brazilian plants. He also transformed the garden of the house he constructed for himself in São Paulo in 1944 into a 'small laboratory'; quoted in Anelli, p. 92.

the old styles but also stop thinking in them', in order to achieve their task 'in this age of petty capitalism': 'the construction of a house as comfortable and cheap as possible'.[102]

Over the following years, Warchavchik designed a series of houses which, in a manner befitting an ideology of hybridity, were celebrated not for the purity of their Modernist principles, but for their synthesis of 'tropicalism and discipline'.[103] Their gardens of cacti and palms, praised by Mário de Andrade, were designed by Mina Klabin Segall Warchavchik (1896–1969), Gregori's wife, who came from a rich industrial Paulista family and was well acquainted with the proponents of Brazilian Modernism. Through her pioneering work, she is responsible for the rehabilitation of the flora earlier Europeanizing tastes had marginalized.[104] From this point onwards, tropical gardens became the hallmark of Brazilian architectural Modernism, providing evidence of a continuation of the traditions of the old domestic patriarchal architecture observed by Freyre.[105] With reference to Warchavchik's houses, Gio Ponti commented in *Domus* in 1933 on the great adaptability of 'the forms of the architecture of rationalism . . . to hot countries, magnificently framed by tropical vegetation'.[106] The architect and critic Renato Anelli proposes that Warchavchik's gardens did not function as mere background to the Modernist forms; he believes that the latter were at times distorted in order to achieve a fusion of background and figure.[107]

Gregori Warchavchik is also to be credited with the first garden terraces – another feature that would become characteristic of Brazilian Modernism in the following years. Tropical flora was, for Warchavchik, a complement to the new architecture in the way plaster mouldings were to the architecture of the past. He even recommended covering the façades of the houses on São Paulo's prestigious Avenida Paulista with vegetation.[108] Flávio de Carvalho accompanied his 1928 entry to the competition for the Columbus Memorial Lighthouse in Santo Domingo, Dominican

Republic, with an allusion to the native Marajoara from Marajó island in the Brazilian state of Pará, whose pottery had inspired a number of Modernist decorative artefacts, arguing that 'The Marajoara were freed from all academic restrictions and inspired themselves in the simplicity of nature and in the virile strength of the tropical forest.'[109]

Warchavchik's first house (1927–28) was built for himself and his wife on Rua Santa Cruz in the Vila Mariana suburb of São Paulo. Recognized as the first Modernist house in Latin America, it represented an attempt to promote the image of the new architecture, rather than the materials, construction methods and skills, which, to its designer's regret, had not yet become available in Brazil. It was probably because of its disguised load-bearing brick walls and hidden pitched and tiled roof that Lúcio Costa spoke of the 'attractive romanticism of the house in Vila Mariana'.[110]

Warchavchik's second house, on Rua Itápolis in the affluent garden suburb of Pacaembú, São Paulo, for Dr Cândido da Silva, was opened to the public in March and April 1930. This *Exposição de uma Casa Modernista* featured specially designed garden and furniture, artworks by Brazilian Modernists as well as a small bronze by Jacques Lipchitz, cushions by Sonia Delaunay and carpets from the Bauhaus. Although the architect's own purist manifesto of 1925 had made no reference to any of the familiar elements of *brasilidade*, the local press reported that the Casa Modernista admitted 'over 20,000 people to the most complete exhibition of modern Brazilian art'.[111] And, in the leaflet handed out to visitors, the educationalist Anísio Teixeira noted: 'In this land we are all foreigners . . . Warchavchik is Russian, and never have I had a stronger impression of a Brazilian house than when . . . I visited his home with the strong clear lines, constructed completely in cement, iron and glass, within a frame of gigantic national cacti.'[112] In the consciousness of their nationalist Brazilian audience, these indigenous giants became an Antropofagist tool that devoured not only the cosmopolitan architecture but its foreign authorship too.

Another Brazilian element of the house is said to have displeased Le Corbusier, who visited it in 1929. Warchavchik attested that, upon seeing the internal walls and ceilings painted in various colours, Le Corbusier remarked: 'Il vous manque du blanc.'[113] Nevertheless, Le Corbusier invited the Russian architect to represent South America on CIAM. In 1930, upon the request of Sigfried Giedion, CIAM's secretary-general, Warchavchik sent a report to CIAM's third meeting in Brussels, part of which was published in *Cahiers d'Art*. This was the first article on modern Brazilian architecture to appear in a foreign journal.[114] Alberto Sartoris included Warchavchik's houses in his *Gli Elementi dell'Architettura Funzionale* of 1931, with contributions by Filippo Tommaso Marinetti, Le Corbusier and the Italian architect Lina Bo Bardi (1914–92).

102 Warchavchik, 2000, pp. 620–21. Warchavchik's article appeared first in Italian under the title 'Futurismo' in the Paulista periodical *Il Piccolo*, on 14 June 1925. On 1 November 1925 it appeared in Portuguese in the Rio broadsheet *Correio da Manhã*, entitled 'Acerca da arquitetura moderna'. During the Semana de Arte Moderna of 1922, the two small exhibitions of architecture had displayed neocolonial designs. **103** Mário de Andrade, quoted in Fraser, 2000a, p. 168. **104** A precedent had already been set by the French hydraulic engineer and amateur botanist Auguste François-Marie Glaziou in the renovation of public squares and parks in Rio, commissioned by Emperor Dom Pedro II. Glaziou had mixed non-native plants with those he collected himself in his numerous expeditions in the hinterland of Brazil; Vaccarino, 2002, p. 211. **105** 'The Brazilian garden', argued Freyre, 'as long as it kept to its Portuguese tradition, was one in which the human, practical quality predominated, reminiscent of the Chinese. In contrast to the formal French or Italian type, it was irregular, varied, full of surprises'; Freyre, 1986, p. 152. **106** Gio Ponti, quoted in Anelli, p. 86. **107** Anelli, p. 88. **108** Fraser, 2000a, p. 167. **109** Flávio de Carvalho, quoted in Vaccarino, 2002, p. 215. **110** Lúcio Costa, 'Muita construção, alguma arquitetura e um milagre' (1951), in Lúcio Costa, 1997, p. 167. **111** Martins, 2000, p. 579 and p. 584, n. 19. **112** Anísio Teixeira, quoted in Fraser, 2000a, p. 168. It is worth noting that, at the time, half of the adult population of São Paulo was foreign born. **113** 'White is lacking' – a rather surprising remark from Le Corbusier, who had already used colour extensively himself at his Pessac project (Quartier Moderne Frugès, 1924–26). The comment is reported by Costa, who was given the story by Warchavchik; Lúcio Costa, 'Gregori Warchavchik', in Lúcio Costa, 1997, p. 72. **114** Martins, 2006, pp. 27, 187, n. 26.

Gregori Ilitch Warchavchik, Warchavchik House on Rua Santa Cruz, Vila Mariana, São Paulo, 1927–28

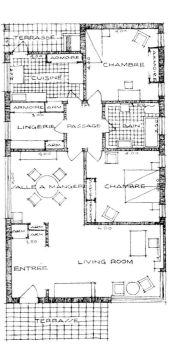

Gregori Ilitch Warchavchik, Dr Cândido da Silva House on Rua Itápolis, Pacaembú, São Paulo, 1930; street elevation and ground floor plan

The presence of Frank Lloyd Wright added prestige to the inauguration of Warchavchik's Nordshield House on Rua Tonelero, Copacabana (1931, demolished 1954), which was also opened to the public and hailed as 'the first Modernist house' in Rio de Janeiro. The local press reported that the American architect predicted: 'With a little effort and imagination, directed on the path along which Mr Gregori is moving, Brazil could have its own modern and rational architecture.'[115] In the city that became the epicentre of the 1930s state-sanctioned cultural *renovação*, Warchavchik collaborated with Lúcio Costa on the Alfredo Schwartz House on Rua Raul Pompéia, in Rio de Janeiro (1932, demolished), also the scene of the debut roof garden of Roberto Burle Marx, the landscape architect who would be acclaimed by the American Institute of Architects as 'the real creator of the modern garden'.[116]

According to Costa, he and Warchavchik first used colour externally in the Schwartz House and in the group of workers' houses they designed in the same year in Gamboa, Rio de Janeiro: brown and salmon pink, in the first; brown and green, in the second.[117] The Brazilian architects' subversion of the mythologized white walls of architectural Modernism had, notwithstanding Le Corbusier's comments on the Casa Modernista, been preceded by Le Corbusier and Pierre Jeanneret's application of colour on the exterior of their Weißenhofsiedlung houses in Stuttgart in 1927. But it is the association with local precedents, the strong colours of colonial city mansions described by Freyre, and 'the shacks of saffron and ochre among the greens of the hillside favelas, under cabraline blue', of Oswald de Andrade's Pau-Brasil manifesto, that must have pleased Tarsila do Amaral.[118] She had earlier gone through the experience of rediscovering colour herself: 'In Minas I found the colours that I had adored as a child. Afterwards they taught me that they were ugly and provincial. I followed the dull routine of refined taste . . . But later I avenged myself for that oppression, introducing them in my paintings: very pure blue, violet pink, bright yellow, still green.'[119] Freyre would later express his approval of Costa's 'assimilation of those Moorish and Arabic colors that the Portuguese so quickly adopted in the arts from his nearest non-European neighbor.'[120] Costa's application of bold colour on the exterior of Rio's first bourgeois apartment blocks in Parque Eduardo Guinle (1948–54), Freyre argued, demonstrated that he had successfully 'associat[ed] his modernism with the Moorish, Portuguese, Brazilian tradition of freely using tropical, vivid

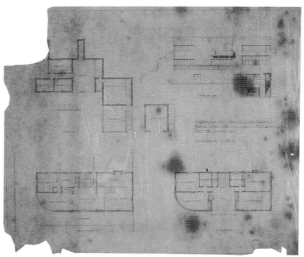

Gregori Ilitch Warchavchik, Nordshield House on Rua Tonelero, Copacabana, Rio de Janeiro, 1931, demolished 1954

115 Frank Lloyd Wright, quoted in Irigoyen, p. 151.　**116** Vaccarino, 2000a, p. 9.　**117** Lúcio Costa, 'Gregori Warchavchik', in Lúcio Costa, 1997, p. 72.　**118** Freyre, 1986, p. 158; Oswald de Andrade, 1989, p. 310. **119** Tarsila do Amaral, p. 587.　**120** Freyre, 1964, pp. 12–13. See also Gilberto Freyre, 'Color and Anticolor in the Forming of Brazil' (1963), in Freyre, 1974, pp. 6–7.

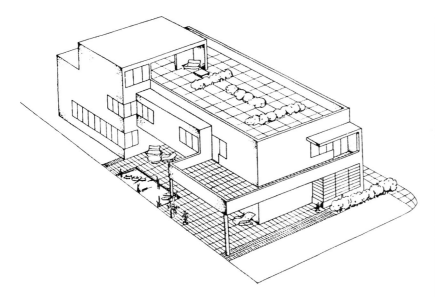

Gregori Ilitch Warchavchik and Lúcio Costa, Schwartz House on Rua Raul Pompéia, Rio de Janeiro, 1932, demolished

colors, and not only the conventional blues and greens of tiles (*azulejos*) with religious motifs'.[121] The new architecture was slowly finding its national colours and, faithful to the Antropofagist strategy, was using them to contaminate dull Old World prototypes.

Roberto Burle Marx is known to have come to an appreciation of the Brazilian ingredients of his art during a European sojourn. In the Dalhem Botanical Gardens of Berlin in 1928 he discovered the 'disquieting beauty of cacti'.[122] In this 'extraordinary garden', Burle Marx saw, 'for the first time, a large quantity of Brazilian plants being used for landscape design purposes. We Brazilians were not using these plants', attested Burle Marx, 'because we considered them vulgar'.[123] Cacti and other succulent plants were darlings of European Modernists, even in countries like Denmark. For his first public gardens, created in 1934–36 in the city of Recife – 'the milieu of . . . [Freyre's] *Casa grande e senzala*', as Burle Marx pointed out – he favoured the *mandacarus* cacti, which had framed Tarsila do Amaral's *Abaporu*. 'The cacti corresponded to our flora of the *caatinga*,' Burle Marx explained, 'the arid region of our Northeast, made famous by Euclides da Cunha in the book *Os sertões*' that identified the poverty-stricken Northeast region with the real, pure Brazilian world.[124]

The twenty-six-year-old Burle Marx named his second garden in Recife Euclides da Cunha Square (1935). For this cactus garden

Roberto Burle Marx, Euclides da Cunha Square cactus garden, Recife, 1935

he undertook several excursions to bring plants from the dry *caatinga*. At the water gardens of Casa Forte (1935), another old square of Recife, he used, for the first time, the Amazonian water lily (*Victoria regia* or *Victoria amazonica*) with giant floating leaves and huge fragrant flowers that change colour as they close through the night, from white to pink to deep carmine. A heated pond with Amazonian water lilies had been the main attraction of the exoticist Brazilian Pavilion at the Exposition Universelle of 1889 in Paris.

121 Freyre, 1963, pp. 234–35. Though Freyre does not name Costa's apartment blocks, he is probably referring to the Edifícios Nova Cintra, Bristol and Caledônia, in Parque Eduardo Guinle, which later provided a model for the residential *superquadras* of Brasília. Several elements used there – vivid colours, blue-and-white ceramic tiles, lattice-work (*muxarabi*), open ceramic blocks (related to the *combogó* of North African origin) for increased privacy in balconies – were extremely popular among Brazilian Modernist architects. **122** Bardi, 1964, p. 14. **123** Burle Marx, 2003, p. 298. **124** Hamerman, pp. 169, 167.

Roberto Burle Marx, Casa Forte water garden, Recife, 1935

In the decades after his first experiments, Roberto Burle Marx made extensive use of traditional crafts like lattice-work and, most frequently, ceramic glazed tiles – both reminders of Portugal's Arab heritage. Freyre saw in Burle Marx 'an artist whose boldness as an experimentalist [was] moderated by his conviction that the patriarchal past of Brazil was creative and not negative'.[125] In accordance with contemporary strategies of Brazilianization, Burle Marx's gardens were welcomed for their de-Europeanization and re-Orientalization of the Brazilian landscape. In Freyre's nationalist scheme, it was the Oriental element of Brazilian architecture and landscape that had been endangered by nineteenth-century Westernizing modernization. The 'forms and colors of the Orient' had stamped the Brazilian landscape for long centuries, he argued; they had become the distinguishing forms and colours of the Brazilian mixture. For Freyre, the trees from Asia and Africa that

had been acclimatized in Brazil were the trees of the traditional patriarchal landscape: the Indian coconut palm, the mango, the jackfruit, the tamarind or the cinnamon tree of Ceylon, which 'rival the native ones in luxuriance and productivity'. The landscape of Brazil, that is, had been successfully hybridized, and not even the nativist cult of the indigenous had championed native trees and plants, wrote Freyre.[126]

It was this mixed botanical geography of Brazil that in the next decades would be re-created in Burle Marx's gardens and would become the legitimate physical framework and companion – an indispensable element – of Brazilian Modernist architecture, 'combining tropical experience with European science'.[127] The most celebrated import to Brazil, the imperial palm (*Roystonea oleraceœ*), introduced in the Botanical Garden of Rio de Janeiro by Prince Dom João VI in 1808, became known as the Brazilian

125 Freyre, 1963, p. 253. Moorish *azulejos* were first imported into Portugal from Seville at the beginning of the sixteenth century. Although their name is usually associated with the Portuguese word for blue, 'azul', it is of Arab origin. According to one theory, it derives from 'al zulaicj', Arabic for a small, smooth, polished stone.   **126** Freyre, 1986, pp. 291–94. At the stucco ceilings of the imperial summer palace of Petrópolis (1845–50), Porto Alegre –

the nineteenth-century Brazilian artist 'known for introducing Brazilian motifs into painting and architecture' – had combined classical models with 'pineapples, cashew-fruit, *araçás*, Brazil cherries (*pitangas*), and guavas'. In the garden, the Frenchman Jean-Baptiste Binot had mixed Brazilian varieties with 'Australian palms, Indian cedars, *incensos*, and Madagascan trees'; Schwarcz, 2004, p. 177.   **127** Freyre, 1963, p. 21.

Imperial palm alley, Rio de Janeiro Botanical Garden. Imported by Prince Dom João VI in 1808, the imperial palm (*Roystonea oleraceæ*) became known as the Brazilian columnar order.

columnar order. Imperial palm colonnades were a favourite of both nineteenth- and twentieth-century landscape gardeners in Brazil, who, according to José Lins do Rego, deployed 'the rigorous discipline of palm alleys to tame the exuberance of tropical vegetation'.[128]

Apprehensively, Pietro Maria Bardi reports that 'Neutra had said to Roberto [Burle Marx]: "I find no roots of the past in your art, which is absolutely original".'[129] Richard Neutra's remark reflected the persisting view of Brazil as the land of the future, the tabula rasa, the ideal receptacle of all things new and modern. Remembering the time when she first arrived in Rio de Janeiro from

the Old World in 1946, Lina Bo Bardi echoed Goethe's description of America as a land with 'no ruined castles': 'I met some amazing people: Oscar Niemeyer, Lucio Costa, Candido Portinari, a group of intelligent and formidable young people, and on top of that there were no ruins in Rio.'[130] Lina Bo Bardi met the leaders of the group of Brazilian architects and artists who had embarked on the process of giving material form to Brazil's future. From their point of view, the task weighing on their shoulders was twofold: to construct the future in agreement with the sanitized and legitimized version of the past, and to furnish what would eventually become Brazil's mythical past – in short, to build the glorious monuments of the land of the future. It may be partly as a result of this aspiration that today Brazil's twentieth-century monuments, primarily in Brasília, still function as universal sources of futurist imagery.[131]

In a text published in 1936, which in many ways set the agenda for the development of Brazilian architectural Modernism, Costa defended the 'Reasons of the New Architecture' against the accusation of 'internationalism'. He argued that the internationalization of architecture is not a new phenomenon; it started at the time of the Renaissance and 'culminated in the classicism of the 18th century and the academicism that followed it'. He proposed the Modernist architecture of reinforced concrete – 'linked . . . to the purest Mediterranean traditions' – as a better medium of national expression than any form of Westernizing internationalist classicism.[132] Brazilian Modernist architects like Lúcio Costa severed their ties with this past of Westernizing classicism but they still appealed to the Mediterranean *Ursprung* of Western civilization. To the nationalist project they contributed their versions of Brazilian architectural history and tradition as well as a new architecture, characterized by a desire for emancipation from Western prototypes, strengthening local historical continuity. Costa even argued that the aesthetic possibilities of Modernist architecture attuned it with that of the colonial tradition on account of the affinities between buildings in reinforced concrete and those in wattle and daub, especially since both distinguished between load-bearing and space-defining elements.[133] Reyner Banham commented on Brazil's '*national* style of modern architecture' that it carried the Corbusian forms 'to a degree of freedom so marked and so personal that the Italian critic Gillo Dorfles has with some justification termed it Neo-Baroque'.[134]

Belle époque propaganda had promoted Brazil as a 'new country without history or traditions, where a new nation is rising

128 Rego, p. 10.   129 Richard Neutra, quoted in Bardi, 1964, p. 12.
130 Lina Bo Bardi, quoted in Olivia de Oliveira, p. 230. Goethe's poem
of 1827 cited in Honour, p. 248.   131 See also Maak, pp. 69–76.
132 Lúcio Costa, 2000, p. 628. The text was developed over the previous
couple of years.   133 Niemeyer, on the other hand, saw wattle and
daub as being as rigid as steel construction, in contrast to the plastic freedom allowed by reinforced concrete.   134 Banham, 1975, p. 39.

without any aristocracy or any prejudices'.[135] In 1924, Blaise Cendrars echoed the enthusiasm:

SÃO PAULO
I adore this city
São Paulo has a place in my heart
Here there is no tradition
No prejudice
No ancient or modern
All that matters is this furious appetite this absolute confidence this optimism this daring this toil this labour this speculation which construct ten houses an hour in all styles . . .
With no concern other than to keep up with the statistics to plan for the future comfort utility increase in value and to attract massive immigration
All countries
All nations[136]

Yet the first half of the twentieth century witnessed the Brazilians arduously constructing their version of their national past. While foreign sojourners continued to admire and envy Brazil for being a land free of oppressive traditions and haunting venerable ruins, Brazilians were keenly weaving the threads binding Modernist efforts with the images of colonial, patriarchal Brazil. In fact, Brazil was not a land without history or prejudice but her history was hardly perceived as a burden by those devoted to the moulding of her future in the sense that they did not fear their deeds would prove them unworthy of their illustrious ancestors. In twentieth-century Brazil, confidence in the future emerged as a consequence of a new confidence in the past.

Brazilian Modernist artists rejected the efforts of their immediate predecessors and conservative contemporaries who wished to modernize Brazil in a manner that would render it dependent upon a foreign history and a domineering culture. But these Modernists spared no effort in the construction of a national past in the image and likeness of an anticipated national future and vice versa. In this sense, the Brazilian nationalist Modernist project perceived no conflict between past and future, tradition and modernity. On the contrary, the invention of a tradition recognizable by all Brazilians as their own was a prerequisite for Brazil's entry into the world of modern nations. Debate focused on the legitimacy of different versions of the national past or on the direction of the future, but past and future were not perceived as antagonistic. They were imagined concurrently and in similar terms.

The Brazilian tradition is a Modernist product, configured with the tools of the Antropofagists, which also served to configure the modern image of Brazil, her people and landscapes, art and architecture. In a relatively short period of time, and at an admirably consistent pace, the Brazilian project of nation- and culture-building moved from 'the identification of specificity [to] the specification of identity and ultimately [to] the speciation of identity'.[137] The widespread and intensified practice of a meticulously specified identity led to the consolidation of the specifics of Brazilian culture.

135 Rodrigo Octávio, quoted in Skidmore, 1993, p. 102.   **136** Blaise Cendrars, 'Landscape (1924), in Cendrars, 2000, p. 613.   **137** Friedman, p. 81.

Chapter Two

Oscar Niemeyer and
the Birth of Brazilian Architectural Modernism

The English barber Wallace Green has been credited with the invention – somewhat unintentional – of the beach towel, in 1902 on the beach of Copacabana.[1] Sea bathing, a trend originating in England, had already been popular with royals in Brazil for a century, but Copacabana Beach had become increasingly accessible to common mortals and adventurous aviators, with modern technology conquering the obstacles of nature. The first tunnel through the mountains to Copacabana Beach was opened in 1892 (Túnel de Copacabana, renamed Túnel Alaor Prata), giving access by horse-drawn streetcar. On 1 November 1901 an electric car ran through it for the first time. The Túnel do Leme, part of Rio's triple project of sanitation, beautification and circulation, was cut through the Morro da Babilônia between 1904 and 1906.

One of the aims of the 'civilizing' urban operations of Mayor Francisco Pereira Passos, previously chief engineer for the Commission of City Improvements, was the conquest of the bay for the benefit of the city.[2] The modernizing projects included the opening of the long and panoramic Avenida Beira Mar along Guanabara Bay, joining Avenida Central to Praia Vermelha; a quay for transatlantic ships; and the construction and urbanization of the now legendary Avenida Atlântica – the great seaside promenade along Copacabana's curved, sandy ocean beach. With the expansion of the city and its services towards the southern beaches (*zona sul*) in the first half of the twentieth century, Avenida Atlântica became the centre of social activity for the wealthy, elegant elite, in the way the central Rua do Ouvidor had been in the second half of the nineteenth century.[3] It was in 1912 that a French poet, Jeanne Catulle Mendès, granted Rio de Janeiro the title 'La ville merveilleuse'.[4]

195   Avenida Beira-mar, Botafogo.   Rio de Janeiro.

Avenida Beira Mar along Guanabara Bay, Rio de Janeiro, completed under the administration of the engineer Francisco Pereira Passos, Mayor of Rio de Janeiro from 1902 to 1906

If, as Gilberto Freyre postulated, 'the rise of the street' and the re-Europeanization of Rio de Janeiro characterized the Brazilian nineteenth century, twentieth-century Rio was marked by the rise of the beach and the modernization and Brazilianization of the city in accordance with contemporary definitions of things Brazilian. Gradually, the beaches became the new 'zones of fraternization' between the 'social extremes' that Freyre had found in Rio's nineteenth-century streets.[5] Lúcio Costa has argued that Le Corbusier's 'lyrical' proposal for the city of Rio de Janeiro,

1 Castro, 2004, p. 218. Gilberto Freyre noted that 'Sea bathing is a recent habit of the gentry or bourgeoisie in Brazil, who, in colonial days and the early days of independence, preferred to bathe in the river'; Freyre, 1986, p. 146.   2 As a young engineer, Francisco Pereira Passos had also been responsible for the second leg of the railroad to the summit of the Corcovado Mountain, completed in 1885.   3 In 1900 Rio de Janeiro had a population of about 900,000, having grown from a mere 275,000 in 1872.   4 Castro, 2004, p. 179. 'Cidade maravilhosa' was the title of a

1935 carnival marchinha with words and music by André Filho, which in 1960 was chosen as the city's anthem. When the capital was transferred to Brasília, 'Cidade maravilhosa' assured Brazilians that Rio remained the 'heart of [their] country, Brazil . . . the altar of [their] hearts / That happily sing'; Castro, 2004, p. 91. The population of Copacabana reached 20,000 by 1910, 185,650 by 1960, and 237,559 by 1970; Evenson, 1973, p. 14. By 1940, Copacabana had also replaced Lapa as the centre of Rio's bohemian nightlife and music scene.   5 Freyre, 1986, pp. xxiv–xxvii.

View of Rio de Janeiro from the Pão de Açúcar, 1920s

The cosmopolitan seafront neighbourhood of Copacabana, 1920s

32091

Le Corbusier, sketch of his proposed elevated inhabited 'majestic highway' extending through the city of Rio de Janeiro and connecting with a bridge to Niterói, presentation panel used in his talks at the Associação dos Arquitetos, Rio de Janeiro, 1929, FLC 32.091

Above and below. Oscar Niemeyer's studio at the top floor of Edifício Ypiranga, popularly known as Mae West, at 3940 Avenida Atlântica, Copacabana, designed by Mário Freire in 1935

Oscar Niemeyer in the intimate study of his Copacabana studio, 2003

presented during his 1929 visit, addressed both the city's increasingly pressing housing problem and the phenomenon of all Cariocas 'swarming the *zona sul* for an open view'. His 'theoretical', 6-kilometre-long, serpentine inhabited viaduct offered views towards the ocean and towards the mountains.[6] Avenida Atlântica and Copacabana Beach feature in the first two sentences of *The Curves of Time: The Memoirs of Oscar Niemeyer*, published in 1998, and written on the top floor of the handsome, ten-storey Art Deco proto-modern Edifício Ypiranga, popularly known as Mae West, at 3940 of Avenida Atlântica – Niemeyer's studio for more than half a century, with a breathtaking view of the ocean at Copacabana.

A Brazilian Carioca in the way Joan Miró was an 'international Catalan', Niemeyer was born and raised in an ancestral house with a large veranda on Rua Manoel Passos in the Laranjeiras area

6 Lúcio Costa, 'Presença de Le Corbusier' (1987), in Lúcio Costa, 1997, pp. 148–49.

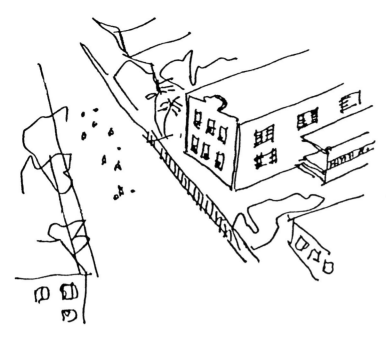

The house where Oscar Niemeyer was born. Rua Manoel Passos, Laranjeiras, Rio de Janeiro

of Rio de Janeiro.[7] He treasures all that remains of this house: 'four old wall tiles' and his own fond memories of it. In the late 1920s the extended family that inhabited the old house at Laranjeiras moved to Rio's fast-growing cosmopolitan seafront neighbourhoods – Ipanema, Copacabana and Leblon – where fashionable modern apartments soon began to replace the old single-family houses.[8]

In the 1930s and 1940s, when the *mestiço* paradigm reigned unchallenged, Gilberto Freyre praised and encouraged the practice of sunbathing, which helped white Brazilians fake the colour of the charming mulatto, bringing the Brazilian 'races' closer together and promoting what he viewed as a 'healthy mixture'. In his typical autobiographical introduction, Niemeyer begins by stressing his Brazilianness in accordance with the national ideology of ethnic amalgamation, based on Freyre's ideal:[9]

> I shall start by remembering my origins. My name ought to be Oscar Ribeiro Soares or Oscar Ribeiro de Almeida de Niemeyer Soares [Filho], but the foreign name prevailed and I became known as Oscar Niemeyer. My ethnic roots are diverse, something I find particularly gratifying. Ribeiro and Soares are Portuguese names, Almeida is Arabic, and Niemeyer is German. Not to mention the blacks or Indians who, unknown to us, may also have been part of our family.[10]

According to Brazilian national ideology, all families have 'a foot in the kitchen'; that is, partial black or Amerindian ancestry from the family's *senzala* (slave quarters). 'I am . . . a mestizo,' emphatically asserts Niemeyer, 'as mestizos are all my Brazilian brothers'.[11]

Miscegenation is central to Brazilians' self-definition, and so it is to Niemeyer's. It also plays a central role in his architecture.

Perhaps the most celebrated feature of Copacabana Beach is its elegant mosaic pavements. For these and the pavements of Avenida Central, in 1905–06 Pereira Passos imported both skilled craftsmen and stone from Portugal – white limestone and black basalt, known as *pedra portuguesa*. The Portuguese craftsmen followed patterns typical of the distinctive paving of Portuguese walkways – *calçada à portuguesa* – developed following the completion in 1848 of Lisbon's Praça Dom Pedro IV or Rossio, entirely covered in alternating black-and-white waves composed of small stones cut and laid by hand. Brazilians, however, allege that the sinuous black-and-white stripes of Copacabana allude to the waves of the sea as well as to the emblematic Amazonian riverscape. More specifically, they are seen to refer to a natural mixing process: the confluence of the mineral-deficient black currents of Rio Negro, which drains from the old granite rocks of the highlands to the north, with the silt-laden waters of Rio Solimões, which flows from the young Andes. Over several kilometres the two rivers preserve their respective colours.

In Manaus, the Praça São Sebastião in front of the extravagant Teatro Amazonas (1893–96), built by the rubber barons, is paved with black-and-white flowing curves in *pedra portuguesa*, recalling Lisbon's Rossio. But in popular belief, the flowing curves of

7 The street was later renamed after Niemeyer's grandfather, Antônio Augusto Ribeiro de Almeida (1838–1919), attorney general of the republic, and later minister of the Federal Supreme Court. Niemeyer lived in this house until the age of twenty-one. His family had a summer cottage on Copacabana Beach. **8** Niemeyer, 2000b, pp. 11–19. Ipanema replaced Copacabana as Rio's fashionable neighbourhood only in the late 1960s, when the latter became overcrowded and its reputation and quality of life went into decline. **9** Freyre defined the Brazilian as 'a European with Negro or Indian blood to revive his energy'. He insisted that 'Every Brazilian, even the light-skinned fair-haired one, carries about with him on his soul, when not on soul and body alike – for there are many in Brazil with the mongrel mark of the *genipap* – the shadow, or at least the birthmark, of the aborigine or the Negro'; Freyre, 1956, pp. 68, 255. **10** Niemeyer, 2000b, p. 6. Also, for example, Niemeyer, 1985, p. 71. Note Niemeyer's distinction between the names that are supposedly Brazilian (Portuguese and Arabic), and the foreign (German) name, which did not feature in the colonial mixture. Later in his autobiography, Niemeyer mentions the genealogist Galdino Duprat, 'who insisted that [Niemeyer] was related to the [Morubixaba] Indian chief Araribóia, whose son, so he said, had married an Almeida girl, supposedly a family relation'; Niemeyer 2000a, p. 121. It is not known why the name Niemeyer prevailed. Perhaps, Niemeyer followed the example of Juscelino Kubitschek, president of Brazil from 1956 to 1961, who, although his family name was Oliveira, adopted the Czechoslovakian name of an ancestor in order to 'stand out among the field of Brazilian politicians, mostly carrying Portuguese names'; Skidmore, 1999, p. 144. 'In Brazil', Niemeyer says elsewhere, 'a foreign name like mine is much easier to remember. Names like Ribeiro and Soares are very common in my country'. Then he adds: 'Today, I have the tendency to return to my true origins. I prefer my full family name, even though it may be difficult to find place for such a long signature . . . In any case, we [Brazilians] are all of different origins, so it is of no importance whether the name is of Latin, Slavic, Germanic or Arab origin. Even the Japanese, who immigrated later than the Europeans or the Arabs, carry names which do not surprise us. *We have assimilated them*. What matters is that we all speak the same language, and that we have *the same conception of our tropical civilization*. Thank God, to use a popular expression, we don't have ethnic conflicts, this racial hatred, this xenophobic spirit that we see resurfacing in Europe. Ours is a more open mentality. Brazilians have always been generous, they don't have religious or race prejudices. Consider, for example, the fusion of Catholicism and African syncretism in *macumba*'; Niemeyer, 1993c, p. 185, my emphasis. **11** Niemeyer, 2004, p. 134.

VOCÊ ESTÁ RECEBENDO UM PEQUENO PEDAÇO DA HISTÓRIA.

PRAIA DE COPACABANA · 1957

Copacabana Beach with its original *pedra portuguesa* pavement of 1905–06, postcard, 1957

Teatro Nacional de Dona Maria II and Praça Dom Pedro IV or Rossio paved in *pedra portuguesa*, Lisbon, completed 1848

View of the confluence of the mineral-deficient black currents of Rio Negro with the silt-laden waters of Rio Solimões near Manaus, Amazonas

Teatro Amazonas and Praça São Sebastião paved in *pedra portuguesa*, Manaus, Amazonas, 1893–96, photograph of 1945

Manaus depict the 'meeting of the waters' – the sensual movements of the jungle – also painted on the main curtain of the Teatro Amazonas by Crispim do Amaral (in Paris). Somewhat ironically, Manaus's *calçada à portuguesa* has been incorporated in the Brazilian Antropofagist tradition, hailed as 'the first great modern Brazilian public monument', bringing together nature and art and foreshadowing the 'jungle and school' of the Pau-Brasil movement.[12]

Roberto Burle Marx's renovation and extension of the pavements of the promenade along Copacabana Beach (Calçadão de Copacabana, 1969–72) retained the original pattern – only accentuating the curves – preserving the memory of the jungle and the colonial metropolis in the 'marvellous city'. Popular imagination extended the symbolism of Burle Marx's mosaics on the opposite side of the beachfront and on the islands at the centre of the avenue to include Brazil's celebrated racial confluence: the red, black and white stones are regarded as symbolic of the three 'races' that have shaped Brazilian culture. In a further ingenious

12 Paulo Herkenhoff, 1995, p. 239; Oswald de Andrade, 1989, p. 311.

Above, Roberto Burle Marx, mosaic pavements (*calçadões*) along Avenida Atlântica, Copacabana Beach, Rio de Janeiro, 1969–72; below, Roberto Burle Marx, lawn of the Museum of Modern Art with two different colours of *Stenotaphrum secundatum* grass, Aterro do Flamengo, Rio de Janeiro, 1954–61

Brazilianization of the stone waves, on the lawn of Affonso Eduardo Reidy's Museum of Modern Art (Aterro do Flamengo, Rio de Janeiro, 1954–61), Burle Marx re-created the Portuguese stone motif using two different colours of *Stenotaphrum secundatum* grass. His translation of the familiar wavy pattern effected a tropicalization of the Portuguese import, which now literally grows on Brazilian soil, symbolically uniting Brazil's two emblems: the biggest river in the world and her most beautiful flora.

On 13 August 1923, one year after the birth of Brazilian Modernism at the Semana de Arte Moderna, the historicist Louis XVI style Copacabana Palace opened its doors to the glamorous, the rich and the famous, including Frank Lloyd Wright during his 1931 Brazilian visit, when he incited 'rebellion' against 'the old [Beaux Arts] forms'.[13] The sumptuous hotel was built with cement

13 Frank Lloyd Wright, quoted in Irigoyen, p. 139.

from Germany and marble from Carrara, and everything else was imported from Europe too, from the chandeliers to the chef. Following European resort fashion, it accommodated a casino, and epitomized the 'tropical *belle époque*' and the *joie de vivre* embodied in things new, progressive and entertaining. It soon brought to Hollywood what was to become the world's most famous beach, full of *dolce vita avant la lettre* all year round. In the musical *Flying Down to Rio* (1933, directed by Thornton Freeland and featuring the first dance of Fred Astaire with Ginger Rogers), an ultra-modern and probably unintentionally comic spectacle of flight-and-dance was staged above Copacabana Beach, with dancing and acrobatics performed by gravity-defying, silk-clad girls fastened to the wings of flying Pan-American clippers.

The palace on the beach, which brought together glamour, pleasure and modernity, was designed in 1917 by the French architect Joseph Gire, who had found inspiration in the French Riviera hotels – the Negresco in Nice and the Carlton in Cannes. Gire was also responsible, with Elisiário da Cunha Bahiana and engineer Emilio Henrique Baumgart, for the twenty-four-storey *A Noite* newspaper building (1928), at the time the tallest reinforced-concrete building in the world, 102.5 metres high, dominating the centre of Rio.[14] The massive *A Noite* tower stood at the north end of Avenida Central on Praça Mauá (formerly Largo da Prainha), dedicated to the pioneer of Brazilian industrialization Irineu Evangelista de Souza, viscount and baron of Mauá. It housed the powerful Radio Nacional broadcasting station and became the most prestigious business address in the city. From its rooftop terrace, one could enjoy the entire panorama of Guanabara Bay. Lúcio Costa argues that it represented the first instance of a conscious pursuit of the integration of form and structure, which was fully realized at the Ministry of Education and Public Health.[15] In 1932, Costa opened an office in the *A Noite* tower, in partnership with Gregori Warchavchik, with Carlos Leão (1906–83) as an associate. It was at this office that, three years later, Oscar Niemeyer appeared 'with a recommendation card from Banco Boavista',[16] in the hope that they 'would assuage some of [his] doubts as an architecture student', and with the 'goal . . . to become a good architect'. At this office, Niemeyer 'learned to respect [Brazil's] colonial history, to appreciate beautiful Portuguese buildings . . . honest beyond reproach'.[17]

RIO DE JANEIRO   HOTEL COPACABANA

Joseph Gire, Copacabana Palace, Avenida Atlântica, Copacabana, Rio de Janeiro, 1917–23

Praça Mauá, formerly Largo da Prainha, with A *Noite* newspaper tower by Joseph Gire with Elisiário da Cunha Bahiana and engineer Emilio Henrique Baumgart, 1928, and Avenida Central towards zona sul, photograph of 1941

14 The longest-span reinforced-concrete bridge at the time was also built in Brazil (Santa Catarina), in 1931. **15** Lúcio Costa, 'Muita construção, alguma arquitetura e um milagre: Depoimento de um arquiteto carioca' (1951), in Lúcio Costa, 1997, p. 167. **16** Lúcio Costa, interview with Mário Cesar Carvalho, published in *Folha de São Paulo* (1995), in Lúcio Costa, 1997, n.p. **17** Niemeyer, 2000b, p. 24. As Costa was not in a position to offer paid employment, Niemeyer offered to work without payment.

The Ministry of Education and Public Health Building: An Architectural Manifesto of Brazilian Modernity

At the end of Copacabana Beach known as Leme, in a former plantation house on Rua Araujo Gondim, Fazenda do Leme, the young Roberto Burle Marx lived with his parents. In 1932, his experimental garden beds attracted the attention of Lúcio Costa, his neighbour and former tutor at the Escola Nacional de Belas Artes (ENBA), who invited him to design the garden of the Alfredo Schwartz House in Copacabana. As a guest at the Copacabana Palace, the governor of Pernambuco, Lima Cavalcanti, saw the garden of the Schwartz House and invited Burle Marx for an interview at the hotel. He offered Burle Marx the position of director of parks at Recife, a role he fulfilled from 1934 to 1936. Back in Copacabana, Burle Marx was offered another collaboration by Costa, on the seminal Ministry of Education and Public Health building (1936–44) – the project that 'gave Brazilian architecture the initial momentum it needed', according to Niemeyer.[18] The building was the fruit of a collaboration between a number of architects who would play a key role in the development of Brazilian Modernist architecture over the ensuing years of intensive production: Lúcio Costa, Carlos Leão, Affonso Eduardo Reidy, Jorge Moreira (1904–92), Ernani Vasconcellos (1909–88) and Oscar Niemeyer, with Le Corbusier acting as a consultant in 1936.

Niemeyer was a student at the francophile Escola Nacional de Belas Artes from 1929 to 1934, and so, like Burle Marx, was there during Costa's short-lived but long-remembered reformist directorship, from October 1930 until September 1931. Costa had added a 'Functional Course' to the Beaux-Arts curriculum, which had proven extremely successful but had also provoked explosive opposition from the Beaux-Arts majority at the school. It was attended by those future Modernist architects whom Costa described as 'a purist battalion dedicated to the impassioned study of Walter Gropius, Ludwig Mies van der Rohe and especially Le Corbusier'.[19] Costa had also appointed Warchavchik as professor, with Affonso Eduardo Reidy as his assistant. The latter, a 1930 graduate of the school, had been working as a trainee since 1929 with Donat-Alfred Agache (1875–1934), on the Directive Plan for the City of Rio de Janeiro (1926–30).

Already as a student, Reidy had felt the need to 'revolt . . . [against] the false orientation stimulated by the school'.[20] In 1931, he won, with Gerson Pompeu Pinheiro, a competition for the Albergue da Boa Vontade (Shelter of Good Will, Bairro da Saúde, Rio de Janeiro) – a building recognized as a pioneer of the new architecture. Reidy built two further Modernist houses in Rio – at Urca (1933) and at Ipanema (1935), again with Pinheiro – before entering the 1935 architectural competition for a headquarters for the Ministry of Education and Public Health. Created by Getúlio Dórtico Vargas in 1930, the ministry was intended to reform educa-

Lúcio Costa, Carlos Leão, Affonso Eduardo Reidy, Jorge Moreira, Ernani Vasconcellos and Oscar Niemeyer with Le Corbusier as consultant; Ministry of Education and Public Health, Rio de Janeiro, 1936–44; view of south elevation

18 Niemeyer, 2000b, p. 25.   **19** Lúcio Costa, quoted in Deckker, pp. 15–16. The ENBA was the successor of the Imperial Academy of Fine Arts, founded in 1826 by the creation of the French Artistic Mission that came to Brazil in 1816. The school was reformed in 1890, having been renamed ENBA in 1889. On the advice of the poet Manuel Bandeira and Rodrigo Melo Franco de Andrade, Francisco Campos, Getúlio Vargas's first minister of state for education and public health, appointed Lúcio Costa director of the ENBA and entrusted him with the task of the school's reform. Costa's controversial new course aimed to '"save" the young' (letter from Lúcio Costa to Le Corbusier, 26 June 1936, in Lissovsky and Moraes de Sá, p. 93). Following his so-called 'Revolutionary Salon' – the Salão Nacional de Artes Plásticas of 1931, which exhibited the work of the Modernist pioneers for the first time – Costa was forced to resign in September 1931, sparking a student revolt and a strike that lasted for almost a year.   **20** Affonso Eduardo Reidy, quoted in Bonduki (ed.), 2000, p. 12. Reidy remained a professor at the school until 1933.

tion and health care – 'the first duty of a revolution which was made to liberate Brazilians'.[21] Based on Le Corbusier's Centrosoyus project in Moscow with Pierre Jeanneret (1927–28), which had been published in the local *Revista de Arquitetura*, Reidy's scheme was rejected, as were the schemes of Costa and Leão, and Vasconcellos and Moreira. The entry of Archimedes Memória (1893–1960) – Costa's successor at the ENBA and architect of the Municipal Council of Rio de Janeiro, where the Ministry of Education was first housed – was selected by the jury.

However, the thirty-two-year-old Mineiro minister of education, Gustavo Capanema, whose Cabinet was staffed with many prominent Modernist intellectuals, including Mário de Andrade, was not satisfied with the 'horrible', artless winning proposal for a ministry responsible for 'questions of art'.[22] With the support of Marcello Piacentini, Mussolini's chief architect, Capanema refused to go ahead with Memória's conservative scheme.[23] The 'Manifesto of the Pioneers of the New Education: Educational

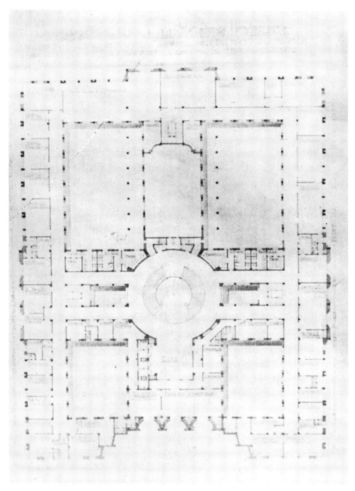

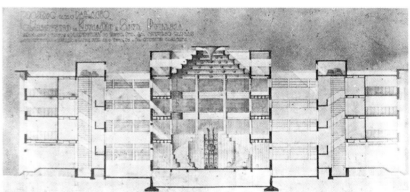

Archimedes Memória, competition entry for the Ministry of Education and Public Health, first prize, 1935

21 Francisco Campos, quoted in Azevedo, p. 451.   **22** Capanema, p. 124. Capanema explains the delicacy of the situation, especially considering that Professor Memória was a very influential figure: a highly regarded architect, director of the ENBA, and personal friend of the president.   **23** In 1935, Capanema invited Piacentini, who was responsible for the University City of Rome, to submit a design for Rio de Janeiro's Cidade Universitária.

Reconstruction in Brazil', published in Rio de Janeiro and São Paulo in 1932, had formulated national education policy in accordance with 'plans for an urban and industrial civilization'. The objective was to bring education in line with 'the social and economic transformations brought about by mechanical inventions which governed natural forces and had revolutionized our habits of work, of recreation, of communication and of exchange'. The institution presiding over this programmatic reconstruction of public education, 'by means of an organic and synthetic view of modern theories of education', could not afford to adopt the historicist styles that lined Rio's newly carved boulevards with 'architectural carnival'.[24] But neither could it embrace the architecture of those who supported colonial models but were seen to have broken the 'bonds between the beautiful and the useful', favouring 'excessive adornment'.[25] Such decoration, furthermore, recalled the Baroque architecture associated with the Catholic Church, exactly when the latter was fiercely opposing educational reform.

In a way that marks Brazil's ambivalent relation to her colonial past, the site proposed by the French planner Donat-Alfred Agache for a federal district was that of the Morro do Castelo. It was on this hill that the Portuguese city of São Sebastião do Rio de Janeiro grew up in 1567, following the victory of Estácio de Sá (1520–67) against the French and their Indian allies. The hydraulic blasting of the hill under Mayor Carlos César de Oliveira Sampaio in 1920–21 had advanced the project for the clearance of the city of all vestiges of provincial colonialism, initiated following the arrival of the Portuguese court in the city in 1808, and intensified after independence.[26] This process saw the transformation of Rio de Janeiro into a 'tropical Paris' by a series of French or French-educated architects, beginning with Auguste-Henri-Victor Grandjean de Montigny (1776–1850), 'an architect of genius' according to Euclides da Cunha.[27] In 1816 the French Artistic Mission came to Rio, invited by King João VI to the 'European' capital of the largest colonial empire in the world to 'help propagate the beaux-arts taste in Brazil, and to perfect the techniques of [local] craftsmen'.[28]

In the nineteenth century, Neoclassical architecture was a reaction against Portuguese colonialism, perceived as suitable for the 'European' nation of independent Brazil. The early twentieth-century reappraisal of colonial architecture signified emancipation from European domination through a return to local tradition. In 1922, the first Centennial of Brazilian Independence was celebrated on the site of the Morro do Castelo with an international fair. Visitors were received in a mixture of pavilions, some classicizing in style, others in the nationalist neocolonial style, which declared that industrial Brazil need not dress like Paris to impress the world of civilized nations.

In the early years of the Vargas administration, however, the Ministry of Education and Public Health became a patron of the architecture of the twentieth-century European avant-garde, through a school building programme that formed part of the reformist movement, vigorously opposing the supporters of neo-colonialist architecture. Health and education buildings around the country referenced Walter Gropius, Italian Razionalismo, Le Corbusier, Rob Mallet-Stevens or Hannes Meyer, exploring the formal and technical possibilities of the new architecture within a framework of limited material resources, prioritizing function, economy and social transformation. Architects like Luís Nunes de Souza, leader of the ENBA student rebellion against Costa's dismissal in Recife (Military Brigade Hospital, Alberto Torres Rural School, 1935–37), José Maria da Silva Neves in São Paulo (School Complex Viscount de Congonhas do Campo, 1936), and Enéas Silva in Rio de Janeiro (República Argentina Municipal School, 1935) were among the protagonists of this early Brazilian architectural Modernism.[29] In the footsteps of Le Corbusier, the Paulista architect Carlos da Silva Prado expressed his commitment to 'the revolution of construction as a means to avoid a social revolution'.[30]

Eneas Silva, República Argentina Municipal School, Vila Isabel, Rio de Janeiro, 1935

24 'Manifesto of the Pioneers of the New Education' (1932), quoted in Azevedo, p. 455.   25 Monteiro Lobato, quoted in Azevedo, p. 310.   26 São Sebastião do Rio de Janeiro was founded in 1565 between the Morros Cara de Cão and Pão de Açúcar. It became capital of the colony in 1763. Rio de Janeiro became capital of the United Kingdom of Portugal and the Algarve in 1815 and then of the United Kingdom of Brazil, Portugal and the Algarve in 1816. The idea of razing the Morro do Castelo and Morro do San Antônio was conceived by José Maria Bomtempo in 1825, based on the belief that it would improve ventilation and sanitation for the city, opening it to sea breezes; Freyre, 1986, p. 199. The operation was completed in 1959. See also Ermakoff, p. 236.   27 Euclides da Cunha, quoted in Azevedo, p. 291. Grandjean de Montigny had also organized the architecture course at the Academia Imperial de Belas Artes.   28 La mission artistique française et les peintres voyageurs, quoted in Vidal, p. 33.   29 Luís Nunes's Water Tower (1937), in the historic context of Olinda, with a dance floor beneath it, was called the 'first modern Folly' by the Architectural Review; Architectural Review, 1944a, p. 69. Joaquim Cardozo, the poet and engineer who would soon distinguish himself through his collaboration with Niemeyer, was responsible for the sculptural parabolic arches supporting the access ramps at Nunes's Alberto Torres Rural School at Recife.   30 Carlos da Silva Prado, quoted in Segawa, 2002, p. 52.

Vargas's centralism, in contrast to earlier federalism, enforced the supremacy of Rio de Janeiro, the seat of the omnipotent president. Under the directorship of the Baiano educational reformer Anísio Spínola Teixeira (1900–71), the Department of Education of the federal district of Rio de Janeiro constructed twenty-eight school buildings.[31]

The Vargas administration's sympathy towards Italian Razionalismo may also be related to the authoritarian state's adoption of models from Mussolini's Fascism: Giuseppe Terragni's Casa del Fascio in Como (1932–36) had literally expressed Mussolini's view of Fascism as 'a house of glass'. The architecture of Terragni and Alberto Sartoris had also been promoted in Brazil through the pages of *Belvedere*, the art review launched by Pietro Maria Bardi in 1929. Brazilian architectural historiography has generally overlooked or marginalized this heroic period, on account of its loyalty to rationalist European prototypes, opting to stress, instead, the importance of the movement initiated by the Ministry of Education building, which challenged the catechisms of 'the dressed man' and strove to accommodate the rational and the national.

The champion of conservative neocolonialism, José Mariano Filho, held this early Modernist architecture, which served Brazil's populist regime, accountable for the vulgarization and 'Sovietization of Brazilian architecture'.[32] In 'Reasons of the New Architecture' of 1936, the 'converted' Lúcio Costa responded to Mariano Filho's criticism of the new, socially minded 'Jewish, communist architecture' that was destroying national traditions.[33] But, rather than denouncing the anti-Semitism and anti-communism of the critics, Costa was trapped into empty rhetoric on the ethnic origin of Modernism, insisting that 'there is nothing exceptional or particularly *Judaic* . . . about the internationalism of the new architecture . . . nothing Germanic . . . [nothing] Slavic . . . [and] nothing of Nordic mysticism'.[34] Costa elaborated his defence of the new architecture on the basis of its affinity with local traditions, perhaps also seeking to distance himself from formulae associated with Hitler's 'crystal-clear functionalism' and Mussolini's Razionalismo: 'the only true expression of Fascism'.[35]

In March 1936, the 'master who liberated modern Brazilian architecture', according to Niemeyer,[36] was appointed by Capanema architect of the new headquarters for the ministry, which had assumed the task of shaping the 'novo homem, Brasileiro e moderno' ('new man, Brazilian and modern'). While contemporaneous public buildings like the Ministry of Finance (Wladimir Alves de Souza and Enéas Silva, Rio de Janeiro, 1936–43) did not hesitate to don academicist gowns, Capanema shared the 'revolutionary' intentions of the young architects' rejected competition entries, and requested 'something courageous, interesting . . . advanced' and Brazilian.[37] Niemeyer notes that Capanema 'encouraged writers, artists and intellectuals, in gener-

al, to demonstrate a Brazilianism and refuse to imitate foreign imports'.[38] Costa sensed that this was a unique opportunity to forward the cause of the new architecture, and quickly decided that the best course of action would be to unite the Modernist battalion against the powerful conservative forces that had prevailed over his reformist spirit at the ENBA. He persuaded Capanema to commission, instead, a team consisting of all the architects who had submitted progressive entries. Oscar Niemeyer 'practically demanded his inclusion in the team and, later on, equality of terms with the other architects'.[39]

Costa had subscribed to Pevsner's view of Modernism as historically inevitable. The new technology of reinforced concrete represented the new machine age, but architecture lagged behind. In tune with Corbusian machine-age rhetoric, in his archi-

31 Although the National Education Plan, which introduced the principle of education as a subjective right, was made part of the constitution of 1934, Teixeira's vision of a free, mandatory, secular and high-quality system of basic public education was never realized. His efforts to democratize and secularize state-led education were criticized by the clergy and reactionary politicians and in 1935 he was removed from his post. In protest, Heitor Villa-Lobos resigned from his position as director of artistic and musical education in the federal district. Teixeira returned to public office in 1947. See Cury, pp. 509–20.   32 José Mariano Filho, in Segawa, 2002, p. 66. Mariano Filho's racial bias is apparent from his 1941 paper (with fellow Rotary Club members Alberto Pires and Americo Campelo) on 'The Problem of the "Favelas" of Rio de Janeiro', presented at the First Brazilian Congress of Urbanism in Rio de Janeiro: 'The tendency of the blacks to isolate themselves from white civilization, to which they don't want to be subjugated, is a current observable fact in South American republics. Among us, it is manifested in an ostensible way, due to the absence of coercive measures. Back to its rural expression, it satisfies violent impulses from the unconscious. The return to primitive life enables the blacks to satisfy their racial tendencies, their fetishist practices, their dances and the *macumba*'; cited in Outtes.   33 José Mariano Filho, quoted in Williams, p. 57.   34 Lúcio Costa, 2000, p. 627–28, emphasis in the original.   35 Adolf Hitler, pamphlet accompanying the 1931 exhibition of the Milanese gruppo 7 in Rome, opened by Mussolini, quoted in Weston, 1996, pp. 170, 172.   36 Niemeyer, 1955b, p. 3.   37 Capanema, p. 125. See Cavalcanti, 1995. As he wrote to Vargas on 14 June 1937, Capanema conceived the Ministry of Education building and the statue of 'do homen, do homen brasileiro', which appeared already in the 1938 model of the headquarters, as 'complementary'; Cavalcanti, 1995, p. 78.   38 Niemeyer, 1993c, p. 59.   39 Lúcio Costa, 1950, p. 2.

tectural manifesto of 1936, 'Reasons of the New Architecture', Costa postulated that it was essential for 'industry to take over construction and produce all the elements that are missing in order to achieve the same degree of perfection as the bodies of cars'. This was the year Ferdinand Porsche designed the Volkswagen touring car. But Costa observed a 'total disagreement between art, in the academic sense, and technology', and made a plea for 'the revision of plastic and traditional values', necessitated by 'the radical transformation of all the old construction processes'. He argued that the 'independent bone structure' and demise of 'support walls' that the new technology of steel and reinforced concrete had brought about indicated the way architecture should develop: the transformation of the south wall (in the case of the southern hemisphere) into 'a simple pane of glass'; 'free' walls that 'slide beside the indifferent columns . . . stop at any distance . . . undulate'; 'freedom of the ground plan'; façades with 'no dependence on, or relation with, the structure'; 'shift of the colonnades . . . from outside the building in, leaving the façades . . . absolute freedom of treatment . . . continuous windows'; and, finally, 'a plastic value never reached before, which brings [architecture] to pure art in spite of its purely utilitarian starting point'.[40] The Ministry of Education building presented Costa with the ideal opportunity to put theory into practice. The report that accompanied the Brazilian team's first scheme in 1936, clearly stated that 'its fundamental principle is the independence of the "skeleton" . . . and the wall', and celebrated the resulting 'elasticity'.[41]

But Costa, the Abbot Suger of Brazilian Modernist architecture, felt that the responsibility and the difficulties of a project of that scale were 'enormous'.[42] As Zilah Quezado Deckker points out, Costa had not seen any Modernist buildings in Europe and had no experience with large buildings.[43] Actually, he had built nothing since 1932. Despite Capanema's initial refusal, Costa persuaded Vargas himself to invite Le Corbusier back to the city whose 'violent and sublime' landscape he had sought to 'improve . . . by that faultless horizontal' of his 'majestic highway' and 'the big architectural beltline carrying it'.[44] Costa saw Le Corbusier as the Brunelleschi of the twentieth century.[45] Niemeyer confirms that his influence on him and his generation was truly 'immense'.[46] Le Corbusier pressed for a commission because 'the profession of being a prophet ha[d] started to weigh heavily on [his] shoulders'.[47] He was officially invited to give a series of lectures and informally to act as a consultant to the project for the Cidade Universitária.[48] Once in Rio de Janeiro, he was given a similar role on the Ministry of Education building, for which Lúcio Costa and his team had already prepared a *parti*. The latter rejected the inner courtyard solution prescribed by the original competition brief and clearly displayed the influence of Le Corbusier's Centrosoyus building.

Le Corbusier arrived on the Zeppelin *Hindenburg* on 13 July 1936. Descriptions of his audacious 1929 proposal for Rio de Janeiro abound in references to his intention to conquer and dominate the 'famous site'.[49] Unaware of Lúcio Costa's participation in the commission that had recently approved the Agache plan for the Castelo federal district, Le Corbusier sought an opportunity to raise his first major public building on a more dominant site than the one prescribed for the Ministry of Education.[50] In order to make the most 'of the natural splendours of Rio, object of world admiration', he sketched a proposal for an alternative site near the airport on the Praia de Santa Luzia, formed with the debris from the Morro do Castelo.[51] Le Corbusier's scheme was based on a single eight-storey horizontal block on *pilotis*, with *pans de verre* on the south side and *brises-soleil* to the north. Panoramic views of Guanabara Bay and Pão de Açúcar feature prominently in the internal perspectives of this scheme.

As it proved too difficult to acquire this new site, on 13 August 1936, two days before his departure, Le Corbusier delivered a proposal for the Castelo site, which he never published: a ten-storey office block on low *pilotis* along Avenida Graça Aranha, and an auditorium linked to the horizontal block with an intermediate volume. The *pans de verre* faced north-east, receiving the hottest sun, while the south-west side was partially covered with *brises-soleil*. The scheme included a row of imperial palm trees. According to Costa and Niemeyer, it was primarily Le Corbusier's first scheme, for the site on Avenida Beira Mar (near Reidy's Museum of Modern Art, 1953–68), that served as the basis for the

40 Lúcio Costa, 2000, pp. 624–26. 41 Ministry of Education project team, cited in Bonduki (ed.), 2000, p. 52. 42 Lúcio Costa, interview with Mário Cesar Carvalho (1995), in Lúcio Costa, 1997, n.p. See also Bardi, 1984, pp. 74–76. 43 Deckker, p. 32. 44 Le Corbusier, 1991, pp. 242–45. 45 Lúcio Costa, 2000, p. 624. 46 Niemeyer, 1993c, p. 61. 47 Le Corbusier, quoted in Deckker, p. 33. 48 The new university campus would house the Universidade do Brasil, Brazil's model university, which emerged from the reorganization of the Universidade do Rio de Janeiro (URJ), Brazil's first university, founded in 1920. 49 Le Corbusier, 1991, pp. 242–45. 50 Tsiomis, 2006, p. 21. 51 Report from Le Corbusier to Capanema, 10 August 1936, in Lissovsky and Moraes de Sá, p. 109. In a letter to Capanema of 5 May 1936, Le Corbusier insisted that he could not stay in Rio for long 'purely to give lectures to students', and that he ought to 'have the opportunity to create works of architecture, small or large, but significant'. Archimedes Memória protested against the invitation of Le Corbusier, so 'closely linked to Soviet Russia'; quoted in Tsiomis, 2006, pp. 23, 24.

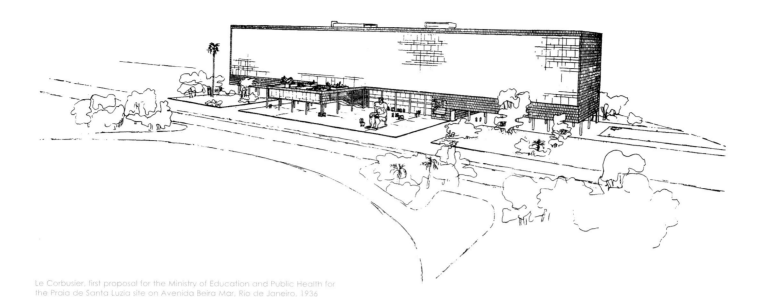

Le Corbusier, first proposal for the Ministry of Education and Public Health for
the Praia de Santa Luzia site on Avenida Beira Mar, Rio de Janeiro, 1936

final project developed by the Brazilian team.[52] Costa has often repeated, however, that Le Corbusier's most important contribution to Brazilian architecture was his awakening, so to speak, of Niemeyer's genius. 'Brave Oscar [with] his beautiful perspectives', who had read Le Corbusier's work 'as if it were Holy Scripture', was the foreign guest's draughtsman for the duration of his visit, always at his disposal.[53] Costa is convinced that this collaboration had a catalytic impact on the young Niemeyer, who later proposed for

the Ministry of Education a scheme based on Le Corbusier's sketch for the Praia de Santa Luzia site.[54]

The Ministry of Education and Public Health was recognized as one of the first regional interpretations of the Modern Movement. Built on the Esplanada do Castelo, it was also one of the first buildings to embody the Modernist reappraisal of the Portuguese colonial heritage in accordance with the principles of 'Cannibalism. The permanent transformation of the Tabu into a totem.'[55] Local

52 Lúcio Costa has repeatedly expressed his anger at Le Corbusier's false claim of authorship of the final project for this seminal building. Vol. 3 of Le Corbusier and Pierre Jeanneret's *Œuvre complète 1934–38*, published in 1939, included a controversial sketch by Le Corbusier and a photograph of the model of the final project (p. 81). On 3 July 1937, Costa wrote a letter to Le Corbusier, including the drawings and a photograph of the model for the final project for the Ministry of Education building, and asking for Le Corbusier's approval: 'Oscar, who following your departure turned into the star of the group, is the principal responsible for [the building] and awaits with great emotion, like all of us, the OK of Jehovah'; in Cecília Rodrigues dos Santos et al., p. 180. Costa is convinced that the sketch published in 1939 was made by Le Corbusier with the 'intention' of 'proving authorship', on the basis of the photograph of the model. The controversial sketch was included in a 1950s exhibition of Le Corbusier's work in São Paulo. Costa wrote to the curators, 'alerting them to the fact that it constituted a *false testimony*' and demanding its 'replacement with the original sketch for a low and long building destined for Beira-Mar – for this one, did really serve as the basis of our new project'; Lúcio Costa, 'Relato pessoal' (1975), in Lúcio Costa, 1997, p. 137, emphasis in the original.
  In 1946, the same sketch, plans and photographs of the completed building – the only completed building – was included in vol. 4 of Le Corbusier's *Œuvre complète 1938–46*. The Brazilian team was acknowledged and Le Corbusier was credited as 'Architecte consulté' (pp. 80–89). On 27 November 1949, Costa wrote to Le Corbusier: 'your current interpretation of the facts is no more that of 1937. In fact, on 13 September 1937, after you saw the definitive plans of the project, you wrote to me: "Your building for the Ministry of Education and Public Health seems excellent to me . . . It is free of the barbarisms we often see in other modern works that do not know what harmony is . . . It will be like a pearl in the Agachean manure. My compliments, my 'OK' (as you requested)"'. In the same letter, Costa noted that Le Corbusier always dated his sketches, but the controversial sketch bears no date (the publication dated the sketch 1936–37). He also asserted that Le Corbusier's project for 'a different site, near the airport, served [the Brazilian team] as compass and reference. And we want to link your name definitely to this historic

building, which is owed above all to Oscar Soares [Niemeyer]'; in Cecília Rodrigues dos Santos et al., pp. 199–200.
  In vol. 4 of the *Œuvre complète*, Le Corbusier confirmed that 'the plans for a building on a site along the coast were adapted to a restricted site, a solution which afforded certain advantages such as liberation from the ground by means of pillars and the sun-breaker which allows a position contrary to traditional usage', but also claimed credit for 'a decisive intervention in his capacity as landscape artist'. He also included an extensive quotation from Philip L. Goodwin's introduction to the catalogue of the 1943 *Brazil Builds* exhibition. The English text included an incomprehensible reference to 'his [Le Corbusier's] work at Bella [sic] Horizonte' (p. 82). Goodwin's original text reads as follows: 'LeCorbusier's [sic] theories have been interpreted with special brilliance in the Ministry of Education and in the work at Belo Horizonte'; Goodwin, p. 81.
  A passage from Niemeyer's memoirs deals with Le Corbusier's appropriation of the final design for the Ministry of Education: 'The old master was going too far.' But, rather surprisingly, he adds: 'our alterations, which appeared in that photo, were of little consequence in relation to his original concept. We have always acknowledged the Ministry of Education design as being the work of Le Corbusier. On the commemorative plaque we wrote: "In accordance with the original sketch by Le Corbusier." In architectural vocabulary, the sketch is the original outline, the basic idea, the architectural invention.' Niemeyer's attempt to dissociate himself from the creation of the Ministry of Education has to be considered in light of his setting the beginning of his own creative output at Pampulha (1940–43), which he refers to immediately following the above: 'My own architecture was to begin later, with my design for the Pampulha complex'; Niemeyer, 2000b, p. 61. In the context of the same incident, Niemeyer has declared: 'In Brazil, we immediately understood that [Le Corbusier] was a great architect, perhaps the greatest of the twentieth century, but he lacked ethics.' Niemeyer, 1993c, p. 62. **53** For example, Lúcio Costa, 'Presença de Le Corbusier' (1987), in Lúcio Costa, 1997, p. 152: the quotation is from a postscript to a letter from Le Corbusier to Lúcio Costa, 21 November 1936, in Cecília Rodrigues dos Santos et al., p. 178; the second quotation is from Niemeyer, 2000b, p. 60. **54** Niemeyer, 2000b, pp. 60–61. **55** Oswald de Andrade, 2000, p. 591.

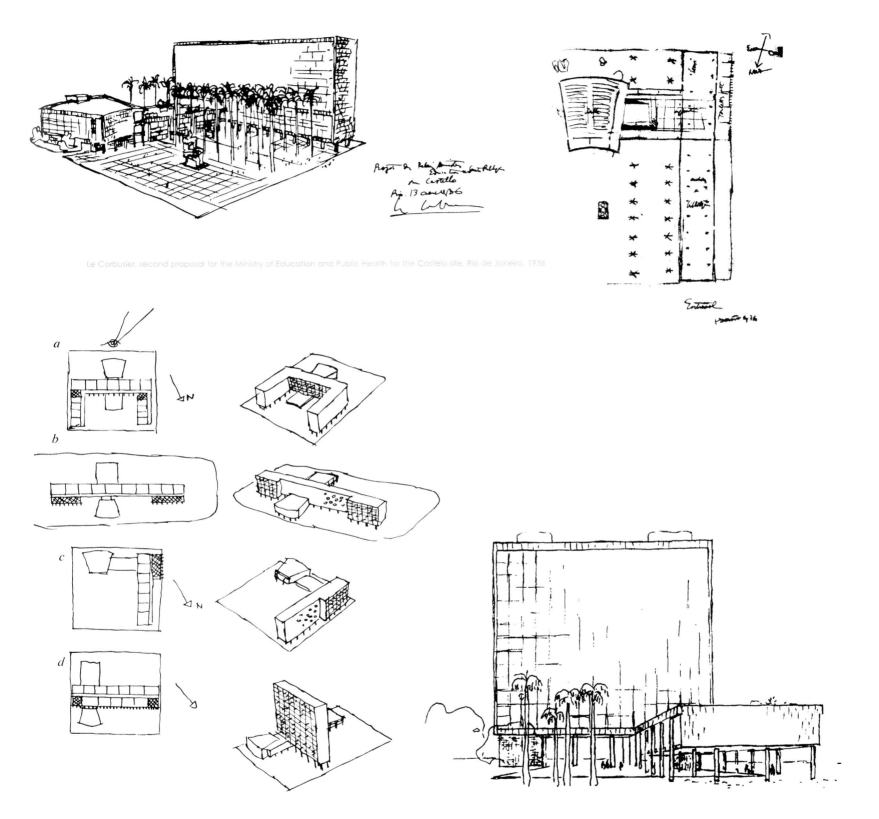

Le Corbusier, second proposal for the Ministry of Education and Public Health for the Castelo site, Rio de Janeiro, 1936

The evolution of the design for the Ministry of Education and Public Health, 1936–37:
a first scheme by the Brazilian team; b first scheme by Le Corbusier; c second scheme by Le Corbusier; d final scheme by the Brazilian team

Lúcio Costa's sketch of the completed building for the Ministry of Education and Public Health

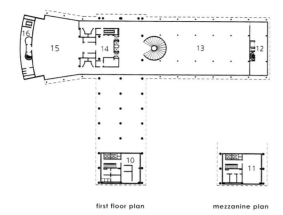

first floor plan   mezzanine plan

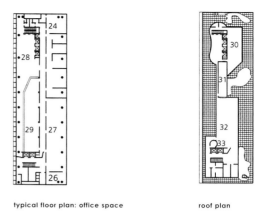

typical floor plan: office space   roof plan

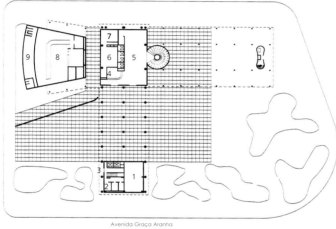

Avenida Graça Aranha

ground floor plan

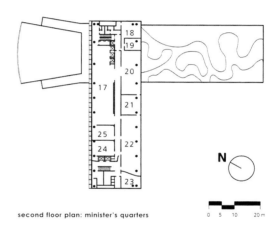

second floor plan: minister's quarters

N

0 5 10 20 m

1	reception (today bookshop)	
2	plant room	19 secretary's office
3	staff entrance	20 meeting room
4	reception	21 general secretary's office
5	public entrance lobby	22 office space
6	minister's entrance	23 reception
7,9,10	services	24 press room
8	treasury	25 staff room
11	storage	26 director's office
12	administration	27 office space
13	exhibition gallery	28 elevator lobby
14	meeting room	29 reception
15	auditorium Gilberto Freyre	30 minister's restaurant
16	projection room	31 kitchen
17	minister's lobby	32 staff cafeteria
18	minister's office	33 building administration

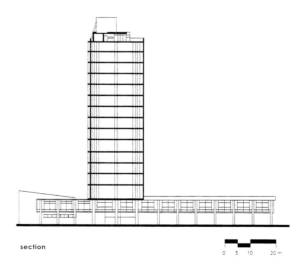

section

0 5 10 20 m

Lúcio Costa, Carlos Leão, Affonso Eduardo Reidy, Jorge Moreira, Ernani Vasconcellos and Oscar Niemeyer
with Le Corbusier as consultant, Ministry of Education and Public Health, Rio de Janeiro, 1936–44

Portuguese architectural traditions had been expelled from the city a century earlier.[56] Now they were redefined as being predisposed to polyphonist mixing and added to the Antropofagist totemic structure to contribute to the Brazilianization of Modernist architecture. Ironically, it was another foreign architect, Le Corbusier, who was called to grant legitimacy to modern Brazil's reconciliation with her colonial past in its redefined form, and who encouraged the seminal rapprochement. Later, Capanema would argue that the architecture of Le Corbusier and the Baroque cities of Minas Gerais shared a harmonious balance between 'beauty, functionality, and form'.[57] In Costa's view, Le Corbusier was 'sensitive to regionalism and cosmopolitan at the same time', and therefore an appropriate mediator between Brazil's local past and her international future.[58]

In 1925, Le Corbusier had declared decoration a 'charming entertainment for savages'.[59] In 1936 Costa reiterated: ' "adornment" is, in a way, a barbarian vestige'.[60] From 3–13 July 1935, one year before his second Brazilian visit, Le Corbusier hosted an exhibition of 'primitive art' in his Parisian apartment and studio, and spoke of the 'art of being able to group objects together . . . an expression of modern sensitivity towards the past, towards exoticism, and towards the present'. Le Corbusier and the art collector Louis Carré combined 'primitive' works from exotic lands with works by Henri Laurens, Fernand Léger and Le Corbusier himself, including a reproduction of the ancient Greek sculpture *Moscophore*, which Le Corbusier had 'restored' to its 'primitive' polychromatic state.[61] In Paris, he rehearsed his new art of grouping 'primitive' with advanced technology in his Petite Maison de Weekend at Celle-St-Cloud, Paris (1935), and in Brazil he found the opportunity to mix the local exotic with the European modern to produce a work of architecture in the same vein. The local 'primitive' that the Brazilians had rejected was granted legitimacy by the European master, who proposed an exoticist mixture.

Upon his departure, the Brazilian architects would take the suggestion one step further, radicalizing the 'primitive' and 'savage' elements of their land and culture, challenging and contaminating the European hegemonic model with the irreverent tropical, along the path delineated by the early Antropofagists, producing an innovative form of expression rather than a composite vision. To employ the terms of the myth at the basis of 'Cobra Norato' ('Black Snake', 1931), the poem of the Antropofagist movement's co-founder Raúl Bopp, the Brazilian (Amazonian in Bopp's poem) youth who worked at the Ministry of Education building seduced and conquered the great snake of European Modernism, entered its skin and, with this new body, embarked on a penetrating discovery of the unknown Brazilian world, symbolized by the jungle and all things 'exotic'.

Lúcio Costa confirms that it was Le Corbusier who recommended the use at the Ministry of Education of *azulejos*, vitrified

tile murals linked to the Portuguese hybrid tradition, and the local granitic gneiss, the colour of 'burnt straw', that the foreign architect had seen in Rio's nineteenth-century Neoclassical buildings and likened to leopard skin. This stone, Costa notes, was greatly favoured by Grandjean de Montigny but hardly used in colonial times, when other granites, similar to those found in Portugal, were considered nobler. In fact, gneiss was used for all external stone cladding at the Ministry of Education, except for the columns, which were sheathed in japuraná granite, which has a similar light pink colour with black veins but a finer grain. Lioz, a limestone from Portugal was used for the floor, staircase and columns in the ground-floor lobby.

Nineteenth-century buildings of Rio de Janeiro featuring the local granitic gneiss

Costa also points out that the *a posteriori* cladding of Neoclassical buildings with *azulejos* and ceramic ornaments, all of them imported from Oporto (where the largest part of the Santo Antonio factory's production was destined for export to Brazil), granted a degree of grace to the 'dry, excessively serious' and 'cold' architecture of Neoclassicism, and fostered its integration into the landscape and the traditional estates (*chácaras*). He notes that Le Corbusier was attracted by the practicality of the solution employed at the majority of city mansions at the time of his visit, as he was sensitive to things that had become too familiar for the Brazilians to take notice. But Costa also charged the nineteenth-century practice with radical qualities. For the Neoclassicism of Montigny and his Portuguese precursors, Costa

56 During the first phase of Rio's architectural Europeanization, when the city was raised to the status of royal capital, the chief of police, Paulo Fernandes Vianna, appointed by King João VI, banned the colonial Mozarabic window trellis, seen as incompatible with the city's modernization. Vianna also discouraged low, single-storey houses. **57** Gustavo Capanema, quoted in Williams, p. 213. **58** Lúcio Costa, 'Presença de Le Corbusier' (1987), in Lúcio Costa, 1997, p. 146. **59** Le Corbusier, 1987c, p. 85. **60** Lúcio Costa, 2000, p. 626. **61** Le Corbusier, quoted in Sbriglio, pp. 57–60.

postulates, represented a 'violation...an *imported* rupture... somewhat like the introduction of modernism' – probably a reference to the rather insufficiently acknowledged early Brazilian Modernism of the school building programme, which preceded the state-sponsored Ministry of Education and Public Health.[62]

The Modernists' self-conscious adoption of the colonial tiles, Costa insinuates, also pays tribute to an intuitive contamination and hybridization of the imposed European style by anonymous nineteenth-century Cariocas, which turned *azulejos* into signifiers of cultural resistance against foreign imports. Costa underlines the functional role of the *azulejos* in a climate where high humidity easily stains rendered walls.[63] In the heat of the summer, the tiles convey a pleasing sensation of coolness, while they also help break up the mass and solidity of volumes. Beyond this justification for the survival of elements of colonial architecture on the basis of function, however, Costa extended to the nineteenth century the interpretation of Brazilian culture as a European legacy transformed by the particular conditions of the New World. He thus endowed defensive climatic responses to particular geographic conditions with the ability to undermine nineteenth- and twentieth-century imported dictates. The Modernists' conscious mixing of the materials of Neoclassicism with those of colonial architecture reversed the Neoclassical break with the colonial past and reestablished a sense of historical continuity through the radical transformation of a taboo of both orthodox Modernism and Brazilian nationalism.

In May 1943, the *Architectural Review* admired the Modernist Brazilian architects' extensive use of *brises-soleil*, which enabled them to create 'surfaces within the limitations of the twentieth century idiom just as flickeringly alive as the stucco and woodwork at [the Baroque churches of] Salvador'.[64] A few months later, however, the March 1944 issue of the same journal described the Ministry of Education's north façade, entirely shielded with *brises-soleil*, as an 'enormous "honeycomb"', and compared it to the 'primitive types of bee-hive dwellings' sketched by Jean-Baptiste Debret (1768–1848) during his travels in Brazil in 1820. The monumental Modernist building was pronounced 'a technically rather more highly developed example of the tree-house in [Debret's] drawing'. Debret's sketches were published as 'a fitting companion' next to the photographs of the building Le Corbusier wished to have fathered.[65] Yet the 'primitive'-inspired element of the Ministry of Education was not its sophisticated, climate-responsive envelope but its architectural application of the Antropofagist strategy of cultural resistance and empowering irreverence. Costa referred to the symbolic significance of the building in clear Antropofagist terms, emphasizing that it 'demonstrated the capacity of the native genius to absorb and assimilate invention'.[66] The Antropofagists reinvented not the dwellings of the Brazilian 'primitives' but the Corbusian evangelizing vocabulary

M i n i s t r y
The Ministry of Education and Health, Rio de Janeiro. Architects, Lucio Costa, Oscar Niemeyer, Afonso Reidy, Carlos Leão, Jorge Moreiro and Ernani Vasconcelos ; Le Corbusier, Consultant. Begun about 1937, still under construction. The Minister of Education and Health has certainly inspired the construction of a remarkable building. Most striking is the enormous "honeycomb" that shields the north side of the building. The north and south elevations are entirely of glass, the narrow east and west walls and the columns supporting the main block are veneered in pinkish-grey granite. The low block contains the auditorium and exhibition halls and is faced with specially designed blue and white tiles, which also form a great mural at the base of the west wall of the main building. The roof structures enclosing water tanks and lift apparatus have boldly curved outlines and are covered by vitreous blue tiles. Debret's quaint drawing of the primitive types of bee-hive dwellings he saw on his travels in 1820 is a fitting companion to this building, which might be described as a technically rather more highly developed example of the tree-house in the drawing.

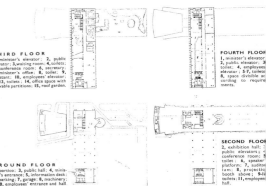

THIRD FLOOR
1, minister's elevator ; 2, public elevator ; 3,waiting room ; 4, toilets ; 5, conference room ; 6, secretary ; 7, minister's office ; 8, toilet. 9, assistant ; 10, employees' elevator ; 11-13, toilets ; 14, office space with movable partitions ; 15, roof garden.

FOURTH FLOOR
1, minister's elevator ; 2, public elevator ; 3, toilet ; 4, employees' elevator ; 5-7, toilets ; 8, space divisible according to requirements.

GROUND FLOOR
2, portico ; 3, public hall ; 4, minister's entrance ; 5, information desk ; 6, parking ; 7, garage ; 8, machinery ; 9-10, employees' entrance and hall.

SECOND FLOOR
2, exhibition hall ; 3, public elevators ; 5, conference room ; 6, toilet. 6, speaker platform ; 7, auditorium ; 8, projection booth above ; 9-10, toilets ; 11,employees' hall.

The Ministry of Education and Public Health compared to the 'primitive types of bee-hive dwellings' sketched by Jean-Baptiste Debret during his travels in Brazil in 1820; *Architectural Review* 45, no. 567, March 1944, special issue on Brazil, p. 76

of open floor plan, free façade, *pilotis*, curtain walls and roof gardens.

The Ministry of Education building constitutes the first complete application of Le Corbusier's 'Five Points of a New Architecture'; but these were combined with local materials, allusions to the Brazilian landscape and Baroque monuments, sensuous curves, and bold colours related to the 'Moorish and Arabic

62 Lúcio Costa, 'Presença de Le Corbusier' (1987), in Lúcio Costa, 1997, pp. 146–47, emphasis in the original. Le Corbusier also produced some abstract sketches for the *azulejo* murals, but these were not implemented. **63** Costa echoes Fernando de Azevedo's article of 1926 in a São Paulo newspaper; Azevedo, p. 310. **64** *Architectural Review* 93, no. 557, May 1943, p. 134. **65** *Architectural Review*, 1944a, p. 76. **66** Lúcio Costa, 'Ministério da Educação e Saúde 1936' (n.d.), in Lúcio Costa, 1997, p. 128.

colors [of] the Portuguese'. In a resourceful architectural application of Modernist collage techniques, all solid walls and columns were sheathed in stone, monochrome small *pastilha* tiles or hand-painted *azulejos*. This kind of 'camouflage architectural' was not strange to Le Corbusier, who had already in 1932 referred to his own 'pictorial interventions' as aiming to 'destroy' 'the quality of pure and functional architecture': 'I admit the mural not to enhance a wall, but on the contrary, as a means to violently destroy the wall, to remove from it all sense of stability, of weight, etc.'[67] Luiz Recamán has also argued that Le Corbusier's 'Five Points' were used by the Brazilian team 'in a way that contradicts the reforming and planning ideals with which they were originally conceived'. In Brazil, Recamán maintains, 'it was a question of overcoming that error, common to almost all modern architecture, that had tied – with no means of mediation – the social dimension of architecture to its autonomous form'.[68]

Cândido Portinari, detail of hand-painted *azulejos* on the freeform volume that anchors the Ministry's lower block and provides access to the minister's rooftop garden

The nationalization of Corbusian imports to serve ideological and environmental requirements was of paramount importance. The *brises-soleil* were related to the Moorish shading devices of colonial architecture, like the *muxarabi* Costa first admired in Diamantina and the pierced concrete screens or ceramic *combogó* already used in other examples of Brazilian Modernist architecture.[69] Here, the horizontal *brises-soleil* – which Niemeyer claims as his own design contribution and which were painted blue following Costa's suggestion – were employed to ensure that the Ministry of Education building would be spared the problems that had befallen Le Corbusier and Pierre Jeanneret's Cité de Refuge (Paris, 1929–33) and Pavillon Suisse (Cité Universitaire, Paris, 1930–31), with their unprotected, south-facing glass façades.[70] The detailing of the windows ensured cross-ventilation, and the *brises-soleil* were also made adjustable to respond to the shifting rays of

Rio's tropical sun and to allow users control of their environment. This solution also granted the façade a playful appearance, a dynamism and plastic instability that was in line with Burle Marx's decolonized, 'open-ended' gardens, and was critical of rigid Modernist forms and plain, static surfaces.[71]

To this day, no air-conditioning system has been installed in the Ministry of Education building, except in the first-floor auditorium (named Auditorio Gilberto Freyre). With the fixed, can-

Muxarabi balcony of an eighteenth-century colonial house known as Casa do Muxarabi, today housing the Biblioteca Antônio Torres, Diamantina, Minas Gerais

67 Letter from Le Corbusier to Vladimir Nekrassov, 1932, quoted in Colomina, 1996a, p. 174. **68** Recamán, p. 114. **69** In 1922, Costa was particularly impressed by the extensive *muxarabi* on the façade of the eighteenth-century house of Chica da Silva in Diamantina. Lúcio Costa, 'Diamantina' (n.d.), in Lúcio Costa, 1997, p. 27. Later, Niemeyer would compare the *brises-soleil* to the volutes of Baroque art. He is reported to have pointed out that the two devices 'fulfil the same role . . .; they give protection from the sun while at the same time avoiding straight lines'; Beauvoir, p. 566. **70** Curtis, 1986, pp. 102–4. Le Corbusier 'acknowledged in the *Œuvre complète 1938–46* that Centrosoyuz would have been better with *brise-soleil*; these were added to the Armée du Salut in 1946, along with new glazing systems to Centrosoyuz and the Pavillon Suisse to make them inhabitable'; Deckker, p. 185. **71** Vaccarino, 2000b, p. 43.

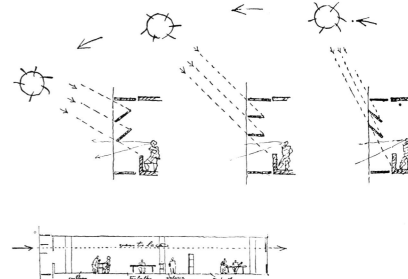

tilevered, 50-centimetre-deep concrete grid that holds the manually operated, movable horizontal blades at a distance from the floor slabs, and the three asbestos blades (four on the second floor) fitted at the upper part of each floor section, adequate shading is ensured throughout the year, while views remain unobstructed. With the addition of a fourth blade, the greater height of the minister's floor was also successfully disguised. In the following decades, these adjustable *brises-soleil* would become the distinguishing refrain of Brazilian Modernist architecture, pointing to strategies of appropriation and recontextualization of both native traditions and foreign contributions, and highlighting the transcultural importance of key elements in the visual language of Brazilian Modernism.

For the first time at the gardens of the Ministry of Education (1938–44), Roberto Burle Marx translated an abstract painting into a tropical space for leisurely promenade. As Jacques Leenhardt notes, the most surprising element of Burle Marx's original gouache

Roberto Burle Marx, painting for the minister's rooftop garden, 1938, gouache

Jardin suspendu atop the lower block of the Ministry and public, street-level garden, both designed by Roberto Burle Marx, 1938–44

for the minister's *jardin suspendu* is that 'the green colour is hardly visible'.[72] Burle Marx applied the same strategy at contemporaneous projects for the Associação Brasileira de Imprensa (ABI, Brazilian Press Association Headquarters), designed by Marcelo, Milton and Maurício Roberto (1936–38), and, most significantly, for Brazil's twentieth-century front door, Rio de Janeiro's Santos Dumont Airport, designed in 1937, again by Marcelo, Milton and Maurício Roberto. Echoing familiar Modernist rhetoric, Costa argued that the Modernist architecture of reinforced concrete was 'linked . . . to the . . . reason of Greeks and Romans'.[73] Burle Marx's tropical gardens rooted the architecture of the Ministry of Education in Brazil's green infernal paradise. Thanks to Rio's tropical climate, they did not take long to mature and complement the architecture. In 1947, 'looking up at the building from below',

towards the minister's rooftop garden with its *Reclining Girl* by Celso Antônio and *Woman* by Adriana Janacópulos, Claude Vincent of the *Architectural Review* had 'the mysterious feeling of some strange jungle rising fantastically into the sky and bringing the rain clouds down to the level of the two blue funnels which enclose the lift shafts and the water cisterns of what is still the most beautiful skyscraper in Rio'.[74]

Through a strategy of radicalization of Brazil's undomesticated and irrational or Dionysian side, the Ministry of Education building brought about a carnivalization of the colonial 'civilization' of the jungle and of the nineteenth-century desire for a Europeanization of Brazil's virgin forest. Furthermore, Burle Marx's 'lusty' gardens, to borrow Stamo Papadaki's term,[75] voiced a critique of the architecture of educational reconstruction in Brazil and, generally, of the reductive functionalist formulae and moralism of technological rationalism, reintroducing the natural, the pleasurable and the poetic into the architectural programme. Thenceforth, the gardens of Roberto Burle Marx would play a key role in the architecture of Niemeyer and the other Brazilian Modernists, epitomizing the desire to transgress the rules of pleasureless, artless and prosaic functionalist architecture.[76] Niemeyer would become the most prominent exponent of this radicalization of extra-functionalist spaces.

The Brazilian architects moved the volume Le Corbusier had positioned along Avenida Graça Aranha to the middle of the site to allow unimpeded views towards the bay, and rotated it by 90 degrees to achieve a north–south orientation. Most importantly, the move to the centre of the site allowed the height of the building to be increased, thus reducing its footprint and freeing up a ground-floor civic space that was made accessible from all streets surrounding the site. Le Corbusier had blocked passage across the site by introducing a glazed enclosure on the ground floor. Realizing the importance of a civic space at the centre of the city that could be criss-crossed throughout the day by employees of the surrounding government buildings, the Brazilian architects extended their scheme across the site to the south and the southeast to incorporate the eighteenth-century Church of Santa Luzia as an *objet trouvé* in the Ministry of Education's extensive landscaped gardens.[77] A desire to emphasize the 'building's splendor' was also offered as a justification for these modifications, and 'ceremonies of a cultural character, in accordance with the Ministry's objective' were foreseen for the 'large esplanade'.[78]

72 Leenhardt, p. 188. Burle Marx worked also as an assistant to his former tutor, Cândido Portinari, in creating the *azulejo* murals of the Ministry of Education building.   **73** Lúcio Costa, 2000, p. 628.   **74** Vincent, 1947, p. 172.   **75** Papadaki, 1960, p. 19.   **76** Niemeyer and Burle Marx have not always got along well. Nevertheless, Niemeyer chose to work with Burle Marx because 'he is the best in his line of business'; Vollers, p. 13.   **77** Sadly, a car park has now taken the place of a large part of the garden, compromising the original scheme.   **78** Ministry of Education project team, 'The Definitive Solution' (1938), in Bonduki (ed.), 2000, p. 55.

The Brazilian team elongated the Corbusian *pilotis* of the sixteen-storey office block considerably from 4 meters to 10, attuning them to the verticality of the tower with which they replaced Le Corbusier's low-lying volume, freeing the ground further and offering a true Corbusian liberated terrain back to the city. This modification also allowed the lower block to cross under the vertical slab without compromising the clarity of either volume. The jungle-crowned perpendicular block preserves its orthogonality at the garden end, stopping short of the line of the site to the south for fear of jeopardizing the continuity, penetrability and fluidity of the civic square that unites the monument with the city. A small volume with a plan in the shape of an 8, nestling within the space of the *pilotis*, anchors this block. It was added after the completion of the building to provide access to the minister's rooftop garden for maintenance. Like all the other volumes within the *pilotis* (apart from that at the point of intersection of the two blocks) – the treas-

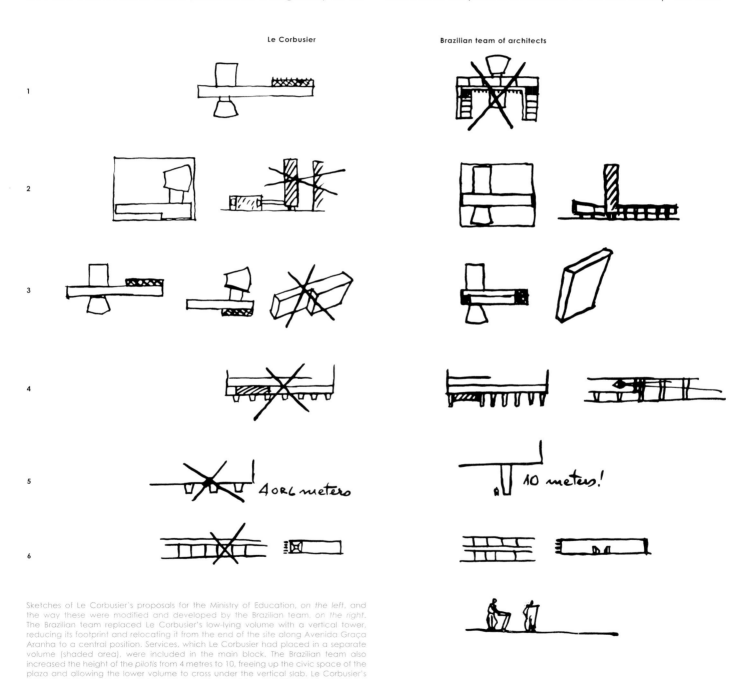

Le Corbusier   Brazilian team of architects

Sketches of Le Corbusier's proposals for the Ministry of Education, *on the left*, and the way these were modified and developed by the Brazilian team, *on the right*. The Brazilian team replaced Le Corbusier's low-lying volume with a vertical tower, reducing its footprint and relocating it from the end of the site along Avenida Graça Aranha to a central position. Services, which Le Corbusier had placed in a separate volume (shaded area), were included in the main block. The Brazilian team also increased the height of the *pilotis* from 4 metres to 10, freeing up the civic space of the plaza and allowing the lower volume to cross under the vertical slab. Le Corbusier's single-loaded corridor was replaced by a central corridor with offices on both sides.

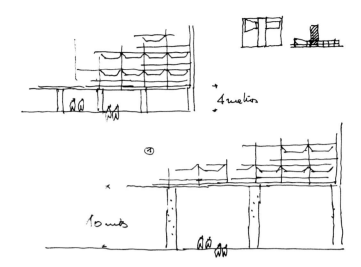

ury and plant room under the first-floor auditorium to the north; the reception (today a bookshop), staff entrance and services to the west; and the circular staircase leading to the first-floor exhibition gallery and auditorium – its solidity is undermined by its cladding in ornamental hand-painted blue-and-white *azulejos* designed by Cândido Portinari and manufactured by Osirarte, under the direction of the artist Paulo Cláudio Rossi (1890–1959).

The slender columns of the two-storey block continue uninterrupted on the outside of its curtain wall, thus appearing as high as those supporting the tall office prism, which retreat behind the curtain wall from the second floor upwards. In this way, all the public spaces of the complex – those in the public plaza and those contained within the two-storey horizontal block (the auditorium, exhibition hall, information desk and public lobby) – are united within the dramatic space of the monumental colonnades. Discreetly connected to the first-floor slab by corbels, the columns of the two-storey volume appear relieved of their load-bearing duty, entrusted with a consciously expressive role that, in the next decades, would become the hallmark of Niemeyer's work. The part of the horizontal volume that projects to the south and houses the exhibition gallery thus appears weightless, suspended in mid-air, producing the 'kind of aesthetic sensation', so novel at the time, that, in Sigfried Giedion's words, 'results when the relation between load and support is no longer traditionally obvious'.[79]

The *pilotis* of the two blocks serve to provide shade, rain shelter and structure to the public open-air space without interrupting movement through it. The more robust, soaring colonnade supporting the office prism, with its peripheral columns sited slightly inboard of the edge of the plan, also acts as a portico, defining and protecting the passage between the public entrance at the intersection of the two blocks and the richly decorated small volume to the west. Niemeyer dwells on the 'free-floating and monumental' columns of the office block, taking credit for the 'modification of Le Corbusier's original design [which gave] the building a more free-flowing style'. He continues: 'the columns undeniably gained integrity, as people moved around them highlighting their scale and splendour.'[80] As already noted, it is significant that Niemeyer attributes his first transformation of the Corbusian means of formal expression to a desire for a 'free-flowing style', 'lightness', monumentality and splendour – all qualities in excess of a func-

79 Giedion, 1949, p. 417.   80 Niemeyer, 2000b, p. 67.

tionalist fulfilment of programmatic requirements.[81] Organic forms appeared in the ground-floor civic space, the second-floor minister's quarters and garden, the fourth-floor public library, and on the roof of the building, with dining pavilions and gardens enjoying an open view to the sea. Visible from a distance, the water tank and free-form elevator tower clad in blue *pastilha* tiles were designed by Niemeyer with the roofscape of surrounding buildings in mind. They recall the ocean liner stacks that would soon appear atop Le Corbusier's Unité d'Habitation in Marseilles (1947–53), while also paying homage to Rio's celebrated natural skyline with its distinct mountain peaks.[82]

Niemeyer recalls the first meeting of the Ministry of Education architects with Le Corbusier, in 1936, when Niemeyer regarded the European guest as 'an architect-genius come down from heaven'.[83] But the Brazilian Modernists' irreverent approach towards their European visitor might be more aptly described by a line from Hans Staden's sixteenth-century travelogue: 'Here comes our food hopping towards us.'[84] The Brazilian architects invited and welcomed Le Corbusier's proposals and ingested them to strengthen their own architecture. At the same time, and most importantly, their conscious 'transformation of the Tabu into a totem' undermined the dominating strategy implied in the foreign catechizing import. The Ministry of Education stands at the beginning of a process that denounces the repressive hierarchy of the allegedly rational, Euclidean orthogonality of the European master – 'where the orthogonal is supreme, there we can read the height of a civilization', were Le Corbusier's words – exposing its cultural bias. For Le Corbusier, 'rational forms, with their basis in geometry' are the forms of 'Classicism' as opposed to 'Barbarism'.[85] Infecting the Cartesian volumes with the crooked lines of the 'pack-donkey' that Le Corbusier had abhorred in his *City of Tomorrow*, ironically, the Brazilians paid homage to his conversion to the 'wavy lines' of the 'violent and sublime' native landscape during his 1929 Brazilian visit.[86] As is often pointed out, Antropofagist critical devouring 'implies a gesture of acknowledgement'.[87] These 'wavy lines' aimed to ally Brazilian and European architecture 'as equal with equal', in the same way that they 'had allied' the Nambikwara leader and Lévi-Strauss in 1938.[88] From the Ministry of Education building onwards, these wavy lines would become the embodiment of the Brazilian 'revolt against reason' that so infuriated Pevsner.[89]

Valerie Fraser argues that Burle Marx's rooftop garden, which resembles an aerial view of a tropical wetland landscape, may

View from the portico towards the Ministry's public entrance at the intersection of the two blocks

Ministry of Education and Public Health: rooftop terrace with minister's restaurant and free-form elevator tower clad in blue *pastilha* tiles, and garden by Roberto Burle Marx

have been inspired by Le Corbusier's lyrical description of the views that fascinated him during his 1929 flight over Argentina, especially those of the meanders of the Paraná and Paraguay rivers 'in these endless flat plains'. In *Précisions*, Le Corbusier repeatedly employed the image of sinuous river curves as a metaphor for 'the incoherent loops of the meanders of an outworn civilization', against which is directed the rationality of the 'machine age'.[90] Fraser offers a convincing reading of the 'meandering anarchy of Burle Marx's design as a . . . deliberate celebra-

81 Niemeyer, 1993c p. 61.   **82** These nautical allusions may be the reason the building was called 'Capanema-Maru' by its contemporary critics. *Maru* were the Japanese ships that were often seen in Rio's harbour at the time: *Correio da Noite*, 2 October 1945, in Lissovsky and Moraes de Sá, p. 209.   **83** Niemeyer, 2000b, p. 69.   **84** Staden, p. 80.   **85** Le Corbusier, 1987b, pp. 36–37.   **86** Le Corbusier, 1987b, pp. 5–6: Le Corbusier, 1991, p. 244.   **87** Vieira, p. 109.   **88** Lévi-Strauss, 1965, pp. 287–93.   **89** Pevsner, 1972, p. 426.   **90** Le Corbusier, 1991, pp. 4, 17, 154.

Roberto Burle Marx, minister's rooftop garden, original version featuring organically curved areas surfaced in stones of various colours and textures, photograph of 1944

tion of the irrational meander coexisting with the straight lines of Le Corbusian modernity'.[91] Unfortunately, following a modification of the garden in the 1970s, much of the original river-bank effect was lost. Around the planted amoebae, Burle Marx's original scheme featured organically curved areas in stones of various colours and textures – like highly polished white marble and textured green jade – sadly, all replaced by white limestone (*pedra portuguesa*).

With their emphasized verticality and upward thrust, the granite-clad columns of the Ministry of Education rhyme with the tall palms standing on the urban square landscaped by Roberto Burle Marx, that Carioca icon 'in whose shade', Freyre notes, 'the first secondary schools [of Brazil] sprang up, the first library, the first bank'.[92] Inside the building, the cylindrical columns clad in sucupira wood are also made to look tall and continuous, effortlessly piercing the floor slabs. Emilio Henrique Baumgart, the distinguished engineer of the *A Noite* tower, where he also had his office, avoided beams, using for the first time in Brazil a system of double slabs and inverted capitals (*Pilzdecken*), which gave clear ceilings. In his memoirs, Niemeyer describes his frequent visits to the Botanical Garden as a young architect, where 'the imperial palms . . . caught my attention with their tall, elegant, and stately trunks reaching skyward'.[93] Palmic colonnades featured first in Le Corbusier's proposals, then on the final project of the Brazilian

team. In contrast to these, however, Burle Marx's palms follow no rigid line, being freely positioned in the planted amoebae of the public street-level garden, which includes five symbolic pau-brasil trees, a *Bombacacea*, and Bruno Giorgi's statue, *Juventude Brasileira*. When viewed from the street, the public square or the windows of the first-floor exhibition hall, the similarity between the granite-clad column trunks and those of the palms, rising across a common visual field, is striking.

The granite-clad columns of the Ministry's *pilotis* rhyme with the tall palms on the urban square landscaped by Roberto Burle Marx

Ministry of Education and Public Health: first-floor exhibition gallery overlooking the public square

91 Fraser, 2000b, pp. 180–93, quotation on p. 189.   **92** Freyre, 1986, p. 4.
93 Niemeyer, 2000b, p. 19.

Allusions to the icons of the Brazilian landscape are also found inside the building. In the gallery space, the shiny black linoleum floor casts up reflections of the black steel mullions of the curtain wall and the sucupira-clad columns in the same way that the black waters of the Rio Negro mirror the veins of vegetal growth on its banks. The detailing of the curtain wall and the circular columns rising next to it merge with the landscaped gardens outside the building, bringing the latter into a relationship with the internal

space. In the second-floor lobby of the minister's quarters, Niemeyer's free-form carpet with its organically curved areas of earthy colours set against a shiny black linoleum floor recalls the emblematic Amazonian riverscape while also echoing Burle Marx's roof-garden patterns.[94]

A copy of one of the celebrated prophet statues at Congonhas by Aleijadinho was also installed in the reception hall of the minister's quarters. But it is in the public space of the *pilotis* that Brazil's venerable Baroque monuments are most powerfully evoked. The sturdy stone columns against the *azulejo-clad* walls bring irresistibly to mind the cloisters of Franciscan convents in the Brazilian Northeast, such as the seventeenth-century Convento de Nossa Senhora das Neves e da Ordem Terceira de São Francisco in Olinda, Pernambuco, the oldest Franciscan monastery in Brazil, or the early eighteenth-century Convento de São Francisco in Salvador, Bahia.

The Ministry of Education building successfully integrated architecture, urbanism, landscape architecture, art and politics. Capanema heralded it as 'a great architectural monument . . . a work of art and a house of work'.[95] The well-equipped and pleasant Euclides da Cunha Library on the fourth floor serves local high-school pupils. At the rooftop restaurant, special meals used to be organized for the purpose of teaching underprivileged children table manners. Among its many innovations, the Ministry of Education building introduced open floor plans with office spaces divided by low partitions, and standardized furniture and fittings. The designers' attention to practical considerations, fine materials and meticulous detailing were matched by high-quality craftsmanship. Organizing the building as a *Gesamtkunstwerk*, the ambitious minister initiated what Niemeyer sees as 'a revival of the old practice of integrating art and architecture',[96] commissioning Brazilian artists: Cândido Portinari, Bruno Giorgi, Celso Antônio and Adriana Janacópulos. Jacques Lipchitz's *Prometheus Unbound* on the north façade of the auditorium – unfortunately mistakenly cast at one-third of the intended size – is the only exception.[97] They created artworks and furniture specially for the building, thus mounting a further assault against a functional rejection of art and luxury.

Niemeyer has since spoken of a 'symbiosis between structure and decoration', explaining that it is at the early design stage that he may conceive a wall of granite, or one covered with a tapestry, bas-reliefs or *azulejos*. Artworks and furnishings, he affirms, can-

First-floor hall above the Ministry's public entrance lobby with sucupira-clad columns and wall, overlooking the entrance portico; at the centre of the spiral staircase, *Reclining Girl* by Celso Antônio, originally in the minister's rooftop garden

Second-floor lobby of the minister's quarters with free-form carpet designed by Oscar Niemeyer, and Cândido Portinari's mural *Jogos infantis (Children's Games)*

94 Sadly, much of the effect was lost following a restoration in the 1990s, when the linoleum floor of this space was replaced by a dark grey carpet. **95** Gustavo Capanema, quoted in Deckker, p. 44. **96** Niemeyer, 'Prefácio', in Cavalcanti (ed.), 2000, p. 7. Le Corbusier, too, had promoted the integration of 'contemporary sculptures . . . to play a dazzling role in the architectural symphonies'; Le Corbusier, 1991, p. 58. **97** Lipchitz was recommended by Niemeyer himself. Niemeyer says that, at the time, Lipchitz 'was the sculptor who worked in close association with Le Corbusier', which no doubt was the reason for the recommendation; Niemeyer, 2000b, p. 137.

The soaring japuraná-clad *pilotis* of the Ministry of Education and Public Health against Cândido Portinari's *azulejo* murals, *below*, evoke the cloisters of Franciscan monasteries in the Brazilian Northeast: *above*, monastery of Nossa Senhora das Neves e da Ordem Terceira de São Francisco, Olinda, Pernambuco, 1585, reconstructed from 1654; cloister with eighteenth-century columns and blue-and-white *azulejos* (1734–45) representing scenes of the life of St Francis of Assis

Euclides da Cunha Library on the fourth floor of the Ministry of Education and Public Health

not be introduced into a building as afterthoughts, but should always be considered at the design stage in relation to the function of each project or space.[98] Populating the architectural stage with artworks has allowed Niemeyer to tap into the theatrical dimension of architecture, initiating a performance that makes it easier to engage the spectator and invite participation. Gilles Deleuze recognized a Baroque sensitivity in this modern pursuit of 'a unity of arts as "performance," [which seeks] to draw the spectator into this very performance'.[99] Niemeyer 'define[d] the architect's role as coordinator of a building's furnishings and of the selection of artworks'. For 'This is the creative act, the highly sought-after integration of art and architecture.' In the 1980s, in an article arguing that he should be the one to select the artworks for his Memorial for America Latina in São Paulo, he 'shamelessly affirm[ed] his position as the [Brazilian] architect who has included the largest number of artworks in architectural designs', always 'with a view to the indispensable unity and beauty of the work'. Referring to the Ministry of Education building, which introduced the practice, he affirmed:

> I have always followed Capanema's example. Whenever possible, I have invited artists to collaborate on my designs . . . I never forgot them, even when I was working abroad. In the Old World [Brazilian artists'] work is integrated into my architectural designs as examples of Brazilian creativity and culture.[100]

Cândido Portinari has been one of Niemeyer's principal artist collaborators. His contribution to the Ministry of Education building

reflects the growing interest at this time in the popular classes, who were invited to take part in the world of Brazilian modernity under construction. For the meeting room adjacent to the minister's office he created a series of frescoes representing the principal economic cycles of Brazilian history through the labours of multi-ethnic workers. The construction of the building aiming to foster Brazil's image of cultural *renovação* coincided also with a time when Brazilian intellectuals intensified promotion of a favourable image of their country as 'the ideal land for a true community of people representing very diverse ethnic origins . . . [a country that] offers the most scientific and human solution to the problem of mixing races and cultures – a problem so acute among other peoples'.[101] In 1935 Gilberto Freyre had issued a 'Manifesto Against Racial Prejudice'. Although a belief in the virtues of so-called whitening persisted and racial relations in Brazil had changed little in the 1930s and 1940s, the Brazilians comforted themselves with the idea that their situation was preferable to both that of the old industrialized world of Nazi Germany and that of the United States, which continued to practise racial segregation.

Granted landmark status in 1947, the Ministry of Education and Public Health became a symbol and manifesto of Brazilian modernity and an architectural synthesis of all the legitimate ingredients of *brasilidade*: 'caravels / canoes / slave-ships', to use

Ministry of Education and Public Health: meeting room adjacent to the minister's office, with Cândido Portinari's frescoes representing the principal economic cycles of Brazilian history

98 Niemeyer, 1993c, pp. 27–31. **99** Deleuze, p. 123. **100** Niemeyer, 2000b, pp. 136–39. **101** From the manifesto issued by the Brazilian Society of Anthropology and Ethnology in 1942, cited in Skidmore, 1993, p. 207.

the symbolic terms of Guilherme de Almeida's poem 'Raça' ('Race', 1925). Functioning as 'a machine for remembering', in Carlos Eduardo Dias Comas's apt formulation, it reflected the new style in which the Brazilian nation was imagined and the fact that this style had been granted official approval by the Brazilian state.[102] Monumentalizing the officially promoted image of Brazilian *mestiçagem*, it offered an architectural expression of hybridization as a reflection of what Florestan Fernandes called Brazil's 'myth of racial democracy' soon after its consolidation. Like the much-vaunted myth itself, the Ministry of Education building embodied a utopia that disguised an all-too-obvious reality of asymmetrical racial and socio-economic relations.

Following Costa's 'self-imposed ostracism' in 1939, Niemeyer assumed the leadership of the Ministry of Education team, while Costa concentrated all his energy on his duties as director of research at the Serviço do Patrimônio Histórico e Artístico Nacional (SPHAN).[103] From 1937, a new law, inspired by Gustavo Capanema, had given the Ministry of Education and Public Health a broader cultural role, and the influential minister requested renaming it the Ministry of National Culture.[104] The building was inaugurated on 3 October 1945. A year earlier, Sigfried Giedion had already included it in his essay 'The Need for a New Monumentality'.[105]

Oscar Niemeyer: Early Works and Projects

The innovations introduced by Brazilian Modernist architects during the 1930s and 1940s were not only responses to local conditions and particularities but also expressions of a critical point of view towards European and North American Modernism. But they were generally reviewed by contemporary critics as responses to the problem of environmental control. The sunbreak or *brise-soleil*, often also functioning as wind- and rain-break, appeared in many variations: with fixed or movable louvres in a range of materials and configurations, jalousies, openwork screens of ceramic (*combogó*) or perforated concrete blocks, lattice-work (*muxarabi*) and so on. This feature was singled out as the architectural element that epitomized a Brazilian architecture attuned to regional climatic realities and traditions. As an architectural device defined through natural conditions rather than industrial production – the state of underdevelopment of Brazilian industry encouraged low-technology solutions – the sunscreen was adopted by the Brazilians as the symbol of their imaginatively subversive tropicalization of European Modernism.

At the opening of the 1943 *Brazil Builds* exhibition at the Museum of Modern Art in New York, Philip L. Goodwin, the museum's co-designer with Edward D. Stone (1938–39) and director of the architecture department, explained that the exhibition was stimulated by MoMA's 'keen desire to know more about Brazilian architecture, especially their solutions for the problem of controlling heat and light on large exterior glass surfaces'.[106] In the accompanying catalogue, which devoted six pages to the development of the sunbreak, Goodwin announced: '[Brazil's] great contribution to modern architecture is the control of heat and glare on glass surfaces by means of external blinds.'[107] Such solutions would soon appear on modern buildings as far apart as Lisbon, Athens, Royan, Conakry in Guinea, Mopti in Mali, London, Havana and Tel Aviv.

Modern Brazilian architecture was first introduced to the French public in 1945 through an article in *L'Architecture d'Aujourd'hui* on the *brise-soleil*, showcasing the completed Brazilian Press Association and Ministry of Education buildings, together with models of two skyscrapers for Algiers by Le Corbusier and Pierre Jeanneret.[108] Graphic abstractions of *brises-soleil* featured also on the covers of the September 1947 and August 1952 issues of *L'Architecture d'Aujourd'hui*, both dedicated to Brazil. In 1956, Henrique Mindlin noted that aluminium *brises-soleil* were being mass produced in São Paulo.[109] Gilberto Freyre commented with approval on Goodwin's linking of the Modernist Brazilian sunblinds to the colonial *rótula*, a type of jalousie, satisfying needs for sun protection as well as for 'the privacy which Brazilians have enjoyed for centuries'. For Freyre, the modern variations of the 'external blinds that the French call *brise-soleil* and the Portuguese *quebra-sol*' exemplified the Brazilian Modernist architects' 'conviction that the patriarchal past of Brazil was creative and not negative'.[110] To take advantage of views towards the park, Lúcio Costa turned the climatically unfavourably oriented façades of his celebrated luxury apartment blocks – Edifícios Nova Cintra, Bristol and Caledônia, in Parque Eduardo Guinle, Rio de Janeiro – into a gridded fabric composed entirely of variations of the sunbreak: vertical *brises-soleil*, different kinds of pre-cast ceramic grilles, latticed panels, *combogó* and so on.[111]

In the first monograph on Oscar Niemeyer, published in 1950, Stamo Papadaki contrasted North American 'technological' answers to the problem, resulting in buildings with artificially controlled environments totally 'free' of their natural surroundings, with the Brazilian 'plastic solutions', which 'enrich the architectural vocabulary' and provide 'the inhabitant with more than a mini-

102 Comas, 1998a, p. 130.   **103** Lúcio Costa, 'Relato pessoal' (1975), in Lúcio Costa, 1997, p. 138. In 1985, following Niemeyer's request, the minister of education, Marco Maciel, named the Ministry of Education building Palácio Gustavo Capanema as a 'tribute . . . to the man who made it possible to build that magnificent work, that unique manifestation of creative freedom and the emblematic landmark of the new Brazilian architecture'; quoted in Niemeyer, 2000b, p. 27.   **104** Williams, pp. 62, 73. In the early 1950s, it was renamed Ministry of Education and Culture.   **105** Giedion, 1984, pp. 53–61.   **106** Philip L. Goodwin, quoted in Deckker, p. 89. **107** Goodwin, pp. 81–84.   **108** Calsat, pp. 22–23.   **109** Mindlin, p. 11. **110** Freyre, 1963, pp. 251–53; the first quotation is from Philip L. Goodwin. **111** These apartment blocks impressed Lewis Mumford; Lewis Mumford, 1956, p. 84.

Lúcio Costa, Edifícios Nova Cintra, Bristol and Caledônia, Parque Eduardo Guinle, Rio de Janeiro, 1948–54: *left*, close-up of Edifício Caledônia with pre-cast ceramic grilles and vertical *brises-soleil*; *right*, view of the apartment blocks' park façades composed of colourful variations of the sunscreen

mum or "sufficient" living environment'. Notwithstanding a conditioning of these formal transformations 'by the vestiges of colonial baroque', Papadaki emphasized a direct engagement with the natural environment. This was expressed in the trapping and channelling of freshening breezes, maintenance of 'minimum barriers' between indoor and outdoor areas, generous 'use of architectural space as much as landscapes', so as to counteract humidity and high temperatures, and careful selection and framing of views of the local landscapes, 'ranging from fantastic to magnificent'. In the 'Foreword' to the same monograph, Lúcio Costa, on the other hand, presented Niemeyer's work as 'clear evidence of the unlimited artistic possibilities of new construction techniques' – a position that Niemeyer himself has maintained throughout his career, emphasizing his orientation towards the future rather than the past.[112]

In the volume first published in 1995 celebrating his lifetime's work, Costa included drawings of Niemeyer's first 'personal project' while still employed at his office. It is for an unrealized university club (1936–37), part of the project for the Cidade Universitária of Rio de Janeiro. Both Costa's ill-fated plan for the university campus and the collaboration between Costa and Niemeyer prefigured Brasília. The first house designed by Niemeyer, for Henrique

Xavier (1936, unbuilt), dramatically framed the spectacle of nature, art – a reclining female figure was prominently positioned on the first-floor veranda – and everyday domestic life. A solid vertical volume occupying one-third of the façade was to act as a gigantic *brise-soleil*, shading ground- and first-floor open-air living areas and a recessed second-floor enclosure. Bound by two party walls, left and right, this cubic formal composition could have been a unit in Le Corbusier's 'Plan Obus' proposal for Algiers (1930), published in *La Ville radieuse* (1935) and presented in his fourth Rio lecture, on 10 August 1936.[113] With luxurious gardens on all four levels, the narrow house on stilts, which Papadaki compared to a 'dwelling tree',[114] dissolved barriers between interior and exterior spaces, questioning the universality of solutions like Le Corbusier's Maison Citrohan (1922), and producing an appropriately localized response to the demands of Le Corbusier's 'Manual of the Dwelling', published in *Vers une architecture* (1923).

In the following years, Niemeyer designed another two modest houses (both unbuilt): a weekend house for M. Passos (1939) in

112 Papadaki, 1950, pp. h–j; Lúcio Costa, 1950, p. 1.   113 Le Corbusier, 2006, p. 136.   114 Papadaki, 1960, p. 14.

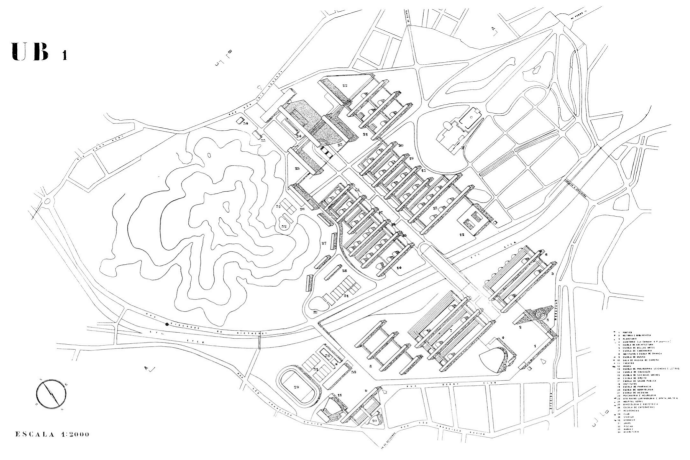

UB 1

ESCALA 1:2000

Lúcio Costa with Affonso Eduardo Reidy, Oscar Niemeyer, Firmino Saldanha, José de Souza Reis,
Jorge Moreira and Angelo Brunhs. Cidade Universitária, Rio de Janeiro, 1936–37, unrealized

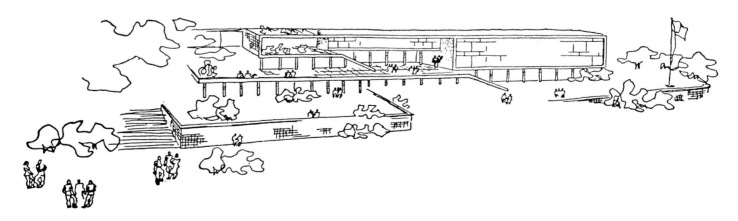

Oscar Niemeyer, University Club, Cidade Universitária, Rio de Janeiro, 1936–37, unrealized

first floor plan

third floor plan

cross section

1 garden
2 covered garden
3 service area
4 living room
5 terrace garden
6 void
7 bedroom
8 study

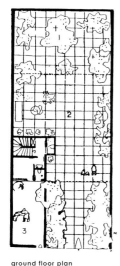

ground floor plan

second floor plan

perspective

Henrique Xavier House, 1936, unbuilt

Miguel Pereira, Rio de Janeiro state, and a small country house for Oswald de Andrade and Tarsila do Amaral (1938) in São Paulo state. Both houses feature inward-sloping pitched roofs, derived perhaps from Le Corbusier's project for the Maison Errazuris on a coastal site in Chile (1930) or his house at Mathes (1934–35), but also applying the inverted-pitch solution of colonial examples. The M. Passos House is clearly indebted to colonial farmhouse models, with exposed rubble stonework, timber loggia and more outdoor than indoor living space, sheltered from rain and sun, cross-ventilated and in direct contact with its natural surroundings.

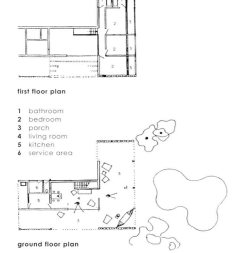

first floor plan

1 bathroom
2 bedroom
3 porch
4 living room
5 kitchen
6 service area

ground floor plan

M. Passos Weekend House, Miguel Pereira, Rio de Janeiro state, 1939, unbuilt

The unrealized weekend house for Oswald de Andrade and Tarsila do Amaral, on the other hand, with its dynamic profile, privileges formal invention as a means of escaping the bondage of the colonial past. It consists of three areas of increasing size. The central area, under a low concrete vault that recalls Le Corbusier's Maisons Monol of 1919 and their descendent, the Petite Maison de Weekend at Celle-St-Cloud, is divided into two with a rubble masonry wall, which continues into the open-plan living area to shield the kitchen and the bathroom above. The porch at the front – twice the area of the service yard at the back – is dominated by a large mural, the centrepiece of the façade, highlighted and protected by a vaulted roof. The mural in the surviving model recalls Tarsila do Amaral's *Abaporu*. In the house for the pioneer Antropofagist couple – 'Tarsiwaldo', as Mário de Andrade used to call them – utility is subservient to art, Niemeyer suggests. A meandering walkway gives the approaching visitor oblique glimpses of the mural, then turns abruptly to meet the corner of a large paved orthogonal area in front of the artwork, commanding stasis, permitting contemplation from an appropriate distance, before continuing into the porch. The pitched roofs of the two asymmetrical volumes that flank the mural point towards the centre of the composition, highlighting the centrality of the artwork and directing the viewer's attention towards it. In the larger volume, part of the living room is a double-height space. Here a spiral staircase leads to the second level, with two bedrooms under the highest point of the roof and a small oblique balcony overlooking the entrance area and mural.

The entrance to the house is found under the porch: a casual unmarked opening in the glazed perimeter of the living area sits opposite the open side of the garage. This underplaying of the front door, combined with a sophisticated choreography of the approach towards a building through an elaborate sequence of carefully composed spaces and vistas, eliciting diverse responses from the moving body, which is frequently required to change direction, constitutes a constant feature of Niemeyer's designs. Entering a building, Niemeyer suggests, is not a matter of abruptly crossing a clearly marked and directly targeted opening on a boundary between interior and exterior space, but, rather, a slow process of gradually passing from one state of spatial consciousness to another, supported by a long sequence of mediating spaces. This mediation process is more important than the final act of crossing the threshold, effecting the demise of the door's traditional dividing and confrontational roles. Niemeyer's slowly accessed, inviting open doors are also commensurate with a climate that favours outdoor living in semi-open areas, like the verandas and loggias of the colonial patriarchal houses described by Jean-Baptiste Debret, protected and well-ventilated, ensuring cool air is channelled to the interior of the house through large openings.[115]

Niemeyer's first independent commission, for the charitable organization Obra do Berço, on the shores of the Lagoa Rodrigo de Freitas in Rio de Janeiro (1937), adopted similar principles, although it fulfilled a much more complex programme, including a day nursery, medical facilities for poor mothers and pregnant women, an auditorium and administration quarters.[116] The ground floor is accessed through a small garden and a semi-open loggia that acts as an extension of the waiting space. The larger of two cubes of accommodation dominates the composition, defined by a symphony of vertical adjustable *brises-soleil*, which create for the institution a dynamic, constantly varying but memorable abstract image, comparable to a large advertising board where movement adds to the ability to grab attention. Niemeyer had

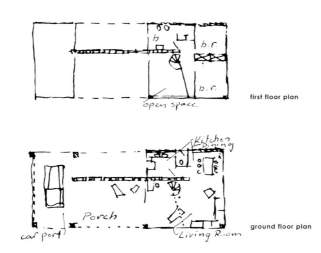

Weekend House for Oswald de Andrade and Tarsila do Amaral.
São Paulo state, 1938, unbuilt

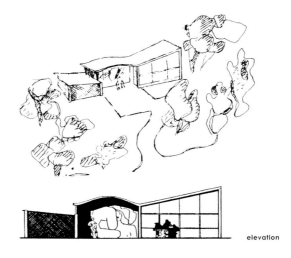

115 Jean-Baptiste Debret, quoted in Freyre, 1943, p. 100.   **116** Under Vargas, such private organizations received subsidies and became semi-public agencies responsible for a series of social initiatives.

originally proposed 'a concrete grid' similar to the egg-crate panel used at the Brazilian Pavilion at the 1939 New York World's Fair, with the horizontal elements tilted forward.[117] Upon his return from the United States, however, where he had been working with Lúcio Costa on the design of the Brazilian Pavilion, Niemeyer found that 'unjustifiable modifications' had led to the installation of horizontal fixed concrete louvres, totally ineffective on this western façade, 'where the rays of the sun are almost horizontal'. After the building had been completed, Niemeyer had these louvres replaced, at his own expense, with the present vertical ones, 'similar to those used for the ABI building' but adjustable.[118]

The report of 1938 on the 'definitive solution' for the Ministry of Education building pays tribute to the 'experiments' with alternative brise-soleil solutions at the Obra do Berço.[119] The latter's verti-cal asbestos sunbreaks are contained within a large concrete frame that appears to be attached to the white cube like a gigantic screen or billboard, arranged in three horizontal bands corresponding to the three floors above the pilotis and visible from the wide road by the lagoon. Displaying a remarkable understanding of visual strategies to seduce the eye in an increasingly consumerist urban context, Niemeyer broke the continuity of the blue-edged brises-soleil in the middle row and positioned there, to the right of the centre, a smaller white frame two-thirds the height of the band and itself divided into two horizontal rows – an opaque one below, which acts as a balcony balustrade, and a hollow one above. On the flat white surface of the balustrade, the only solid surface at the outermost limit of the building, appears in blue the name of the philanthropic institution, Obra do Berço,

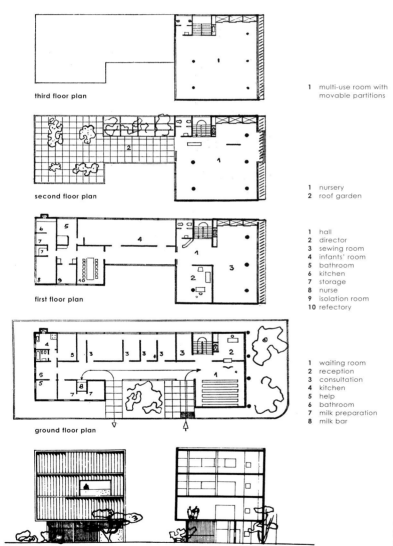

third floor plan

1 multi-use room with movable partitions

second floor plan

1 nursery
2 roof garden

first floor plan

1 hall
2 director
3 sewing room
4 infants' room
5 bathroom
6 kitchen
7 storage
8 nurse
9 isolation room
10 refectory

ground floor plan

1 waiting room
2 reception
3 consultation
4 kitchen
5 help
6 bathroom
7 milk preparation
8 milk bar

street (west) elevation   **cross section**

Obra do Berço, Rio de Janeiro, 1937

Obra do Berço: close-up of street (west) elevation with vertical asbestos sunbreaks pivoting on steel frames

117 A photograph of a model showing this first solution may be found in Niemeyer, 2004, p. 358.   **118** Oscar Niemeyer, quoted in Petit, 1995, p. 23. Niemeyer refers to the ABI Headquarters as the 'first important modern work, elaborated by a Brazilian architect'; Niemeyer, 2004, p. 148.   **119** Ministry of Education project team, 'The Definitive Solution' (1938), in Bonduki (ed.), 2000, p. 56.

directing the traveller's eye to Niemeyer's first constructed work, and anticipating Robert Venturi's message.

Before the completion of the Ministry of Education, Lúcio Costa had already married elements of Modernist architecture with typologies and *in-situ* archaeological remains from Brazil's golden age in his appropriately hybrid Museu das Missões (1937), designed in collaboration with Lucas Mayerhofer and Paulo Thedim Barreto in the Brazilian president's homeland, São Miguel das Missões, Rio Grande do Sul. In 1938, it was decided to build a new, state-financed hotel in Ouro Prêto, repository of Brazil's pre-eminent national treasures. Costa advised the minister of national culture to reject Carlos Leão's proposal, arguing that 'a "neo-colonial" fake . . . has nothing to do with the true spirit of the old constructions'.[120] Instead, he proposed for Ouro Prêto's hillside an uncompromisingly modern structure from the hand of Niemeyer.[121] Following Costa's advice, influenced by the protests of local and national preservationists, Niemeyer modified his original design, replacing, for example, a planted flat roof with a single

Carlos Leão, Grande Hotel de Ouro Prêto, Ouro Prêto, Minas Gerais, 1938, unrealized proposal

Ouro Prêto with Niemeyer's Grande Hotel de Ouro Prêto, Minas Gerais, 1939

pitch and adding tiled surfaces and lattice-work elements similar to those found in the region's colonial windows and balconies.[122]

Stamo Papadaki commented favourably on 'the tiles of the sloping roof, the occasional use of stone from the nearby Itacomi Mountain and the adoption of the same colors which are predominant in the town,' noting that these features 'contribute to an organic blending of this building with its historical setting while avoiding narrow applications of dead styles'.[123] A new, latticed *brise-soleil*, developed for this building and related by Freyre to the colonial *rotulas*, contributed to the rich patterning of the façade, while also carrying polysemic qualities, endowing familiar traditions with new meaning.[124] The Costa-inspired conciliatory formu-

la of Niemeyer's Grande Hotel de Ouro Prêto (1939) established a precedent, henceforth followed by SPHAN, which was responsible for the approval of new construction in the historic city. Unfortunately this eventually led to the promotion of a homogenizing, hybrid, 'simplified colonial' idiom, without the sophistication of

120 Lúcio Costa, quoted in Williams, p. 112. **121** See Cavalcanti, 1995, pp. 153–70. **122** The planted flat roof would probably have been less obtrusive than the final implementation. See all three solutions in Motta, p. 112. In this article, Motta also discusses the idealization and purification process that Ouro Prêto underwent in order to comply better with its venerable, eighteenth-century image. The most recent case of an 'elimination of the *bastard* aspect' from a building in Ouro Prêto was that of the Cine Vila Rica, antiquated by Costa himself in 1957; Motta, emphasis in the original. **123** Papadaki, 1950, p. 23. **124** Freyre, 1963, p. 252.

Grande Hotel de Ouro Prêto: main (south-west) façade overlooking the colonial town with the ramp *in the foreground*

Grande Hotel de Ouro Prêto: latticed *brises-soleil* in front of the kitchen window and *muxarabi* screens for the bedroom balconies

Niemeyer's touch, baptized by local builders 'estilo Patrimônio' ('Heritage style').[125]

As the Grande Hotel is built at the edge of the city, it offers space for parking, concealing the cars of its guests behind its lush garden with a raised pool area. A long ramp leads to the inconspicuous yet unambiguously pre-announced entrance. From the intimate space of the shaded ground-floor open porch, the visitor can enjoy views back to the garden. Raised on *pilotis*, the first-floor restaurant veranda and glazed lobby area, with furniture by Brazilian designers like Sergio Rodrigues and Michel Arnoult, command panoramic views of the eighteenth-century historic town. The seventeen duplex suites, accessed on the second floor, have double-height living areas with access to private trellis-protected, west-facing verandas, enjoying views towards the town. The private living areas boast Adolf Loos's and Le Corbusier's favourite 'humble' yet 'noble' Thonet bentwood chair, model no. 9, featured in Le Corbusier and Pierre Jeanneret's Pavillon de L'Esprit Nouveau for the *Exposition des Arts Décoratifs et Industriels Modernes* in Paris in 1925 and subsequent Corbusian houses. Freestanding wooden spiral staircases lead to the bedroom and bathroom areas, which bulge slightly out in a curve, enlivening the double-height wall and increasing intimacy of scale at the entrance area beneath it. Through the arrangement of these

125 Motta, p. 113.

Grande Hotel de Ouro Prêto: first-floor lobby area with Mole armchairs designed by Sergio Rodrigues in 1957

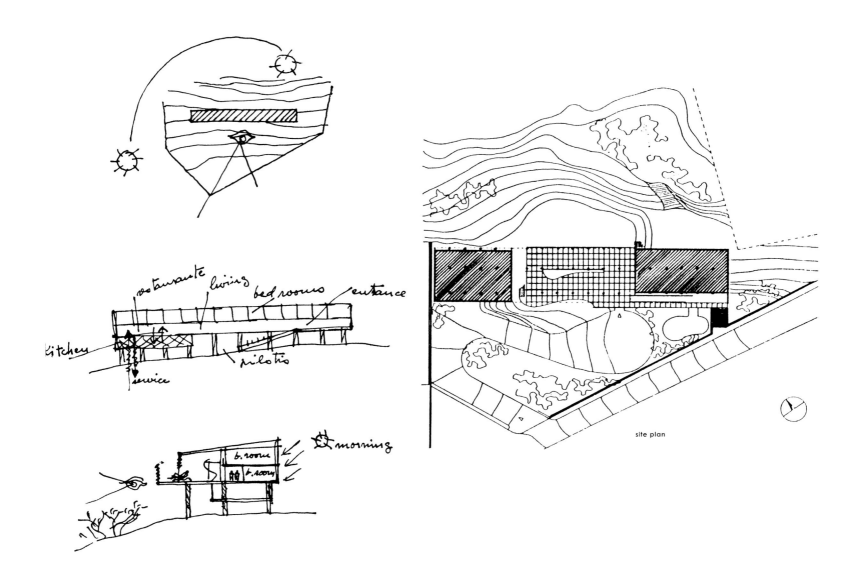

site plan

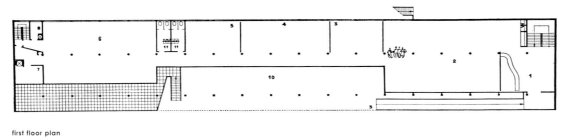

first floor plan

1 reception
2 main lobby
3 writing room
4 reading room
5 displays
6 dining room
7 pantry
8 linen
10 open to terrace below
11 toilets

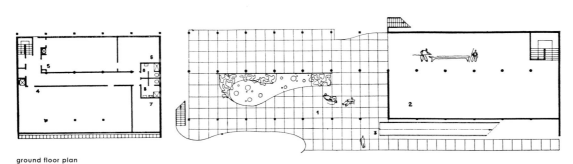

ground floor plan

1 sheltered terrace
2 game room
3 ramp to main entrance
4 kitchen
5 laundry
6, 7 personnel
8 toilets

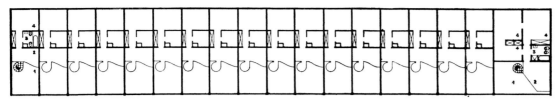

third floor plan

1 upper part of living room
2 balcony
3 bathroom
4 bedroom

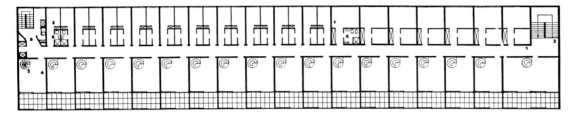

second floor plan

1 corridor
2 guests' staircase
3 service staircase
4 private living room
5 spiral staircase to bedroom
6,7 bedroom
8 bathroom

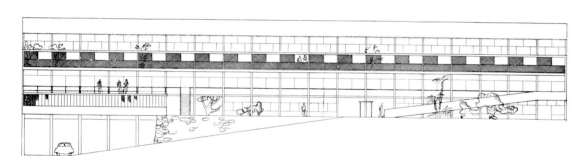

elevation

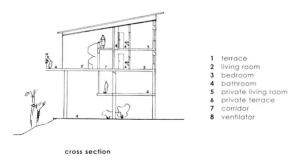

cross section

1 terrace
2 living room
3 bedroom
4 bathroom
5 private living room
6 private terrace
7 corridor
8 ventilator

Grande Hotel de Ouro Prêto, Ouro Prêto, Minas Gerais, 1939

immeuble-villa-inspired units under the pitched roof, Niemeyer optimized use of the available space, dispensing with the need for a corridor on the top floor, while also enlisting the benefits of morning sun for the bedrooms and cross-ventilation for the entire suite.

Niemeyer employed the benefits of this section for two dwelling types – C-1 and C-2 – at a staff housing development for 4,000 people (1947) at the Aeronautical Technical Centre in São José dos Campos in the state of São Paulo, as well as for some apartments in the Conjunto Juscelino Kubitschek in Belo Horizonte (1951-70). He applied the same section to the basic, cross-ventilated dwelling unit of a hotel-cum-apartment building on a heroic scale proposed for Petrópolis in 1950 but never built. In these, as well as in the other projects that followed the Ouro Prêto hotel, shading devices and pitched roofs still appear, but they have been emancipated from colonial precedents.

The hybrid architecture of Niemeyer's Grande Hotel de Ouro Prêto satisfied its principal aim of confirming the message formulated by Costa's earlier treasure house of national culture: that in

Brazil there was no conflict between modernity and tradition. From its seat on the eighth floor of the uncompromisingly modern Ministry of Education, SPHAN publicized the alliance between tradition and modernity. Aleijadinho's celebrated statue shared the space of the reception hall of the minister's quarters with Portinari's mural *Jogos infantis* (*Children's Games*) and Niemeyer's sinuous curves. Soon, however, Niemeyer rejected the path of reconciliation and continuity indicated by Costa in favour of an Antropofagist quest for an innovative form of expression.

While the Lusophile Costa continued working in close proximity with the colonial prototypes, which, for him, represented a Brazilian architectural tradition, Niemeyer consciously began to invent a new, post-colonial, truly national and modern Brazilian tradition through the creation of a body of works to suit his vision of 'the past of tomorrow'.[126] At SPHAN, Costa became increasingly involved in a process of reifying selected national memories, and his architectural work favoured faithful translation and montage. Interestingly, while the idealization of Brazil's cradle of colonial civilization was in progress, the so-called Dodsworth works, named after Henrique Dodsworth, appointed head of the municipality by the Estado Nôvo, were underway in Rio de Janeiro. Between 1941 and 1944 around six hundred buildings were demolished for the sake of the opening of Avenida Presidente Vargas, proposed by the Agache plan. Among these were some jewels of colonial ecclesiastical architecture, including the church of São Pedro dos Clérigos with carved work by the celebrated mestizo Mineiro artist Valentim da Fonseca e Silva, known as Mestre Valentim (1745–1813), and the churches of São Joaquim, São Domingos, Bom Jesus and Nossa Senhora da Conceição.[127]

Developing at a safe distance from the canonization of national architectural traditions, Niemeyer's later work invested memory in innovation. To Niemeyer, the colonial architecture was a foreign architecture, 'a transposition of Portuguese architecture. . . . in Brazil'. He has often repeated:

> In architecture and in culture, in general, we stand with open arms for new solutions, because we have no past. We must create the past of tomorrow. Tomorrow, our work will constitute the Brazilian past, and it must be a past better than the one we received from Portugal, which may be good but is not ours. For this reason, Brazilian architecture is made with lots of freedom. We are not afraid of making mistakes. We have to create something different. . . . You may like [my architecture] or not, but you could not say you ever saw anything like it before. This is what matters.

And this is what Niemeyer aimed at, once he had completed his apprenticeship with Costa. Le Corbusier's recognition of his inventive powers is put forward by Niemeyer as evidence of recognition of both his success and his emancipation from Le Corbusier, his second mentor.[128]

The Brazilian Pavilion at the 1939 New York World's Fair

Early in his career, Niemeyer acknowledged the lessons of the colonial past. But he was also eager to destroy the Otherness of this tradition. He demanded that the process of creating a truly Brazilian heritage was clearly independent from foreign models of the past and of the present. His last collaboration with Costa was on the creation of an 'architectural form which would translate the expression of the Brazilian environment . . . preferably contemporary'. This was the criterion applied in 1938 by the competition jury for the Brazilian Pavilion at the 1939 New York World's Fair, in which President Vargas took a personal interest. Lúcio Costa's competition project was awarded first prize for its 'espirito de brasilidade', and Niemeyer's second for its technical competence, which to him became increasingly important, symbolizing Brazil's modernity and progress.[129] The jury complimented both architects for not employing standard International Style solutions, clearly promoting an architectural representation of Brazil's distinct national character. Then Costa invited Niemeyer to collaborate on a new scheme, also sharing his fee with him:

> I took Oscar with me to New York, in order to work on a new project for the Brazilian Pavilion . . . Because I had noticed that, after the visit of Le Corbusier, in 1936, which I initiated, his creativity and his extraordinary capacity for invention had been quickly affirmed. I understood then that this was the time for him to flower and become recognized on the international scene. . . . It was a matter of *defending the good cause of architecture*.[130]

The two architects spent almost a year in New York. During this collaboration, Costa recognized in Niemeyer 'artistic vanity and professional pride which [he regarded as] the inevitable mark of the real creator'.[131]

Designed by Costa and Niemeyer and executed in collaboration with Paul Lester Wiener, the Brazilian Pavilion in Flushing Meadow Park embodied an image of Brazilian modernity and state-led modernization. In the context of contemporary Brazilian architecture, it represents a rare instance of experimentation with emerging programmatic and spatial values by exploring the possibilities of a steel structure. Impressed by the finished pavilion, Mayor Fiorello LaGuardia awarded Niemeyer the keys of the city of New York. As 'a fine example of the "modern" vocabulary', the

126 Niemeyer, 1988b, p. 185.   **127** A total of 1,225 buildings were demolished in the process of Rio's Europeanization, which began with Mayor Pereira Passos's civilizing measures of 1902–06: Underwood, 1992, p. 55. **128** Niemeyer, 1988b, p. 185.   **129** Deckker, p. 55.   **130** Lúcio Costa, 'Pavilhão do Brasil: Feira Mundial de Nova York de 1939' (n.d.), in Lúcio Costa, 1997, p. 190, emphasis in the original.   **131** Lúcio Costa, 1950, p. 2.

pavilion influenced the decision by Wallace Harrison (designer, with Max Abramovitz, of the Fair's Theme Center) to include Niemeyer in the Board of Design for the United Nations Headquarters in New York, in December 1946.[132]

Costa reported that they eschewed monumentality and lavishness in favour of simplicity, purity and equilibrium – qualities he considered appropriate to the size of the site and the 'still poor' country the pavilion represented. The pavilion maximized the potential of its location to express the fair's theme – the 'World of Tomorrow'. It confronted its monumental French neighbour with a public open plaza on Rainbow Avenue, merging its ground-floor entrance area with the street and subtly lifting an edge of the plaza carpet to connect smoothly to the broad sweeping ramp dominating the pavilion's open-air foyer. Casually gesturing towards those turning into Rainbow Avenue from the curved Garden Way, the sinuous ramp allowed pedestrian traffic to flow effortlessly into the upper-floor esplanade leading to the double-height exhibition area, enlivened by a free-flowing mezzanine slab that seemed to float in mid-air, and the auditorium with its hyperbolic plan. Along Rainbow Avenue to the south, the ramp formed a portico, oblique to the entrance. Moving under the ramp towards the entrance, the visitor was greeted by a an exotic bird house on the right, while also being able to catch glimpses of the substantial garden to the rear – separated from the river only by a walking path – and the rolling fields beyond.

Visitors were led through the intricately laced, semi-transparent ground floor towards the seductive tropical garden, dominated by a large free-form lagoon with Amazonian water lilies (*Victoriae regiae*), recalling the Brazilian Pavilion at the Exposition Universelle of 1889 in Paris. As Comas points out, the arrangement of this floor, with its 'recessed peripheral columns alternately exposed or hidden' represents 'the first instance of a frank external disclosure of the free-plan mechanism, not to be found in the work of Le Corbusier, quite possibly a development of an insinuation made by Mies in the Barcelona Pavilion', to which the Brazilian Pavilion's steel columns also owe a debt.[133]

Once inside the L-shaped ground floor, the visitor could take the longer route to the left, slowly strolling along the curved wing by the bank of a pond, on the other side of a glazed wall, sampling Brazilian delicacies at the restaurant: coffee, *guaraná*, *yerba matte* tea, hot chocolate. This route culminated in Brazil's ultimate space of temptation and pleasure: a dance floor with open views to the Epicurean garden. Here, another icon of tropical Brazil was awaiting the visitor: the Bahian costumed 'lady in the tutti-frutti hat', singer Carmen Miranda (Maria do Carmo Miranda da Cunha, 1905–1955), who would intoxicate Hollywood in the next decade. The pavilion's music director, Walter Burle Marx (1902–

132 Dudley, p. 7.   **133** Comas, 1998c, p. 52.

Lúcio Costa and Oscar Niemeyer, Brazilian Pavilion at the 1939 New York World's Fair, Flushing Meadow Park, New York: views of south façade protected with egg-crate sunscreen

1990, Roberto's brother), conducted the New York Philharmonic in several premieres of works by Antropofagist composers Heitor Villa-Lobos and Camargo Guarnieri (1907–1993).

Alternatively, on entering the pavilion, the visitor could move along a line of steel columns, straight across the space and out to the garden, arriving at the centre of a precisely staged tropical world marked by a snake pit, which corresponded to the internal dance floor in size and form. With the rear elevation fully glazed,

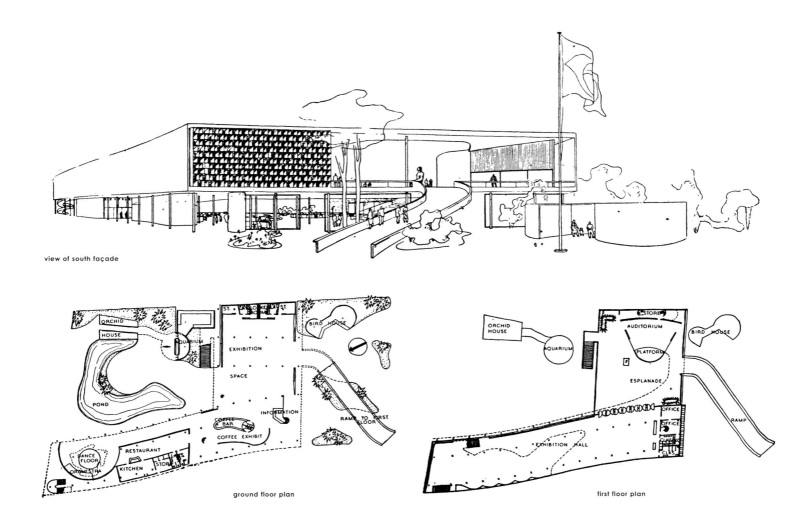

view of south façade

ground floor plan

first floor plan

Brazilian Pavilion at the 1939 New York World's Fair: exhibition hall with free-flowing mezzanine

the lush beckoning garden, which included an aquarium and an orchid house, was visible from all parts of the pavilion and even from across the Lagoon of Nations, infusing Brazil's 'Pavilion of the New Spirit' with a Dionysian *espirito de brasilidade*. This served to position firmly at the heart of Brazil's constructed modern image an open world where luxury, sensual pleasure and abundance are natural qualities. And these were the qualities associated with indigenous Brazilian societies by both colonialist discourse and anticolonialist Antropofagists. Oscar Niemeyer would wholeheartedly adopt them to energize his future architectural work, con-

scious of the fact that this adversarial choice would turn him into a polemic critic of canonical Modernist dogma and its puritanical mores.

Costa explained that the Brazilian Pavilion adopted a language of 'grace and elegance', lightness and spatial fluidity, open plan, curves and free walls, which he termed 'Ionic', contrasting it to contemporaneous stern Modernist architecture, which he termed 'Doric'.[134] His compositional principles,

134 Lúcio Costa, quoted in Papadaki, 1950, p. 59.

rehearsed in his 'Reasons of the New Architecture' of 1936, were confidently applied: walls and floor slabs sang their freedom from the light yet rigid steel structure. The southern façade was protected with an egg-crate sunscreen, and the pavilion's overall openness and lightness that contrasted the Brazilian Pavilion to its Old World neighbour received wide acclaim. Its 'refutation of the dogmas of the industrial designers' was noted, as were its strategies for 'produc[ing] the maximum enjoyment'.[135]

On the solid surfaces away from the garden, the pavilion prominently displayed works of art, which also received the critics' attention. These were images of Brazil's regionally, ethnically and racially diverse society: *favelas*, black Baianas, *jangadeiros*, mulattoes, *gaúchos* and so on, painted by Cândido Portinari. It is reported that it was precisely because of its Afro-Brazilian subject matter that Portinari's *Café* (1935, Museu Nacional de Belas Artes, Rio de Janeiro), a portrait of the Afro-Brazilian rural proletariat, had received Second Honorable Mention from the Carnegie Institute (Pittsburgh, PA) in 1935, the artist's first award outside Brazil, but had been rejected by the Brazilian Embassy in Washington and excluded from the collection sent to the 1937 Paris World's Fair.[136] Although not unanimously, two years later, Portinari was hailed in the United States as 'the foremost interpreter of that great force who is daily growing articulate – the Negro of the Americas.'[137] Costa argued that 'In an industrial and culturally developed land like the United States and in a fair in which countries richer and more "experienced" than ours are taking part, [Brazil] could not be reasonably thought to stand out through ... expertise.'[138] Portinari's images served to export the Brazilian utopia of racial democracy and 'the argument that Brazilians' alleged lack of discrimination made them morally superior to the technologically more advanced countries where systematic repression of racial minorities was still practiced'.[139]

The *Architectural Review*'s special number of March 1944 on Brazil celebrated the country's 'miraculously effective' melting pot and her mulatto artists, pronouncing Brazil, in 'this negation of colour and racial distinction ... ahead of North America and even of the other Spanish American countries'.[140] In the text prefacing the first published survey of *Modern Architecture in Brazil*, by Henrique E. Mindlin (1956), Sigfried Giedion recycled Gilberto Freyre's romantic interpretation of Brazilian slavery and presented Brazil's Modernist architectural forms as shelters of her golden

utopia: 'Unlike the USA, Brazil has solved the difficult racial problem: in the beautiful housing estates of Pedregulho negroes and Norwegians are living side by side.'[141]

Ten years after the New York World's Fair, Niemeyer's unbuilt 1949 project for a monument in Rio to Rui Barbosa, the jurist-politician who wrote the constitution for Brazil's newly formed republic in 1890, put forward a wide, polished black marble walkway with a statue of Justice. Past a soaring white obelisk the walkway led to a space under a large concrete shell, where viewers would find themselves surrounded by a colourful mural depicting the life of the man who was the champion of national equality in the international arena. Barbosa headed the Brazilian delegation to the Second International Peace Conference at the Hague, in 1907. In 1919 he had optimistically spoken of Brazil as a 'leveling' society where 'the vestiges of slavery are constantly diminishing in a fusion of all races'.[142] Niemeyer's juxtaposition of powerful black and white elements leading to a colourful panorama may be seen to hint – unconsciously perhaps – at the need for an affirmation of

Monument to Rui Barbosa, Rio de Janeiro, 1949, unrealized; photomontage with model on site

135 From the US *Magazine of Arts*, cited in Deckker, pp. 60–61. **136** Daryle Williams notes that 'The question was not official racism per se: *Café* was in the permanent collection at the National Museum of Fine Arts, and Portinari's mural series at the Ministry of Education told the national history through the labors of nonwhite workers. The overriding concern was audience. On domestic soil, Brazilians enjoyed access to official spaces that included, at a minimum, some recognition of Brazil's multiethnic character. On foreign soil, however, the steering committees who organized narrated Brazilianness abroad most often consciously tried to censor blackness and manual labor on the principle that foreign eyes needed to see a white and civilized Brazil'; Williams, p. 214. Cândido Portinari and Celso Antônio had been invited to exhibit at the Brazilian Pavilion at the suggestion of Lúcio Costa. **137** Robert C. Smith, assistant director of the Hispanic Foundation at the Library of Congress, quoted in Williams, pp. 219–20. **138** Lúcio Costa, quoted in Deckker, pp. 56–57. **139** Skidmore, 1993, p. 209. Brazil's reputation would be tarnished by evidence that surfaced in the 1950s and 1960s, later suppressed by the military dictatorship. **140** Sousa-Leão, p. 62. **141** Giedion, 1956, p. ix. This statement appeared first in Giedion's 1953 text on Brazilian architecture; Giedion, 1982, p. 95. The Pedregulho Social Housing Complex (1947–58) in Rio de Janeiro was designed by Affonso Eduardo Reidy. **142** Rui Barbosa, quoted in Stam, 1997, p. 65.

the distinct but equally valued identities of the members of Brazilian society and recognition of existing divisions, as opposed to stressing a common racial identity, cultural mélange and fictional multiracial integration.

'Positive Images' of Brazil and Brazilian Architecture in the United States and Europe

Upon entering the first-floor exhibition area of the 1939 Brazilian Pavilion, visitors found themselves in the 'Hall of the Good Neighbor'. The Good Neighbor Policy between the United States and its Latin American neighbours had been proclaimed in 1928 by President Herbert Hoover and warmly embraced by Franklin D. Roosevelt's administration in 1933. In 1940, President Roosevelt was convinced that increased investment in Latin America was necessary 'in order to develop sources of raw materials needed in the United States'.[143] Culture and education were seen as powerful instruments of foreign policy. The millionaire Republican politician and industrialist Nelson Rockefeller headed the Office of the Coordination of Inter-American Affairs (OCIAA), established in 1940. This agency promoted economic measures of 'goodwill' among the Latin American republics, systematically exported 'the American way of life' to the large emerging Latin American consumer market, and disseminated 'positive images' of Latin American nations in the United States. Roosevelt had explained his 'new approach . . . to these South American things. Give them a share. They think they are just as good as we are, and many of them are.'[144]

During World War II, the United States intensified calls for 'the Americas for the Americans', focusing on preventing Axis infiltration in the Americas – which German and Italian cultural diplomacy had fostered – and trying to mobilize Brazil to the Allied cause.[145] Brazil supplied raw materials – iron and rubber – to the United States, and was the largest consumer market in the area. Most importantly, the strategic 'Brazilian Bulge' made air routes across the Atlantic possible. Within the context of the political project of pan-Americanism promoting 'hemispheric solidarity', the New York Museum of Modern Art with the Pan-American Committee of the American Institute of Architects started preparations in 1942 for the already mentioned exhibition of Brazilian architecture, 'Colonial and Modern', *Brazil Builds*.[146] The museum had advanced the 'International Style' with its hugely influential exhibition of 1932, which had travelled across the United States for two years. But, following the departure of Philip Johnson in 1934, MoMA had turned its attention away from the doctrine of universality, towards regional, especially American topics. Brazilian architecture offered an excellent example of that 'naturalization' of 'European doctrines' touted by the 1938 MoMA director John McAndrew at the opening of the *Three Centuries of American Art* exhibition in Paris.[147]

In August 1942, after five Brazilian ships were torpedoed by German submarines a few miles from the coast, Brazil declared war on Italy and Germany and sent an expeditionary force to the Italian front. In October of the same year, *Life* published the first photographs following exhibition director Philip L. Goodwin's return from Brazil. It declared Brazil 'a paradise for young architects'. Goodwin had found Rio 'quite lovely in a Paris-cum-Los Angeles way', stayed in the fashionable – although neither colonial nor Modern – Copacabana Palace, and relied on his Brazilian contacts to show him the country's architecture. Costa acted as his guide on both Modern and colonial architecture. The press release of the exhibition echoed its director: 'The Brazilian Government leads all other national governments in the Western Hemisphere in its discriminating and active encouragement of modern architecture.'[148] Hardly any mention was made of the various eclecticist ministry headquarters constructed at the same time in Brazil's capital. Back home, the exhibition review in the *A Gazeta* of São Paulo brandished the title of Celso's 1901 chauvinist paean 'Why I Am Proud of My Country'.

The aim of the MoMA exhibition, which in the course of three years travelled to forty-eight American cities,[149] was to show the 'future ally['s] . . . charming old and inspiring new buildings'. In typically Modernist fashion, the architecture of the nineteenth century was equalled to a 'disease' and rejected. Probably on the basis of Costa's interpretation, Brazil's new architecture was linked to the colonial, which was viewed as being much more homogeneous than it really is. As the emphasis of the exhibition was on what was presented as 'a genuine national character', it privileged the eighteenth-century architecture of 'the Church . . . Gold . . . [and] the Negro slave'.[150] In this way MoMA paid homage to the African element in Brazil's cultural heritage, which other

143 Franklin D. Roosevelt, quoted in Augusto, p. 358. **144** Franklin D. Roosevelt, quoted in Deckker, p. 96. **145** From a 1938 nationwide radio broadcast by Fiorello LaGuardia, mayor of New York City, quoted in Deckker, p. 97. **146** From MoMA's statement of intentions, issued in May 1942, quoted in Deckker, p. 113. Nelson Rockefeller had been president of MoMA from 1939 to 1941 and contributed a grant to the exhibition. **147** See Eggener, 2006, pp. 249–51. **148** Philip L. Goodwin, quoted in Deckker, p. 148. In his review of the exhibition catalogue, John Summerson also praised Brazil's enlightened government patronage of modern architecture, which he believed sprang up 'quickly and naturally' and without

resistance, contrasting Brazil to England, 'where a few private houses and a playground for quaint birds are almost the only representatives of advanced architectural thought'. England's civil servants, he suggested, 'would certainly commit hari-kari rather than be seen entering a Board of Education building remotely resembling Rio's'; Summerson, p. 135. **149** Cavalcanti, 2004, p. 55. **150** Goodwin, pp. 7–8, 25, 18. In 1944, a special number of the *Architectural Review* on Brazil echoed Goodwin: 'Brazil has three dominant colours: white, gold and black, symbolizing the three powerful influences of the country: the Church, Gold and the Negro'; Sousa-Leão, p. 60.

'goodwill' initiatives at the time suppressed.[151] It was also in 1943 that Gilberto Freyre's *Casa grande e senzala* was published in English, with a title that reflected its romanticization of the relations between *The Masters and the Slaves* in Brazil.

In the following two decades, Brazilian Modernist architecture gained international recognition, primarily stimulated by the MoMA show. Kenneth Frampton notes that the editors of the international architectural periodicals of the period, in the United States and in Europe, 'displayed an uncommon penchant for Latin American [primarily Brazilian] architecture'.[152] Oscar Niemeyer was acknowledged among the leaders of the 'first national style in modern architecture', and his projects featured regularly in journals like *Progressive Architecture*, the *Architectural Forum*, the *Architectural Review* and *L'Architecture d'Aujourd'hui*, together with the work of the other prominent architects of Brazil's 'strong native school'.[153] The May 1944 'one-man number' of the *Architectural Review* featured buildings by Niemeyer, 'possibly the most brilliant of contemporary Brazilian architects'.[154]

The December 1946 issue of *L'Architecture d'Aujourd'hui*, dedicated to post-war reconstruction in France, contained a jubilant article by Le Corbusier. As well as celebrating his contract, 'signed by the Minister', for a 'unité d'habitation Le Corbusier' in Marseilles, Le Corbusier also praised the application of CIAM doctrine in Josep Lluís Sert and Paul Lester Wiener's 'model' plan for Brazil's new Cidade dos Motores, based on the achievements of the Ministry of Education and the project for Rio's Cidade Universitária.[155] In the same issue the poet and friend of Le Corbusier Pierre Guegen announced that Niemeyer was moving away from 'the triumph of the Straight line' and 'the monumental Cartesianism' of the Ministry and the 'Le Corbusian school', towards 'the affirmation of his own originality' in 'the triumph of the curve' demonstrated by his Pampulha Church of São Francisco de Assis. Celebrating the 'boldness of young countries', he contrasted the 'originality' of Niemeyer's architecture to the persisting academicism of French ecclesiastical architecture.[156] The same journal's September 1947 special issue on Brazil reported on the exhibition of recent Brazilian architecture at the Galerie Maeght in Paris, attended by Brazilian architects Rino Levi, Carlos Frederico Ferrera and Vital Brazil, and by Roberto Burle Marx.

The enormous influence of this Brazilian 'revelation' on the architects of the post-war reconstruction of Royan in France has already been noted in the Introduction. Gilles Ragot confirms a lasting influence on an entire generation of Bordeaux architects.[157] Five years later, the August 1952 issue of *L'Architecture d'Aujourd'hui* was also a special number on Brazil, eliciting an enthusiastic response from its readers.[158] In his *A Decade of New Architecture*, published in 1951, Giedion remarked that the Ministry of Education 'not only marked an important point in the development of South American architecture, it has also had a far-reaching influence on the design of large buildings all over the world.'[159] In 1956, Reinhold, the publisher of Stamo Papadaki's second monograph on Niemeyer, *Oscar Niemeyer: Works in Progress*, reported 'record sales . . . of 1,900 copies in just one month'.[160] Le Corbusier wrote Niemeyer a letter of congratulations.[161]

Niemeyer's pioneering group of works at Pampulha near Belo Horizonte featured triumphant in the publication that accompanied the 'goodwill' promotion of modern Brazilian architecture. *Brazil Builds* opened with a full-page colour photograph of Niemeyer's casino at Pampulha and 'the new city of Belo Horizonte' was the first sight of human habitation mentioned in the book's 'Introduction'. The section on Pampulha was introduced with a photograph of 'dramatic stalagmites . . . cones of earth left by the contractor', who dug deep into Brazil's earth to open the 'modern highway to the new city of Belo Horizonte' in the southern state of Minas Gerais. New roads marked new beginnings, for Brazil as well as for Niemeyer, who never tires of repeating: 'My architectural oeuvre began with Pampulha, which I designed in sensual and unexpected curves'.[162]

151 It is important to note here that both in Brazil and abroad what was disseminated was a kind of hyper-real image of the Indian, the black and the humble poor. As long as these images remained confined within the sphere of culture and folklore, they were positive and highly valued, but, when they threatened to become real and thus acquire political meaning and potentially power, they were perceived as negative and were censored. In 1944, Walt Disney's *The Three Caballeros* celebrated the Baiana *tias* – invariably black 'aunties of Bahia' – the matriarchs of Rio de Janeiro's neighbourhood known as Little Africa, who became central figures in the formation of Rio's samba schools of carnival. Disney's exotic Baianas were all lily white; the entertaining sound of African instruments was 'detached from black bodies'; Stam, 1997, pp. 85, 119.   152 Frampton, 2000, p. ix.   153 Banham, p. 36; *Architectural Review*, 1944a, p. 77. Generally, the publication of Niemeyer's works in the US periodical *Progressive Architecture* preceded publication in the European journals.   154 *Architectural Review*, 1944b, p. 114. In 1953, Giedion referred to Costa as 'the most tender violin' and to Niemeyer as the 'blinding talent' of Brazilian architecture; Giedion, 1982, p. 96.   155 Le Corbusier, 1946, p. 3.   156 Guegen, pp. 54–55.   157 Ragot, 2003b, p. 124.   158 The following issue reported that the journal received numerous congratulation letters; *Architecture d'Aujourd'hui* 23, nos 42–43, September 1952, n.p.   159 Giedion (ed.), 1951, p. 134.   160 *Reinhold News* 5, no. 7, August 1956. Papadaki sent complimentary copies of his book to Berthold Lubetkin and Le Corbusier among others.   161 Letter from Le Corbusier to Oscar Niemeyer (15 July 1956), in Portuguese in Cecília Rodrigues dos Santos et al., p. 287.   162 Niemeyer, 2000b, p. 163.

Chapter Three

Curves of Transgression:
The Architectural Complex of Pampulha

From the early nineteenth century, the idea of reversing the coastal orientation of Brazil's colonists was associated with achieving the goal of true independence and national integration. To this end, opening up new roads and founding new, rationally ordered cities became key instruments of renewal and modernization. Planned cities guaranteed the formation a new national order – social, economic and political – based on progress, industrialization and modernization. The capital of Minas Gerais was transferred from Ouro Prêto to the new city of Belo Horizonte, inaugurated on 12 December 1897. Later Cuiabá was replaced as capital of the state of Goiás by the pioneer frontier city of Goiânia, laid out in 1933 and formally inaugurated in 1942. These were both landmark events in the process that culminated in the building of the nation's new capital, Brasília, inaugurated on 21 April 1960.

Originally named Cidade das Minas (City of Mines), Belo Horizonte, as it was renamed in 1901, was a modern city at the centre of Brazil's lucrative mining industry, planned in 1894 largely on the model of Washington, D.C. In the early 1940s, Minas Gerais governor Benedito Valadares and his appointed Belo Horizonte 'hurricane mayor' (1940–45), Juscelino Kubitschek, planned to modernize Belo Horizonte and inject it with new prosperity. Having sought the advice of Donat-Alfred Agache, who proposed expansion with a view to solving the housing shortage, the politicians opted instead for the creation of a centre for tourism and leisure, bespeaking contemporaneous bourgeois visions of a modern way of life.[1] The new suburb of Pampulha was located in an area already marked for development by Kubitschek's predecessor, Otacílio Negrão de Lima, near the airport, where a dam and water reservoir had been inaugurated in 1938. Kubitschek envisaged linking it directly to the centre of Belo Horizonte via a major new 8.5-kilometre-long highway, 25 metres wide within the city and 125 metres wide in the rural periphery, 'a real boulevard like those [he] had seen in Paris'.[2]

Kubitschek had his own medical practice in Belo Horizonte's first skyscraper, the ten-storey Edifício Ibaté by Ângelo Murgel (1935), and inhabited a house equipped with the latest modern comforts. For Pampulha he launched an architectural competi-

tion but, disappointed with the 'conventional style' of the entries, like Gustavo Capanema before him, he approached Niemeyer for a 'modern' proposal on the basis of Rodrigo Melo Franco de Andrade's recommendation. The mayor was highly 'impressed by [Niemeyer's] innovative ideas'; most of all by the 'absolutely revolutionary conception' of the church Kubitschek had already decided to dedicate to St Francis, patron of the eighteenth-century church near the house of his birth in Diamantina.[3] Kubitschek's commission perfectly suited Niemeyer's own career programme: 'I want to turn [Pampulha] into a lovely neighborhood, unlike anything in the entire country', were the ambitious mayor's words. With the same enthusiasm that he would later dream of the 'most beautiful capital of the world', Kubitschek marvelled in Pampulha at 'the most beautiful quarter in the world!' During construction the two men visited the site frequently 'by motorboat to see the buildings reflected on the lake'.[4] Ever since Pampulha, Niemeyer's romance with water has been constant; water reflections are a crucial motif of his architecture, which is submitted to the constant scrutiny of its own reflection as well as to the scrutiny of the spectator's eye. At Pampulha, water provided what Gaston Bachelard calls 'a marvellous instrument of narcissism', appropriate for a modern luxury resort – a locus of pleasure without sin – and for an architecture consciously distancing itself from the socialist ideals of the European Modernist pioneers.[5]

Although he joined the Brazilian Communist Party in 1945, throughout his career, Niemeyer has maintained the position that architecture, with no means of controlling production, cannot bring about social change in the context of a capitalist econom-

1 Lemos, pp. 230–31.   2 Juscelino Kubitschek, quoted in Souza, p. 195.
3 Souza, pp. 184–95. Niemeyer had already been introduced to Benedito Valadares by Gustavo Capanema when the former 'was planning to build a casino in a remote suburban district of Belo Horizonte nicknamed Acaba Mundo (End of the World). On that occasion [he] met Juscelino "JK" Kubitschek, then a candidate for city mayor'; Niemeyer, 2000b, p. 61. 4 Juscelino Kubitschek, quoted in Niemeyer 2000b, pp. 62, 70; Niemeyer 2000b, p. 62.   5 Bachelard, p. 24.

ic infrastructure.[6] His architecture has remained conscious of its ideological subservience to the model of bourgeois and capitalist modernization that Brazil adopted, in a way that, as Manfredo Tafuri has shown, the romantic European avant-gardes were not.[7] In a 2005 interview, Niemeyer emphasized the contrast between his and Le Corbusier's approach: '[Le Corbusier] thought . . . that architecture can change life . . . I don't agree at all with that view. I believe exactly the opposite is true. It is life that influences architecture.'[8]

From an ideological point of view, Niemeyer's architecture moved closer to the architectural aesthetics propagated by Henry-Russell Hitchcock and Philip Johnson's 1932 *Modern Architecture: International Exhibition* at the Museum of Modern Art in New York and their almost concurrent book *The International Style: Architecture since 1922*. Niemeyer espoused the idea of architecture as high art for clients who could afford it and governments who would sponsor it, rather than as an agent of social reform. Having rejected the false morality of functionalism, from Pampulha onwards Niemeyer's experiments advocated the autonomy of artistic work, offering richness of material form as an alternative to De Stijl's 'richness of spirit', subtly undermining the 'new poverty' of mechanical civilization.[9]

In a 1982 interview, Johnson affirmed his unshaken belief in the importance of the 1932 MoMA exhibition as an assault against the social agenda of the early Modern Movement:

> The last sentence in our book is the only important one – 'We have an architecture still' – because the functionalists denied it. We wrote that book in a fury against the functionalist, German Social Democratic worker's approach to architecture as a part of social revolution. We thought that architecture was still an art; that it was something you could look at; that, therefore, architects should not be worried about the social implications, but about whether the work looked good or not.[10]

Niemeyer's aesthetic preoccupations subscribed to this view, but he also renounced the sterile codification and homogenization of an international modern style, the 'monotonous and repetitive architecture, which was so easy to create that it quickly spread from the United States to Japan'.[11] His formal investigations followed the 1921 motto of the Paulista Antropofagist poet Menotti del Picchia, professing 'maximum liberty within the most spontaneous originality'.[12] He did, however, ascribe a social function to the beautiful in architecture, the most public of the arts, which lies outside the production cycle: 'I do not know why I have always designed large public buildings. But, because these buildings do not always serve the functions of social justice, I try to make them beautiful and spectacular so that the poor can stop to look at them, and be touched and enthused. As an architect, that is all I can do.'[13]

Kubitschek's urban dream of a new age for the 'Beautiful Horizon' coincided with Niemeyer's dream of an innovative Brazilian architecture of 'spectacle . . . plastic freedom and . . . inventiveness', at a distance from the Cartesian order of Belo Horizonte. At this idealized 'starting point of [his] career', with full deliberation, Niemeyer embarked on a process of shaping a personal architectural manifesto as well as a founding architecture.[14] His activist and utopian spirit was fuelled by the desire to shake off the colonial yoke and ensure a clear start for Brazilian architecture, free of foreign dependencies. His vision was of an architecture destined to establish a kind of visual mythology for Brazil, superseding all the architectural myths that preceded it. In this sense, Niemeyer's *oeuvre* holds the position of founding fiction; his unshakeable emphasis on 'invention' springs from the conviction that his primary aim was to give birth to the modern architectural 'identity documents of the Brazilian nation'. Later he explained: 'I made use of the limitless resources of reinforced concrete to enter a universe of curves, truncated planes, oblique façades, and divers [sic] supports . . . a world of strange, unforeseen forms, of which all the essentials are now part of the vocabulary of Brazilian architecture.'[15]

Niemeyer was not alone in his vision of a future Brazilian antiquity.[16] He had the virtually unconditional support of Lúcio Costa and all other participants in the process of composing a national

6 'I do not believe in socialist architecture in a capitalist country. It tends to be paternalistic; or worse, it perversely intends to mitigate struggles around old, hard-fought-for demands'; Niemeyer, 2000b, p. 162. In his 'Acceptance Speech' for the 1988 Pritzker Architecture Prize, Niemeyer spoke of 'architecture, a practice that has held me fast over the years, to my drawing board, at the beck and call of governments in compliance with the ruling classes, indignant at the misery that weighs upon a world socially unjust, a misery ignored, which our profession is powerless to better'; Niemeyer, 1988a. Together with Luis Carlos Prestes, Niemeyer left the Communist Party in 1990. 7 See Tafuri. 8 'Les courbes vitales d'Oscar Niemeyer', 2005, p. 50. 9 See Tafuri, p. 95. 10 Philip Johnson, quoted in Colomina, 1996b, p. 203. 11 Niemeyer, 2000b, p. 170. In his 1966 introduction to Robert Venturi's *Complexity and Contradiction in Architecture*, Vincent Scully confirmed Niemeyer's anticipation of 'that cataclysmic purism of contemporary urban renewal . . . in which Le Corbusier's ideas have now found terrifying vulgarization'; Scully, p. 9. 12 Menotti del Picchia, quoted in Inês Palma Fernandes, p. 16. 13 Niemeyer, 2000b, p. 163. 14 Niemeyer, 2000b, pp. 169–70, 62. 15 Oscar Niemeyer, quoted in Petit, 1997, p. 91. In an article published in

Módulo, Niemeyer clearly stated: 'Brazilian architecture did not spring from, neither was it inspired by, the Portuguese architecture transported here in the colonial period . . . Brazilian architecture did not originate with the Ministry of Education and Health, designed by Le Corbusier in 1936 . . . it sprang from the works at Pampulha, the [building of the] Associação Brasileira de Imprensa, and the other buildings that were designed and constructed in the 1940s and 1950s.' Although he did acknowledge the importance of 'pioneer' experiments like the houses of Lúcio Costa, Marcelo Roberto and Gregori Warchavchik, he suggested that these had 'no local characteristics'. He recognized the 'modern movement initiated by Luis Nunes in Recife, with the collaboration of Fernando Brito and Joaquim Cardozo', but, apologizing for his lack of modesty, insisted that it was 'primarily with the works of Pampulha' that an architecture emerged in Brazil with 'new characteristics, freer, lighter and more creative'; Niemeyer, 1977a, p. 36. 16 With great delight, Niemeyer frequently cites Le Corbusier's exaltation of Brazil's future archaeological treasures when he expected the imminent destruction of Brasília after the military coup of 1964: 'Brasília will disappear. But what great ruins we are going to have!' For example, in Niemeyer, 1988b, p. 187.

Brazilian heritage. From 1937, Costa was the leading authority at the Serviço do Patrimônio Histórico e Artístico Nacional (SPHAN) on the documentation, registration and conservation of historic and modern architecture; the Ministry of Education building was listed in 1945. But Brazil's first listed modern monument was Niemeyer's Pampulha Church of São Francisco de Assis, made part of the national high art canon in 1943, one year after its completion. The Pampulha complex included a casino, a dance hall and restaurant, a yacht club, a golf club, and a hundred-room hotel (unbuilt), distributed around an artificial lake. A weekend retreat for the mayor was also constructed near the lake.

Rethinking Spectacle and Luxury

The centrepiece of the Pampulha complex and the first building constructed was the Casino (1940–43), built with the structural engineer Joaquim Cardozo and set on a promontory jutting out into the lake. It is approached via a ceremonial ascending drive, wrapping around Roberto Burle Marx's luxurious garden with a central pond, large swathes of tropical colour and organically curved banks. This approach celebrated the modern motor car, possession of the casino's privileged pre-war clientele in the same way that Le Corbusier's Villa Savoye (1928–31) had a decade ear-

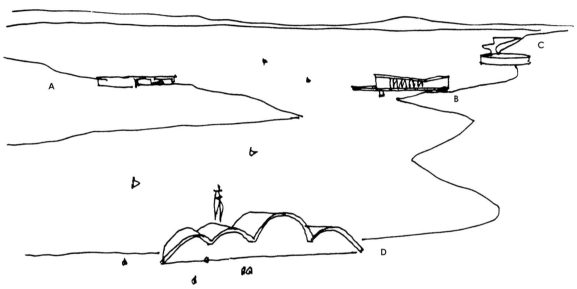

The lake of Pampulha with Niemeyer's buildings on its shores, Pampulha, Belo Horizonte, Minas Gerais, 1940–43

A Casino
B Yacht Club
C Casa do Baile
D Church of São Francisco de Assis
E pier
1 to Belo Horizonte
2 to airport

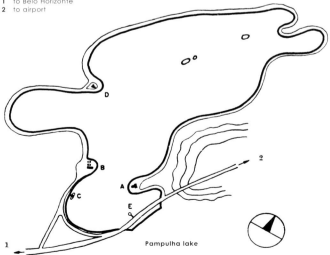

Pampulha lake

Casino, Pampulha, Belo Horizonte, Minas Gerais, 1940–43: view from across the lake; landscape design by Roberto Burle Marx

Casino: view of entrance (east) elevation and garden designed by Roberto Burle Marx

lier. Kenneth Frampton considers the casino 'the ultimate neo-Corbusian building of Niemeyer's early career . . . a transposition of Corbusier's Villa Savoye', but does not fail to notice the 'greater clarity' with which Niemeyer articulated the columns within the casino's prism. With narrow cantilevers on all four sides of the building, Niemeyer avoids the tension and awkward detailing at the points where the Corbusian villa's circular columns meet the first-floor external walls with no cantilevers on the north-east and south-west sides. Visible beams have also been avoided at Pampulha. Frampton rightly contrasts the 'Villa Savoye [that] stands aloof in the landscape' to the casino's profound responsiveness to its promontory.[17] Richard Weston is unequivocally in favour of the casino, 'in which the freedom of planning and dynamism of form make Le Corbusier's first moves in that direction look tentative'.[18] Elsewhere, he has commented that, in works like the Pampulha complex and the Brazilian Pavilion at the 1939 New York World's Fair, 'Niemeyer brought a brio and fluidity to the

Corbusian syntax, which anticipated the master's own late work.'[19]

The extravagant double-height foyer behind the sober glazed façade is the focal point of the casino, at the heart of its main orthogonal volume. This refined, theatrical space stimulates the senses with its luring pink-tinted mirror-clad walls, evoking memories of the early twentieth-century deluxe cabarets and casinos of Rio's Lapa. The floors are of polished travertine and parquet. A sophisticated system of catwalks – corridors, gaming and lounging galleries, curved viewing balconies, spiral staircases and lethargic, apparently free-standing ramps – features milky-green Argentine-onyx-clad balustrades with stainless-steel handrails. Every night, these catwalks joined their sparkling reflections in the mirrors and the glass curtain walls to form ever-unfolding sumptuous

17 Frampton, 2004, p. 43.   18 Weston, 2002, p. 105.   19 Weston, 1996, p. 192.

streamers, gracefully enveloping the adventurous beau monde of Brazil's new city of banking and industry. The first-floor L-shaped gaming gallery overlooking the foyer is reached via a straight double ramp running parallel to the main façade. Halfway up, a gallery affords views towards the foyer below as well as towards the privileged balcony of the casino-cum-society-theatre. Brushed stainless-steel sheathing accentuates the elegance of the circular columns, which appear effortlessly to pierce rather than support the concrete slabs, their long slender bodies rising uninterrupted, clearly independent of the walls, at times connected to intermediate levels by corbels. Their smooth, reflective surface is an affront to their solidity, while their fragmented reflection in the mirrored wall panels subverts their utilitarian role.

If the planning and space articulation point towards the Corbusian villa, the prioritization of the aesthetic in the casino's lavish interior points towards a Miesian sensibility to fine materials, praised by Lewis Mumford in 1949 as 'an early departure' on the part of the Modern Movement pioneers from 'one-sided absorption in expressing technical processes'.[20] But, in contrast to Mies van der Rohe, whose interiors intend to induce a spiritual aesthetic experience and a contemplative state of mind, Niemeyer mobilizes every material effect to boost the vibrancy and splendour of the environment, energize a bodily experience and conjure an electrifying atmosphere fit for glamorous gala parties rather than meditation. To appreciate the full effect of this luminous foyer as seen from the top-level inward-turned gaming gallery, it should be imagined in full swing, all reflective surfaces reverberating with the bright lights of a night of gambling fever, complemented by a floating choir of silk organza tulle flounces, fine chiffon drapes and shimmering taffeta ruffles. The casino's gambling tables were equally luxurious, but gambling was banned in Brazil and the opulent casino was forced to close as early as 1946. Niemeyer laments its 'poor taste' conversion to an art gallery as well as the alterations suffered by the other buildings around the lake.[21]

The front (east) elevation of the casino presents a simple composition of framed *pans de verre*, relieved by a solid wall surface, revetted with japuraná granite and divided into six bays by japuraná-clad columns. Four columns rise uninterrupted in front of the steel-and-glass façade, their verticality accentuated by closely spaced steel mullions. The last three columns support the opaque wall of the gaming gallery. The ground-floor glazing is discreetly lifted onto a solid base and turns the corner with a soft curve – the only curve on the external envelope of this volume, more visible when the volume above it casts a curved shadow. The independent columns and curved glazing – 'slid[ing] beside the indifferent columns', following Costa's prescription – underline

20 Lewis Mumford, 1949, p. 173.   **21** Niemeyer, 2000b, p. 107.
22 Lúcio Costa, 2000, p. 625.

Casino: views of the luxurious double-height foyer with ramps, balconies and galleries featuring Argentine-onyx-clad balustrades and columns and handrails sheathed in brushed stainless steel

compositional freedom as a hallmark of modern architecture.[22] The decorative, mass-produced tiles on the base of the curved glazing continue along the covered terrace to the south, introducing an element of domesticity in this intimately scaled part of the composition, which contrasts with the imposing four-bay portico of the principal façade.

The canopy that marks the entrance to the casino defines a large area of arrival between the end of the driveway and the entrance. Yves Bruand calls attention to the 'irregular form' of the entrance canopy, 'whose apparent instability confers dynamism'

to the composition.[23] Its trapezoidal white slab rests on a thin steel V-shaped support on the left and tails off to the right in a curve supported by twin steel columns to gesture towards a semi-reclining bronze nude female figure – August Zamoisky's *Carmela*. Her presence is more strongly felt during the night, when the curves of her female body are clearly outlined against the brilliant façade. Figures like this, most often by the sculptor Alfredo Ceschiatti, would grace many a Niemeyer building thenceforth.

The casino's restaurant-nightclub, which prided itself on its 'revolutionary menu' is housed in a smaller but higher volume, ovoid in plan, on the side of the lake.[24] It is invisible from the front, with a ground-floor bar area that flows onto a terrace overlooking the lake, with steps down to the waterfront. The fully glazed drum above is supported on *pilotis* and crowned by a high, stone-clad cornice concealing stage equipment. A service spine along the north side of the prism links the two main volumes of the composition. It contains dressing rooms on the ground floor and a staircase leading to the backstage of the restaurant. An onyx-clad narrow spiral staircase leads from the grand foyer to the mezzanine gallery, which gives access to the powder room. At the opposite end of the spine, past the ramp that leads to the gaming floor, the gallery splits into two ramps, slowly descending into the restaurant, along its curved walls. A shallow bay adds play to the parapet of the mezzanine gallery, alleviates congestion near the spiral staircase, and highlights that these are not mere circulation routes but principally viewing platforms.

To the right of the casino's orthogonal prism, a lower T-shaped volume, recessed so as not to compromise the severe orthogonal front glowing seductively in the night, contains ancillary spaces. It houses the kitchen on the first floor, supported on two irregularly shaped, smaller volumes containing toilets and an office space, tile-clad so as to subvert their solidity. The kitchen is serviced via a free-standing spiral staircase by the loading bay, set between the prism and the service rooms. Access to the restaurant is via the service spine, along a corridor behind the mirror-clad wall. The effect of the juxtaposition of the three loosely connected elements of the building is best appreciated from the lake; the curvilinear restaurant volume dominates the ingenious composition from this side. The dining area is also accessible directly from the garden on the side of the lake, via a staircase that tails off the ovoid drum.

The centrepiece of the restaurant is a glowing, etched glass dancing floor, lit from underneath. Other notable features include a stage area with an undulating wall faced with peroba-do-campo wood panels and a row of sound-absorbent, padded-and-tufted, satin-upholstered vertical louvres. Noting the 'sensorial provocation' of such materials in Mies van der Rohe's Tugendhat House (1928–30), Bernard Rudofsky spoke of fetishism.[25] Frampton commented that the casino's 'exoticism, bordering on decadence, removes us totally from the polychromatic painterly character of the Purist ethos'.[26] He also criticized the sophisticated plan of Niemeyer's 'hedonistic' casino, especially the restaurant 'with its complex accessways', for having 'established not only the routes but also the class roles of the various "actors" [of 'such an under-developed society'] divided between clients, entertainers,

23 Bruand, p. 111.   **24** Souza, p. 197.   **25** Bernard Rudofsky, quoted in Scott, p. 69.   **26** Frampton, 2004, p. 44.

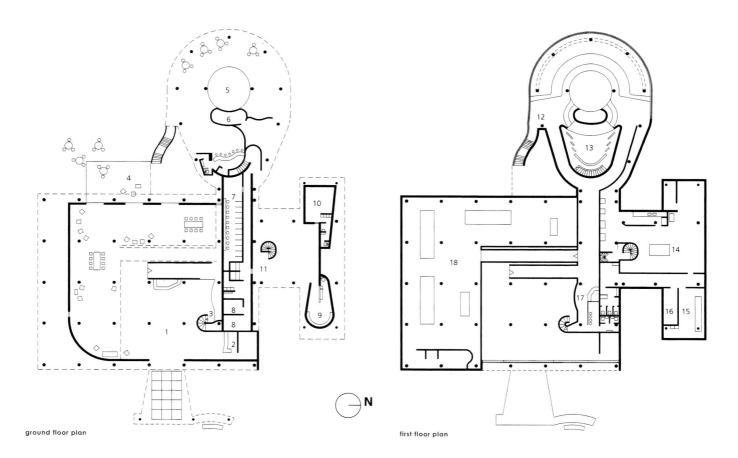

ground floor plan

first floor plan

N

1 foyer
2 cloakroom
3 entrance to powder room
4 terrace
5 dance floor
6 storage
7, 8 dressing rooms
9 staff room
10 manager's office
11 staff staircase
12 restaurant
13 stage
15 staff dining room
16 storage
17 bar
18 gaming gallery

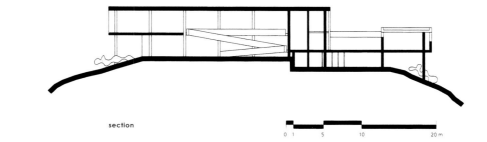

section

0 1   5   10   20 m

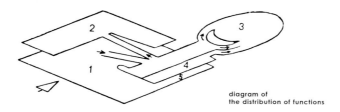

1 foyer
2 gaming gallery
3 restaurant-nightclub
4 service
5 performers' dressing rooms

diagram of
the distribution of functions

Casino, Pampulha, Belo Horizonte

and serving staff'.[27] It would be hard to find anything exoticist in the casino, but it is also questionable whether a kitchen serviced by the front door or the elimination of a stage entrance would have been interpreted as signs of a more democratic architecture.

The Pampulha complex aimed to serve an affluent modern Brazilian society, which had the means and the time to practise sports during the day and pursue other diversions during the night. It announced that the Brazilian *dolce vita* was moving from Rio's beaches to the lakeside of Brazil's booming city of industry and modernization. Undoubtedly, Niemeyer's luxurious casino did not attempt to question the mechanisms of bourgeois pleasure; on the contrary, it glorified and spectacularized it. But Niemeyer's architecture of spectacle and luxury also points towards what Theodor Adorno calls 'the other side of luxury'; that is, 'the use of parts of the social product which serve not the reproduction of expended labour, directly or indirectly, but of man in so far as he is not entirely under the sway of the utility principle'.[28]

As Stamo Papadaki noted, the 'acceptance of the non-functional as a legitimate architectural task' in Niemeyer's 'architecture of pleasure' marked 'a turning point in the modern architectural movement'.[29] In his 1939 article on 'The Dangers and Advantages of Luxury', Sigfried Giedion had already identified a 'reaction against the strictly functional', linking it to 'our need for luxury, splendour and beauty'. Dwelling on the 'pointlessness' of the pillars and the 'flowing glass' of Frank Lloyd Wright's Administration Building for the Johnson Wax Company in Racine, Wisconsin (1936–39), he conceded that these devices produced a 'magic effect' in the hall, which brought to his mind images of luxuriant Amazonian lilies. Although Giedion did not name Adolf Loos, what he proposed was a revision of the puritanical doctrine of the Viennese. 'Luxury', Giedion concluded, 'does not simply mean waste of material [and "wasted capital", as for Loos], but only makes sense when it broadens emotional experience by means of a new discovery.'[30]

With Niemeyer, beauty transgressed the limits of utility and profitability, and luxury was identified with pleasure. What may be considered his major contribution to the architecture of the twentieth century is exactly this: his introduction of pleasure as a legitimate architectural pursuit, and of a space for the luxury experience of pleasure as a legitimate part of the architectural programme. Ironically, in this sense, his architecture of luxury

Casino: view over the garden designed by Roberto Burle Marx

27 Frampton, 1992, p. 255. **28** Adorno, 1984, p. 86. **29** Papadaki, 1960, pp. 21–22. **30** Giedion, 1939, pp. 36– 38.

acquired a political dimension, which lies in its role of disturbing pre-established structures and conservative ideologies or, following the Antropofagist formula, in its 'transformation of the Tabu into a totem'.[31]

Pleasure and Beauty versus Rationality and Utility

Before the Portuguese discovered Brazil, Brazil had discovered happiness . . . Down with the dressed and oppressive social reality registered by Freud – reality without complexes, without madness, without prostitutions and without penitentiaries, in the matriarchy of Pindorama.

Oswald de Andrade, 'Manifesto Antropófago'

On 9 November 1889, a ball was held at the blue-green neo-Gothic palace on the Ilha Fiscal of Rio de Janeiro. Three thousand invitations had been sent and the palace was lit by thousands of candles. In Brazilian history, the Ilha Fiscal Ball has come to symbolize the end of the monarchy, which became official only five days later. Joachim Maria Machado de Assis remembers that, at nightfall, every Carioca ran to the beach to see 'the basket of lights in the middle of the quiet darkness of the sea'.[32] This historic image of inappropriate ostentation and luxury may have been in the mind of Niemeyer when he placed the Casa do Baile (1940–43), with structural engineer Albino Froufe, opposite the brightly lit casino, investing the latter with political ambiguity.

Niemeyer's Modernist basket of lights is, perhaps, both an expression of Lampedusan pessimism before all things that

change in order to remain the same, and an optimistic foretelling of the end of the bourgeoisie – that is, the end of capitalist class society. The Casa do Baile, a dance hall and restaurant, recognized play, luxury and aesthetic pleasure as not belonging exclusively to the bourgeoisie. While the casino was aimed at the indulgent, chauffeur-driven, upper echelons of society, the House of Dance, on a little island reached by a footbridge, addressed the samba-loving working classes.[33] During the night of the Ilha Fiscal Ball, ordinary Cariocas danced to the tunes of a police band in the square in front of the City Palace, opposite the island. In a reversal of the historical image, Niemeyer gave to the working classes of Belo Horizonte an exclusive island for their balls. At the same time, the two buildings reflected the alliance between the industrial bourgeoisie and the urban working class, fostered by Vargas's economic and social policies.

On a much more modest scale than the casino, the Casa do Baile, defined by its undulating concrete canopy, its sophisticated choreography of fluid interior and exterior spaces and dance floors, and its emphasis on festivity and pleasure, is perhaps the most delightful of the Pampulha structures. Together with the Church of São Francisco de Assis, also on the lake shore, it offered Niemeyer the opportunity to

challenge the monotony of contemporary architecture, the wave of misinterpreted functionalism that hindered it, and the dogmas of form and function that had emerged, counteracting the plastic freedom that reinforced concrete introduced. I was attracted by the curve – the liberated, sensual curve suggested by the possibilities of new technology yet so often recalled in venerable old baroque churches.[34]

Further, Niemeyer explains:

I deliberately disregarded the right angle and rationalist architecture designed with ruler and square to boldly enter the world of curves and straight lines offered by reinforced concrete . . . This deliberate protest arose from the environment in which I lived, with its white beaches, its huge mountains, its old baroque churches, and the beautiful suntanned women.[35]

The Casa do Baile consists of a circular dance-and-restaurant space, invoking the circle formation or *roda* of all traditional Afro-Brazilian dance, to which a crescent of service rooms is attached. The concrete roof slab flows freely out into a serpentine canopy that meanders along the sinuous contours of the shoreline of the island. It is faced in white marble with pink and black veins, while

No. 77. Rio de Janeiro.   Ilha Fiscal.

Adolfo José Del Vecchio, Ilha Fiscal neo-Gothic palace, Guanabara Bay, Rio de Janeiro, 1881–89

31 Oswald de Andrade, 2000, p. 591.   **32** Joachim Maria Machado de Assis, quoted in Schwarcz, 2004, p. 325.   **33** Its distance from the city and lack of public transport, however, made access difficult for the working classes.   **34** Niemeyer, 2000b, p. 62.   **35** Niemeyer, 2000b, pp. 169–70.

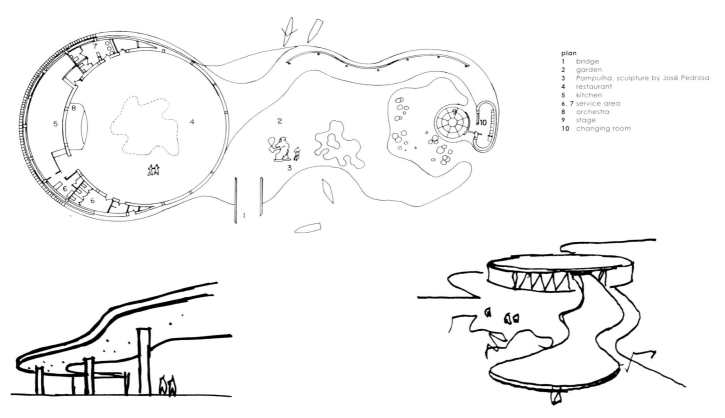

plan
1   bridge
2   garden
3   *Pampulha*, sculpture by José Pedrosa
4   restaurant
5   kitchen
6, 7   service area
8   orchestra
9   stage
10   changing room

Above and opposite. Casa do Baile, dance hall and restaurant, Pampulha, Belo Horizonte, Minas Gerais, 1940–43

the circular columns that support it are sheathed in japuraná granite of similar but slightly darker colour. The concrete canopy playfully covers an outdoor dining area, framing the view of the lake, then 'whips its tail into the water' to embrace a small bandstand set against the tiled curve of a dressing room, with an organically curving lily-pond proscenium.[36]

This was the first time Niemeyer used an undulating *marquise* – a dynamic canopy-in-motion – to unite the elements of a composition and emphasize movement. A similar element, yet without the fluidity of Niemeyer's canopy, had appeared in Affonso Eduardo Reidy's unexecuted project for a refreshment bar in the public gardens of Praça Afonso Vizeu in Tijuca, Rio de Janeiro (1939). Niemeyer has often explained that he designs with a moving spectator in mind in pursuit of the typically modern multi-perspectival space, following 'the lesson of Arab architecture' championed by Le Corbusier, who also contrasted the ever-shifting point of view to the 'fixed theoretical point' of Baroque architecture.[37] The symphony of the circular columns – which embrace the steel-and-glass drum of the restaurant and then break free and disperse to join the tireless, absorbing and liberating curves of the capricious *marquise* – is carefully composed to offer the stimulat-

ing experience of a multitude of ever-changing, fluid perspectives. The white underside of the *marquise* reflects the sparkling light of the lake waters.

The free-flowing *marquise*, confronting the spectator with its regular irregularities, has proved a useful, flexible and economical device for articulating space and experience, appearing in multiple forms in Niemeyer's subsequent works. In this building more than in any other, however, its allusion to the curves 'on the body of the beloved woman', especially the 'desired, baroque woman, full of curves, like the mulattas painted by . . . Di Cavalcanti', is most poignantly evocative.[38] The Casa do Baile intended to offer its guests a kind of pleasure that is all physical and corporal. It

36 Goodwin, p. 188. In photographs from the 1940s and 1950s the external paved area is covered in uniform white *pedra portuguesa*. The black-and-white curves of Copacabana Beach were applied to the entire hard-paved area at a later stage, boosting the dynamism of Niemeyer's canopy-in-motion; see Wajnberg, and Underwood, 1994b, figs 28 and 29. It has not been possible to establish whether the black-and-white *calçada à portuguesa* was part of Burle Marx's original project. The uniform pavement was recently restored.   37 Le Corbusier with Jeanneret, 1999, vol. 2, p. 24.   38 From Niemeyer's 'O Pema da Curva' ('Poem of the Curve'), in English in Niemeyer, 2000b, p. 3; Niemeyer, 1975a, p. 33. See also Niemeyer, 2000b, p. 54. Michael Hanchard speaks of 'an African-derived corporal aesthetics for a national standard of beauty' or the "Africanization" of the female bodily aesthetic' in Brazil; Hanchard, pp. 68, 78, n. 4.

energizes, and is experienced by, the dancing body moving through and thereby activating its spaces, gliding smoothly through the restaurant, stepping on the polished parquet of the dance floor for a frenzied samba, leaning over the curves of the tiled parapet to look at the glamorous lights of the busy casino across the lake, stepping off the dance floor, slightly dizzy by the lily pond and the scented garden, carefully crossing the narrow arching bridge that slows the moving body, while taking it away from the bouncy island of music and dance, back to the world of solid ground and the static, mundane straight lines of Modernist rationalist mythology.

It has been said of samba that 'the secret of its fascination lies in the syncopations, the deviations from the norm'.[39] Daryle Williams notes that, despite the efforts of the Estado Nôvo Department of Press and Propaganda to reform it as 'a musical genre and social signifier, samba remained a vehicle of resistance to state intervention into cultural production and commercialization. It remained a vehicle for resisting the official versions of renewal.'[40] In a similar way, Niemeyer's temple to samba served as the outspoken foreteller of his forthcoming 'O Poema da Curva' ('Poem of the Curve') – his answer to Le Corbusier's 'Le Poème de l'angle droit' ('Poem of the Right Angle', 1955) and potent counterstatement to the Modernist canon of rationalist

straight lines and right angles that 'issued from a European ethical tradition'.[41] In his *Précisions* (1930), Le Corbusier compared the tropical landscape of 'rain forests' and 'majestic rivers' to 'the veinings of rotting bodies . . . Forms that, below and close up, give sensations of nobility, exuberance, the opulence of life . . . seen from the sky, seem nothing but mold.'[42] Niemeyer's poem-manifesto celebrates and claims inspiration from precisely this landscape, which both fascinated and disturbed the European visitor:

> I am not attracted to [right] angles or to the straight line, hard and inflexible, created by man. I am attracted to free-flowing, sensual curves. The curves that I find in the mountains of my country, in the sinuousness of its rivers, in the waves of the ocean, and on the body of the beloved woman. Curves make up the entire Universe, the curved Universe of Einstein.[43]

Niemeyer is explicit about his 'tropicalization' of all he learnt from Le Corbusier, his 'liberation' from the influence of the European master, and his launching of a 'new' architecture 'in the dimensions of Brazil' – an architecture of 'imagination' and 'invention', with a repertoire of curves and tropical motifs imagined as eminently Brazilian and epitomizing sensuality, eroticism, irrationality, laziness and *dolce vita*.[44] Against the efforts of the Vargas regime to regulate samba and encourage the *samba exaltação*

Casa do Baile's free-flowing *marquise*

39 *Brazil*, p. 125.　**40** Williams, p. 86.　**41** Niemeyer, 1993c, p. 66.
42 Le Corbusier, 1991, p. 7.　**43** Oscar Niemeyer, 'O Poema da Curva', in English in Niemeyer, 2000b, p. 3.　**44** Niemeyer, 1993c, pp. 66–74.

– 'compositions which extolled the virtues of hard work, moral rectitude, and patriotism' – bohemian *sambistas* subverted state-commissioned sambas 'by alternative stanzas glorifying *malandragem* and other forms of social deviancy'.[45]

Niemeyer's popular Casa do Baile adopted a similar strategy in its resistance and Dionysian subversion of catechizing architectural discourses. Its call to hedonism and programme of epicurean pleasure were put forward to the working classes as means to overcome the oppression of labour – means denied to them by the functionalist, puritanical denunciation of pleasure. As Adorno has shown, Loos treated pleasure 'according to the bourgeois work ethic, as wasted energy'.[46] Precisely in this marginalized area of the beautiful and the pleasurable, Niemeyer recognized the possibility for a new aesthetics as well as a new cultural and social order, echoing Oswald de Andrade's revalorization and radicalization of the ludic life of imagined native Brazilian communities.

Having rejected steel construction for its uncompromising rigidity, Niemeyer found in reinforced concrete an ideal means of self-expression and liberation from the tyranny of technocratic reason and practical necessity.[47] *In-situ* cast concrete was also a construction material suitable for a building industry based on the abundance of low-cost and relatively unskilled *in-situ* labour. It was precisely these buildings in reinforced concrete, where Niemeyer married sculpture and structure, that prompted Pevsner to speak of 'innovations in the use of concrete'. However, he pointed out that 'their effect on architecture as an art has indeed been a revival of radical individualism'. Reiterating the old Eurocentric interpretation of the Brazilian exotic as irrational, Pevsner lamented Niemeyer's 'desire for novelty of form', which 'appeared purely and simply as a revolt against reason'. Effectively, he dogmatically posited familiar orthogonal formalism as rational and curvaceous formalism as irrational. Pevsner spoke of 'mannerisms', 'irresponsibility', 'fabulous' but also 'frivolous' structures, for which he held accountable Brazil's late conversion to Modernism and her 'most irresponsible' Baroque heritage. He also speculated that it may have been Brazil that forced 'into the open the irrational traits of [Le Corbusier's] character', which would soon become manifest at Notre-Dame-du-Haut at Ronchamp (1950–55): 'the most discussed monument of a new irrationalism'.[48] Somewhat ironically, Pevsner foreshadowed the Brazilian poet Haroldo de Campos who, from the 1960s onwards, would stress bilateral flow and appropriation of sources, the Antropofagist mutual feeding between Brazil and Europe. Niemeyer quotes Henri Matisse, another scandalizing champion of frivolous decorativeness, to insist: 'My

Casa do Baile's dynamic canopy-in-motion

curves are not crazy; they have a meaning', beyond practical utility, we may add.[49] His curves are not irrational; rather than negating rationality, they pose a rational, direct confrontation to limiting conceptions of the rational.

At the Casa do Baile, Niemeyer's concrete 'Poem of the Curve' amounted to an architectural translation of the verses of the mulatto 'pope' of Brazilian Modernism, Mário de Andrade:

Free verse
Free rhyme
Victory of the dictionary . . .
the Substitution of the Intellectual Order for the
    Subconscious Order
Speed and Synthesis
Poliphonism[50]

The Casa do Baile proposed the substitution of the orthogonality of reason for the sensual curves of the African female dancing body. It celebrated the Brazilian Dionysian spirit associated with the 'irrational', African element of Brazilian culture, and all things exotic, sensual, festive, luxurious, popular, wild.[51] Lush tropical nature, vibrant colours and feminine curves were all mobilized to cannibalize and erode the aesthetic prejudices of hard-edged rationalism without, however, denying its nutritive properties. Niemeyer's programmatic carnivalization of the functionalist par-

45 Williams, pp. 85–86.   **46** Adorno, 1979, p. 35.   **47** Niemeyer, 1987b, p. 159.   **48** Pevsner, 1972, pp. 425–31. Pevsner's criticism of 'the new anti-rationalism of the 1950s' was included in a new last chapter added to the Jubilee edition of his book.   **49** Oscar Niemeyer, quoted in Petit, 1995, p. 403. Niemeyer quoted Matisse in a text he prepared for an exhibition of his work (Turin, Bologna, October 1987): 'Mes courbes ne sont pas folles!'; Niemeyer, 1987a, p. 163. **50** Mário de Andrade, 'A escrava que não é Isaura', cited in Williams, p. 41.   **51** In 1953, for example, Giedion wrote: 'the influence of the Negro is evident in a certain irrationality, which is also closely related with the tropical character of the whole country'; Giedion, 1982, p. 95.

adigm adopted a mantra: 'My work is not about "form follows function," but "form follows beauty" or, even better, "form follows feminine".'[52] By opting for ornate, fluid and mutable forms, Niemeyer was opting for things feminine, epitomizing sensuality, as opposed to things austere, straight, fixed and static, traditionally associated with the male, with productivism and a narrowly conceived rationality.[53] His instrumentalization of the feminine Other is part of the same liberatory, Antropofagist radicalization of that which is perceived to be negative, the eroticized tropical Other that is perceived to be irrational and amoral.

It has often been noted that the Portuguese and, by extension, the European image of Brazil was, from the beginning, erotic. In the legendary Portuguese phrase, 'beneath the equator there is no sin'.[54] In the words of Amerigo Vespucci, the Brazilian Indians 'should be considered Epicureans rather than Stoics'.[55] His *Mundus Novus*, first published in Paris in 1503, described in salacious, though not credible, detail the excessive lasciviousness of Indian women.[56] Jan Van der Straet's sixteenth-century image (engraved by Theodore Galle, 1589) of Vespucci's first encounter with America depicts the continent that bears his name as a passive, naked, voluptuous and vulnerable female beauty, rising from her hammock. As Richard Parker has demonstrated, the Brazilian cannibal of European thought was also highly eroticized. But the 'emphasis on the native women, on the pleasures and products of their bodies, on their unrestrained sensuality and their easy seduction of the European male is [also] crucial in the configuration of Brazil's own myths of origin'.[57]

For Gilberto Freyre, the 'milieu in which Brazilian life began was one of sexual intoxication', of unbridled sensuality and uninhibited sexuality. The Portuguese, Freyre explained, 'always was inclined to a voluptuous contact with the exotic woman. For purposes of racial crossing, miscegenation.' The successful mixing of the third race – the African – was also accomplished, according to Freyre, in 'an atmosphere of sexual intoxication' and moral laxity, created by 'the economic system of monoculture and slave labor'.[58] Sensuality – especially the female sensuality associated with the body of the African woman or the *mulata* – and the notion of

Brazil as a strangely sensual, exotic land with what Parker calls 'the hidden tradition of a licentious past' continue to play a key role in definitions of *brasilidade* to this day, and are also firmly at the centre of that most Brazilian of festivals: carnival.[59]

In 1925, Le Corbusier had insisted: 'It seems justified to affirm: *the more cultivated a people becomes, the more decoration disappears.* (Surely it was Loos who put it so neatly.)'[60] For Adolf Loos, ornament with its erotic origins was typical of primitive cultures, peasants and women, who 'have no other means to fulfil their existence'.[61] Panayotis Tournikiotis notes Loos's 'sentimental erotic approach' to the decoration in 1903 of the bedroom of his nineteen-year-old wife Lina with integrated bed and floor coverings of white angora sheepskins. His unsolicited house of 1927 for Josephine Baker also featured 'unusually erotic spatial manipulations'.[62] As Barbara Hooper has argued, for Le Corbusier, the feminine, especially the primitive feminine, 'represents what disfigures the orthogonal forms of modern architecture'.[63]

The association of the ornamental with impurity and excess has long implied an association with the decadent and the feminine, and architecture's responsibility to defend itself against the impurity of the body – primarily the female body – has, at least since the Renaissance, implied a detachment from bodily pleasure and a repression of sexuality.[64] Oswald de Andrade posited an 'unsublimated sexual instinct [as] the revenge of the matriarchs . . . the sublime limit of the cannibalistic metaphor that symbolizes a Brazilian utopia that is carnal'.[65] Niemeyer used feminine curves and apparently superfluous, sensual ornament as means to resist that fear of the body – especially the female body – which he recognized in the functionalist rationality of architectural Modernism. Eroticized curves also served to subvert the hegemonic Eurocentric rationalist order of modern masculinist civilization that austerity of form and restraint of self-expression valorized. To the 'intellectual beauty . . . beneath sensory beauty' that Le Corbusier and Amedée Ozenfant associated with 'Europe, inheritor of Greek thought [that] dominates the world', Niemeyer counterposed the intoxicating beauty of corporeal dynamism, the beauty of 'the savages [who] like loud colors and the noisy

52 Oscar Niemeyer, quoted in Metz, p. 35. **53** It is worth noting that Le Corbusier, too, had contrasted angular forms and curves in terms of gender, speaking of 'strong objectivity of forms . . . *male* architecture . . . limitless subjectivity . . . *female* architecture'; quoted in Curtis, 1986, p. 115, emphasis in the original. He 'characterized the Citrohan descendants as "male" architecture, standing square and rigid against the landscape. The Monol lineage, on the other hand, was "female", with low vaulted spaces blending into the setting'; Curtis, 1986, p. 210. **54** 'It is an idea that has been traced as far back as the writings of the austere Dutch historian Gaspar von Barlaeus, in the seventeenth-century chronicle *Rerum per Octennium in Brasilien*'; Parker, p. 136. **55** Amerigo Vespucci, quoted in Parker, p. 12. **56** Honour, p. 8. **57** Parker, p. 19. **58** Freyre, 1956, pp. 83, 161–62, 350. **59** Parker, p. 160. See also Freyre, 1986, pp. 380ff, on the myth of the 'sex appeal of the mulatto woman' to whom 'a kind of permanent "sexual superexcitation" had been attributed . . . which would make her abnormal and, from the point of view of European and Catholic morality, dangerously amoral'. As late as 1996, in a survey of twentieth-century Latin American Art, the Brazilian scholar Ivo Mesquita unblinkingly declared: 'Brazilians are the result of a mixture, even the

promiscuity of all these races'; Mesquita, p. 202. **60** Le Corbusier, 1987c, pp. 85–87. **61** Loos, p. 287. See also Tournikiotis, pp. 23–27. Tournikiotis argues that, despite widespread interpretations following the French publication of Loos's famous manifesto 'Ornament and Crime' (first published in *Les Cahiers d'Aujourd'hui* in June 1913 and reprinted in the first issue of *L'Esprit Nouveau* on 15 November 1920), Loos 'did not insist on the suppression of all architectural ornament; it is clear that he does not compare "the superfluous" ornamentation of the Secession (and generally of Art Nouveau) with the "grammar" of classical ornament – of which, on the contrary, he approved and which he practiced'. According to Tournikiotis, 'Loos gave women the right to ornament, for erotic signification'; Tournikiotis, pp. 23, 26. **62** Tournikiotis, pp. 36, 98. Beatriz Colomina argues that 'Loos's raid against ornament is not only gender-loaded but openly homophobic'; Colomina, 1996b, p. 38. **63** Hooper, p. 62. **64** Bloomer, pp. 168–69. See also Mark Wigley, 1992: 'The threat of ornament is its sensuality . . . [Alberti] explicitly identified ornament with sexuality. The woman's use of decoration and makeup is condemned because its dissimulation calls into question her chastity'; Wigley, 1992, p. 355. **65** Oswald de Andrade, quoted in Jackson, p. 103.

sound of tambourines', in the Brazilian spirit of the 'Manifesto Antropófago', which 'refuses to conceive a spirit without a body'.[66] In Niemeyer's drawings, a female nude, *Pampulha* by José Pedrosa (commissioned but never installed, today at the garden of the casino), greeted the guests who crossed the bridge to Pampulha's island of dance, and helped focus attention on and engage the unwittingly devalued human body.

In the sixteenth century Hans Staden escaped his savage Tupinambá Indian captors. In the 1971 film *Como era gostoso o meu francês* (*How Tasty Was My Little Frenchman*), set in sixteenth-century France Antarctique on Guanabara Bay, the primitive colonized Tupí woman – coloured, tattooed, naked – finally eats the enslaved colonizer man – civilized, French, white, dressed – in an ultimate inversion – carnivalization – of normative discourses relating to race, gender and Old/Third versus New/First World.[67] Questioning the premises of the European binary model of civilization versus savagery, the image of Sebiopepe's (the French captive's native wife) deglutition of her tasty Frenchman is preceded by a quotation from a report on European genocide.

Le Corbusier said the beautiful mulatto girl whose memory accompanied him on his way back to Europe told him she was 'a seamstress', but '[Di] Cavalcanti said that she was a cook'.[68] In the Brazilian Portuguese word 'comer' there is a linguistic convergence between eating and sexual possession. Le Corbusier appeared convinced that it was the aeroplane, the ultimate machine of modern civilization, that offered him the pleasure of 'enter[ing] into the body and the heart of the city'.[69] But it was in the manner of the primitive savage of the jungle that his 'drawing-room' ideas and forms were ingested and ultimately subverted. 'I do not deny that it is an excellent thing to keep an element of the savage alive in us – a small one,' he had earlier conceded.[70] Following his second visit to Brazil in 1936 and the international recognition of Brazil's architectural achievements, during and after World War II, Le Corbusier repeatedly expressed frustration and resentment with regard to what he perceived as the inadequate acknowledgement of his contribution to the success of Brazilian architecture, protesting the 'nationalization of [his] thought'.[71] Although in his *Précisions* he had displayed his acquaintance with the Brazilian ideology of cultural cannibalism, what Le Corbusier had not foreseen then was that he himself would eventually take the position of the 'captured warrior' and, unavoidably, the 'meal' would have to be preceded by the killing of the 'sacred enemy. To transform him into a totem.'[72] Like the tasty little Frenchman, devouring the European architect meant his destruction as well as his transformation and incorporation into the captors' tribal body.[73]

Brazilian Modernist architects borrowed extensively from each other, especially during the years when they were shaping the visual language of Brazilian Modernism, collectively exploring its possibilities. At Francisco Bolonha's Thermal Baths Pavilion (1946) for the newly discovered sulphur springs in the town of Araxá, also in the state of Minas Gerais, the corporeal curves of the Casa do Baile reappeared to embrace the bathing bodies. Bolonha's bathing pavilion is clearly derived from Niemeyer's dance pavilion. It consists of a free-form *marquise* anchored on a section of a steel-and-glass cylinder at one end, and following the contours of a peninsula jutting out into an artificial, free-form lake, set in a park landscaped by Burle Marx. The undulating steel-and-glass screen provides shelter from the easterly winter wind, only partially enclosing the pool area and standing independent of the slender circular columns. For the pavement around the mineral water pools, Burle Marx used motifs inspired by the animal fossils discovered during excavation.[74]

Niemeyer directed much of his criticism of functionalist dogma against the Bauhaus 'that Le Corbusier used to call the paradise of mediocrity', turning, instead, towards the past, the

Francisco Bolonha, Thermal Baths Pavilion, Araxá, Minas Gerais, 1946

66 Le Corbusier and Amedée Ozenfant, quoted in Colomina, 2002, p. 151; Oswald de Andrade, 2000, p. 591. **67** The film was made by Cinema Novo father Nelson Pereira dos Santos. France Antarctique was a French colony established in 1555 by Nicholas Durand de Villegagnon on Guanabara Bay, around Rio de Janeiro (founded in 1565). The French colonists were expelled from the region in 1567. Interestingly, the 'film was rejected by the Festival in Cannes, land of bikinis and semi-nude starlets . . . because of its non-voyeuristic normalization of nudity'; Stam, 2003, p. 217. See also Young. **68** Le Corbusier, quoted in Calif, p. 571. **69** Le Corbusier, 1991, p. 235. **70** Le Corbusier, 1987c, p. 85. **71** From a letter from Le Corbusier to P. M. Bardi, 18 October 1949, in Portuguese in Cecilia Rodrigues dos Santos et al., p. 199. See also Deckker, pp. 172–87. Le Corbusier's protests must have surprised the Brazilians who had attended his 1929 lectures, in one of which Le Corbusier argued: 'we give our ideas willingly, we use, we recuperate, we exploit . . . Ideas are in the public domain. To give one's idea, well, it is simple; there is no other solution than that! Besides, to give an idea is not only pain or loss. One can find deep satisfaction, which will not be vanity, in seeing one's idea adopted by others. In fact, there is no other purpose to ideas. It is the very basis of solidarity'; Le Corbusier, 1991, p. 237, emphasis in the original. **72** Le Corbusier, 1991, p. 16; Oswald de Andrade, 2000, p. 592. **73** See Peña, pp. 191–99. **74** The project was published in the 1947 special numbers of the *Architectural Forum* and *L'Architecture d'Aujourd'hui*, dedicated to Brazil; *Architectural Forum*, 1947, pp. 68–69; and *Architecture d'Aujourd'hui*, 1947, pp. 76–77. Rather curiously, this project has not featured in any of the major publications on Brazilian Modernism.

exemplary works of 'Palladio, Brunelleschi, and the other Italian masters'.[75] The outline and tripartite division of his small building for a golf club (1940–42), to the west of the lake at Pampulha, recall his 1938 unrealized house for Oswald de Andrade. By recycling the form of a project with a completely different programme, Niemeyer assaulted the two prescriptive design theories he had attributed to the Bauhaus and dismissed: namely, that 'the plan [should be] elaborated from the inside to the outside', and the 'inconceivable proposal of studying a project for each type of building'. Oblivious to Le Corbusier's assertion that 'the Plan is the generator', Niemeyer stressed the Swiss-French architect's 'tendency for the unreal', demonstrated 'already in 1928', when Le Corbusier 'called attention to Gaudi's raving architecture'. According to Niemeyer, 'less is more . . . contradicted the versatile

spirit of the reinforced concrete'. He is convinced that the author of Ronchamp 'was the only one to understand the problem' and eventually be converted to an architecture of plastic freedom.[76]

More, richly decorated spaces for lounging, partying and dining for the leisure class of Belo Horizonte were provided in the yacht club (1940–43), with structural engineer Joaquim Cardozo. Its visually powerful butterfly roof, also featured in the Weekend House for Juscelino Kubitschek in Pampulha (1940–43) and the Charles Ofair House in Rio de Janeiro (1943, unbuilt), was indebted to Le Corbusier's unbuilt Errazuris House in Chile and had already been applied by Niemeyer in his earlier projects for the M. Passos and Oswald de Andrade houses. Over the next decades, this asymmetrical, inward-sloping roof would become a favourite of Brazilian architects.

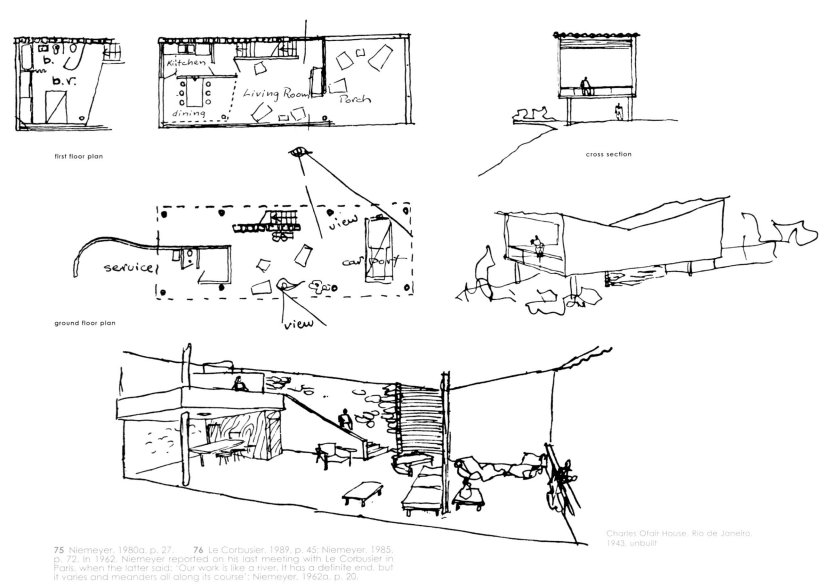

first floor plan

ground floor plan

cross section

Charles Ofair House, Rio de Janeiro, 1943, unbuilt

75 Niemeyer, 1980a, p. 27.   **76** Le Corbusier, 1989, p. 45; Niemeyer, 1985, p. 72. In 1962, Niemeyer reported on his last meeting with Le Corbusier in Paris, when the latter said: 'Our work is like a river. It has a definite end, but it varies and meanders all along its course'; Niemeyer, 1962a, p. 20.

The yacht club is equipped for aquatic and land sports. Boat shelter, changing rooms and other service areas are all accommodated on the ground floor, in an assemblage of tiled volumes of various shapes asserting their independence from the *pilotis*. This arrangement strengthens the impression of a floating *piano nobile*, containing the privileged social spaces enjoying an elevated prospect over the lake. The boathouse projects beyond the upper volume on the sides facing the lake and the garden, but its walls are dressed in ornamental *azulejos*, which undermine their solidity, they are recessed under the streamlined deck of the *piano nobile* and disengaged from it by clerestories. The forecastle deck shoots well beyond the hull of the boathouse, extending a large marble-paved terrace over the water, for outdoor dining at the bow of the metaphorical ship. The long sweeping lines breathe life into the nautical theme, and features like the incline of the solid terrace parapet on the lakeside reinforce the effect. The starboard of the glazed east elevation is the most evocative in this respect, with the dynamic lines of the roof suggesting movement, and the straight slim ramp anchoring the stern.

The two principal spaces on the first floor correspond to the two sides of the inverted gable, and feature a rich palette of materials: corduroy wood panelling, parquet floors and columns clad in ribbed anodized aluminium. Both have balconies to the west, overlooking the pool, protected by two bands of adjustable *brises-soleil*. The dynamic modulation of light and shade through blue-edged, vertical *brises-soleil* on this façade is enriched through the curving of the plane of *brises-soleil* at the balcony of the lounge in the forecastle. Part of the ceiling of the restaurant curls down to form a free-standing wall, which partly separates the two spaces, and acts as acoustic shell for the orchestra. The larger space to the south is a lounge dominated by a large mural by Cândido Portinari.

Upon entering the first-floor vestibule, club members are greeted by another mural, this time by Burle Marx, who also contributed flamboyant flower arrangements and is responsible for all the evocative landscaping of the Pampulha complex. His contribution to the ensemble cannot be overestimated. The bold graphics of the solid-colour patterns of his gardens, the carefully

Yacht Club, Pampulha, Belo Horizonte, Minas Gerais, 1940–43; main (east) façade

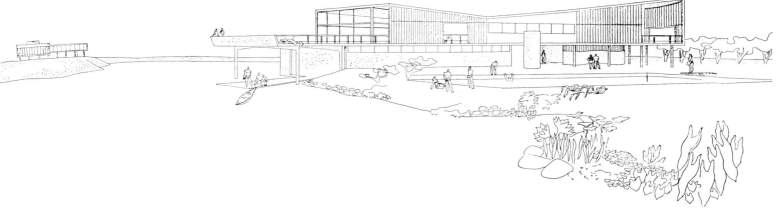

View of the yacht club´s north and west façades with the casino across the lake

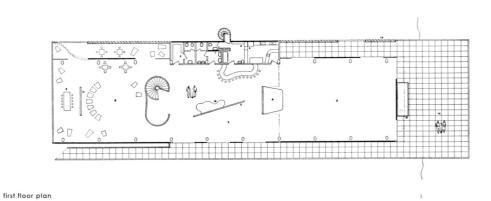

first floor plan

1	vestibule
2	mural by Cândido Portinari
3	dining room
4	orchestra
5	lounge
6, 7	toilets
8	kitchen
9	bar
10	pool
11	mural by Roberto Burle Marx
12	terrace

N

ground floor plan

1	ramp
2	laundry
3	barber shop
4, 6	male changing rooms
7	boat house
8	female changing rooms
9	waiting room
10	office
11-14	first aid

Yacht Club, Pampulha, Belo Horizonte

Yacht Club: view of the northern end of the west façade with the restaurant terrace facing the casino across the lake.

Yacht Club: west elevation facing the swimming pool

laid motifs on the paved areas, his minutely worked out syntheses of free forms and diverse cultural references, all spring from a fierce imagination, combined with a deep understanding of the architecture with which they collaborate and into which they so frequently offer unexpected insights. In a climate where outdoor living and its protection from harsh elements are of paramount importance, Burle Marx's outdoor rooms are not a mere complement to the architecture but an essential part of it. At Pampulha, the tropical gardens amplify the architectural call to hedonism and the desire to exceed functionalist constraints, transforming into a totem this useless world of sensual pleasure that Modernist puritanical attitudes treated as taboo. As Bernard Tschumi notes, in a 1977 text that draws attention to the fact that 'the ancient idea of pleasure still seems sacrilegious to modern architectural theory', 'Built exclusively for delight, gardens are like the earliest experiments in that part of architecture that is so difficult to express

Left and below, Yacht Club: external and internal views of the vertically pivoting louvres that protect the first-floor lounge

with words or drawings; pleasure and eroticism. Whether romantic or classical, gardens merge the sensual pleasure of space with the pleasure of reason, in a most useless manner.'[77]

Integrating Structure and Formal Concept

Catering for the pleasures of Catholic Brazilian flesh had to be balanced by a provision for penitence. The Church of São Francisco de Assis (1940–42), built with structural engineer Joaquim Cardozo, consists entirely of two concrete shells, clad with small (1.5 × 1.5 centimetre) blue *pastilha* tiles: a parabolic vault that shelters narthex, choir gallery and nave; and an undulating vault defining the high altar under its highest parabola, with the sacristy and auxiliary spaces on either side. In the first, 1955 issue of *Módulo*, the architectural journal founded by Oscar Niemeyer in Rio de Janeiro, the structural engineer and poet Joaquim Cardozo (1878–1978), with whom Niemeyer enjoyed a most fruitful and effective collaboration, starting at Pampulha, wrote that the Pampulha church 'inaugurated a new style in modern Brazilian architecture'. He also listed its precedents: the arched bridges of Robert Maillart, the celebrated vaulted hangars of 1924 at Orly by Eugène Freyssinet (illustrated in Le Corbusier's *Vers une architecture*) and the plans of Erich Mendelsohn.[78] To these may be added the vaulting of the Walnut warehouse in Casablanca (1915) by Auguste Perret (1874–1954), similar to that of his Church of Notre Dame in Le Raincy (1922–23), and the parabolic arches, to some degree rhetorical, supporting the ramps of the Alberto Torres Rural School in Recife by the Brazilian Modernist pioneer Luís Nunes (1908–1937). Carlos Eduardo Comas has also gathered precedents from the local Baroque tradition of Minas Gerais, especially the T-plan chapels and the works of Aleijadinho, noting that the typology of the Pampulha church (single nave, narthex, single bell tower) is consistent with the Franciscan tradition.[79]

Niemeyer could not have been unmoved by Erich Mendelsohn's early concrete sculpture for the Einstein Tower in Potsdam (1920–24), and must have recognized an affinity between his concerns and Mendelsohn's postulate of 'functional dynamics'. Already in 1923, the 'born revolutionary' Mendelsohn had boldly declared: 'The primary element is function. But function without a sensual component remains construction.'[80] Mendelsohn and Serge Chermayeff's De La Warr Pavilion – a 1935 seafront pleasure palace at the English resort of Bexhill-on-Sea, conceived to serve the democratization of the early twentieth-century leisure industry – must surely, with its elongated deck lines and dynamic spiralling staircase, have attracted Niemeyer's attention at the time when he was developing an architectural vocabulary of fluid curves and nautical allusions. Mendelsohn and Niemeyer share a messianism that made them refuse to acknowl-

edge forerunners and reject all available codes. They also share a belief in the potential of reinforced concrete as the building material of innovative artistic expression. Helping to overcome the traditional limits of support and load, reinforced concrete offered a new, previously unknown freedom in architectural design. Niemeyer pushed the freedom of plastic expression in reinforced concrete far beyond the achievements of Mendelsohn.

At the São Francisco church, the technology of reinforced concrete enabled Niemeyer to merge walls and roof into a single

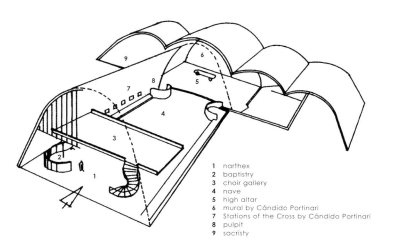

1 narthex
2 baptistry
3 choir gallery
4 nave
5 high altar
6 mural by Cândido Portinari
7 Stations of the Cross by Cândido Portinari
8 pulpit
9 sacristy

Church of São Francisco de Assis, Pampulha, Belo Horizonte, Minas Gerais, 1940–42: isometric drawing; view from across the lake

77 Tschumi, p. 86.   **78** Cardozo, 1955, p. 6. Niemeyer referred to Joaquim Cardozo as 'the most cultured Brazilian I know'; Niemeyer, 1961, p. 6.   **79** Comas, 2002a, p. 213.   **80** The Dean of Ann Arbor University introduced Mendelsohn to the students as a 'born revolutionary' in 1941; Zevi, 1999, p. xiv. For the Mendelsohn quote, see http://www.architectureweek.com/2001/0124/culture_1-2.html.

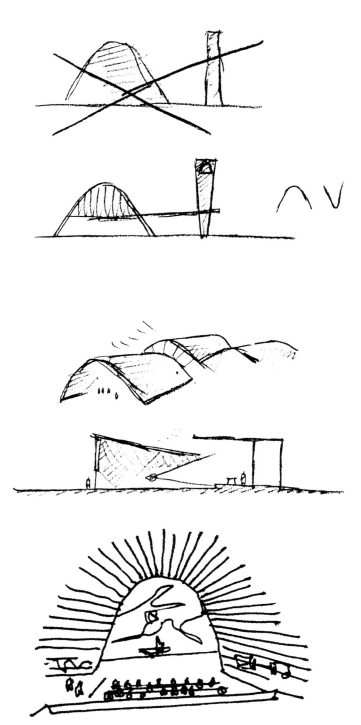

element. The structural parabolic vaults became form- and space-defining elements, anticipating his explicit proclamation of the aim of fully integrating structure and formal concept in the 1950s. Cardozo justified the centrality of the vault in Niemeyer's work on the basis of Giedion's assertion: 'from the beginning of architecture the vaulting problem has always brought forth the higher architectural expression of every epoch.'[81] Cardozo added that 'the progressive transformation of the vault' resulted in a great variety of curved roof forms. In the same article, he acknowledged the formative influence of the French engineer Bernard Lafaille, structural engineer of Le Corbusier's Unité d'Habitation, with his imaginative space-enclosing surfaces.[82] For decades, Niemeyer's inventive structural proposals relied on Cardozo's enthusiastic verification of his sculptural surface structures. In 1956, Giedion confirmed his expectation 'that in the very near future Brazilian architects will play their part in the task of evolving the vaulted form of our period . . . different from that of *all* foregoing periods'.[83]

In his seminal text of 1936, 'Reasons of the New Architecture', Lúcio Costa highlighted the 'independent bone structure' and separation of the functions of 'walls and supports' brought about by modern technology as 'the secret of all new architecture' and of its radical transformation.[84] Early Modernist buildings, from Gropius's Bauhaus in Dessau (1925–26) to Le Corbusier's Villa Savoye in Poissy, took advantage of and emphatically displayed the liberation of the building's envelope from structural constraints. The Brazilian Ministry of Education building deployed the same formula. At this stage of the development of the new architectural language, however, the two systems of spatial definition – formal and structural – remained indifferent to each other. For Le Corbusier, the domain of 'pure invention' of the architect as 'plastic artist' is the domain of 'profile and contour' and it is 'free of all constraint', utilitarian and structural; it is the domain where the architect's whim has free rein, where 'the engineer is effaced and the sculptor comes to life'.[85] Niemeyer's pursuit of free composition went one step further, seamlessly reintegrating structural, spatial and formal coordinates, taking full advantage of modern technology, in particular of 'the limitless resources of reinforced concrete', to subvert a formula that was by then mainstream, and to expand the formal and conceptual limits of Modernist architecture. For Niemeyer, the domain of 'pure invention' of the architect

81 In his 1950 article on Alvar Aalto, Giedion wrote: 'The solution of the problem of spanning space has always been indicative of the creativeness of a period'; Giedion, 1950, p. 79.   **82** Cardozo, 1955, pp. 7–8. **83** Giedion, 1956, pp. ix–x, emphasis in the original. Pevsner, on the other hand, ridiculed Niemeyer's 'structural acrobatics'; Pevsner, 1972, p. 426. **84** Lúcio Costa, 2000, p. 625.   **85** Le Corbusier, 1989, p. 218.

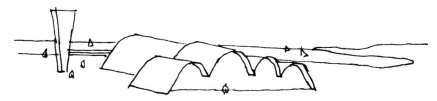

Church of São Francisco de Assis, Pampulha, Belo Horizonte

became the domain of the structure's 'profile and contour', and it remains 'free of all constraint'.

Cardozo emphasized the 'disappearance of the wall' at the Church of São Francisco de Assis, the irregularity of all the forms of the church, and the way each line of the composition is set askew, linking Niemeyer's 'almost magical space' with the Brazilian ecclesiastical Baroque of the eighteenth century. Cardozo's interpretation echoes Niemeyer's contemporaneous definition of his architecture through a discourse of dissent: one that decentres, disrupts, destabilizes and sets askew all that is dominant. Cardozo speaks of the Pampulha church as 'an exuberant demonstration of non-verticalism [averticalismo]'; that is, an architectural essay against the verticalism that 'has been the characteristic of powerful forms in the past' – all the more important in the case of a programme that has traditionally given rise to the concretization of the vertical axis mundi.[86]

Perhaps Cardozo's remarks imply that, in Brazil, heaven and earth meet on a sensual coastal curve. The rejection of verticality as the means to achieve visual power, combined with a preference for light and fluid forms, playful irregularity, bold silhouettes and dynamic asymmetries, renders Niemeyer's architecture commensurate with a Brazilian landscape where visual power lies in sinuous contours, meandering rivers, aquatic horizons and uncontrollable tropical growth, in the voluptuous curves of luxurious beaches and Baroque monuments. Burle Marx's gardens of 'horizontal structural surfaces' and arabesque patterns became an ideal companion to Niemeyer's forms of expressive plasticity, and to what Freyre described as a Brazilian 'Catholicism, which so delights the senses'.[87] Here, their humility seems fit for the church of St Francis.

The plan of the church suggests a Latin cross. The positioning of the entrance wall beside the lake suggests that the chapel

Church of São Francisco de Assis: street (west) elevation with azulejos by Cândido Portinari representing scenes from the life of St Francis

86 Cardozo, 1955, p. 6.   **87** Giedion, 1956, p. x; Freyre, 1956, p. 255.

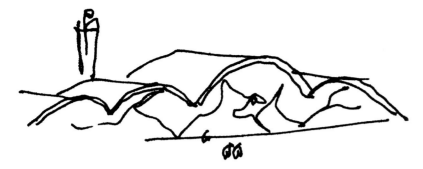

Church of São Francisco de Assis: view of street (west) elevation

addresses the pleasurable promenade along the water, rather than the road that passes the chapel's richly decorated, blind wall. On this side a garden obliges the viewer to stand at a distance from the illuminated west façade of the church to appreciate the striking, hand-painted, blue-and-white *azulejos* by Cândido Portinari, representing scenes from the life of St Francis, which announces the church to those who approach from the street or pass by in a fast-moving car. The overhanging vaulting is outlined with a fascia of japuraná granite. Turning to enter the church, the visitor is obliged to slow down, find the relatively narrow meandering path, walk by the side of the church but not too close to it, careful not to step on the slightly raised planted areas, guided by the flowing curves of Paulo Werneck's abstract *pastilha* mosaics on the lower part of the main vault, which echo the low travelling clouds in the tropical blue sky. Throughout the building, materials have been carefully selected and artworks exquisitely integrated so as to enhance the spatial experience. The quality of workmanship is of the highest order.

Church of São Francisco de Assis: detail of Cândido Portinari's hand-painted *azulejo* mural on the street (west) elevation

Church of São Francisco de Assis: detail of Paulo Werneck's *pastilha* mosaic on the main vault

Depending on which side they come from, pilgrims are greeted by a latticed, inversely tapered bell tower or a free-standing blue cross at the opening in front of the church by the lakeside – still paved in white *pedra portuguesa*, still on the profane side of things. They are then invited to step on the polished white marble floor with free-form patterns in black basalt, which interrupts the lakeside promenade in front of the church's 'wall of light'.[88] They advance towards the sacred space of São Francisco in stages, through a series of thresholds, finally moving under the entrance canopy, which slopes from the bell tower down, slightly below the entrance lintel, held on elegantly curved V-shaped steel poles. The polished marble floor extends up to the bell tower, under the *marquise*, which links the elements of the composition, imparting dynamism to the elevation and articulating a kind of external narthex, a place to stop before crossing another, more important threshold.

When the large, sliding, glass panes are open, the black-and-white basalt-and-marble floor flows uninterrupted, uniting interior and exterior spaces. The two sliding sections of the glass wall are indistinguishable from the other four fixed panes, as is the case with the Casino and Casa do Baile. At the Church of São Francisco, too, conventional doors have been abolished and replaced by long entrance sequences that blur the boundaries between interior and exterior space, allowing one to flow gradu-

88 Unfortunately, the beautiful black-and-white pavement under the *marquise* of the Church of São Francisco de Assis was badly disfigured as a result of restoration work in 2005, when a long and wide strip of glass was inserted in the basalt-and-marble floor, as part of a new external lighting installation; see photograph in Introduction, p.14.

ally into the other. As already noted in Chapter Two, precisely choreographed entrance sequences, embodying a fluid narrative of movement, stressing transition rather than sudden change from one kind of condition or space to another, are a defining characteristic of Niemeyer's buildings.

The principal lines of the lake elevation of São Francisco de Assis – the parabola of the vault, the oblique line of the *marquise* and the tapering wall of the bell tower – have been highlighted with japuraná granite revetments. The same material has been employed to trace the outline of the lower vaults. Upon entering into the parabolic vault of the church, the visitor recognizes familiar elements. On the left is the baptistery, defined by a low free-standing wall with *azulejos* by Portinari depicting the Baptism of Christ on its external, concave side, and four bronze bas-reliefs of Adam and Eve by Ceschiatti on its convex side. The choir gallery with its undulating parapet recalls Baroque prototypes. The nave, illuminated by Portinari's fourteen Stations of the Cross, directs the worshipper towards the high altar, lit mysteriously from above in typically Baroque fashion. Against customary practice, the choir gallery is positioned away from the curtain wall, at a distance equal to the width of the external narthex. A white concrete flat hull vessel adrift, it is held in mid-space by slender circular columns, isolated from the wood-panelled vault and extending its capriciously twisting staircase into the narthex. The internal narthex under the lofty vault is brightly lit via both the lower glazed area of the east façade and, more playfully, through the light-blue vertical *brises-soleil* above. The luminosity of the narthex is reinforced by the light-reflecting *azulejos* on the graciously curving baptistery wall and the angled gallery parapet, as well as by the polished white circular columns and the white marble spiral staircase.

Beyond the slender columns, upon crossing the second threshold under the gallery and emerging into the nave, the space gets darker and the cerejera-wood panelling of the vault imbues it with warmth. This is a space apart from the bright world outside the

Church of São Francisco de Assis: view of entrance from narthex

Church of São Francisco de Assis: view of lakeside (east) elevation with precisely choreographed entrance sequence

church, which filters through into the narthex. Only the polished marble-and-basalt floor carries a memory of familiar, profane ground inside the nave. The nave narrows and its vault descends towards the altar, which is raised on a platform two steps higher than the nave, with its vault higher and slightly wider than that of the nave at the point where it meets the transept.

The light that falls on the high altar wall and the *azulejo*-clad pulpit enters from a lantern at the point where the vault of the nave slots into that of the altar. The high altar wall bears a mural

Church of São Francisco de Assis: narthex with baptistery featuring Cândido Portinari's *azulejo* mural of the Baptism of Christ and Alfredo Ceschiatti's four bronze bas-reliefs of Adam and Eve, and choir gallery with Portinari's *azulejos* on its parapet

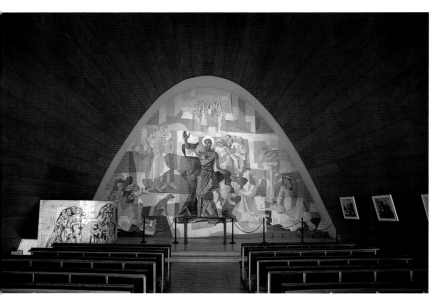

Church of São Francisco de Assis: high altar mural, Stations of the Cross and pulpit *azulejos* by Cândido Portinari; nave vault panelled in cerejera wood

by Portinari, its warm, earthy colours contrasting with the cold blues of the *azulejos*. It depicts Christ as the saviour of the ill, the poor and, most importantly, the sinner. The Pampulha worshipper had no reason to be fearful, and initially the chapel contained no confessional.[89] Here, Niemeyer's irreverence extended to the dictates of the Roman Catholic Church. Born to a devoutly Roman Catholic family, a 'non-believer' himself but with 'respect for religion', Niemeyer has clearly stated that his innovative design 'with its many curves' aimed at 'challenging . . . the religious rigidity of that period'.[90] Borrowing the forms of industrial architecture for the celestial dome, Niemeyer's intention, like Auguste Perret's before him, was not to desecrate ecclesiastical space but to consecrate the reinforced-concrete structures of utilitarian programmes, elevating them to the privileged realm of high art. Nevertheless, the forward-looking Church of São Francisco de Assis was considered sacrilegious and provocative by the conservative church authorities of Minas Gerais, whose reaction was violent and prolonged. At one stage it was even proposed to demolish the heretic structure and replace it with a replica of a church from Ouro Prêto. Consecration was refused until 1959.

Integrating Form, Site and Programme

Niemeyer's Resort Hotel at Pampulha (1943, unbuilt), with a highly ambitious programme including a public basement cinema, was also to be located on the lake front. Its linear 100-guest-room wing followed the curve of its access road, creating a protective barrier for the deployment of a multitude of low-lying spaces on its small peninsular setting. The lakeside two-storey guest rooms, entered at second-floor level, enjoy uninterrupted views over the landscaped garden and the lake, while those facing the avenue are equipped with vertical *brises-soleil*. For the first time here, Niemeyer shaped his building as an integral part of the landscape, maximizing the potential of its location. The programme develops as a topographical event and an exploratory experience, while a series of diverse unprogrammatic spaces for uninstructed occupation is introduced. The sophisticated interweaving of closed, open and semi-open spaces maximizes integration of landscape and programme, producing an environment where architecture and nature become intrinsically connected: the contours of the built areas merge with those of the terrain; the roof terrace melds with the garden; the *marquise* threads together interior and exterior

89 A confessional has been accommodated behind Ceschiatti's bronze panel of Adam and Eve's expulsion from paradise. Fifteen years after the Pampulha church, Alvar Aalto would include the crosses of the two thieves alongside that of Christ at the Church of the Three Crosses, Vuokkseniska, Imatra, Finland (1957–59).   90 Oscar Niemeyer, in Petit, 1995, p. 58; Niemeyer, 1985, p. 72.

spaces, then shreds into ramps reaching down to the lake; verandas extend to form piers or branch out to morph into amoebic lounging areas surrounded by tropical vegetation. This unexecuted project reflects Niemeyer's confident handling and interweaving of spatial and programmatic requirements, applying his newly developed formal strategies to a project of a much larger scale than all the other buildings around the lake of Pampulha.

In 1986, the Pampulha complex was granted national landmark status. It has become Belo Horizonte's most visited attraction. Niemeyer remarks that 'it was said to have launched an innovative architectural style that eventually spread throughout the world. "It is the only independent branch of contemporary architecture," said the architect Marc Emery, director of *L'Architecture d'Aujourd'hui* in Paris'.[91] In the years following Pampulha,

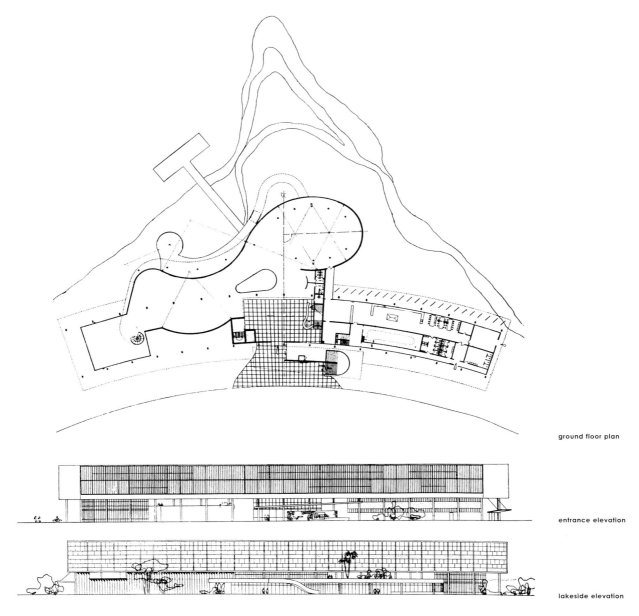

ground floor plan

entrance elevation

lakeside elevation

Resort Hotel, Pampulha, Belo Horizonte, Minas Gerais, 1943, unbuilt: on the ground-floor plan, the wide stairs near the entrance lead to the public basement cinema; the rooms facing the avenue are protected with vertical louvres

91 Niemeyer, 2000b, p. 108.

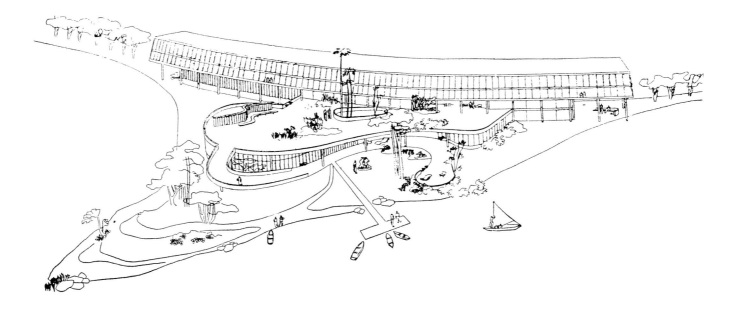

View of the Pampulha hotel from the lake: public rooms with roof garden, *in the foreground*, and guestroom wing, *in the background*, along the greatest dimension of the triangular site

Resort Hotel, Pampulha: indoor-outdoor lounge areas with a central pear-shaped atrium and a ramp at the rear leading to the roof garden above

Niemeyer designed a number of large-scale sports, leisure and recreation complexes which remained on paper: a restaurant and boathouse at the Lagoa Rodrigo de Freitas, Rio de Janeiro (1944); the Fluminense Yacht Club at Botafogo Beach, Rio de Janeiro (1945); a hotel at Nova Friburgo in the state of Rio de Janeiro (1945). The most eloquent unexecuted project from this period, however, is his 1948 proposal for an extension to the celebrated Ministry of Education and Public Health in Rio de Janeiro,

accommodating two auditoria, with capacity for 600 and 2,500 spectators respectively.

Echoing Abbé Laugier's dictum that 'an architect must be able to justify by reason everything he does', Niemeyer attests to the fact that, although intuition and delight in a particular shape or form guide his design, he has always sought a practical justification too: 'I carried on like this for many years, always searching for a different shape and then explaining it afterward.'

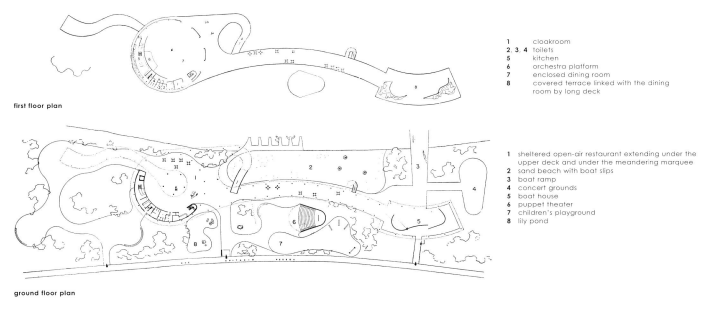

first floor plan

1	cloakroom
2, 3, 4	toilets
5	kitchen
6	orchestra platform
7	enclosed dining room
8	covered terrace linked with the dining room by long deck

ground floor plan

1	sheltered open-air restaurant extending under the upper deck and under the meandering marquee
2	sand beach with boat slips
3	boat ramp
4	concert grounds
5	boat house
6	puppet theater
7	children's playground
8	lily pond

Restaurant and Boathouse at the Lagoa Rodrigo de Freitas, Rio de Janeiro, 1944, unbuilt

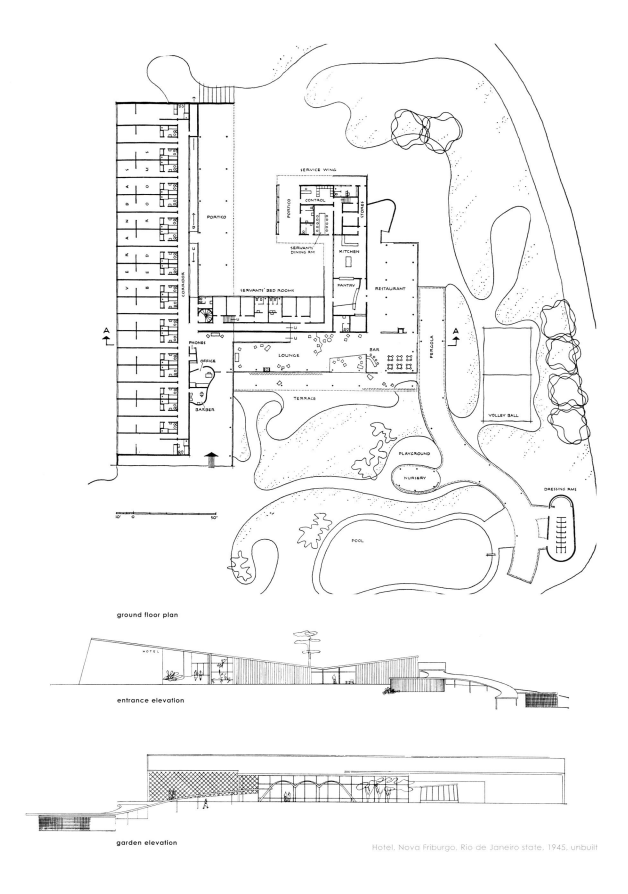

ground floor plan

entrance elevation

garden elevation

Hotel, Nova Friburgo, Rio de Janeiro state, 1945, unbuilt

Every time I designed a curved block standing alone on a site, for instance, I presented it with accompanying sketches showing that the existing curved topography itself had suggested it. When I designed inclined facades, I likewise explained that these were intended to provide greater solar protection or exposure; when I designed an auditorium shaped like an ink blotter, I was addressing the problem of interior visibility . . . In this way I defended my architecture and my fantasies, creating new forms and architectural elements that over time were added to the plastic vocabulary of our architecture, which was often used by my colleagues.[92]

Perhaps, it would be more appropriate to view Niemeyer's avoidance of preconceived solutions and his a posteriori justification of formal choices as a testing of his initial experimental, seemingly improvised formal proposals. But his statement clearly also indicates that he found it necessary to explain his 'fantasies' in familiar 'rational' terms instead of defending a deliberate process of invention of programmatic solutions and spatial concepts, unprejudiced by familiarity and habit, and a self-conscious desire to extend the familiar limits of form and function.

In the case of the new double auditorium for the Ministry of Education, with its dramatic curvilinear structural ribs opening into a fan, Niemeyer produced a series of working sketches that present his 'explanation' or justification of the proposed solution in terms of optical angles, suggesting that the profile of his building was determined by the desire to allow unrestricted views towards the Brazilian Modernist monument. There is no doubt, however, that Niemeyer intended the two volumes to be viewed together. The low, undulating form of his auditoria building, with a curving ramp gracefully lifting the visitor up to a viewing platform, contrasts dramatically with the Corbusian slab of the Ministry of Education. In no way does the newcomer overshadow the host. Yet Niemeyer's imposition of his revolutionary sensual curves on the site that initiated a critique of the unforgiving straight lines of strict functionalism was intended as an affirmation of a definite schism. In a photomontage produced by Niemeyer to show his

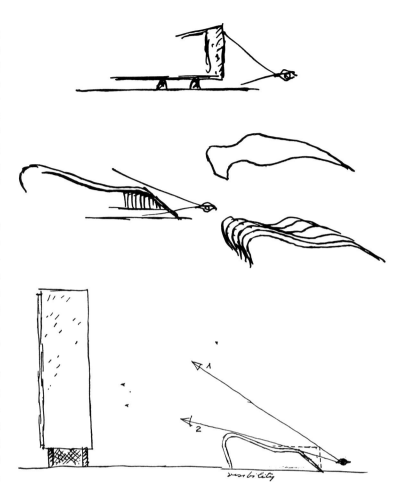

Proposal for a double-auditorium extension to the Ministry of Education and Public Health, Rio de Janeiro, 1948, unbuilt: working sketches

proposed extension next to the constructed building, his restless David assumes what appears to be a confrontational pose against the erect and indifferent Goliath. To the site of the functional and beautiful Ministry of Education, Niemeyer wanted to add an element of shock. Architecture, he argues, must be 'functional, beautiful, and shocking'.[93]

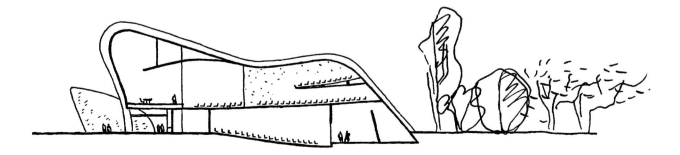

92 Niemeyer, 2000b, p. 170.   **93** Niemeyer, 1994a, p. 28.

Double-auditorium extension to the Ministry of Education and Public Health: longitudinal section showing the two auditoria with stages at opposite ends

Double-auditorium extension to the Ministry of Education and Public Health: photomontage with model on site

From the 'old building', he retained the decorative *azulejos* and *brises-soleil*, which feature prominently in his 'new addition'. But he also clearly posited his liberating Brazilian contours as a synthesis *de novo* rather than an evolution based on European prototypes. The added spectacle serves to bring home the two vital messages of his curvilinear forms: first, that they define his architecture as a counterstatement to the rigid, angular forms of European Modernism, demystifying its socialist, rationalist and functionalist pretensions in the process; and second, that they underscore the primacy of the native landscape and, by association, the authority and authenticity of local Brazilian culture.

With remarkable consistency, in so many of his texts, Niemeyer repeats that he aims at the unexpected, the spectacular, the surprising, the variable, the uplifting and the awe-inspiring. He sees these as the ingredients of the beautiful, which he lists through Charles Baudelaire: '*L'inattendu, l'irrégularité, la surprise et l'étonnement sont une partie essentielle et une caractéristique de la beauté.*'[94] The 'free-flowing style' of his spectacular addition to the seminal Rio de Janeiro site represents Niemeyer's attempt to complete the project that gave birth to the architecture of Brazilian Modernism, consolidating its meticulously specified ingredients.

94 'The unexpected, irregularity, surprise and astonishment are an essential part and characteristic of beauty'; Charles Baudelaire, quoted in Niemeyer, 2000b, p. 168, emphasis in the original. Niemeyer's notion of 'spectacle' is also indebted to Le Corbusier, who spoke of the 'architectural spectacle' offered to the visitor who embarks on his prescribed *promenade architecturale*. With reference to the Villa Savoye at Poissy, Le Corbusier wrote: 'In this house it's a question of real architectural promenade, offering constantly changing views, unexpected, sometimes astonishing'; Le Corbusier and Jeanneret, 1999, vol. 2, p. 24.

Chapter Four

Challenging Established Hierarchies in the Post-War Brazilian Metropolis

Architecture worthy of human beings thinks better of men than they really are. It views them in the way they could be according to the status of their own productive energies as embodied in technology. Architecture contradicts the needs of the here and now as soon as it proceeds to serve those needs – without simultaneously representing any absolute or lasting ideology.

Theodor W. Adorno, 'Functionalism Today'

At a dance held in honour of Emperor Dom Pedro II in 1848, more than sixty ladies appeared exhibiting the national colours on their dresses – the green and yellow of the royal houses of Bragança and Habsburg – and with a sprig of coffee bush in their hair.[1] The states of Rio de Janeiro, São Paulo and Minas Gerais were the major coffee producers of the Brazilian Empire, and by the mid-nineteenth century the prosperous coffee industry of the Southeast had replaced the sugar industry of the Northeast as the backbone of the Brazilian economy. Under the Old Republic (1889–1930), Brazil enjoyed a virtual monopoly over the world coffee market (78 per cent in 1906–10). Coffee dominated the export trade (53 per cent in 1908), and the coffee *fazendeiros* (coffee plantation owners) controlled the economy.

As the oligarchy of the *senhores de engenho* (sugar plantation and mill owners) declined, the 'República do café-com-leite' ('Coffee-and-milk republic') was increasingly dominated by the political alliance of the two richest and most populous states: the coffee-producing state of São Paulo and the dairy producing state of Minas Gerais. The 1930 schism between the Paulista and Mineiro elites over the presidential succession propelled Minas Gerais to the cause of *gaúcho* Getúlio Vargas's Aliança Liberal. With military intervention, the revolution of 1930 wrested power from those with coffee interests, although Vargas did not antagonize the planters. The collapse of coffee markets during the Great Depression in the 1930s, the deteriorating trade balance, import controls and currency depreciation stimulated Brazil's domestic economy.

In 1928, Cassiano Ricardo's poem 'Martim Cererê' saluted Brazil's urban industrial future. In 1929, two films, Adalberto Kemeny and Rodolfo Rex Lustig's *São Paulo, A symphonia da metrópole* (*São Paulo: Symphony of a Metropolis*) and José Medina's *Fragmentos da vida* (*Fragments of Life*, based on a tale by the American O. Henry), celebrated the growing city, its skyscrapers, elevators and industrial parks, 'defying the clouds, bearing in that uncontrolled urge the sweat of humble workers'.[2] In the 1930s and 1940s, accelerated industrialization and economic diversification, population explosion and internal migration brought rapid urban growth and an expansion of the industrial middle class and the urban proletariat. The locus of power shifted from the landed gentry to the urban industrial bourgeoisie. The *fazendeiro* Vargas denied agricultural workers (85 per cent of the workforce) the benefits conferred to the urban working class through paternalistic labour legislation and welfare programmes. The industrial workers, largely literate and thus part of the electorate, became a privileged minority (2.5 per cent of the population in 1950), acknowledged as a vital segment of the Brazilian economy and society.

Between 1929 and 1937, industrial output increased by nearly 50 per cent and in 1938 it was more than double that of agriculture. But Brazil was still a neocolonial debtor nation. Industrial self-sufficiency and protection of the country's natural resources were seen as necessary in order to guarantee Brazil's sovereignty, economic independence and achievement of world-power status. From 1935, European rearmament demands were high, and Brazilian production of iron ore quintupled in the 1940s. Latin America's first integrated steel complex, Volta Redonda, went into operation in 1946 on the site of a former coffee plantation in the Paraíba Valley in the state of Rio de Janeiro, roughly midway between the iron mines of Minas Gerais and the steel market of exchange for military cooperation – Vargas hailed the steelworks

1 Schwarcz, 2004, p. 136.   **2** Caption from *Fragmentos da vida*, cited in Bernadet, p. 555. Adalberto Kemeny and Rodolfo Rex Lustig's *São Paulo, A symphonia da metrópole* was inspired by Walther Ruttman's *Berlin, Die Sinfonie der Großstadt* (*Berlin: Symphony of a Great City*) of 1927.

Adalberto Kemeny and Rudolf Rex Lustig, 1929, *São Paulo. A symphonia da metrópole* (São Paulo: Rex)

Brazil's participation in World War II and nationalist campaigns to develop Brazilian-owned steel and petroleum industries fostered national unity, pride and confidence in the country's economic future. Economic nationalism inspired cultural nationalism. Almirante (Henrique Foreis Domingues), 'the most respected producer in Brazilian radio' in the 1940s, rallied Brazilians to the preservation of the nation's 'authentic' cultural traditions and sought to curtail the impact of imported cultural innovations, particularly from the United States. He proclaimed: 'Brazilians now have confidence in the things that other Brazilians produce. They are confident that our industry has completely surpassed that of foreign countries.'[4] But despite rapid urban growth, in the 1950s more than half of all Brazilians continued to live in the impoverished countryside. Most of them were illiterate and therefore barred from direct participation in the political process.[5] When they gravitated to the city, they joined the shadow economy as domestic servants or street sellers and lived in self-built shacks in the rapidly expanding, insalubrious *favelas* or *cortiços* typical of São Paulo.

Building in the Socially, Racially and Spatially Segregated City

The concentration of production and surplus labour in the cities strengthened the influence of the privileged, fast-expanding middle class, which included some second-generation European immigrants and the affluent urban elite, controlling commerce, banking and industry, usually linked to the old patriarchal *latifundios* and positioned at the top of the new social hierarchy. In the cities with the largest share of the national industry, these high-income earners lived in fashionable, multi-storey apartment blocks, which, alongside prestigious office blocks, quickly transformed the skylines of Brazil's major urban centres.[6] In *Fragmentos da vida*, there was an ironic discrepancy between the futuristic city described in the captions and that of reality in 1929 projected on the screen. The 'progress and promise' of the former acquired concrete form in the following decades, when Brazilian cities were rapidly 'becoming full of skyscrapers, dotted with squares [characterized by] the refinement and taste of the inhabitants and their economic assertion'.[7]

As Niemeyer observed, however, the new structures of the Brazilian cities, including those by his own hand, 'reflect the social disequilibrium of the country with a majority of its citizens living in the most miserable quarters'.[8] The high social and racial segregation of cities like Rio de Janeiro reached the silver screen with

'as the symbol of Brazil's economic emancipation'.[3] With electrical power already in foreign hands, the nationalists rallied to the cry 'o petróleo é nosso!' ('the oil is ours!') against the *entreguistas* (an epithet applied to those who hand over national wealth to foreign interests), who favoured modernization with the help of international investment. In 1953, under Vargas's second administration (1951–54), Petrobrás was established as a state monopoly of all petroleum resources and their exploration.

3 Wirth, p. 1.   **4** McCann, p. 474; Almirante (Henrique Foreis Domingues), quoted in McCann, p. 477. Since the 1920s, the United States had replaced Great Britain as Brazil's main trade partner.   **5** In 1945, a mere 16 per cent of the population was registered to vote, rising to 25 per cent by 1962; Burns, 1970, p. 330.   **6** In 1951, Lúcio Costa related the late appearance of the apartment block in Brazil to the availability of cheap 'domestic' labour long after the abolition of slavery, continuing until World War II; Lúcio Costa, 'Muita construção, alguma arquitetura e um milagre' (1951), in Lúcio Costa, 1997, p. 160.   **7** Caption from *Fragmentos da vida*, cited in Bernadet, p. 555.   **8** Niemeyer, 1956b, p. 12.

Nelson Pereira dos Santos's first two realist features, *Rio 40 graus* (*Rio 40 Degrees*, 1955), banned by the Rio chief of police precisely for its 'negative' portrayal of the federal capital, and *Rio Zona Norte* (*Rio Northern Zone*, 1957). Ironically, the spatialization of the federal capital's socio-economic inequities inverted the social hierarchy: the *favelas*, clinging on the granite hills surrounding the *zona sul*, look down on the privileged spaces of the Carioca cosmopolitans inhabiting the elite neighbourhoods by the beach.

Niemeyer's own house on Rua Carvalho de Azevedo, Fonte da Saudade, Rio de Janeiro, was designed in 1942. In contrast to common practice (still current) in the houses of the Brazilian middle and upper classes, it has no service entrance separate from the so-called 'social' or 'public' entrance – something that allegedly made it particularly difficult to sell the house a few years later.[9] Raised on *pilotis* on a hill with a magnificent view across the Lagoa Rodrigo de Freitas to the south, Niemeyer's version of the Corbusian Maison Citrohan, with its single-pitch, red-tiled roof projecting over the veranda and wooden sliding jalousies, originally deep blue, currently bright yellow, recalls Le Corbusier's rhapsodic description of the houses of the black Carioca *favelados*.[10]

Built on a small site, the four levels of the house unfold along a *promenade architecturale*, guided by a gently rising ramp affording plunging views of the lush, shaded garden and lagoon. Running along the house's main axis, the ramp begins, apparently unsupported, by the external wall of the ground-floor service area. This wall, originally blue and currently bright yellow, greets the visitor and directs them towards the ramp, mediating between the house and the garage with a curve that underscores its independence from the slender columns of the *pilotis*. A low, smoothly undulating, retaining rubble wall marks the limit of the cool garden to the right, a short flight of stairs below the entrance level, sharply dropping towards the lagoon.

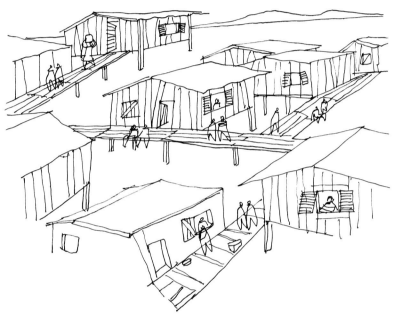

Sketch of squatter settlement or *favela* in mid-twentieth-century Rio de Janeiro with wooden houses and walkways on *pilotis*

Niemeyer House on Rua Carvalho de Azevedo, Fonte da Saudade, Rio de Janeiro, 1942: the first house Niemeyer built for his family on a hill with a magnificent view across the Lagoa Rodrigo de Freitas

Still today, the bare brick houses of the *favelas* built by the urban poor on Rio de Janeiro's hillsides or *morros* contrast with the white structures of the planned city or *asfalto*, reflecting Rio's social and spatial segregation.

9 Personal communication with the house's current owner, Ms Elbasette Camara, who bought the house from Oscar Niemeyer in the 1950s.
10 See Chapter One, p. 19.

The *pilotis* come in a variety of sections: circular around the garage and by the first flight of the ramp, square at the rear, north-eastern side of the house, and oval for the columns to the south towards the lagoon. These four sturdiest and longest columns of the house appear to emerge through the thick vegetation, as if the tropical garden had always been there, and Niemeyer was careful to step lightly in it for fear of disturbing its natural equilibrium. To use Le Corbusier's words, 'the natural ground remains, the poetry is intact'.[11] The oval columns continue above the cantilevered balcony with much slimmer, square sections, visible along the first-floor west and south elevations. The discrepancy is most clearly displayed at the south-west corner of the house, where an oval *piloti* leads to a square free-standing column, slightly off the corner of the covered terrace hollowed out of the first floor.

One level higher, on the west elevation, a long, horizontal, dark-blue, wooden frame has been inserted, creating the impression of a ribbon window, especially when the dark-blue jalousies slide open in front of the recessed parts of the wall. With the south bedroom window detailed in a similar fashion, when its jalousie is open the vertical support, somewhat disconcertingly, disappears from sight. A further wilful inconsistency has been introduced on the south elevation at second-floor level, where the two middle vertical supports have been painted dark blue and are thus visually incorporated within the large wooden opening and deprived of their solidity.

On plan additional inconsistencies appear in the irregularity of the columnar grid, with deviations that are not the result of structure or utility constraints. Most notably, the circular *piloti* at the north-west corner of the house appears randomly positioned away from the corner, farther along the rear, north elevation. The middle row of *pilotis* begins with two columns that define the limits of the garage, and is then shifted to the outer side of the ramp,

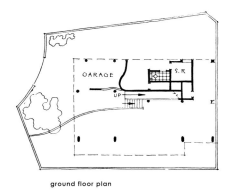

ground floor plan

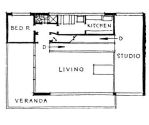

first floor plan

second floor plan

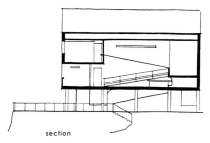

section

Niemeyer House on Rua Carvalho de Azevedo, Rio de Janeiro

11 Le Corbusier, 1991, p. 49.

where the two circular columns supporting the first flight are connected to it by corbels that obscure their structural role; one of these two columns steps casually down to the garden.

Arrangements like this, as well as the general apparent informality of the *pilotis*, undermine geometric and structural clarity and subvert the reading of a regular grid, contributing to an effect of lightness and spatial freedom. At the same time, the seemingly haphazard, spontaneous assembly of irregular structural elements, together with the unusually strong colours, the pitched roof and cantilevered balcony negotiate an encounter between the sophisticated, self-conscious Modernist white cube and the Brazilian people's makeshift, fragile dwellings of necessity and deprivation, perched on the steep *morros* of Rio de Janeiro. It is tempting to read Niemeyer's hillside house as an attempt to sketch a vision of a *mestiça* domestic architecture to suit the mythical, 'beautiful, wheat-coloured Brazil' with which he identifies, dispelling the disturbing reality of 'social disequilibrium' that belies the cherished illusion.[12]

The entrance to the house is found at the end of the second flight of the ramp, well concealed from both street and garden and typically uneventful. Once through the door and on into the living room on the left, the Spartan Modernist interior is dominated by the intoxicating panorama of the lagoon, the sea and the mountains, admitted through the continuous window to the south. A west-facing bedroom for Niemeyer's cousin Milota, who had always lived with his family, is also found on the first floor. On the opposite side of the double-height living space, the long ramp becomes a space-articulating device, leading to a studio on the mezzanine and to two bedrooms on the second floor without ever losing sight of Rio's natural landmarks.

A simple, polished wood balustrade is fitted to the first flight of the ramp, minimizing its visual impact and helping to integrate this spatial intruder into the living space. The lower, outer side of the ramp is faced with the same peroba do campo wood, as are the cupboard units perpendicular to the ramp, which form a parapet between the living room and raised studio space. From an alcove in this parapet projects a rectangular table with V-shaped steel-tube support, served by Thonet bentwood chairs, model no. 9, also found in Le Corbusier's Parisian apartment at 24 rue Nungesser et Coli (1931–34). The table brings to mind Charlotte Perriand's table for the gallery in Le Corbusier and Pierre Jeanneret's Villa La Roche, Paris (1923–35).

The wall with the door to the living room, which continues as the outer side of the ramp leading from the mezzanine to the bedrooms, is painted a warm brown (*havana*), also recalling the burnt umber of the much steeper ramp in the Villa La Roche gallery. The

volume of the two second-floor bedrooms along the west side of Niemeyer's house overhangs the space of the bright living room, reducing its height and light, and increasing its intimacy at the point of entry. A screen of open ceramic blocks (*combogó*) was added later on the outer side of the first-floor covered terrace, further reducing light and heat from the west and increasing privacy

Niemeyer House on Rua Carvalho de Azevedo: view of south elevation overlooking the lagoon

Niemeyer House on Rua Carvalho de Azevedo: view of the living room with continuous south-facing window and Bruno Mathsson's bentwood-and-webbing chairs

12 From Ary Barroso's samba for the carnival of 1939, 'Aquarela do Brasil', perhaps the most popular song ever written in Brazil and also the theme song of Walt Disney's *Saludos Amigos* (1943); Niemeyer, 1956b, p. 12.

Niemeyer House on Rua Carvalho de Azevedo: views of the living room with ramp leading to the studio on the mezzanine

in the terrace overlooking the street. The floors of the living room and ramp are covered with black linoleum, against which was laid a cow hide, again recalling Le Corbusier's own apartment. The relatively austere interior was complemented by Bruno Mathsson's bentwood-and-webbing lounge chairs, similar to Alvar Aalto's designs, and probably seen by Niemeyer in 1939 in New York at the Museum of Modern Art or the Swedish Pavilion at the World's Fair.

David Underwood interprets Niemeyer's appropriation of the 'popular type' of the hillside shanty for the use of 'only the upper classes' as a 'monumentalization of the vernacular', which 'serves to legitimize the elite conquest of the usual realm of the *favelados*'.[13] *Pace* Underwood, Niemeyer's aesthetics of randomness and utilitarian simplicity steered clear of the romanticization of poverty and social marginalization that such appropriations usually effect, contesting the myth of the picturesque *favela*. His interest in Rio's black vernacular coincided with a time when the 'very dirty and disreputable nigger neighborhoods' of the city featured in the Brazilian press as a source of potential major international embarrassment.

It was in 1942 that Orson Welles was filming *favelas* and Afro-Brazilian carnival and samba for his ill-fated 'pan-American documentary' *It's All True*, largely finished but never released, and partially reconstructed in 1993. Welles was 'well attuned to the power and intelligence of what Robert Farris Thompson calls "black Atlantic civilization", and therefore well prepared to appreciate

the black contribution to Brazilian culture'. But the Rockefeller Committee of the Coordination of Inter-American Affairs (OCIAA) strongly advised him to avoid showing to North American audiences 'sequences . . . in which mulattos or mestiços appear conspicuously' and to omit 'any reference to miscegenation'. Both US authorities and the Vargas government objected to 'nigger singing and dancing'. The local press expressed uneasiness with Welles's portrayal of Rio 'as though [it] were another Harlem', and insisted that he should show Brazil 'to the world as a civilized nation', excluding 'all the negative elements of [the] land'. Walt Disney's *The Three Caballeros* (1944) offered a solution: it celebrated black Baiana *tias* – aunties from the Northeast state of Bahia, invariably black matriarchs linked to African religions and samba – in an innocently exotic, lily-white incarnation, detaching the entertaining sound of African instruments from the black bodies that would have spoiled the Hollywood spectacle and shocked its audience.[14]

But rather than 'whitening' the architecture of the shanties while preserving their exotic appeal, Niemeyer's valorization of the excluded 'aesthetics of bricolage' articulates his and Brazil's utopian and frustrated longing for genuine social and interracial

13 Underwood, 1994b, p. 38.   **14** Production manager Lynne Shores, quoted in Stam, 1997, p. 127; Stam, 1997, p. 122; memorandum from the Rockefeller Committee of the Coordination of Inter-American Affairs (OCIAA) to RKO, Lynne Shores, *Meio Dia*, quoted in Stam, 1997, pp. 125, 127, 129. Welles's project was denounced as 'communist'; Stam, 1997, p. 122.

dialogue and equality. Only a few years after Vargas's Estado Nôvo had rejected Mário de Andrade's proposal to catalogue and register works of popular culture, Niemeyer's Antropofagist architecture united the popular with the erudite, the European with the African, arguing for the centrality of the marginalized and excluded. In his 1924 'Manifesto de la Poesia Pau-Brasil', Oswald de Andrade had demanded 'black women in the Jockey Club'.[15] At a time when black people were still not allowed into the Cassino da Urca, Niemeyer denounced an architecture of segregation and granted entry to the domestic workers of his house – most likely black – through the front door.[16] Although it may not have overtly challenged social hierarchy, Niemeyer's house, built at a distance from 'the impertinent beach-going socialite set', may be interpreted as an attempt to grant legitimacy to the voice of those socially and politically incapacitated members of Brazilian society who are allowed no right to speak.[17] Paying homage to the disempowered and stigmatized architecture of poverty and marginality, Niemeyer's house revealed the dignity of these makeshift dwellings in a manner that would find followers in subsequent decades, notably Lina Bo Bardi and João da Gama Filgueiras Lima, known as Lelé (1932–).[18]

Niemeyer posited the peripheral, urban, popular black architecture of the *morros* – 'from which come all moral and material miseries and all vices' according to one of the founders of the Instituto Central de Arquitetos do Brasil – as a legitimate, central source of inspiration for modern Brazilian architecture, but thereby risked rendering it into a commodity for consumption, like other black cultural practices such as music and dance.[19] But he also claimed for 'the filthy *favela* huts infesting the lovely edge of the lagoon' a status in Brazil's historic past and present equal to that of the 'venerable old baroque churches', thus empowering the subaltern architecture of practical necessity.[20] Niemeyer established a continuity with the Corbusian 'black disorder' of the architecture of the oppressed 'no good half-breeds', including it in the process of building an image of modern Brazil.[21] He thus deployed its force to contaminate – although not sever – the hegemonic bourgeois Modernist model and open up its field of significance. Architects like Lina Bo Bardi and Lelé would later take things forward, seeking to open up a space in which the significance and aesthetic power of that Other architecture could resonate.

In the Heart of the Business District: 'Lift shafts, skyscraper cubes, and the compensating laziness of the sun'

In his 'Foreword' to the first monograph on Oscar Niemeyer in 1950, Lúcio Costa stressed Niemeyer's ability 'to transform, without any apparent effort, as with a mere wave of a wand, the most strictly utilitarian program into a plastic expression of the purest refinement'.[22] Niemeyer himself argued that, in the 1940s and 1950s, Brazilian architecture was 'in search of plastic expressions', having overcome 'the stage of orthodox functionalism'.[23] His design for the headquarters of the Banco Boavista (1946–48), in the heart of Rio's emerging financial district, was selected by its chairman, the Baron de Saavedra, from three submitted proposals, as 'the most daring and most beautiful'.[24] This was the first time Niemeyer dealt with a programme that had to be precisely inserted into a tight urban grid, with a pre-established size and massing. The large office building on this relatively small site was subject to rigid planning restrictions, in accordance with Donat-Alfred Agache's plan (1926–30). It faces onto three streets: the monumental Avenida Presidente Vargas, from which the first three floors had to be set back to allow for an arcade required by the Agache plan; Rua Teofilo Ottoni to the rear; and the extremely narrow Rua Quintada. Niemeyer himself kept an office for many years on the top floor of the building, the bank itself occupying five floors.

Turning limitations into creative possibilities, Niemeyer came up with a number of innovative solutions to enliven the fourteen-storey monolith. When completed, the all-glass building was such a novelty that it provoked not only humorous press coverage but also mistrust among the Boavista clientele, who feared for the safety of their investments. Niemeyer's 'kick at convention', to quote the 1948 journalist of *O Globo*, was predominantly a kick at the solidity that until then had been regarded as both a functional and symbolic requirement of such a programme. With orientation on his side, he raised the bank's most transparent façade, the curtain wall of the south elevation, on the prestigious new Avenida Presidente Vargas, opposite Rio's largest colonial monument, the eighteenth-century church of Nossa Senhora da Candelária, which marks the end of the avenue. On this elevation, fixed stone *brises-soleil* were employed only on the crowning floor, containing

15 Oswald de Andrade, 1989, p. 310. **16** Stam, 1997, p. 124. **17** Niemeyer, 2000b, p. 28. **18** Lelé's naked brickwork Church of Nossa Senhora de Alagados at the Alagados *favela* of Salvador, Bahia, specially commissioned for the visit of Pope John Paul II on 7 July 1980, adopted an aesthetics of scarcity while avoiding both caricaturing mimicry and patronizing sentimentality. **19** Marcelo Mendonça, from a paper Mendonça presented in 1931 at the Primeiro Congresso de Habitação in São Paulo. The paper argued that 'the slums . . . must be demolished'; cited in Outtes. **20** 'Each time the robust and handsome fiancé of "del Rio" [Orson Welles] points his cameras at the so-

called "picturesque" spots of the city, we feel a slight uneasiness . . . Instead of showing him our possibilities, [his Brazilian advisors] let him film, to his delight, scenes of no-good half-breeds . . . and the filthy *favela* huts infesting the lovely edge of the lagoon': from Gatinha Angora's article of 20 May 1942, in *Ciné-Radio Jornal*, cited in Stam, 1997, p. 129. **21** Le Corbusier, 1948, p. 46; Gatinha Angora, quoted in Stam, 1997, p. 129. **22** Lúcio Costa, 1950, p. 3. The quotation in the subheading is from Oswald de Andrade, 1989, p. 311. **23** Oscar Niemeyer, quoted in Papadaki, 1950, p. 5. **24** Baron de Saavedra, interview with *O Globo*, 14 September 1948, cited in Banco Boavista, p. 7.

the employees' club and medical treatment rooms. The granite-clad circular columns of the loggia rise behind this south-facing curtain wall, effortlessly penetrating slab after slab with no visible beams, overriding the reflected image of the Baroque Cande-lária. Here, as elsewhere, the columns are the element that has received Niemeyer's special attention; made to appear almost

entirely relieved of their structural burden, they are ascribed instead the role of structuring an aesthetic experience.

Speaking of the elongated, 'free-floating' columns of the Ministry of Education and Public Health, Niemeyer has recalled Auguste Perret's exhortation: 'One has to make the supports sing.'[25] Henceforth, he spared no effort in his indefatigable formal experimentation with his buildings' vertical supports, against the odds of gravity and always to this end: that they appear to bear their loads effortlessly; that they break free of bondage and sing without losing breath, articulating ever-variable spatial experiences. In a process that culminated in Brasília, the lightness of Niemeyer's columnar supports increased in tandem with an increase of their aesthetic and spatial role. From Brasília onwards, they often became the central, if not the sole, form-defining and space-articulating element, underscoring Niemeyer's consistent pursuit of the integration of structural and spatial components.

On the pattern of the Ministry of Education building, the north elevation of the bank, on Rua Teofilo Ottoni, is lined with horizontal, light-blue, adjustable wooden brises-soleil, set within a dense and deep concrete grid to ensure adequate shading. With the viewer on the narrow Rua Quintada in mind, Niemeyer set in motion also the western façade of Banco Boavista, shielding it in vertical, adjustable wooden brises-soleil within a larger, shallow concrete grid, so as not to crowd the foreshortened view of this kinetic panel from the street. Foreshortening as well as considerations of light absorption guided the decision to graduate the colour of these sunshades, from white on the first floor to deep blue at the top. In this way, the building's upper part gains definition and the light-coloured sunshades allow more light to be reflected in the lower floors, while foreshortening diminishes the perception of colour variation. It is not so much the need for protection against the sun as that for privacy that is answered by the brises-soleil on this façade. Its solid crown is interrupted at the centre by a pierced screen in front of a small, top-floor garden.

The most remarkable feature of the exterior of the bank building was also reserved for the lower part of this west elevation beside the narrow, slow street, where the relation with passers-by is most intimate. With uncompromising rigour, Niemeyer undertook here a faithful translation of Costa's vision of 'free' walls 'slid[ing] beside the indifferent columns, . . . undulat[ing]'.[26] A three-storey wall of translucent glass blocks undulates past the circular columns, standing indifferent at its inflection points. The junctions where the mezzanine is held by these columns are made almost

Banco Boavista Headquarters, Rio de Janeiro, 1946–48: glazed south façade on Avenida Presidente Vargas and brises-soleil-shielded west façade on Rua Quintada

25 Auguste Perret, quoted in Niemeyer, 2002, p. 67. In September 1936, on his way from Buenos Aires back to Europe, Auguste Perret had stopped in Rio de Janeiro and given a lecture at the Instituto Nacional de Música, invited by the Ministry of Education and Public Health. He had also commented on the design for the Ministry of Education building.   26 Lúcio Costa, 2000, p. 625.

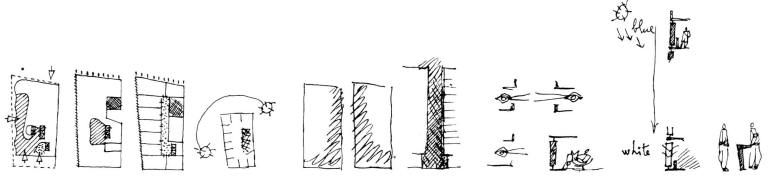

Sketches showing three distinct types of circulation for customers, personnel and tenants, and light and privacy requirements satisfied through the use of *brises-soleil*

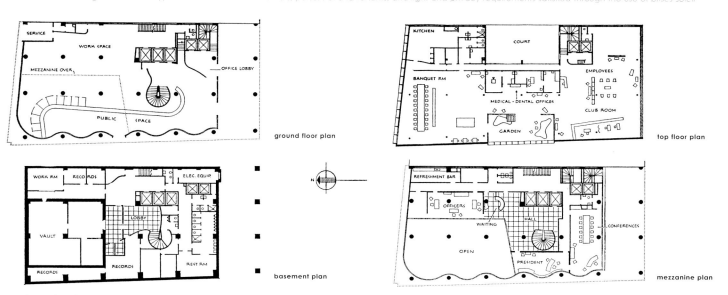

ground floor plan

top floor plan

basement plan

mezzanine plan

Banco Boavista Headquarters, Rio de Janeiro

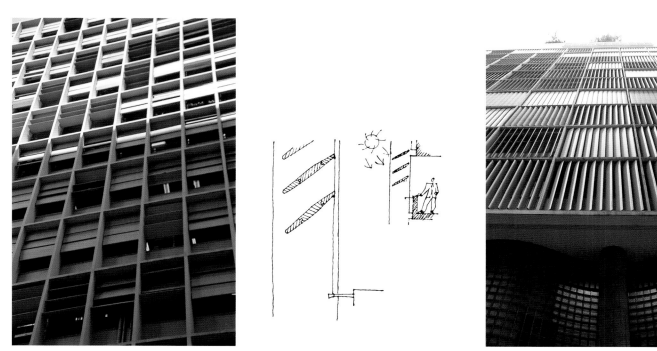

Banco Boavista Headquarters: sunscreen of north façade on Rua Teofilo Ottoni; sketch of wooden adjustable louvres; west façade on Rua Quintada

Banco Boavista Headquarters: *above*, view of the banking lobby under the mezzanine; *below*, studies for the undulating three-storey glass-block wall 'slid[ing] beside the indifferent columns'

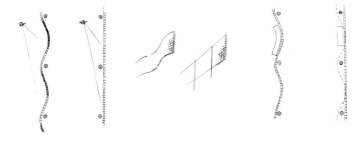

invisible. Always eager to justify his designs on practical grounds, Niemeyer claimed that this undulating membrane offered greater stability, while also allowing for a better arrangement of furniture and richer light effects in the interior of the banking lobby. For Boavista's clients, Niemeyer staged a modern banking drama. A triple-height, brightly lit, polished-marble environment awaited the confident banking classes at a time of rapid economic growth. For those waiting to be served, undulating benches were fitted along the glass-block wall.

From his office on the glazed mezzanine, enlivened by a Cândido Portinari mural, the bank's chairman could survey the glamorous lobby. But it is also the experience of the anonymous passers-by on the insignificant Rua Quintada, which the planners judged unworthy of a loggia, that Niemeyer's sculptural arrangement dynamizes. Surprise is most effective where it is least expected: on the narrow pavement, pedestrians are suddenly entertained by a sparkling, breathing wave, a notional loggia in motion. The limits of the city turn liquid where they are expected to be tight. At the corner with Rua Teofilo Ottoni, a solid shield bearing an energizing mosaic with wavy patterns by Paulo Werneck covers the lower part of the wall as it curves indifferent to the column

at the corner, before straightening out to embrace the two columns on the north side. This is no more the Corbusian building 'seen as in a showcase', but a building that joins in with the life and scale of the small street and moves along with its pedlars. For Niemeyer, streets are not Le Corbusier's outdated relics of the past, 'independent of buildings'.[27]

Niemeyer and his contemporary Brazilian Modernists, like the brothers Marcelo and Milton Roberto, composed numerous elevations in the course of the following years that fully exploited the functional, formal and aesthetic potential of sunbreaks, achieving 'endless incidental variety within an orderly frame'.[28] In low-cost

27 Le Corbusier, 1991, pp. 58 and 62.   **28** Papadaki, 1960, p. 18.

Banco Boavista Headquarters: views of the lower part of west elevation along Rua Quintada bearing a mosaic by Paulo Werneck at the corner with Rua Teofilo Ottoni

buildings like that for the plant and headquarters of O Cruzeiro Publishing Company, Rio de Janeiro (1949), the need for sun protection provided an opportunity to alleviate the mundane character of the office block and give it visual interest. Using minimum means to maximum effect and possibly inspired by Le Corbusier's project for business-centre skyscrapers in Algiers (1938–42), Niemeyer broke the two-dimensionality of the north elevation of O Cruzeiro, set on a main street, by composing a kind of bas-relief panel with two different sizes of adjustable horizontal sunbreaks, some of them jutting forward beyond the frame.

At the twenty-storey Edifício Montreal in São Paulo (1950), on a prominent, irregular site at the sharp intersection of two main roads (Avenida Casper Libero and Avenida Ipiranga), opposite Praça Alfredo Lessa, Niemeyer opted for dense, deep, horizontal, perforated sunbreaks, three to a floor, reduced to one around the corner, in response to the articulation of the adjacent façade on Avenida Ipiranga. The headquarters of the Banco Mineiro da Produção (today Banco do Estado de Minas Gerais) in Belo Horizonte (1953), built with structural engineer Werner Müller, are set on a similarly shaped plot. Here the horizontal fins, fixed to the transoms of the north elevation, stop at the corner of the building, leaving the south-west glazed façade unprotected, with opening windows for ventilation. Around the corner, the transition from one façade treatment to the other has been handled with notable elegance: avoiding an abrupt change along a harsh vertical line, as in his working model, Niemeyer allowed every second fin to

O Cruzeiro Publishing Company Plant and Headquarters, Rio de Janeiro, 1949: model showing the north elevation on the main street with two different types of adjustable louvres, and the east elevation on the side street shielded with a concrete honeycomb sunscreen

wrap around the corner and continue along the south-west façade's delicate skin of curtain walling for the length of four window panes, thus making the two elevations appear gracefully entwined. As at the Edifício Montreal, halfway up the tower's stra-

ground floor plan

1 entrance
2 lobby
3 shops
4 restaurant
5 plant room
6 bar
7 kitchen

typical floor plan

1 lobby
2 office/showroom space
3 toilets

Edifício Montreal, São Paulo, 1950: view from Praça Alfredo Lessa

Edifício Montreal, São Paulo

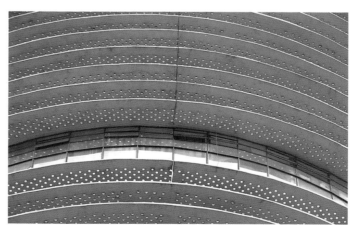

Edifício Montreal: the vertical brises-soleil visible on the black-and-white 1950s photograph, *left*, were eliminated following restoration work in 2004, *top right*; *bottom right*, close-up of perforated sunbreaks

ta, a momentary suspension moderates the upward thrust. The State Library in Belo Horizonte (1955) is enveloped by a precisely orchestrated symphony of playful vertical aluminium *brises-soleil*, austere perforated screens, deep horizontal concrete fins and exposed glazed panels.

The even expression of the south-west elevation of the Edifício California in São Paulo (1951), on the pedestrian Rua Barão de Itapetininga, has been achieved though the repetition of a series of horizontal elements: the perforated sunshade at the top of each floor, the deep void of the loggia, the perforated balustrade

Banco Mineiro da Produção, Belo Horizonte, Minas Gerais, 1953

State Library, Belo Horizonte, Minas Gerais, 1955

and the concrete floor slab. The two perforated panels – sun-shade and balustrade – are identical, of equal width with the void of the loggia and fixed so as to allow a margin between them and the floor slab, thus emphasizing the horizontality of the composition. There is no hierarchy between the components of the façade, which is perceived as a large striped screen on Y-shaped columns, with a rhythmical pattern of light and shadow, rather than as an assemblage of individual elements. The building has an open-V-shaped plan, with a second elevation on the perpendicular Rua Dom José de Barros, also a pedestrian street in São Paulo's commercial district. An internal shopping arcade has undulating shopfronts. Inside the building an abstract *pastilha* mosaic by Portinari animates the blind wall by the reception area and stair-case leading to the basement. Perforated panels like those found on the façade are also used for the dropped ceiling by the shop-fronts, hiding services and distinguishing the internal shopping 'street' from the central space of the reception area, which serves

as a lobby for the offices above. The transition between the two types of ceiling is elegantly negotiated around a row of sturdy cir-cular columns dividing the two areas.

Also in the heart of São Paulo's retail and commercial district, the fully glazed, twenty-storey Edifício Triângulo (1954) – named after its plan – occupies a prow-like position at the intersection of two narrow pedestrian streets – Rua Quintino Bocaiuva and Rua José Bonifácio. Floating twelve storeys above the surrounding rooftops, it refers unmistakably to that Modernist favourite, the ocean liner, with smooth lines and rounded corners; a streamlined exterior with continuous bands of glass and steel between the expressed slim concrete floor decks; the top three glazed storeys recessed; and a white triangular funnel-like lift-and-water tower set further back, at an angle to the roof edge. At ground-floor level, on Rua José Bonifácio, between shopfronts, a wall featuring a blue-and-white figurative mosaic by Emiliano Di Cavalcanti curves towards the entrance of the building and past the thresh-

Edifício California, São Paulo, 1951; south-west elevation on Rua Barão de Itapetininga

Edifício California, São Paulo, 1951; shopping arcade with *pastilha* mosaic by Cândido Portinari

Edifício Eiffel, São Paulo, 1955; view from the Praça da Republica

Edifício Triângulo, São Paulo, 1954

old, where a second, thematically related mosaic by Di Cavalcanti beckons the visitor to descend to the underground lobby.

On the other hand, the elevation of the residential upper storeys of the Edifício Eiffel, also in São Paulo (1955) on Praça da República, gestures towards the individuality of the apartments behind the horizontal patterns between the expressed concrete floor decks, suggesting the threatening chaos of the private domestic world in the middle of the ordered business district. The façade is composed of two alternating patterns, each consisting of sliding glass panes with a brow of horizontally pivoting windows, tinted glass spandrels and perforated solid sunscreens, all with horizontally oriented proportions. The grid pattern of the perforated screens is aligned with the transoms. The precisely controlled composition of the façade canvas, together with the articulation of the three volumes of the building – a twenty-two-storey one in the middle with two ten-storey wings attached to its sides at an angle, like open arms – temper the verticality of the Eiffel, creating a focal point on the busy square. The three residential volumes are raised on a white plinth on stilts. This is aligned with the street edge and its narrow sides are curved to articulate the connection with the adjoining buildings. The white plinth is punctuated by a series of small square windows, heightening its horizontality. Always striving for lightness, Niemeyer set the circular columns of the *pilotis* back from the perimeter wall of the white volume, which appears to float over the permeable shopping arcade.

Building for 'One World':
The United Nations Headquarters in New York

In the notes he was assigned to take in lieu of minutes during the forty-five meetings of the Board of Design for the United Nations Headquarters in New York, George A. Dudley describes the board's response to Niemeyer's 'Scheme 32'.[29] The design was presented at the thirty-second of these meetings, on 25 April 1947 on the twenty-seventh floor of the RKO Building at the Rockefeller Center:

> It literally took our breath away to see the simple plane of the site kept wide open from First Avenue to the [East] River, only three structures on it, standing free, a fourth lying low behind them along the river's edge.
>
> The solution Niemeyer had in his head and developed in five days was, in his own words, 'to maintain the tall building required by the program; then the Councils and the Assembly completely separated, Councils next to the river and the Assembly at the [south] edge of the area. In this way a huge square of the United Nations was created: a large civic square, which would give the plot the necessary importance.' . . . 'In plan, it is simple, with quick connections to all meeting halls, and open out over the river. You want it to fulfill the program – to have the meeting rooms on the river . . . – and yet you want the beauty of the esplanade.'
>
> He had also said, 'Beauty will come from the buildings being in the right space!' The space he found was an open, yet unified, level sweep for the whole site, extending cleanly from First Avenue and its backdrop of Tudor City's cliffs over to the East River, which carried the same plane to the Long Island Shore.
>
> . . . Four simple masses, composed as one, placed delicately in his 'right space,' the site and river joined, each enhancing the other, achieved dignity and potential monumentality.
>
> . . . The comparison between Le Corbusier's heavy block and Niemeyer's startling, elegantly articulated composition seemed to me to be in everyone's mind. As different as night and day, the heaviness of the block seemed to close the whole site, while in Niemeyer's refreshing scheme the site was open, a grand space with a clean base for the modest masses standing in it. Internally, having separate areas for the

29 On the Board of Design consultants, see Dudley, pp. 32–43.

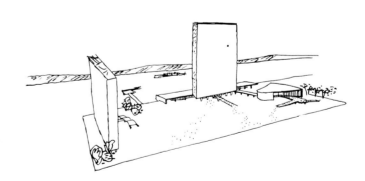

Niemeyer's 'Scheme 32' for the United Nations Headquarters, New York City, 1947: preliminary analysis of the site, programme analysis and studies in search of the best location for the various building elements of the complex; perspective sketch of the final project with the assembly hall (1) near the south end of the site, the council chambers behind the secretariat (2), overhanging the East River, and the delegations building (3) at the north end of the site, along its narrow side. Niemeyer emphasized that in this solution all major buildings, each with its own characteristic form, would be fully visible from any point on First Avenue, while the 'United Nations Square', a central open civic space, would be created at the heart of an institution with the vision of building 'one world'.

Assembly and the other meeting-hall functions, each in its own building, channeled circulation into a more easily recognized flow pattern, rather than the contained set of intersecting spaces in Le Corbusier's unitary block.[30]

Niemeyer was the Board of Design's youngest member. His proposal for the East River site, purchased through a gift from John D. Rockefeller, Jr., father of Nelson Rockefeller, met with enthusiastic approval from the other members of the board, with the exception only of Le Corbusier, who eventually 'blew his top and shouted: "He's just a young man; that scheme isn't from a mature architect."' Later he qualified his disapproval of Niemeyer's scheme: 'Oscar is a true artist, but not so much an architect.' In his *carnet de poche*, Le Corbusier sketched a reclining nude resting on her elbow, representing his own 'Scheme 23', which, according to the note, was 'beau', in contrast to Niemeyer's 'Scheme 32', which was 'médiôcre' [sic]. To represent the latter, he sketched the body of the same nude 'violently dismembered, the decapitated torso floating unsupported, the severed legs akimbo'.[31] Dudley recorded:

> Niemeyer had been quietly elated when his project was 'approved by unanimity,' Le Corbusier's calling it 'a correct and elegant project,' but, as he wrote later, he felt [Wallace] Harrison's decision [to approve Niemeyer's scheme] had not pleased Le Corbusier: 'I could notice that, as soon as we left, when he said: "Oscar, let's meet early tomorrow!" Next day he proposed me to change the Assembly's position: "It is hierarchically the main element and should be in the center of the terrain." I did not agree; it would again divide the square. However, I decided to comply with him and together we submitted project 23/32. Of course, I could have resisted, but I was young and to remain solidary with Le Corbusier and his hopes seemed to me the best to do.'[32]

More recently, Niemeyer has expressed regret for having given in to Le Corbusier's pressure.[33] The United Nations Headquarters building was built on the basis of this 'amicable compromise' scheme.[34] Niemeyer still feels 'a bit sad' for the loss of his

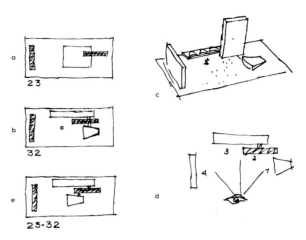

United Nations Headquarters: **a** Le Corbusier's 'Scheme 23'; **b**, **c** and **d** Niemeyer's 'Scheme 32'; **e** 'amicable compromise' 'Scheme 23/32'

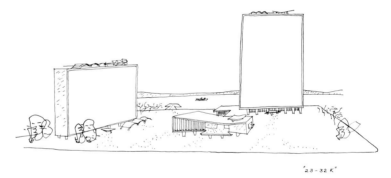

'23-32 K'

United Nations Headquarters: 'Scheme 23/32' that resulted in the much regretted loss of Niemeyer's monumental 'United Nations Square'

30 Dudley, pp. 234–36. On the day of his arrival in New York, Sunday 9 March 1947, before he joined the other members of the Board of Design, Niemeyer met Le Corbusier upon the latter's demand. Le Corbusier 'request[ed] [him] not to submit any solution of [his] own and to collaborate in his project. "You can create a commotion," [Le Corbusier] warned'; letter from Niemeyer to George Dudley, 12 November 1985, cited in Dudley, p. 110. Wallace K. Harrison, who as director of planning headed the Board of Design, and his partner Max Abramovitz tried to persuade a reluctant Niemeyer to move on his own. Niemeyer decided to submit his own project only after Le Corbusier prompted him: 'make the project'. Later, Niemeyer noted: 'When my project was ready I wrote on it: 'This is my idea but I advise my colleagues to examine again Le Corbusier's plan.' It was not exactly what I was thinking. The big block that Le Corbusier had imagined in fact did not please me, but I was not wishing to compete, the important thing for me was to remain at his side'; Dudley, pp. 137, 223, 230. **31** Le Corbusier, quoted in Dudley, pp. 240, 259; Dudley, p. 266. **32** Dudley, p. 273. Following Niemeyer's agreement to collaborate with Le Corbusier on a compromise scheme, 'Le Corbusier had cleared the air, finally, with his "memory of good-bye to Scheme 23." Niemeyer did not speak up in the same way about his Scheme 32, since it was accepted that 32 was clearly the principal progenitor of . . . 23/32'; Dudley, p. 286. 'Scheme 23/32' was developed with Vladimir Bodiansky (special consultant to the board, who worked primarily with Le Corbusier) and Ernest Weissmann (special consultant to the board for Yugoslavia). **33** Niemeyer adds that he also regrets the modifications this compromise scheme suffered subsequently, which were all too easily accepted by Le Corbusier, who 'absolutely wanted his project approved, no matter at what price'; Niemeyer, 1993c, pp. 69–71. In

the piece he contributed to vol. 7 of Le Corbusier's *Œuvre complète*, written in 1963, Niemeyer referred to the episode as an 'occasion, to my great satisfaction, to manifest the esteem and respect which we all owe [to Le Corbusier] in remaining by his side during the evolution of the work and by refusing the distinctions and honors which I knew could only belong to him'; Niemeyer, 1999, p. 9. **34** Dudley quotes from his diary: 'Pact between Le Corbusier, Weissmann, Bodiansky, Niemeyer . . . [who] signed an agreement with each other pledging themselves not to claim individual authorship for the plan'; Dudley, p. 405, n. 9. In a letter to Stamo Papadaki of 20 June 1950, with regard to the monograph Papadaki was preparing, Niemeyer insisted: 'In the text of the United Nations, my preoccupation is to present primarily my own contribution, but avoiding any word that might displease my colleagues of the UN committee. In this sense it appears to me more correct placing in the book (as we will do with the collaborators of all the other projects) the names of all architects that formed the United Nations Commission as responsables [sic] for the definitive plan, of which we can use a photo of the construction.' In his letter to Niemeyer of 4 August 1950, Papadaki explained: 'The UN was quite a headache. As soon as I had organized the material I presented it to the "proper authorities" for checking up and to receive their blessing. I met with an explosion. Their idea was that all designs were the result of a collaboration and that no one had the right to put his name under the scheme . . . the publication of scheme 32 was finally "approved". However, a compromise had to be done: the elimination of scheme 23 and 23-32 . . . I thought that in doing so I acted in the best interest of all concerned (maintaining thus the reputation you have here as a "good boy" in distinction to the enfant terrible in Paris)'; in Stamo Papadaki Papers.

generous 'United Nations Square', which he had imagined filled with people, with his signature easy ramps reaching forward to lift delegates to the parabolic General Assembly and to the conference rooms and council chambers in the Secretariat tower. A civic platform was to extend towards the horizon and there was to be an imposing free-standing sculpture, as in the eloquent perspectives of board member Hugh Ferriss. In contrast to Le Corbusier, who had declared 'L'Assemblée est Le Roi!', Niemeyer had wished to grant monumental proportions not to any of the UN buildings but to this open civic space, which would embody the newly formed institution's vision of bringing about 'one world'. But he admits to no feeling of bitterness over his act of loyalty towards Le Corbusier.[35] The jacket for the record of the last interview Le Corbusier gave, on 15 May 1965, was designed by Niemeyer and dated 5 September 1965, a week after Le Corbusier's death.

Soon after his election as director of planning on 15 December 1946, Wallace K. Harrison had told George Barrett of the New York Times that 'the basic problem [was] not to try to symbolize the United Nations in some highly imaginative design, but to construct a Capitol where the world representatives can work efficiently and in comfort'. After the first thirty meetings of the Board of Design, Sunday's New York Times quoted Niemeyer:

> [the UN] is an organism to set the nations of the world in a common direction and give to the world security. I think it is difficult to get this into steel and stone. But if we make something representing the true spirit of our age, of compression [sic] and solidarity, it will by its own strength give the idea that it is the big political effort, too.[36]

Throughout the design process, Harrison struggled to ensure harmonious collaboration among the members of the Board of Design.

While in New York, Le Corbusier had explicitly assured a worried Harrison on several occasions that he agreed with the idea of working in a team and presenting the resulting project with no specific authorship attribution. Throughout the design process, he was the most vocal on this point, going as far as inviting the members of the board to sign a memorandum he prepared, stating that the final report of the board 'will leave personalities in the shade, stress only the team itself'.[37] Nevertheless, Le Corbusier's campaign to be identified as the sole author of the building commenced a year after he left New York in July 1947. As Dudley notes, 'The sketch he and others used in later publications of his work is made from the East River and gives an appearance of resembling both the revised Niemeyer Scheme and the final built form.' The date given to this sketch is also contestable.[38]

Niemeyer has consistently presented the UN as the product of teamwork, while Dudley's published records aver that 'the strongest impact on the group was made by the clarity of thinking

and design sensitivity in Niemeyer's scheme . . . "the only scheme that [got] complete satisfaction",' in Harrison's words.[39] Despite Le Corbusier's insistence on a continuing role in the design process for the United Nations Headquarters after the conclusion of the conceptual design effort on 9 June 1947, the approved 'Scheme 23/32' was carried forward by Wallace Harrison and Max Abramovitz, then a partnership. In some ways, the theatricality of the interiors of the realized building pays tribute to Niemeyer's sensitivity. In 1959, Alfred Hitchcock found in the sensual curved balconies of the General Assembly public lobby a dramatic stage set for a murder scene in North by Northwest. A remark by Paul Rudolph, although dismissive, may have pleased Niemeyer: he

United Nations Headquarters, based on the approved 'Scheme 23/32', carried forward by Wallace Harrison and Max Abramovitz

described the building as 'not really a product of the international style but rather a backdrop for a grade B movie . . . with Rita Hayworth dancing up the main ramp'.[40]

In 1949, Oscar Niemeyer was elected honorary member of the American Academy of Arts and Sciences. In 1953, he was selected for the position of dean of the Harvard Graduate School of

35 'Regarding Le Corbusier, he never mentioned the 23-32 project, but I remember, months later, having lunch in his apartment, he looked at me and said: "You are generous." And I realized that, a bit late perhaps, he was remembering that morning in New York, when, to be attentive to him, I put my design, the one that the Architects Commission had chosen, aside'; Niemeyer, 2004, p. 164. According to Oscar Nitzchke, who was present, Niemeyer said goodbye to Wallace Harrison with the following words: 'You were fair with Le Corbusier, whose actions were unfair toward you!'; quoted in Dudley, p. 329.   **36** Dudley, pp. 32, 224.   **37** Dudley, p. 251, from meeting 34, 30 April 1947. On 18 April, Le Corbusier had declared: 'Each one of us can give to Mr Harrison the assurance that all will work anonymously'; Dudley, p. 213.   **38** Dudley, pp. 379–80. See also Le Corbusier, 1997, pp. 22–30.   **39** Dudley, p. 342. During World War II, Wallace Harrison had worked in Nelson Rockefeller's Office of the Coordination of Inter-American Affairs.   **40** Paul Rudolph, quoted in Haw, p. 50.

Design. But his Communist Party membership meant that he was refused a visa to enter the United States and he was unable to take up his position at the university Richard Nixon had dubbed the 'Kremlin on the Charles'.[41] Inspired by Niemeyer's architecture for Brasília and the house he built for his family at Canoas, Rio de Janeiro (1952–53), in 1964, the politically progressive couple Joseph and Anne Strick commissioned Niemeyer to design a house in Santa Monica, California. According to Anne Strick, their 'choice of Niemeyer was not only an aesthetic one, but, in part, a way of thumbing our noses at the whole McCarthy era because it seemed so reprehensible that a man, simply because of his political views, could be prevented from working in this country'. The Stricks and Niemeyer never met and the design of the house was carried out entirely by correspondence.[42] In 1967, Niemeyer applied again for a visa to travel to the United States, following a commission for a multi-unit business centre on Claughton Island near Miami (unbuilt). His application was refused again.

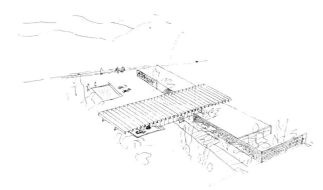

Joseph and Anne Strick House, Santa Monica, California, USA, 1964

Business Centre, Claughton Island, USA, 1967, unbuilt

41 Ernesto Rogers, the second choice, declined, and CIAM president Josep Lluis Sert took up the position. Niemeyer had already been refused entry to the US in 1946, when he had been invited to teach at Yale. **42** PCR Services Corporation for City of Santa Monica Planning Division, p. 5. **43** Niemeyer, 1998, p. 44. **44** See Caldas and Alcadipani. **45** Drexler, p. 8. **46** Hitchcock, 1955, pp. 11, 30, 28–29, 12, 36.

In the early 1970s, Niemeyer finally visited the United States after 'a highly prestigious person . . . managed to obtain a visa for a fifteen-day visit'. Upon arriving in New York, he went to visit the United Nations Headquarters. At a press interview he declared: 'I'm glad to visit this building for which I have contributed as an architect and I'm glad to know that Communist China has joined the UN as a member nation.' His American companion warned him that he would not be granted a visa extension. 'Sure enough, I left the country 15 days later.'[43]

A High-Density Domestic Environment at the Centre of Brazil's Industrial Metropolis

Despite declining North American geopolitical and market interests in Brazil and Latin America after World War II (the OCIAA was shut down by President Harry S. Truman in 1946), Brazil's intensified industrialization from 1930 to the late 1950s was marked by an economic and technological dependence on the United States that influenced Brazil's social and cultural fabric.[44] With the post-war shift of the centre of representation of the 'civilized world' from the Old World of Europe to the 'First World' of the United States, Brazil's booming industrial centres turned towards the North American model of modernization, progress and 'rational organization' of industry. And Brazil's urban middle class modelled its living and working patterns on those of the United States.

In the catalogue of the 1955 MoMA exhibition on *Latin American Architecture Since 1945*, Arthur Drexler drew the public's attention to Latin America's 'predominantly "modern" cities', anticipating the future appearance of US cities.[45] Henry-Russell Hitchcock celebrated the unrivalled modernity of Latin American cities, where the 'new architecture . . . belongs specifically to the age of the airplane', acknowledging the North American influence evident in the vertically rising city centres and noting that 'the skyscrapers rise thicker today in Mexico City or São Paulo than in most cities of the United States'. He singled out Brazil as the country with 'the most solidly established modern tradition' and pronounced Rio's Santos Dumont Airport 'perhaps the most beautiful in the world'. For Hitchcock, São Paulo, 'the center of activity of the most intensely personal talent in architecture, Oscar Niemeyer . . . epitomizes the incredibly rapid transformation of the architectural scene in the last fifteen years'.[46]

The state of São Paulo, Brazil's chief exporter (50 per cent in 1912), had played the leading role in the coffee-dominated economy of the nineteenth century, and its influence extended to national and international politics. Prudente José de Morais Barros, Brazil's first civilian president (1894–98), had been the first republican governor of São Paulo. With the transfer of capital from coffee to industry and a manufacturing industry already growing during the first decades of the twentieth century, São Paulo, the region with the best transportation facilities, became Brazil's industrial giant and economic powerhouse. Ford launched its first assembly line in 1921 and General Motors in 1925. Between 1905 and 1930, the city of São Paulo tripled its population to 822,400. Its first reinforced-concrete skyscraper, the thirty-storey Edifício Martinelli, rose to 130 metres in 1929, surpassing Rio's *A Noite* tower, completed one year earlier. It was designed by the Lacombe Brothers and was crowned by a four-storey mansion with private elevator and garden for its Italian immigrant owner, Giuseppe Martinelli.[47]

According to Oswald de Andrade, during the 1932 São Paulo constitutional revolt against the Vargas regime, 'windows waved with flags and walls with posters'.[48] Although the revolt failed and political activists like the painter Tarsila do Amaral were imprisoned, Ramos de Azevedo's twelve-storey 'Gold for São Paulo' building (1935), was financed by the Paulistas' generous donations for the cause of the civil war, mostly in gold jewellery. Built as a headquarters for the Santa Casa da Misericórdia hospitals, it cast

the Paulista state's waved flag in concrete as a permanent invocation of Brazil's wealthiest 'nation's' identity and heroism.

Claude Lévi-Strauss reported that, already in 1935, 'the people of São Paulo liked to boast that their city was expanding at the rate of a house every hour'.[49] In 1947, the thirty-six-storey Edifício Sede do Banespa, by Plínio Botelho do Amaral with Franz Heep, renamed Altino Arantes in 1960, rose 161 metres and referenced the Empire State Building. With luxuriously finished interiors, from 1947 to 1962 it was the tallest reinforced-concrete structure in the world. By 1950, São Paulo boasted 47 per cent of national industry, rising to 54 per cent by 1960. It employed half of Brazil's factory workers and produced half of its gross domestic product and more than half of federal revenues. In 1953, it became a metropolis – Brazil's largest urban nucleus, with 2.7 million inhabitants overburdening its services. In the 1950s, it saw 21,600 new constructions, almost double that of the previous decade, while it boasted 6,000 streets and 170,000 cars. With high literacy rates, the affluent São Paulo possessed, also, a powerful and influential electorate.

Oscar Niemeyer's first building for the birthplace of Brazilian Modernism was designed in 1951, the year when the construction rate reached four-and-a-half buildings per hour and also the year of the first São Paulo International Art Biennale. The imposing 140-

Av. São João   São Paulo - Brasil   Fotolabor 186

São Paulo, Avenida São João, postcard, 1950s: the three tall buildings in the middle are, *from left to right*, the Banco do Brasil, 1955, 143 metres; the Edifício Sede do Banespa, 1939–47, 161 metres; and the Prédio Martinelli, 1929, 130 metres, the tallest building in São Paulo until 1947.

Ramos de Azevedo, 'Gold for São Paulo', headquarters for the Santa Casa da Misericórdia hospitals, São Paulo, 1935

47 In 1934, Commendatore Martinelli sold the building to the Italian government. In 1943, with Brazil joining the Second World War against the Axis, all Italian properties were confiscated by the Brazilian government, including the Edifício Martinelli. In the 1950s it was squatted by poor families, and in 1992 it was listed by the Instituto do Patrimônio Histórico e Artístico Nacional (Institute for the Protection of the National Historic and Artistic Heritage, IPHAN).   **48** Mehrtens, p. 164.   **49** Lévi-Strauss, 1965, p. 101.

metre-high Edifício COPAN, constructed 1953–66, under the supervision of Carlos Lemos, director of Niemeyer's São Paulo office, remains the largest structure ever built in Brazil and the largest residential building in the world, with 5,000 residents in 1,160 apartments (from 25 to 150 square metres), 107 employees and 20 elevators. It was constructed on a 11,500-square-metre piece of land in the city centre, bought by the Companhia Pan-Americana de Hotéis e Turismo (COPAN, Pan-American Hotel and Tourism Company) from the Santa Casa da Misericórdia and two private owners of a group of nineteenth-century 'German style' houses, known as Vila Normanda. The development project was conceived as an urban centre after Raymond Hood's Rockefeller Center model, aiming to 'expand the possibilities of social life and

Edifício COPAN, São Paulo, under construction: *left*, in 1957 with one of the nineteenth-century 'German style' houses of Vila Normanda still standing; *right*, in 1959

commerce of fine products'. It was marketed as a prime investment opportunity on a location where land prices were rising rapidly. The founding shareholders' marketing literature compared its anticipated landmark status for São Paulo to that of the Eiffel Tower in Paris. The COPAN building remains São Paulo's definitive landmark, with its own postcode. From the beginning, the budget catered for the highest quality of construction materials and finishes, and the project received US technical and financial cooperation.

Niemeyer went through three different schemes for the COPAN, all of which included two volumes: a curvilinear one and a rectangular one.[50] A gigantic open-S-plan block of thirty-two residential floors atop a mixed-use commercial space at street level was juxtaposed with a smaller, twenty-five-storey rectangular hotel block for three thousand guests. The hotel was eventually

replaced by a building designed by Carlos Lemos for the Bradesco Bank, the COPAN building's owner from 1957.

The S-plan block, winding its way through the irregularly shaped site, was internally divided into six vertical units with various apartment types for a range of incomes. Both blocks were raised on *pilotis*, seemingly standing on floating, free-form platforms joined at first-floor level, similar to those proposed in Niemeyer's two unrealized schemes for the gigantic Quitandinha-Petrópolis hotel-cum-apartment development (1950 and 1953). The terrace platforms united the two blocks, while also mediating between their upper-floor private spaces and the public spaces near the street, flowing into the ground-floor area of the complex. In the two- or three-storey-high areas beneath these platforms retail,

50 See all three schemes in *Architecture d'Aujourd'hui*, 1952, pp. 120–21, 135.

leisure and recreation spaces, including the hotel lobby, were accommodated in a series of free-form, double-height pavilions, articulating a labyrinthine arcade. The combination of activities was intended to ensure that the complex remained active throughout the day, seven days a week, and to stimulate the participation of the local population as well as tourists.

Edificio COPAN, São Paulo, 1953–66: photomontage with model of first scheme on site

Edificio COPAN, final version of the original scheme: photomontage with model on site

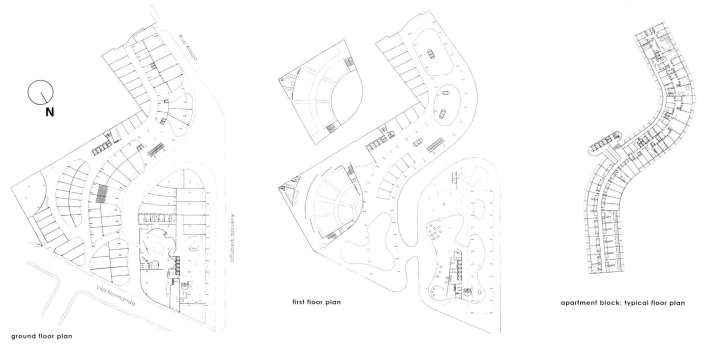

N

ground floor plan

first floor plan

apartment block: typical floor plan

Edificio COPAN, final version of the original scheme: ground-floor plan with shopping streets, hotel lobby and nightclub directly at the rear; first-floor plan with restaurant connected to the hotel, theatre and lobbies of the apartment block; typical floor of the apartment block with semi-detached elevator-and-stair tower serving approximately half the length of the building where the apartments are accessible through a central corridor, and separate elevators in groups of two serving larger apartments, also linked to the central tower through an open emergency corridor to the south (three separate spiral-stair towers were also eventually added to the residential block)

curvilinear retail pavilions, guardrails – are kept in check, set back in darker colours, allowing the bright, flowing horizontal ribbons of the terrace platform and deck slabs to wrap freely around the building, strata tying the various formal and programmatic elements together, while maintaining the porosity of the building's public base. An external staircase, replacing a more elegant ramp in Niemeyer's model and leading to the first-floor terrace, articulates another link with the street. Its generous landings are claimed by users as places for informal contact, for a rest in the sun or as viewing platforms. Between the two blocks, a central pedestrian street is open to the sky, while narrower, covered streets are articulated under the residential block.

51 In the 1970s, the loggias and terrace area were enclosed and given to commercial use. Plans for recovering the original use of these areas are currently under way.

As the large residential block in its realized form snakes from higher to lower ground towards Vila Normanda, one and then a second free-form deck are inserted beneath the large first-floor terrace platform, creating loggias with deep overhanging soffits. The inserted deck slabs, the terrace platform and the first slab above are emphatically delineated at the boundary of the building.[51] All other elements – columns, the external membranes of the

The free-form platform of the COPAN building plays a role similar to that of the *marquise* Niemeyer employs in so many of his projects, uniting the various spaces in the intricately laced public areas that address the city, while also serving to distance from the level of the street the private spaces above. The amoebic *marquise* is aligned with Vila Normanda and with Avenida Ipiranga along the west elevation of the sober, recessed bank block. Extending beyond the outline of the residential block, it provides a sunny terrace, a private beach along the entire undulating façade, encouraging sociability and a sense of community. On this level, under the raised *pilotis*, are located the lobbies of the residential block with a theatre to the south.

The external treatment of the playful volumes in the shopping arcade – a meticulously detailed collage of glazing, timber-slat cladding and white-render panes heightened by window displays – contrasts sharply with the homogeneity of the façades of the block above, encouraging leisurely circulation through the free-flowing spaces. Never exposing a hard edge to the surrounding urban landscape, the polychrome volumes invite the city to permeate the arcade with its eighty-two commercial units. Movement through the winding internal streets awakens a sense of discovery appropriate for a shopping arcade, with new possibilities unfolding around every corner. In the original scheme, access to a street-level nightclub was located on a wide internal street, with the bridge between the two terrace platforms marking and protecting its entrance.

In Niemeyer's original scheme, featured on the cover of the July 1953 issue of the *Architectural Review*, which compared it to the Rockefeller Center, the large amoeba of a restaurant invaded the space of the first-floor *pilotis* of the Imperator Hotel.[52] Its largest area flowed beyond the outline of the rectilinear block, opposite the concave part of the residential block. Another variant of the free-form *marquise* was introduced here. The concrete roof slab of the restaurant followed neither the contours of its walls, nor those of the platform beneath it – a composition that anticipated the polymetric rhythms of Niemeyer's second house for his family at Canoas. In an arrangement prefigured at the Casa do Baile at Pampulha, the restaurant roof slab swung away from the enclosed volume, into a serpentine thread wending its way through the large hotel terrace to embrace a smaller bar and shade part of the open-air dining area. Both inside and outside the restaurant, the structural columns appeared scattered at random, underscoring the fluidity of the free curves, unrestricted by geometry, utility or gravity.

Photographs of the original model show that both the hotel terrace and that of the residential block were imagined paved in black-and-white stone, with amoebic patterns similar to those at the Pampulha church flowing in and out of the space of the *pilotis*. Under the residential block, a free-form volume responded to

that of the restaurant across the bridge linking the two first-floor platforms. Without the eloquent programmatic and unprogrammatic spaces of the restaurant area, an essential point of dialogue between the two blocks and programmes was lost. But the street-level arcade was realized, inscribing the city centre with a much-needed, highly animated urban site with a buzzing ambience, very popular until the late 1970s, when São Paulo's fashionable nightlife started drifting towards the 'safer' suburbs. Today, life is slowly returning to São Paulo's centre and therefore also to the COPAN building.

Questioning the Hierarchies of the Gendered City

At a time of explosive urban growth in Latin America, suburban residential developments like Luis Barragán's Gardens of El Pedregal, outside Mexico City (1945–53), lured those who could afford it to flee the city and retreat into suburbia, although the working men would always return to the city centre for business. In 1944 Sigfried Giedion had called for a rethinking of cities beyond their conception 'as mere agglomerations of jobs and traffic lights'.[53] By the time the Edifício COPAN was built, São Paulo already had a number of leafy, low-rise, low-density garden cities outside the increasingly crowded urban core, realized from 1912 through to the 1920s. English architects Barry Parker and Raymond Unwin's Jardim América was the first and best-known of these. At a time when residential apartment buildings were associated with the *cortiços* housing the poor, the COPAN building's high-density domestic environment, right in the centre of the technocratic city, configured a site of resistance to urban flight and the 'bourgeois utopia' of North American picturesque suburban enclaves, insulated from the workplace.[54]

It was on the last of Niemeyer's three schemes for the COPAN complex that the curvilinear volume became the dominant one, all the more powerful amid the cylindrical towers and hard-edged skyscrapers of downtown São Paulo. Its dynamism is accentuated by continuous, horizontal, shadow-casting *brises-soleil*, three per storey. Catherine Séron-Pierre suggests that the 'monumental, stratified wave provokes a real rupture in the brutal, repetitive landscape of the city'.[55] At the very least, it articulates a site of tension. Presenting the Paulistas with an alternative model of urban, and implicitly social, organization, the exuberant residential COPAN building challenged the post-war American, masculine order of the vertical city, bringing into the middle of the white-collar arena a site of pleasure and *dolce vita* cast only a few years earlier in the idyll of the new suburb of Pampulha. The free-flowing

52 'Brazilian Preview', cover and p. 233.   **53** Giedion, 1984, p. 59.
54 See Fishman.   **55** Séron-Pierre, p. 77.

The gigantic wave of the Edifício COPAN in the midst of the hard-edged-skyscraper cityscape of downtown São Paulo: *left*, photograph of 1971; *right*, today

curves of the COPAN building were not confined to the street level or the interior of the site, as in the shopping galleries of Niemeyer's previous urban interventions. The gigantic wave of the residential block raised its sinuous curves high above street level, engaging with the right-angled office landscape, tempering verticality with sensuous horizontality, impregnating the American city with a new spirit.

The deep, glazed-concrete sunbreaks were constructed together with, and fastened to, the reinforced-concrete structure of the building. They fulfil both shading and aesthetic requirements, producing a foliated effect that gives the building its distinct image, imparting palpability and movement to the static grid of the city and rendering its façade soft and permeable, in sharp contrast to the forbidding and impenetrable steel-and-glass surfaces of dogmatic, homophonic skyscrapers. Changing weather, light and shadow further animate the horizontally striated, highly textured north-west elevation, which is never perceived as a single plane like the façade of a typical office block. The built version of the COPAN building's three-dimensional façade, in which the slender vertical elements – recessed and clad in grey-blue *pastilha* tiles – have almost totally disappeared, especially from the viewpoint of the street below, is considerably more effective than that of the model, stressing horizontality, inviting the eye to surf along the undulating blades of the great concrete wave. The striation of the façade is twice syncopated by the omission of two rows of *brises-soleil*, at the fifteenth and twenty-third floors – a ges-

ture that further heightens horizontality, intensifies movement along the flowing horizontal grooves, and undermines the solidity of the softly gliding huge volume, imbuing it with the energy to embrace and consume the rigid, vertical city.

At the beginning of the twentieth century, Adolf Loos established the polarity between a 'horizontal line: the reclining woman' and a 'vertical line: the penetrating man'.[56] In his own apartment, he established a sharp distinction between the sober comfort of the living room, which he associated with his ideal of the English gentleman, and the sensuality of 'das Zimmer meiner Frau'.[57] The COPAN building's irrational thrusting curves contrasted sharply with the 'cold, hard, unornamental, technical image' of the contemporaneous, gleaming, twenty-four-storey Lever House by Gordon Bunshaft for Skidmore, Owings, & Merrill (1950–52) – the first New York City curtain-wall skyscraper to define the North American corporate capitalist landscape.[58] The hygienic headquarters of the world's biggest manufacturer of soap and detergent represented 'a maximum of technical ingenuity with a minimum of dissent' and, in the eyes of Pevsner, an example of architectural 'evolution' as opposed to the Brazilian 'revolution'.[59] At a time when Taylorist zoning was promoted by city planners as the solution to all urban ills, the COPAN building emphatically positioned in the city centre the peripheral realm of domestic, tropical, feminine curves, cannibalistically transforming prevailing images of the virile city. On 18 October 1956, Flávio de Carvalho paraded the streets of downtown São Paulo sporting his polemic 'new look'

56 Loos, p. 277. **57** Schorske, p. 167. **58** Ockman, 1996, p. 195. Zilah Quezado Deckker notes the resemblance as well as the significant differences between the Lever House on the one hand, and the Brazilian Ministry of Education and Public Health and the United Nations Headquarters on the other; Deckker, p. 176. In 1988, the Pritzker jury split its architecture prize between Niemeyer and Gordon Bunshaft. Ada Louise Huxtable justified the decision as follows: 'The award acknowl-

edges the quality and importance of two parallel and complementary contributions. Bunshaft and Niemeyer represent the opposite sides of the modernist coin – the rational and the romantic, the powerful and the poetic . . . Together, these two architects summarize and signify the range and character of the modern movement'; Huxtable. **59** Godfrey Hodgson, quoted in Ockman, p. 195; Pevsner, 1972, pp. 431–33.

Affonso Eduardo Reidy, Pedregulho Social Housing Complex,
Rio de Janeiro, 1947–58

although close to downtown Rio, rose at a safe distance from the business district.[60] Its sinuous curves were, furthermore, related to the capricious curves of Rio's mountains and thus conveniently confined to the world of natural imagery and private, segregated domesticity. Alvar Aalto's 'attempt to free architecture from the threat of rigidity', the undulating Baker House Dormitory for the Massachusetts Institute of Technology in Cambridge (1947–48), had also been built at a safe distance from the city centre, by the Charles River, in the kind of picturesque surroundings for which Le Corbusier saw the choice of the curve to be justified.[61] The source of Aalto's design had also been firmly located in nature, more precisely, in 'the curved contours of the Finnish lakes'.[62]

Le Corbusier found the source of Niemeyer's curves, too, in the 'mountains of Rio' – a comment Niemeyer treats with a certain nonchalance, preferring to privilege instead the femininity of his sinuous lines.[63] His high-density domestic complex introduced into the rational order of the city the curves of 'confusion' and 'rectitude' Le Corbusier had denounced a few years earlier in 1947 in his When the Cathedrals Were White: 'Let's not graft plastic forms' on cities, obstructing their clear, liberating 'checkerboard'.[64] In

of skirt, blouson and sandals for the 'new man of the tropics', first presented in 1952.

Until then, Niemeyer had proposed curving slabs for programmes associated with leisure in non-urban locations such as the Pampulha and Quitandinha-Petrópolis complexes. Affonso Eduardo Reidy's serpentine block for the Pedregulho Social Housing Complex, with engineer Carmen Portinho (1947–58),

60 The Pedregulho Social Housing Complex was awarded first prize at the Second São Paulo Biennale in 1953 by a jury presided over by Giedion. Reidy worked as an architect at the federal district City Hall from 1932. He designed the Pedregulho Social Housing Complex as head architect of the Department of Popular Housing from 1946. He also employed serpentine slabs in his unrealized Catacumbas Housing Complex by the Lagoa Rodrigo de Freitas (1951), and the Marquês de São Vicente Housing Complex (1952, only partly realized), both intended to be offered at low rent to families living in Rio's *favelas*. **61** Le Corbusier, 1987b, pp. 208–9. With regard to the curved wall of the Pavillon Suisse at the Cité Universitaire, Paris, Le Corbusier pointed out that it 'gives a suggestion of tremendous extent, seems to pick up, by its concave surface, the whole surrounding landscape'; quoted in Curtis, 1986, p. 177. **62** Giedion, 1949, p. 472. In his 1951 revisit of *The*

International Style, Henry-Russell Hitchcock argued that Aalto's MIT dormitory, which 'most people . . . tend to assume . . . was . . . consciously breaking with the rigidities of the International Style', was really a reaction 'not against the International Style, but against the vulgar parodying of its more obvious aspects – the "Drugstore Modern" – which had become ubiquitous in the previous decade'; Hitchcock, 1993, p. 148. More recently, Richard Weston wrote that, at Cambridge, Aalto's MIT dormitory 'suggests the meandering form of the Charles River', or, more generally, 'the presence of nature – "freedom's symbol" – in man's world'; Weston, 1995, p. 114. **63** Niemeyer writes: 'Le Corbusier said once that I had Rio's mountains in my eyes. I laughed. I prefer to think like Andre [sic] Malraux, who said: "I keep inside myself, in my private museum, everything I have seen and loved in my life" '; Niemeyer, 2004, pp. 148–50. **64** Le Corbusier, 1947c, pp. 49–50.

The City of Tomorrow and Its Planning (1929), Le Corbusier had banished the curve from the city, where there is no place for 'happy-go-lucky heedlessness'. For a city where 'order' and 'absolute exactness' are paramount, he proposed the right angle and 'the straight line; it is the proper thing for the heart of the city. The curve is ruinous, difficult and dangerous; it is a paralyzing thing.' Convinced that 'a modern city lives by the straight line', Le Corbusier had urged: 'We must have the courage to view the rectilinear cities of America with admiration.'[65]

As Mark Wigley remarks, at least since Leon Battista Alberti's fifteenth-century treatise *On the Art of Building*, 'the house is literally understood as a mechanism for the domestication of (delicately minded and pathologically embodied) women'.[66] The COPAN building's actively heroic, freely undulating, sensual form decidedly invaded the urban core of Latin America's premier industrial and financial centre, assaulting its rigid grid and contesting the dichotomy between the private, emotionalized and sexualized feminine world of home and pleasure and the public, masculine world of work and power, articulating the possibility of a rethinking of the gender polarities of the North American city. Although it did not resolve existing dichotomies, it introduced a rupture that problematized them.

There is no intention here to suggest that Niemeyer was overtly defending a feminization of urban space. Nevertheless, his Antropofagist feminization of canonical Modernist blocks and the implanting of an imposing, curvaceous feminine giant right at the pivotal heart of the male-dominated, rectilinear business centre of the city implicitly challenged prevailing assumptions about the gendering of city structures and spaces and the invisibility of women in the profoundly patriarchal Brazilian society of the 1950s. Like the early Modernist European models, the American erect skyscraper was not rejected; it was contaminated with the sensual movements of the jungle and the Dionysian rhythms of feminine curved horizons. The juxtaposition of the dominant 'Aphrodisiac curves'[67] of the COPAN building and the submissive rectilinear bank slab suggested a questioning of the hierarchy implicit in gendered city symbolism, through a reversal – carnivalization – of the asymmetry of gendered signifiers of domination and oppression.

The curvaceous residential block of the COPAN complex dominates the submissive rectilinear block designed by Carlos Lemos for the Bradesco Bank, replacing a hotel of similar form and proportions in Niemeyer's original scheme, photograph of 1977

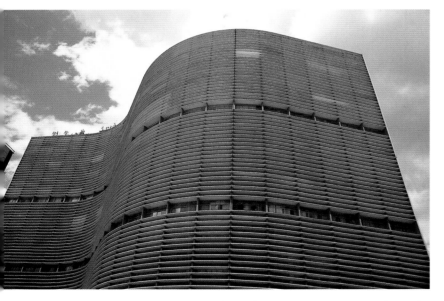

The striated north-west façade of the Edifício COPAN invites the eye to surf along the undulating blades of the great concrete wave.

Although in *The City of Tomorrow and Its Planning* Le Corbusier had banished the curve from the city, in 1929 he had proposed for the city of Rio de Janeiro a curvilinear 'immense expressway' on which he raised his *immeubles villas* 'from 30 to 100 metres' above the ground. Perhaps his solution was inspired by the towering Arcos da Lapa viaduct, built as an aqueduct in 1750 and converted in 1896, which crosses the centre of the city, and serves the hill of Santa Teresa. His 'earthscraper', he argues, was inspired by the topography of Rio, 'striking from hill to hill and stretching hands from one bay to the next', striving 'to dominate the enchanting site'.[68] Barbara Hooper observes that the 'primitive female body' that Le Corbusier abjected returned in the 'curvilinear lines that [he] first use[d] in spaces he view[ed] as outside and other': in Rio de Janeiro, in Chandigarh, in Algiers and in Notre-Dame-du-Haut at Ronchamp.[69] Upon arriving in Rio, he had felt simultaneously

65 Le Corbusier, 1987b, pp. 10–12. **66** Wigley, 1992, p. 332. **67** Freyre, 1956, p. 275. **68** Le Corbusier, 1991, pp. 242–44. See Le Corbusier's sketch of his inhabited motorway in Chapter Two, p. 45. **69** Hooper, p. 63.

enchanted and threatened by the 'universally proclaimed beauty' of the city, with its 'disorderly green flame' conjuring images of 'green hell'. He admitted that he first thought it a 'waste' of time trying to plan anything for Rio, fearing that 'everything would be absorbed by this violent and sublime landscape'. His 'big architectural beltline' was designed to 'connect the city rapidly with the high hinterlands of the healthy plateaus', enabling an easy escape from 'this magical sight' that threatened to devour the rational creations of the European mind.[70]

Niemeyer, on the other hand, brought into a city that faced no threat from nature the exuberant forms associated with destructive (feminine) disorder and the violent tropical jungle in order to destabilize the technoscientific image of gleaming, bureaucratic, orthogonal rationality. His exaltation of the feminine Other confronted the leaden lines of the 'ideology of monotonous vacuity' that Ernst Bloch held responsible for the 'undernourishment of the [architectural] imagination', with the exorbitant 'ornamental force' of a liberating sculptural form.[71]

Towards a Critique of Hegemonic Identity

Before construction of the COPAN building had begun, Niemeyer grafted the plastic form of a luxury apartment building onto the city of Belo Horizonte. This prominent landmark boasts, among its former illustrious residents Tancredo Neves, governor of Minas Gerais and the first elected civilian president of Brazil after the twenty-one-year military dictatorship from 1964 to 1985 (elected 15 March 1985, he died thirty-eight days later). The Edifício Liberdade (1954–60), later renamed Edifício Niemeyer and built with structural engineer Sérgio Marques de Souza, is proudly perched on Praça da Liberdade.[72] This is the highest and one of the most privileged spots of the city, designed at the end of the nineteenth century as the civic centre of the new capital of Minas Gerais and remodelled in 1920, with the Beaux-Arts Governor's Palace (Palácio da Liberdade, 1898), the state secretariats, imperial palm colonnades and gardens inspired by Versailles.

On a triangular plot at the junction of three main roads, by the open square, surrounded by relatively low-rise buildings and opposite the Governor's Palace, Niemeyer's assertive residential tower dominates the urban space. Its entirely free form leaves no doubt as to Niemeyer's intention to hoist high the colours of his defiant rejection of the ideological and formal constraints of orthodox Modernism. It bespeaks his refusal to adopt the simplified and 'easily assimilable language' of the International Style, which increasingly dominated the metropolises of the 1950s, 'intimately connected with forms adaptable to commercial exploitation', favouring instead an eroticized curvaceous world of sophisticated luxury and sensual pleasure.[73] At the same time, anchoring this pri-

Praça da Liberdade, designed at the end of the nineteenth century as the civic centre of Belo Horizonte, the new capital of Minas Gerais, remodelled in 1920, postcard, 1920s

vate world in the heart of the city, Niemeyer subverted the image of the civic centre as stable and authoritarian, choosing instead dynamism, elasticity and malleability.

The biomorphism of the plan recalls Mies van der Rohe's visionary unbuilt glass skyscraper of 1922. Yves Bruand points out the resemblance, but also the two projects' distinct material qualities.[74] Most importantly, Mies's dematerialized glass structure points towards a lofty Platonic ideal free from its carnal prison, while Niemeyer's concrete plasticity evokes a dynamic, sensuous reality that is all earthly and corporeal. Lauro Cavalcanti also observes that 'Mies's tower had an absolute vertical orientation that is not the case with Niemeyer's'. The dynamism and 'provocative rhythm' of the Liberdade tower's concave and convex curves are accentuated by the addition of thirty-six deep, impressively thin, horizontal sunbreaks – three per floor – which follow the contours of the floor slabs.[75] They add a sense of movement, which can be fully appreciated by the viewer moving along Avenida Brasil in a car or strolling in the open square from which the tower is always visible, its shape constantly mutating.

The *brises-soleil* wrap around the entire building, stressing the formal priority of the flowing contours, obliterating the dichotomy between solid and void on the external envelope. They function as sunshades on the glazed part of the façade, but continue along the solid wall, where the play of light and shadow underscores aesthetic concerns that transgress the original utilitarian intent of the device. Penetrating its skin, they turn into shelves

70 Le Corbusier, 1991, pp. 234–44.   **71** Ernst Bloch, p. 46.   **72** The building was renamed Edifício Niemeyer to honour Oscar Niemeyer's brother, Paulo Niemeyer, a surgeon who saved the life of the building's chief contractor. Each one of the twelve floors contains two apartments, one of 185 square metres and a smaller one.   **73** Tafuri and Dal Co, vol. 2, p. 340. **74** Bruand, p. 161.   **75** Cavalcanti, 2003, p. 237.

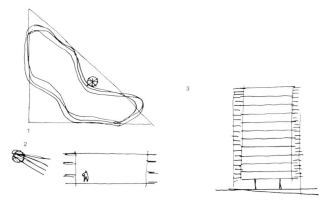

inside the building. Taking full advantage of the prominence of the site, Niemeyer enhanced the grace and coquetry of his apartment block by commissioning Athos Bulcão (1918–) to decorate the solid external walls. Bulcão's ornamental cement tiles create a bold, black-and-white, leopard-skin-like pattern that makes the curved surface pulsate in the shifting sunlight.

A link to the striated, streamlined forms of Erich Mendelsohn's 1920s work may also be worth exploring. The major chords of

Mendelsohn's tension-filled volumes glorified speed and efficiency, the machine-driven dynamism of modern industrial production and the power of consumerism that sustains it. Niemeyer's soft, voluptuous curves, on the other hand, breathe in tempo with a relaxed human body, aimlessly gliding for the unproductive pleasure of movement and dance. Whereas Mendelsohn's horizontal, electrifying rhythms receive their stimulus from the modern metropolis and ultimately remain restricted within a rigid geometry, the unhurried pace of Niemeyer's fluid forms refuses to adapt to the laws of the productivist city. Relaying the energy and magnetism of its fulsome curves to its surroundings, the block attempts to pacify, as it were, the destructive powers of the industrial-technological metropolis.

The Edifício Liberdade may also be seen to bear a superficial resemblance to the organicized skyscrapers of Norman Bel Geddes's 'Futurama', his 1939 streamlining spectacle of progress looking thirty years into the future of the United States. Niemeyer would have seen the diorama at the General Motors Pavilion, at the 1939 New York World's Fair. But Bel Geddes's autopia was specifically targeted to promote the Reichsautobahn-inspired superhighways of a technology-driven future, boosting car sales in the process. The curvilinear skyscrapers flanking the split 'highways of tomorrow', like the colourful cars that populated the models of

Edifício Liberdade: the tower's concave and convex curves accentuated by thirty-six horizontal concrete sunbreaks, which continue along the solid wall clad with Athos Bulcão's block-and-white cement tiles

the stage and product designer, were employed to popularize images of the automobile age and boost consumer confidence.[76] Niemeyer's apartment block for Belo Horizonte called into question the 'performance principle' and the ordered, rationalist technological image of the metropolis, offering playful movement as an alternative to efficient circulation, unrolling before the public an architecture that proposed pleasure as an aesthetic pursuit – of no 'exchange value', in Henri Lefebvre's sense – rather than pleasure as the satisfaction of consumer needs.

Outside the amoeba of the plan, where the Liberdade block seems to fold into a curl, rises the building's only vertical element: a cylindrical stair tower, its white-rendered surface enhancing the impression of a deep fold. The undulating mass of the Liberdade building is elevated from the steeply sloping site on bare-concrete slabs, defining parking bays and contrasting with the smooth, white, rendered underside of the amoeba hovering overhead and extending beyond the first concealed concrete deck in line with the *brises-soleil*. This gives the onlooker the impression that the entire residential volume rests on this paper-thin, concrete saucer, recasting the Corbusian 'completely new value in architecture:

Edifício Liberdade: the white cylindrical stair tower nestles in the deep fold of the tower.

the *clean line of the underside of a building*. A building seen as in a showcase on a display support, *entirely* legible.'[77] The sensuous interplay of textures continues at the entrance lobby, nesting among the slim concrete slabs. This light, penetrable box is formed of a curved glass-block wall, a solid wall clad in thin pink stone slats and a clear glass wall, underscoring spatial fluidity and inviting

76 See Burgess. 77 Le Corbusier, 1991, p. 58, emphasis in the original.

entry into the apartment block. Ever unwilling to impose a door that firmly divides the private from the public domain, Niemeyer cut the entrance to the Liberdade block into the minimally detailed glass plane.

Niemeyer justified the intoxicating and transgressive Otherness of his version of Modernist architecture, purged of its dogmatic roots, in terms of its 'conformity with the Brazilian climate and our fantastic tropical nature'.[78] But his Dionysian subversion of Modernism's European ancestry and rationalist catechism is also grounded in an 'African-derived corporal aesthetics' that, as Michael Hanchard has argued, underlies the Brazilian 'national standard of beauty' and, like samba, is associated with sexuality and sensual pleasure. Commenting on the 'pervasiveness of the "Africanisms" in Brazilian daily life', Hanchard suggests that Afro-Brazilian cultural practices in Brazil are 'at once residual and dominant'. They are residual, Hanchard postulates, as

> national practices . . . manipulated for their symbolic resonance by Brazilian elites to display the heterogenic cohesiveness of Brazilians; they are dominant in that they are suffused in an almost transracial way throughout the norms and values of civil society . . . The 'Africanization' of the female bodily aesthetic is one of Brazil's distinctive features,

exemplifying the dominating presence of Afro-Brazilian culture.[79]

In Niemeyer's work, curvaceous form functions as a metaphor for the eroticized female body. And this is imagined as an Africanized body, 'shaped in the baroque style we favored'.[80] His Antropofagist violations of Modernist rectangularity and rigidity of form were achieved through the feminization of Cartesian geometry, but also through its Africanization. They may be interpreted as attempts to graft on the Brazilian urban tissue agents of transformation that both extend to architecture the integration of symbolic African elements of Brazilian national cultural practice and subvert the dominance of the white presence in the Brazilian bourgeois public and civic space.

The time when the 'A[f]rodisiac curves' of the Edifício Liberdade were rising to grace the civic centre of Belo Horizonte was also the time when a new picture of the reality of Brazilian race relations was emerging, following extensive field research sponsored by the United Nations Educational, Scientific, and Cultural Organization (UNESCO).[81] This originally aimed to demonstrate the virtues and success of the Brazilian model of 'harmonious' racial relations, especially as a counterexample to Nazi racism and US segregation laws. Growing evidence, however, exposed what later would be labelled the Brazilian 'myth of racial democracy' and its disguise of discrimination practices, revealing persistent racial antagonisms and inequality.

Whether consciously or unconsciously, by turning black corporeal aesthetics into the primary means of expression at his residential tower for the primarily white bourgeoisie, Niemeyer challenged contemporaneous aesthetic conventions; but he also voiced recognition of all the invisible Afro-Brazilian women working in the tower's luxury apartments.[82] Although there is no intention to suggest that his was an overtly anti-racist architecture, it is important to stress that the feminine and African element in Niemeyer's work is not simply tolerated or opportunistically appropriated to enrich an architecture for the white social elite. Through an architectural 'transformation of the Tabu into a totem', it becomes the dominant and most dynamic trait of his *mestiça* architecture, instrumentalized to corrode white city centres with black corporal aesthetics.[83] In this way, Niemeyer's architectural *mestiçagem* may be seen as effecting an inversion of the racial hegemony that the official Brazilian ideology of ethnic amalgamation hypocritically concealed.

Mediating between Private Building and Public Ground

I still think Niemeyer is a great architect . . . the whole seamless project starts there. The whole idea of the ramp and the manipulated ground. It is very peculiar. The unfortunate thing about it is that this was all done in the 1950's [sic] and 1960's [sic], and not much more has been done in the last twenty or thirty years.

Zaha Hadid, *El Croquis*, no. 103 (2001)

With reference to his work of the 1950s, primarily in the booming states of São Paulo and Minas Gerais, Niemeyer stated with assurance that he was 'forced [by the circumstances] to make improvisation [the] basic element' of his architecture. He explained the 'great variety of forms' that characterize this production on the basis of the 'absence of a large building industry with prefabricated assemblies and parts', an absence that 'encourages the development of a wealth of individualistic architectural forms and

78 Niemeyer, 1997a, p. 10.   **79** Hanchard, pp. 68, 78, n. 4.
80 Niemeyer, 2000b, p. 54.   **81** This research project originated in an earlier one that focused on social change in Bahia, jointly undertaken by Columbia University and the state of Bahia; Skidmore, 1993, p. 215.
82 In the 1980s, studies still demonstrated that 'the largest single job opportunity for Afro-Brazilian women continued to be that of domestic servant'; Lovell, p. 149.   **83** Oswald de Andrade, 2000, p. 591. Although a vocal critic of racism, Niemeyer remains a firm advocate of the valorization of miscegenation and multiracial integration, to the point of criticizing the formation of a separate Afro-Brazilian identity and political mobilization among Afro-Brazilians. In 1977 he referred to 'negative practices, such as the group Black-Power, which emerged in *zona norte* [of Rio de Janeiro] as 'racist and alienated', holding accountable for these the housing policies that had led to residential segregation and created 'real ghettoes and marginalization'; Niemeyer, 1977a, p. 39.

solutions'.[84] But he also saw formal speculation, plastic virtuosity and imaginative spatial experimentation, combined with innovative engineering, as originating in a heightened awareness of the plastic possibilities offered by reinforced concrete and a desire to question known solutions, take risks and adventurously explore untrodden ground.

Niemeyer's Conjunto Juscelino Kubitschek in Belo Horizonte was designed in 1951 with structural engineer Joaquim Cardozo to provide a variety of residential units for permanent and temporary accommodation. Its thirty-six-storey tower, the city's third tallest structure at 100 metres high, was completed in 1963. Niemeyer dynamically manipulated and foliated the ground, drawing threads from the fabric of the city, and weaving the base of the new buildings into it, treating the street level as a three-dimensional plastic network of spatial incidents and activities that smoothly merge building and ground. In doing so, he clearly moved away

from Modernism's emphatic separation of these two elements. Diametrically opposed to the Corbusian sterilized ground of *pilotis*, symbolizing air and light but remaining bereft of activity, the amoebic platforms of Niemeyer's urban residential blocks mediate between the public and the private domain, at some points hovering above street level and at others growing out of the ground and then splitting into fluid terraces that in turn rip and tear into ramps and bridges. These new artificial terrains are conceived in a three-dimensional manner. They aim not to free but to multiply and animate the living ground of the urban complex, articulating, layering and dynamizing its communal living spaces while allowing for different degrees of interaction between public and private space.

Contrary to commonly held views, Niemeyer's buildings cannot be easily separated from their ground. Rather than primarily isolated sculptural buildings in pristine settings, they are complex

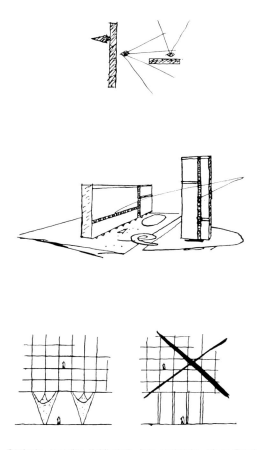

Conjunto Juscelino Kubitschek, Belo Horizonte, Minas Gerais, designed 1951, constructed 1953–70, incomplete; the buildings of the complex are arranged on the site so as to create the minimum obstruction of views; the repetition of certain features of the façades aims to achieve a sense of unity; bulkier stilts are chosen for being less obstructive at the pedestrian level

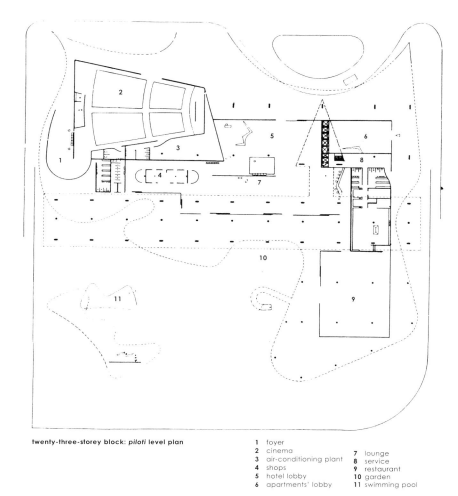

twenty-three-storey block: *piloti* **level plan**

1	foyer		
2	cinema	7	lounge
3	air-conditioning plant	8	service
4	shops	9	restaurant
5	hotel lobby	10	garden
6	apartments' lobby	11	swimming pool

84 Niemeyer, 1956b, p. 12.

Conjunto Juscelino Kubitschek: model

Conjunto Juscelino Kubitschek: view of lower block, crowned by a continuous flowing space given to recreational functions, with open terraces on both ends of the floor

spatial actors, actively participating in the moulding of the urban public and semi-public space, investing the boundaries between the city and the private building with a calculated ambiguity. His high-rise buildings do not rest on weak bases. On the lowest levels Niemeyer slots uses closer to the life of the street and the city, such as shopping arcades and restaurants. Higher up, on platforms

emancipated from the rectilinear grid of the city, he arranges lobbies, restaurants, gardens, swimming pools, cafés, cinemas and so on – activities close to the everyday life of the residents yet not entirely private, freely occupying the space of the *pilotis*, flowing beyond it onto sunny terraces.

The private space of Niemeyer's urban housing blocks is never abruptly cut off from the city, raised 'on a [Corbusian] display support'. Ever-new configurations emerge within the spaces of his *pilotis*, which are never allowed to raise brazen barriers, to mark limits or draw sharp dividing lines between public and private space. The complex three-dimensional landscape formations that penetrate the *pilotis* ensure a constant flow of city life through the pleats of the block bases, valued as vital oxygen-carrying blood that guarantees the good life of the residents. In this sense, Niemeyer's perception of the crucial role of *pilotis* in guaranteeing a healthy living is radically different from that of mainstream Modernist housing paradigms, which reject the city in favour of sun, air and greenery, equate health with hygiene, and deploy *pilotis* to distance the clean domestic world from the filthy and dangerous city and from dirty soil.

Kubitschek's visionary 'Eiffel Tower of Belo Horizonte' aimed to house 4,000 of its middle-class citizens in thirteen apartment types (from 38 to 190 square metres), sharing generous collective areas and services. Construction continued until the early 1970s, but the collective areas remained incomplete or accommodated functions that were never intended as part of the programme for the residential complex such as a police station. Niemeyer came forward with a number of inventive solutions. The first row of columns along the narrow side of the tall tower, on the side of the street, has been eliminated at street level and replaced by reinforced-concrete brackets that spring from the second row of columns, thus freeing the space beneath the curved terrace and offering it back to the city, at the same time drawing the pavement into the space of the complex. In a further extension of his columnar repertoire, ever eager to decrease congestion and increase spatial fluidity at *piloti* level, Niemeyer shaped the mighty atlantes of the twenty-three-storey block in the form of trifurcated stilts (with an expansion joint), each supporting two spans, with one span between consecutive stilts. The concrete bearing walls between dwelling units provide flush walls and ceilings, while dispensing with the need for columns above *piloti* level.

In his famous crushing review of modern Brazilian architecture in 1953, Max Bill would hold these 'walls entirely of reinforced concrete pointlessly confused with the columns' as an example of an 'awesome muddle of construction systems' and 'anti-social waste'.[85] Stamo Papadaki, on the other hand, noted that this solution had proven economical in Tecton's low-cost housing

85 Bill, 1954. See a slightly longer version of the speech in Bill, 2003.

Conjunto Juscelino Kubitschek: street-level *pilotis* of the vertical, thirty-six-storey block

Conjunto Juscelino Kubitschek: trifurcated stilts of the horizontal, twenty-three-storey block

schemes in London, and in the Nantes-Rezé Unité d'Habitation by Le Corbusier, A. Wogenscky, B. Lafaille and I. Xenakis (1953–55).[86] Totally free of structural components, the top floor of the low block of the Conjunto Kubitschek was designed as a continuous, fluid space with stage, dance floor, bar and lounge areas, and terraces at both ends.

To the 1957 *Interbau Exhibition* at Berlin's Hansaviertel on Altonaer Straße – a showcase for socially motivated, post-war architecture, particularly housing – Niemeyer contributed an eleven-floor apartment block with *pilotis* and basement level. Ten single-level apartments were proposed for each of nine 72-metre-long floors, with dual east–west aspect. A complex vertical circulation system was devised, with a semi-detached tower containing two elevators and a ramp serving the basement, ground floor, fifth floor (seventh in the original scheme) and roof, and five stairs each serving two apartments on each floor. Each stairway has an independent entrance on a platform inserted between two rows of V-shaped columns at ground level and accessed via a gentle ramp. Niemeyer thus achieved increased privacy while also dispensing with the need for long corridors. As far as possible, corridors were also eliminated inside the apartments.

The original scheme – developed during two weeks Niemeyer spent in Berlin in February 1955 – envisaged a large paved collective space in front of the residential block, populated with sculptures, canopies and so on. This space led to sculpturally expressive secondary structures with recreational facilities, enabling the life of the block to flow into the common areas of the Hansa quarter and establish links with surrounding blocks. Niemeyer considered collective spaces essential, justifying multiple-housing units. The entire seventh floor of the block was dedicated to communal uses, including lounging spaces, an auditorium, a banquet room, a game room and balconies along the entire length of the block on the east and west sides. These were eventually condensed to half of the fifth-floor area, allowing for an extra row of apartments along the block's east side on this floor.

Niemeyer's original sketches also indicate that he envisaged communal semi-open areas in the space between the V-shaped *pilotis*, with a wide ramp connecting these spaces to the open piazza. Sadly, like all other Modernist paradigms for the Hansaviertel, Niemeyer's block was encaged within oxygen-giving greenery, its domestic world allowed only minimal contact with the green terrain. Tellingly, Niemeyer's generous catwalk ramp, gesturing out towards the open public square and providing an almost ceremonial route towards the block and a small spectacle in the square, was turned parallel to the row of columns and attached to the residential body, reducing it to a mere access device. The façades of the building were also significantly modified: the apartments were provided with west-facing balconies while the terrace of the communal floor was enclosed behind glass. Finally, the block was crowned with a heavy, blind, concrete wall concealing utility rooms, sacrificing the original scheme's

86 Papadaki, 1956, p. 50.

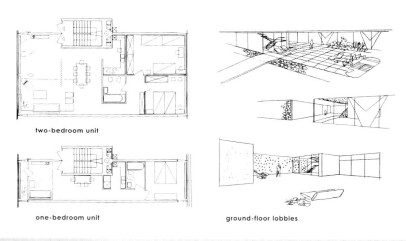

two-bedroom unit

one-bedroom unit

ground-floor lobbies

rooftop

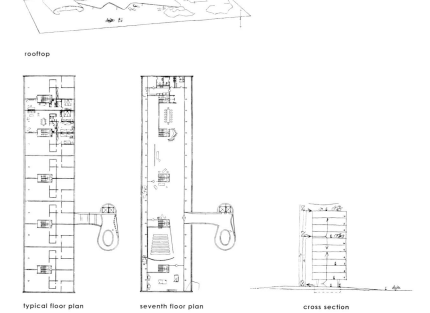

typical floor plan

seventh floor plan

cross section

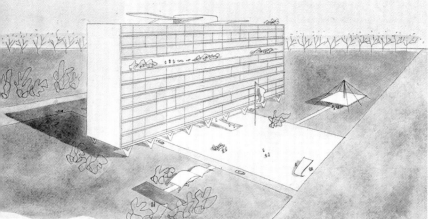

communal roof terrace with its gardens, children's pool and play area, and the sculptural, fluid forms of a vaulted gymnasium with a sinuous *marquise*. In 1959, the *Architectural Review* praised 'the superb finish of the *pilotis* to Oscar Niemeyer's flats at Hansa, 22, [taking] great and uneconomic care over workmanship, choice of cement samples, even choice of cement colour'.[87]

Dialogical Formal Compositions and the Integration of Structural and Spatial Coordinates

Working closely with structural engineers, Niemeyer experimented in numerous projects with intricate combinations of parabolic arches and hovering platforms, sharply oblique supports and slender, continuous structural elements seamlessly mutating from one function to another, in a perpetual quest for lightness and for the total integration of space and structure. To this phase belong the various vaulted structures he designed in the 1940s and 1950s, like those he placed on the roof of his UN Headquarters Secretariat and the Hotel Regente Gávea on the beach at Rio de Janeiro (1949, unbuilt), or the wide parabolic vault of the small airport terminal in Diamantina (1954), with structural engineer Werner Müller, with one-third of its width splitting and curling to form an entrance canopy.

87 Eastwick-Field and Stillman, p. 392.

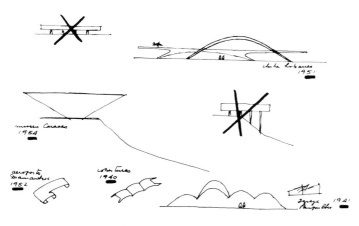

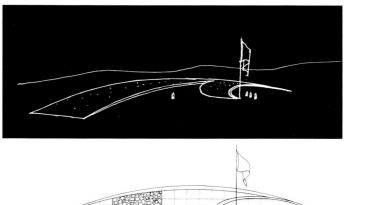

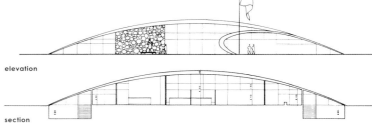

elevation

section

Niemeyer dedicated one of the thirteen panels he prepared for the 1965 exhibition *Oscar Niemeyer: l'architecte de Brasilia* to his vaulted structures (Musée des Arts Décoratifs, Palais du Louvre, Paris, curated by Jean Petit and Guy Dupuis).

Airport Terminal, Diamantina, Minas Gerais, 1954, unbuilt: excavation at both ends of the building achieves an interior height of 2.20 metres at the lowest point of the baggage-handling areas

Yves Bruand observes that this was a period of renewed interest in the revolutionary structures of Robert Maillart, following a commemorative exhibition in Geneva that stimulated a number of publications ten years after the Swiss structural engineer's death.[88] Similar forms appear in the work of other Brazilian architects of the time, like the vaulted structures on the roof of Affonso Eduardo Reidy and Jorge Moreira's competition winning project for the Headquarters of the Rio Grande do Sul Railway Central Administration in Porto Alegre (1944), or those featuring in Reidy's unexecuted industrial complex for the Sydney Ross Pharmaceuticals Company in Rio de Janeiro (1948). Niemeyer's unbuilt Lebanese Club in Belo Horizonte (1955) features a twin-vault superstructure from which a raised platform was partially hung, while the Diamantina Youth Club (1950), with its interlocking roof arch and

Lebanese Club, Belo Horizonte, Minas Gerais, 1955, unbuilt: the vaulted pavilion accommodates a restaurant on the ground floor and lounges on the first floor; game rooms are located in a semi-detached single-storey pavilion.

88 Bruand, p. 157.

raised jutting platform, appears to touch the ground only lightly and temporarily, resembling a grasshopper ready to pounce and take flight.

With all the structural elements at the periphery of the building clearly delineated outside the glass membranes that enclose the vast free spaces of the Diamantina club, Niemeyer achieved maximum transparency, lightness and dynamism, fully integrating the building's structural and spatial coordinates. 'By the time the structure was finished', he would later explain, 'architecture and structure were there as two things that must be born together and that together enrich each other.'[89] The concise expression of the two interlocking reinforced-concrete elements of the composition and their apparent precariousness create a tension, as if their meeting were no more than a fleeting encounter that the visitor is lucky to witness. The roof insect seems to be ready to fly off at any moment, or the skating board below it to slide away and continue on its smooth ride. Stasis, this building asserts, is only momentary, if not entirely an illusion.

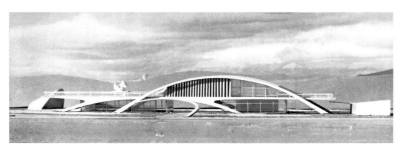

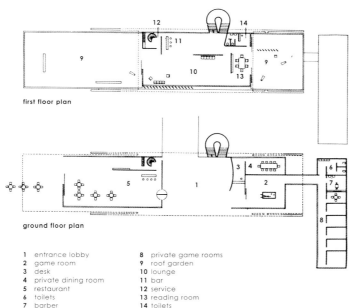

first floor plan

ground floor plan

1 entrance lobby	8 private game rooms
2 game room	9 roof garden
3 desk	10 lounge
4 private dining room	11 bar
5 restaurant	12 service
6 toilets	13 reading room
7 barber	14 toilets

Diamantina Youth Club, Diamantina, Minas Gerais, 1950; kitchen and services are located in a basement

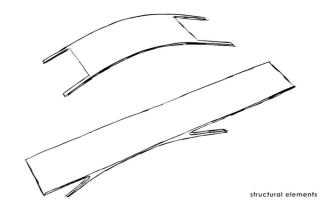

structural elements

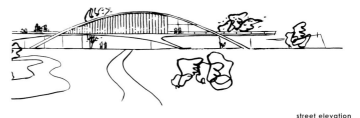

street elevation

Diamantina Youth Club

In the first issue of *Módulo* (1955), Joaquim Cardozo reflected on the latest tendencies of Brazilian architecture,

> manifested in large surfaces made into true concrete *sheets*. I say *sheets* because they form thin layers that suggest an intimate lightness, resembling envelopes of hot-air balloons and dirigibles. They are surfaces of variable form and inclination that advance and widen, retreat or narrow down as they participate in a vibrating, nearly magical space, comparable only with the spatial expression of the baroque.[90]

Niemeyer has often acknowledged the invaluable contribution of structural engineers to modern Brazilian architecture's quest for ongoing invention. The term 'structural acrobatics' is customarily used in a derogatory sense, but Niemeyer utterly enjoys the challenge of ordering fabulous tiptoeing structures.[91] His quest for an architecture 'capable of arousing surprise and emotion' relies on a sensitivity to reinforced concrete's structural potential, and the resulting spatial and aesthetic implications, as well as on an almost Brunelleschian penchant for risky experiment. Architectural spectacle in Niemeyer's work means a precisely choreographed

89 Niemeyer, 2000b, p. 163.   **90** Cardozo, 1955, p. 6, emphasis in the original.   **91** The Italian structural engineer Pier Luigi Nervi defined 'technical acrobatics' as follows: 'an ambitious formal research that, utilizing the possibilities of techniques and materials, achieves the indispensable equilibrium through the play of actions and reactions that are not evident and do not become a visible part of the architectural composition. The resistant systems of these structures at times constitute true technical acrobatics'; Nervi, 1959, p. 55. See also Nervi, 1962, p. 4, where Nervi spoke of 'exhibitionist acrobatics'.

aerial dance performed by exquisitely trained concrete acrobats. The seductive power of works that, like the Diamantina club, shun the earth and flirt with the skies, is the result of a persistent struggle against the forces of gravity defied by acrobats. The Diamantina club is one of Niemeyer's most graceful and handsome structures, sadly in a state of dereliction today.

The Diamantina Youth Club is currently in a dilapidated state

There is no building type or programme, however utilitarian, that Niemeyer considers unworthy of imaginative experimentation with new forms of plastic expression in reinforced concrete. Without compromising function, he uses every opportunity to test new design manoeuvres, thereby transforming utilitarian carcasses into graceful dancers. The Duchen Factory in Parque Novo Mundo, São Paulo (1950–51), was built with architect Helio Uchôa and structural engineer Joaquim Cardozo. The constraints and limitations of the programme for this pasta and biscuit factory were translated into a 300-metre-long block, composed of reinforced-concrete double vaults at 10-metre intervals, with two spans of 18 metres each. The roof slab is curved along the contours of the double vault, improving the distribution of southern light, which enters from windows at the point where the two vaults – of unequal heights – meet. The architectural language of the factory suggests industrial mass production. The supervisor's glazed office on the mezzanine has an open view towards the whole working area. The Duchen Factory was awarded first prize for an industrial building at the first São Paulo International Art Biennale in 1951. The jury was led by Sigfried Giedion.

Overlooking the Lagoa Rodrigo do Freitas, on the opposite shore from Niemeyer's own house and from his first built work, the Obra do Berço, rises the Sul America Hospital (1952–59). It was built with architect Helio Uchôa and structural engineer Morales Ribeiro for the employees of the Sul America Insurance Company and the Lar Brasileiro Bank, with a capacity of 280 beds and was, at the time, the best-equipped surgical centre in South America. It is

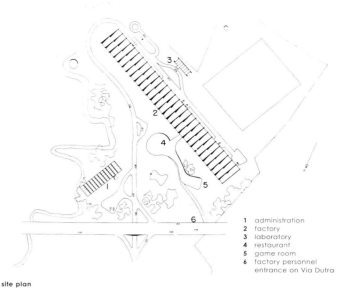

1 administration
2 factory
3 laboratory
4 restaurant
5 game room
6 factory personnel
  entrance on Via Dutra

site plan

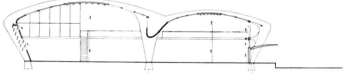

cross section

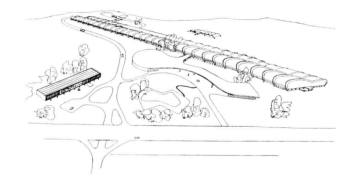

Duchen Factory, Parque Novo Mundo, São Paulo, 1950–51

a ten-storey structure supported on elegant bifurcating columns like those that first appeared in the unrealized schemes for the Quitandinha-Petrópolis residential block. These are set against Athos Bulcão's first abstract mural in blue-and-white tiles, which effaces the wall and underscores the strength of the concrete pillars. The east-facing patient rooms – on five floors – are provided with deep loggias, offering sun protection and allowing uninterrupted views towards gardens designed by Roberto Burle Marx and the lagoon beyond. The west-facing administration spaces are protected behind honeycomb brick *combogó* and vertical adjustable *brises-soleil*.

The large, sober, rectilinear block housing the hospital's main facilities is set in a dialogue of contrasting geometries with a much smaller chapel composed of what appears as a single, continuous structural element, echoing the skyline of the Sumaré mountains in the background. The profile of the volumes of the chapel recalls Reidy's school and gymnasium for the Pedregulho Social Housing Complex, inspired in turn by the vaulted church at Pampulha. Niemeyer's 'feat of structural magic', to use Underwood's formulation, achieves a heightened effect of lightness.[92] While Reidy's gymnasium sits comfortably on the earth, sheltered under its concrete vault with arches falling gently to the ground, Niemeyer's hospital chapel is held in mid-air between a pair of slender concrete arches. At the point where the two parabolae reach the swampy ground, wild concrete shoots spring up to lift the chapel's second volume, which slots into the vault of the first. The roof of this volume sweeps gently upwards, stretching towards the peak of Rio's Mount Corcovado. The sharply oblique end supports accentuate the upward thrust, affirming the weightlessness of the chapel. Vertical *brise-soleil* meshing and minimally detailed glazing compose a façade with no solid parts, underscoring the lightness of the floating chapel, which cannot be accessed from the ground, but only through a bridge from the hospital block.

Set against the uniform screen of the west façade of the principal hospital block, the capricious white outline of this secondary

92 Underwood. 1994a, p. 39.

element of the programme attracts the viewer's attention, becoming the protagonist of the composition. Underwood notes that 'Niemeyer inverted the logical hierarchy of several of his works of this period'. At the State High School (today Milton Campos College) in Belo Horizonte (1954, structural engineer Z. Gable), the independent curving structure of the auditorium contrasts with the simple rectangular volume of the main classroom block. Carnivalizing conventional programme hierarchies, Niemeyer turned the 'secondary' space of the auditorium into 'the primary focus of aesthetic exploration: the functional periphery becomes the aesthetic center'.[93] At the same time, this gesture suggests a decentring of conventional educational priorities, shifting a space where theatre and play are the key elements to the centre of the learning experience.

The auditorium's eye shape alludes to Niemeyer's justification of the selected form on the basis of optimum visibility, accommodating speaker and audience in the minimum useful enclosure while also helping to integrate all functional requirements – and transgress them. A sequence of events unfolds along the elastic concrete band of a ramp gently lifting pupils off the ground to a small external sloping foyer, then looping overhead to lead them through a glazed wall into the vaulted space of the auditorium, finally folding back towards the ground at a sharper angle. Niemeyer had envisaged a sculpture of a reclining nude for the sloping balcony opposite the ramp. Luckily, the sculpture was not realized and this unprogrammatic and apparently useless space under the overhanging vault has become a favourite shaded corner for pupils, who perch along its excitingly strange oblique surface, waiting for classes to begin or having a snack during breaks.

Similar principles apply to the Corumba Secondary School in the state of Mato Gross (1953), with structural engineer J. Alvariz,

State High School, Belo Horizonte: classroom protected with adjustable *brises-soleil*

State High School, Belo Horizonte: the independent structure of the auditorium is the focal point of the architectural composition.

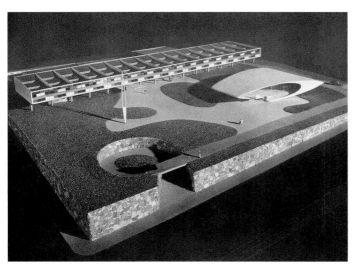

State High School (today Milton Campos College), Belo Horizonte, Minas Gerais, 1954: model

93 Underwood, 1994b, p. 77.

where the entrance foyer is found between the two distinct volumes of the auditorium and the gymnasium. These three spaces form the school's central pavilion, while a simple rectilinear block housing classrooms and teachers' offices lies lower, at the end of a covered passage connecting the two structures. A narrower passage off the classroom block leads to a further separate pavilion at the rear, containing a canteen, medical facilities and toilets. The programme of an automobile service station in São Paulo (1952) has also been accommodated in two distinct structures connected by a low covered passage: one contains customer facilities, defined by five barrel vaults overhanging a perforated curtain wall, which underlines the clarity of the structural line; this contrasts with a longer, flat canopy for the petrol pumps and lubrication pits, resting on K-shaped columns. Near the road, an attention-seeking boomerang-shaped pylon holds a jutting canopy.

Recognizing structural engineering as a major formative force in his work, Niemeyer took pains to ensure that space-articulating and structural elements coincided, striving for precision and clarity in their expression and bringing structure into sharp focus. The Hotel Tijuco in Diamantina, Minas Gerais (1951, structural engineer Joaquim Cardozo), commissioned by Minas Gerais governor Juscelino Kubitschek, was built on a steep slope overlooking the eighteenth-century city that Niemeyer deeply admired for its 'unity and harmony', still a diamond-mining centre surrounded by rocky hills at the edge of the *sertão mineiro*. In accordance with the principles established by the Serviço do Patrimônio Histórico e Artístico Nacional (SPHAN) for architectural interventions in historic settings, the Hotel Tijuco is a bold, uncompromisingly modern,

two-storey structure, partly raised on transverse, asymmetrical, V-shaped stilts, their outer arms extending to support the overhang of the roof slab. At the level of the first-floor loggia, the supports are incorporated into the walls dividing the guest rooms. The inward-canted east façade highlights the skilful integration of structural and spatial coordinates, while also ensuring sun protection for rooms and terraces. The profile of the interrupted roof slab echoes the sloping terrain; along a central corridor it is lowered to provide all twenty-four rooms with cross-ventilation.

Economy of means characterizes also the second structure Juscelino Kubitschek commissioned for his birthplace, the Júlia Kubitschek School in Diamantina (1951), built with structural engineer Werner Müller and honouring the politician's mother, who had been a schoolteacher in Diamantina. The two-storey school is also situated on a sloping terrain and utilizes an inverted trapezoid profile similar to that of the Hotel Tijuco. The distinct structural solutions employed for the two levels reflect distinct spatial requirements. The semi-open refectory and glazed hall, with open views towards the colonial town and graced by a painting by Di Cavalcanti (1954), are accommodated within the space of the *pilotis*. The oval-section columns are set on the grid of the upper-level classrooms and clad with octagonal grey-blue *pastilha* tiles. A row of eight classrooms is contained within the upper volume, along a single-loaded corridor reached via a linear ramp rising along the rear wall of the large hall. The first-floor slab overhangs the *pilotis*. Sharply angled concrete brackets springing from the cantilevered first-floor slab support the overhanging roof, which protects the classrooms against the sun throughout the day. The

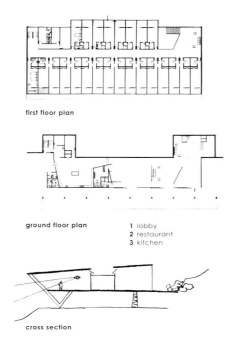

first floor plan

ground floor plan

1 lobby
2 restaurant
3 kitchen

cross section

Hotel Tijuco, Diamantina, Minas Gerais, 1951: *above*, view of street (east) façade

brackets and the first-floor and roof slabs are also outlined in grey-blue.

The bold outline of the upper volume and its formal, structural and material unity dictate its reading as the focal point of the composition. The free-standing *combogó* and perforated screens protecting the spaces within the *pilotis* stop short of the first-floor slab so that the upper volume appears to hover weightless, clearly separating the flight-thirsty vessel from all that belongs to the earth. The only architectural element allowed to project beyond the upper volume is a small concrete canopy – also painted grey-blue – marking the main entrance, which is, typically, no more than an opening in the ground-floor glazing. Of a trapezoid shape that accentuates its directionality, this canopy appears to glide unsupported beneath the first floor. Smooth and slightly curled upwards, it resembles a sheet of paper that flew out of a classroom and is dancing in the wind of the *sertão*.

The school's tiled surfaces, the *combogó* screen protecting the offices and medical dispensary, the rear rubble retaining walls, the large sheltered outdoor space of the refectory behind the colonnade, the perforated screen, the gently sloping, overhanging roofs and the ventilators above the upper-level glazing – all serve clear functional requirements. But they may also be read as overt references to the architecture of Brazil's colonial past, establishing a connection with the historic town. Both the Hotel Tijuco and the Júlia Kubitschek School are long, low structures along the lines of the patriarchal *casas grande* of the Brazilian interior, with their long sequence of rooms, 'more like monasteries than like private residences'.[94]

But in contrast to the authoritarian 'big houses' of the feudal plantations, set behind high walls and embodying rootedness, conservatism, permanence and an attachment to the soil, centred around a sedentary life and 'the imposing bulk of the Portuguese matron . . . fat and slow-moving', Niemeyer's hill-perched, dynamic structures despise stability and earthiness.[95] They evoke images of flight, allude to lightness, openness and emancipation, pleading for a break with a past that was also centred around 'the infamous trade', and claiming for Brazil a place in the world of modernity, freedom from oppression, social reconciliation and justice – all that Niemeyer yearned for during these years of optimism.

These two innovative structures became a source of inspiration for Affonso Eduardo Reidy's Brasil-Paraguai School, in Asunción in Paraguay (1952) as well as for one of the boldest and most beautiful buildings of Brazilian Modernism, the Museu de Arte Moderna (MAM) in Rio de Janeiro, also by Reidy, with structural engineers Carmen Portinho and Emílio Baumgart. It was 'A new form / before the ancient sea', set in the exuberant pleasure gardens of Roberto Burle Marx and framed by the spectacle of the Carioca landscape on the site that had so enchanted Le

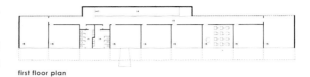

first floor plan

ground floor plan

1	entrance		
2	hall	8	teachers' room
3	terrace	9-12	dental and medical dispensary
4	refectory	13	toilets
5	kitchen	14	ramp
6	secretary	15	corridor
7	head teacher	16	classrooms

cross section

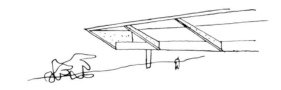

Júlia Kubitschek School, Diamantina, Minas Gerais, 1951: the section allows cross-ventilation and additional daylight; *above*, view of west façade

94 Freyre, 1963, p. 233.   95 Freyre, 1986, p. 29.

Affonso Eduardo Reidy, Museum of Modern Art, Rio de Janeiro, 1953–68

Corbusier in 1936.[96] Although much more earth-bound, one of Le Corbusier's last buildings, the Maison de la Culture at Firminy (1961–65), would also adopt the inverted trapezoidal profile a decade later.

'Jungle and school': Celebrating the Foundational Encounter between European and Indigene

In 1951, on behalf of the city of São Paulo, the Italian businessman and cultural patron Francisco 'Ciccillo' Matarazzo commissioned Niemeyer to design a series of structures for the celebration of the fourth centennial of the foundation of the city in 1954 at Ibirapuera Park (1951–2005, in collaboration with Zenon Lotufu, Eduardo Kneese de Melo and Helio Uchôa with their associates Gauss Estelita and Carlos Lemos). The old, wooded municipal park, an area of 180 hectares, provided the site for the city's new focus of cultural activity, hosting large-scale exhibitions and fairs as well as a variety of cultural events, such as the São Paulo International Art Biennale (Bienal Internacional de Artes Plásticas). In contrast to Le Corbusier's 'attempted . . . conquest of America' in the form of a symbolic battle between nature and city or 'nature and the product of the work of men', Niemeyer's festive park for São Paulo proposed a close collaboration between archi-

tecture and nature in the spirit of the Pau-Brasil dialogue between 'jungle and school'.[97]

From the early days of Brazilian Modernism, nature was identified with, and symbolized by, the tropical jungle: the feared and awe-inspiring, bloodthirsty and paradisiacal 'Land without Evil' of Portuguese colonizers, the Other of early European travellers, and the Brazilian Modernists' privileged locus of native *brasilidade*. In 1923, Mário de Andrade urged Tarsila do Amaral: 'Tarsila, Tarsila, go back within yourself . . . Leave Paris! Tarsila! Come to the virgin forest.'[98] Niemeyer's original scheme for the commemorative Ibirapuera Park envisaged a tropicalized Modernist complex – a vast park designed by Roberto Burle Marx with scattered architectural events united by a concrete polypoid *marquise*. This defined a grand sinuous esplanade with limbs spreading languorously through the park, linking all the main buildings: the Pavilion of Industry, the Pavilion of Nations, a restaurant by the lake (not constructed), the Pavilion of States, and via a raised walkway (not constructed) the domed Pavilion of the Arts and an auditorium.

Unfortunately, Burle Marx's gardens were not realized and the preliminary plan was significantly 'mutilated', as the designers put it.[99] 'In view of the urgency of the project' important structures such as the entrance pavilion were entirely omitted.[100] Nevertheless, the ensemble of the Ibirapuera Park reflects Niemeyer's vision of the incorporation of the 'architecture of the school' into the body of nature, with modern white structures set in green surroundings, thick green lawns strewn with colourful flowers on the banks of a sinuous lake, swarming with visitors whizzing on skateboards under the long-limbed *marquise* or resting in hammocks in the shade of evergreen trees, recalling the sixteenth-century Jesuit fathers' descriptions of a 'very healthy and fresh land, with good waters'.[101] Here, as elsewhere, gardens of leisure and pleasure underscore the amorous implications of the tropical milieu, emblematic of Niemeyer's transgression into forbidden territories beyond the boundaries of the functionalist utopia.

Official São Paulo city history has long indulged the myth of the peaceful coexistence of Indians and colonizers during the first three hundred years of colonization in the area. Indians and *mamelucos* (of mixed European and indigenous ancestry) far surpassed Europeans in number, indigenous influence on the Portuguese was strong and a common language or *língua geral*, based on Tupí-Guarani, was spoken until the middle of the eighteenth century. Subjugation and exploitation of the Indians, however, started immediately after the foundation of São Paulo's precursor, Vila de São Vicente, in 1532, and continued at São Paulo

96 From the poem 'MAM' (Museu de Arte Moderna), by Carlos Drumond de Andrade (1956); in Bonduki (ed.), 2000, p. 181. **97** Le Corbusier, 1991, pp. 18, 245; Oswald de Andrade, 1989, p. 311. **98** Letter from Mário de Andrade to Tarsila do Amaral, 15 November 1923, cited in Herkenhoff, 1995, p. 243. **99** Papadaki, 1956, p. 127. **100** Letter from Oscar Niemeyer to Stamo Papadaki, 6 August 1953. In the same letter, Niemeyer

insists that Papadaki's publication of the work should include a photograph of the model of the original scheme and notes: 'I am sure that this is an honest and decent work. Le Corbusier wrote me praising the auditorium very much and Leger [sic] did likewise'; in Stamo Papadaki Papers. **101** Quoted in http://www.saopaulo.sp.gov.br/ingles/saopaulo/historia/colonia.htm.

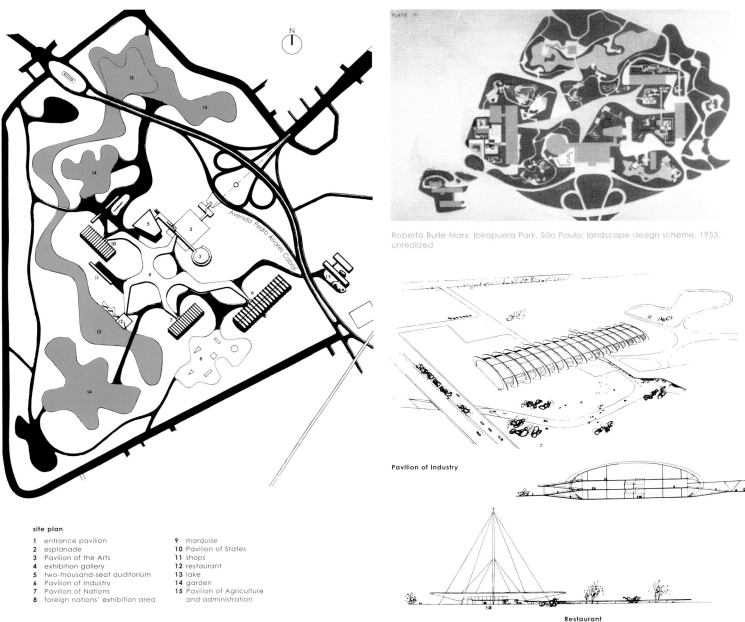

Roberto Burle Marx, Ibirapuera Park, São Paulo: landscape design scheme, 1953, unrealized

Pavilion of Industry

Restaurant

Fourth Centenary Exhibition of São Paulo, Ibirapuera Park, São Paulo, 1951–2005; original scheme, 1951

site plan

1 entrance pavilion
2 esplanade
3 Pavilion of the Arts
4 exhibition gallery
5 two-thousand-seat auditorium
6 Pavilion of Industry
7 Pavilion of Nations
8 foreign nations' exhibition area

9 *marquise*
10 Pavilion of States
11 shops
12 restaurant
13 lake
14 garden
15 Pavilion of Agriculture
　　and administration

de Piratininga through Jesuit 'pacification' and Christianization and violent *bandeirante* conquests and enslavement.[102] Although the name and birthday of the city link it to the Jesuit Colégio São Paulo – a seminary for the catechism of the large local Indian population, founded in 1554 in the Piratininga Plateau, with an inaugural mass held on 25 January, St Paul's day – a typical European–indigene foundational romance also features in the mythology of the city.

The Portuguese sailor João Ramalho, survivor of a shipwreck in 1510, is said to have been the first white man on the shore of São Paulo. Ramalho and the Guaianás Indian princess he married, Portira, daughter of the tribal chief Tibiriçá, represent the symbolic parents of the city, shadowing the symbolic parents of Brazil: the Indian Iracema (an anagram of America) and the Christian

102 The greatly idealized and mythicized *bandeirantes* were seventeenth- and eighteenth-century slave hunters and prospectors, who led predatory *bandeira* (literally 'flag') expeditions, which included large numbers of enslaved Indians and *mamelucos*, and later African slaves and mulattoes. They originated primarily in the coastal regions of São Paulo and reached far into the backlands, opening up the interior, and were thus seen as major contributors to Brazilian unity. They regularly destroyed Indian villages, massacring and capturing Indians and selling them as slaves to the sugar plantations.

Aerial view of Ibirapuera Park as constructed for the celebration of the fourth centennial of the foundation of São Paulo in 1954: the Pavilion of Nations, *at bottom left*, with the Pavilion of States, *to its right*; the Pavilion of Industry opposite the Pavilion of Nations; the domed Pavilion of the Arts, *at the centre*; beyond, across the tree-lined Avenida Álvares Cabral, the Pavilion of Agriculture.

explorer Martins in the Romantic Indigenist novel *Iracema* (1865) by the Conservative senator José de Alencar (1829–77).[103] They also parallel the real-life symbolic progenitors of the *mestiço* nation: Paraguaçu, daughter of the chief of the Bahian Tupinambás, and the Portuguese cartographer and painter Diogo Álvares Correia, renamed Caramuru and, according to legend, 'King of Brazil'.[104] By some uncanny coincidence, while the Ibirapuera complex was under construction in 1952, Brazil was shaken by a case sensationalized by the media, which transformed into a melodramatic Romeo-and-Juliet affair the relationship between the *gaúcho* Ayres Câmara Cunha and a young Kalapalo Indian woman, Diacuí Canualo Aiute, whose legal union was initially refused by Diacuí's official guardian, the Serviço de Proteção aos Índios. The modern-day demystification of Alencar's 'honey-lipped virgin' did little, however, to alter the image of the Indian as a pillar of Brazilian *mestiçagem*.[105]

In a way that complied with official versions of Brazilian history, the celebrations of the fourth centennial of 'the fastest-growing city in the world' were centred on a 'return to origins' or a 'nostalgia [*saudades*] for origins', to use Vinícius de Moraes's later description of Brasília, highlighting Brazil's (and São Paulo's) foundational encounter between European and indigene.[106] The valorization of the local *caipira* (rural) culture stimulated regional pride, alerting Paulista *quatrocentões* – landowner families who traced their roots to the beginning of colonization – to the destruction of the last remains of the city's *bandeirista* architectural heritage, representing 'the strength, talent and courage of Paulista origins'.[107] Like the commemoration in 2000 of Brazil's five hundredth anniversary, the four hundredth anniversary of São Paulo was commemorated with images of Portuguese caravels arriving in a tropical paradise, setting in motion the process of happy race mixing (*mestiçagem*). The vast Ibirapuera Park – bearing a name of Indian origin, and, uncannily, located on Avenida Pedro Álvares Cabral – was colonized by a small fleet of modern reinforced-concrete ships: the Pavilion of Nations, the Pavilion of States, the Pavilion of Industry and the Pavilion of Agriculture. The domed Pavilion of the Arts bears a Tupí-Guarani name, 'Oca' ('Home'), paying homage to the city's indigenous heritage. Victor Brecheret's massive stone sculpture *Monumento às Bandeiras*, inaugurated one year before the celebrations, and Galileo Emendabili's *Obelisco dos Heróis de 32* (a monument to the heroes of São Paulo's constitutional revolt against the Vargas regime in 1932) helped unite all key protagonists in the city's official history.

As the structural engineer Joaquim Cardozo affirmed in a text accompanying an early publication of Niemeyer's original scheme, the intention of the complex was 'to communicate . . . the importance and the degree of technical and industrial development of this great state during its four centuries of existence'.[108]

Although the technically ambitious original proposals were superseded by more conventional ones, the idea of a peaceful coexistence, a synthesis even, of industry and nature, like that envisaged by Oswald de Andrade, remained at the centre of the tropicalized Modernist ensemble.[109]

The paired 150 m-long blocks of the Pavilion of States and the Pavilion of Nations, much simplified from the original design, were intended for exhibitions of plastic art from the twenty Brazilian states and from other participating nations respectively. They hosted the São Paulo Art Biennale in 1953 and 1955. Positioned at right angles to each other, they have identical plans and sections, with an enormous 5-metre-high hypostyle hall measuring 140 × 42 metres in the cantilevered upper storey, and a 5-metre-high ground floor, partly sunk 2 metres below ground level. The 10 × 10-metre columnar grid of the exhibition halls ensures maximum flexibility in the use of space. A considerable part of the sunken section of the ground floor was left open to be used as a bar.

All three levels are connected by long ramps supported by a single, V-shaped, concrete column, minimizing visual interference. The sharp curve of the level change on the ground floor – introducing into the exhibition space a liquid viewing platform – and the prominently positioned ramps highlight the visitors' central role in the exhibition space. Members of the public are gently enticed to stroll in three-dimensional space, as it were, wandering vertically as well as horizontally and granted unique and ever-changing views of the exhibits. These gestures enhance the spatial experience while also maintaining a sense of spectacle from the original scheme for an independent shell enveloping a free-standing, multi-level structure. They also foster the idea of a collective experience of art. With a view to preserving maximum spatial clarity, ancillary functions have been delegated to the basement.

The two blocks have different façades, reflecting their different orientations. The large glazed panel of the north-east elevation of the Pavilion of States is protected with a deep honeycomb sunscreen featuring perforated horizontal sunbreaks. The rear elevation has vertical, adjustable louvres. Today it houses the Companhia de Processamento de Dados do Município de São Paulo

103 It has been argued that, 'Once combined with the concept of miscegenation, Alencar's mythology acquired an ideological force that reached far beyond the Indianist movement itself, for this notion of a conciliatory, collaborative relationship between races, on the basis of a history of social and sexual contact. is the first manifestation of the most influential tradition of thinking about race relations and national identity in Brazil to date: a tradition of *mestiço* nationalism'; D. Treece, quoted in Guzmán, p. 101. **104** The last foundational romance was celebrated at Salvador's quincentennial carnival; Stam, 2003, pp. 206–7. **105** For a full discussion of the Diacuí case, see Guzmán, pp. 92–122. **106** 'The fastest-growing city in the world' was the slogan of the celebrations. 'Paisagem de oxigênio, silêncio e saudades das origines'; Moraes, 1961. **107** Sampaio. **108** *Ante-Projeto da Exposição do IV Centenário de São Paulo*, 1952, n.p. **109** In his essay entitled 'O novo humansimo científico e tecnológico' ('The New Scientific and Technological Humanism'), commissioned by the Massachusetts Institute of Technology to celebrate its centenary in 1961, Lúcio Costa stressed that 'Scientific and Technological development are not in opposition to Nature, of which they are in fact the hidden face'; Lúcio Costa, quoted in *Lúcio Costa 1902–2002*, p. 58.

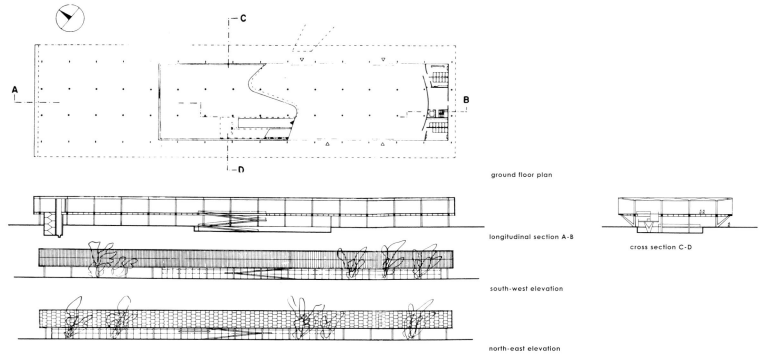

ground floor plan

longitudinal section A-B

cross section C-D

south-west elevation

north-east elevation

Pavilion of States, Ibirapuera Park: dotted lines on the ground-floor plan indicate the cantilevered first floor and its connection with the *marquise*

Pavilion of States, Ibirapuera Park: *above*, view of main (north-east) façade with free-standing columns and tapering brackets, and honeycomb sunscreen featuring perforated horizontal sunbreaks; *right*, close-up of perforated sunbreaks

(PRODAM). The Pavilion of Nations is fully glazed. It was renamed Pavilion Manoel da Nóbrega in 2004 and it houses the Museu Afro Brasil. The upper storeys of the two pavilions read like fragile industrial vessels lifted off the ground by slender bamboo-like columns with long, sharply angled brackets sprouting like branches from the base of the vertical stems to support the precariously balanced hulls. Closer observation of columns and brackets reinforces the analogy: the visible lines that have resulted from their casting in stages evoke the growth nodes of tropical bamboo culms, while the diameter of the slender brackets progressively diminishes as they shoot away from the upright cane.

All of the exhibition buildings are sober structures veiling adventurous interiors. The most striking of all is that of the large

Pavilion of Nations, Ibirapuera Park: view of main (south-east) façade with the *marquise* connected to the cantilevered first floor

The rigorously rectilinear building is rendered strange internally, where the lofty space of the central nave is animated by the capricious contours of long side galleries that shun the regularity of the columnar grid, instigating interplay between the different, visually communicating levels and encouraging the kind of peripatetic exploration that would find its full realization in Frank Lloyd Wright's Solomon R. Guggenheim Museum (New York, 1944–57). At the north-east end of the nave, a tree-like column, its trunk seemingly embraced by a large liana plant, provides a focal point. Its limbs support the spectacular horseshoe-shaped ramp that takes visitors to the upper exhibition galleries. The double-ribbon balustrades of the ramp and the free-flowing balconies combine to create the spectacle of endlessly unfurling carnival serpentines, encircling the viewers in this festive interior. To a certain extent, the interior of the Pavilion of Industry, with the liquid contours of its upper-storey slabs, may be seen as a reinvention of the interior of the Brazilian Pavilion at the 1939 New York World's Fair. At Ibirapuera, Niemeyer's pre-announced 'aesthetic of fluidity', to

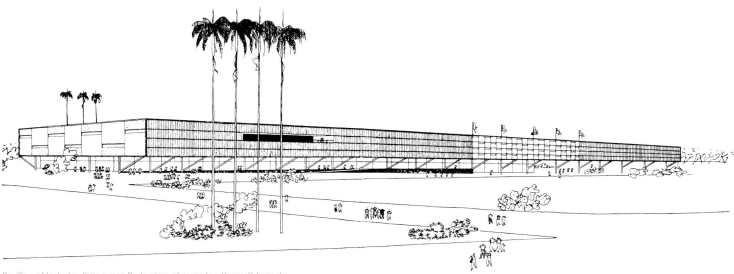

Pavilion of Industry, Ibirapuera Park: view of main (north-west) façade

Pavilion of Industry, measuring 250 × 50 metres. At the opposite end of the site from the Pavilion of Nations, it was originally intended for the display of machinery and manufactured products and today houses the Art Biennale. The north-west elevation is partially glazed, and partially protected by vertical aluminium adjustable *brises-soleil*. At variable distances from the gently sloping ground tapering brackets branch off external circular columns to support an overhanging upper volume. At the lower end of the slope the long vessel of industry, supported on thin open *pilotis* on a 10 × 10-metre grid, occupies the space of a tree canopy 8.6 metres from the ground.

use Gilbert Luigi's term,[110] soars to a climactic high. A set of escalators, in the centre of the building, and an external, free-standing, linear ramp set perpendicular to the building provide additional opportunities for languid vertical promenading, theatrical stages turning ordinary pedestrian traffic into a continually unfolding, extravagant spectacle.

The Pavilion of Agriculture, an annex of the Ministry of Agriculture intended to house permanent services, is situated outside the main grounds of the park and accessed via an under-

110 Luigi.

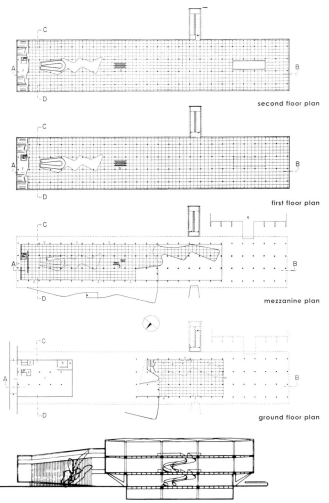

second floor plan

first floor plan

mezzanine plan

ground floor plan

cross section

Pavilion of Industry, Ibirapuera Park: the gridded areas on the plans indicate enclosed space; a free-standing ramp, *on the left of the cross-section*, links all four levels

Pavilion of Industry, Ibirapuera Park: view through north-west curtain wall with vertically pivoting, aluminium *brises-soleil*

Pavilion of Industry, Ibirapuera Park: exhibition galleries with horseshoe-shaped ramp and free-flowing balconies

pass. Today it houses the Departamento Estadual de Trânsito de São Paulo (DETRAN). The bifurcating stilts of its *pilotis* enabled free planning of the light-filled public-access levels on the ground floor and mezzanine, and are translated into the regular columnar structure of the eight upper floors. Nautical references – decks, railings, roof stacks – are prominent. The recessed, white-tiled mezzanine deck is set off against the polished black ground floor, which reflects the elegant, horseshoe stair that energizes the public hall. The mezzanine slab branches out beyond the limits of the box, mutating into a free-form *marquise* that tails off into an external stair helix. Under the *marquise* is found a restaurant, bar and waiting room.

The twenty-first-century reappraisal of the domed Governor Lucas Nogueira Garces Pavilion of the Arts (reopened in 2000, fol-

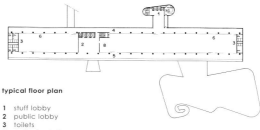

typical floor plan

1	stuff lobby
2	public lobby
3	toilets
4	staff circulation
5	public circulation
6	office
7	storage
8	principal's office

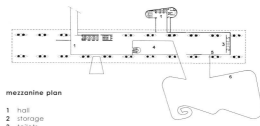

mezzanine plan

1	hall
2	storage
3	toilets
4	open to ground floor
5	lecture room
6	roof terrace

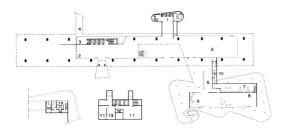

ground floor and basement plan

1	stuff lobby	6	bar
2	public hall	7	kitchen
3	entrance for high functionaries	8	restaurant
4	passage to garage	9	lounge
5	exhibition area	10-14	services and storage

Pavilion of Agriculture, Ibirapuera Park: the V-shaped *pilotis* on the periphery of the building transfer the loads carried by two columns to a single point on the ground, allowing freedom of planning for the ground floor and mezzanine

lowing extensive renovation by Paulo Mendes da Rocha) found in it 'a sublime anticipation of what is today the organic fashion in architecture, the "blobmeister" tendency that has seen certain – not necessarily young – architects harking back to the architecture of those heroic years'.[111] The space under the cupola, 76 metres in diameter and 18 metres high, was intended for exhibitions of sculpture on four levels, one below ground level, and is illuminated by a series of thirty porthole windows near the base of the dome.

Here, too, Niemeyer has orchestrated a spectacle of a slowly unfolding catwalk, where works of art and spectators mingle under the protective white dome, which remains always present yet ever out of reach. A wide, horseshoe-shaped ramp connects all levels, leading the visitor to the centre of each platform. The first-floor slab is hexagonal and the second-floor one rectangular, both with concave sides. Their thickness diminishes progressively towards their edges in the interests of an appearance of lightness,

[111] Casciani, 2003, p. 92.

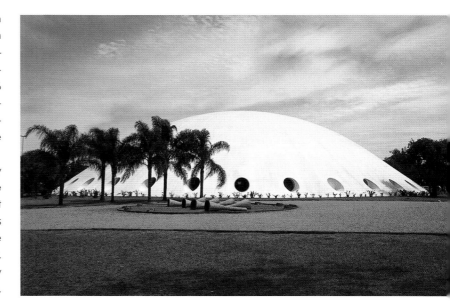

Pavilion of the Arts (Oca), Ibirapuera Park, reopened in 2000, following extensive renovation by Paulo Mendes da Rocha

Pavilion of the Arts (Oca), Ibirapuera Park: four tiers of exhibition space linked through dramatically unfolding ramps, *above*, view from basement level; *opposite*, view from entrance (ground-floor) level

Pavilion of the Arts (Oca), Ibirapuera Park: concrete plates of various configurations appear to float in mid-space: portholes near the base of the dome admit daylight

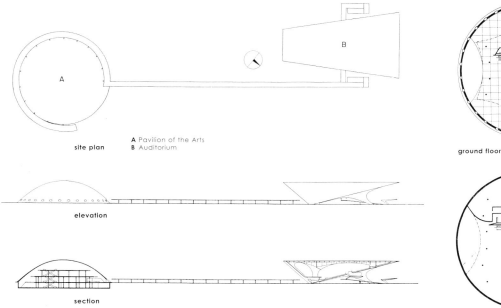

site plan

A Pavilion of the Arts
B Auditorium

elevation

section

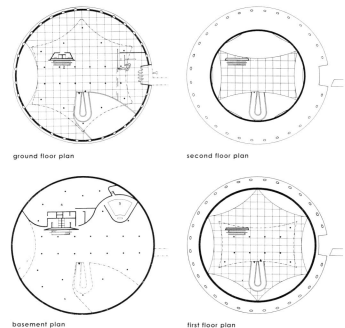

ground floor plan

second floor plan

basement plan

first floor plan

and the fact that their corners actually do touch the dome has been skilfully concealed so that they appear to scorn gravity and float in mid-space. The ramps – of equal thickness to the thin edges of the platforms and with the same slick railing – enhance the impression of a continuous, weightless, extruded concrete plate that is split, bent, folded and unfolded, turned and twisted in different directions, as it journeys through the space of the cupola. When filled with visitors in perpetual motion, the dynamic catwalks spring into action, granting a central position in the Pavilion of the Arts to the spectacle of art viewing, calling attention to the relationship between spectator and art object. The expansive whiteness of the indirectly lit dome lends an eerie quality to the interior of this spaceship of art, helping the viewer to enter into a contemplative frame of mind befitting a utopian world of art, which from the highest platform appears infinite and totally Other to the world of reality.

It comes as a surprise to discover that the integrity of the dome has been compromised and the entrance to the pavilion is found at ground-floor level, through a vertical glazed surface. This represents an unusual choice for Niemeyer, who might be expected to have provided an entrance carved into the ground with an underground passage through which the visitor emerges into the space of the pavilion – like, say, at the cathedral of Brasília – or at least an opening that reconstitutes the surface of the dome when closed, as at the auditorium of Niemeyer's French Communist Party Headquarters in Paris. Had the Ibirapuera Pavilion of the Arts been designed according to the original proposal, the entrance would have been located exactly at the point where the raised walkway reaches the pavilion to become a ring-like ramp around

the dome. With the walkway omitted, the violation of the purity of the dome became frustratingly conspicuous.

Planned for the city's 450th anniversary in 2004 but opened in 2005, Niemeyer's last building for the Ibirapuera Park is an eight-hundred-seat convertible auditorium, a smaller and simpler version of the two-hundred seat one in his scheme of 1951. The sober, white, concrete wedge is energized by a red, undulating, upward-thrusting steel canopy that marks the entrance, then curls towards

Auditório Ibirapuera, Ibirapuera Park, opened in 2005: *above*, view of the foyer with red-carpeted ramp that tangoes with Tomie Ohtake's red sculpture; *below*, close-up of steel entrance canopy

the ground to form the recessed opening, in dialogue with veteran local artist Tomie Ohtake's swirling red sculpture inside the building, which tangoes with Niemeyer's grand, white-and-red curving ramp. The wall behind the stage of the auditorium opens to offer the audience on the red carpet a view to the park, while also allowing a larger audience on the grass outside to enjoy concerts. A free concert is performed every Sunday. The basement contains a VIP room, a government-funded music school, café and dressing rooms.

In 1926, Mário de Andrade's Macunaíma, the hero of the major novel of Brazilian Modernism of the same name (1926), born in the virgin jungle, defended the cosmic laziness and humanism of the 'Amazons against the nascent materialism of São Paulo's industrial modernization'.[112] Ibirapuera Park functions as a much-

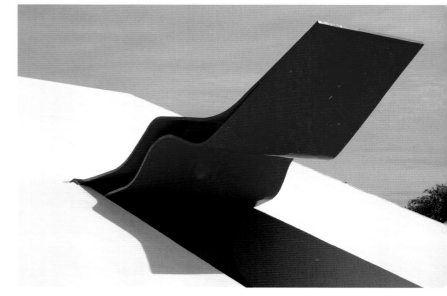

112 Jackson, p. 97.

Auditório Ibirapuera, Ibirapuera Park: view from the stalls through the convertible rear wall that opens the stage to a large audience in the park

inspired by the discovery of Brazil, the milieu of Michel de Montaigne's ideal republic of the native Indians of Brazil, 'a nation' with 'no occupation but that of idleness'.[115] This vision was radicalized by Oswald de Andrade, who portrayed the indigenous Brazilian social model, 'based on the full enjoyment of leisure', as superior to the European.[116] In the modern Brazilian vision of the future conjured up by Gilberto Freyre, industrial development does not antagonize nature, which, in Brazil, is always associated with leisure and unproductive pleasure. On the contrary, the absolute triumph of the machine inaugurates the age of leisure, anticipated by the Brazilians with 'their disdain for systematic work and an exaggerated fondness for dance, music and idleness... who have developed pure leisure (or unproductive idleness) almost to a form of art'.[117] Stressing that, in Brazil, nature is not perceived as an enemy to be kept outside the house, José Lins do Rego underlined the humanizing effect of gardens in modern Brazilian cities: 'The *catingas* of the Sertao... the Amazonian forest, the mountains of Minas Gerais, and the pampas of Rio Grande do Sul enter the heart of the city, and climb up its skyscrapers to help modern man to be more human... to be something other than a mere *machine à vivre*.'[118]

appreciated, hugely popular oasis in the midst of the megalopolis aptly described in Caetano Veloso's song 'Sampa' (an acronym for São Paulo, 1978):

> the reverse of the reverse
> of the reverse of the reverse
> of the oppressed people in the rows of *favelas*
> of the power of money
> that creates and destroys beautiful things
> of the horrid smoke that rises and turns out the stars.[113]

The dissonance created by the rectilinear exhibition machines of modern industrial São Paulo in a garden filled with longing for a Virgilian age of unsurpassable happiness and inexhaustible leisure for love was resolved in the wandering *marquise*, fusing into a single device architecture and nature which, to remember William Kent, 'abhors a straight line'.

Oswald de Andrade's 'Manifesto Antropófago' had insisted: 'Before the Portuguese discovered Brazil, Brazil had discovered happiness.'[114] As already remarked, in Brazilian Modernism, gardens invoke and appropriate the visions of the Garden of Eden

Ibirapuera *marquise* (named Marquise José Ermírio de Moraes in 2000), Ibirapuera Park: much abbreviated in its final realization, the *marquise* defines a sinuous, long-limbed esplanade, links major buildings and provides flexible, unhierarchical, unprogrammatic space for appropriation by users

113 In English in Casciani, 2003, p. 90.   **114** Oswald de Andrade, 2000, p. 592.   **115** Montaigne, p. 100. In their idyllic world, Montaigne noted, 'the whole day is spent in dancing'; Montaigne, p. 101. According to Gilberto Freyre, 'those Brazilians who have African blood or are predominantly African in their culture... tend to reduce everything to dance, work and play alike, and this tendency, apparently becoming more and more general in Brazil, is not solely the characteristic of an ethnic or regional group'; Freyre, 1974, p. 32.   **116** Shohat and Stam, p. 309. The authors point out that the 'Dadaists too had called for "progressive unemployment" and André Breton's Surrealist "rules" had forbidden regular work'; Shohat and Stam, p. 309.   **117** Gilberto Freyre, quoted in Evenson, 1973, p. 210. This point of view echoes Situationist thinking. But

John Maynard Keynes also imagined that the richer societies become, the more time they will be able to dedicate to leisure. For Le Corbusier, too, leisure was 'the true occupation' of the (urban) 'civilisation machiniste', which he imagined would reduce the working day to six or even four hours. His third 1936 lecture in Rio de Janeiro, on 7 August, was entirely dedicated to this subject; Le Corbusier, 2006, pp. 96–117. As Yannis Tsiomis points out in his notes to the lecture, Le Corbusier referred in his *La Ville radieuse* to leisure as 'a social danger', stressing the importance of its transformation into a 'disciplined function' of the city. Tsiomis observes that Le Corbusier's vision of organized leisure reveals 'also a Fordism and a new capitalist logic, [based on the notion of] the worker as consumer'; Tsiomis, 2006, p. 36.   **118** Rego, p. 12.

Adept at employing grand gestures to question established hierarchies, at Ibirapuera Park Niemeyer monumentalized the space of the sinuous *marquise* – a space outside the architectural programme – radicalizing idleness and turning the 'useless', unproductive space of the vast, covered esplanade into the central space of the celebrations of the four hundredth anniversary of Brazil's industrial capital. This unprogrammatic space in-between became the central focus of the design and the unifying element, revealing the large scale and urban dimension of Ibirapuera Park.[119] Pointing to a utopian ludic life, it also prefigured the idea of an age of pure leisure achieved through industrial development. In 1964 Lúcio Costa also celebrated this idea at the Brazilian Pavilion of the thirteenth Milan Triennale, where he staged a utopian Brazilian world of tropical beaches (in Marcel Gautherot's black-and-white photographs covering one wall of the room) and futuristic architecture (represented by Gautherot's images of Brasília on the opposite wall), inhabiting it with fourteen colourful hammocks and a few guitars and inviting visitors to 'relax' ('riposatevi').[120] Although the Ibirapuera *marquise* was much abbreviated in the final realization, its innovative spatial conditions and sense of surprise and spectacle sustain its popularity among young and old city dwellers, who flood Ibirapuera Park on Sundays and demonstrate their immense capacity for improvising ever-new temporary uses for this most flexible, unhierarchical and empowering of spaces. In Brazil, it is a popular saying that every city craves its beach; in São Paulo, a great part of the beach needs to be covered for protection against the city's notorious drizzle.

The amplification of this programmatically peripheral space underscores Niemeyer's commitment to the redemption of the 'pleasure principle' that functionalist moralizing ideologies repressed. His sensuous contours cast in reinforced concrete and his ambitious structures atop adventurously shaped columns, evoking images of natural, wild growth, articulate the desire to bring together the worlds of 'jungle and school', industry and undomesticated nature. He thereby paints an image of that utopian Brazilian 'blend of reason and emotion' sung by Freyre – a world of Apollonian and Dionysian elements.[121]

Lúcio Costa, Brazilian Pavilion at the thirteenth Milan Triennale, 1964

Eurocentric Reactions to 'jungle growth in the worst sense'

In 1951 and 1953 respectively, the first two São Paulo Art Biennales, the second with an international architecture section, served to publicize the latest trends in Brazilian architecture. The 'magnet of São Paulo, the bonanza-city of contemporary architecture', drew 'the masters from Europe and North America', stimulating mixed reactions to 'a vigorous movement' (Walter Gropius) with 'a growing architectural maturity' (Ernesto Rogers). The majority of foreign visitors found it difficult to come to terms with what they perceived as an 'effort to make a show' (Hiroshi Ohye), remaining ambivalent as to whether the 'exuberance' that was the hallmark of the Brazilian 'fantasy of functionalism' (John Summerson) was to be valued as 'a wonderful quality' or condemned as 'too much freedom of the imagination' (Hiroshi Ohye). Ernesto Rogers, editor of *Casabella*, reported 'exaggerated, arbitrary, and diametrically opposed judgements' ensuing from 'a certain overbearing novelty in [the modern Brazilian buildings'] appearance', and 'a new kind of liberty . . . [at times] degenerate[ing] in licence and caprice.'[122]

One year earlier, Costa had written that the Brazilian architects' innovative formal vocabulary did not represent a search for 'originality' for its own sake, but 'the sacred obsession of all truly

119 A large, meandering *marquise* was also the central unifying element of Niemeyer's 1953 version of his Quitandinha-Petrópolis residential complex (unbuilt), set in a green park; published in Papadaki, 1960, pp. 89–90. **120** Lúcio Costa, 'XIII Trienal de Milão: "Tempo livre" Pavilhão do Brasil: RIPOSATEVI' (1964), in Lúcio Costa, 1997, pp. 408–9. 'Free Time' was the theme of the thirteenth Milan Triennale. **121** Freyre, 1970, p. xxiii. **122** 'Report on Brazil', 1954.

creative artists to unveil the world of forms not yet revealed'.[123] Nevertheless, the Paulista 'thick *pilotis*, thin *pilotis*, *pilotis* of whimsical shapes lacking any structural rhyme or reason, disposed all over the place ... born of ... the spirit of decorativeness' prompted Max Bill to inveigh against 'spectacular buildings', which for him represented 'anti-social academicism ... utter anarchy in building ... jungle growth in the worst sense'.[124] Effectively, Niemeyer's most ardent detractor took the side of those limiting 'old-fashioned' formulae that Lewis Mumford had described four years earlier as 'a new kind of academicism, in which a very limited system of architectural forms takes the place of the classic five orders'.[125]

A retrospective of Bill's work, at the São Paulo Museum of Modern Art in 1950 had inspired Brazil's Concretist movement, and the following year he had been awarded first prize for his sculpture *Tripartite Unity* (1947–48) at the first São Paulo Biennale. He presented his scathing criticisms of Brazilian architecture in a talk delivered on 9 June 1953 at the Faculty of Architecture and Urban Development of the University of São Paulo, published in 1954 in the *Architectural Review*'s 'Report on Brazil'. To this day, Bill's dis-

dainful comments have been uncritically repeated countless times, to the point of ennui.[126] Brazil's foreign guest argued that in Europe he 'might well' have addressed 'artistic questions and [spoken] of beauty from the point of view of defending art against pure rationalism'.[127] In his book on Robert Maillart's bridges a few years earlier (1949) he had celebrated the synthesis of art and technique. He was convinced, however, that, in Brazil, such talk would reflect 'the most terrible academic unrealism'. For Brazil was too poor to indulge in aesthetics – a domain Bill would rather keep exclusive to the Old World.

The Swiss artist's snobbish and deeply insulting attitude enraged Niemeyer, perhaps reminding him of his grandmother's similar approach towards those she assumed inferior, which he deplored from an early age. 'Take that cloth off your head,' Niemeyer remembers her bursting out at the housemaid, 'Colored folk don't wear such things.'[128] In the first issue of *Módulo* (March 1955), Niemeyer declared: 'we are a young people with a cultural tradition still in the making. Naturally, this exposes us to the criticism of those who consider themselves representatives of a superior civilization ... Nevertheless, we are simple and confident in our work.'[129] Responding to debates regarding the extent to which architecture ought 'to cease to be one of the arts, but instead to provide, with the maximum economy and efficiency, a diagrammatic background as anonymous as the motor car', Niemeyer affirmed: 'We consider architecture a work of art.'[130]

Owing to its social content and regardless of its typically Brazilian architectural language and veritable indulgence in what Bill elsewhere frowned upon as superfluous decorative display, Reidy's Pedregulho Social Housing Complex was held by the Swiss artist and all other foreign guests to be exceptionally successful.[131] Yet Bill extended his invective to the Ministry of Education, which Gropius, also in the 'Report on Brazil', lauded as 'a landmark of modern architecture'.[132] Max Bill protested that this building had not 'been conceived in proper organic relation to the conditions of the country'.[133]

In an interview published in a popular Brazilian journal in 1953 he attacked the *azulejos* of the celebrated Ministry of Education as 'useless' and 'anti-architectural' and derided 'the exaggerat-

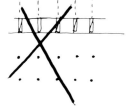

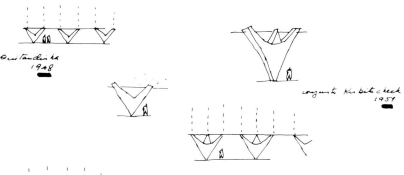

Niemeyer dedicated one of the thirteen panels he prepared for the 1965 exhibition *Oscar Niemeyer: l'architecte de Brasilia* to his 'whimsical' *pilotis* (Musée des Arts Décoratifs, Palais du Louvre, Paris, curated by Jean Petit and Guy Dupuis).

123 Lúcio Costa, 1952, p. 7. **124** Bill, 1954, pp. 238–39. It is said that it was the *pilotis* of Niemeyer's Edifício California that prompted Bill's remark. **125** Lewis Mumford, 1949, p. 174. **126** In 1971, Bruno Zevi commented on Bill's 'very harsh' and 'un-diplomatic' criticism, but proceeded to assert his own disapproval of Brazilian architecture's 'extrovert taste', its 'mania for glass façades' and their 'antidote' in the form of *brises-soleil*, its exuberance, fantasy, barbarian disorder and so on. Without revealing the reasoning behind his judgement, Zevi pronounced Brazilian architecture an architecture of 'escape' and 'uncertainty', in 'a country with no permanent values and no stable economy'; Zevi, 2003, pp. 163–66. **127** Bill, 1954, pp. 238–39. **128** Niemeyer, 2002, p. 8. **129** Niemeyer, 1955a, p. 47. **130** Richards, 1950, p. 179; Niemeyer, 1955a, p. 47. **131** Lewis Mumford, on the other hand, raised doubts about Pedregulho's 'somewhat over-dramatized primary school and gymnasium'; Lewis Mumford, 1956, p. 85. **132** Gropius and Gropius, 1954, p. 237. **133** Bill, 1954, p. 238.

ed individualism' and 'excessive baroquism' of the Pampulha complex.[134] Bursting out against the Brazilian 'pioneers', whom he judged 'devoid of all decency and of all responsibility', he reproached them for 'barbarism', 'whimsicalities' and disregard for the social purpose of architecture, denouncing precisely that defence of artistic freedom against rigid ideologisms with which he would have sided on European ground. He eulogized Mies van der Rohe, 'whose work refuses to be rational or functional, yet is characterized by an unequalled aesthetic and technical perfection', but assailed the Brazilians for the 'folly' of 'self-expression'.[135] Measuring Brazil 'with a Swiss yardstick', as Mrs Gropius put it, Bill rejected the Brazilians' claims to art and beauty, and found them guilty of overstepping their measure, and taking 'jungle growth' outside their 'splendid natural conditions'.[136] Somewhat surprisingly, he attributed to '"the latest Paris fashion" as set in the workrooms of Le Corbusier' the Brazilian 'baroque' distortions of form and pursuit of 'sensation', but hastened to add that Le Corbusier's ideas have 'sometimes been misunderstood' in Brazil.[137]

The three members of the architecture jury at the 1953 São Paulo Biennale, Alvar Aalto, Walter Gropius and Ernesto Rogers, did not fully share Bill's views. Aalto had already clearly expressed his own opposition to narrow notions of building economy and, on this occasion, he promptly wrote to Niemeyer to express his disapproval of Bill's polemic: 'today, I put the last shovel over Max Bill.'[138] Nevertheless, Bill's antagonistic moralisms still echoed in Pevsner's 1961 analysis of 'the new post-modern anti-rationalism' and 'anti-functionalism' that he diagnosed in Niemeyer's work as well as in Le Corbusier's Notre-Dame-du-Haut at Ronchamp and Chandigarh Secretariat (1953), in Jørn Utzon's Sydney Opera House (1957–73) and in Hans Scharoun's 'old Expressionism'.[139]

Critical voices were also raised among Brazilians. The gaúcho Demétrio Ribeiro (1916–2003) criticized modern architecture for remaining 'isolated from the people and reserved to bourgeois landowners'.[140] In two articles, entitled 'Le Corbusier and Imperialism' (1951) and 'The Roads of Modern Architecture' (1952), the Paulista João Batista Vilanova Artigas (1915–85), who would play a leading role in Brazil's architectural scene over the following decades, pronounced modern architecture an instrument of state propaganda and demagoguery, serving commercial interests and 'reinforcing the penetration of imperialism'.[141] In 1952, Eduardo Guimarães, editor of Arquitetura e Engenharia, warned against a 'form-creation fever' that threatened to undermine the excellence of Brazilian architecture.[142] The following year, however, in an article published in L'Architecture d'Aujour-

d'hui, Mário Pedrosa (1900–81), internationally acclaimed art critic, curator of the second São Paulo Biennale and co-founder of the Trotskyist Liga Comunista do Brasil, with his brother-in-law, the French Surrealist poet Benjamin Péret, presented his politically charged interpretation of, and optimistic forecasts for, 'The Modern Architecture of Brazil'.[143]

Pedrosa suggested that modern architecture in Brazil was free of 'primitivism' and 'ideological nationalism', and thus different from contemporaneous Brazilian literature, music and political writing. He emphasized Lúcio Costa's concern for the reconciliation of art and technique and, most importantly, Costa's noble aim, shared by his fellow Brazilian Modernist architects, of 'making the benefits of industrialization accessible to the majority'. Guided by a 'revolutionary spirit', this 'purist group' behind the 'miracle' of the Ministry of Education, argued Pedrosa, benefited from the political conditions of the totalitarian Estado Nôvo, 'utilizing the absolute powers of the dictators . . . without renouncing their own [democratic and socialist] ideas'. Pedrosa compared the nature of the patronage of the 'all-powerful governors' behind the 'magnificent caprice' of Pampulha to that of seventeenth- and eighteenth-century absolutist princes, despots like Louis XIV invoked also by Le Corbusier, who longed for an era when immense projects could be realized at command. Pedrosa spoke of the 'initial faustian deal of the new architecture with the dictatorship', and highlighted Reidy's Pedregulho as the emblematic fruit of Brazil's democratic era. Pedrosa also linked Niemeyer's sinuous curves to the colonial tradition, and particularly to the Baroque churches of Minas Gerais – realizations of 'the creative genius of the people' – holding the architect of Pampulha as a worthy successor to the eighteenth-century Portuguese stonemason José Pereira Arouca, but cautioning against what he perceived as a tendency to shed programmatic restrictions. Finally, the Brazilian critic proclaimed Burle Marx's concession of 'citizenship to the plebeian plants' as a further indication of Brazilian Modernism's reconciliation with popular traditions, and praised the integration of the arts in the new architecture for turning attention away from individual artists and transforming art into a 'practical and effective activity'.[144]

Lúcio Costa's response to Max Bill – in an interview published in Manchete on 13 June 1953 – dwelt on questions of formal expression, defending the conception of architecture as high art and answering Bill's 'prejudiced' critique of the azulejos and Baroque influences of the Ministry of Education. Costa expressed his unreserved agreement with all the praise Pedregulho had deservedly received but hastened to add: 'All Brazilian architecture in its cur-

134 Max Bill, quoted in Hugo Segawa, 2002, p. 109.   135 Bill, 2003, p. 121.   136 Gropius and Gropius, p. 237. In contrast to Bill, in 2004 Edwin Heathcote recognized in Brazilian architecture 'a terrific development of that vein of socialist Modernism in which public buildings are as extravagantly beautiful as the villas of the wealthy'; Heathcote, 2004, p. W18.   137 Bill, 1954, pp. 238–39.

138 Alvar Aalto, quoted in Niemeyer, 2004, p. 158.   139 Pevsner, 1961, pp. 230–40.   140 Demétrio Ribeiro, quoted in Segawa, 2002, p. 113.   141 Artigas, 2003a, pp. 195–96.   142 Eduardo Guimarães, quoted in Lara, 2001, p. 155. In 1954, Guimarães argued for 'the inclusion of the common man as the architect's client'; Lara, 2001, p. 156.   143 Pedrosa, 2003a.   144 Pedrosa, 2003a, pp. 98–105.

rent state, including Pedregulho, owes its existence to Pampulha, a building complex for the capitalist bourgeoisie.'[145]

In his second monograph on Oscar Niemeyer, published in 1956, Stamo Papadaki commented on the hegemonic discourse of the 'Report on Brazil':

> We learn here that all there is left for the designer to do now is to learn the rules of the grammar as they are established. And Brazilian architects were found, according to the same report, to abuse the grammar without fully comprehending its rules . . . It is true, however, that a Japanese architect, Hiroshi Ohye, was able to detect and express with words the 'state of exuberance' which exists in Brazil.
>
> Now, why will such exuberance not make an ideal climate for architecture? This question should have been at the basis of any attempt at serious evaluation of Brazilian buildings; it was assumed, instead, that our world must be a grey one, our problems average and our language conforming to the style of financial reports. The distress resulting from the impact of such exuberance . . . permeates every criticism and every comment; and it is exuberance which became the real evil spirit, the villain behind the scenes. We could only hope that such an attitude was the result of a passing postwar fatigue and of the emotional impasses that this fatigue had created. The rights to lyricism cannot be clothed with grammatical canons . . . The findings of the new psychology in depth, the current desire to implement humanity in a continental scale and the growing understanding of aspirations in terms of global regions, rather than in sizes of parochial units alone, will further enhance the chances for an exuberant, even heroic architecture. The progressive dematerialization that we witness in the recent buildings of Niemeyer . . . points [to] the dawn of a still greater lyrical outburst.[146]

Niemeyer's own response focused on a contextualization of the Brazilian architecture of self-expression and individualism that so disturbed socially minded Europeans. He admitted that 'the lack of human content is the main reason for the shortfalls of modern [Brazilian] architecture, reflecting . . . the social contradictions of the environment in which it develops'. Social disequilibrium, the lack of an effective social basis and of large-scale planning, combined with the lack of a powerful industry with prefabrication systems, Niemeyer argued, have resulted in an architecture characterized by 'inconsistency . . . a carefree attitude towards economy, and a variety and richness of form'. He concluded: 'We refuse to follow an architecture cold and rigid – of European persuasion – just like we reject a 'social architecture' under current conditions. The first course would deprive our architecture of what is fresh and creative in it, while the second would make it deceptive, artificial and demagogic.'[147]

Denouncing social-housing 'ghettoes' for reproducing spaces of 'discrimination and poverty', Niemeyer proposed instead mixed housing, where 'rich and poor live together'.[148] An architecture with socialist pretensions, he firmly believed, cannot function as an agent of social reform in capitalist society; on the contrary, it would constitute a betrayal of genuine social struggle, concealing social deprivation behind a functionalist socialist façade, fetishized in the service of political demagoguery. In 1965, Ernst Bloch agreed with Niemeyer on both fronts. He condemned 'the lack of fantasy, still being artificially produced', supporting the quest for innovation and an architecture that exposes the fragmentation of social reality rather than offering the illusion of coherence. Doubting the value of Neue Sachlichkeit rationality, he commented: 'The question remains unanswered as to whether . . . the unornamented honesty of pure functional form might not itself turn out to be a fig leaf behind which a lack of honesty in the remaining relations lies concealed.'[149] In creative experimentation and expressionism, Bloch and Niemeyer saw a radical possibility for social critique that may, in the long term, function as a lever for social reform.

145 Lúcio Costa, 2003, pp. 181–84.   **146** Papadaki, 1956, pp. 9–10.
147 Niemeyer, 2003b, pp. 184–88. Although in this text Niemeyer does not refer explicitly to Max Bill's talk, it is fairly clear that he responds to the criticism of the Swiss artist. Hugo Segawa points out that, unfortunately, the Brazilian architectural review *Módulo* reacted to criticism from abroad with attempts to 'disqualify the critic rather than the criticism'; Segawa, 2002, p. 110. See also Niemeyer, 2003a, pp. 123–27. In an article published in *Módulo* in early 1957, Niemeyer also criticized what he considered inappropriate uses of popularized elements of modern Brazilian architecture, such as the various devices of solar control, cladding materials, V-shaped columns, free forms and inclined façades. Illustrating his points with sketches, he argued that, at times, especially in so-called 'modern houses', these elements were employed without a proper understanding of their 'practical or functional purpose', without a sense of proportion and so on: Niemeyer, 1957, pp. 5–10. Twenty years later, Niemeyer lamented the 'invasion of our cities, parks, hills and beaches' by private apartment blocks, which he held responsible for the degradation of Brazil's urban environment, 'ostensibly disrespectful of man and nature'. With nostalgia, he evoked the 'enthusiasm of the 1940s', when Brazilian architects believed in the possibility of 'the minimization of private property and its substitution with collective complexes, with parks, swimming pools, schools, clubs, etc'; Niemeyer, 1977a, p. 38.   **148** Oscar Niemeyer, in 'O arquiteto da paz'.   **149** Ernst Bloch, quoted in Heynen, p. 124. In the following decade, Brazil's dictatorial state used the provision of mass housing 'as a soothing balm to [the masses'] civic wounds'; letter from Sandra Cavalcanti, future chair of the Banco Nacional de Habitação (BNH), to dictator Castelo Branco (1964–66), quoted in Arantes, p. 187.

Chapter Five

Dwelling in the 'New World in the Tropics'

The sites of public memory in the twentieth century are no longer public buildings ... the twentieth century is from the beginning, and as it closes, obsessed with the house ... virtually all architects of this century have elaborated their most important architectural ideas through the design of houses ... To architects, the house has the appeal of the experiment ... The house becomes a laboratory for ideas.

Beatriz Colomina, 'The Private Site of Public Memory'

The more conservative countries always favour the maintenance of tradition, which can only be justified in the case of the individual house, a type of structure which represents but an 'accident' in the new architectural era.

In reality, the bourgeois dwelling, no matter how luxurious, will never be able to express our era. It will be the buildings of collective interest that will come to represent contemporary architecture: schools, hospitals, theatres, stadia, sports clubs, collective housing, etc.

Oscar Niemeyer, 'Pampulha: l'architecture'

The 'one-man number' of the *Architectural Review* for May 1944 featured Niemeyer's recently completed works: the Pampulha complex, his own house on Rua Carvalho de Azevedo and the Cavalcanti House in Rio de Janeiro (1940), 'which out-Swedes the Swedes in charm'. The theme of the issue was described as 'the integration of contemporary architectural practice with eighteenth-century Landscape Theory'. Viewing twentieth-century Brazilian architecture through a persistently neocolonialist, Eurocentric perspective that asserts the primacy of the Western canon and seeks to establish Brazil's debts to European centres of civilization, the British periodical presented the Cavalcanti House as an emphatic example of modern designers' 'debt to Lord Burlington and his followers':

There is for instance the variety, sensitiveness and apparent casualness of the planting which, applied though it is to the small suburban villa, remains a direct product of Picturesque theory. There is, too, the plan itself which so obviously practises those principles of free-planning (Sharawaggi) which were given their first try-out in the gardens of William Kent. As to the courtyard ... Sir Uvedale Price would have blushed with pleasure to see the variation in textures between the different materials of the elevation, the creeper clinging nostalgically to a column, the door tucked away behind a shrub and another column, the shaggy tufts of grass popping up between the flagstones.[1]

In the context of Brazil's Modernist cultural theory and practice, it seems appropriate to speak of a real, twentieth-century Brazilian 'Garden Revolution' rather than a 'direct product' of European theories. For Brazil's Modernist turn towards the 'virgin jungle' represented a deliberate turn away from Europe to embrace Brazil's tropical Otherness, which took the form of an Antropofagist devouring and remixing of the European legacy. As already noted, Roberto Burle Marx, perhaps the worthiest successor of William Kent – the 'true father of modern gardening' – was acclaimed in Brazil for his de-Europeanization and re-Orientalization of the Brazilian landscape.[2] His tropical gardens injected Modernist 'machines for living in' with the Dionysian spirit of *brasilidade*, playing a role in the Other Modernist architecture of Brazil that was as vital – if not more so – as that of the *azulejo* murals and various sunscreening devices responding to functional as well as aesthetic requirements.

Burle Marx's vertical gardens or living *xaxim*, totemic columns composed of epiphytic bromeliads, orchids or philodendrons embedded in metal, cork or tree-fern structures, 'colonize[d] the air space' of skyscrapers and other urban environments. They reinterpreted popular traditions and the natural phenomena of the Brazilian forest in an effort 'to exorcise or challenge modernization and its practices of environmental destruction'. As Rossana Vaccarino points out, Burle Marx also progressively included archi-

1 *Architectural Review*, 1944b, pp. 134, 113, 130.   2 Alexander Pope, quoted in Panofsky, 1995, p. 131. For Burle Marx, see Chapter One, pp. 38–41.

tectural elements in his gardens: free-standing walls with concrete relief patterns or *azulejo* murals that contributed to his chromatic scheme; sinuous canopies and running benches; trellises made of concrete lattice-work or ceramic grilles that guaranteed sun and wind control. Burle Marx's syncretic designs mixed these structures with compositions of indigenous and non-indigenous tropical plants – 'artificial ecological associations', as he called them. Afro-Brazilian folklore and reinvented traditional Portuguese crafts such as black-and-white *pedra portuguesa* pavement mosaics, were also incorporated to create a modern, *mestiço* Brazilian landscape.[3]

Dionysization and hybridization extended far beyond the gardens of Brazilian Modernist architecture. Unlike Lord Burlington and his austere Palladian designs for Chiswick House (1723–29), Niemeyer imbued his structures with the intoxicating rhythms of tropical nature, bringing together the diverse traditions of Europe and Brazil in irreverent Antropofagist mixtures, producing an endless variety of artificial architectural associations. Like other houses designed by Niemeyer, the Cavalcanti House combines modern with rustic materials and techniques, and programmatic spaces that respond to both modern and traditional living patterns: a reinforced-concrete frame and dry granite-chip walls; a lethargic pitched roof with deep overhanging eaves clad in red terracotta tiles beside freely undulating walls; stucco white and deep-blue wall surfaces; a garage and vegetable garden. The free plan of the house exploits the possibilities offered by modern construction, while its spatial articulation and material palette link it to local colonial precedents.

Kenneth Frampton sees both the Cavalcanti and Niemeyer's own house as 'neo-vernacular dwelling[s]', failing to discern the contrast between the two designs. To start with, the large

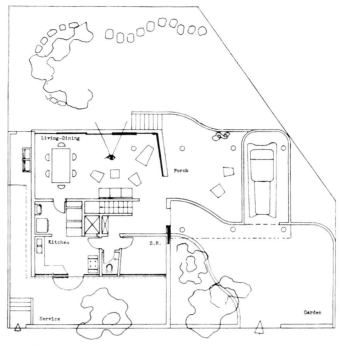

ground floor plan

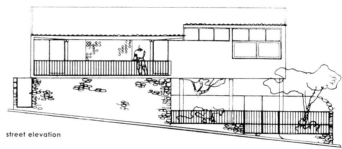

street elevation

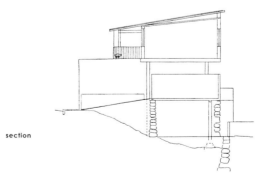

section

Left and above, Cavalcanti House, Rio de Janeiro, 1940

3 Vaccarino, 2002, pp. 220–21, 230–31.

Cavalcanti property has two clearly distinct entrances from the street. The principal, wider entrance is found at the centre of the iron railing that marks the permeable limit of the lower half of the property, inviting views towards an entrance courtyard and the mountains and the lagoon in the distance. The upper half of the property presents a solid, one-storey-high masonry front to the street, which conceals the kitchen and service quarters beyond the vegetable garden. At the top end of the dry granite-chip wall, a wooden door leads to the narrow service yard on its axis, four steps below street level, at the side of the house, past the vegetable garden to the right.

Instead of the spatial fluidity, apparent informality and seemingly random assemblage of irregular structural elements of the contemporaneous Niemeyer House, the Cavalcanti residence has a conventionally ordered plan. A number of gestures like the deep-blue wall undulating past the slender white structural *pilotis*, the free-standing column in the living room, or the oblique wall between living room and porch express spatial freedom as a benefit of modern technology, but do not compromise clarity. And while the Niemeyer House acknowledges the informal architecture of the *morros*, the Cavalcanti House is primarily indebted to those rural, 'beautiful old Portuguese buildings' that Niemeyer first 'learned to . . . appreciate' at the studio of Lúcio Costa: 'so sober and rigid, with their thick walls of stone or *taipa de pilão* (gravel-clay wattle), their gently sloping slate tiles contrasting with their whitewashed walls'.[4]

A precisely orchestrated sequence of spaces stages the passage from public to private living areas, leading gradually from the tarmac of the street, through the house, out to the luxuriant garden, which merges with the fantastic Carioca landscape. The light, iron railing separates the street from the flagstone-paved courtyard that provides access to the garage and the house itself, flanked by tropical border planting. The free-standing, deep-blue wall defines the path towards the main door of the house, concealing and thus protecting the privacy of a covered, 'wide veranda that [functions as] an extension of the living room, in the Portuguese style' of Niemeyer's 'favorite colonial farmhouse'.[5] A short flight of steps down from the veranda at the rear of the house unfolds the family's private garden, informally laid out and commanding ravishing views towards Rio's celebrated mountains and the lagoa. Internal and external living areas are entirely turned towards the view, with the kitchen and service areas insulating them from the street.

A book Niemeyer published in 2005, entitled *Casas onde morei* (*Houses Where I Lived*), visits the houses he has inhabited during his long life.[6] In his memoirs and other texts he refers frequently to these houses, of which he has fond memories, weaving together memory and spatial experience, nature and architecture, evoking what Stamo Papadaki refers to as 'the taste for the "good life" which permeates Brazil', where 'nature is not an enemy and man's earthly condition does not depend wholly on his inevitable death'.[7] When he reminisces about the houses he has lived in, it is almost exclusively their exterior spaces and views that Niemeyer revisits: the veranda of the house where he was born, 'where the family gathered' after dinner; the house of an uncle who 'settled . . . under the trees . . . like Robinson Crusoe'; or the mountain retreat he built for his father, which he observed 'becoming almost an extension of the garden'.[8] The architect, photographer and writer G.E. Kidder Smith, who travelled to Brazil with Philip L. Goodwin in 1942, collecting material for the 1943 *Brazil Builds* exhibition at the MoMA, was astounded by Rio's 'thick jungles tumbling into the very city itself . . . [and] gardeners . . . employed not to culture but control. There is a steady "back-to-the-city" movement on the part of the local vegetation', he observed, and added: '[Brazil's] architecture is bound up in [her] physical conditions, and at its best expresses them admirably.'[9]

Dwelling in a World where 'nature is not an enemy'

In Niemeyer's houses, the garden is not regarded as an appendix to the house: on the contrary, it is as if the house were built to support the full enjoyment of the tropical garden and the natural landscape, which lies beyond the property's boundaries but is always skilfully integrated into the design. The relation between the house and the marvellous landscape beyond is markedly different from that pursued by Le Corbusier, for example. For the latter, the landscape needed to be limited, framed, geometrified, in order to be enjoyed through carefully positioned openings on the garden walls or intricately detailed windows on the house walls. With a grand *mise en scène*, in his Rio lectures of 1936 Le Corbusier demonstrated precisely how the Carioca landscape 'framed all around . . . enters the room'.[10] His spectator contemplates the landscape tableau from an armchair at the centre of a single-point perspective, protected by the architectural enclosure.

Closer to Charlotte Perriand in her Weekend Waterside House of 1934, Niemeyer seeks continuity between architecture and natural landscape – the gardens or terraces of his houses meld with the environment. Rather than defence perimeters, the various built elements of Niemeyer's houses are treated as sites for opportunist encounters between nature and artifice. Semi-open spaces like those within *pilotis* do not separate living quarters from gardens but mediate between open gardens and enclosed spaces, inviting the gardens to penetrate into the buildings. The description of his father's weekend house at Mendes (1949), a two-hour

4 Niemeyer, 2000b, p. 24. **5** Niemeyer, 2000b, p. 121. **6** Niemeyer, 2005. **7** Papadaki, 1960, p. 9. **8** Niemeyer, 2000b, pp. 7, 10, 28. **9** Kidder Smith, p. 78. **10** See Casali, pp. 63–73, quotation on p. 70.

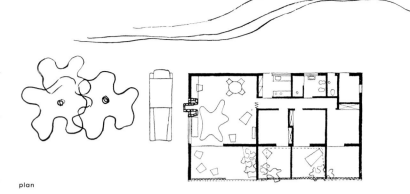

drive from Rio, reveals Niemeyer's penchant for privacy, simplicity of accommodation and, above all, communion with nature:

> I had a house built in the Mendes area for my father, but the place won me over, too. It was a quiet location in the Rio de Janeiro mountains, free from unexpected encounters and the impertinent beach-going socialite set. I picked a small lot on the road to Vassouras through which flowed a pleasant stream that, at the time, was swollen by seasonal rains. In just one month I built the house, making use of an old chicken coop that I split up into living room, bedrooms, kitchen, and so forth. The roofing was made of asbestos tiles and the facade was covered by a wooden trellis. The little house shaped up nicely as the creepers flowered, becoming almost an extension of the garden, homey and picturesque.

> As I had intended, I spent carnival and other holidays there for several years. Through the low, horizontal living-room window, we could see the rapidly growing garden: the lawn, the clumps of bamboo trees, the bridge over the stream, the enormous *tecomas* – gift from Nature that became our national tree – and the path winding up to the side road . . . the bamboos were pretty and I would lie there in a hammock, peering between the branches at the infinite spaces beyond, imagining myself in the desert like Saint-Exupéry, riding on the back of this old planer, roaming among the stars.[11]

plan

The trapezoidal profile of this modest, compact, single-storey house, framed by the soft ridge lines of the hills, expresses its east-ward orientation towards a view of rolling land. All rooms are arranged in a line, with service rooms at the rear, behind the bed-rooms, where the ceiling is at its lowest. The solid, whitewashed side walls and roof project forward to contain a row of terraces. On the north elevation a narrow horizontal slit is balanced by a vertical chimney in rustic rubble stone projecting from the white-washed wall. The two central bedroom terraces are open to the sky and all three are fully screened with a wooden lattice, less dense at the top, which defines the oblique plane of the east ele-vation, divided into five bays. The living-room terrace is fully cov-ered and only partially screened. Entering the terrace through the second, open bay, which the creepers were encouraged to reduce to human height, the visitor faces a solid wall. Typically, the house entrance is unmarked and uneventful, diagonally opposite the open bay, through the glazing on the living-room wall, con-cealed behind the first-bay trellis, which ensures protection from the sun.

Prominently situated on the banks of the artificial lake of Pampulha, the weekend house for Juscelino Kubitschek (1943) is

11 Kidder Smith, pp. 28–29.

Weekend House for Niemeyer's father, Mendes, Rio de Janeiro state, 1949

set back from and raised higher than the street, which it greets with a garden designed by Roberto Burle Marx in a predominant purple hue. Walking towards the house or away from it, the visitor soon becomes aware of the precise orchestration of constantly changing views. Through the opening in a minimal low railing, a flagstone-paved driveway curves as it rises towards the garage at the lowest, left end of the house, then branches to the right to form ramps that give access to the house through two casual openings in the glazed façade. These glass doors that open out to the raised terrace are characteristically unconventional points of entry into the house; as in other houses by Niemeyer, there is no marked, solid 'front door' defending the interior and representing the private owner. The conservatory behind the glazed façade is separated from the living room by a latticed screen. This sheltered belvedere and the elevated terrace with a tall palm enjoy views towards Burle Marx's garden, with his signature great sweeps of colour, flowing curves and still water surface multiplying the effect of the striking forms of the plants in the organically shaped, rock-studded beds. From the vantage point of the terrace, with its uninterrupted views towards the lake, the garden appears to merge with the surrounding landscape.

The plan of the Kubitschek House mirrors that of the weekend house for M. Passos. The bedrooms, directly above the garage, are accessed via a short flight of steps from the living room on the middle level. The internal latticed screen, parallel to the lower, glazed part of the façade, protects the living room against excessive heat while also discreetly guaranteeing privacy. A new variation of the *brise-soleil* has been inserted above the curtain wall, under the inward-sloping, asymmetrical pitched roofs. A dense row of untreated tree branches acts as sunscreen, forming a dark frieze that underscores the building's bold, white outline and grants it an appearance of lightness. When viewed from the street, the house appears to have been conceived as an essential part of the garden, adding depth and textural contrasts, not unlike one of the free-standing ornamental walls with abstract geometric patterns that Burle Marx would soon begin to introduce into his polyphonic landscapes. The domestic courtyard to the rear of the building is adorned with Paulo Werneck's abstract, blue-and-white *pastilha* wall mosaic, set against Alfredo Volpi's *azulejo*-paved floor and echoing the free curves of the lawns.

Over the following decades, in descriptions accompanying a number of domestic schemes, addressed to his clients and always entitled 'necessary explanation', Niemeyer consistently emphasized the virtues of simplicity, lightness and transparency, a pleasant and welcoming atmosphere, and, most importantly, harmonious integration with garden and nature, 'as appropriate'.[12] He also frequently listed the elements he gladly borrowed

12 Presentation folios, Oscar Niemeyer Foundation Archive.

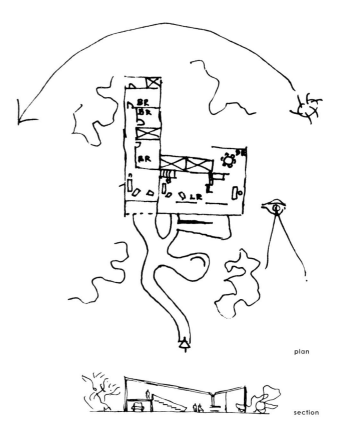

plan

section

Weekend House for Juscelino Kubitschek, Pampulha, Belo Horizonte, Minas Gerais, 1943; garden designed by Roberto Burle Marx

Weekend House for Juscelino Kubitschek: view of main elevation with ramp leading to the living-room terrace

from colonial *fazendas*: their horizontality, the way they spread over the terrain, their large verandas, whitewashed walls with windows painted in bright colours and traditional ceramic roof tiles. His sketches and drawings were always furnished, however, with modern furniture of his own design and populated with oft-topless women and men enjoying themselves by the pool.

Niemeyer's early domestic commissions combine features indebted to colonial prototypes with modern construction methods and the spatial fluidity that these made possible, which came to characterize modern, informal, open living. The interplay between indoor and outdoor spaces is at once modern and evocative of the way of living in Brazil's rural patriarchal dwellings. Many of these early Niemeyer houses were designed for the urban, bourgeois, modern descendents of the Portuguese aristocracy of the colonial country manors.

At the centre of the house for Francisco Inácio Peixoto at Cataguases (1943, structural engineer Albino Froufe), there is a three-dimensionally open, common living space with interconnected living, dining and music areas that unfold over three levels and overflow to covered porches on two levels. From the twelve-seat dining table at the centre of the composition, the eye can roam freely through the various spaces and across the terrace to

the gardens and landscape beyond. Only the study, at first-floor level, can be closed off, but it also opens out to the veranda. The skilful sequencing of spaces brings to mind the Loosian concept of the *Raumplan* (space plan). Secondary functions are accommodated along the perimeter of the plan, with the bedrooms on the first floor in a line along the north side, protected by adjustable *brises-soleil*. The house is entered from the street through a deep portico under the bedroom wing, but is clearly turned towards the view to the rear over sloping gardens, which coincides with the favourable southern orientation. The pitched, tiled roof oversails the veranda, and before it reaches the latter's outer line it is connected to a long, two-storey-high canopy, jutting out beyond the veranda and running parallel to the south elevation, protecting the part of the ground-floor terrace that borders the garden. The slender, round steel columns that support the giant canopy on the garden side betray an effort to minimize interruption of the views towards the landscape, contrasting with the sturdier, square columns on the internal side of the canopy.

With gardens by Roberto Burle Marx, furniture by Joaquim Tenreiro, sculpture by José Pedrosa and paintings by Cândido Portinari, the Peixoto house became a veritable 'manifesto of modern sophistication'. Arguably, it was the industrialist Francisco

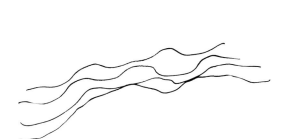

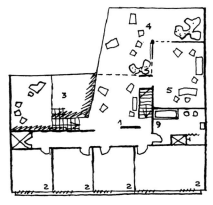

first floor plan

1 living room
2 bedroom
3 void
4 porch
5 study
9 bathroom

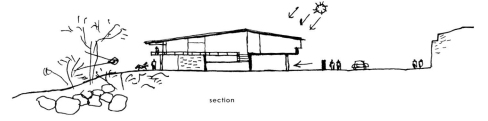

section

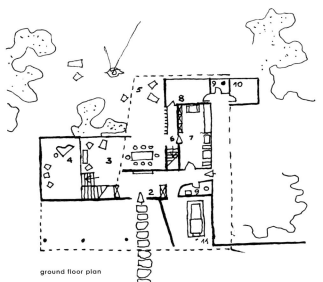

ground floor plan

1 street entrance
2 entrance hall
3 living room and dining room
4 music room open to living room
5 porch
6 service corridor
7 kitchen
8, 9, 10 service quarters

Francisco Inácio Peixoto House, Cataguases, Minas Gerais, 1943

Francisco Inácio Peixoto House: view of living space on three levels from the intermediate level

Francisco Inácio Peixoto House: view of the rear of the house with two-storey-high canopy and terraces overlooking the sloping gardens by Roberto Burle Marx

Inácio Peixoto, a founding member of the Modernist literary review *Verde* in 1927, who by commissioning Niemeyer to design his private residence initiated the remarkable production of Modernist art and architecture in this small but at the time prosperous city of twenty thousand inhabitants in the forest of Minas Gerais. Lauro Cavalcanti suggests that Cataguases 'found in the new architecture an instrument for constructing an identity free of the provincialism that characterized the Minas Gerais interior'.[13] Architects like Francisco Bolonha, Aldary Henrique Toledo, Gilberto Lyra de Lemos, Carlos Leão, Edgar Vale and Flávio de Aquino, and artists like Cândido Portinari, Anísio Medeiros and Paulo Werneck contributed to the creation of the largest complex of Modernist buildings in any small Brazilian city. Niemeyer himself designed the Boys Academy at Cataguases (1946), today the Manuel Inácio Peixoto State School, for three hundred pupils, half of them boarders, inviting Portinari to create for the entrance hall what would become one of his most celebrated murals: *Tiradentes*, a pictorial narrative of the deeds of the 'protomartyr of independence'.

The interpenetration of house and garden was exploited further at the house for Prudente de Morais Neto in Gávea, in Rio de Janeiro (1943–49), based on a design originally intended for a Pampulha site. The sketch and model of the Pampulha scheme show a screen – mostly glazed – dividing the site into two parts. The garden is continuous on both sides of the screen, which stops short of the side walls of the property to allow for passage from the open area of the garden to its more secluded counterpart. The final project, on a sloping Rio de Janeiro site, preserves the fundamental idea of a promenade that begins in the garden and continues through the house, culminating in privileged viewing points over the garden. The house featured in the *Architectural Forum*'s 1947 special issue on Brazil, which reported that Brazil's best residential buildings 'show standards which are, if anything, superior to [those in the United States]', and made particular reference to 'careful attention to proper orientation and breeze . . . space standards . . . construction . . . [and] site planning . . . of very high order'.[14] Upon entering the site of the Prudente de Morais Neto House, the visitor follows an ascending path that makes a U-turn through the garden, proceeding alongside a retaining, serpentine, rubble-stone wall that links to a semicircular wall of the house. Walking around this, the visitor finds the entrance – a simple sliding opening in the glazing between the semicircular wall and a volume to the rear that contains service rooms.

Superimposed on the L-shaped ground floor is a U-shaped upper floor. Through the small lobby, the visitor enters the double-height living and dining room at the heart of the plan, which continues to the right under the first-floor bedroom wing. The promenade continues up a ramp leading from the living room to a gallery in front of the bedrooms. From the bedrooms, the visitor moves on to a balcony suspended by cables from the roof slab, the cables creating an oblique plane along which movable blinds roll down from the top. Having changed direction nine times already, the visitor who has reached this balcony enjoys a view towards the garden, which has already been experienced at a more intimate scale.

A second route, on the axis of the house entrance, leads through the living room out to a secluded garden, protected from the north by the rising mountain mass, from the west by the rear

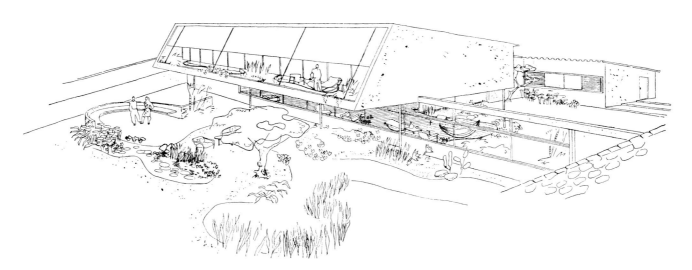

Prudente de Morais Neto House: perspective of original scheme designed for a site at Pampulha in 1943, later adapted for a sloping site in Rio de Janeiro; the overhanging, east-facing, first-floor balcony is suspended by cables from the roof

13 Cavalcanti, 2003, p. 397. See also Couto.   **14** *Architectural Forum*, 1947, p. 93.

volume of the house, and from the east by a free-standing screen that is the continuation of the glazed wall of the living room. Between this screen and the northern property wall, a passage leads back to the belvedere in front of the living room, overlooking the open garden. The volume that contains the bedrooms is lifted on slender, tubular steel columns and extends above part of the secluded garden terrace, enhancing the intimacy of this space, as well as above part of the belvedere. Protected by the generous overhang of the bedroom wing, the full-height glazing of the living room slides away to unite indoor and outdoor living areas. From the dining room, a door leads to a staircase that gives access to the most private and acoustically insulated room of the house: the study on the perimeter of the rear volume, with windows surveying the rear yard.

The precise articulation of multiple intricate routes from garden to house and back, the non-hierarchical agglomeration of walls, screens, partitions and living areas that could belong to the garden or the house, and the integration of functional and environmental requirements generate a fluid residential landscape. Traditional distinctions between inside and outside are blurred, and the integration of house and garden, artifice and nature is maximized. In the tropical climate of Rio, these spatial arrangements guarantee privacy and protection from sun and rain without impeding full enjoyment of the house's most precious spaces, which remain cool and shaded, taking advantage of the temperate sea breeze and in direct contact with luxurious tropical nature.

Niemeyer's tropicalization of the modern house went a long way beyond the early Brazilian Modernist addition of tokens of tropical vegetation to conjure instead a dwelling with fragile, dis-

soluble boundaries between nature and building. His rejection of the traditional, easily identifiable, assertive front door embodies a rupture with the Brazilian past of the patriarchal mansion, while also proposing a daring adaptation of modern European models to the conditions of the tropical environment, allowing the landscape to penetrate the house and the house to flow freely out into the garden. It symbolizes the conscious denial of the ultimate artificial defence mechanism against a nature that is not perceived as obstacle or threat but is welcomed as the desirable place to dwell in the tropics.

The outline of the bedroom wing dominates the image of the Prudente de Morais Neto House, and its balcony suspended on tension steel wires re-creates the experience treasured by Niemeyer of lying in a hammock in the midst of a tropical garden, 'peering between the branches at the infinite spaces beyond'. Niemeyer repeated the gesture in a number of other residential schemes, raising the bedroom quarters on stilts over an intricately laced, semi-transparent ground floor, with a suspended balcony surveying a tropical garden. Their design recalls the Brazilian Pavilion at the 1939 New York World's Fair, but the relation between building and garden in the residential examples is significantly different; in fact, inverted. Where the World's Fair pavilion functioned as a gate towards the Dionysian garden it embraced, in the case of the houses, it is the garden's role to introduce the visitor to a domestic world, mediating between the city and the house. In this sense, the houses also challenge Eurocentric images of tropical, 'undomesticated' nature as hostile and dangerous, welcoming the 'jungle' as the ideal garden in the tropics, insulating the private retreat from the 'impertinent' bourgeois public.

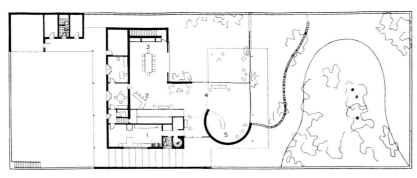

ground floor plan

1 kitchen
2 bar
3 dining room
4 living room
5 study

first floor plan

1, 2, 8 dressing room
3   study
4   void
5, 6   bedroom
7   master bedroom

Prudente de Morais Neto House, Gávea, Rio de Janeiro, 1943–49

Needless to add, such urban retreats embraced by lush tropical gardens were, and still are, accessible only to the privileged Brazilian bourgeoisie, who supplied Niemeyer with commissions for private villas where large gardens allowed for greater openness in the house.

Avoiding short, direct access routes and requiring the visitor to trace the gardens' meandering paths, Niemeyer appears to suggest that this intimate, indulgent exploration of domesticated

The unbuilt house for minister of education Gustavo Capanema in Gávea, in Rio de Janeiro (1947), is a long, low building bound on its two narrow sides by masonry walls. The glazed screen of its ground floor, under the metaphorical sleeping hammock, is set back from the building line, and an irregular semi-open space is carved out of the living room to configure shady spaces with varying degrees of shelter and to enhance the lightness of the structure.

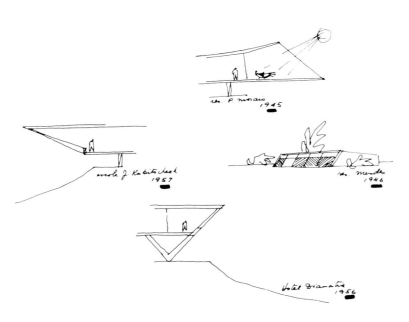

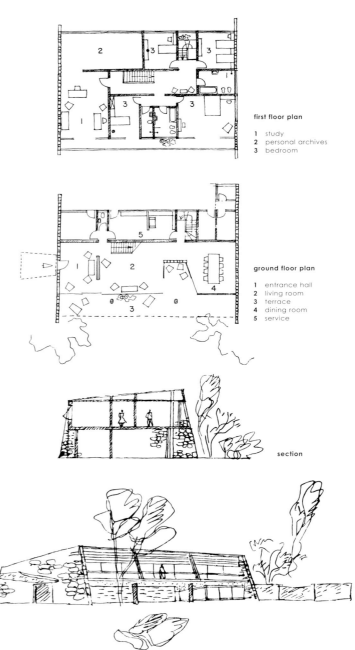

first floor plan

1 study
2 personal archives
3 bedroom

ground floor plan

1 entrance hall
2 living room
3 terrace
4 dining room
5 service

section

Gustavo Capanema House, Gávea, Rio de Janeiro, 1947, unbuilt

nature is necessary in order to appreciate a whole set of different qualities celebrated from the high terraces of his houses. The backward-leaning plane of their principal façades accentuates the belvedere effect. In Niemeyer's houses, the garden becomes an essential component of the Corbusian 'machine for making eyes see' the landscape. In contrast to Corbusian precedents, however, such as the Villa La Roche, Niemeyer's *promenade architecturale* threads through house and garden without transforming large areas into circulation space. Instead, Niemeyer's circulation areas are integrated into the living space, which unfolds vertically as well as horizontally and always in dialogue with the landscape. Movement is essential to the spatial experience; but it organizes and enhances rather than dominating and consuming the living space of the house.

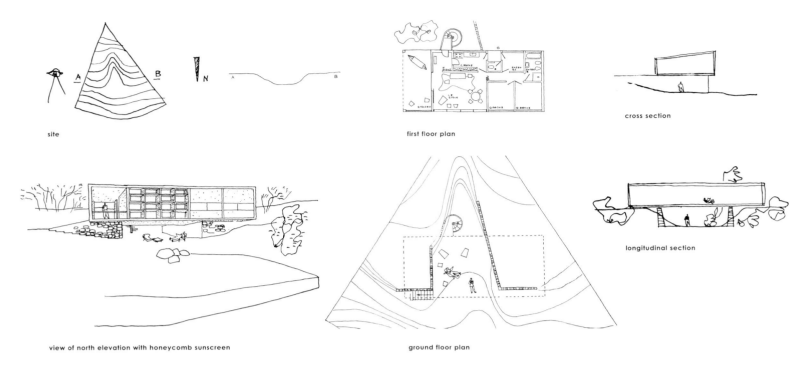

site

first floor plan

cross section

view of north elevation with honeycomb sunscreen

ground floor plan

longitudinal section

House for an anonymous client, Rio de Janeiro, 1949, unbuilt

The highly unusual site of a house at Rio de Janeiro for an anonymous client (1949), which also remained on paper, offered Niemeyer the opportunity to simplify this theme further. An orthogonal prism with a sloping roof that lends it a pronounced orientation towards the view to the north rests on two retaining rubblestone walls, which follow the contours of the site, totally unrelated to the geometry of the prism. The concrete prism is suspended over the valley at the centre of the plot and is accessed by a spiral staircase at the rear of the house, outside the orthogonal structure. It contains a veranda, living and sleeping quarters, arranged in sequence and protected by a variety of sunscreens, which reflect the organization of the plan and variable privacy requirements on the vertical plane of the north elevation. The hollow centre of the site under the prism forms a large porch for outdoor living. Niemeyer's meticulous specification of how the house might be inhabited indicates how greatly he valued this porch space. The upper-floor plan shows a hammock hung at the rear – the coolest, southern side of the semi-enclosed veranda, where it would benefit from a through-breeze.

Niemeyer also raised the house for Léonel Miranda in Gávea, in Rio de Janeiro (1952), above Burle Marx's landscaped garden with free-form pool to ensure good views for all rooms. This is a large version of the weekend house at Mendes, lifted up on *pilotis* and accessed via two ramps. At the side of the house, an unruly, sinuous concrete *marquise* juts out a few centimetres below the main volume to mark the entrance, resting on a slender steel column, seemingly randomly positioned, and a free-standing, rubblestone wall that projects at an angle from the rear of the house. A

Léonel Miranda House: garden (north) façade with ramp leading to the first-floor terrace

second rubble-stone wall screens the garden from the entrance area.

The black-carpeted, more formal ramp spirals languidly inside the glazed, curvilinear enclosure of an entrance area under the *pilotis* to arrive at the living room, which is slowly revealed to the ascending visitor. Along the way, it captures views towards the lush tropical garden. The planting invades the *pilotis*, embracing the glazed enclosure. Part of the curved steel-and-glass wall reap-

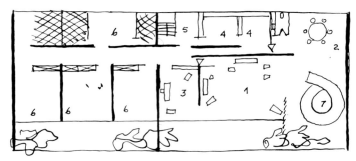

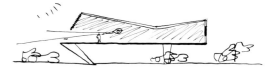

first floor plan	1	living room		
	2	dining room	5	stair
	3	study	6	bedroom
	4	kitchen	7	ramp

cross section

Léonel Miranda House, Gávea, Rio de Janeiro, 1952

pears higher up on the garden elevation, piercing a perforated canted screen to channel light down to the entrance area. From the north-facing terrace, a second, marble-paved ramp descends to the garden, coiled around an existing tree. The latticed, canted façade and sharply angled front row of tapered columns, clad in jade-green *pastilha* tiles, emphasize the turn towards the view, the cardinal composition principle of the design.

Expression is balanced with utility: the white, perforated screen shields the upper third of the oblique plane in front of the two bays of the living-room veranda, ensuring protection from the high sun and maximum views, while the screening of the lower two-thirds of the plane in front of the bedrooms guarantees shading as well as maximum privacy and adequate ventilation. Inside the living room the walls panelled in peroba do campo and the tropical-wood floorboards glow warmly in the filtered light that fills this space, lending it an atmosphere of intimacy. The house's rich array of carefully selected fine materials and high-quality workmanship are typical of Niemeyer's domestic projects.

Léonel Miranda House: *above*, view of the *pastilha*-clad side wall of the house with freeform entrance canopy, and part of the garden façade with the glazed enclosure of the ramp projecting at the top; *below*, marble-laid ramp leading from the garden to the first-floor terrace

Léonel Miranda House: *above*, view of north-facing living room and terrace protected by latticed screen; *in the foreground*, spiral ramp descending to the ground-floor entrance area; *below and opposite*, ground-floor entrance hall with black-carpeted ramp leading to the first-floor living room

Léonel Miranda House: view of living room with walls panelled in peroba do campo; in the foreground, spiral ramp descending to the ground-floor entrance area

His most promising house project among those never built was designed for a wealthy American client at the time Niemeyer's international reputation had reached a peak. A large set of sketches, drawings and a model for the Burton Tremaine House at Santa Barbara, California (1947) show him running the gamut of the glamorous vocabulary he had been developing over the previous years. The resulting scheme for this privileged beachfront property is closer to those for the Pampulha and Nova Friburgo resort hotels than to any of his contemporaneous domestic projects, which appear modest in comparison. In the first publication of Niemeyer's works, Papadaki dedicated eight pages to this house scheme for a contemporary art collector and noted: 'Climatic conditions and local exuberance produced the design of this California residence which could be considered a unique example for "total living": facilities for unlimited lounging with occasional fresh water or ocean bathing.' Niemeyer's first decision was to avoid any major solid structure on the ground in order to optimize spectacular views towards the Pacific Ocean, about 5 metres below site level, and to transform the site into a garden of pleasure and delight with a non-linear narrative of architectural events, an 'elaborate system of "pas perdus"', in Papadaki's words.[15]

The horizontal upper volume with a backward-leaning façade turned towards the sea contains the master suite and a guest wing. These intimate domestic spaces are positioned at the centre of Burle Marx's extensive grounds. Raised on slender *pilotis*, they overlook the rear garden with a large free-form pool – complete with a statue at one end – and an amoebic pond. They also enjoy privileged views towards the front garden and the ocean. The rigidity of this floating volume is relieved by latticed screens and rows of *brises-soleil* that shade the large verandas along the two long sides. It is balanced by independent curvaceous structures: a meandering *marquise* on the ocean side and a three-vault triple garage on the landward side. At its centre, the floating horizontal volume is lightened by a large, roofed terrace the full width of the first floor, which separates the master suite from the three guestrooms and offers panoramic views towards land and ocean. This terrace extends beyond the orthogonal structure and then morphs into the deliciously frivolous *marquise* that undulates parallel to the shoreline, sheltering and uniting activities at ground-floor level and celebrating open-air living in the warm climate of California.

Between the *marquise*-cum-catwalk and the *pilotis*, a second swimming pool, protected from the ocean winds, provides the privileged viewpoint for an elaborate perspective that narrates Niemeyer's vision of a life of endless pleasure at this house: open sunbathing platforms with palm trees; a bar under the *marquise*

15 Papadaki, 1950, p. 182.

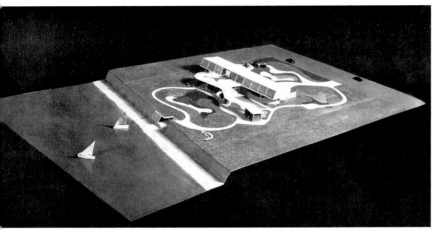

Burton Tremaine House, Santa Barbara, California, USA, 1947, unbuilt: model

Burton Tremaine House: view from the street

protected by a windscreen that allows views towards the sculpture garden and the sea; an area with free-standing partitions for art displays against a *brise-soleil* screen; an intimate sheltered salon; and a raised dance floor or orchestra platform. A small, free-standing, orthogonal service wing below the master suite, within the space of the *pilotis*, is the solid structure that anchors the house at one end of the longitudinal section. A small, double-curled volume containing washroom facilities and skilfully combining utility with formal play brackets the spectacle that develops under the *marquise*, without obstructing views from the pool to the sea. Three stairs, each of a different configuration, connect the two levels of the house: one leads directly to the upper-floor terrace by the master suite; the second arrives by the guestroom wing; and the third, halfway along the free-flowing *marquise* and outside its outline, ascends to the upper floor from the garden between house and beach. On the cross-section the storyline begins with the private beach; about 1 metre up, a small lounging niche is hollowed out of the slope just below ground level.

The house presents a more sober, vertical elevation towards the landside, with a projecting canopy leading the pedestrian towards the entrance. The geometric clarity of this elevation and the axiality of the canopy are subverted at ground-floor level, where, once within the space of the *pilotis*, the visitor finds the entrance wall receding at an angle, pointing towards the open-air areas of the house, enticing the newcomer to turn and take the light-hearted route towards the zone of play, luxury and seduction. A large garden insulates the house from the street. The Burton Tremaine House scheme was published in the issue of *Arts and Architecture* for March 1949 and was included in the 1949 exhibition *From Le Corbusier to Niemeyer: 1929–49*, at the Museum of Modern Art in New York, but was never built. Richard Neutra was commissioned to design a new scheme.

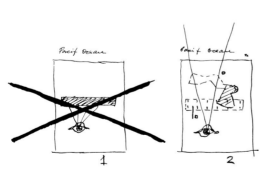

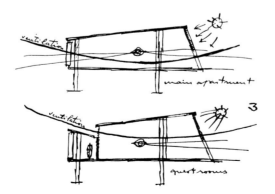

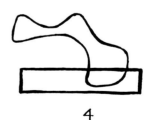

Burton Tremaine House: 'explanation' of the design process

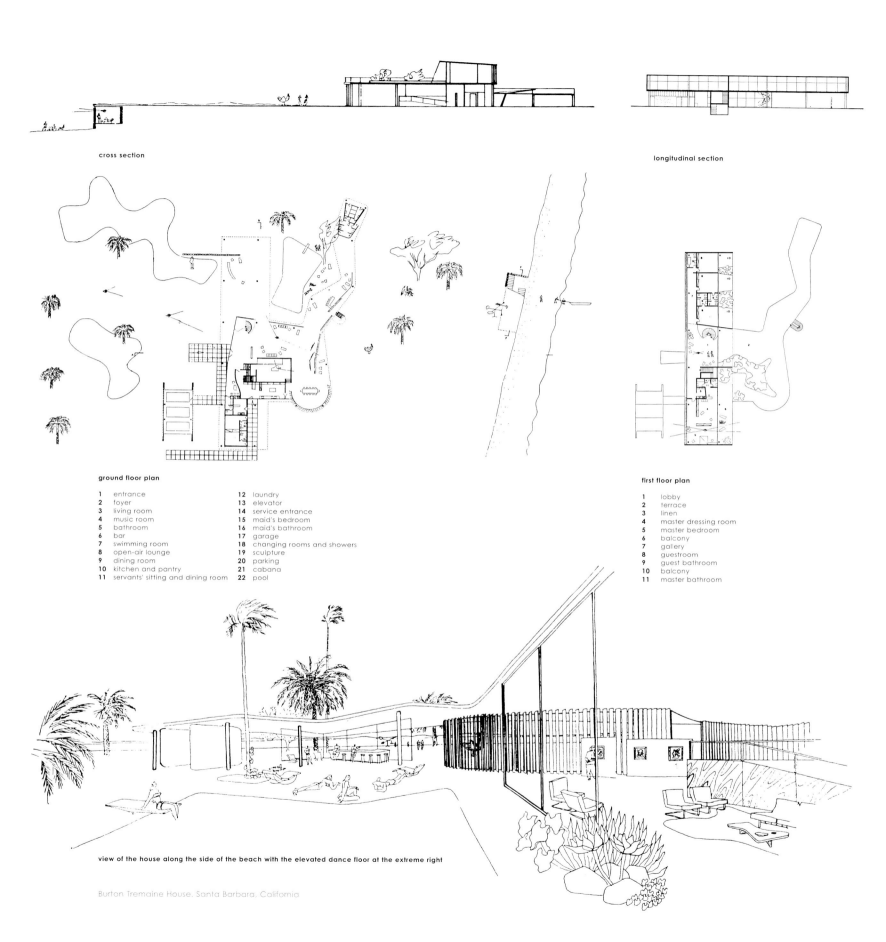

cross section

longitudinal section

ground floor plan

1	entrance	12	laundry
2	foyer	13	elevator
3	living room	14	service entrance
4	music room	15	maid's bedroom
5	bathroom	16	maid's bathroom
6	bar	17	garage
7	swimming room	18	changing rooms and showers
8	open-air lounge	19	sculpture
9	dining room	20	parking
10	kitchen and pantry	21	cabana
11	servants' sitting and dining room	22	pool

first floor plan

1	lobby
2	terrace
3	linen
4	master dressing room
5	master bedroom
6	balcony
7	gallery
8	guestroom
9	guest bathroom
10	balcony
11	master bathroom

view of the house along the side of the beach with the elevated dance floor at the extreme right

Burton Tremaine House, Santa Barbara, California

Similar themes were exploited in 1953, at the B. Pigmatary House for a São Paulo site, with architect Helio Uchôa and structural engineer Joaquim Cardozo (unbuilt). Papadaki described the design as another 'attempt to achieve a background for total living in a modern fragmentary, "granular" world', which took 'the form of a faraway island, reminiscent of the one described by Sir Thomas More'.[16] In More's utopian world, inspired by Amerigo Vespucci's enthusiastic accounts of the 'New World', 'there is indeed nothing belonging to the whole town that is both more useful and more pleasant' than its gardens, cultivated 'with great care' to be 'both so fruitful and so beautiful'.[17] At the Pigmatary House, the site has been cultivated to receive an ambitious programme, broken down into groups of functions assigned to separate volumes or folds of the ground, minimizing the impact of the building on the landscape.

The sloping terrain of the garden is incised to accommodate a small amusement complex, including bowling alley, gymnasium, turkish bath, dressing rooms, bar and lounging areas and sheltered swimming pool. The intermediate level of the house coincides with the level of the street and develops in two parallel wings with intimate, open-air spaces in-between. The shorter, wider wing containing living and dining room overlooks the graded layers of the garden. The longer wing is set back from the street, with a linear sequence of kitchen and service rooms and a private study suite with separate entrance. A large entrance hall cuts across and connects the two wings, also acting as an acoustic buffer between study and services. From the entrance hall, a linear ramp leads to the lowest level, while two separate staircases serve the master suite and guestroom zone on the upper level, atop the long wing of the house, with balconies overlooking the garden, partially protected by vertical *brises-soleil*. A second, spiralling ramp descends from the landscaped terrace on the roof of the amusement area to the lower level of the garden beside the large outdoor pool, partly sheltered by the terrace. The tunnel garage disappears into the hill across the street.

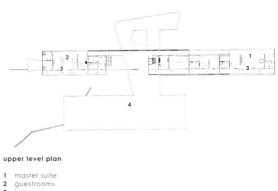

upper level plan

1 master suite
2 guestrooms
3 balcony
4 terrace

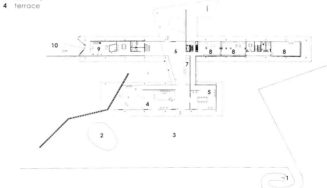

street level plan

1 ramp
2 open to lower level swimming pool
3 landscaped terrace
4 living room
5 dining room
6 entrance hall
7 ramp
8 kitchen and service wing
9 study
10 study entrance

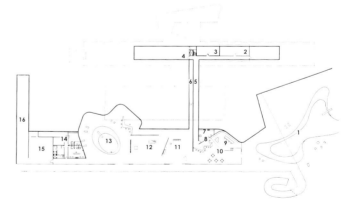

lower garden level plan: amusement complex

1 outdoor swimming pool
2 food storage
3 mechanical equipment
4 wine cellar
5 service passageway
6 passageway
7 kitchen
8 bar
9 raised orchestra stand
10 dining room
11 lounge
12 game room
13 sheltered swimming pool
14 turkish bath, dressing room
15 gymnasium
16 bowling alley

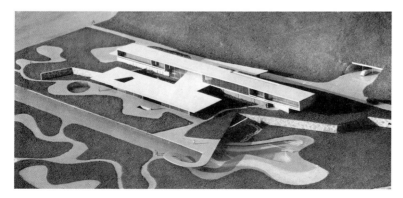

Above and right, B. Pigmatary House, São Paulo, 1953, unbuilt

16 Papadaki, 1956, p. 182.   **17** More.

Manipulating House and Setting to Achieve a Unified Whole

Also in 1953, Niemeyer designed a house for Ermiro de Lima in Rio de Janeiro (unbuilt), partially cut into a hill to minimize the footprint of the building and maximize the potential of topography and views. His own private residence was also under construction in the densely forested São Conrado area of Rio de Janeiro. Niemeyer quotes Le Corbusier with approval: 'The ideal thing is a shack with a pool beside it.'[18] Perched high on a dramatic steep site between the towering mountains of the Serra do Mar, with magnificent views downhill towards the ocean, the Casa das Canoas, undoubtedly his domestic masterpiece, appears at first sight to consist of no more than a concrete, free-form *marquise* with a pool amid a tropical garden that merges seamlessly with a fantastic landscape.[19] Niemeyer describes the house as 'modest,

without entrance hall, simple as . . . they should all be'.[20] His conscious decision to inhabit Brazil's chaotic and undomesticated natural landscape did not involve an attempt to tame it: 'I did not touch the terrain,' Niemeyer insists.[21] He has also said of the house:

> My concern was to design this residence with complete liberty, adapting it to the irregularities of the terrain, without changing it, and making it curved, so as to permit the vegetation to penetrate, without being separated by the straight line. And I created for the living rooms a zone of shade, so that the glazed walls wouldn't need curtains and the house would be transparent as I preferred.[22]

David Underwood sees the drive up the long and winding Estrada das Canoas as 'a sort of elite *subida do morro* (ascent to a *favela*)'.[23] Obliged to leave the car at a parking bay, the visitor

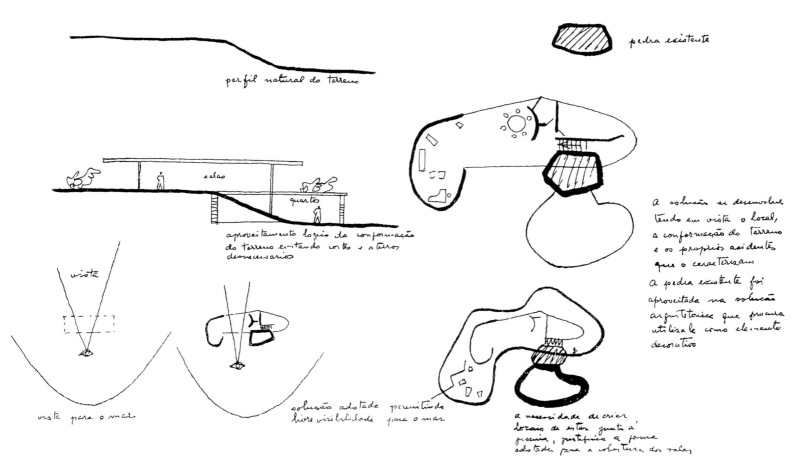

Niemeyer House at Canoas (Casa das Canoas), São Conrado, Rio de Janeiro, 1950–53: 'explanation' of the design process

18 Niemeyer, 1994a, p. 29. Niemeyer says this was a statement Le Corbusier made once when they were together in New York. 19 Currently, the Casa das Canoas belongs to the Oscar Niemeyer Foundation and is open to the public. Niemeyer now lives in an apartment in Rua Prudente de Morais in Ipanema. 20 Niemeyer, 2005, p. 24. 21 Oscar Niemeyer, in Wajnberg. 22 Oscar Niemeyer, quoted in Underwood, 1994b, p. 79. 23 Underwood, 1994b, p. 82.

enters the shady tropical garden on foot, through a gate, then turns left to descend a gently curving ramp towards what appears to be a clearing cut into the mountainside. Typically, the approach to the house is neither direct nor axial. Water, a huge granite boulder and the low horizon of the thin roof slab configure a Carioca landscape in miniature, beckoning from a distance and anticipating the wondrous spectacle that lies still out of sight. Moving into the porch under the meandering canopy, the visitor passes through a casual opening in the glazing into the relatively dark interior of the house, to be drawn by the light out again

through the rear opening diagonally opposite, into a second, smaller porch and on to the large veranda, where a spectacular view awaits the initiated and holds them captive.

In the vein of the Casa do Baile and more successfully than at the Alberto Dalva Simão House (1954), both at Pampulha, the house at Canoas is defined by the floating concrete canopy, which neither encloses space nor determines spatial hierarchy. When the floor-to-ceiling glass doors slide open, uniting inside and outside space, the visitor finds under the reassuring canopy a universe of structural and space-defining elements, forms and mate-

Casa das Canoas. Niemeyer's 'ideal ... shack with a pool beside it'; view of the pavilion from the ramp that descends from the entrance gate towards the house set in what appears like a clearing cut into the mountainside

rials that bring to mind Mies van der Rohe's German Pavilion for the Barcelona International Exhibition of 1929. The openness, spatial fluidity, slender steel columns piercing the ceiling, subdued luxury, reflective surfaces and, most notably, the horizontal axis of symmetry that renders the plane of the ceiling a reflection of the floor betray Niemeyer's debt to the Barcelona Pavilion. The horizontal symmetry captures the viewer's attention when standing by the shallow pool looking through the Canoas pavilion between the curve of the roof and the sharp line of its shadow underfoot. Mies's project for a 50 × 50-foot square glass house (1950–51) and his Farnsworth House in Plano, Illinois (1946–51), and Philip Johnson's Glass House at New Canaan, Connecticut (1949), the last two exhibited at the first São Paulo International Art Biennale in 1951, are the other obvious precedents of the house at Canoas, amazingly free of Corbusian recipes.

Alberto Dalva Simão House, Pampulha, Belo Horizonte, Minas Gerais, 1954

Casa das Canoas: view from the porch under the marquise towards the entrance and through the pavilion's 'zone of shade' towards the rear opening and the veranda overlooking the ocean

Niemeyer's sketches reveal that his initial gesture was to place a semi-transparent prismatic pavilion on the mountainside, permitting cross-views towards the ocean. But rather than Johnson's path of conformity, he chose reinvention for a tropical context. Faithful to his ideology of mixed ancestry and Antropofagist hybridization, Niemeyer proceeded to infect the classical pavilion with the organic, spontaneous architecture of the *morros*, mixing Western achievements in the field of domestic architecture with tropical exuberance and lessons from Brazil's colonial past and popular present. It is not surprising that, free of the restrictions imposed by a client's programme, Niemeyer composed his own house primarily of the sensual female curves traditionally associated with the *mulata*, the Brazilian woman of mixed European and African origin who embodies the eroticization of miscegenation. Since Gilberto Freyre, this eroticized miscegenation has been firmly located in the Brazilian family house – the powerful signifier and

machine of unrestricted racial and cultural mixing. For Niemeyer the privileged candid curve signals emancipation from both the Euro-Modernist canon and the local patriarchal tradition, to some extent invented by twentieth-century conservationists like Lúcio Costa.

Niemeyer eagerly points out that he did not touch the terrain at Canoas, yet his claim that he adapted the house 'to the irregularities of the terrain' is slightly misleading. Rather than producing a house that represents a rendering of the topographical profile, he exploited the site's contours, disposing living and sleeping quarters on separate floors. Pulling the external membrane of the mountain over the house's private quarters, he concealed this lower level and formed a straight-edged terrace with uninterrupted sea views. To the side of the house, the terrace edge and lower-floor plan follow the contours of the ground. Effectively, Niemeyer adapted both terrain and programme to the requirements of his design. His primary concern was not the integration of the house into the natural setting in the sense of making the house almost indistinguishable from its environment, but the manipulation of both house and setting in order to achieve a unified whole. The architecture is not directed against nature, but neither is the natural landscape incorporated as found in the design.

Reverence towards nature and perceptive engagement with topography do not imply unquestionable submission: 'Man intervenes in Nature,' Niemeyer says, 'turning it into the theater of his illusions.'[24] At Canoas, the semi-transparent pavilion that expresses the 'ideal . . . shack with a pool beside it' owes its apparent simplicity to the fact that it is displayed on a new, artificial terrain, simpler than the natural one. This new, planar ground economically effects a transformation of both topography and programme. The architect's effort has been carefully concealed, so that the secluded glade appears found or natural. The gently sloping site has been transformed into a platform at the edge of a cliff. Its primary purpose is to provide a neutral, frictionless plane for the display of Niemeyer's idealized tropical dwelling, reduced to a bare ideogram: a gliding *marquise* by a pond and a granite boulder amid dense tropical forest. The sophisticated simplicity of the composition and the majesty of the site conspire to invest the particular house with archetypal resonance.

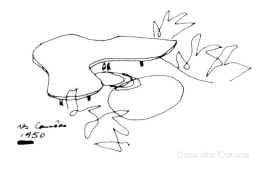

Casa das Canoas

Under the *marquise*, to the left of the entrance opening, an ovoid curve embraces the sitting area, the darker and most intimate area of the house, delimited by a rectangular, beige-coloured rug. The view to the sea is wittily framed on this wall: a small vertical opening is positioned at sitters' eye level, perhaps a token homage to Le Corbusier. This is the only opaque external wall, rendered and painted green on the outside and internally panelled in streaked peroba do campo wood, polished to a warm red-brown finish. The same material is used for the shallow arc to the right of the rear opening, which defines an alcove for a round dining table of Niemeyer's design (1972), with Thonet model no. 9 chairs on a circular green rug, evoking a similar arrangement at Mies's Tugendhat House.

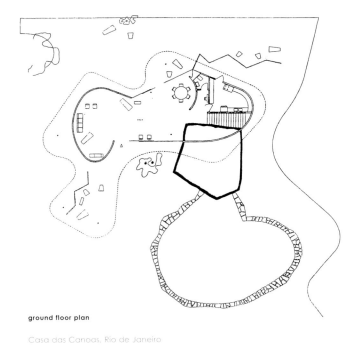

ground floor plan

Casa das Canoas, Rio de Janeiro

24 Niemeyer, 2000b, p. 123.

lower floor plan

The concern to reveal external walls and internal partitions as independent planar elements rather than constituents of volumes is satisfied with tectonic confidence. The dining arc screens off the two enclosed spaces: a kitchen, contained within the western loop, which also embraces a staircase, and a toilet positioned between kitchen and dining alcove so as not to compromise the impression of a free-standing, curving plane. Perforated hollow-brick zigzag screens define sitting areas in the porch and rear veranda, also screening off a small court for the kitchen (the veranda screen was later replaced by a solid, white, low curved wall). The kitchen wall by the internal stair is also defined as an independent plane, its full thickness revealed as it protrudes beyond the point where it meets the perpendicular white wall with the door to the kitchen. It is highlighted with a dark green-blue polished plaster that reflects the surrounding thick green foliage and the silhouette of Alfredo Ceschiatti's reclining figure at the top of the stairwell beside the granite boulder. This wall is the only vertical element in the composition, linking the two levels of the house.

In contrast to the Farnsworth House, at Canoas transparency has not been achieved at the cost of privacy but neither has it been compromised. The cave-like, cellular, lower floor that is kept out of sight contains four bedrooms, three bathrooms and a small study area at the bottom of the stair, which is devoid of views, lit as it is by a narrow vertical slit and a row of high, circular clerestory windows. The walls of the bedrooms are painted oxblood red. Three bedroom windows project out of the rear wall, emphatically imposing a double frame on views towards thick foliage. According to Underwood, they present 'a parody of the Corbusian approach', but they are more likely inspired by Alvar Aalto's bedroom-window bays for his Villa Mairea in Noormarkku (1938–41).[25]

Mies's Farnsworth House was also a source of inspiration for Lina Bo Bardi's private residence and first built work, her magnificent Casa de Vidro (House of Glass) in São Paulo (1950–51). 'If you observe nature through the glass walls of the Farnsworth House, it assumes a meaning deeper than when you stand outside,' Mies claims.[26] Bo Bardi's house, partially elevated on thin steel stilts, is penetrated via a light, steel staircase. A muscular tree surging upwards through the central patio, and the forest surrounding the glazed living room and library, its canopy asserting its primacy above the delicate curve of the roof, reassure the visitor that nature has not been left behind.

At Canoas, Niemeyer sought an even closer relation with nature, making the house porous, allowing a huge grey granite boulder to syncopate the curve of the pool, penetrate the glass

Casa das Canoas: view from the entrance towards the dining alcove, panelled in streaked peroba do campo, and the staircase between the green-blue kitchen wall and the granite boulder. The dining table is of Niemeyer's design (1972), and the reclining female figure at the top of the stairwell by Alfredo Ceschiatti.

25 Underwood, 1994b, p. 79.   **26** Mies van der Rohe, quoted in Blaser, p. 20.

Casa das Canoas: study area at the bottom of the stair with Rio. Oscar and Anna Maria Niemeyer's version of the Corbusian 'machine à se reposer', designed in 1978

Casa das Canoas: bedroom window projecting out of the rear wall

pleted' the composition, Niemeyer says, framing the hovering concrete roof slab, and intensifying the effect of the house as a minimal, horizontal, free-floating, sheltering plane.[27]

Although nature has been permitted to inhabit the Canoas House, it is not allowed to run wild; Burle Marx's hand is clearly visible. While Ceschiatti's figure reclines inside the house, many other sculptures inhabit the garden. In 1948, the Brazilian correspondent of the *Architectural Review*, Claude Vincent, commented with approval and not a little surprise on the Brazilian

> idea of sculpture as a necessary adjunct to architecture . . . so generally accepted that no architect waits until he has finished his project before calling in the sculptor . . . a state of affairs practically unknown in modern Europe, where a 'collectors' [sic] attitude to sculpture, of regarding it merely as a subsequent embellishment to existing buildings, has so long prevailed.

Her examples included Niemeyer's commissions for the gardens of the houses he was designing at the time.[28] At Canoas, an abstract architecture of improvisation and spontaneity is balanced by figurative sculpture; nature is populated by art and technology. The materials of the architectural intervention – concrete, steel and glass – are self-consciously modern, products of technology. But rather than a reconciliation between art and nature, 'jungle and school', what is pursued is a condition of coexistence articulated as a syncretic resolution of what is traditionally perceived as a relationship of conflict.[29]

27 Oscar Niemeyer, in Wajnberg. **28** Vincent, 1948, p. 206. **29** Oswald de Andrade, 1989, p. 311.

Lina Bo Bardi, Casa de Vidro, São Paulo, 1950–51

wall and intrude into the living space and stairwell, lifting a structural column on the way. Shade-loving plants grow by the rock and by the glass wall, outside as well as inside the house. Refuting Adolf Loos's notion of the house as a defence perimeter, Niemeyer opts for an architecture that collaborates with rather than harnessing nature's irrational forces – in Brazil, always associated with things indigenous. At Canoas, it is as if boulder and vegetation grew naturally at the centre of the composition after the house had been built. The trees planted around the house 'com-

The Dancing Curves of Canoas

The domestic ideogram of Canoas brings to mind Mies van der Rohe's saying: 'We have taken away . . . everything we could take away, and what is left, sings,' or, in Niemeyer's case, 'dances'.[30] Forging the architectural equivalent of polyrhythmic samba, Niemeyer set his curves in multiple metres, apparently unrestricted by geometry, utility or gravity. Samba has been described as 'a complex dialogue in which various parts of the body talk at the same time, and in seemingly different languages. The feet keep up a rapid patter, while the hips beat out a heavy staccato and the shoulders roll a slow drawl.'[31] Similarly at Canoas three separate, interacting rhythms are articulated in the walls, white roof slab and black structural columns, which appear to be scattered at random inside or outside the house. The zigzagging lines of the black-tile floor follow yet a different rhythm, allowed to overflow onto the stone pavement, enhancing the effect of fluidity and confirming that all limits have been dissolved, all devices of separation made penetrable. The strong beat sounded by the sinuous roof slab is suspended in the 'zone of shade' underneath it, where the weaker beats of the tubular steel columns, curved and straight screens and floor patterns are accentuated. The polymetric, vertical layering of rhythmic lines in open-ended dialogue sets the composition in perpetual motion, 'pushing the *plan libre* to new extremes of freedom', achieving a hitherto unknown lightness.[32] The shadow cast by the roof slab introduces yet another, ever-changing rhythm that follows the path of the sun and brings to the fore the dimension of time.

In the 1950s, European visitors to Canoas were accustomed to an architecture that may be seen to reflect the predominant harmonic and melodic progression of European music, and were not used to practising a synchronic reading of simultaneous patterns

The interacting rhythms of the polymetric Casa das Canoas: view from the entrance porch under the sinuous roof slab towards the pool

30 Mies van der Rohe, quoted in 'Mies in America', 1989, p. 193.
31 Browning, p. 2.   **32** Weston, 2002, p. 108.

Casa das Canoas: view from the rear veranda towards the south-west end of the pavilion overlooked by the legendary, 842-metre-high gneiss rock known as Pedra da Gávea. The free-standing white curved wall screens off the kitchen court.

that appear to contradict each other. They found the polymetric architecture of this unique house incomprehensibly complex, arbitrary and incoherent, echoing European perceptions of the simultaneous patterns of polymetric Afro-Brazilian music. Barbara Browning's comment on European perceptions of cacophony applies to both music and architecture: 'The problem', she sug-

gests, is 'not the indirection of the music but the misdirection of the listening.'[33]

The *Architectural Review* of October 1954 reported that Niemeyer's new house was at 'the centre of discussion in Sao Paulo' among foreign visitors at the 1953 Art Biennale.[34] In his 1956 monograph, Papadaki wrote that

> their experience as guests [at Canoas] must have been unbearable . . . the result was thunderous. We heard about 'incoherent relationship between the ground floor and . . .' 'poorly ventilated mezzanine,' the lack of similarity to a 'Pompeian house,' up to a definition that 'Art consists in making an idea as clear and objective as it can be made,' obviously referring to the technique of writing military dispatches.[35]

'The air was still full of Max Bill's accusations,' Mrs Gropius recalled when she and her husband visited the house.[36] Walter Gropius resorted to the animalizing colonialist trope, naming Niemeyer 'Paradiesvogel'. He may have been alluding to King Vidor's filmic North American–indigene romance *Bird of Paradise* (1932), in which a South Seas native woman (Dolores del Rio) embodies a land both idyllic and dangerous for mortals, and an infernal punishment awaits the transgressive exotic.[37] Gropius also criticized the house for not being 'multipliable'.[38] He probably saw Niemeyer's experiments as no more than 'masterful distractions, not subject to reproduction outside the remote reality in which they have their roots', exactly as Manfredo Tafuri and Francesco Dal Co saw Alvar Aalto's work.[39] The following year, Gropius praised the 'Japanese house' as 'really prefabricated', most likely thinking of the seventeenth-century Katsura Imperial Villa at Kyoto.[40] Lewis Mumford, too, who saw Niemeyer's house at the 1955 Museum of Modern Art exhibition on *Latin American Architecture Since 1945*, found its 'adventurous' architecture unconvincing. He criticized 'its too fluent periphery', and thought that the whole house 'has been sacrificed to the upstairs living room; so much was given up for the sake of aesthetic whimsery that the result may not be sound architecture,' he opined.[41]

For Henry-Russell Hitchcock, the house at Canoas represented 'the most extreme statement of [Niemeyer's] special Cariocan [sic] lyricism'.[42] Like the Casa do Baile, the Casa das Canoas put forward rhythm and dance as the ultimate transgressions of utility. Its emphasis on movement constitutes its most notable departure from its precedents. With few lines and a precise choreography, it fully exploited Niemeyer's innovations of the previous years, while in some ways it also looked forward to his future work in Brasília. It was at this house that a euphoric Juscelino Kubitschek visited Niemeyer one September morning in 1956, soon after he assumed the Brazilian presidency. While driving back to the city, the politician 'eagerly' spoke to the architect about his most audacious scheme: 'I am going to build a new capital for this country and I

33 Browning, p. 10. One German critic went as far as to talk of Niemeyer's house as 'kitsch'; Klotz, p. 107.   34 'Report on Brazil', 1954, p. 235.   35 Papadaki, 1956, p. 69.   36 'We did not think them quite justified,' she added; Gropius and Gropius, p. 236.   37 See Shohat and Stam, p. 143.   38 Walter Gropius, quoted in Niemeyer, 1985, p. 72. 39 Tafuri and Dal Co, p. 338.   40 Postcard from Walter Gropius to Le Corbusier, June 1954, cited in Dal Co, p. 389.   41 Lewis Mumford, 1956, pp. 84–85.   42 Hitchcock, 1955, p. 170.

want you to help me . . . Oscar, this time we are going to build the capital of Brazil.'[43]

Ernesto Rogers also visited the house at Canoas in 1953 and described it as 'a confession of [Niemeyer's] sins':

I doubt that I shall ever forget that scene: the sun was just dipping below the horizon, leaving us in a dark sea of orange, violet, green and indigo. The house repeated the themes of that orgiastic countryside (incense and the hum of insects): a vast rhapsody beginning in the roof vibrated down the walls and their niches to finish in the pool, where the water, instead of being neatly dammed up, freely spread along the rocks of a kind of forest pool.[44]

A rhapsody of curves also defines Niemeyer's Nara Mondadori Holiday House, at the luxury Côte d'Azur resort of Saint-Jean-Cap-Ferrat (1968–72).[45] More than thirty years earlier, the architect Flávio de Carvalho had treated the Europe of his travels as an exotic Other in *Os ossos do mundo* (*The Bones of the World*, 1936). Niemeyer employed an architectural repertoire associated with Europe's imagined Other landscape of Dionysian exuberance and excessive luxury to exalt a European exotic landscape. Free canopies snake through lush vegetation; open-air ramps-cum-catwalks spiral against a blue sky; undulating walls decorated with colourful glazed tiles from the hand of Athos Bulcão frolic with the golden light of southern France; fresh- and salt-water pools, meandering past circular islands of lotus, water lilies and papyrus, flirt merrily with the ocean. At Cap Ferrat, Niemeyer's luxuriant architecture of playfulness, elation and rejuvenation, light, water and luscious scents celebrates a European landscape famed for its seductive allure. Emphatically different, his Edmond de Rothschild House for a desert site near Caesarea, north of Tel Aviv (1965, unbuilt), and the Federmann House in the austere landscape of Herzliya, Israel (1964, unbuilt), are the only two introverted domestic environments from Niemeyer's hand, with shady, freely shaped courtyards surrounded by high walls, open to Israel's cloudless skies.

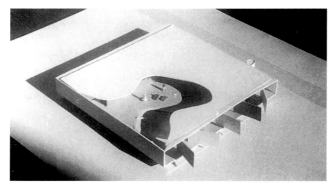

Edmond de Rothschild House for a desert site near Caesarea, north of Tel Aviv, Israel, 1965, unbuilt

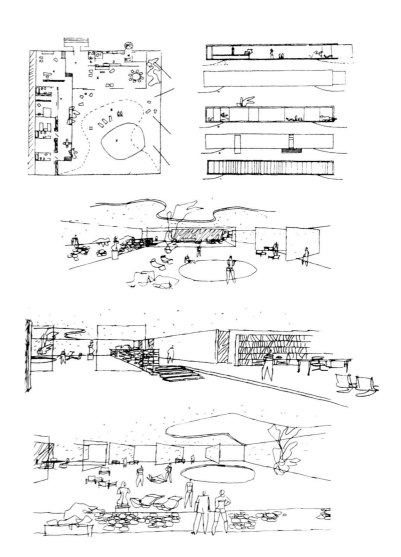

Edmond de Rothschild House, Caesarea

A Moment of Stasis for Contemplation

No other house by Niemeyer implicates the drama of the physical landscape in its formal concept more directly than the holiday house for Edmundo Cavanelas in Pedro do Rio, a two-hour drive from Rio de Janeiro (1954). It is graced with stupendous gardens by Roberto Burle Marx, which conspire with the surrounding landscape to produce a unique setting. Brazil's national composer

43 Juscelino Kubitschek, quoted in Niemeyer, 2000b, p. 70. Kubitschek was democratically elected in early October 1955 and, following a 'preventive' military coup, took office on the prescribed date, 31 January 1956. **44** Rogers, p. 240. In the same text, Ernesto Rogers notes: 'When I visited this house I was with Lucio Costa, who after having been considered for many years the Allah of Brazilian architects, decided (in a gesture of unheard-of and, perhaps, excessive modesty) to become Oscar's Mohammed, his most devout and generous prophet.' **45** The Nara Mondadori House was restored and unfortunately modified by Peter Marino in 1998.

Edmundo Cavanelas House, Pedro do Rio, Rio de Janeiro state, 1954

Heitor Villa-Lobos had tried composing melodies on the outlines of the mountains of the Serra da Piedade in Minas Gerais (*Melodia da montanha*, 1938), and Frank Lloyd Wright had designed Fallingwater in Bear Run, Pennsylvania (1935–39) 'to the music of the stream'.[46] In a very large property in a drained alluvial valley cradled by a pair of barren mountainsides, Niemeyer hung the roof of a single-storey pavilion from four triangular reinforced-concrete corner pillars, composing a second, artificial valley to amplify the voluptuous chorus of the mountain ridges.

The masterly gesture resonates with Niemeyer's almost instinctive sense of place and deep understanding of the relations between the forms of the natural landscape and those of his art. Responding with a lightness of touch to a spectacular setting with no flat horizon, his tent-like structure ensures that the ground remains the only horizontal element of the composition, intimating that human habitation is, ultimately, only temporary. Avoiding hubris, Niemeyer chose for this striking rural setting a low-key

vocabulary of sobriety and humility in preference to festivity and irreverence, including the spectacle of nature within the living landscape of the house rather than attempting to compete with it. The soft curve of the oversailing roof, with edges lifted up to the sky, suggests an act of prayer or thanksgiving, inspired by majestic scenery. Serene and expressive, the slightly asymmetrical structure also evokes the Indian hammock – a celebrated symbol of *brasilidade* – floating at ease, composed of double steel lattice beams acting as cables, with a corrugated steel cover, its underside finished in striped Finnish pine (except in the bathroom, where there is a suspended perforated cement ceiling).

In the 'zone of shade' under the suspended great sail, the plan is organized in three parts. To the south, by a blind stone-clad wall, is an open car port paved in black *pedra portuguesa* that

46 Frank Lloyd Wright, quoted in Weston, 2002, p. 134.

extends to the terrace to the west of the house, differentiating the car route from the adjoining living-room terrace in white *pedra portuguesa*. At the centre a transparent, orthogonal, open living area with through views towards the gardens and the mountain scenery on either side is surfaced in smooth white marble on an irregular pattern that echoes the stonework on the walls. To the north a wider, opaque, almost square wing contains the kitchen, with a door to the garden, three bedrooms turned towards the forested mountainside, and two bathrooms. Two entirely stone-clad solid masonry walls affirm their status as independent Miesian planes, extending beyond the limits of the tent, claiming their place in the physical landscape. The vertical one to the south penetrates the roof, incorporating a fireplace and concealing the chimney flue. The second, long wall separates the two wings of the house, screening off the T-shaped corridor of the private accommodation, and projects beyond the roof overhang to the east of the house to separate the kitchen yard from the living-room terrace beside the garden with a pool.

A low honeycomb brick screen, originally painted white like the lime-washed brickwork and timber weatherboarding of the bedroom wall behind it, shields the kitchen yard, adding texture to the east elevation. Its pattern echoes the checkerboard lawn around the orthogonal swimming pool, laid out by Burle Marx with two colours of *Stenotaphrum secundatum* grass, accentuated by square beds of carmine *Iresine herbstii* and golden yellow *Helichrysum petiolatum*. Looking towards the house from this garden, the eye moves fast along the straight line of the colourful beds, lingers on the reclining figure by Ceschiatti (the same as those found inside the house at Canoas and by the pool at Niemeyer's house in Brasília), then passes over the roof to surf leisurely along the ridge of the mountains in the distance.

The central section of the west elevation is a rendered solid brick wall, which defines the sitting area, centred on an ortho-

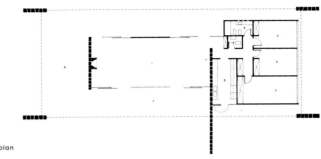

plan

1 living and dining room
2 bedroom
3 bathroom
4 toilet
5 kitchen
6 car port
7 terrace

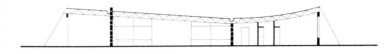

longitudinal section

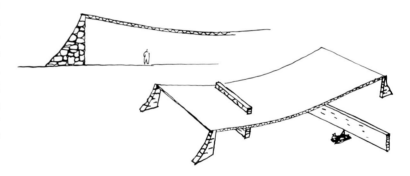

Edmundo Cavanelas House, Pedro do Rio

gonal rug. It is flanked by full-height glazing that slides away to unite inside and outside lounging spaces. Large roof overhangs offer protection against the sun. The dining table stands next to the long, horizontal, stone-clad wall, with easy access from the kitchen on the other side. The approach to the house is via a slowly descending, palm-lined driveway commanding a view of the entire valley with the house at the centre. Typically, the house has no main entrance door. Its public area may be entered through any of four identical, large openings apparently randomly positioned in the glazing.

Surrounded by precisely elaborated gardens and gently cascading mountains, scattered with a variety of native plants, the small dwelling looks like a modest garden pavilion, a parenthesis in the fantastic landscape. The west elevation, with the clear brush-stroke of the roof and the abstract geometric pattern formed by

Edmundo Cavanelas House under construction

glazed and solid wall sections painted in different colours (originally black for the bedroom wall and yellow for that of the sitting area), is incorporated in the huge canvas of the garden. The gentle undulations, broad sweeps of colour and sinuous curves of flowerbeds, lawns, pathways and languid pond seep into the mountainous landscape, to which the Cavanelas house pays homage. Howard Adams observes that Burle Marx's painterly gardens 'effect a "bifurcation" of the viewer's perceptions between the plant specimen close at hand and the distant vista'.[47] Viewed from the high vantage point of the driveway, the Cavanelas gardens present a stunning example of this effect, and Niemeyer's design is a fully complicit participant in Burle Marx's strategy.

This house is a typical example of Niemeyer's hugely underestimated attention to detail and rigorous integration of formal and material concerns. Challenging Modernist architectural conventions of 'honest' material expression and, like Alvar Aalto, obvious-

Edmundo Cavanelas House: view from the driveway

Edmundo Cavanelas House: *left*, view from the living room towards the checkerboard lawn to the east of the house, laid out by Roberto Burle Marx with two colours of *Stenotaphrum secundatum* grass, with reclining figure by Alfredo Ceschiatti; *right*, west elevation with car port

ly familiar with Modernist painting's collage techniques, Niemeyer juxtaposed, for example, quintessentially Modernist sliding glass screens with the elaborate stone overlay found in so many of his projects, alluding to colonial prototypes. He sheathed in this vernacular material design elements that he employed in exemplary Modernist fashion, such as the free-standing walls. He dressed concrete and brickwork in uniform stonework. He applied variable surface materials, textures and colours to identical solid masonry to construct a carefully calibrated hierarchy of composition elements, define spaces or blur the boundaries between exterior and interior, tradition and modernity, nature and artifice. Cladding in stone the four concrete piers and two principal walls, Niemeyer

underlined their prominence over the other solid masonry members of the house and granted them a more 'natural' appearance. They are the elements of the architectural intervention that extend beyond the artificial valley of the roof, mediating between architecture and natural landscape.

Similar planning strategies notwithstanding, in contrast to the Canoas, Burton Tremaine, Alberto Dalva Simão and Nara

47 Howard Adams, quoted in Treib, p. 53. The current owners of the house, Marta and Gilberto Struncki, have invested a great deal of effort to meticulously restoring the house and garden, especially the latter, which had suffered years of neglect. Their efforts were rewarded by a stroke of luck when they discovered Ceschiatti's statue at an antique shop. The statue has now returned to its original position.

Edmundo Cavanelas House: detail of stone cladding applied externally and internally on a pattern frequently employed by Niemeyer

Edmundo Cavanelas House: detail of marble-paved floor in the living room

Mondadori houses – where the emphasis is on narrative and dancing movement and the surrounding landscape is appreciated through exploration, gradually revealing its various aspects – the Cavanelas house suggests a moment of stasis for contemplation. Moreover, in Pedro do Rio the landscape is present in its entirety from the beginning. In the carefully composed canvas, the ephemeral and temporal is forcefully juxtaposed with the permanent and timeless. And, as in the paper cut-outs of Henri Matisse, 'the eternal presence of the image unites with the fleeting grace of the ornament'.[48]

Niemeyer's unexecuted project for a house in Norway (2000) also proposed a pause for the contemplation of 'the beauty of the surrounding landscape'. Niemeyer speaks of 'integration' with the landscape, but rather than hiding his concrete vaulted structure among the folds of the mountainous site, he boldly raised it on high so as to take in fully the stunning views, immersing its inhabitants in the experience of nature.[49] Whether in fluid motion or at contemplative rest, all Niemeyer's houses assume a central position in their natural setting, creating a sense of syncopation that emphasizes the need to listen to the rhythms of nature, drawing the eye from the built structure to the total environment.

Sérgio Buarque de Holanda observed that the 'city built by the Portuguese in America . . . is insufficient to disturb the scene of nature, and her silhouette is intertwined in the line of the landscape'.[50] Niemeyer remarks that, in Brazil, 'architecture and design came from Portugal'.[51] He has never disavowed the colonial plantation manor that Freyre had firmly positioned at the centre of Brazil's national consciousness as a legitimate source of inspiration, but he has always been quick to add that Brazilian architecture has developed in its own ways, independent from, and even against, its colonial past – a development to which his own work has contributed significantly. According to de Holanda, early colonizing adventurers occupied the land of Brazil according to 'the spirit of Portuguese domination . . . which was less concerned with building, planning, or laying foundations, than with exploiting the easy riches that were available there for the taking'.[52] Niemeyer's domestic choreographies embrace post-colonial ideals and aspirations for partnership with the land and laying the foundations of a sustainable dialogue with nature.

It can hardly be stressed strongly enough that Burle Marx's magnificent gardens were indispensable to the realization of the vision of a post-colonial dwelling in the 'New World in the Tropics', clearly distinct from that of the Old World colonizers.[53] The gardens of this 'painter in plants' both integrate and reveal the character and ambitions of architectural interventions. 'A garden is not a copy of Nature,' Burle Marx liked to repeat. 'It is an organization of elements that exist in Nature. And that may be a work of art'.[54] His gardens temper the impact of tropical nature and epitomize the desire to cultivate the land and transform it artfully into a legible, human-scale, domesticated landscape in which to dwell pleasurably. They rarely follow the natural lay of the land; they invest in its riches in order to make of previously ruthlessly exploited nature a cultural artefact and an invaluable resource of useless delight and sensual pleasure.

48 Labrusse, p. 85.   **49** Niemeyer, 2002, n.p.   **50** Sérgio Buarque de Holanda, quoted in Martins, 2003, p. 65.   **51** Niemeyer, 1988c, p. 25.
52 Sérgio Buarque de Holanda, quoted in Martins, 2003, p. 65.   **53** *New World in the Tropics* is the title of a book by Gilberto Freyre; Freyre, 1963.
54 Treib, p. 53; Roberto Burle Marx, in Leftel.

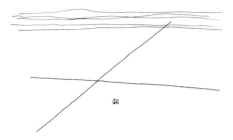

Chapter Six

Brasília: The President's Plantation or the Second Colonization of Brazil

Who was it that invented Brasília?
it was Dr Costa
it was Dr Costa
on the 21st of April
two months after Carnival

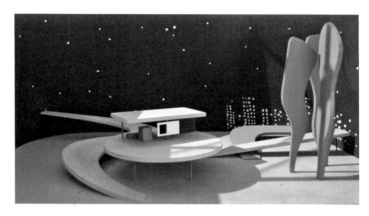

While Brasília, the long-awaited new capital of Brazil, was 'rising up from the middle of nowhere' *Orfeu do Carnaval* or *Orphée Noir* (*Black Orpheus*) was lighting up the silver screen.[1] Released in Brazil in 1959, *Orphée Noir* was French director Marcel Camus's version of the very successful musical play *Orfeu da Conceição* by the poet and composer Vinícius de Moraes (1918–80), which had opened at the Teatro Municipal in Rio de Janeiro on 25 September 1956, directed by Léo Jusi.[2] The allegorical stage set for *Orfeu da Conceição* was designed by de Moraes's friend, Oscar Niemeyer, and was dominated by his signature sweeping ramps leading up the Morro da Conceição.[3] The score for the play had been written by Antônio Carlos (Tom) Jobim, 'the pope of Brazilian modern music' according to Ronaldo Bôscoli, who had recommended him to the poet when the latter was looking specifically for someone modern.[4] Tom Jobim with de Moraes and Luiz Bonfá wrote the soundtrack to the motion picture, which sold millions of records. In 1957, only a year before the film was produced, Rio had been enraptured by João Gilberto's musical invention in the form of 'Hô-ba-la lá' and 'Bim-bom', the latter reproducing 'the rhythm of the washerwomen's hips when they passed by carrying bundles of laundry on their heads'. The new beat that the genius Bahian guitarist had brought to Rio was first called *samba moderno* but eventually became famous as *bossa nova*.[5]

Orphée Noir brought to an international audience not only the gliding groove of *bossa nova* but also the bucolic utopia of the happy black *favelados* who sing, dance and play their guitar all day, oblivious to poverty and chores. At the start of the film, Orpheus and Eurydice appear on an ancient frieze that bursts into life to reveal a colourful group of musicians dancing up a Rio hill. Following the well-practised Antropofagist method, Vinícius de Moraes had transported the legendary Old World couple into the

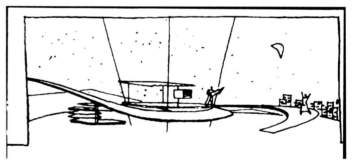

Stage set for the musical play *Orfeu da Conceição*, written by Vinícius de Moraes, directed by Léo Jusi and opened at the Teatro Municipal in Rio de Janeiro on 25 September 1956

The epigraph to this chapter is a paraphrase of the first verses of a 1934 parodic *marchinha* (carnival march) by Lamartine Babo, entitled 'História do Brasil': 'Who was it that invented Brazil? / it was Mr Cabral / it was Mr Cabral / on the 21st of April / two months after Carnival' ('Quem foi que inventou o Brasil? / Foi seu Cabral / foi seu Cabral / no dia 21 do abril / dois meses depois do carnaval'), cited in José Miguel Wisnik, p. 558 in English, p. 563 in Portuguese.   **1** Niemeyer, 2000b, p. 98. Produced in 1958, by Sacha Gordine, *Orphée Noir* won the Cannes Palme d'Or in 1959 and a Golden Globe (1959) and Academy Award (1960) for Best Foreign Film.   **2** In 1959, *Orphée Noir* was hailed in Brazil as 'a wondrous documentary'; Huret. But Vinícius de Moraes 'didn't like the film at all because it had betrayed the original, he said. All the Brazilians I meet blamed Marcel Camus for having given such a facile and untruthful picture of their country'; Beauvoir, p. 547.   **3** The theatre play *Orfeu da Conceição* was awarded first prize at a competition held in 1954 in the context of the celebrations of the four hundredth anniversary of São Paulo.   **4** *Orfeu da Conceição* gave Vinícius de Moraes one of his first opportunities to write song lyrics. When the musical play moved to São Paulo, 'the set was transported by truck, but mysteriously, it never arrived in São Paulo, nor did it return to Rio'; Castro, 2000, p. 82.   **5** Castro, 2000, p. 105.

211

'religious outpouring of the [Brazilian] race', carnivalizing the ancient Greek myth, Brazilianizing and Africanizing it through a baptism in the exotic waters of the 'marvellous city' and its most vibrant neighbourhoods on the *morros*.[6]

De Moraes, who described himself as the 'blackest white man in Brazil', is reported to have had the idea of a black Orpheus during a conversation with the American writer Waldo Frank.[7] The two writers had been exploring Rio's sites of black culture in early 1942, and Frank drew analogies between black pagan festivals and the neglected, Dionysian side of ancient Greek culture. Upon reading the myth of Orpheus at the house of the architect Carlos Leão, de Moraes sketched out his 'Carioca black tragedy' in one night as a 'homage to the Brazilian black'.[8] Orpheus who, according to the Greek philosopher Proclus, was the principal in the Dionysian rites and played Apollo's lyre, provided de Moraes with an ideal character in whom to unite the native with the foreign, the savage with the civilized, in the manner of the Brazilian Antropofagists yet also in the tradition of European primitivism.[9]

Camus's film distanced itself from its highly symbolic predecessor, *Orphée* (1949), the second film in the Orphic trilogy of the Parisian avant-garde cinematic poet Jean Cocteau (1889–1963), who had frequented Tarsila do Amaral's studio. Camus diligently included the blind prophet figure, the fortune-teller Mira, Hermes the messenger, Cerberus, the maenads and so on – all in Brazilian roles and robes. In his film, however, the Antropofagist practice was turned into a powerless cliché. Rather than a critical appropriation and mixing of 'civilization and savagery', *Orphée Noir* is centred upon a picturesque portrayal of the modern savage for the entertainment of the civilized.[10] What in the hands of the Brazilian Modernists had been a strategy for decolonization, cultural empowerment and subversion of the European models, Marcel Camus light-heartedly transformed into a tool for romanticization of the poor and the primitive Other, for aesthetization and commodification of the stereotypical image of popular Brazil, a glamorous repackaging of Brazilian folklore for consumption by Hollywood-bred audiences. Camus's idealized, humble *favelados*, inhabiting a purified, idyllic shanty town, are presented in the same way as the innocent, happy natives of sixteenth-century chroniclers and the carefree blacks of the curious European artists who made the pilgrimage to the *favela* hills of Rio de Janeiro from the early days of the twentieth century.

Camus's immortalized hero is not Cocteau's avant-garde poet but a Brazilian popular samba musician whose tunes have the power to make the sun rise. The mythologization of the *favelas* and their characters – especially the *sambista de morro*, the national character par excellence – and the glorification of carnival and Rio's spectacular landscape had been initiated in Brazil long before Camus's film was produced. From 1937 to 1945 Getúlio Vargas's Estado Nôvo had been a keen promoter and exporter of Brazilian popular culture with a view to attracting tourists, promoting national unity and identity, and turning people's attention away from the dark side of the dictatorship. Football, samba and the samba schools of Rio's carnival received official support. In the 1950s and 1960s, Rádio Nacional achieved a national consolidation of urban popular music, especially samba. In 1958, Pelé led the Brazilian football team to its first World Cup victory, which was celebrated with dancing in the streets. Breno Mello, who played Orpheus in Camus's film, was a football player. By then, a number of films had already transformed the *favela*, cradle of the national tune, into 'the site for idealized dreams of a beautiful and dignified poverty. The clichés of the "noble savage" . . . were applied to the "noble poor".'[11]

Orphée Noir exported the exotic New World Other, living in a perfect climate, in the same way that sixteenth-century French sailors returning from France Antarctique had brought Tupinambá and Tabajara Indians to Rouen to participate in 'Brazilian festivals', specially staged to enchant Henry II (1550) and later Charles IX and Catherine de' Medici with their court (1562).[12] Among those observing the real, naked natives swinging in hammocks or engaging in tribal warfare was the philosopher Michel de Montaigne, who subsequently wrote 'Des Cannibales'.

Orphée Noir, which proved extremely popular, perpetuated fantasies about an exuberant land where exotic beauty, joy and sensuality are plentiful. Once again, Brazil was portrayed as a lost paradise, inhabited by beautiful *mulatas* swaying their hips seductively up the Morro da Babilônia. Signs of a rather naïve optimism were abundant but signs of modernity had been carefully eradicated. As Jean-Luc Godard pointed out at the time, even the city's means of public transport had been replaced by outdated ones to match Rio's filmic primitive inhabitants. Godard, who had visited Rio de Janeiro the year before, particularly disapproved of Eurydice's arrival in the city via a primitive boat rather than at the small airport of Santos Dumont, 'the most beautiful [airport] in the world'.[13] The Ministry of Education, already almost twenty years old, did feature in *Orphée Noir*, but in silent isolation, totally devoid of people, portrayed as a site of alienation that Eurydice crosses quickly to reach the noisy, colourful carnival crowds and eventually the happy land of the *morro*.

The filmic tale of the immortal, illiterate *sambista* brought to the world the shuffling beat of *bossa nova*, born in the nightclubs

6 From Oswald de Andrade's 'Manifesto da Poesia Pau-Brasil'. Oswald de Andrade, 1989, p. 310.   7 Vinícius de Moraes, quoted in Stam, 1997, p. 113.   8 Vinícius de Moraes, text on the sleeve of *Orfeu da Conceição*, long play 10", music by Antônio Carlos Jobim, lyrics by Vinícius de Moraes, Odeon MODB 3056, 1956; Moraes, 1960.   9 'I began to reflect on the life of blacks in Rio and to Hellenize their experience', wrote Vinícius de Moraes, quoted in Stam, 1997, p. 168.   10 Blaise Cendrars, quoted in Calil, p. 568.   11 Bentes, p. 129.   12 For France Antarctique, see Chapter Three, p. 103, n. 67.   13 Jean-Luc Godard, quoted in http://www.geocities.com/Hollywood/9400/ofilme.html. Last accessed March 2004.

and bourgeois apartments of Rio's *zona sul*, at a time of national euphoria and heedless optimism. But the optimism that pervaded Brazil in the late 1950s was not that of the trapped poor who escape reality through daydreaming. Brazil was in the process of constructing her bright future with real bricks and mortar or, rather, steel and concrete. Her optimism was based on a forward-looking, democratically elected government, vigorously pursuing political stability, innovation and ambitious programmes for rapid economic development, aggressive industrialization and modernization. In *Orphée Noir*, the stammering rhythm of *bossa nova* accompanied images of a bucolic utopia on the hills of Rio, which appeared to preserve a rural way of life. At the same time, the heart of the Brazilian nation was set on a new, urban utopia. At the Planalto Central, Brazil's central highlands, hammers were pounding ceaselessly to build 'the most beautiful capital in the world'.[14] 'Invented' in a beachfront apartment in Leblon, it was envisaged as a city uncompromisingly modern, which would inaugurate 'the New Age of Brazil'.[15]

The Utopia of Decolonization, National Unity and a Great Destiny

Brasília was both a new and an old, long-cherished utopia. From the official and highly symbolic – however mythical – date of its inception in 1789, the idea of a new Brazilian capital was associated with the goal of achieving independence from the Old World and fulfilling Brazil's exalted destiny.[16] The notion of a Brazilian city of the future had been at the centre of the preoccupations of the Paulista Modernists (née Futurists) of the early twentieth century. For Oswald de Andrade 'Never was any human conglomeration so irrevocably bound to Futurism of action, industry, history and art as São Paulo. What are we, inevitably and unavoidably, if not Futurists – this people of a thousand origins, carried here with their failures and hopes in a thousand ships?' Ronald de Carvalho extolled the 'great virgin world, full of exciting promise', and 'a people in gestation'.[17]

To the *futuristas* in the avant-garde centre of Brazil in the 1920s, São Paulo was the 'city of the future'. But to all Brazilians who yearned for a future radically different from the past as well as

from the present, the epicentre of a truly liberated and emancipated, unequivocally modern Brazil was a city not yet built. Early in 1926, Fernand Léger wrote to Le Corbusier that he had recommended him to 'one of his Brazilian admirers, Mr [Paulo] Prado', when the latter spoke of the project for an 'entirely new city to be constructed' in Brazil. A few months later, Blaise Cendrars informed Le Corbusier of the Brazilian government's intention to ask Congress for approval of the necessary funds for the construction of the federal capital, 'a city of one million souls: PLANALTINA, in a region still virgin'.[18]

The building of Brasília in the 1950s signified the realization of the old dream of opening up the vast unexplored interior of the country, claiming her legendary natural and material riches, and of unifying the two Brazils, the urban Brazil of the coast, which embodied the European legacy, and the rural one of the hinterland, the truly Brazilian one, as predicted by Euclides da Cunha. Da Cunha's epic of 1902, *Os Sertões*, had been based upon 'the bold and inspiring conjecture that [the Brazilians] are destined to national unity'.[19] President Juscelino Kubitschek's audacious transfer of the capital from the coast to the untapped interior marked Brazil's settling of her promised land on the central highlands, as stipulated in the First Republican Constitution of 1891 and reiterated in those of 1934 and 1946.

Washington Luís, president from 1926 to 1930, coined the motto 'to govern is to construct roads', and in 1928 he had celebrated the completion of the Rio–São Paulo highway as the major achievement of his administration.[20] Kubitschek's government opened over 17,000 kilometres of new roads and 'highways of national union', some through regions hitherto unmapped, connecting Brasília with the rest of the country, while also making Brazil the world's seventh largest automobile producer (somewhat ironically, an industry concentrated almost entirely in the area of greater São Paulo and in foreign hands). Brasília was built on the macroeconomic assumptions that it would help diffuse modernization and development in the surrounding region, and that its invigoration of labour-intensive activities – such as road and public-work construction – would induce the incorporation into the market of large marginalized segments of Brazilian society.[21] Kubitschek anticipated a 'new order' that would guarantee the

14 Juscelino Kubitschek, quoted in Niemeyer, 2000b, p. 70.   **15** Lúcio Costa, ' "Ingredientes" da concepção urbanística de Brasília' (n.d.), in Lúcio Costa, 1997, p. 282, emphasis in the original.   **16** That the transfer of the capital to the interior constituted one of the goals of the 1789 movement for independence belongs to Brasília's mythology rather than history. It was put forward by Professor Horácio Mendes in the journal *Brasília*, no. 40, dedicated to the inauguration of the city, but remains unsubstantiated. It is nevertheless promoted by the Historical Museum of Brasília: Vidal, p. 287. The first known document containing a proposal for the transfer of the imperial capital to a new city, named 'Nova Lisboa' and located in the interior of the country, is the text of a speech by William Pitt, given in the British Parliament in 1807 or early 1808 (published in 1809, but its authenticity has been contested). Pitt's concern was for British commercial interests. In 1813 and again in 1818 Hipólito José da Costa argued for the transfer of the Brazilian capital to the interior of the country, the region of Goiás, on the basis of Brazilian interests. His articles appeared in the first newspaper that opposed the Portuguese administration of Brazil, *Correio Braziliense*, published irregularly in London from 1808 to 1822. Arguing for the interiorization of the capital and the population of the Brazilian territory, Hipólito José da Costa spoke of a 'terrestrial paradise': Vidal, pp. 36–43.   **17** Oswald de Andrade; Ronald de Carvalho, quoted in Franco, p. 110.   **18** Letters published in Portuguese in Cecília Rodrigues dos Santos et al., pp. 41–42, upper case in the original. See also Tsiomis, 2006, p. 17. On Blaise Cendrars, see Chapter One, pp. 26–27.   **19** Cunha, p. 481, n. 5.   **20** Garcia, p. 11.   **21** See Farret, pp. 137–48.

integration of millions of isolated Brazilian citizens in the poor interior of the country, a better life for all and a fairer distribution of Brazil's 'riches'.[22]

In the interior of Brazil, far away from the tropical coastal paradise, da Cunha and his sertanist literary predecessors had found the real, pure, authentic Brazil. *Os Sertões* had revealed the prophesy of a singer who is blind like the shamans of antiquity: 'a thousand flocks shall run from the seacoast to the backlands; and then the backlands [*sertão*] will turn into seacoast and the seacoast into backlands [*sertão*] . . . and the earth some place shall find itself in heaven.' The prophesies associated with the old Portuguese Sebastianist cults and transplanted to Brazil were written down in notebooks found in Canudos by da Cunha. The latter nationalized the apocalyptic sayings of the popular mystic of the backlands, Antônio Vicente Mendes Maciel or Antônio Conselheiro, who led his band of followers into the desert and established his city of the elect at the Vasa-Barris River, known as Arraial de Canudos.

Da Cunha reported that these nineteenth-century settlers saw Canudos or Belo Monte 'as the first broad step of the stairway to heaven'. Their social rebellion brought the nation's attention to the simple folk who humiliated the police unit sent against them in 1896, and to their long, heroic struggle against the 'furiously raging' federal army until their massacre and their settlement's violent devastation in 1897, witnessed by da Cunha.[23] In 1889, the historian Capistrano de Abreu found in the interior of the country 'the consolidator of Brazilian nationality and the unifier of the nation'.[24] And in the decades that followed the publication of da Cunha's epic, which identified the villain with the cities on the coast, the identification of the interior with the Brazilian Brazil was popularized.

For more than a century the belief had been cultivated that, for the prophecies to be realized and Brazil to fulfil her independent destiny, she had to turn her back on the coastal centre of the Portuguese maritime empire, renouncing the Portuguese habit of 'clinging to the coast like crabs' described in 1627 by the Franciscan Frei Vicente do Salvador, the first historian of Brazil. Already in 1813, a Carioca newspaper had urged: 'We are no longer these crabs . . . but a people which has projected itself into the heart of the continent, which has taken its territory virilly in its hands and is preparing to be, in a short while, one of the four great nations of the universe.'[25]

In 1823, Paulo Ferreira de Menezes Palmiro dedicated to José Bonifácio, the pre-eminent leader of the era of independence, the first project for Brazil's new continental capital, named Cidade Pedrália, in the honour of Emperor Dom Pedro I.[26] It was followed by Imperatória (1839–78). Petrópolis was also perhaps inspired by José Bonifácio's proposal for a new capital 'called Brasilea or Petropole', and was built by German immigrants and slaves in

record time (1844–50), in a plantation area in the 'alpine' province of Rio de Janeiro. But this was a new 'European' city, built for Dom Pedro II's 'delight and protection', soon to become his favourite retreat.[27] On 30 August 1883, the Italian missionary friar and future patron saint of Brasília, Dom Giovanni Bosco, had one of his oft-repeated dreams. 'Between parallels 15 and 20 there was a long and wide depression, in the vicinity of a lake. Thus spoke a voice, over and over again: "when they come to explore the riches buried in these mountains, here will rise the promised land of milk and honey, of unconceivable wealth." '[28] The prophecy of Dom Bosco endowed Brasília with a mystical origin too; the choice of the site for the new federal capital was guided by divine revelation.

In 1912, Gustavo Barroso published his *Terra do Sol* (*Land of the Sun*), singing the praises of the backlander, and in 1942 Cassiano Ricardo's *Marcha para o Oeste* (*March to the West*) romanticized the *bandeirantes*' explorations of the untrodden interior in search of gold, precious stones and slaves, as well as the socio-political organization of the Brazilian West, where 'There is no preoccupation with class and position . . . no preoccupation about color, creed or origin'.[29] *Bandeirante* activity in the seventeenth and eighteenth centuries was seen to have been a major contributor to territorial expansion and national unity. Getúlio Vargas had been hailed by Ildefonso Escobar as the heir of the restless *bandeirantes*, announcing plans for a 'March to the West', aiming for a modern, industrial Brazil that would also be national and nationalist, away from the cosmopolitanism of the coast.

But it was Juscelino Kubitschek who sallied forth into the unknown Brazilian central plateau, aiming for pioneering growth and the realization of the national multi-ethnic and egalitarian utopia, carving 'highways of national union'. Marching towards the area demarcated by law (no. 1803) as 'Future Federal District' (on the basis of the recommendations of the Luiz Cruls Commission, 1892–93, and the Polli Coelho Commission, 1946–48, approved by Congress on 5 January 1953), Kubitschek assumed the role of the messiah of the Canudos prophet, heralding national unity and territorial integration: 'there will be . . . one shepherd and

22 Kubitschek, 1960, pp. 2–3.   **23** Cunha, pp. 135, 143, 475. Sebastianism is the Portuguese messianic belief in the return of Sebastião I, king of Portugal from 1557 to 1578, to restore the Portuguese nation to its former greatness. Sebastianism persisted into the nineteenth century. **24** Capistrano de Abreu, cited in Burns, 1970, pp. 352–53.   **25** *Correio Brasiliense*, quoted in Shoumatoff, p. 60.   **26** For a discussion of Cidade Pedrália and the projects that followed it, see Vidal, pp. 60–107. **27** Schwarcz, 2004, p. 176.   **28** Dom Giovanni Bosco, quoted in http://www.infobrasilia.com.br/bsb_h5i.htm#sonho. Last accessed May 2004.   **29** Cassiano Ricardo, quoted in Burns, 1970, p. 353. For the *bandeirantes*, see Chapter Four, p. 165, n. 102.

one flock only', 'preaching sermons at the gates, making towns in the desert'.[30]

In symbolic terms, Kubitschek's bold decision to move the capital to the unknown hinterland may be compared with Hernán Cortés's burning of his ships at the beginning of his expedition to the interior of Mexico in 1519. Brasília signified a new beginning as well as the culmination of independent Brazil's efforts to become a coherent, integrated and emancipated modern nation, represented by a city built by Brazilians at the centre of the *Land of the Future*, as Stefan Zweig had dubbed Brazil.[31] Brazil's centre of gravity was finally moving away from the old centre of colonial power. From the ports of the colonial coastal towns, Brazil's riches had been exported for centuries. The Brazilians who favoured the interiorization of the capital favoured an interiorization of their land's legendary resources; that is, their exploitation for the benefit of Brazilians themselves.

In the early twentieth century, many were those who had praised the riches awaiting the brave who ventured *Through the Brazilian Wilderness* (1914), the title of former US president Theodore Roosevelt's account of his own guided adventure of 1913. Roosevelt described the 'vast open spaces', 'clear and fresh' air and seemingly 'limitless' landscape of Brazil's central plateau, echoing the local prophets: 'Surely, in the future this region will be the home of a healthy, highly civilized population.'[32]

Kubitschek did not harbour another vision of a fabled El Dorado in the rainforest. Neither did he lead an expedition to cover the 1,000 kilometres from the coast to the site selected for Brasília. The first construction materials for Brazil's new capital in the semi-arid scrubland, 1,000 metres above sea level, in the state of Goiás, came in Air Force planes. And so did the president's 'Michelangelo', Oscar Niemeyer, having hastily closed his Copacabana office to dedicate himself entirely to the transformation of 'a huge and dismal patch of wilderness' into the acropolis of the new Brazil, the place where a new utopia would become concrete reality.[33]

On 2 October 1956, Juscelino Kubitschek visited the site of Brasília for the first time, with Oscar Niemeyer and the war minister, General Henrique Teixeira Lott, and predicted 'a new dawn' for Brazil. On 2 December 1956, construction work started at Brasília's vital point of contact with the rest of the vast country: the airport, which was to have the largest runway in Brazil. The 'first airport in the world specially designed for the age of jets', serving 'the first city planned from the air' was inaugurated on 2 April 1957.[34] Independence Day, 21 April 1960, commemorating the martyrdom in 1792 of Tiradentes, the anniversary of Brazil's discovery and the date of Rome's foundation, was the date set by law for the inauguration of the capital that symbolically marked the completion of the second discovery of Brazil, by the Brazilians themselves. The Herculean task had to be accomplished within Kubitschek's five-year term of office, since, by law, the president could serve only a single term; that is, Brasília had to be completed within three years, one month and five days of the selection of its masterplan.

Brasília, frontier capital: map showing the distances between Brasília and other major Brazilian cities

30 Juscelino Kubitschek, quoted in Burns, 1970, p. 337; Cunha, p. 135. On 8 June 1953, Getúlio Vargas established the Comissão de Localização da Nova Capital Federal (Commission for the Location of the New Federal Capital) with General Aguinaldo Caiado de Castro as president. In August and September 1953, Aerofoto, a Brazilian photogrammetric company, surveyed the area using aerial photography. On 20 April 1954, the firm of Donald J. Belcher & Associates of Ithaca, New York, was contracted to select five alternative sites for a capital city of 500,000 inhabitants, within the greater area established in 1953. The results of their study were submitted to Marechal José Pessoa Cavalcanti de Albuquerque (1885–1959, known as Marechal José Pessoa), new president of the Comissão de Localização da Nova Capital Federal. The site finally chosen on 15 April 1955 by the Pessoa Commission 'was precisely the spot which had been so favourably described by Dr. Glaziou and recommended by the Cruls report sixty-one years previously. It lay 25 kilometres southeast of the town of Planaltina where, in 1922, President Epitácio Pessôa had dedicated a monument to the new capital. The present Federal District of 5,814 square kilometers lies between the parallels of 15° 30' and 16° 03' and is bound on the east and west by the rivers Descoberto and Prêto . . . Within the Federal District, the city itself occupies a roughly triangular site originally bounded by two rivers, the Bananal and Gamma, which converged to form the Paranoá. Subsequently, the Paranoá was dammed, creating a 15-square-mile artificial lake surrounding the site of the city', Evenson, 1973, pp. 110–12, quotation on p. 112. See also Vidal, pp. 175–88. 31 Although it is often said that Brasília lies at the geographical centre of the country, it is rather the case that its position marks the demographical centre of Brazil. *Land of the Future* is the subtitle of Stefan Zweig's 1941 book on Brazil; see Chapter One, p. 35. 32 Juscelino Kubitschek, quoted in Shoumatoff, p. 31; Theodore Roosevelt, quoted in Evenson, 1969, pp. 19–20. 33 Niemeyer, 2000b, p. 70. 34 Israël Pinheiro, quoted in Dos Passos, p. 76. Niemeyer writes: 'I accompanied JK on his first flight to the site . . . It was a three hours flight. I confess I did not have a good impression of the site. Far away from everything, it was an abandoned, empty land. But JK's enthusiasm was such, and the purpose of driving the progress inward was so valid that we all ended up agreeing with him.' Niemeyer, 2000a, p. 35.

The Utopia of Order and Progress

The relocation of the federal capital to the desolate red earth of the *cerrado* or tropical savannah of central Brazil aimed to materialize a modern national centre purified of and distanced from both the colonial past and the socio-economic problems of the present. Paradise on earth was to be realized through an escape from lands infested with problems that it would be easier to run away from than to solve.[35] The impoverished *sertão* was the symbolic centre of both the true Brazil of the hinterland and the country's hunger, misery and social injustice. Together with the real urban *favela* – not the ideal land of *Orphée Noir* – the burning sands of the rural *sertão* became identified with the Brazilian underbelly, the loci of disillusion with positivism, of social inequality, and of modernity's failure to reach those it had promised to save.

Still today, the *sertão* and the *favela* are Brazil's rural and urban sites of poverty, violence and marginality, 'two sides of the same coin', holding privileged positions in the Brazilian imaginary. They are historically connected too: *favelas* acquired their name from Morro da Favella as Rio's Morro da Providência was christened after Mount Favella in Canudos by the soldiers who settled there in protest against unpaid wages following their return from the campaign against the Canudos rebels. Mount Favella was the birthplace of many of the girls who came with the soldiers. Subsequent migrants from the arid backlands to Brazil's urban centres settled in *favelas* which, for some time, retained a semirural character. It has been suggested that in the *favelas* of Rio 'the remnants of Palmares and Canudos, that is, the heirs of the greatest rebellions of slaves and north-eastern peasants in the country, have survived and multiplied'.[36] By 1957 the *favelas* housed a quarter of Rio's population, harbouring potentially 'large forces of riot and rebellion' according to officials and the upper classes.[37] Kubitschek's relocation of the capital to the *cerrado* signified a desire to re-create an orderly centre of power far away from the impoverished *sertão* and from the 'unsightly' *favelas*.[38]

Brasília, the 'perennial dream of Brazilian patriots' in the words of the nationalists of the 1920s, the city conceived to do justice to the Republican slogan 'Order and Progress', befitting positivist Brazil, was designed to be a city without *favelas*.[39] 'It is very important to avoid the mushrooming of hovels ... it is up to the Urbanizing Company ... to provide decent and economic accommodation for the entire population', proposed Lúcio Costa in the 'Report' that accompanied his winning entry for the masterplan of Brasília.[40] Costa may have envisaged a new seat of power without the disorder of the *favelas*, but the building of Brasília required large numbers of immigrant workers and most of these were *nordestinos* (from the Northeast, 43 per cent, according to a 1959 census), escaping the drought-ridden *sertão*.[41] They arrived in waves as soon as construction began at Brasília, and they continued to flock into the city for decades after its inauguration.

> In March 1958, about ten thousand *flagelados* [victims of calamitous drought] began to leave the Northeast in a great diaspora. About half of them, barefooted, emaciated, with only the rags on their backs and a few crusts of bread, descended on Cidade Livre [the city where the *candangos* who laboured to build Brasília lived] and created Brasília's first *favela*,

which they strategically christened Sara Kubitschek Town after the president's wife.[42]

Brasília was to stay clear of the problems of big cities, and the poor *favelados* were, initially at least, expected to depart once they had built the city of a magnificent future, from which they were banished. In contrast to other cities envisaged by the European avant-garde movements of the early twentieth century, Brasília was not conceived as a metropolis for large masses, where the individual is absorbed by the perfect city-machine. It could be argued that an architecture aiming at representing ideas of mass production, governed by 'a formal law equally valid for each ele-

35 Kubitschek argued that 'Brasília ... permitted the Congress to act freely and to rule quietly without social disturbances or pressures. This by itself justifies Brasília'; quoted in Inês Palma Fernandes, p. 139. **36** Lúcia Nagib, 2003, pp. 158, 160. **37** Anthony Leeds, quoted in Epstein, p. 7. Interestingly, the *favelas* were built on the same hills that had hosted the resistance of the Tupinambás and few remaining French colonists against the Portuguese colonizers in the sixteenth century. **38** In the imagination of the builders of Brasília, the *cerrado* of central Brazil was identified with da Cunha's mythologized *sertão* rather than the real, impoverished *sertão*. This identification was so strong that, in his account of his experience at Brasília, Niemeyer repeatedly refers to the land where the capital was built as 'sertão' rather than 'cerrado'; Niemeyer, 1960. Cf: 'Rio seems to have turned its back on its own country ... Rio is a lavish show-window which hides from public view the poor, backward, and forgotten *sertão*, and in order that the attention of the state be drawn to the *sertão* – to the jungle, the mighty grasslands, the untold potential riches, and to the lean but strong *sertanejo*, the forgotten man of the back country – the seat of government must be established in the heart of Brazil's vast territory, so that it surveys the whole national panorama, so that it will be within reach of all the classes and all the regions'; Penna, n.d., n.p. **39** Burns, 1968, p. 68. **40** Lúcio

Costa, 1966, p. 16. In his 1944 call for 'the reconquest of monumental expression', Sigfried Giedion had announced: 'The civic center of the coming period will be surrounded by greenery, it will never be a neighbor to slums'; Giedion, 1984, p. 59. **41** Epstein, p. 141. **42** Shoumatoff, p. 58. Its inhabitants were eventually moved to Brasília's first satellite town, Taguatinga, planned by NOVACAP (Companhia Urbanizadora da Nova Capital do Brasil) outside the lakeshed, 25 kilometres from the Plano Piloto. Other *favelas* followed, however. According to Costa's original plan, satellite towns were to be built only after the Plano Piloto had been completely occupied.
The Núcleo Bandeirante was a temporary settlement outside the Plano Piloto, approximately 15 kilometres from the intersection of the two axes of the city, where land was made available for Brasília's workmen. It consisted primarily of wooden shacks and provided residence as well shopping and entertainment facilities. It was renamed Cidade Livre (Free City) because it was exempted from taxes. By 1960, it had 12,000 inhabitants, and in June 1961 the National Congress declared it a satellite town with its original name reinstated. Costa opposed the legitimization of the Cidade Livre, and never stopped campaigning for its eradication.
In tribute to the pioneering workmen of Brasília, its early citizens called themselves *candangos*.

Núcleo Bandeirante, renamed Cidade Livre, Brasília

Juscelino Kubitschek in Hotel Brasília, Núcleo Bandeirante (Cidade Livre), 8 December 1956

Candango in Núcleo Bandeirante (Cidade Livre), 1956

Avenida Central, Núcleo Bandeirante (Cidade Livre), 1957–60

ment', as envisaged by L. Hilberseimer in 1927, would have been a more suitable representation of Kubitschek's programme of intensive industrialization.[43] Yet the new, smoothly functioning seat of the Brazilian national government, at the demographic centre of the country, was intended to remain close to the Platonic and Aristotelian ideal of a small polity, reaching a population of a mere 500,000 by the year 2000, exactly the same number as that envisaged for Le Corbusier's Chandigarh (1951–65).[44] This city 'of the human scale', of a much lower density than Le Corbusier's Ville Radieuse of the early 1930s, was also in accordance with the post-

war doctrine of CIAM (the Congrès Internationaux d'Architecture Moderne).[45] Brasília was envisaged as the small, symbolic capital of a multi-centred Brazil, appropriate for a democratic regime, and also as an isolated city, where riots would be easier to control.[46]

The diplomat J. O. de Meira Penna argued that Brasília, far removed from the coast and its sinful diversions, possessed the 'physical [and] mental climate' that was needed to establish 'a small and efficient civil service, capable of coping with the urgent problems of a growing colossus'. Although the Brazilian flag has

43 L. Hilberseimer, quoted in Tafuri, p. 106. **44** Cf: 'Chandigarh is a Government city with a precise goal and consequently a precise quality of inhabitants. On this presumption, the city has not to be a big city (metropolis) – it must not lose its definition'; Le Corbusier, *Statute of the Land*, quoted in Sagar, p. 369.

As a result of real-estate prices (the highest in Brazil) and property taxation policy (the highest in the federal district), Brasília's Plano Piloto and its periphery developed asymmetrically. In 2000, the population of the federal district had exceeded two million, while the Plano Piloto accommodated a mere 198,422 inhabitants; Holanda et al., p. 25. In his 1987 document 'Brasília Revisited', Costa raised the potential population of the Plano Piloto to one million. Although the federal district grows at an annual demographic rate of 3.41 per cent, Brazil's highest, the number of residents in the Plano Piloto is falling every year; Batista et al., p. 175. **45** Maria Elisa Costa insists that the distinguishing features of Brasília – the *'superquadras . . . monumental scale . . . [and] symbolic aspects'* – have 'no connection to Ciams'. 'Everything', she emphatically posits, 'is much nearer to the Brazilian soul.' Betraying the persistent national (at least Carioca) identification of things Brazilian with things Carioca, she later adds: 'Brasília is "*carioca*"'; Maria Elisa Costa, 2002, p. 254. **46** It was in the administration of Castelo Branco, first military president after the 1964 coup, that the city was consolidated as the de facto capital, and its isolation from the masses of the Brazilian population played a key role.

'Ordem e Progresso' emblazoned across a night sky as seen from Rio de Janeiro, it was believed by many at the time that real order and progress could not be appropriately administered from the old, coastal capital. In Rio, Penna argued,

> serving the state seems merely an easy way of life, a peculiar but congenial form of social welfare. Rio breeds a parasitical bureaucracy . . . A resort town, surrounded by the seductions of nature and steeped in a luxurious atmosphere, a Cythera where one basks in the sun, swims in the cool waters and enjoys the pleasures of life with nonchalance.[47]

Located 1,000 kilometres away from the old capital's crowded, unhygienic *favelas* and 80 kilometres of opulent strand, a small and beachless Brasília was expected to nurture an efficient governmental mechanism, free from corruption and closer to the problems of the country as a whole.[48] The idea of a sanitary new capital as a means to escape the ills of a seaport had already been with the Portuguese chancellor and royal crown advisor Veloso de Oliveira in 1810, when he had advised the court to settle in a 'location free from the confusion of the clamorous multitudes of people indiscriminately thrown together'.[49] Ironically, it was the decolonized Brazilians who would eventually seek to escape the evils of Rio.

In September 1956, on the insistence of the Institute of Brazilian Architects (IAB), and against Le Corbusier's advice,[50] NOVACAP (Companhia Urbanizadora da Nova Capital do Brasil), a governmental body specially founded to undertake all work in relation to the grandiose project of the transfer of the capital, with Oscar Niemeyer appointed director of the Department of Architecture and Urbanism, announced a competition for all architects, engineers and urbanists with a licence to practise in Brazil.[51] Its brief was considered by William Holford, chair of the jury, 'perhaps, the simplest ever issued for a competition of this size', giving the candidates immense freedom and placing priority on political symbolism and aesthetics.[52] The deadline for submissions was 11 March 1957.

The twentieth-century colonization of the remote Planalto Central retraced the steps of the Portuguese colonizers of the sixteenth century. Lúcio Costa's winning Plano Piloto (Pilot Plan), in the form of a cross, re-enacted the sixteenth-century discovery and appropriation of Brazil, first christened Ilha de Vera Cruz or Island of the True Cross by Dom Manuel I. This second arrival on new land, by the Brazilians this time, followed the pattern of the Portuguese colonization and fecundation of land deemed virgin. In 1955, Marechal Pessoa, president of the Comissão de Localização da Nova Capital Federal (Commission for the Location of the New Federal Capital), had proposed Vera Cruz as an appropriate name, 'representing . . . the historical continuity of [Brazil], civilized through the centuries in the shadow of the holy rood'.[53] Costa's plan 'arose from the elementary gesture of one who marks or *takes possession* of a place: two axes crossing at right angles', like the *cardo* and *decumanus* of colonial Roman cities. These axes formed 'the sign of the cross itself', which had featured on the sails of Pedro Álvares Cabral's ships when they landed in Brazil in 1500, on the first flag that Portugal raised over Brazil, the 'Order of Christ', and on the flag decreed in 1822 for the kingdom of Brazil. In the 'Report' supporting his entry, Costa was explicit: 'Founding a city in the wilderness is a deliberate act of conquest.' His was 'a gesture of pioneers acting in the spirit of their colonial tradition'.[54]

Like Gilberto Freyre before him and Henrique Mindlin in his 1956 survey of *Modern Architecture in Brazil*, Costa situated the beginning of Brazilian civilization 'at the moment at which the Portuguese navigators stepped out of their caravels and into the feminized, Indianized water-bodies of coastal Brazil'.[55] Loyal to his struggle for a rehabilitation of the colonial heritage in the Brazilian cultural consciousness, Costa's act of conquest confirmed the re-Cabralization of Brazil, which Oswald de Andrade had wished to de-Cabralize, and the reintegration of the Church with the state, initiated by Vargas and evoked in the constitution of 1934. 'Catholicism was in reality the cement of our unity,' wrote Freyre in 1933.[56] 'The Cross of Christ has always been the seed of our nation-

47 Penna, n.d., n.p.   **48** When asked if he could live in Brasília, Lúcio Costa replied, from his Leblon apartment: 'Me? . . . Never. I'm a true son of Rio . . . I'm too *comodista*, addicted to the comforts here . . . That indolence . . . The beach at your door . . . no, I could never give it up'; Shoumatoff, p. 43. After his first visit to the site of Brasília, in 1957, Costa did not return to the city he 'invented' until 1974 for the 'First Seminar for the Study of the Urban Problems of Brasília', organized by Senator Cattete Pinheiro. See Costa's address, 'Lembrança do Seminário: Senado, Brasília' (1974), in Lúcio Costa, 1997, pp. 316–17.   **49** Veloso de Oliveira, quoted in Evenson, 1973, p. 106.   **50** Evenson, 1973, p. 118. In a letter to Hugo Gontier, consul general of Brazil in New York, Le Corbusier referred to competitions as 'democratic cowardice' (10 May 1955). On behalf of Marechal José Pessoa, Hugo Gontier invited Le Corbusier to 'give opinion commission Brazilian architects for planning said capital' (Telegram from Hugo Gontier to Le Corbusier, 2 June 1955). On 24 June 1955, Le Corbusier wrote to Pessoa of his wish to create Brasília's 'Plano Piloto'. He also wrote to the French president, Vincent Auriol, asking him to intercede in his favour with Juscelino Kubitschek. Finally, Marechal Pessoa decided against Le Corbusier's involvement in the project; Vidal, pp. 195–97.   **51** Kubitschek had 'insisted' that Niemeyer undertook the task, but Niemeyer refused. He 'considered [Affonso Eduardo Reidy] the most qualified for the task . . . He was the most experienced in urbanism

problems among us, once as a City Hall architect he had elaborated various projects of this kind'; quoted in Bonduki, p. 23. See also Niemeyer, 2000a, p. 36. As a trainee, Reidy had worked as a trainee with the French urbanist Donat-Alfred Agache on the Directive Plan for the City of Rio de Janeiro. Together with Roberto Burle Marx, in 1954 he had been part of Marechal Pessoa's group working on the demarcation of the new federal district. The competition brief for the masterplan of Brasília led to disagreement within the Institute of Brazilian Architects, which prompted Niemeyer's resignation from his post as vice-president. Some Brazilian architects like Jorge Moreira and Reidy refused to enter, protesting the conditions under which the competition was held; Vidal, p. 217. Reidy and Burle Marx proposed 'to call in Le Corbusier, who had already come forward to offer his services to Kubitschek by letter'; Tsiomis, 1997, p. 78.   **52** Holford, 1957, p. 397.   **53** Marechal José Pessoa, quoted in Vidal, p. 189. Two axes crossing at right angles had also defined the plan of Vera Cruz, proposed in 1955 by the Pessoa Commission (drawn by engineers Raul Pena Firme, José de Oliveira Reis and Roberto Lacombe, all three professors of urbanism). As Laurent Vidal points out, Vera Cruz was planned for the specific site chosen by the Pessoa Commission, in contrast to all earlier plans for the new capital, which were drawn without reference to any particular site; Vidal, p. 190, plan on p. 191.   **54** Lúcio Costa, 1966, p. 12.   **55** Williams, p. 244.   **56** Freyre, 1956, p. 45.

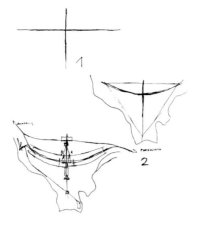

Lúcio Costa, the first sketches illustrating the 'Report' supporting his Plano Piloto:
1. Basically [the idea proposed] arose from the elementary gesture of one who marks or takes possession of a place: two axes crossing at right angles; the sign of the cross itself (figure 1).
2. It was then sought to adapt this cross to the local topography, the natural drainage of the area and, in short, to the best position possible; to achieve this one of the axes was curved in order to contain it within the equilateral triangle which limits the urbanized area (figure 2).
(Lúcio Costa, 1966, pp. 12–13)

The crossing of the two axes at Costa's Plano Piloto on the earth of the cerrado, 1957

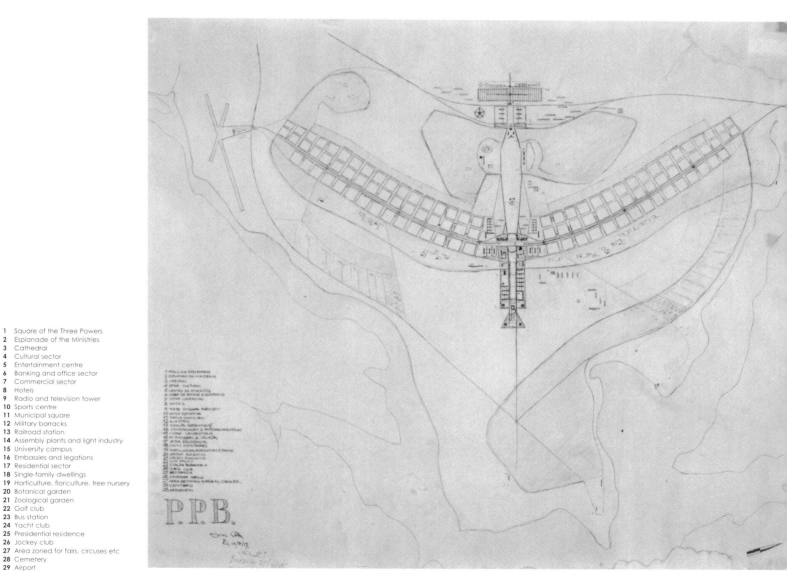

1 Square of the Three Powers
2 Esplanade of the Ministries
3 Cathedral
4 Cultural sector
5 Entertainment centre
6 Banking and office sector
7 Commercial sector
8 Hotels
9 Radio and television tower
10 Sports centre
11 Municipal square
12 Military barracks
13 Railroad station
14 Assembly plants and light industry
15 University campus
16 Embassies and legations
17 Residential sector
18 Single-family dwellings
19 Horticulture, floriculture, tree nursery
20 Botanical garden
21 Zoological garden
22 Golf club
23 Bus station
24 Yacht club
25 Presidential residence
26 Jockey club
27 Area zoned for fairs, circuses etc
28 Cemetery
29 Airport

Lúcio Costa, Plano Piloto (Pilot Plan), winning entry to the competition for the masterplan of Brasília, 10 March 1957

al unity,' reiterated Kubitschek in 1958, thus linking his efforts to those of the sixteenth-century Jesuit fathers who first ventured inland seeking recruits.[57] A replica of the statue of Nossa Senhora da Esperança (Our Lady of Hope, today at the Church of Santa Maria, Belmonte, Portugal) that accompanied Cabral in his voyage of discovery was later installed in the cathedral of Brasília.

In a later explanation of his plan, still in the spirit of a Cabralian conquest, Costa was careful not to exclude Brazil's indigenous population from this second colonizing force and the *caput mundi* of Brazil's multi-ethnic utopia. The 'shape of my plan', he suggested, is 'exactly' that of the Amazonian Indian's drawn bow about to shoot an arrow: the Brazilian capital, that is, fused within its primary form the colonial legacy and the noble qualities of the brave native Indian warriors.[58] And the planner's arrow was aimed at the wilderness of the interior.

On sixteenth- and seventeenth-century European maps, Brasilia is a name applied to the country as a whole.[59] It was proposed as the name for the new national capital 'in the center of Brazil' in 1822, and endorsed by José Bonifácio in 1823.[60] A symbolic foundation stone had been laid in Planaltina on 7 September 1922, the centenary of independence, in the *annus mirabilis* of the Modernist poet Mário de Andrade and birth year of all things modern Brazilian, including the Communist Party. But Kubitschek's building of a runway was the decisive act of taking possession of the new territory, recognizing the cardinal importance of communication links with the nation Brasília aimed to unite. The inauguration of the airport preceded the celebration of the first official Catholic mass on 3 May 1957 at the highest point of the city, and the erection of a wooden cross there – acts that repeated the ritual followed by Pedro Álvares Cabral and his men in Porto Seguro. The latter held the second mass on Brazilian soil on 3 May 1500, when the Tupiniquin Indians allegedly expressed their submission to the Christian faith. Kubitschek chose the date for its symbolism and invited the cacique of the Carajá Indians to the mass that marked the second birth of Brazil under the sign of the cross and confirmed the subjugation of the indigenous population.[61]

The large, temporary, open-air chapel with a monumental altar for the statue of the mestiza Nossa Senhora Aparecida,

patron saint of Brazil, was the first structure designed by Niemeyer for Brasília. Its light, hyperbolic canopy acknowledges the tent of the biblical tabernacle and prefigures the sweeping curves of the Roman Catholic churches Niemeyer designed for Brasília in subse-

Juscelino Kubitschek with the Carajá cacique at the first official Catholic mass held in Brasília on 3 May 1957

Above and below, open-air chapel for the first official Catholic mass, Brasília, 3 May 1957

57 Juscelino Kubitschek, quoted in Inês Palma Fernandes, p. 152. **58** Lúcio Costa, quoted in Shoumatoff, p. 39. **59** For example, Theodor de Bry, 1592, *Americae tertia pars memorabilê provinciae Brasiliae historiam continês* (Frankfurt); Petrus Bertius, 1616, *Tabularum Geographicarum Contractum* (Amsterdam); Willem Janszoon Blaeu, 1635, *Atlas Novus* (Amsterdam); Guillaume and Jean Blaeu (eds), 1640, *Le Theatre du Monde ou Nouvel Atlas* (Amsterdam); and Kaspar van Baerle, 1647, *Rerum per Octennium in Brasilia* (Amsterdam: I. Braeu). **60** Henrique Luttgardes Cardoso de Castro, quoted in Evenson, 1973, p. 106. **61** Vidal, pp. 268–70. During the 1950s, the Indian communities of the Mato Grosso *cerrado* were particularly hard hit by western frontier expansion, increased white settlement and land speculation, when a number of villages came under siege and suffered brutal attacks by cattle ranchers and armed bands. In 1982, Mario Juruna, a member of one of these Xavante Indian communities, became Brazil's first and only indigenous person to be elected to Brazil's National Congress (representing Rio de Janeiro); Garfield, pp. 287–304.

quent years: the Chapel of Nossa Senhora de Fátima (1957–58), the Metropolitan Cathedral of Nossa Senhora Aparecida (1958–71, refurbished in 1987) and the Military Cathedral of Nossa Senhora da Paz (1991).

The Chapel of Nossa Senhora de Fátima, in Superquadra South 308, was the first permanent church constructed in Brasília. It was inaugurated on 28 June 1958 with the wedding of the daughter of Israël Pinheiro (1896-1973), the man who oversaw the construction of Brasília as second president of NOVACAP (and Brasília's first mayor). Set in parkland in the residential sector, it is defined almost exclusively by its tapered catenary-curved roof canopy, seemingly borne entirely by three tapering concrete pillars. The tent-like elements of the roof and triangular concrete supports are emphasized, painted white, while the mass of the deeply recessed, horseshoe wall – mostly in shade – dissolves under the uniform cladding of blue-and-white ceramic tiles, designed by Athos Bulcão and featuring a white dove and a star of Bethlehem, presiding over the birth of Brasília. Recessed into the horseshoe, a wide wooden door folds away against the side walls, preventing the definition of a volume that might undermine the primacy of the triangular, upward-sweeping concrete roof.[62] The crown-like

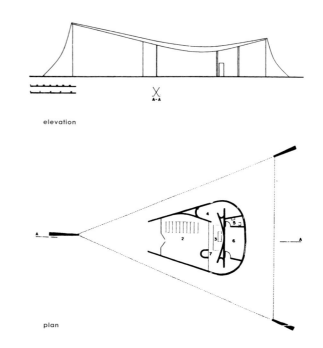

elevation

plan

Above and below. Chapel of Nossa Senhora de Fátima, Entrequadra Sul 307/308, Brasília, 1957–58

62 Having seen a model of the Chapel of Nossa Senhora de Fátima, Pier Luigi Nervi remarked: 'it is impossible to conceal our wonderment at such a daring technical feat . . . the fact that the pylons are anchored to a concrete sheet of such limited curvature brings horizontal tensions into play, and therefore moments of interlocking at the base of the pylons that raise legitimate doubts regarding the possibility of actually building this design'; Nervi, 1959, p. 55.

Above and below left: Metropolitan Cathedral of Nossa Senhora Aparecida, Brasília, 1958–71, refurbished in 1987

Military Cathedral of Nossa Senhora da Paz, Brasília, 1991

dome of Brasília's cathedral – the only part of the sanctuary above ground – may also be read as an allusion to a tent structure, recalling the nation-unifying mass of the modern Brazilians who took full possession of Brazil's territory.

In his fifth lecture during his visit to Rio de Janeiro in 1936, Le Corbusier proposed an airport in place of Agache's Capitol for Rio: 'A Capitol is good, but it's old,' he declared; 'an airport is new'.[63] The shape of Costa's Plano Piloto, in which the transverse arm of the cross is curved, is most often likened to that of an aeroplane. Costa suggested that the curve came about by the adaptation of his original line to the local topography. But it is, perhaps, the resemblance to an aircraft that suits best Kubitschek's industrial utopia.

Commercial aviation had begun in Brazil in 1927. Over the three decades preceding the construction of Brasília, surface and air transportation and communication networks had been crucial for the welding of Brazil into a unity and the central control of the nation. The aeroplane was now also lending its shape to the keystone of Kubitschek's project for a brave new Brazilian world of order and progress, where the two projects of domination, that of Christianity and that of modernity, were brought together.[64] The Christian metaphor was already put forward by Costa in the 'elementary gesture' of his plan: the 'sign of the cross'. 'JK's vision', says Niemeyer, 'and mine, too – was . . . of a modern and up-to-date city, one that would represent the importance of our country'.[65] Costa's masterplan envisaged Brasília as the 'capital of the

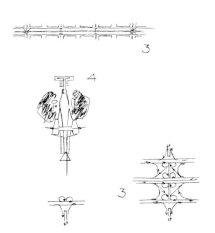

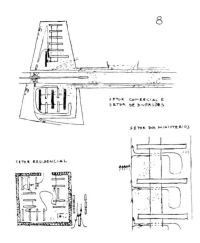

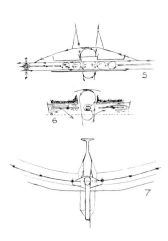

Lúcio Costa, sketches illustrating the 'Report' supporting his Plano Piloto;

3. To apply to the urbanization plan the principles of modern road-building techniques – including the elimination of intersections – the curved axis, which corresponds to the natural means of access, was made the trunk line for circulation, with central lanes for speeding vehicles and service lanes for local traffic. Along this axis the bulk of the residential sectors has been placed (figure 3).

4. In harmony with this residential concentration, the civic and administration centers, the cultural, entertainment and sports centers, the municipal administration facilities, the barracks, the storage and supply zones, the sites for small local industries and the railway station automatically fell into place along the transverse axis, which thus became the main or monumental axis of the system (figure 4). Next to the intersection of the axes, but appertaining functionally and in terms of urbanistic composition to the main axis, the banking and commercial sectors have been placed, as well as the offices for private business and the liberal professions and the ample areas set aside for shopping centers.

5. The intersection of the main and the highway-residential axes, the former being on a lower level,

called for the creation of a great platform where only parking and local traffic would be permitted and which logically suggested the location of the entertainment center for the city, with cinemas, theatres, restaurants, etc. (figure 5).

6. Traffic going through to other sectors passes along the lower ground level under the platform in one-way lanes, the platform being closed on the narrow ends but open on the two broader sides: a large part of this covered area is used for parking and the interurban bus station has been placed there and is accessible to passengers from the upper levels of the platform (figure 6). When the transversal axis reaches the platform, its central speed lanes go underground, beneath the lower ground level at which local traffic continues to circulate and which slopes gently down until it levels off with the esplanade in the ministerial sector.

7. Thus, and with the introduction of three separate clover-leaf turnoffs from each lane of the highway axis and the same number of lower level crossings, automobiles and buses circulate both in the central and the residential sectors without any intersections whatsoever. For truck traffic a secondary, independent road system with grade crossings and good traffic signals was established but without

crossing or interfering in any way with the main system, except above the sports sector. This secondary system has access to the buildings of the commercial sector at basement level, goes through the civic center on the lower plane and is reached through galleries at ground level (figure 7).

8. With the general network for automotive traffic thus established, independent paths for local pedestrian traffic were created in both the central and the residential sectors, ensuring free circulation for those on foot (figure 8). This separation of automotive and pedestrian traffic was not, however, carried to a systematic and unnatural extreme for it must be remembered that today the automobile is no longer man's irreconcilable enemy; it has been domesticated and is, so to speak, a member of the family. It only becomes 'dehumanized' and re-acquires its menacing and hostile aspect to pedestrians when incorporated into the anonymous mass of traffic. A certain degree of separation is therefore necessary but under certain circumstances and for mutual convenience co-existence is at times indispensable.
(Lúcio Costa, 1966, pp. 13–14)

63 Le Corbusier, 2006, p. 140.   **64** Hector Babenco's film *At Play in the Fields of the Lord* (1991) features an aeroplane flying over the Amazon and casting its shadow on the water in the form of a cross. It thus establishes a similar link between these two projects of domination: Stam, 1997, p. 328. (I do not mean to suggest that there is a consciously intended parallel with Brasília in Babenco's film).   **65** Niemeyer, 2000b, p. 72.

The introduction to the catalogue of the 1943 Museum of Modern Art exhibition *Brazil Builds* begins with a survey of the country from a 'shining silver airplane'. On the occasion that marked the welcoming of Brazil into the world of modernity, the evocation of the modern device 'rush[ing] over the great river Amazon' suggested the possibility of taking possession of the impenetrable and unsettled jungle. 'In an airplane', exhibition co-designer Philip L. Goodwin wrote, 'one can see hundreds of years of a nation's building in a few days.'[70] Le Corbusier had discovered a 'territorial' scale flying over South America on his 1929 visit, conquering Rio from the air with his 'immense . . . majestic highway', designed on a flight over the city, accompanied by Mayor Antônio Prado Júnior (brother of Le Corbusier's benefactor Paulo Prado).[71]

Brazil's colonial cities were founded on ports that facilitated control of exports; Costa's aeroplane-shaped, skyway-and-highway-accessed city permitted colonization of the interior and promoted the domestic distribution of Brazil's produce. The *Architectural Review* of 1944 had predicted that 'if the country becomes air-minded, its development may step up to the speed of the aeroplane'.[72] This was precisely the aim of Costa's plan: to bring to the entire nation the modern architecture that the 1943 MoMA exhibition had celebrated, thrusting the whole of Brazil into the modern era represented by that architecture, which he had done so much to pioneer, and by this formidable machine. Brasília's aeroplane-shaped plan has become one of the most enduring icons of modern city planning and a persistent advert for the modernity of the Brazilian capital.

Representing a rare historic realization of the Functional City defined by CIAM, significantly, Costa's plan has also given prominence to the airborne view of Brasília, reinforcing its status as a utopian urban order. Costa himself designed the city's Television Tower (1957, constructed 1959–61 and 1965–67), which further promotes Brasília's aerial view, offering it to all its inhabitants and visitors, turning the city intelligible. Ironically, in this way, the capital of Claude Debussy's 'century of the aeroplane' also pays homage to the old capital of Rio de Janeiro which, from its very early days was portrayed from above.[73] In 1840 Rio became the first city in the world to be photographed from the air;[74] in 1885, four years

highways and skyways', which is another way of saying the capital of a modern, unified nation with a strong centralist government.[66] And it should not be forgotten that petrol was an important symbol of economic nationalism.

But Costa did not grant the new seat of power an aircraft landing-deck at the centre of the city, like those proposed by Antonio Sant'Elia's Città Nuova (1914) and Le Corbusier's Ville Contemporaine pour trois million habitants (1922).[67] Instead, the plan of Costa's Brazilian civitas of the air age evoked, and symbolically embodied, the modern machine par excellence, thus celebrating Brazil as the country of the aviation pioneer Mineiro Alberto Santos Dumont (1873–1932). The plan became 'a symbol . . . of a nation capable, by its own efforts and inventions, of raising itself to a level of progressivism where the impact of its technical advances would be felt throughout the world'.[68] The venerable Futurist device, to which Le Corbusier had dedicated twenty-two pages in his *Vers une architecture*, came to land at the centre of the country and the nation, thus turning the whole of Brazil into a Ville Contemporaine.[69]

66 Lúcio Costa, 1966, p. 16. **67** The airport was also monumentally positioned on a river island in Le Corbusier's 1929 sketch for Buenos Aires; Le Corbusier, 1991, p. 202. **68** Freyre, 1970, p. 277. **69** Le Corbusier, 1989, pp. 105–27. It seems likely that Le Corbusier flew in an aeroplane for the first time during his first Latin American visit in 1929. **70** Goodwin, p. 17. **71** Le Corbusier, 1991, pp. 242–43. Following his flights over Latin America, Le Corbusier started thinking of urbanism in terms of a 'fifth façade', and in 1935 he wrote a small book dedicated to the aircraft, 'symbol of the New Age'; Le Corbusier, 1987a, p. 6. See also Tsiomis, 2006, p. 20. See Le Corbusier's sketch of his inhabited motorway in Chapter Two, p. 45. **72** Sousa-Leão, p. 59. In the catalogue of the 1955 MoMA exhibition on *Latin American Architecture Since 1945*, Henry-Russell Hitchcock wrote: 'Today, there is perhaps no part of the world where air traffic is so vital, bringing all the South American countries into close contact with the outside world and, almost more significantly, with each other. Building materials rarely travel by air, but most architects do and their ideas as well.

The São Paulo airport is the third busiest in the world, seventy flights a day linking it with Rio de Janeiro alone'; Hitchcock, 1955, p. 12.
In 1956, J.O. de Meira Penna wrote: 'it is the "air age" that is fast changing the geopolitical map of the planet. Air transportation has much to do with the convenience and feasibility of building a new capital in the Central Plateau of Brazil. Ours will be the first capital built in the new air age and it is symbolic of the fact that the site was chosen on the basis of aerial surveys'. But he also noted: 'Goiania might in a sense be considered the first city of the air age, a city carved out of the jungle around an airport. Its very site was selected by aerial inspection and photoanalysis. And although it is now linked with Minas Gerais by railway and an all-weather road, its main connection with the outside world is still by air.' Penna, n.d., n.p. **73** Dawn Ades notes 'the predominance of panoramic views' in representations of the Brazilian landscape in general by the artists of nineteenth-century expeditions to Brazil; quoted in Martins, 2003, p. 69. **74** Castro, 2004, p. 13.

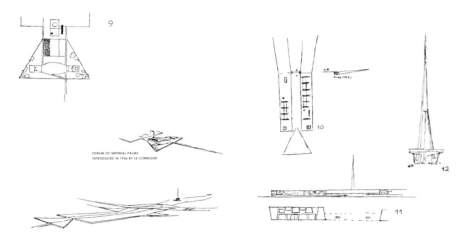

Lúcio Costa, sketches illustrating the 'Report' supporting his Plano Piloto:

9 . . . The most outstanding buildings are those which will house the governmental powers and, because these are autonomous and three in number, the equilateral triangle seemed the elementary form most appropriate to enclose them . . . A terraced triangle was therefore created, slightly higher than the neighboring areas which are reached by the highway leading to the residential districts and the airport (figure 9) . . . The [Congress at the apex of the triangle] faces a broad esplanade set out on a second terrace, rectangular in shape . . . Along this equivalent of the English mall – broad sweeping lawns to be used by pedestrians, processions and parades – the various ministries and autonomous agencies were placed (figure 10) . . .

10 . . . On the front face of the platform [at the central intersection] the cinemas and theatres have been concentrated, the pattern chosen being low and uniform so that they form a single, harmonious and continuous architectonic whole . . . the full height of the respective façades can serve for the installation of illuminated signs and advertisements (figure 11) . . . The tower of the radio and television station . . . has been integrated as a plastic element in the general composition of the project (figures 9, 10, 11 and 12) . . .

12 . . . [The radio transmitter tower] is envisaged as a triangular structure standing on a monumental base of concrete and having above the floor level of the studios and other installations, a metal superstructure with an observation tower halfway up (figure 12).
(Lúcio Costa, 1966, pp. 14–15)

before the Eiffel Tower was completed, Rio had steam trams carrying tourists to the summit of Mount Corcovado to admire the famous bird's-eye view; and its Santos Dumont Airport had been revered for two decades as 'the most beautiful in the world and certainly the most conveniently located . . . one of the two major buildings that called attention to the development of a brilliant Cariocan [sic] school of modern architecture'.[75]

Where in Rio, however, it is the wondrous natural landscape that is to be marvelled at, its sinuous bays, hovering hills and forested mountain ranges, inlets, islands and the vast blue Atlantic, overpowering any structure designed by human hand, Brasília's aerial image and landmarks are entirely of human creation. Costa assumed that Brasília's visitors would arrive by aeroplane and ensured that they would be greeted by a clear, rational, two-dimensional image of a planned, unified city, which the flat pictorial surface of the landscape made easier to achieve. With its few, sharp lines, clear geometric shapes, low-lying structures and large-scale open spaces, Brasília was designed to be read from an aerial perspective, not as a city born of nature, 'not as a dynamic habitat, but as a deposit of human intentionality, as a planned text'.[76] The clear, symmetrical plan of the new capital quickly produced a legible image that privileged potentiality over reality, ensuring that the foundational acts of its inventors were cast 'in the form of imperishable signs'. Aerial reconnaissance was conscripted to advance the message that Brazil's new seat of government was a fact on the ground and guaranteed the rapid dissemination of the technologically sponsored, symbolic representation of Brasília.

Niemeyer's symbolic forms for Brasília's main buildings faithfully followed the prescriptions of the Plano Piloto, producing clear, memorable signs for each institution of Brazil's democratic govern-

ment, also fully embracing the plan's symbolism in their allusions to images of flight. For Costa and Niemeyer knew what the Uruguayan writer Angel Rama would later formulate with reference to the Baroque cities of Latin America's primarily Spanish conquerors: 'the permanence of the whole depended on the immutability of the signs themselves – on the words that transmitted the will to build the city in accordance with the stipulated norms – and also on the diagrams that translated the will into graphic terms.'[77]

Steam tram carrying tourists to the summit of Mount Corcovado, postcard, 1911

75 Hitchcock, 1955, p. 12.   **76** Saint-Amour, p. 352.   **77** Rama, p. 6.

View of Rio de Janeiro from Mount Corcovado

The automotive emphasis of Costa's plan for a city originally intended to have not one traffic light was consistent with both the new direction of Brazil's industrial development and Le Corbusier's visionary city plans. Already in 1925, the latter had named his plan for the sanitization of Paris after an automobile manufacturer, Gabriel Voisin, one of the two sponsors of the Pavillon de L'Esprit Nouveau for the *Exposition des Arts Décoratifs et Industriels Modernes* in Paris. And more than a decade before Costa's Plano Piloto, Josep Lluís Sert and Paul Lester Wiener had responded with their Cidade dos Motores (1944, conceived by Atílio Correia Lima in 1943) to a commission for a new, model industrial town of twenty to twenty-five thousand inhabitants, attached to Vargas's ambitious National Factory of Motors.[78] Sert and Wiener's plans had brought 'profound joy' and 'extreme pleasure' to Le Corbusier.[79]

The Functional City of CIAM promised redemption from all the problems of the chaotic, overpopulated, haphazardly grown, disorderly, uncontrollable cities of the past that, in Le Corbusier's

words, had 'become inhuman, hostile to man, dangerous for his physical and moral health'.[80] Brasília joined the Swiss architect's '*march towards order*', opposing chaos with order, history with progress, formlessness with precisely controlled form, uncontrollable change and mutation with permanence and stability.[81] It was conceived as the comprehensive, rational urban order of the machine era. Fleeing the inefficient and parasitical bureaucracy and social problems of the old capital would guarantee the modernization of public administration, as well as protection from 'elements of indiscipline and disorder, which have there the ideal conditions for subversion', according to Israël Pinheiro.[82] In an exact reversal of Affonso Eduardo Reidy's injunction – '[the city's] planning should result of regional planning' – Costa's 'Report' hailed a city that would be 'not the result of regional planning, but the cause', in accordance with the objectives of Kubitschek's utopian project for a new capital that would function as a pole of development for the whole of Brazil.[83] Serving the president's political aspirations, Costa's triumphantly imposed monumental layout was

78 See Rovira, pp. 114–27. **79** Le Corbusier, 1947a, p. 97. **80** Le Corbusier, quoted in Peter, p. 144. In his *The City of Tomorrow and Its Planning*, Le Corbusier showed a picture of Paris and posed the question: 'Is this a picture of the seventh circle of Dante's Inferno?'; Le

Corbusier, 1987b, p. 284. **81** Le Corbusier, 1987b, p. 16, emphasis in the original. **82** Israël Pinheiro, quoted in Epstein, p. 29. **83** Affonso Eduardo Reidy, quoted in Bonduki, 2000, p. 24; Lúcio Costa, 1966, p. 12.

'more than strictly functional', promising a city with a 'lyrical value', to 'be contemplated not only during a rapid flight but also from a helicopter stopping in mid-air', in the manner imagined by Sert, Léger and Giedion in their 1943 essay on monumental architecture and city planning.[84]

The Utopia of a Society of Equality and Justice

> Brasília is not the city of the future, for our society is still that of the past.
>
> Oscar Niemeyer, *Niemeyer par lui-même*

From the radical beginnings of CIAM, modern architecture and urbanism had been linked to the realities of industrial production and to the revolutionary intention to change society. For Costa, it held the promise of 'establishing, at last, for *the masses* an *individual* standard of living worthy of the human condition'.[85] Since Menezes Palmiro's early nineteenth-century project for Cidade Pedrália, the project of a new Brazilian capital had also been associated with the project of shaping a new, urban Brazilian society. Costa's original intention was to 'allow for gradations proper to the present regime', but 'avoid questionable and undesirable stratification'. Nevertheless, despite his original belief that 'state ownership of the land would guarantee a more democratic urban spatial structure', the segregated spatial structure of the federal capital and the discontinuity of its urban fabric reflect – magnify even – the problematic situation that characterizes Brazil as a whole. As Frederico de Holanda et al. phrase it: 'Brazil is one of those countries in which the state has been most strongly captured by dominant classes [and families], in order to support their own interests.'[86]

Already in 1961, Costa wrote to the president of NOVACAP complaining about the way the latter dealt with Brasília's increasing social problems.[87] Nevertheless, the propaganda published by the latter in 1963 insisted on the 'inexistence of social discrimination' and 'perfect social coexistence' in the capital's residential areas, ignoring the fact that these already extended far beyond those prescribed by the Plano Piloto, especially for the lowest social strata. For NOVACAP, the utopia was built and in the time of a generation it would encompass the whole of Brazil: 'thus is [sic] raised, on the plateau, the children who will construct the Brazil of tomorrow, since Brasília is the glorious cradle of a new civiliza-

tion.'[88] Eventually, in 1985, Costa designed a series of affordable housing blocks (*quadras econômicas*), three storeys high on *pilotis*, built on the periphery of the Plano Piloto along the routes that lead to the satellite towns. Six new residential areas, two with *superquadras* in the Plano Piloto, were also demarcated in Costa's 1987 'Brasília Revisited' document, presented to José Aparecido de Oliveira, federal district governor from 1985 to 1988.

For Le Corbusier, 'the platform of a bus is a democratic spot where the men in flat caps and the gentlemen in raglans pile in together'.[89] At the centre of the Plano Piloto, where the Monumental Axis and the Highway-Residential Axis intersect, Costa located the road platform, a multi-layered megastructure for all kinds of traffic, vehicular and pedestrian, and the bus platform, which eventually proved too small for interstate buses and

Bus platform at the intersection of the Monumental Axis and the Highway-Residential Axis

remained a local bus terminal. Offering an opportunity for viewing the city's Monumental Axis from on high, Costa's bus platform, at the centre of Brasília, carried the message of the city, which for him represented 'a crossroads where the roads of the country intersect'.[90] With good reason, David Epstein, on the other hand, sees Brasília's bus platform as symbolic of the city's inequality and strong class segregation, which is spatial as well as social and economic and the result of political decisions rather than market forces.[91]

The problems resulting from Brasília's class stratification tarnished its utopian credibility right from the start. Lúcio Costa had been adamant: 'Everyone who works in Brasília must live *in Brasília* and not at a distance of 20 kilometres, in "pseudo-satellite-

84 Sert, Léger and Giedion, p. 30.   **85** Lúcio Costa, 'Considerações sobre arte contemporânea' (1952), in Lúcio Costa, 1997, p. 258, emphasis in the original.   **86** Holanda et al., pp. 20, 28.   **87** See Epstein, pp. 83–84.   **88** Journal of Companhia Urbanizadora da Nova Capital do Brasil, quoted in Holston, pp. 20–21.   **89** Le Corbusier, 1987c, p. 42.   **90** Lúcio Costa, 'Restez chez vous' (n.d.), in Lúcio Costa, 1997, p. 315. Costa repeated the symbolic gesture in his 1976 proposal for the new capital of Nigeria.   **91** Epstein, p. 94.

1 Gama
2 Taguatinga
3 Suburban lots
4 Núcleo Bandeirante
5 Sobradinho
6 Planaltina

Brasília and satellite towns existing by 1967

on the building of the capital, published in *L'Architecture d'Aujourd'hui* in 1960 as 'Mes expériences à Brasília', stresses that Brasília should be a city of 'free, fortunate men without racial or social discrimination'.[97] The new capital of Brazil endorsed the utopia of the architectural movements of the early twentieth century, which

> consisted in obstinately hiding the fact that the ideology of planning could be realized in building production only by indicating that it is beyond it that the true plan can take form; rather, that once come within the sphere of the reorganization of production in general, architecture and urbanism would have to be the objects and not the subjects of the Plan.[98]

William Holford, too, valued Costa's plan primarily as 'the supreme manifestation of architecture as a social art'.[99] Niemeyer soon recognized the impasse and regularly laments the fact that 'Brazil's social conditions run counter to the spirit of the Pilot Plan'. He firmly believes that 'the solution for such [social] problems is beyond the reach of architects and architecture'.[100]

Nevertheless, 'we can always dream a little', he would state in the 1980s, 'and present our modest proposal for the city of the future'.[101] In his 1964 proposal for the city of Negev at the heart of the Israeli desert, Niemeyer turned towards the small medieval cities by which 'we are all still enchanted' – the cities destroyed by 'the large metropolis'.[102] In contrast to Brasília, Negev was also planned as 'multipliable' along major routes to allow for 'organic and disciplined' growth.[103]

His 1979 article on the 'City of Tomorrow' reads as an implicit critique of Brasília. Although he remains faithful to ideas about zoning and large green urban spaces, Niemeyer's revised urban utopia is that of 'a smaller city, a city at a more human scale, destined for the human being rather than the machine'. Unlike Brasília, it is a vertical city of high urban concentration, like Negev, tailored to pedestrian use. Of course, Niemeyer's 'ideal city' is also a socialist urban utopia: 'a city without rich and poor'. He is confident that his is 'a dream that will come true in the future'.[104] For Negev's housing blocks he insisted on no 'distinction of class or means . . . no best or worst flat, nor the old "public housing" whose name already suggests capitalist discrimination'.[105] As for Brasília, in an interview in 1998 he admitted that it 'was a city constructed as a showcase of capitalism – everything for a few on a world stage'.[106]

towns".'[92] On the day of its inauguration, Brasília already had eight satellite towns, 'justified by a sanitation discourse'.[93] In 2000, the Plano Piloto housed about 10 per cent of the population and provided about 76 per cent of all jobs in the metropolitan area. Some of the people who work in Brasília live more than 60 kilometres from the Plano Piloto. The ratio of passengers to kilometres in Brasília is 1:2, '*circa 4 times less than in other Brazilian metropolises of similar size . . .* [which] implies the most expensive bus fares in the country'.[94] Nevertheless, some continue to see the bus platform through rose-tinted spectacles as the ideal 'meeting of the population' imagined by the city's visionary architects, who, at least during Brasília's early days, believed their Modernist creation capable of producing a new Brazilian reality and collective social order.[95]

Through their involvement in the creation of Brasília, Costa and Niemeyer opted for architecture rather than revolution, thus granting the city the political role envisaged by Le Corbusier. Niemeyer was convinced that Le Corbusier's city plans were based on 'a premise of equality and justice'.[96] Niemeyer's much-cited article

92 Lúcio Costa, 'O urbanista defende sua cidade' (1967), in Lúcio Costa, 1997, p. 302, emphasis in the original.   93 Batista et al., p. 172.
94 Holanda et al., pp. 24–25, emphasis in the original.   95 Peralva, p. 61.
96 Niemeyer, 1955b, n. 1, p. 3.   97 Niemeyer, 1960.   98 Tafuri, p. 100.
99 Holford, 1960b, p. 17.   100 Oscar Niemeyer, quoted in Brayne; Niemeyer, 1966, p. 21. As early as 1967, Costa, too, recognized that Brasília could not but reflect the problems and contradictions of Brazil; Lúcio

Costa, 'O urbanista defende sua cidade' (1967), in Lúcio Costa, 1997, p. 301.   101 Oscar Niemeyer, quoted in Krohn, p. 37.   102 Niemeyer, 1965b, pp. 1–12.   103 Niemeyer, 1968, p. 44.   104 Niemeyer, 1979e, p. 80.   105 Niemeyer, 'Plan of the Town of Negev', in *Oscar Niemeyer: Notebooks of the Architect*, n.p.   106 Oscar Niemeyer, quoted in Niesewand, p. 40. In the same interview, Niemeyer says that he regrets the fact that his 'medieval dream' for the city of Negev was not realized.

The Nationalist Utopia

The new capital was to act as the catalyst for Brazil to fulfil her destiny, rising to world power status, a nineteenth-century imperialist ambition that, in the twentieth century, was shared by public opinion, intellectuals, popular press and politicians, encouraged by similar predictions emanating from Europe and the United States.[107] Internationally acclaimed Brazilian architecture was expected to help new Brazil fulfil its old goal. On 6 December 1952, the popular magazine *Manchete* included a six-page report entitled 'Brazil: Architectural Power', and in August 1954 it hailed Niemeyer's 'Ibirapuera [Park]: Brave New World'.[108] Kubitschek inherited a well-developed orientation towards, and an enduring romanticization of, the future, with a strong sense of national purpose. However, Brazil's marginal role in post-war world affairs and the shift of US interests towards Europe and Asia led to a sense of isolation that increased as the Cold War intensified. With the return to a participatory democratic system and growing leftist sentiment, the Brazilian public turned inwards, uniting under the banner of nationalism and passionately debating popular issues of domestic importance such as petroleum policy and industrialization.

The firm belief in industrialization as the primary means to true economic and political independence was well established by the time Kubitschek rose to power and shared by technocrats, politicians and the general public. The economic policies of the previous years had prepared the ground for his administration's march towards national 'development and order', orchestrated in 'the pure air of the plateau', away from 'the atmosphere impregnated with sea air, burnt oil and cynical sensualism'.[109] The developmental nationalism and state interventionism of earlier years gave way to the national developmentalism (*nacional-desenvolvimento* or *desenvolvimentismo*) of Kubitschek's Programa de Metas – 1956/1961 (Programme of [30] Goals). This attracted private and foreign investment and stimulated impressive real economic growth (7 per cent from 1957 to 1961), coupled, however, with a soaring budget deficit, a depreciating currency and a galloping inflation rate. Brasília became the 'synthesis goal' or, in Costa's words, the 'keystone' of the arch constructed by Kubitschek, keeping all other stones in place.[110]

Vargas's nationalism had already set a trend for the popularization of economic development and top-down social change without political strife. The visionary Kubitschek promised 'fifty years' progress in five', and pronounced 'The construction of Brasília symbolic of our efforts to provide the nation with a foundation on which to build the future'.[111] 'President bossa nova' had served as mayor of one of the first modern Brazilian cities, Belo Horizonte, geometrically ordered by the engineers Aarão Reis and Francisco Bicalho and built in the last decade of the nineteenth century. The success of the capital of the state of Minas Gerais as a centre for banking and industry, and his dam- and road-building projects as governor from 1951 to 1955 of this most important inland state gave Kubitschek the confidence to 'build a federal capital that will unite the whole nation' by becoming its 'crossroads'.[112] He and his collaborators were keen to present the project as entirely Brazilian: 'We imported neither architects nor town-planning experts to design Brasília. We planned and built it with our own native talents – Niemeyer and Lúcio Costa – and the laborers who erected it, from the contractor down to the "candango" . . . were all our own people.'[113] NOVACAP, it was triumphantly declared, had only one shareholder: the Brazilian nation. Building construction materials were almost exclusively Brazilian. And even the trucks that carried them were made in Brazil.

Costa proudly referred to Brasília as an 'original, native, Brazilian creation'.[114] But the report that accompanied his masterplan made no effort to denounce what the much younger Brazilian architect Paulo Mendes da Rocha (1928–) would later call 'the dominance of the Old World'. According to the latter, 'A person who lands in America will always make the same thing: build a city with the entire memory of the European city.'[115] This memory pervades Costa's 'Report'. European (or Europeanizing) precedents parade through the text: 'the English mall' is presented as the model of the broad esplanade between the two rows of ministries, reminiscent of the mall in Washington, D.C.; 'Piccadilly Circus, Times Square and the Champs Elysées' serve as paradigms for the capital's entertainment centre, 'Rio's Rua Ouvidor' and 'Venetian "vielas"' for the cultural sector, and for the proposed cemeteries are prescribed 'headstones . . . in the English tradition'.[116] 'I was greatly influenced by French eighteenth-century

107 'A. A. Berle, the United States Assistant Secretary of State, speaking to-night, said that . . . Brazil alone . . . in the next generation, will be not merely a great South American country, but a world Power if she so chooses.' *The Times*, February 8, 1944, cited in *Architectural Review*, 1944a, p. 59.   **108** *Manchete*, quoted in Lara, 2001, pp. 131–32. **109** J. O. Meira Penna, quoted in Epstein, p. 30. Between 1955 and 1961, industrial production grew by 80 per cent.   **110** Juscelino Kubitschek; Lúcio Costa, quoted in Shoumatoff, p. 38.   **111** Juscelino Kubitschek, quoted in Epstein, p. 31. Kubitschek's critics spoke of 'fifty years' inflation in five'; Skidmore, 1999, p. 148.   **112** Juscelino Kubitschek, quoted in Dos Passos, pp. 65, 67.   **113** Kubitschek, 1966, p. 7. Kubitschek here ignores the fact that the American Raymond Concrete Pile Company was contracted to erect the steel frames of the ministries and the dam. 'The awarding of this lucrative contract to foreigners, just as Brazil was struggling to realize its own steel-producing potential, was bitterly criticized in the Congress. Only the personal appearance of Niemeyer, who explained that the Americans had been hired for reasons of time and economy, placated the critics'; Shoumatoff, p. 46. From the beginning of his term of office, Kubitschek had openly welcomed foreign investment. Promising to 'control Communism in Brazil', in 1956, he had secured a $35 million steel loan from the United States and announced: 'No matter how busy I may be, any foreign investor who comes to Brazil will find my door open'; Spade, p. 15.   **114** Lúcio Costa, ' "Ingredientes" da concepção urbanística de Brasília' (n.d.), in Lúcio Costa, 1997, p. 282.   **115** Paulo Mendes da Rocha, quoted in Spiro, p. 255.   **116** Lúcio Costa, 1966, pp. 14–16. Costa has repeatedly referred also to the precedent of China's architecture and dramatic ground configuration (based on a set of 1904 photographs he had seen), and to the 'beautiful axes and perspectives' of Paris [and Belo Horizonte] in the 'classico-baroque tradition'; for example, Lúcio Costa, 'Eixo Monumental' (n.d.), in Lúcio Costa, 1997, p. 304.

Steel-frame ministry slabs under construction, Brasília, photograph of 1958

urbanism,' asserts Costa. Brasília is a Brazilian invention, 'corresponding to a Brazilian reality and sensibility, which it represents, but it is also of French intellectual descent'.[117] Niemeyer, too, in his search for an architecture for Brazil's new capital, turned to 'the Piazza San Marco in Venice, the Palace of the Doges and the Cathedral of Chartres', aiming to achieve the kind of 'architectural unity which is invariably a source of beauty . . . in the ancient cities of Europe'.[118]

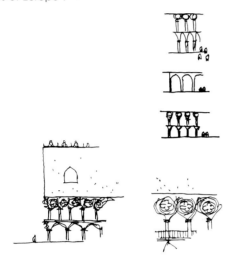

Sketches of the Palace of the Doges in Venice, which 'surprised' Niemeyer 'by its admirable lightness', offered him an 'example of what [his own] architecture defended', and inspired his 'Socratic dialogue' with 'a rationalist architect':
  – 'What do you think about this palace?'
  – 'Magnificent!'
  – 'And what about its carved columns?'
  – 'Very beautiful!'
  – 'But you, a functionalist, would still prefer them to be simpler and more functional?'
  – 'That's correct.'
  – 'But if they were, there wouldn't be this splendid contrast of the columns so full of arabesques and the plain wall which supports them.'
  – 'That's true.'
  – 'So you must agree that when a shape creates beauty, it has in beauty its own justification.'
(Niemeyer, 1998, p. 21)

The primary criterion applied by the jury who on 16 March 1957 selected Costa's entry for the new federal capital was monumentality: ability to express 'the grandeur of a nation-wide desire', a 'functional city' with a ceremonial governmental centre, and with 'its own personal architectural style'.[119] 'The Need for a New Monumentality' – the title of Sigfried Giedion's essay of 1944 – had re-entered architectural debate already a decade earlier, especially in relation to symbolic civic representation.

Giedion had singled out Rio's Ministry of Education for moving towards *the reconquest of the monumental expression . . . beyond functional fulfillment*', and as an exceptional case of enlightened patronage where 'creative contemporary artists were allowed to participate in a Community task'.[120] Sert, Léger and Giedion's 'Nine Points on Monumentality – A Human Need' had been formulated in 1943 and debated at CIAM's sixth meeting in Bridgewater, U.K., in 1947. Through the collaboration of architects, planners and artists, the authors argued, modern monuments can 'satisfy the eternal demands of the people for translation of their collective force into symbols'.[121] Costa and Holford had both been invited to contribute to the 1948 symposium 'In Search of a New Monumentality', hosted by the *Architectural Review*.[122]

Costa's Plano Piloto clearly reflected the Modernist rehabilitation of civic and cultural centres as the city's 'brain and governing machine' and satisfied demands for 'areas especially planned for public gatherings, the main monuments constituting landmarks in the region, and symbols of popular aspirations'.[123] The reconciliation of Modernism and monumentality had been apparent in Sert and Wiener's Cidade dos Motores as well as in Le Corbusier's 1945 plan for St-Dié in northern France. The latter, with its open-platform civic centre and free-standing buildings, 'each emanat[ing] its own social atmosphere', in Giedion's words, prefigured Costa's Monumental Axis.[124] Costa's own unrealized plan for Rio de Janeiro's Cidade Universitária (1936–37), with its monumental esplanade flanked by uniform school buildings, is the indisputable antecedent of Brasília's Plano Piloto.

Costa's 'bow and arrow' plan dazzled the competition jury with its 'artistic unity', and was described as 'clear, direct and fundamentally simple, as exemplified by Pompeii, Nancy, Wren's London, Louis XV's Paris'.[125] Costa defended his Brasília as the result of pure, unsolicited inspiration – perhaps revelation – and, despite the minimal description and apologetic prelude of his 'Report', his scheme was adjudicated fit to take its place among the historic cities of the (Old) world, as appropriate for the capital of a country that saw itself as an up-and-coming world power.[126]

The Pessoa Commission had also stressed the importance of a monumental scale for the new capital and, in its plan for Vera Cruz (1955), it proposed a monumental Avenue of Independence with the Congress at its central and most elevated point. The ground configuration of Costa's Monumental Axis from east to

117 Lúcio Costa, 'O urbanista defende sua cidade' (1967), in Lúcio Costa, 1997, p. 303. Costa also refers to 'the "old" Corbusian principles of the Ville Radieuse'.   **118** Oscar Niemeyer, quoted in Evenson, 1975, p. 498; Niemeyer, 1959b, n.p.   **119** William Holford, quoted in Evenson, 1975, p. 480.   **120** Giedion, 1984, pp. 54–56, emphasis in the original. This is the only modern building mentioned favourably in Giedion's text, which included an illustration of the Ministry of Education's north elevation.   **121** Sert, Léger and Giedion, p. 29.   **122** 'In Search of a New Monumentality', 1948, pp. 117–28.   **123** Josep Lluis Sert, quoted in Eric Mumford, p. 152.   **124** Sigfried Giedion, quoted in Eric Mumford, p. 152.   **125** Holford, 1960b,

pp. 11–13; 'Minutes of the Committee for Judging the Pilot Plan of Brasília', cited in Evenson, 1975, pp. 478–79. See Lúcio Costa's unrealized plan for Rio de Janeiro's Cidade Universitária in Chapter Two, p. 74.   **126** Costa's plan was selected by five of the six jurors. 'Paulo Antunes Ribeiro, the juror who represented the Brazilian Institute of Architects, dissented, calling Costa's proposal far too slight even to merit consideration'; Epstein, p. 49. The other members of the jury were: Israël Pinheiro (non-voting chairman), Luiz Hildebrando Horta Barbosa (Society of Engineers), Oscar Niemeyer (NOVACAP), Stamo Papadaki (architect), William Holford (town planner, chair) and André Sive (town planner).

west, its dramatic changes of level and carefully controlled broad vistas, together with its remarkable generosity of open space, produced the desired effects. The monumental emphasis of the plan reaches its height in the vast, open, unprotected spaces of the triangular Praça dos Três Poderes (Square of the Three Powers), at the eastern tip of the Monumental Axis, and in the 'broad sweeping lawns' of the ceremonial esplanade, 'based on the English lawns of [Costa's] childhood', leading to the imposing Congress.[127] Costa imagined this esplanade between the two rows of ministries filled with people: a space of grandiose proportions, open to the vast sky of the highlands, to host 'pedestrians, processions and parades'.[128]

These open spaces satisfy the demands of the eighth congress of CIAM on 'the Heart of the City' at Hoddesdon, near London (1951), while also representing a rupture with colonial Brazilian cities, which significantly lacked civic spaces of grand proportions. Most importantly, Costa's privileged open spaces fulfil a vision first conceived by Menezes Palmiro, who positioned at the heart of his Cidade Pedrália, in front of the royal palace, an enormous civic square measuring 660 × 660 metres, thus dedicating the most imposing monument of the Brazilian capital to the young Brazilian nation.[129] 'The Square of the Three Powers is the Versailles of the people,' affirmed Costa, aiming to satisfy what Giedion had exposed as the devalued 'demand for *shaping the*

View of the Monumental Axis with the triangular Praça dos Três Poderes at its eastern tip and the ceremonial esplanade leading to the imposing National Congress; in the distance, the Lake Paranoá

127 Lúcio Costa, ' "Ingredientes" da concepção urbanística de Brasília' (n.d.), in Lúcio Costa, 1997, p. 282. The three powers are: the executive, represented by the Presidential Palace; the legislative, represented by the National Congress, and the judiciary, represented by the Supreme Court.   **128** Lúcio Costa, 1966, p. 14.   **129** See Vidal, pp. 74–75.

Juscelino Kubitschek and Lúcio Costa locating
the Monumental Axis of Brasília, April 1957

The triangular Praça dos Três Poderes under construction, 1959: the Presidential Palace and the Supreme Court
at the base of the triangle, and the National Congress at the apex

emotional life of the masses'.[130] Ironically, it became the seat of
an authoritarian dictatorship just four years after its construction,
and remained so for twenty-one years.

Niemeyer's skill was mobilized to populate this brave new
Brazilian world, especially its Monumental Axis – the fuselage of the
city containing its government buildings – with awe-inspiring architectural works to make the world marvel: 'Oh wonder, how many
goodly creatures are there here, how beauteous mankind is, oh
Brave New [Brazilian] World that has such [buildings] in't.'[131] In
1958, Aldous Huxley travelled from Ouro Prêto to Brasília on 'a dramatic journey across time and history'. His words justified
Niemeyer's efforts, as he spoke of 'a journey from Yesterday to
Tomorrow, from what has ended to what will begin, from old realizations to new promises.'[132]

Costa's plan for the city that he conceived as the 'symbol of
the identity of the [Brazilian] nation' aimed beyond a mere '*march
towards order*', to achieve the Corbusian 'more perfect order . . .
[a] work of art'.[133] The competition jury applauded it precisely as
'a work of art'.[134] From the beginning, the city was conceived as
an architectural scheme in the narrow sense, a piece of design
imposed on a landscape with little consideration for the latter
beyond its visual characteristics. The new capital was conceived
as a new Brazil, a reinvented 'Island of the True Cross', a green
island in the middle of the barren red earth. 'I found the Planalto,

that horizon without limit, excessively vast,' stated Costa. 'It was
out of scale, like an ocean, with immense clouds moving over it.
By putting a city in the middle of it, we would be creating a landscape.'[135] For Costa and Niemeyer, Brasília presented the ideal
site on which to give form to the Brazilian world *ex novo* and *ex
nihilo*, fulfilling what Niemeyer saw as their task: 'to create today
the past of tomorrow'.[136]

For the president, the city planner and the architect, Brasília
was no less than an all-wish-fulfilling insular utopia, a sheltering paradise, with the ebullient Kubitschek its Prospero-like magician, a
retreat with little concern for the wicked world outside its shores.
Costa's plan, like the Pessoa Commission's plan for Vera Cruz,
gave final definition to the island of the half million blessed: its
declared aim was to

> take possession of the place – in the manner of the conquista-
> dores or of Luis XIV – to impose an urban structure capable to
> receive a capital within a short period of time. In contrast to
> the cities which conform, and try to adjust themselves, to the
> landscape, at the point where the desert of the *cerrado* and
> an immense sky meet, like at high sea, *the city created a
> landscape*.[137]

Niemeyer would later recall Costa saying that in Brasília 'my architecture is the landscape'.[138]

130 Lúcio Costa, 'Saudação aos críticos de arte' (1959), in Lúcio Costa,
1997, p. 299; Giedion, 1984, p. 57, emphasis in the original.
131 William Shakespeare, *The Tempest*.   **132** Aldous Huxley, quoted
in Shoumatoff, p. 53. Huxley may also be referring to his dystopian
tomorrow. In his *Brave New World Revisited*, published in the same year,
he wrote: 'The nightmare of total organization . . . has emerged from the
safe, remote future and is now awaiting us, just around the next corner';
Huxley, p. 363.   **133** Lúcio Costa, 'Brasília 57–85: Do plano-piloto ao
"Plano Piloto" ' (n.d.), in Lúcio Costa, 1997, p. 326; Le Corbusier, 1987b,
pp. 16, 23.   **134** 'Minutes of the Committee for Judging the Pilot Plan
of Brasília', cited in Evenson, 1975, p. 478.   **135** Lúcio Costa, quoted in
Shoumatoff, p. 43.   **136** Niemeyer, 2000b, pp. 128–29.   **137** Lúcio
Costa, 'O urbanista defende sua cidade' (1967), in Lúcio Costa, 1997,
p. 303, emphasis in the original. According to Maria Elisa Costa, Brasília's
plan was conceived literally at high sea, during a twelve-day journey
from New York to Rio de Janeiro, 'in the middle of the Atlantic Ocean,
with the same 360° stretch of horizon as the Central Plain'; Maria Elisa
Costa, 2002, p. 248.   **138** Oscar Niemeyer, in Wajnberg.

Unlike the other competition participants, Costa made no allowances for scalability, growth and accommodation of new functions beyond the predetermined, rigid outline of the plan, giving birth to the city in her final and finite form, 'as if she had been, from the beginning, fully grown'.[139] His refusal to set foot on the site until the completion of the project was a conscious decision, aiming to protect the purity of the original design. The selection of Costa's finite, relatively small city was also politically motivated, ensuring an appearance of completeness and permanence at Brasília's inauguration and the irreversibility of the capital transfer afterwards.[140] The New World inside Brasília, observes the sociologist Francisco de Oliveira, is protected by an invisible wall in the form of a large green belt, thus turning Brasília into the 'only medieval city of Brazil'.[141] Its elevation to the status of World Heritage Site in 1987 on the basis of Costa's report supporting the application by the governor of the federal district, José Aparecido de Oliveira, confirmed Brasília's utopian status and aggravated the situation arising from its finite form, since the Plano Piloto must be preserved intact for future generations, who will not be able to live in it.[142]

Kubitschek shared Niemeyer's ambition to define the features of Brazil's architectural history and tradition for future generations, and to shape the architectural image of an expanding Brazilian civilization. Brasília was the city that would inaugurate the golden age of Brazil, and he entrusted Niemeyer with the task of creating a Brazilian architecture that would rank with the architecture of the venerable golden age of classical Athens and Rome. 'The founding of Brasília as a way to conquer our "hinterland," to attract settlers, to extend westward a civilization seemingly rooted to the coastal strip, was itself a formidable task,' declared Kubitschek. 'But it is the architectural features of Brasília that reflect the high degree of civilization in my country, just as Greek and Latin architecture and sculpture reflected the magnitude of Greek and Roman civilizations.'[143]

The civic architecture of Brasília is in marked contrast to colonial public architecture, characterized by mostly unassuming, plain civic buildings of a domestic scale, like Rio's Palácio Episcopal (1702) and the Paço Imperial (inaugurated 1743), residences of the bishop and emperor respectively. Brasília's 'elevated and somewhat abstract architecture', argued Costa in 1967, 'grants her an enchanting air of irreality and an attractive *sui generis* character; Brasília is truly a capital and not a provincial city,' he affirmed. Loyal to the vision of the 'land of the future', he concluded that, 'despite all her deficiencies', Brasília's 'scale and [architectural] intention correspond to the greatness and destiny of [Brazil]'.[144]

The Arcadia of the Patriarchal Plantation

Following Le Corbusier's teaching, Brasília represented 'a human operation directed against nature'.[145] Costa's 'Report' envisaged 'a park and a city – the Patriarch's century-old dream', for which the nineteenth-century Rousseauist planner of Cidade Pedrália had specified 'plants from the four corners of the earth'.[146] In the dry, silent wilderness of the *cerrado*, a park is a human creation and a technological achievement no less than modern traffic systems. The 'definitive capital of the country' was a machine-age and air-age arcadia, embodying Le Corbusier's concept of a 'a green "Ville Radieuse"' (Ville Verte).

On the eve of Costa's planning of the new capital, Freyre had lamented the 'divorce, so sharp in modern Brazil, between architecture and town-planning', which he diagnosed by the symptomatic disappearance of vegetation from urban areas.[147] The new seat of federal power would rectify this problem. According to Roberto Burle Marx, whose involvement commenced only after Kubitschek's term of office, in Brasília green spaces aim at establishing an 'intimate connection between humans and vegetation', and at achieving 'the *effective integration of the bucolic with the monumental*', which Costa had anticipated a decade before Brasília.[148] The green colonization of the *cerrado* betrays the civilizing intentions of the twentieth-century colonization of Brazil's hinterland by the Brazilian state. Like Major Júlio Frederico Koeler's Petrópolis (1843), the first planned capital of independent

139 Lúcio Costa, 'Brasília 57–85: Do plano-piloto ao "Plano Piloto" ' (n.d.), in Lúcio Costa, 1997, p. 326. Costa's 1976 plan for Nigeria, on the other hand, allowed for future expansion of the city, although to a limited degree; Lúcio Costa, 'Nigéria' (1976), in Lúcio Costa, 1997, pp. 359–60. **140** Penna, 1960, p. 7. **141** Francisco de Oliveira, quoted in Vidal, p. 242. **142** In 1987, Costa produced a document entitled 'Brasília Revisited', which set the rules for the capital's preservation and future development. It referred to Brasília as 'the expression of a certain urbanist concept . . . with a precise filiation, not a bastard city', which has to be protected from 'innovations and fashions'. Costa's rules were integrated in the Constitution of 1987. Lúcio Costa, 'Brasília Revisitada' (1987), in Lúcio Costa, 1997, p. 330. David Crease noted a particular advantage of the completeness and inelasticity of Brasília's masterplan: 'This immediate transition from town to country is one of Brasília's most positive qualities . . . One arrives indubitably, at a definite instant, at the city; one is not slowly engulfed by

mounting evidences of chaos and congestion'; Crease, 1962, p. 262. **143** Kubitschek, 1966, p. 7. **144** Lúcio Costa, 'O urbanista defende sua cidade' (1967), in Lúcio Costa, 1997, pp. 301–2. **145** Le Corbusier, 1987b, p. xxi. 'Scientific and technological development are not in opposition to Nature', Costa also argued, 'of which they are in fact the hidden face – with all its virtual potential'; Lúcio Costa, quoted in *Lúcio Costa 1902–2002*, p. 58. **146** Paulo Ferreira de Menezes Palmiro, quoted in Vidal, p. 79. **147** Freyre, 1963, p. 237. **148** Burle Marx, p. 298; Lúcio Costa, 'Considerações sobre arte contemporânea' (1940s), in Lúcio Costa, 1997, p. 257, emphasis in the original. At the symposium hosted by the *Architectural Review* in 1948, Costa had argued that 'what characterizes the modern conception of urbanism . . . is that it abolishes the picturesque by incorporating the bucolic into the monumental'. And Giedion had prescribed: 'The civic centre of the coming period will be surrounded by greenery'; in 'In Search of a New Monumentality', 1948, p. 127.

Brazil, Costa's Brasília found inspiration in European urban nature.[149] Costa asserted that 'the English lawns of my childhood are the precedence for all the green spaces of Brasília'.[150] Burle Marx said that in Brasília 'the prevailing idea was always to make a "Bois de Boulogne", or a "Hyde Park" of the tropics'.[151]

In accordance with CIAM principles, the federal capital was envisaged by its planner with a large green belt between the Plano Piloto and future satellite towns, also reiterating the proposals for Vera Cruz. Vegetation would complement the architecture of the public buildings and residential blocks, resulting in a city in the image of Brazil in the days of the patriarchal 'park-like plantations' defended by Freyre, the sociologist responsible for the official version of Brazilian history and national ideology.[152] It is perhaps in this sense that Brasília represents 'a Brazilian reality' based on local traditions.[153] Costa himself included among the 'ingredients' of Brasília the 'purity' of the Baroque town of Diamantina, incidentally, the birthplace of Juscelino Kubitschek, but also the colonial town that had stimulated Costa to move away from neo-colonialism and seek the 'true past' of Brazil and its links with modern architecture.[154]

Gilberto Freyre discerned two complementary tendencies that have marked the history and civilization of Brazil. The first he saw represented by 'the *vertical* founders of Brazil' – sugar- or coffee-planters who established themselves on their plantations like feudal lords, inhabiting solid white mansions or *casas grandes*. The second was represented by the '*horizontal* founders' – frontiersmen or pioneers, the *bandeirantes*, Paulistas and later Cearenses (from the state of Ceará) who escaped the 'feudal social organization established on the coast by the sedentary men' and led 'a process of auto-colonization', continuously moving Brazil's frontier.[155] Although Freyre was critical of Kubitschek's Brasília, the capital appears to have embodied both tendencies, colonizing the country's hitherto desolate central plains and establishing a settlement along the lines of the patriarchal colonial plantations. Of early nineteenth-century Brazil, the French naturalist Auguste de Sainte-Hilaire (1779–1853) remarked: 'There was a country called Brazil, but, unquestionably, there were no Brazilians'; that is, Brazil was not yet a unified nation. It was, in the words of another

scholar, the 'king's plantation'.[156] With astonishing similarity, twentieth-century Brasília was a city before it had any citizens; and it very much resembled a president's plantation. Juscelino Kubitschek assumed the role of the modern patriarch-of-the-nation-cum-*bandeirante*.

With reference to the force that bound together the society of colonial Brazil, Freyre wrote that it 'was exerted from above downward, emanating from the Big Houses that were the center of patriarchal and religious cohesion, the points of support for the organized society of the nation'.[157] Modern Brazilian society and politics have also been characterized by intense personalism, paternalism, clientelism, nepotism and populism. A network of family and patron–client relations of dependence helps maintain traditional class hierarchies and social stratification. At all levels of government, 'political program takes second place to personal leadership and image', with the president acting as the patriarch of the nation.[158] Vargas was known as the 'father of the poor' and, while Brasília was being built, Kubitschek performed his patriarchal role, closely following progress, encouraging and supporting his labouring children.

Before even the inauguration of Brasília's airport, a temporary version of the patriarchal–presidential *casa grande* had been built in ten days, from 22 to 31 October 1956, also reminiscent of Niemeyer's weekend house for M. Passos in Miguel Pereira. It was made of wood and called the Catetinho – that is, little Catete, Palácio do Catete being the name of the presidential palace in Rio de Janeiro.[159] At Kubitschek's request, it was classified as a national monument in 1959. A second, larger Catetinho was constructed in Brasília in 1958. It was also a long, orthogonal wooden

Catetinho, temporary presidential residence, Brasília, built in ten days, inaugurated 10 November 1956

149 Petrópolis was constructed in the 'alpine' region of the Serra da Estrela, around 100 kilometres from Rio de Janeiro, as the summer capital of the Brazilian empire, where foreign guests unaccustomed to the tropical heat would be more comfortably accommodated. The German engineer Júlio Frederico Koeler was also the first director of the new colony. By 1860, Petrópolis had become 'a kind of European town', where people thought they lived as if they were "in the civilized world"'; Schwarcz, 2004, p. 179.　　150 Lúcio Costa, ' "Ingredientes" da concepção urbanística de Brasília' (n.d.), in Lúcio Costa, 1997, p. 282. 151 Burle Marx, p. 302.　　152 Freyre, 1963, pp. 237, 240, 246. 153 Maria Elisa Costa, 2001, p. 22.　　154 Lúcio Costa, ' "Ingredientes" da concepção urbanística de Brasília' (n.d.), in Lúcio Costa, 1997, p. 282. The other ingredients were the Parisian *ordonnance*, English lawns, Chinese terraces and US highways.　　155 Freyre, 1963, pp. 67–92 (the title of this chapter is 'Frontier and Plantation in Brazil').

156 Quoted in Skidmore, 1999, p. 25. Auguste de Sainte-Hilaire travelled around Brazil from 1816 to 1822. Lilia Moritz Schwarcz has also compared the governing of the country by the 'café-com-leite' alliance of São Paulo and Minas Gerais during the Old Republic (1889–1930), to that of 'a great coffee plantation'; Schwarcz, 1999, p. 20, n.　　157 Freyre, 1956, p. 7.　　158 Epstein, p. 35.　　159 The Palácio do Catete was designed in 1862 by Gustav Waeneldt as a residence for the barons of Nova Friburgo. It was remodelled by Aarão Reis in 1896 to serve as a presidential residence. Juscelino Kubitschek had chosen for his official residence in Rio the luxurious, eclecticist Laranjeiras Palace (1909–14) by Armando da Silva Telles and Joseph Gire, architect of the Copacabana Palace. It was originally built as a home for Eduardo Guinle, of the family who owned the Copacabana Palace. Since 1975, the Laranjeiras Palace has served as the official residence of the governor of the state of Rio de Janeiro.

Catetinho: kitchen and services on the ground floor, living and working quarters on the first floor; photograph of 1958–60

Catetinho II, Brasília, 1958, photograph of 20 March 1958

building on stilts with extensive lattice-work protecting its long first-floor façade. Before a masterplan for the city had been drawn, Niemeyer had started work on the building that would become the official presidential residence in the new capital, the Palácio da Alvorada (Palace of the Dawn, designed 1956, constructed 30 September 1957–30 June 1958). The site was selected by Niemeyer and Israël Pinheiro, who 'couldn't wait'. They searched in the *cerrado* for 'the proper site, grass hitting our knees', and found it on the edge of Lake Paranoá, on the peninsula which divides the lake into north and south, beyond the eastern tip of the Monumental Axis, at the point where Brasília's sun rises.[160] In accordance with Tupí beliefs, as reported by Michel de Montaigne, 'those who have deserved well of the gods are lodged in that part of the heaven where the sun rises'.[161]

Twentieth-century Brazilian architects like 'Senhor Lúcio Costa', Freyre contended, 'are showing that it is possible to have perfectly modern buildings that are at the same time Brazilian in the way that they retain something of the patriarchal, personalistic, familist past of Brazil'. According to Freyre, 'Brazilian creativeness has its roots in a family system . . . It was . . . this family system that laid the foundations of modern Brazilian architecture'.[162] Surprisingly, having dismissed Brasília as 'un-Brazilian', Freyre failed to recognize the white, monumental, modern *casa grande* of the Palácio da Alvorada, the first permanent structure completed in Brasília.[163] It closely followed the example of 'the long low structure of a typical Brazilian [*casa grande*] of the colonial days', with its 'protective, large verandah, roofed in such a way . . . as to exclude excesses of light and to protect the house against heavy rains', 'famous for its flower gardens', and 'decorated with statues, most of them made in Oporto'.[164] On the south side, the palace of the president is connected by an underground passage to a low-lying servants' building, at right angles to the main building. In contrast to Freyre, Costa did notice with satisfaction the similarities between the Alvorada and the whitewashed house of the eighteenth-century *fazenda* Columbandê in São Gonçalo, Rio de Janeiro state , a favourite at the Serviço do Patrimônio Histórico e Artístico Nacional (SPHAN), with Tuscan peristyle and nineteenth-

Opposite top, Palácio da Alvorada, presidential residence, Brasília, 1956–58; main (east) façade; *opposite bottom,* Fazenda Columbandê, São Gonçalo, Rio de Janeiro state, eighteenth century, photograph of 1960

160 Niemeyer, 2004, p. 176.   **161** Montaigne, p. 101.   **162** Freyre, 1963, pp. 238, 254.   **163** See Skidmore, 1999, p. 167, and Evenson, 1973, pp. 210–11. Freyre was one of the first Brazilians to question why 'these socialist minded architects [should] build a new city for an old-fashioned bourgeois order'. His vision of Brasília as 'an ultramodern city, where leisure would be the dominant note' was not, however, any less utopian than Costa's and Niemeyer's; quoted in Inês Palma Fernandes, p. 319. Freyre criticized particularly the fact that Brasília was planned exclusively by architects instead of a team including eminent international figures such as 'Lewis Mumford . . . Mukerjee or Dioxadis [sic]' – social scientists and ecologists; Freyre, 1968, pp. 175–97.   **164** Freyre, 1963, pp. 233, 235, 240. Niemeyer writes: 'The palace suggested things of the past. The façade's horizontal direction, the wide veranda protecting the building, even the little chapel by the edge of the composition, reminding [sic] our old farm houses'; Niemeyer, 2000a, p. 39. Elsewhere, he draws a comparison between the curves of Brasília and those of 'the baroque churches of Minas Gerais'; Niemeyer, 1998, p. 34.

century palm colonnades, documented following its accidental 'discovery' in 1938.[165]

In his explanatory notes to his domestic projects, Niemeyer frequently refers to his favourite model of the colonial *fazenda* and its pronounced horizontality. In his quest for a national historic precedent and a link with local tradition for what were intended as the most important civic monuments of modern Brazil, he turned again towards the plantation house – the secular building type that had received the most elaborate architectural treatment during colonial times, and that early twentieth-century nationalist ideology had turned into a symbol of native, Luso-Brazilian tradition. As Freyre pointed out, the houses of the 'patrician patriarchy' had a long association with Brazilian ruling power:

> The bureaucracy was not infrequently installed in what had once been patriarchal dwellings, as in the case of the [nineteenth-century] palaces of Catete and Itamaraty in Rio de Janeiro . . . These homes were of such opulence, especially in and around Rio de Janeiro, that the leaders of the republic of 1889 found them a better place to house their main offices than the dwellings of the former Emperor and the princes.[166]

Significantly, Niemeyer, in collaboration with his daughter Ana Maria Niemeyer, furnished the Alvorada exclusively with Luso-

Palácio da Alvorada: view of main reception area along the west side of the building

Brazilian antiques representing Brazil's high-art heritage, and with modern pieces by living Brazilian designers and European Modern masters, privileging Mies's 'modern version of a royal throne'.[167] Nothing was included from the intervening years of detested foreign economic and cultural domination.

In Brasília, architecture and urbanism, along with government rhetoric and city historiography, assumed the responsibility of integrating the national capital into a carefully constructed national history, representing historical continuity. Following the restoration of the Alvorada's interior to its original condition, from 2002 to 2003, under the direction of the Instituto do Patrimônio Histórico e Artístico Nacional (Institute for the Protection of the National Historic and Artistic Heritage, IPHAN), a government publication suggests that its iconic columns bring to mind the hammocks hung in the verandas of colonial mansions.[168] In an attempt to relate the modern to the native, Freyre noted that 'Siegfried [sic] Giedion . . . pointed out the modernity of the hammock', and added: 'It is to be regretted that the initiative of developing ultra-modern types of light, flexible steel furniture from the suggestive curves of the tropical hammock is a European rather than a Brazilian initiative: logically it should be Brazilian'.[169]

With Brasília wholeheartedly joining modern architecture's campaign against the corridor street typical of nineteenth-century cities like Rio de Janeiro, the rural, spatially isolated *casa grande*, the cornerstone of Brazilian tradition, became an appropriate building type for Brazil's new era of spatial conquest. The nineteenth-century transformation of rural, patriarchal, slave-holding Brazilian society into an urban, democratic one had been characterized, according to Freyre, by 'the rise of the street' and the re-Europeanization of cities like Rio de Janeiro.[170] The Palácio da Alvorada stood at the historic moment of a desired further transformation, bringing together the 'settledness' of the Portuguese colonists, embodied in the patriarchal *casa grande*, with the Modernist rejection of the street, and inspiring both a sense of historical rootedness and one of rupture with Brazil's past centred on the old capital. No imposing gate or wall separates the presidential residence from Brasília's citizens and visitors. Iron gates, after all, had been associated with 'British protection' since, in the early nineteenth century, the Portuguese regent Dom João had gates made in England to install at the Quinta da Boa Vista, the second royal residence, in São Cristóvão of Rio de Janeiro. At

165 Personal communication with Maria Elisa Costa, 15 November 2006. See Lúcio Costa, 'Anotações ao correr da lembrança' (n.d.), in Lúcio Costa, 1997, pp. 503–7. Already in 1960 noting Niemeyer's modern reinterpretation of the *casa grande*, Penna wrote: 'It is rather strange that a building so undeniably bold is, in a certain sense, derived from the colonial tradition.' Accepting the official version of Brazilian history as established by Freyre, Penna argued that the *casa grande* was a 'natural' starting point, since these feudal mansions constituted the 'centres of Brazilian civilization during the seventeenth and eighteenth centuries'; Penna, 1960, p. 7. A 1967 documentary film on Brasília also points out that the design of the Alvorada

is based on the colonial *casa grande*: Joaquim Pedro de Andrade. 166 Freyre, 1986, p. xix. These were the nineteenth-century colonial city mansions, which, according to Freyre, 'succeeded the plantation house as the expression of the domination of the Brazilian scene by the patriarchal system' in what he described as the second epoch in the formation of Brazilian society and civilization. Freyre, 1986, p. xviii.   167 Ludwig Glaeser's description of Mies van der Rohe's chromium-plated steel and calfskin Barcelona chair, designed for the German Pavilion at the Barcelona International Exhibition of 1929. Glaeser, p. 11.   168 *Palácio da Alvorada*, n.p.   169 Freyre, 1963, pp. 245–46.   170 Freyre, 1986, p. xxvii.

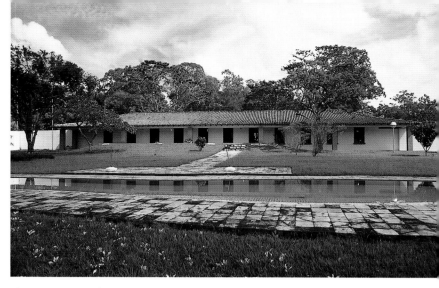

Alvorada, a green lawn of monumental proportions ensures insurmountable distance.

Like the *fazenda* do Columbandê, Niemeyer's Palácio da Alvorada includes a small independent chapel, emphasizing the Christian faith as a permanent accessory of Brazil's ruling authority, while also reflecting 'a family Catholicism, with the chaplain subordinated to the paterfamilias', as in the colonial *casa grande*.[171] The spiralling, marble-sheathed wall that defines the chapel points towards the house, revealing the passage of entry to the relatively dark interior. The colonial plantation traditions explored by Freyre survived independence. Quoting the American sociologist Lynn Smith from the early 1950s, Freyre noted 'that in the best coffee and other modern *fazendas* or plantations of Brazil . . . [the] "point of orientation" continues to be, as in the old patriarchal days, "the casa grande . . . surrounded by well-kept lawns and gardens, which nearly always include a tiled swimming pool".'[172] In the reflective pool of the Alvorada there is a bronze sculpture by Alfredo Ceschiatti, *The Water Nymphs*.

In Brasília, da Cunha's real Brazilian world of the interior provided both the fierce, independent *sertanejos* (people from the *sertão*) who built the federal capital's modern monuments, and models for the successful embodiment of the nation's collective memory and national history in the form of the patriarchal *casa grande* of the feudal sugar plantation. Oscar Niemeyer's own residence in Brasília, built in 1960 near the country club, is a white, characteristically long, one-storey structure, with a tiled roof that overhangs to protect the veranda, and a row of tall windows like those of the Laranjeiras house where he was born, opening to a large lawn to the rear, based on 'the type of old colonial farmhouse that I had always wanted'.[173] It includes a swimming pool of sinuous curves and the ubiquitous reclining figure by Ceschiatti.[174] In 1990, Niemeyer would build a house for the governor of São Paulo, Orestes Quércia, in Pedregulho, São Paulo state, closely following the model of the traditional Brazilian *fazenda*. The squat, whitewashed house with gabled, red-tiled roof, however, is accessed via a long, sinuous ramp that sweeps and swerves through the front garden before it reaches the sheltered veranda. Circular windows, an irregularly shaped pool and, most prominently, a modern chapel standing on the extension of the veranda, to the left of the house, further undermine the historicist elements of the design.

At the Sebastião Camargo Correira House (1985–87), near the lake of Brasília, the emphatic juxtaposition of colonial–traditional and modern forms became the central theme of the design. A long, orthogonal volume with a red-tiled roof and tall blue windows contains sleeping quarters and auxiliary spaces and ad-

Niemeyer House, Brasília, 1960: garden façade with swimming pool

Sebastião Camargo Correira House, Lago Sul, Brasília, 1985–87: above, entrance elevation; below, side elevation

171 Freyre, 1956, p. 7.   **172** Freyre, 1963, p. 242, n. 7, quoting Lynn Smith. See also Burns, 1970, pp. 345–46.   **173** Niemeyer, 2000b, p. 121. **174** 'People tell you he only built it to please his wife'; Dos Passos, p. 132.

dresses the public garden to the side of the house. This is married with an uncompromisingly modern, unruly, flat-roofed volume with extensive glazing, containing reception spaces and jutting out into the garden with, again, an irregularly shaped pool. At the entrance to the house, at the top of six wide steps up from the street, the flat roof plane shoots forward and folds down at a wide angle, origami-like, to form a porch, its angular formation set against the plain walls of the white volume freely zigzagging behind it. On the wall of the red-roofed volume visible from the street, Niemeyer positioned a hybrid smoking bay that combines blue lattice with his signature curves, negotiating the transition between the modern and the traditional.

Among the principal characteristics of Brazilian society, Freyre lists 'hospitality to strangers'.[175] Hospitality was customary in the plantation era, a duty of the patriarchal families. Freyre suggests that it 'was not only an expression of "conspicuous waste" . . . but also a manifestation of the so-called gregarious instinct intensified by isolation'.[176] Like the Palácio da Alvorada, the first-class Brasília Palace Hotel with 105 suites (1957–58, destroyed by fire in 1978, restored in 2006) was designed independently from the city's mas-

terplan, in the neighbourhood of the presidential residence, and received its first guests, the president of Paraguay and his entourage, on 2 May 1958.

For Brazil to fulfil her vision of becoming a world power, it was important to promote her image as a modern country; that is, a country where reason, progress and individual freedom are represented by new forms of communal living. Brasília was to present its guests with the new image of Brazil 'in an age of heroic reawakening', a Corbusian image of 'precision and clarity, speed and correctness'.[177] Costa had foreseen two different itineraries for 'distinguished visitors': one to be followed upon arrival and a second one for their departure. The first one was to be a journey along 'an independent highway which directly connects the airport and the civic center', showcasing Brasília as the modern capital of speed and efficiency. The second one was to 'be made by the residential highway itself which displays the city to advantage'.[178] Costa had thus arranged for the visitor to leave Brazil with an image of 'Beauty' where 'mathematical exactness is joined to daring and imagination'.[179]

The houses of the executive and judiciary branches of government at the Praça dos Três Poderes also follow the model of the patriarchal house. These grand houses of post-slave-holding, democratic Brazil have no 'dovecotes', to use abolitionist writer and statesman Joaquim Nabuco's term for the slave quarters of the patriarchal houses.[180] It may be as a tribute to slave labour and the African slaves' contribution to the Brazilian culture and economy that Niemeyer gave a prominent position to his monumental *Pombal* (*Dovecote*,1961), a 10-metre-tall exposed-concrete structure at the Praça dos Três Poderes. His *Pombal* may have also been intended as a reminder; for Niemeyer recognizes that in Brazil 'We still have slavery because there are two societies. Rich and poor. This must be changed.'[181] The *Pombal* also calls to mind the enlightened Marquês de Pombal, Sebastião José de Carvalho e Melo (1699–1782), despotic ruler of the Portuguese empire in the name of King José I, who 'raised the Indians to the rank of equali-

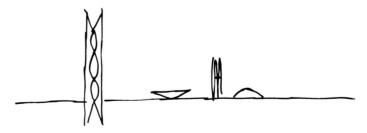

Pombal (Dovecote), 1961, with the National Congress in the distance

Brasília Palace Hotel, Brasília, 1957–58, destroyed by fire 1978, restored 2006, photograph of 1958

175 Freyre, 1956, p. 77.   176 Freyre, 1963, p. 87.   177 Le Corbusier, 1987c, p. 192.   178 Lúcio Costa, 1966, p. 16.   179 Le Corbusier, 1989, p. 18.   180 Joaquim Aurélio Barreto Nabuco de Araújo (1849–1910), quoted in Freyre, 1986, p. 194.   181 Niemeyer, 1988c, p. 25.

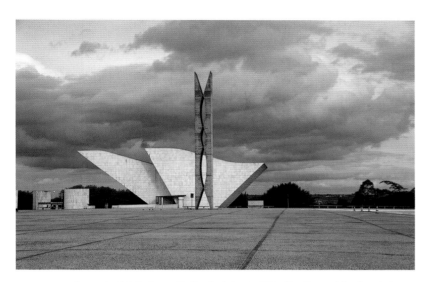

Praça dos Três Poderes with the Panteão da Pátria (Pantheon of the Country)
Tancredo Neves, 1987, and the *Pombal*

ty with all the king's other subjects' and encouraged intermarriage between Portuguese and Indians to foster national unity.[182] Perhaps the *Pombal* was intended as a gesture towards Brazil's third 'race', establishing Indian representation in the 'Versailles of the people' and thus returning to the favoured theme of *mestiçagem*.

It may be argued that, effectively, Brasília as a whole follows the model of the colonial plantation raising a single crop, with the buildings for the ruling family and its dependents prominently displayed, and the serving underclass in separate quarters, satellite towns beyond the garden of the family, coming into the masters' protected world to offer their services and then discreetly disappearing in their modest *senzala* (slave quarters) beyond the city's gates. Lúcio Costa was aware of the persistence of the *senzala* in the separate quarters of the domestic servants of the Brazilian bourgeoisie. He regretted the appearance of Brasília's first *favelas*, which he thought would have been avoided had his original proposal been faithfully realized, offering accommodation in each residential unit at three different levels of affordability. The population of the *favelas* that grew up around the residential quarters was transferred to satellite towns by NOVACAP.[183]

Brasília and its satellite towns, with their corresponding distribution of power and social, racial, spatial and economic segregation, may be seen to represent the third, twentieth-century epoch in the formation of Brazilian society and civilization. Extending Freyre's architectural metaphor, the shanties that in nineteenth-century Brazil had taken the place of the colonial *senzala* were transformed in streetless Brasília into satellite dormitories – planned towns and other settlements on the periphery of the capital – some of which have now grown larger than Brasília and relatively prosperous. The distance between the satellite dormitories and the big house of the government, with its high-ranking loyal servants, was made unbridgeable. In Brasília, there seems to be no realistic provision for Freyre's 'zones' or 'moments of fraternization' between the 'social extremes'.

As early as 1962, *Módulo*, the journal edited by Niemeyer, announced: 'The housing problem is becoming increasingly serious in Brasília.' In order to prevent the proliferation of private houses based on the US suburban 'little-house cult', and to accommodate the need for low-cost housing, Niemeyer proposed two types of prefabricated housing: a seven-storey apartment block and a second, flexible type, composed of a variable number of single, prefabricated, low-cost units with a garden.[184] In 1963, in his speech for the Lenin Prize at the University of Brasília, he condemned the 'discriminatory spirit which predominates in the Federal District', manifested in the satellite towns – 'dormitory cities, a pile of *favelas*'.[185]

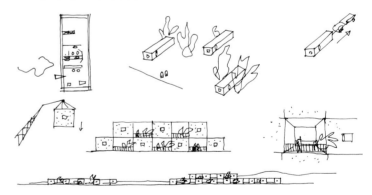

Proposal for prefabricated housing for Brasília, assembled of single units with a garden, 1962

182 Burns, 1970, p. 37. See also Gott, pp. 279–80. Gott calls the May 1755 royal edict attributed to the Marquês de Pombal 'an early example of positive discrimination . . . All this, of course, was too good to be true', Gott comments. 'The white settlers of Brazil rejected the reforms, and they were never put into effect. But to advocate miscegenation rather than extermination was notably more progressive than the policies that would emerge in independent Latin America in the course of the next century.' Policies to assimilate the Indians are also responsible for their cultural extinction – a process initiated by Jesuit missions. **183** Lúcio Costa, 'Restez chez vous', (n.d.), in Lúcio Costa, 1997, p. 314. Costa notes that 'as the architects disagreed [with NOVACAP's decision], they did not cooperate'. **184** Niemeyer, 1962c, pp. 27–37. In 1963, Niemeyer proposed the same system of prefabricated units for student housing for the University of Brasília. **185** Niemeyer, 1968, pp. 28–29. In the same speech, Niemeyer said: 'What has become of our brothers the workers who helped build the city? They who, like us, have humbly

struggled and suffered, perhaps more than we, in this enterprise. What has happened to these brave comrades, the real builders of this capital? That is the question I put to legislators and members of the government when they ask me to say something about Brasília. I should like to point out, although the fact is well known, that our fellow-workers have left the capital city they themselves built and that the houses, schools, nurseries, clubs and ministries that they constructed never in fact in the least belonged to them. As consolation they have only the time-honoured misery upon which exploitation and poverty are based . . . I do not hesitate to warn you that Lucio Costa's master plan is about to be changed. The provisions for public assistance housing have been refused at the very moment when contact between rich and poor would have provided the best guarantee of development for Brasília . . . social discrimination has taken root throughout the capital district . . . I ask you: what measures do we intend to take to put this situation to rights?'; extract in English in *Architecture d'Aujourd'hui*, 1974, p. lxxxiii.

Kubitschek stated that his developmentalist ideology aimed 'to defend our way of life against ideologies which are opposed to our Christian faith and democratic institutions'.[186] Elsewhere he said: 'Brasília was born under the sign of democracy and with the blessing of God.' He christened the *candangos* – the construction workers who built Brasília – 'The Builders of the Cathedral', and dedicated to them a chapter in his memoirs.[187] The priest of Brasília's Metropolitan Cathedral is accommodated in the world of the masters, but remains clearly subordinate, according to tradition and protocol, as Costa emphasized in his 'Report'.[188]

Niemeyer's cathedral evokes Brazil's Baroque national heritage, with the standing figures of the four evangelists clearly alluding to the most celebrated of all Mineiro monuments: Aleijadinho's soapstone statues of the twelve lesser prophets, his last major achievement, in the forecourt or *adro* of the Santuário do Bom Jesus de Matosinhos in Congonhas do Campo.[189] They were modelled, in turn, on the Via Sacra of the Santuário do Bom Jesus do Monte in Braga, Portugal (1723–1837), leading to Carlos Ama-

rante's Neoclassical church (1784–1811) with the statues of the evangelists adorning its façade. Alfredo Ceschiatti's evangelists guard the route to the entrance of Brasília's cathedral. His angels, suspended in mid-air inside the glazed dome, also recall the life-size, cedarwood angels of Aleijadinho's Stations of the Cross (1796–99) in the six chapels that line the ascent to the main church at Congonhas. While Aleijadinho's prophets greet the ascending pilgrim, foretelling the pending sacrifice, Brasília's evangelists, in the previously untouched *cerrado*, herald redemption, deliverance from the tears of colonization and underdevelopment. Armed with the good news, the worshipper descends the entrance ramp and, passing through relative darkness under a channel of purifying water overhead, is reborn in a new world in the nave, accommodating four thousand and filled with light and joy. In Christian terms, the evangelists' message of liberation is also to be understood as a return to a lost paradise or a union with God. Niemeyer's cathedral of the 'Capital of Hope' reinforces the Christian metaphor put forward by Costa in his cross-shaped Pilot

Metropolitan Cathedral of Nossa Senhora Aparecida with Alfredo Ceschiatti's statues of the evangelists guarding the route to the entrance

186 Juscelino Kubitschek, quoted in Vidal, p. 202.   **187** Juscelino Kubitschek, quoted in Inês Palma Fernandes, pp. 201, 199.   **188** Lúcio Costa, 1966, p. 14.   **189** See Chapter One, p. 32.

Above, Aleijadinho (Antônio Francisco Lisboa), Santuário do Bom Jesus de Matosinhos, Congonhas do Campo, Minas Gerais, 1757–90, with statues of the twelve lesser prophets in the adro, 1795–1805

Right top, Via Sacra, Santuário do Bom Jesus do Monte, Braga, Portugal, 1723–1837. The statues of the evangelists on the façade of Carlos Amarante's Neoclassical church (1784–1811) were designed by Manuel Joaquim Álvares and executed by José Domingues in 1808.

Right bottom, Aleijadinho (Antônio Francisco Lisboa), angel, 1796–99, cedarwood, second chapel, Stations of the Cross, Santuário do Bom Jesus de Matosinhos, Congonhas do Campo, Minas Gerais

Below, Metropolitan Cathedral of Nossa Senhora Aparecida: dome with Alfredo Ceschiatti's angels suspended in mid-air and stained-glass panels by Marianne Peretti

Plan for Brasília and brings together the promise of Christian salvation with that of the nation's deliverance from suffering.

Following plantation tradition, Brasília's patriarch is also buried near his *casa grande*. Niemeyer's Memorial for Juscelino Kubitschek was built twenty years after the inauguration of the city (1980–81), at the exact spot where the first mass had been celebrated, at the western tip of the Monumental Axis. Five years after his death, Kubitschek's remains were ceremoniously transferred to this truncated and elongated pyramid designed to eternalize the memory of the city's founder, who has been compared to the Egyptian pharaoh Akhenaton. 'O FUNDATOR' lies in a granite tomb in the mortuary chamber, the only part of the building that receives some natural light, through stained-glass windows designed by Marianne Peretti, under a pebble-shaped dome that marks the holy of holies. Like a shell rounded by the passage of time and the winds of Brasília and curled inwards towards its precious centre, the concrete dome is stripped of all solidity, hovering on the flat expanse of the mausoleum's pyramidal base. The pronounced horizontality of the memorial suggests an eternal *casa grande* under the mythologized clouds drifting across Brasília's sky. Raised on an exposed-concrete stela and embraced by a cres-

cent from the hand of his favourite architect, Kubitschek's figure, by Honório Peçanha, surveys 'Sugarcane Fields Forever'.[190] Niemeyer regards this 28-metre-high structure as the first of his 'protest sculptures', 'simultaneously shelter[ing] and highlight[ing] the former president's statue . . . defy[ing] the dictatorship and its reactionary supporters [by] forcing them to look at Kubitschek's statue every day'.[191]

On Brasília's inauguration day, President Kubitschek presented the new capital to Queen Elizabeth II as 'the dawn of a new day for Brazil'. In his ceremonial speech, he heralded the imminent realization of the Brazilian utopia. Deliberately blind to the realities of life in Brasília and faithful to his idealization of the future, he proclaimed: 'With the New Capital there will come, God willing, an era of abundance and genuine brotherhood which will permit to all Brazilians, without distinction, the enjoyment of the advantages of culture and of progress.'[192] Perhaps John Donne's words from 'The Sun Rising' would have reflected Kubitschek's feelings more accurately: 'She is all states, and all princes, I.'

Brazil's Monument of Hope

While the self-confident tunes of the presidential Palace of the Rising Sun were ascending to grace Brasília's 'landscape of oxygen, silence and nostalgia [*saudades*] for origins', as depicted by Vinícius de Moraes, he and his fellow guest at the Catetinho, Antônio Carlos Jobim, were composing their *Sinfonia da Alvorada* for the city's inauguration ceremony.[193] The architecture of Brasília combines a yearning for, and a reaffirmation of, the romanticized, rural, patriarchal values of Brazilian society with Niemeyer's exacting diction and obsessive experimentalism, continually reinventing his formal repertoire, ever on guard against conformity and mediocrity. Costa interpreted the Brazilian motto 'Order and Progress' as pointing to an integration of a conservative with a progressive spirit.[194] His and Niemeyer's concretization of the dream that was Brasília is pervaded by '*saudades* for origins' – a sort of counterreformist and conservative spirit that aimed to project the values of the past onto a modern, urban, industrial future that was promised radiant and free of *saudades*. Nevertheless, the tone of Niemeyer's architecture is not revivalist; rather than attempting to bring the past to life, he strove to transform it with his magic wand

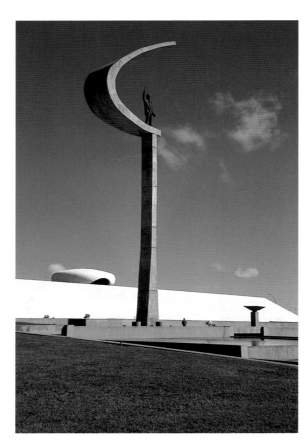

Memorial for Juscelino Kubitschek at the western tip of the Monumental Axis, Brasília, 1980–81

190 The title of a 1972 song by Caetano Veloso.   **191** Niemeyer, 2000b, p. 131.   **192** Juscelino Kubitschek, quoted in Epstein, p. 71. **193** 'Paisagem de oxigênio, silêncio e saudades das origines'; Moraes, 1961. *Brasília – Sinfonia da Alvorada* was released by Columbia in 1961, with Oscar Niemeyer's iconic sketches on its white sleeve. Later it became known as *Sinfonia de Brasília*. In 1960, Oscar Niemeyer passed on to de Moraes the president's wish to create, for the inauguration day of Brasília, a 'son et lumière' type of spectacle at the Praça dos Três Poderes, in collaboration with the French firm Clemançon; text on the sleeve of the LP. The symphony was not performed at the inauguration ceremony. It was eventually performed at the Praça dos Três Poderes in 1986.   **194** Lúcio Costa, 'Bandeira' (n.d.), in Lúcio Costa, 1997, p. 49.

National Congress, at the apex of the triangular Praça dos Três Poderes, with the shallow dome of the Senate partnered with the inverted larger dome of the Chamber of Deputies and the twenty-seven-storey twin towers of the Secretariat, 1958–60. As prescribed by Costa's 'Report', the Congress 'faces a broad esplanade set out on a second terrace, rectangular in shape'. Sérgio Bernardes's flagpole, 1961, is visible between the towers of the Secretariat.

– devouring it and thus assimilating its strengths in the long-practised Antropofagist manner.

'Utopias and the changes they undergo', argue Gregory Claeys and Lyman Tower Sargent, 'both help bring about and are reflections of paradigm shifts in the way a culture views itself.'[195] Since the 1920s, the new capital city had become the privileged locus of Brazilian modernity. From the beginning, it was not expected to reject, but to enshrine, the values of the Brazilian historical past, now regarded through a transhistorical perspective. As Laurent Vidal has amply demonstrated in his masterful study of Brasília, the invention of the capital went hand in hand with a reinterpretation of the history of Brazil as an orderly progression of events, or rather, a succession of heroic personalities resolutely turned towards a single end: the making of Brasília. Brazil's long-wished-for capital became the goal that united all key figures in the nation's official history, from Cabral through Tiradentes, Dom Pedro I and José Bonifácio to Kubitschek, conferring meaning on their actions.

Niemeyer's monuments for Brasília portray a Brazilian nation state proud of its past and confident in the future, at once traditional and modern. They embody this teleological vision of Brazil and Brazilian history, which was popularized to support and legitimize the ambitious project, setting the stage for an ideal future. Brasília presented an image of Brazil and Luso-Brazilian architectural tradition 'condemned to modernity', to use Mário Pedrosa's popular phrase.[196] Through an ultimate act of Antropofagist mixing of diverse ingredients, Brasília, and with it the modern Brazilian state it was created to represent, were born bearing the hallmark of the nation: 'Hybrid from the beginning'.[197] Kubitschek was proclaimed the proud descendent of the Mineiro Tiradentes and Niemeyer the worthy heir of the mulatto Aleijadinho. Their actions gained legitimacy by having their origins firmly established in those of the early national heroes.

On the tabula rasa of Brasília, Niemeyer strove to mould an ideal urban reality through a perfectly orchestrated ensemble of civic buildings. The decisive landmark marking the virgin skyline of Brasília is the National Congress (1958–60), at the apex of the Monumental Axis. Costa's equilateral triangle of the Praça dos Três Poderes, and Niemeyer's monumentalization of the legislature – faithful to Costa's schematic sketch – may correspond to their designers' ideal of parliamentary democracy, but they disguise Brazilian political reality, where the judiciary and legislature are subordinate to the executive power of the patriarch – president. It is the columns of the president's residence, the Alvorada, that feature on the city's coat of arms. Perhaps, Costa and Niemeyer's Capitol for Brasília expressed an anticipation – as Ernst Bloch demanded – of the ideal polis. Niemeyer ensured that the 'panoramic vista' along the Monumental Axis continues 'unimpeded far beyond the building, over the terrace, between the cupolas' and up to the Praça dos Três Poderes, 'the grand open air salon where all citizens will be able to gather'.[198]

195 Claeys and Sargent, 1999, p. 3.   196 Pedrosa's phrase echoed Euclides da Cunha: 'We are condemned to civilization. Either we shall progress or we shall perish'; quoted in E. Bradford Burns, 'Introduction to the Paperback Edition', in Freyre, 1986, p. xlix.   197 Freyre, 1956, p. 81. 198 Niemeyer, 1966, p. 22; Niemeyer, 1979e, p. 80.

" le bâtiment du Congrès, très bas, au niveau du sol,
la vue pénétrant sur l'esplanade, entre les coupoles,
jusqu'à la place des trois Pouvoirs."

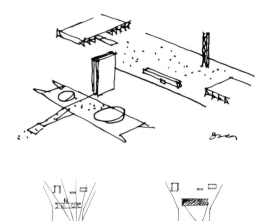

Museum of the City, Brasília, 1958

The major buildings housing the mechanism of Brazilian democracy and power were conceived as 'a symphony of forms which makes the whole group look much richer and much more diversified'.[199] Niemeyer's decision to steer clear of mass and solidity, staging instead a drama 'almost antimonumental in the customary sense', is loyal to the conclusions of the eighth congress of CIAM at Hoddesdon in 1951.[200] In a near reversal of his earlier expressed views, Giedion there admonished: 'there is no excuse for the erection of a monumental building mass', shifting the responsibility for producing symbolic forms to 'creative painters and sculptors'.[201] Originally intended to accommodate no other buildings except the Executive Palace, the National Congress and the Supreme Court, the Praça dos Três Poderes was gradually populated by a number of symbolic structures and sculptures, including the aforementioned *Dovecote* near the Supreme Court; the white-granite-clad Museum of the City (1958), upon Kubitschek's request; the Teahouse (1958), defined by a roofplane that hovers close to the vast horizon of the civic square; the Hall Lúcio Costa (1987), submerged under his 'Versailles of the people'; and, finally, the Pantheon of the Country Tancredo Neves (1987), 'designed to enhance the Três Poderes Square like a white bird',

and dedicated to Brazil's 'President of Hope', the first elected civilian president since 1964, whose death before his inauguration in 1985 caused a massive outpouring of grief.[202]

Niemeyer's Congress does not lack monumentality. Here, monumentality resides in the pronouncement of the horizontal dimension, a self-assured gesture that, while diverging from the norm, is all the more powerful and effective in a landscape that, as Costa emphasized, has no natural vertical elements at all, no mountains or sea, but 360° of horizon and 180° of sky. Le Corbusier proclaimed: 'the eye of the man who sees wide horizons is prouder, wide horizons confer dignity; that is the thought of a planner.'[203] By superimposing the focal point of the city on the perspectival vanishing point, Brasília's Monumental Axis and its prolongation through the twin tower office blocks of the National Congress and beyond the triangular Praça dos Três Poderes towards the lake, accentuate the effect of limitless flat ground. A parallel canopy of fast-drifting clouds is reflected in the waters of Lake Paranoá. Niemeyer translated Brasília's natural landmark, its almighty horizon, into reinforced concrete and turned it into the monumental terrace of the National Congress, the podium of the Brazilian people. A ceremonial ramp lifts the elect onto this new

199 Niemeyer, 1966, p. 22. Cf. the Corbusian 'complex of forms assembled in a precise relationship'; Le Corbusier, 1987c, p. 207.   200 Evenson, 1975, p. 498.   201 Sigfried Giedion, quoted in Ockman (ed.), p. 28. In 1939, Giedion had argued that such a collaboration between architects and artists would enable architects to satisfy 'our need for luxury, splendour and beauty'; Giedion, 1939, pp. 36–37.   202 Niemeyer, 1998, p. 22.
203 Le Corbusier, 1991, p. 235.

civic plane. Beyond Brasília's new, concrete horizon, a 100-metre-high flagpole by Sérgio Bernardes (1961) marks the elusive vanishing point where the ideal city becomes reality.

Like Brazil's ideology of continental destiny and undiminished optimism, the new capital's Monumental Axis extends *ad infinitum* and *in posterum*, preserving the openness of the vista of the future for 'the Capital of Hope'. The salutation first used by André Malraux during his visit of 1959 became the title of the hymn to Brasília sung by schoolchildren:

> In the middle of an untamed virgin land,
> In the most splendorous of dawns,
> Happy as a child's smile,
> A dream transformed itself into reality,
> The most fantastic city came into being,
> Brasília, the Capital of Hope.[204]

In Glauber Rocha's 1964 film *Deus e o Diabo na Terra do Sol* (*Black God, White Devil*), the millennial cult leader Sebastião pronounces: 'God separated heaven and earth; when heaven and earth become one again, you will see the island [of the blest]'.[205]

Brazil's 'tragic carnival'

On the plateau of Goiás, it is easy to lose a sense of scale and distance. Infinity appears accessible. But the Brazil of the space age, and of an age of equality and social justice conjured up by Kubitschek's ambitious programmes, Costa's vision and Niemeyer's undiminishing enthusiasm and insatiable appetite for innovation remained inaccessible – a largely undiscovered country. Like earlier *bandeirantes*, they searched in vain for Lago Dourado – a mythical lake of gold awaiting the adventurous. The *candangos* who constructed the 'kingdom of the *desejado*' (the desired one – King Sebastian) were judged unfit for citizenship. The president's neighbours were carefully selected, like those of Dom Pedro II at Petrópolis.

Niemeyer remembers with nostalgia the days when Brasília was under construction, days of enthusiasm and camaraderie, when *candangos* and engineers lived and worked side by side. 'This was the time of illusions,' he says: 'On the inauguration day, with the President of the Republic, the generals in their full dress uniforms, the deputies dressed to the nines, all state officials and their high-society ladies in their finest jewellery, everything

Candangos in the Praça dos Três Poderes, photograph of 1959–60

changed. The magic was shattered in a single blow.'[206] Niemeyer did not attend the ceremony. In a speech on 'The Contemporary City' he delivered in 1958 at the International Students' Conference in Leningrad and published in *Módulo*, he had posited 'a society free from class distinction' as 'the indispensable basis for the modern city'. But he had also warned that this goal cannot be achieved by the architect or the urban planner. Unless society itself is organized on that basis, 'what was intended for all will become the privilege of a small minority', a mere 'grandiose display of technique and good taste'.[207]

The international architectural community's reception of the 'Kafkaesque nightmare' and 'instant city', as Bruno Zevi called Brasília, turned unfavourable before its completion and increasingly hostile as reports about its 'magnificent parade ground' and 'Orwellian' environment proliferated.[208] Inflation, which had plagued the country since World War II, continued to mount, spiralling upwards following Kubitschek's decision to please the radical nationalists by breaking off negotiations with the International Monetary Fund in June 1959 and jettisoning the economic stabilization programme. Following his election with 48 per cent of the vote on 3 October 1960, President Jânio da Silva Quadros made a radio broadcast focused on the 'terrible' financial situation he inherited: $2 billion of foreign debt due in his presidential term, and over $600 million payable within the first year. Quadros lamented: 'All this money, spent with so much publicity, we must now raise, bitterly, patiently, dollar by dollar and cruzeiro by cruzeiro. We have spent, drawing on our future to a greater extent than the imagination dares to contemplate.'[209] In a markedly different

204 Cited in Shoumatoff, pp. 54–55. **205** *Terra do Sol* was the title of Gustavo Barroso's 1912 ethnographic study of the drought-afflicted Northeast. **206** Niemeyer, 1993c, p. 41. 'Vanity and egoism have returned', Niemeyer declared in a 1968 documentary film. 'And we ourselves are returning to the habits and the privileges of the bourgeoisie that we hate,' he added; Oscar Niemeyer, quoted in Brayne. **207** Niemeyer, 1958a, n.p. **208** A number of critics saw Brasília as a demonstration of the failures of the Modern Movement. Wolf von Eckard lamented: 'Niemeyer and Costa have realized not just their own dream but that of Le Corbusier and a generation of planners and architects who followed him . . . Perhaps . . . they have demolished the dream by this achievement'; quoted in Inês Palma Fernandes, p. 314. For a detailed review of the international and national debate on Brasília, see Inês Palma Fernandes, pp. 294–329. **209** Jânio da Silva Quadros, quoted in Skidmore, 1967, p. 194.

vein, in a 1961 lecture Henrique Mindlin remarked: 'The total cost of Brasilia in its first four years had been only a third of what France was currently paying every year for the war in Algeria.'[210]

Although he declared his commitment to completing the city, Niemeyer reported that 'with the departure of JK, from one day to the next . . . our work in Brasília was paralyzed'.[211] The military coup of 1964 was the final assault on the spirit of optimism embodied in the new Brazil's cloudscraping structures. Like that of Clarice Lispector's fictional chicken, the myth of Brasília could not be sustained for too long: 'one year they killed her and ate her, and the years rolled on.'[212] From 1967, the dictators settled comfortably in Brasília's remote gardens, which served to distance 'the masses from the seat of courtly power'.[213]

In 1967, Glauber Rocha's unsettling film *Terra em Transe* (*Land in Anguish*) appeared as a critique of El Dorado and what its director called the 'tragic carnival' of Brazilian politics, where 'purity rots in tropical gardens'.[214] Rocha's Africanization and carnivalization of the foundational 'first mass' allegorized disenchantment with the illusionism of the populist project and its historicized narratives. The same year, the Paulista architect João Batista Vilanova Artigas placed the concrete slab of his Elza Berquó House in São Paulo on bare tree trunks, protesting 'that all this reinforced concrete technique, which produced the magnificent architecture that we know, was nothing but irremediable foolishness in the face of the political conditions that we lived under'.[215]

The monumental utopia of Brasília found its way into the Antropofagist totemic structure of Tropicália or Tropicalismo, a 1960s and 1970s artistic and socio-cultural movement that articulated a critique of Brazilian society and officially promoted national culture. Envisaging radical transformation, it encompassed in its experimental field realms of cultural practice as diverse as popular music, poetry, visual arts, cinema, theatre, architecture, fashion and media. Caetano Veloso's allegorical Tropicalista flag song 'Tropicália' (1967), brought together 'palhoça' – the mud huts of the *sertão* – with the *bossa nova* of Brasília, the latest national myth ripe for cannibalization, 'the capital of the freakish song-monument I'd raise to our sorrow, our delight and our absurdity'.

Above my head the soaring planes,
Below my feet the trucks and trains,
My nose head on with the highlands,
I lead the movement,
I direct the Carnival,
I unveil the monument in my homeland's central plain.[216]

Brasília was added to the symbols and clichés of *brasilidade*, both celebrated and satirically appropriated. Some critics have even suggested that Tropicália (the movement rather than the song) was directly related to Brasília as a 'mythical double that exists in counterpoint to the real fact of Brasília'.[218] In Gilberto Gil's

'Geléia Geral', the song with lyrics by Torquato Neto featured on the concept album *Tropicália, Panis et Circencis* [sic] (1968), the patriotic emblems of an authentic *brasilidade*, like the 'sweet wicked mulatto woman' and Brazil's 'anil skies', are satirized and provocatively mixed with imported cultural icons ('Sinatra') and industrial products ('Formica'). At the song's climax, the legendary Brazilian 'hospitable friendship' turns into a 'brutality garden', an allusion to Brasília's transformation into a symbol of military power imbued with political violence.[218]

The 1968 military 'coup within a coup' was followed by the darkest years of the dictatorship (1969–74). With the return of democracy in the 1980s, politics was staged in Rio de Janeiro and São Paulo, and 1990s pessimism was aptly expressed in a project for the 'decapitalization' of Brasília and a return of the capital to the real, dynamic centre of the country, along the Rio de Janeiro–São Paulo axis. Nevertheless, Brasília has survived and, like St Petersburg, another city born of political will, today it has a history and a memory and an indigenous generation of citizens who take pride in their 'green city'. According to United Nations statistics, Brasília enjoys the highest quality of life and the highest education level in Brazil. It has become part of the local landscape but also something much larger: a twentieth-century Brazilian icon embedded in the cultural consciousness and as widely recognizable as Copacabana Beach or the statue of Christ the Redeemer atop Mount Corcovado. For the majority of Brazilians who live outside the epic federal capital, its monuments have indelibly marked and updated the visual imaginary of *brasilidade*.

210 Henrique Mindlin, quoted in Evenson, 1969, p. 28. **211** Oscar Niemeyer, quoted in Evenson, 1973, p. 164. **212** Lispector, 1972, p. 52 (this is the last sentence of the short story). **213** Vale, p. 127. **214** Glauber Rocha, quoted in Skidmore, 1999, p. 169. **215** João Batista Vilanova Artigas, quoted in Conduru, p. 78. **216** 'Sobre a cabeça os aviões / Sob os meus pés os caminhões / aponta contra os chapadões meu nariz / Eu organizo o movimento / Eu oriento o Carnaval / Eu inauguro o monumento no planalto central do país'; Veloso, pp. 117–18. The term Tropicalismo was introduced by the journalist Nelson Motta in 1968. The song title 'Tropicália' was borrowed from Hélio Oiticica's Antropofagist installation *Tropicália* (at the exhibition *Nova Objetividade Brasileira*, Museum of Modern Art, Rio de Janeiro, April 1967), which returned to 'the fantastic architecture of the slums', and 'the "myth" of miscegenation'; Oiticica, 2004, p. 178. Oiticica's programme, however, had a much stronger nationalist tone than Tropicalismo, aiming at 'a total "Brazilian" image . . . [and] the downfall of the universalist myth of Brazilian culture, entirely based on Europe and North America, and on an Aryanism which is inadmissible here.' At the same time, Oiticica stressed that 'For the creation of a true Brazilian culture, characteristic and strong, expressive at last, this accursed European and North American influence will have to be absorbed, anthropophagically, by the Black and Indian of our land'; Oiticica, 2004, pp. 178–79. **217** Basuado, p. 18. **218** The term 'geléia geral' ('general jelly') was borrowed from Concretist poet Décio Pignatari, who had borrowed it in turn from Oswald de Andrade. In the Tropicalista song, it serves as an ironic reference to Brazilian hybridity. 'Brutalidade jardim' is a line from Oswald de Andrade's *Serafim Ponte Grande* (1928); Dunn, pp. 244–45, 247, n. 7.

The inverted dome of the Chamber of Deputies on the monumental terrace of the National Congress seen through a grove of buriti palms from the *cerrado*, included in Costa's Plano Piloto as a homage to Le Corbusier

Chapter Seven

Anagrams of Monumentality:
Inversion, Levitation, Hybridization, Dissonance

It is so very easy for us Brazilians to take over the world of imagination and fantasy! Our past is a humble one and every option is open to us . . . It must be so difficult for you people here [in the Old World] to innovate, after spending your whole life around monuments! . . .

We have a different task: to create today the past of tomorrow.

Oscar Niemeyer, *The Curves of Time*

I know what those two [Costa and Niemeyer] wanted: slowness and silence, which is also my idea of eternity. The two of them created a portrait of an eternal city.

Clarice Lispector, 'Brasília' (1962)

Oscar Niemeyer and Lúcio Costa discussing the plans for Brasília at the Ministry of Education and Public Health building in Rio de Janeiro, 1958

In his 1987 document 'Brasília Revisited', Lúcio Costa spoke of the 'four scales' embodied in the Plano Piloto, with first and foremost 'the symbolic and collective, or *Monumental*' scale.[1] From the early stages of planning, monumentality, which had been lacking in the old capital of Rio de Janeiro, was put forward as a requirement for the 'Capital of all Brazilians', celebrating the country's

coming of age. Brasília was envisioned as the stage on which Brazil's great destiny would be enacted, and monumentality was called for to express this collective higher aspiration. Niemeyer's civic architecture for Costa's 'city of the future' was conceived to represent the strength of the country's democratic institutions, to convey permanence and the cohesion of Brazilian society, united under the new symbol of Brasília.

But the monumental character of Brazil's democratic capital was bound to raise controversy. Modernism had shunned monumentality, associating it with the repressive political regimes of the past. Architectural servitude in the totalitarian states of the 1930s had fostered distrust. 'The monumental is anti-democratic . . . the democratic society in conformity with its nature is anti-monumental,' stated Gregor Paulsson in 1948.[2] 'Monumentality in architecture is a form of affirmation; and affirmations are usually made by the few to impress the many,' maintained John Summerson a year later.[3] The monumental architecture of Brasília aimed to project the confidence of the many in a democratic, post-colonial Brazil, faith in a common future – the desire to construct what Josep Lluís Sert, Fernand Léger and Sigfried Giedion termed 'a heritage for future generations', and Niemeyer 'the past of tomorrow'.[4]

As early as 1957, however, Marcelo Roberto, one of the entrants to the competition for the plan of the new federal capital, declared: 'I do not believe that a capital should be a pantheon . . . I cannot accept this nineteenth-century concept of "monumentality".' 'I do not see why in a democracy a city must necessarily be devoid of grandeur', Costa objected.[5] In October 1959, Sibyl Moholy-Nagy belaboured the question: 'Brasilia: Majestic Concept or Autocratic Monument?'[6] Giedion criticized the absence of human scale in Brasília (1960).[7] And the city's

1 Lúcio Costa, 'Brasília Revisitada' (1987), in Lúcio Costa, 1997, p. 331. The other three scales were 'the domestic or *Residential* scale; the entertainment or *Gregarious* scale; and the leisure or *Bucolic* scale', emphasis in the original.   2 Gregor Paulsson, in 'In Search of a New Monumentality', 1948, p. 123.   3 John Summerson, quoted in Evenson, 1973, p. 201.   4 Sert, Léger and Giedion, p. 29; Niemeyer, 2000b, p. 129.   5 Marcelo Roberto and Lúcio Costa, quoted in El-Dahdah, p. 12.   6 Sibyl Moholy-Nagy, pp. 88–89.   7 Tsiomis, 1997, p. 78.

fiercest critic, Bruno Zevi, forthrightly denounced Costa and Niemeyer's Brasília as 'a declaration of cultural failure . . . rhetorical . . . substantially anti-democratic', with a plan of 'classicist character', and 'pseudo-monumental architecture'.[8]

In January 1961, *L'Architecture d'Aujourd'hui* published the two 'new cities' of Chandigarh and Brasília side by side – the Assembly Palace (1952–62) of the former was still under construction – but avoided direct comparisons. In 1980, Kenneth Frampton argued that 'clearly Niemeyer's work became increasingly simplistic and monumental after the publication of the first sketches for Chandigarh . . . mov[ing] closer . . . to the Neo-Classical tradition.' He dated Niemeyer's 'return to Classical absolutes' to his proposed inverted pyramid for the Museum of Modern Art in Caracas of 1954–55.[9] In 1988, Marshall Berman concluded: 'Brasilia's design might have made perfect sense for the capital of a military dictatorship, ruled by generals who wanted the people kept at a distance, kept apart and kept down.'[10] And, at the close of the Modernist century, Richard Weston dismissed the city as 'a lifeless, artificial showpiece',

> the grandest formalist extravaganza of all . . . planned by Lúcio Costa and Oscar Niemeyer as a homage to the Corbusian 'Radiant City' . . . the homage turned out to be a parody and the city a practical and artistic disaster thrown up on the cheap by corrupt contractors and bureaucrats. Niemeyer's ceremonial buildings (1958–63) are built diagrams . . . Max Bill had seen it all coming.[11]

At the time of his first Brazilian visit, the landscape of Rio de Janeiro inspired Le Corbusier's monumental proposals: 'here, man can, once again, realize that which Greece did at the Acropolis, and Rome on the seven hills: seize the landscape by the correct architecture.'[12] Brazil's Ministry of Education and Public Health had been acknowledged as the first work of modern architecture with a symbolic and collective content. Although it did not have the power to harness contemporaneous conservative historicist trends at an international level, it inspired confidence in modern architecture's ability 'to re-create the lost sense of monumentality' in a modern democratic society.[13] Le Corbusier's Capitol complex for Chandigarh (1951–62) – Pandit Nehru's 'temple of the New India' – and Niemeyer's government buildings for Brasília reflected the political and nationalist demands that brought them into being as well as recent critical reassessments of the need for modern architecture to carry symbolic values.

In his *The Culture of Cities* of 1938, Lewis Mumford had proclaimed 'The Death of the Monument' and succinctly expressed the anti-monumentality view: 'The notion of a modern monument is veritably a contradiction in terms: if it is a monument it is not modern, and if it is modern, it cannot be a monument.'[14] His pronouncements of ten years later, however, indicate that his scepticism over the value of the 'static grandeur' of monuments that express a civilization's aim for permanence had been dramatically overturned. At a late contribution to the *Architectural Review*'s symposium on monumentality in July 1948, prompted by Giedion's plea for a new monumentality, Mumford's re-evaluation of the meaning of the monument echoed the attitudes of the builders of Brasília. Mumford boldly argued:

> In essence, the monument is a declaration of love and admiration attached to the higher purposes men hold in common . . . Most ages, to make the monument possible, have (in Ruskin's terms) lighted the lamp of sacrifice, giving to the temple or the buildings of the state, not their surplus, but their very life-blood, that which should have gone into the bare decencies of life for the common man. This fact is responsible for democracy's distrustfulness . . . toward the monument. But, though often painful in the giving, these sacrifices were not without their reward even to the giver . . . Denying the claims of the flesh and the prosperity of the household, buildings of permanent value, enriching the eye, sustaining the spirit, not for a few passing days, but for generations and centuries, actually came forth . . .
>
> But as we approach a high general level of comfort today, the danger is . . . that we forget the function of sacrifice: which means ultimately the arrangement of the good life, not in the order that produces merely physical survival, but in the order that conduces to continued spiritual development . . .
>
> William Butler Yeats's words, to the Dublin philanthropist who wanted to make sure that the common people would enjoy art before he gave any more bequests, should be remembered and heeded. Monumental architecture is to be justified, not in terms of present necessity and popular demand, but in terms of future liberation: to create a 'nest for eagles'.[15]

Lúcio Costa was one of the contributors to the symposium. Ten years later, his Plano Piloto manifested his overriding concern for

8 Bruno Zevi, quoted in Inês Palma Fernandes, pp. 311–12, 334. **9** Frampton, 1992, pp. 256–57. **10** Berman, p. 7. **11** Weston, 1996, pp. 221 (illustration caption), 217–18. **12** Le Corbusier, 'L'Esprit de la Sud-Amérique' (1930–35), in Le Corbusier, 2006, p. 187. **13** Giedion, 1984, p. 55. For a brief review of the debate on monumentality in the twentieth century, see Collins and Collins. **14** Lewis Mumford, 1958, p. 438. **15** Lewis Mumford, 1949, pp. 179–80. The symposium was prompted by Giedion's lecture on monumentality at the Royal Institute of British Architects, London, in 1946. In the early 1950s, criticism of the United Nations project concentrated occasionally on its monumental character; see Collins and Collins, p. 25.

monumental effect beyond functional fulfilment. In the 'Report' that accompanied his winning entry for the masterplan of Brasília he called for

> Brasília . . . not [to] be envisaged merely as an organism capable of fulfilling adequately and effortlessly the vital functions of the modern city, not merely as an 'urbs,' but as a 'civitas,' possessing the attributes of a capital. And, for this to be possible, the planner must be imbued with a certain dignity and nobility of 'intent,' because that fundamental attitude will give birth to the sense of order, utility and proportion which alone can confer on the project as a whole the desirable monumental quality.

And he hastened to clarify the way he understood the meaning of monumentality in a modern democratic society: 'not, let it be clear, in the sense of ostentation, but as the palpable and conscious expression, so to speak, of what is worthwhile and significant'.[16]

The negative reception of Brasília's modern monumentality was not unanimous. Richard Neutra praised the choice of Costa's plan, celebrating the recognition of 'the necessity of form'.[17] Reyner Banham saw Brasília as the 'triumphant' conclusion of the process that began with Rio's Ministry of Education and Public Health. He held the National Congress as an example of 'the Brazilian style . . . pushed to its last extremity of elaboration' and found Niemeyer's 'sophisticated work' for Brasília far superior to Le Corbusier's 'simplicities, almost crudities' at Chandigarh.[18] Alberto Sartoris and Eero Saarinen lauded the harmonious integration of the city's urban planning and architecture. Sartoris regarded Brasília as 'a symbol of its people and of its country, and beyond that, as a symbol of western civilization'.[19]

Early reports on Niemeyer's first building to grace the sky of the city, the Palácio da Alvorada, described it as a 'consciously monumental conception' with 'a nobility of character rarely achieved in a frame-and-glass idiom . . . a slightly grander than domestic scale [10,410 square metres] . . . dignity . . . [a] magnificent suite of reception rooms . . . sumptuous furnishing . . . [and] elegant sophistication'. J. M. Richards concluded his 1959 review of Brasília under construction by emphasizing that, for Brazil, it represented 'a declaration of faith in the future'.[20] 'Brasília's function is to be monumental', suggested George Balcombe in 1961, asserting that the new capital was already 'integrated into Brazilian life as a

whole'.[21] In 1962, two years after its inauguration, David Crease lucidly reported that the city had 'proved to be . . . that focus of national unity . . . which it was its prime purpose to become', confounding Brasília's critics, for 'it works'. On Niemeyer's monumental architecture, he commented that it perfectly complemented the planner's vision, avoiding 'totalitarian bombast and empty gigantism'.[22] And in 1969 Norma Evenson, the first scholar to consider Brasília from within its cultural context, interpreted the dismay of Brasília's critics as springing from their inability to understand an 'aspect of human activity' which, for her, Brasília represents – 'the irrational'. 'Building Brasília', she argued,

> makes no more practical sense than building the Acropolis, the cathedrals or Versailles . . . It embodies the focus for a genuinely enthusiastic common effort. The projects which throughout human history have inspired the most dedication have seldom been the most utilitarian, but more frequently those with strong symbolic meaning. In an underdeveloped country like Brazil, the importance for national pride of such an ambitious showpiece as Brasília should not be underestimated.[23]

Undaunted by adverse criticism, Niemeyer has never recanted his belief in monumentality as an expression of confidence in the historical moment. He has also consistently regarded monumental works as guarantors of posterity. In the old 'monuments of grace and beauty', he notes, 'the functional and utilitarian features are of secondary importance'. What makes for 'immortal' works, like 'the Cathedral of Chartres or the Church of Saint Basil in Moscow', is 'the beautiful, the unexpected, the harmony of the plastic solution'.[24] He deems technical superiority, formal invention, and emotional impact or beauty – a kind of universal beauty he does not attempt to define – as the essential characteristics of permanent contributions to history: 'monumentality never frightened me when a stronger topic justified it. After all, what remains in architecture are the monumental works, the ones that mark history and technical evolution – those that, socially justified or not, still touch us. This is beauty imposing itself on man's sensibility.'[25]

After a journey that took him 'from Lisbon to Moscow' in 1958, a 'self-critical' review of Niemeyer's work appeared in *Módulo* as well as in the daily *Jornal do Brasil*. Without denying the value of his earlier oeuvre, his 'Testimony' intended to illustrate a new direction his work had begun to take since 1955, when he designed the

16 Lúcio Costa, 1966, p. 12.   **17** Neutra, p. 104.   **18** Banham, pp. 151–52. Banham also praised Costa's planning 'in terms that would be generous even on a community that had two Cadillacs in every garage instead of a bus-stop on every superblock'. And he added: 'Compared with this, Corb's Chandigarh seems to hang in an historical vacuum waiting for some unexpected turn of events to validate its extraordinary conception – an Acropolis on the site of a suburban supermarket'; Banham, p. 152.   **19** Alberto Sartoris, quoted in Inês Palma Fernandes, pp. 300–02.   **20** Richards, 1959, pp. 95–104.   **21** 'Conversation in Brasília Between Robert Harbinson and George

Balcombe', 1961, pp. 491, 494, emphasis in the original.   **22** Crease, 1962, pp. 257–58.   **23** Evenson, 1969, p. 28. Evenson also noted 'a notable contrast with Chandigarh. In the Punjab capital, the distinction between the monumental complex and the overall fabric of the city is sharply defined, giving the effect of two separate Chandigarhs . . . In Brasília, although an architectural hierarchy gives emphasis to the governmental complex, there is an essential unity of architectural style and scale throughout the city. Chandigarh is a city containing monuments; in Brasília, the city is a monument.' Evenson, 1973, p. 206.   **24** Niemeyer, 1956a, pp. 41–42.   **25** Niemeyer, 2000b, p. 176.

Caracas Museum of Modern Art. Expressing dissatisfaction with both an architecture 'relegated only to wait upon the whims of the wealthy', showing 'an excessive tendency towards originality', and with an architecture serving 'purely commercial interest[s]', he declared his determination to refuse commissions of this nature henceforth in order to dedicate himself entirely to the design of the government buildings of Brasília, which he envisioned as his 'definitive' work.[26]

This announcement of a clean break may also have been stimulated by a rising feeling among Brazilian architects and critics, including Lúcio Costa, that the 'Brazilian Style' may have run its

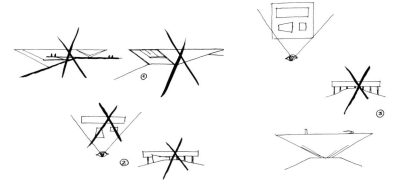

Museum of Modern Art, Caracas: 'explanation' of the design process that led to the development of the museum's form of an inverted pyramid.

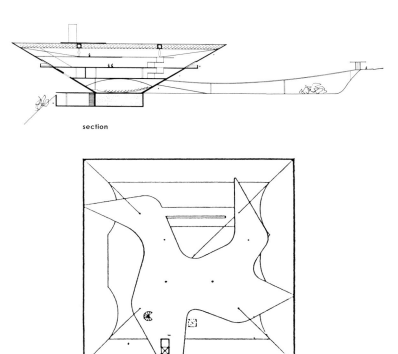

section

mezzanine plan

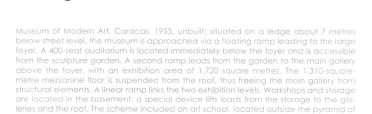

Museum of Modern Art, Caracas, 1955, unbuilt: situated on a ledge about 7 metres below street level, the museum is approached via a floating ramp leading to the large foyer. A 400-seat auditorium is located immediately below the foyer and is accessible from the sculpture garden. A second ramp leads from the garden to the main gallery above the foyer, with an exhibition area of 1,720 square metres. The 1,310-square-metre mezzanine floor is suspended from the roof, thus freeing the main gallery from structural elements. A linear ramp links the two exhibition levels. Workshops and storage are located in the basement; a special device lifts loads from the storage to the galleries and the roof. The scheme included an art school, located outside the pyramid of the museum, dug into the hill below the street and facing the sculpture garden.

Museum of Modern Art, Caracas: 'Our desire', Niemeyer says, 'was to develop a compact form detaching itself clearly from the landscape and expressing in the purity of its lines the forces of contemporary art', and 'to offer to the visitor the surprise and the emotion resulting from a violent contrast between a sealed exterior and an interior flooded with daylight' (Oscar Niemeyer, quoted in Papadaki, 1956, p. 83). In the early 1950s, Niemeyer singled out the Caracas Museum of Modern Art as his 'best work'.

26 Niemeyer, 1958b, pp. 3–6.

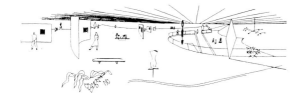

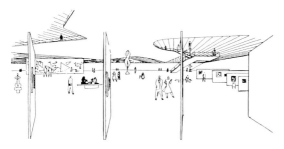

Museum of Modern Art, Caracas: views of the main gallery area and the mezzanine. The mezzanine is hung from the roof by cables and four rhomboidal elements, three of which are visible here. At the time Niemeyer was commissioned to design the museum, Caracas was hosting an exhibition of Alexander Calder's work, which may explain the inclusion of his mobile in Niemeyer's sketch.

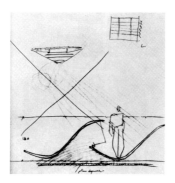

Museum of Modern Art, Caracas: exploration of a system of louvres to create a luminous roof admitting daylight without glare to the galleries

Museum of Modern Art, Caracas: photomontage with model on site showing the roof of the museum with an additional exhibition area of 650 square metres. The largest part of the roof is used to provide controlled daylight to the galleries through a system of two layers of louvres, reinforced concrete on the outside and aluminium on the inside. The latter carry fixtures for artificial lighting.

course and entered a period of routine. Vilanova Artigas was a vocal critic of 'uncritical acceptance of the forms of modern architecture' and submission to commercial interests.[27] In his view, Niemeyer's self-critical review inspired great confidence in the future of Brazilian architecture, 'especially among progressive architects', marking 'the beginning of a new phase in the national architecture [of Brazil]'. Abandoning commercial interests, Artigas postulated, Brazilian 'national architecture' would develop 'at the level of purely cultural manifestation'.[28] In his commentary on Niemeyer's text, which he judged of 'great significance for the Brazilian cultural world', Mário Pedrosa argued that 'the formidable and noble mission of the construction of the utopia of Brasília' offered the leading figure of Brazilian architecture an opportunity to re-establish 'a synthesis of the political and the social with the aesthetic and the professional'.[29] Artigas's unequivocal identification of Niemeyer's work with 'national architecture' and Pedrosa's enthusiastic reception of his change of professional direction betray the extent to which Niemeyer's architecture for Brasília had become the focus of large collective aspirations and a source of national pride.

Effectively, Niemeyer put his architecture exclusively at the service of the state and 'the formidable and noble mission of the construction of the [national] utopia'. He became a civil servant, with a salary of 40,000 cruzeiros.[30] Beginning afresh, he set out a series of 'disciplinary measures' to guide his architecture for Brazil's 'second "call of independence" ', aiming at 'simplicity of plastic form and in balance with functional and construction problems'.[31] He declared a preference for 'compact solutions, simple and geometric', concentrating on 'problems of hierarchy and architectonic character' and pursuing 'unity and harmony amongst the buildings'. Most importantly, Niemeyer explained, these qualities would not be expressed through 'secondary elements but through the structure itself, duly integrated with the original plastic conception'.[32]

His new-found desire for restraint – but 'not . . . false purity' – brings to mind Auguste Perret's concept of the 'banal', which the French architect also conceived in relation to unified large-scale urban schemes and understood as a quality to be achieved 'through having disciplined oneself sufficiently to participate in a narrative larger than one's own circumstances'.[33] Like Perret before him, Niemeyer stressed, however, that, to achieve 'greater purity and simplicity', he would not betray 'the constraints of a modern building programme, nor the use of modern materials'.[34] He would steer clear of 'false purism, monotonous form with an

27 Artigas, 2003a, p. 196.   **28** Artigas, 2003b, p. 240.   **29** Pedrosa, 2003b, p. 242.   **30** This would be about $1,200, but this estimate should be considered as a rough approximation only; the galloping inflation rate of those years makes precise calculation particularly difficult.   **31** Eduardo Kneese de Mello, p. 13; Niemeyer, 1958b, p. 4. **32** Niemeyer, 1958b, pp. 4–5.   **33** Britton, p. 187.   **34** Niemeyer, 1958b, p. 6; Auguste Perret, quoted in Britton, p. 187.

industrial tendency; being aware of the tremendous possibilities of reinforced concrete and keen that this new attitude should not become an insurmountable barrier but, on the contrary, should freely encourage ideas and innovations'. In Brasília, Niemeyer wrote, he had to deal with 'three different problems . . . that of the individual building . . . the monumental building . . . [and] the group as a whole, which, prior to anything else, calls for harmony and unity'.[35]

The architectural form of Brazil's new national centre was not merely an aesthetic matter but a matter of large cultural and ideological significance. Brasília's conception as a concrete symbol of national unity is comparable to the role of the city of Washington as the symbol of the American Union. The Brazilian federal capital did not adopt the classicism of Washington, but architectural coherence was sought and achieved through the adoption of a father architect, the acknowledged hero of Brazil's modern national architecture, with a distinct architectural style. And this was not a personal style but the style in which twentieth-century architects and politicians had sought to imagine the nation – Brazilian *and* modern.[36] In 1955, Niemeyer had already remarked that 'The success of modern architecture in Brazil was such that it rapidly became the architecture of the people. Everybody, whether private developers or the government, desired modern buildings, so as to cause a sensation both here and abroad.'[37] In Brasília, the aim was to produce works speaking of maturity, both for the nation they would represent and for the architect who assumed the burden of representation. Eventually, Niemeyer would acknowledge continuity between his early contributions to the modern 'identity documents of the Brazilian nation' and the architecture of the 'New Capital of a great nation'.[38] In his autobiography he wrote 'Pampulha was the beginning of Brasília.'[39]

As if to underscore this sense of continuity, work on Brasília's government buildings started at the Ministry of Education and Public Health in Rio de Janeiro, in the first-floor exhibition gallery. But in August 1958 Niemeyer moved permanently on site to direct more efficiently the projects under construction, perhaps also already tired of the rough, eighteen-hour car journey between Rio and Brasília, which he nevertheless preferred to flying. He took with him a team of fifteen, 'all friends, all motivated by the same idealism'.[40] Searching for paradigmatic unity and harmony, he turned

Oscar Niemeyer on the west veranda of the Palácio da Alvorada, *circa* 1958

to the old cities of Europe and Brazil's colonial towns. In cities like Lisbon, Ouro Prêto and Diamantina, Niemeyer argued, architects were 'forced, often without realizing it, to repeat the same solutions, use the same materials, and resort to the same design elements'. In the old streets of Rio de Janeiro, like Rua Buenos Aires and Rua Teófilo Otoni, he detected similar characteristics. He then proceeded to contrast these harmonious urban ensembles with 'the cities of today . . . reduced to a conglomeration of structures, some of them of great merit, considered individually, but having nothing in common with one another and presenting . . . a deplorable picture of confusion and lack of harmony'. Niemeyer sought to discipline the buildings of Brasília following the example of the old cities he admired, and hoped that Brasília 'will exercise a salutary influence on Brasilian [sic] architecture, in the field of city planning, by disciplining the use of masses and open spaces and by restoring among architects the concern for unity'.[41]

Somewhat unexpectedly, two years after his self-critical 'Testimony', in 'a statement with no theoretical or erudite pretensions, based merely on his work and his professional experience', he announced: 'I am in favor of an almost unlimited plastic free-

35 Niemeyer, 1958b, p. 5.   **36** With a dose of exaggeration, in an article in the daily *Jornal do Brasil* in 1982 Costa stated: 'The so-called Brazilian contemporary architecture movement is, fundamentally, Oscar Niemeyer. The other architects more or less followed what he did'; quoted in Tinem and Borges, p. 116.   **37** Niemeyer, 1955c, p. 21; in English, Niemeyer, 2003a, p. 125. Again, Perret's idea of the 'banal' comes to mind. As Karla Britton explains, this should be thought of in terms of the medieval derivation of the word, which 'designated something that pertained not to the individual but to a community'; Britton, p. 187. **38** Niemeyer, 1960.   **39** Niemeyer, 2000a, p. 17.   **40** Niemeyer, 1960. In his autobiography, Niemeyer notes: 'The money issue did not

bother me at all. In fact, the experience did me good . . . The greatest joy of all was hiring whomever I wanted to work with me on the new capital. That's why I summoned lots of friends from different professions, whom I hired for the simple pleasure of helping them out, since I knew they were short of money. As it turned out, our team included a physician, a journalist, a lawyer, a goalkeeper from the Flamengo soccer team, and others of even more dubious professional classification. They were all useful to me, and the team became very flexible, the conversation more versatile, the work more complete, with each member contributing according to his own area of specialty'; Niemeyer, 2000b, p. 71.   **41** Niemeyer, 1959b, n.p.

Typical street view in the colonial town of Diamantina, Minas Gerais

Niemeyer found in the old streets of Rio de Janeiro the unity and harmony that characterized Brazil's colonial towns like Ouro Prêto and Diamantina.

dom, a freedom that is not slavishly subordinate to the reasons of any given technique or of functionalism, capable of arousing surprise and emotion by their newness and creativeness.' But he hastened to add:

> Of course, this freedom cannot be used freely. In urban localities, for instance, I am, on the contrary, all for restricting it, rather, for preserving the unity and harmony of the overall plan ... with this end in view, in Brasília, in the urban sections to which I am alluding, regulations are set up to cover volumes, free spaces, heights, facing materials, etc.[42]

Preserving a freedom to experiment with plastic form while, at the same time, controlling and subjugating this freedom to the demands of the larger architectural narrative emerged as Niemeyer's greatest challenge in Brasília.

The Palácio da Alvorada

In 1961, Nikolaus Pevsner compared the 'all embracing unity' of Ouro Prêto to that of Brasília, which he felt 'equally convinced' to defend. In both cities, Pevsner suggested, this unity is not 'totalitarian'. He singled out the Palácio da Alvorada as an example of how 'Niemeyer has grown wonderfully from [his Pampulha] dare-devil naughtiness to the maturity of the President's Palace'.[43] With its sophisticated constellation of associations, the Palácio da Alvorada summarized the objectives of the monumental project of the 'first capital of twentieth-century civilization',[44] and

became Brasília's architectural prelude and crowning glory. In its formal structure it wove together evocations of a colonial way of life with bold classical allusions and modern aesthetic aspirations, filtered through a highly personal interpretation and delivered with the natural fluency and refinement of *bossa nova*. It has been noted that, just as *bossa nova* is music for listening, the Alvorada emphasizes aesthetic pleasure rather than sensual pleasure, which is at the centre of dance music like samba.[45] Niemeyer's works for Brasília – exemplified by the Alvorada – bear a similar relation to his earlier, playful experiments, epitomized by Pampulha's Casa do Baile. And, as with *bossa nova*, the seemingly conservative aesthetic of the Alvorada diverges at closer observation from the norm, subtly subverted by progressive, 'dissonant' elements, which prove all the more powerful for having been incorporated into an apparently classical structure.

The tunes of the Alvorada's iconic white columns are essentially 'Off-Key', to borrow the title of the seminal *bossa nova* masterpiece 'Desafinado' by Tom Jobim and Newton Mendonça (1958), 'a celebration of cultural dissonance in all its forms'.[46] The squatting *casa grande* is, at the very last moment, lifted off the ground, allowed only to tiptoe upon it precariously. Stripped of the colonial *casa grande*'s traditional insignia of power – an imposing portico and grand entrance staircase – the modern presidential *casa grande* is entered at ground or, rather, water level. Instead of the visitor rising to enter the house of the patriarch, the house façade reaches down to welcome the visitor. To dissolve barriers further, a fragile glass membrane replaces the forbidding masonry walls of the plantation house.

42 Niemeyer, 1993b, p. 309. **43** Pevsner, 2002, pp. 266–67. **44** André Malraux. In the speech he delivered in Brasília on 24 August 1959, the French minister of culture commented: 'Modern architecture was up to now an architecture of buildings: it created houses. That some day such an epic individualism should be surpassed, none of its historians had any doubts. But nearly all of them thought that the greater architecture, that which creates cities instead of buildings, would be born in the Soviet Union – and it is appearing right here'; quoted in Evenson, 1973, p. 100. **45** Carvalho, p. 165. **46** Julian Dibbell, 'Foreword', in Castro, 2000, p. xiv.

Niemeyer produced two schemes for this building. It is reported that, upon seeing the first proposal for the presidential residence, an unsatisfied Juscelino Kubitschek demanded 'something that will still be admired a hundred years from now'.[47] To achieve greater simplicity and purity of form, which Giedion held as 'the stamp of any kind of symbolic expression' and monumental effect, in the second and final scheme, Niemeyer accentuated the horizontality of the building, increasing its length and reducing its height and width.[48] He also aligned the presidential chapel with the house, simplified the internal, originally diamond-shaped columns, lowered the entrance, and eliminated the ceremonial ramp and a number of secondary elements like a speaker's rostrum and a fanciful *marquise* on the roof.

Like those of eighteenth-century *fazendas*, the columns of the Alvorada bear no entablature, but they have also been deprived of the solid stylobate that firmly grounded colonial colonnades. Liberated from the weight of the colonial pitched roof and graced with the long curve of the *berimbau* – the instrument that accom-

panies *capoeira* – they appear effortlessly to carry a flat roof that gently curves upwards, amazingly thin (15 centimetres) and infinitely light, seemingly supported by columns that barely touch the ground.

The marble revetment on the short sides of the building conceals the articulation of the roof, making it appear like a single slab. In fact, it consists of three sections: a flat middle slab, tapered towards the edges, resting on and projecting slightly beyond circular concrete columns, flanked by two gently curved canopies over the long verandas. These canopies begin below the level of the main roof, their curved edges visible internally projecting from the circular columns, and reach the height of the central roof slab at the point where they meet the external marble colonnades, which are entrusted only with this small burden. In the preliminary scheme, which had no external gallery, the sculptural outer colon-

47 Juscelino Kubitschek, quoted in Shoumatoff, p. 52.   **48** Giedion, 1984, p. 57.

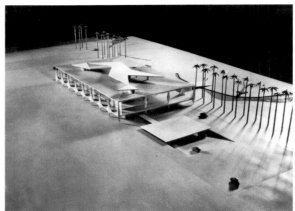

Palácio da Alvorada, first scheme, 1956: model

nades were flush with the glass wall. The introduction of the loggias diminished the colonnades' structural role, but their configuration was retained for its expressive force, with minor alterations that enhanced their elegance. Between the overlapping sections of the roof are hidden concrete beams as well as artificial lighting, so that inside the building the central roof plane seems to levitate above the cloud-like, folding soffits of the canopies and upper-floor galleries.

'The palaces [of Brasília] appeared to scarcely touch the ground. I wanted them floating in the sky of the plateau,' says

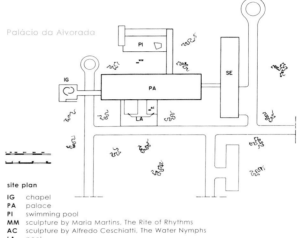

Palácio da Alvorada

site plan
IG chapel
PA palace
PI swimming pool
MM sculpture by Maria Martins, The Rite of Rhythms
AC sculpture by Alfredo Ceschiatti, The Water Nymphs
LA pool
SE servants' quarters

Palácio da Alvorada: aerial view of the west side

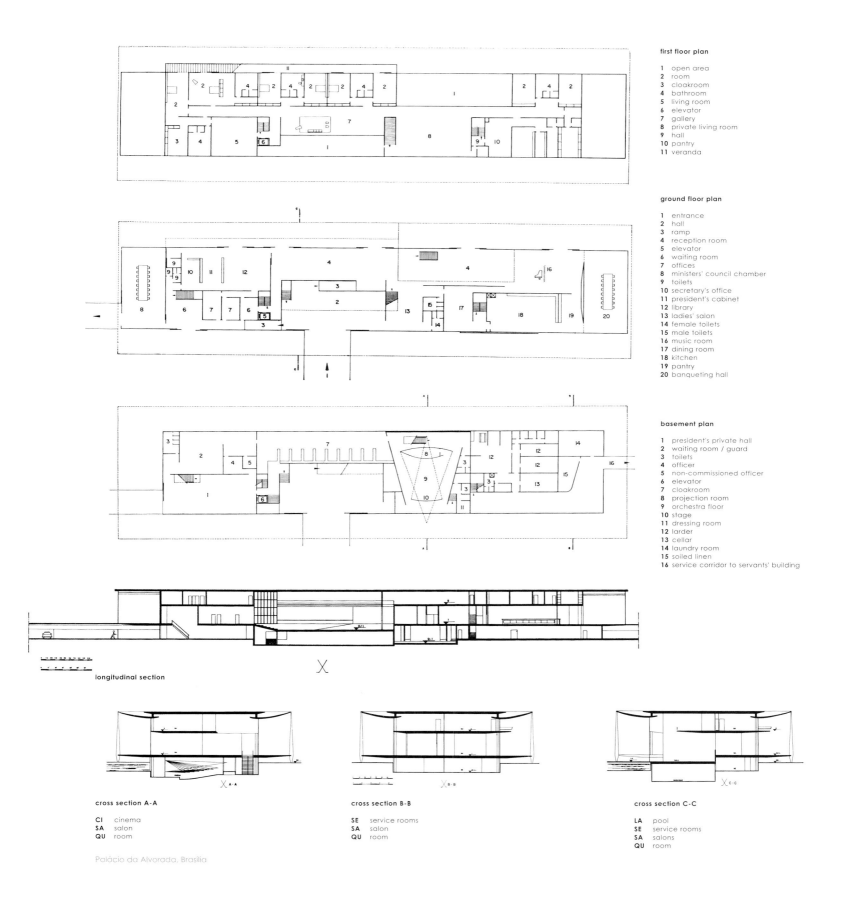

first floor plan

1　open area
2　room
3　cloakroom
4　bathroom
5　living room
6　elevator
7　gallery
8　private living room
9　hall
10　pantry
11　veranda

ground floor plan

1　entrance
2　hall
3　ramp
4　reception room
5　elevator
6　waiting room
7　offices
8　ministers' council chamber
9　toilets
10　secretary's office
11　president's cabinet
12　library
13　ladies' salon
14　female toilets
15　male toilets
16　music room
17　dining room
18　kitchen
19　pantry
20　banqueting hall

basement plan

1　president's private hall
2　waiting room / guard
3　toilets
4　officer
5　non-commissioned officer
6　elevator
7　cloakroom
8　projection room
9　orchestra floor
10　stage
11　dressing room
12　larder
13　cellar
14　laundry room
15　soiled linen
16　service corridor to servants' building

longitudinal section

cross section A-A

CI　cinema
SA　salon
QU　room

cross section B-B

SE　service rooms
SA　salon
QU　room

cross section C-C

LA　pool
SE　service rooms
SA　salons
QU　room

Palácio da Alvorada, Brasília

Niemeyer.[49] The Alvorada columns' skyward thrust has been carefully choreographed through a series of precisely controlled gestures: their meeting of the ground at what appears to be a single point (with the marble revetment detailed so as to reinforce the illusion), their pronounced diminution and hyperbolic intercolumnar spaces, and their evocation of popular Carioca kites. Their sophisticated variable section – sculpted with Brancusian precision – makes their upper part appear extremely slender while also producing continuously changing effects of light and shade. These accentuate the plastic qualities of the white colonnade and give it an air of ethereality and fragility, undermining allusions to permanence, solidity and stability conjured by the initial evocation of the patriarchal *casa grande*. From the verandas the roof overhang appears to be pushed upwards, the columns surging gracefully towards the sky.

Rejoicing in the luminosity of Brasília, light, fluid and powerful, the Alvorada's majestic colonnades are reflected on the highly polished black granite floor of the veranda and in the water of the pool, which illustrious guests cross to enter the palace. According to David Underwood, this reflection 'transforms the colonnade back into an ethereal, dreamlike arcade of classical antiquity, as if to pose and resolve the duality of ancient and modern. The impression is of a classical dream that has become Brazilian reality.'[50] At certain times of day, in the pool and on the polished marble of the platform that precedes it, the reflections of

Palácio da Alvorada: entrance hall: the aluminium-clad circular concrete columns rising behind the glazing along the long elevations support the main roof slab and the flanking canopies that begin below the apparently floating central roof plane and extend over the verandas: the curling soffit of the upper-floor gallery reinforces the effect

Palácio da Alvorada: view of garden (west) and side (south) elevations: the marble revetment on the short sides of the building conceals the articulation of the roof

Palácio da Alvorada: colonnade under construction

49 Niemeyer, 'The Alvorada Palace', in *Oscar Niemeyer: Notebooks of the Architect*, n.p.   **50** Underwood, 1994b, p. 107.

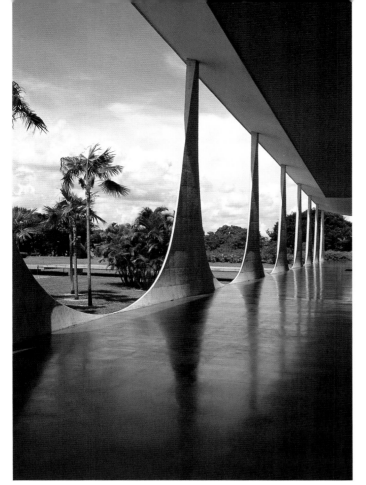

The west colonnade of the Palácio da Alvorada reflected on the black granite floor of the veranda

Niemeyer's columns meet with those of the parallel double row of imperial palms – the Brazilian columnar order that amazed Jean Prouvé with the economy of its structure.[51]

Approaching architecture as an ongoing critical and systematic investigation of ever-new formal configurations, Niemeyer advocated a view of the architectural process as open-ended. He resisted submission to any dogmatic stylistic orthodoxy and long-standing habits of thought, and forcefully distinguished his explorations from a hegemonic lineage of European Modernism and its recent American stylization. He notes:

> As with the Pampulha phase, a feeling of protest possessed me in Brasília. It was no longer the imposition of the right angle that angered me, but the obsessive concern for architectural purity and structural logic, the systematic campaign against the free and creative forms that attracted me and which were viewed as gratuitous and unnecessary... Contemporary architecture was vanishing through its repetitive glass boxes.[52]

Matthew Nowicki, author of the first masterplan for Chandigarh (1950) and special consultant to the United Nations

51 Choay, p. 215.   52 Niemeyer, 2000b, p. 171.

In the first of the thirteen panels Niemeyer prepared for the 1965 exhibition *Oscar Niemeyer: l'architecte de Brasília* at the Parisian Musée des Arts Décoratifs, he proclaimed his sustained commitment to an architecture of 'invention and imagination' and continuous 'experimentation with reinforced concrete', treating the 'formalist' solutions of contemporaneous 'functional architecture' with nonchalant indifference, undaunted by criticism. The novel forms that sprang from his pen over the years before Brasília, Niemeyer declared, had been 'incorporated into the vocabulary of Brazilian architecture.' His work in Brasília aimed to further enrich not only his personal repertoire but that of a distinct national architecture.

Headquarters Board of Design, had already observed a shift from the 'decoration of [physical] *function*' in orthodox functionalism to the 'decoration of *structure*', noting that 'the symbolic meaning of structure has also been rediscovered, and a steel column is used frankly as a symbol of structure even when it is not part of the structure itself'.[53] Niemeyer privileges invention and innovative or symbolic form over a rationalist commitment to the most economical arrangement of structural components and so-called 'honest' tectonic expression that requires structural elements to symbolize the particular structural purpose they serve.

Niemeyer has often singled out the column as the element that received his greatest attention in his works at Brasília. Yet, notwithstanding the great emphasis laid on the column as an independent architectural element, the iconic column of the Palácio da Alvorada was not conceived independently as a piece of sculpture. Beginning with a simple orthogonal box, Niemeyer developed a colonnaded pavilion raised on a floating platform, perhaps a translation of the primitive wooden architecture of the Catetinho into stone, in the tradition of the revered classical temple. He then linked the pavilion's perimetric columns with a single vitalizing pen stroke that became popularly known as 'Oscar's cardiogram', made, unsurprisingly, of fluidly rising and dropping curves. The diamond shape of the iconic columns of the Alvorada emerged graphically, once he had traced the inverted arcade above the floating platform and the shallow arches below, which conceal part of the basement. As a result, the colonnades appear to begin and end with half columns. They insinuate the possibility of exceeding their frame, yet remain remarkably free of tension, favouring a pleasurable resolution of conflict in the Baroque fashion observed by Erwin Panofsky.

Ever fond of sophisticated designs born of a few simple lines, Niemeyer began here, as in many of his buildings, with the two-dimensional elevation, in defiance of the Modernist privileging of the plan. The façade of the Alvorada is most successful in its intention of immediately engaging the spectator, drawing the eye into the fluid dance of its colonnade. Jean Prouvé was a participant at the September 1959 International Congress of Art Critics, which took place in Brasília, the city that struck him as an 'object-lesson in optimism'. His graphic analysis of the main elevation of the presidential palace, surviving in a sketch for his CNAM (Conservatoire national des arts et metiers) lectures, focused on the 'rigid-nodes' of the colonnade, rightly reading it as an integrated, seamless, lace-like structure rather than as a row of independent columns.[54]

The individual column became the object of sculptural refinement at a second stage, and marble cladding reinforced the desired visual effect. 'I remember my pleasure in designing the columns of the Alvorada Palace', Niemeyer writes, 'and my even greater pleasure in seeing them repeated everywhere. It was architectural surprise contrasting with dominant monotony.'[55] Pleased with its eccentric configuration, Niemeyer frequently draws a single Alvorada column next to a column of classical antiquity, a column of the Italian Renaissance and a linear 'modern' column, implying an evolutionary line, while also suggesting that its timeless beauty may be measured against the revered orders of a golden age and outdo them.

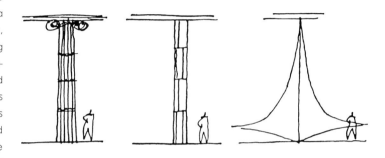

Niemeyer's sketch of a column of the Italian Renaissance, a linear 'modern' column and a column of the Palácio da Alvorada implies an evolutionary line.

Like Walter Gropius, who brought together the Parthenon, the Katsura Imperial Villa and the Bauhaus, Niemeyer proposed his architecture for Brasília as part of the myth of universal architecture. To press the point, he recalls that André Malraux, who compared 'Brasília on its great plateau . . . [to] the Acropolis on its rock', hailed the Alvorada columns as 'the most beautiful columns I have ever seen after the Greek columns'.[56] Responding to Kubitschek's nationalist brief, they were intended to 'reflect the high degree of civilization in [Brazil]'. Hovering between abstraction and figuration and invested with a wealth of metaphors and legends with regard to their origins and associations, they became the emblem of the city that symbolically marked the Brazilian settlement of Brazil. At the 1965 Paris exhibition on Brasília at the Musée des Arts Décoratifs, Palais du Louvre, Niemeyer displayed the columns of the Palácio da Alvorada, the Palácio do Planalto and the cathedral of Brasília free-standing, 'like statuary'.[57]

53 Nowicki, pp. 156, emphasis in the original.   **54** Jean Prouvé, quoted in Cohen, p. 53, and sketch on p. 50. Eero Saarinen and Charlotte Perriand were also among the participants. Niemeyer himself guided their visit to the buildings of Brasília.   **55** Niemeyer, 'The Alvorada Palace', in *Oscar Niemeyer: Notebooks of the Architect*, n.p. For example, E. Stuart Williams's colonnade for the Coachella Valley Savings & Loan Association, Palm Canyon Drive, Palm Springs (1961, today the Washington Mutual Bank), is undoubtedly based on that of the Alvorada, although it lacks the elegance and clarity of the original. Local builders have freely applied the columns of the Alvorada on modest houses throughout Brazil.   **56** André Malraux, quoted in Evenson, 1973, p. 207; André Malraux, quoted in Niemeyer, 2004, p. 178.   **57** Niemeyer, 1963b, p. 8.

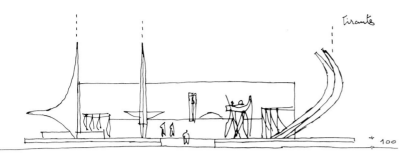

Sketch for the display of the columns of Brasília's major buildings at the 1965 Paris exhibition *Oscar Niemeyer: l'architecte de Brasília*

Niemeyer spares no effort to ensure that the final designs of his buildings appear to have emerged from a few swift strokes spontaneously committed to paper, like Chinese ideograms or ink paintings. He is particularly fond of retracing the 'few strokes' of his buildings, recounting the blessed moment of inspiration that nurtures the myth of the genius, having practised this ideographic technique by trying to capture the forms of nature with his pencil.[58] The ragged lines of these felt-pen retracings, however, do not always accurately reflect a working method that prioritizes fluidity of line, achieved through a continuous tracing and discarding until the painstakingly improvised line is deemed satisfactory in its appearance of effortlessness and spontaneity. In order to achieve a built form filtered to its essentials, ensuring that the constructed building is a literal translation of the apparent ease of these simple calligraphic drawings, from Brasília onwards, Niemeyer strove to underplay or even conceal all architectural elements elaborated at a second stage: 'solutions entailing a wealth of decoration and ornamental elements were discarded . . . We endeavored to achieve a compact and simple form in which the very beauty of its structural proportions could be used as a decorative element.'[59]

Palácio da Alvorada, Brasília

In Brasília, work proceeded at a breakneck pace, and Niemeyer's talent for improvisation may be compared only to Kubitschek's. All major buildings were explored through models, but often 'construction started with only the foundation calculations completed'.[60] Time pressure had its advantages for Niemeyer, keen to preserve the freshness of the initial design solution: 'If there was no time to think, there was also no time to make undesired alterations.'[61]

Niemeyer's essay on 'the question of *form in architecture*' is preceded by an epigraph from Giedion: 'Architecture is ap-proaching sculpture, they are being reconciled; they are ready to be integrated.'[62] He admits that, in Brasília, sculptural effect remained his key concern, to the point that sometimes he wished he were able to do away with programmatic requirements altogether, to preserve undiluted the full aesthetic impact of the building's visually powerful concrete structure.

Late one evening I stood with my work colleagues in front of Brasília's Alvorada Palace, the framework of which had already been freed of props and unleashed in the vastness of the plateau.

I recall saying to them: 'Look how pretty it looks, without door or window frames, without any protective structure, so light and mysterious. It serves no purpose other than that of beauty itself . . . It represents the moment of creation, that is only achieved, theme permitting, when there is complete freedom for creation' . . .

I must confess that it was with a touch of sorrow that I told my companions as we left the building structure: 'Soon, this framework is going to support a building, clad with protective materials, colors and shimmering glass. Illustrious people will inhabit it and turn it into the stage of their lives, hopes, ambitions, happy and sad moments.'

Actually, I had always toyed with the idea of doing sculpture work.[63]

John Soane (1753–1837) went as far as to commission and exhibit imaginary drawings of his buildings in sublime ruins. Eero Saarinen thought his TWA Terminal at Kennedy Airport, New York (1956–62) 'would make a beautiful ruin' even if it remained unfinished.[64] Equally concerned with posterity, Niemeyer contemplates architectural immortality through visions of the beauty of the future ruins of Brasília. Once again, he invokes Auguste Perret, who called attention to the beauty of naked structure through visions of ruins: 'Architecture is that which makes beautiful ruins.' After the coup of 1964, Niemeyer remembers, André Malraux visited Le Corbusier at his studio. A rumour was circulating at the time that the dictators would destroy Brasília. Seeking consolation, Le Corbusier exclaimed: 'They are going to destroy Brasília. Brasília will disappear. But what great ruins we are going to have!'[65]

Counter to established views, reinforced by Niemeyer's rhetoric and often based on little first-hand knowledge and direct experience of his buildings, the final result does not lack sophistication. Once the design is deemed 'complete', total subordination of all architectural elements to the primary ones of the initial abstract schema, guaranteeing the unity and clarity of the composition, is

58 Niemeyer, 2000b, p. 19.   **59** Oscar Niemeyer, quoted in Stäubli, pp. 131–35.   **60** Niemeyer, 1992, p. 133.   **61** Niemeyer, 1998, p. 22.   **62** Niemeyer, 1978a, pp. 9, 8, emphasis in the original.   **63** Niemeyer, 1998, pp. 33–34.   **64** Eero Saarinen, quoted in Merkel, p. 210.   **65** Niemeyer, 1988b, p. 187.

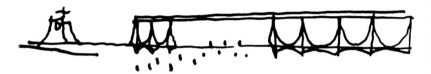

It has been suggested that the colonnade of the Palácio da Alvorada is an inversion of the wooden arches of the colonial market hall of Diamantina

an extremely laborious endeavour, requiring tremendous discipline, virtuosity, exactitude and relentless control of every detail. Needless to say, this quest for a radical reduction of the means of expression, for elimination of everything deemed superfluous or irrelevant, rarely compromises function. What is frequently disobeyed is the rationalist dogma of structural honesty; that is, Niemeyer refuses to submit to the arbitrary rule that the architectural elements of a building that appear – or are habitually perceived – to perform a certain structural function should really do so.

The elegant columns of the Alvorada are certainly not the building's primary means of support, despite their visual prominence and central role in the definition of the palace's ideogram. Their principal function is not structural but what Roland Barthes calls 'the great imaginary function which enables men to be strictly human'.[66] For Niemeyer, they represent 'beauty prevailing over

the limitations of the constructive logic', introducing the irrationality of the aesthetic into the rigour of structure.[67] Giedion spoke of a 'kind of aesthetic sensation that results when the relation between load and support is no longer traditionally obvious'.[68] With his disrespectful subversion of canonized codes of structural expression, Niemeyer undermined the reliable meaning of signs, seeking the kind of aesthetic sensation that results when the familiar relation between load and support is rendered strange. Unrepentant, he wrote: 'All along I laughed . . . about the "mistake" that, hopefully, the prevailing mediocre critics were soon to discover.'[69] The Alvorada's rows of circular structural columns, sheathed in anodized aluminium that understates their solidity are almost invisible from the outside, rising behind the uninterrupted glazing along the long elevations, moving in front of it on the narrow sides of the building.

The garden (west) elevation of the presidential residence presents an unbroken inverted arcade, a synthesis of 'classical nobility with baroque plasticity'.[70] It has been suggested that it derived from an inversion of the wooden arches of the colonial market hall of Diamantina.[71] It also resembles an inversion of the celebrated colonial palm colonnade. The arcade of the Palácio da Alvorada constitutes a second instance in a series of inversions of canonical forms by Niemeyer, beginning with the inverted pyramid for the Museum of Modern Art, in Caracas, which he singled out in the 1950s as his 'best work'.[72] As the latter occupies such an important position in his oeuvre, initiating a dialogue with historic precedents and consecrated historiographic narratives and a literal inversion of dominant forms and codes, he deeply regrets the fact that it was not executed.

Niemeyer's deliberate acts of defamiliarization, targeting forms from the normative tradition of so-called Western civilization, manifest a desire to renew the possibilities of invention from within a culturally powerful and legitimating tradition, as well as a desire for deliverance. Rather than a new vocabulary of forms, in this phase of his career Niemeyer opted for an innovative syntax that does not oppose the canonized vocabulary but absorbs it, masticates it and strategically ironizes it. The irreverent carnivalization – turning upside down – of forms sanctioned by history and tradition undermines all certainties embodied in the familiar, not in order to destroy it but in order to exorcize its demons and break it open to new and unexpected possibilities.[73] It also seeks to assert the autonomy of Brazilian architecture from its European counterparts.

66 Barthes, p. 6. For Niemeyer, the Alvorada columns are the result of 'a perfect integration of the form . . . with the structural system': Niemeyer, 1958b, p. 6.   67 Niemeyer, 1985, p. 74.   68 Giedion, 1949, p. 417.   69 Niemeyer, 2000b, pp. 172–73. In 1959, Pier Luigi Nervi criticized the 'totally arbitrary' structure of the Alvorada, 'as seen in the form of the pylons, in the variations in the spans of the pilasters at the entrance, corresponding to no visible reinforcement of the architrave of the roof, and thus halving the resistant section of the pilasters themselves. And aren't the floor slabs too thin?'; Nervi, 1959, p. 55. The photograph included in Nervi's article indicates that he

was looking at Niemeyer's first scheme for the Alvorada, but the same criticism could have been made for the building as constructed. 70 Underwood, 1994b, p. 107.   71 Sant'Anna, p. 197.   72 Note to an undated letter from Niemeyer to Stamo Papadaki, when the latter was preparing his second monograph on Niemeyer (1956): 'If possible I would like to give the best place in the book to the Caracas Museum that I think is my best work'; in Stamo Papadaki Papers.   73 Always eager to present Niemeyer's works as derivative, Frampton interprets the Caracas project as 'a self-conscious inversion of Le Corbusier's Musée Mondial of 1928'; Frampton, 2004, p. 48.

The principal (east) elevation of the Alvorada, turned towards the city, was skilfully modified to accommodate the entrance, which, although not marked by any element that would compromise the laconic purity of the design, does not lack ceremony. The elimination of a section of the dancing colonnade, which makes it appear as if it had parted, curtain-like, to allow the elect to enter, is a gesture powerful enough to create the necessary impact while preserving an air of casualness and spontaneity that adds to the spirit of hospitality. The entrance to the Palácio da Alvorada is reached via a marble-paved walkway over the shallow pool, connecting the forecourt and the palace. A section of the glass wall, approximately one-fourth of its length, drops to the level of the entrance platform, 1 metre below that of the veranda, bowing to receive the visitor. This section of the wall was further differentiated following a later addition of vertical *brises-soleil* by Niemeyer himself along the two flanking sections of the glazing.

The Mineiro anthropologist and politician Darcy Ribeiro (1922–97) found in the new capital 'the only palaces made by modern architecture'.[74] André Malraux lauded the Alvorada as 'the first successful attempt to renew the theme of the palace residence since Versailles'.[75] Niemeyer admitted that his objective was to design not just 'an important residence, but . . . a true palace, imbued with the spirit of monumentality and nobility'. In line with traditional conceptions, Henry-Russell Hitchcock had listed 'large scale . . . solidity . . . weight . . . dignity and . . . unity' as the means to achieve monumentality.[76] Niemeyer preferred 'lightness and dignity . . . as if [the building] had landed softly on the ground'.[77] In Brasília, 'beauty alone is the guiding, dominating spirit, with its message of grace and poetry', he stated.[78]

Norma Evenson suggests that the 'relatively low, horizontal spaces' found inside Niemeyer's monuments for Brasília may 'be seen to embody a uniquely contemporary conception of monumental space, making no concessions to the visual associations of the past'. She points out that he avoided the 'lofty proportions' traditionally expected of such interiors, and rightly observes that the 'architectural drama of Brasília tends to be primarily external – in the relationship of building to site and in the establishment of large-scale composition'. Evenson is the only critic who has noticed Niemeyer's clear 'departure from traditional monumentality'. In 'the symbolic buildings of Brasília [which] display variations on a theme of lightness and fragility', she perceives 'a poignant awareness of the ephemeral, a melancholy and sophisticated perception of how tenuous is man's grasp of the earth and how transient are his works'. And she goes on to interpret the 'anti-monumental' character and 'insubstantiality of the architecture . . . accentuated against the image of the surrounding wasteland'

Palácio da Alvorada: view of the entrance elevation from the forecourt along the reflective pool

The entrance to the palace of the president, a simple opening in the glazing, reflected in the mirror-clad wall of the entrance hall

as a 'subconscious evocation of the very insecurity and shallowness of Brazilian political institutions'.[79]

The political events that followed the inauguration of the federal capital gave Evenson reason to find in Niemeyer's buildings an omen of Brazil's dismal political future. As far as his intentions are concerned, however, it would be more justifiable to interpret his radical rethinking of monumentality as a reflection of both his

74 Ribeiro, 1992, p. 123.   **75** Underwood, 1994b, p. 111.   **76** Niemeyer, 1958b, p. 6; Henry-Russell Hitchcock, in 'In Search of a New Monumentality', 1948, pp. 124–25.   **77** Niemeyer, 1958b, p. 6.   **78** Niemeyer, 1960. **79** Evenson, 1973, pp. 200–05.

exploratory approach to design – in effect, a critical approach to received ideas – and a desire to celebrate not things already achieved but things about to unfurl. Niemeyer's aesthetics of arrested flight was intended to represent a nation about to take off and fulfil its long-promised great destiny. The architectural challenge of Brasília was to give material expression to Brazil's inexhaustible hope and firm belief in a future as yet immaterial. Uncompromisingly horizontal, floating above the earth of the *cerrado*, the Palace of the Dawn – named so by Kubitschek himself – turned concrete and monumental the physical and metaphorical new horizon of Brasília, awaiting the promised dawn of a new Brazil. Like Marco Polo's Despina, one of Italo Calvino's *Invisible Cities*, Brasília 'receives its form from the desert it opposes'. Here, Niemeyer's 'demonstration of non-verticalism', which Joaquim Cardozo saw nascent at Pampulha, acquired even greater symbolic significance as a statement against the 'characteristic[s] of powerful forms in the past'. Horizontality and ethereality were also presented as the qualities of a Modernist monumentality that is 'part of a universe in which all that is solid melts into air'.[80]

Instead of anti-monumentality, it may be more appropriate to speak of a counter-monumentality that questions and reorders the qualities of the powerful forms of the past. Wrapped in stone, the palaces of the nation's symbolic capital manifest the eternal nature of the democratic processes that brought them into being. But rather than solidity and weight, they propose lightness and grace, underscoring the individuality of their constituent parts – the columns – yet subordinating the individuality of equals to the synthesis of the whole. Rather than affirming the power of the state, Brasília's houses of government aimed to express the ideal harmony of the democratic polis. Their colonnades' upward thrust denotes the collectively embraced utopian aspirations of Brazilian society and culture. On the gold-ceramic-tiled wall inside the Alvorada entrance hall are inscribed Kubitschek's words, uttered on 2 October 1956: 'From this Central Plateau, from this solitary place that will shortly be transformed into the brain centre of the highest national decisions, I cast my eyes once again on the tomorrow of my country, with unshakeable faith and unlimited confidence in the greatness of its destiny.'

The approach to the Palácio da Alvorada is precisely choreographed. From the car park to the north, by the service wing, the visitor turns onto a mundane tarmac road running parallel to the main building. A few metres ahead, a yellow-beige stone path, flanked by lawns, marks the beginning of the ceremonial ap-proach along the double row of tall imperial palms, thinly veiling the indolent white colonnade and anchoring the journey in the world of Brazilian tradition. The walk along the iconic façade is prolonged, since the entrance is strategically positioned off-centre. Past the palm colonnade unfolds a frontal, undisturbed view

of the façade. From here, the visitor turns onto a platform paved in light-grey polished marble, a further change of material in the progression from the humble to the noble. This forecourt, parallel to the building, along the long side of the reflective pool that keeps the viewer at a distance from the façade, is a clear call for pause before crossing the bridge to the house. A second point of stasis is located under the roof overhang. Here there is another platform, smaller than the first, not for active contemplation but for symbolic hesitation before entering the presidential residence. The glazing slides away to reveal the ultimate ceremonial ascent: in a spacious hall is a free-standing wall, revetted with glittering golden tiles designed by Athos Bulcão and reflected in the polished marble floor, the mirror-sheathed partitions, glass, and aluminium-clad columns and mullions. A broad, red-carpeted, shallow ramp, set parallel to the façade, takes the world's dignitaries to the visitors' salon on the raised-ground-floor level.[81] The finishes are exquisite throughout and the detailing sparse so as not to adulterate the beauty and nobility of the materials.

Palácio da Alvorada: entrance hall

As at the nineteenth-century summer imperial palace at Petrópolis, the ground floor of the Alvorada is given over to public life. The main suite of reception rooms runs the full length of the west side of the building, to the south of the entrance hall, facing the garden and the lake and culminating in a double-height banqueting hall with a dining suite by the renowned Brazilian designer Sergio Rodrigues.[82] To the north of the entrance hall are located

80 Calvino, p. 18; Cardozo, 1955, p. 6; Berman, p. 345. **81** Apparently, the dictators who came to inhabit the building in the 1960s interpreted the red carpet as a Communist allusion and promptly changed it to green. The original colour was restored following the return of democracy and the building's extensive restoration from 2002 to 2003. **82** A reassessment of the building's performance in the 1990s led to a number of modifications like the introduction of *brises-soleil* on the east elevation and the transfer of the main cooking facilities to the basement.

the president's private offices and library and, symmetrically to the banqueting hall, a double-height ministers' council chamber, reached also by a separate entrance. The ministers' council chamber is equipped with table and chairs in aluminium and white leather by Charles and Ray Eames, model no. EA 105, designed in 1958. Eames' lounge chairs in rosewood-veneered plywood with black leather upholstery, model no. 670 (1956), populate the basement projection room. Modern classics are combined with pieces designed by Brazilian contemporaries and Luso-Brazilian antiques – a grouping already proposed by Lúcio Costa in his 1930 project for a modern house for Ernesto G. Fontes and justified in his 1939 article on 'Luso-Brazilian Furniture'.[83]

Ludwig Glaeser has interpreted Mies van der Rohe's 'abolition of the solid, rooted supports on which the primeval ruler elevated himself above his subjects', in his Barcelona chair, as a 'democratising gesture which rejected past hierarchical orders'.[84] This democratic throne suited perfectly Niemeyer's programme of democratizing the colonial seat of the patriarchal ruler. In 1929, Mies had offered it exclusively to the king and queen of Spain. In a further democratizing gesture, thirty years later, Niemeyer populated Brazil's presidential residence with twenty-four of these modern thrones. Inside the Alvorada as well as in the extensive gardens are displayed works by modern Brazilian artists: Cândido Portinari, Emiliano Di Cavalcanti, Alfredo Ceschiatti, Maria Martins, Athos Bulcão, Alfredo Volpi, Djanira da Mota e Silva and Franz Weissman. A bronze sculpture by the French sculptor André Bloc is also displayed in the main reception hall.

The state rooms are sumptuous but not ostentatious or pompous, while detailing and workmanship are of the highest quality. Niemeyer's palette of fine finishes is carefully composed: white plaster, mirror and jacaranda-wood panelling, anodized aluminium cladding for the round columns, jacaranda-wood floors, red carpets and bronze balustrades for stairways, and silk curtains. The upper floor, of significantly lower height, contains relatively modest private apartments for the president's family and guests, divided into two groups, which are connected by a gallery overlooking the entrance hall, with a second gallery overlooking the main reception hall. The bedrooms are paraded in sequence along the west side of the building, and the largest group is served by a long balcony projecting beneath the canopy of the veranda, enjoying unobstructed views towards the lake and the extensive gardens. The latter were designed by Yoichi Aikawa, landscape architect to Emperor Hirohito of Japan. The green granite parapet of the bedroom balcony ensures minimal visual interference on the façade.

For the chapel of the Palácio da Alvorada, to the north of the main building, Niemeyer dusted off and reworked an unbuilt project of 1955, published in Stamo Papadaki's second monograph (1956). It is composed of organic curves stemming from the lan-

Palácio da Alvorada: reception room on the raised ground floor

Palácio da Alvorada: banqueting hall with dining suite by Sergio Rodrigues

guage of Le Corbusier's Notre-Dame-du-Haut at Ronchamp. In a 1956 article entitled 'Ronchamp: Le Corbusier's Chapel and the Crisis of Rationalism', published in the same issue of the *Architectural Review* that featured Niemeyer's Museum at Caracas, James Stirling had announced the arrival of 'the most plastic building ever created in the name of modern architecture'. Judging it mannerist, Stirling noted the Ronchamp chapel's 'ethereal quality', its 'weightlessness', 'entirely visual appeal', and

83 Lúcio Costa, 'Mobiliário luso-brasileiro' (1939), in Lúcio Costa, 1997, pp. 463–70.   84 Glaeser, p. 8.

'freedom from the precept of the correct use and expression of materials'.[85] It is probably because of these qualities that it 'is said to mark the beginning of [the Brazilian] influence on the work [of Le Corbusier], something that pleases us [Brazilians] a great deal,' Niemeyer adds.[86]

Subordinating the plasticity of his chapel to the demands of Brazil's modern patriarchal palace and careful to avoid any competition with the leading formal elements of the latter, Niemeyer edited the nautilus-like plan of his earlier scheme to achieve greater lightness and simplicity. His declared intention was to 'enhance, by contrast, the palace's majestic structure', ending the horizontal composition with a relatively timid, upward-surging swirl, culminating in a small cross, the material finishes integrating the ensemble.[87] The sacristy was moved to the basement and the curvilinear walls developed into more sober near-semicircles. The flat roof is set low so that the walls appear to be free-standing, and is visible only above the large opening of the entrance to the south, facing the palace, and the small opening to the north that illuminates the altar.

The chapel that greatly impressed Simone de Beauvoir stands on a square, floating platform, at the same level as that of the main building.[88] The platform tears into a gentle ramp reaching down to the path that leads to the basement. A passageway off the axis of the entrance hyphenates the two platforms, leading to the ministers' council chamber. At basement level, the sacristy is also connected to the main building via a passageway. The plan is ingenious in its simplicity: a narthex is formed between the two

Palácio da Alvorada: view of the chapel to the north of the main building from the passageway that links it to the ministers' council chamber

curving walls; following the large curve into the relatively dark interior, the visitor turns to face the altar, at the centre of the smaller curve, bathed in a northern light from a hidden source. Externally, the tapering walls are faced with the same luminous white marble as the main building's colonnades, contrasting with the internal gilded-wood revetment that recalls the venerated Baroque churches of Brazil. At the point where the two curves come closest, a spiral stair, invisible to worshippers, leads to the sacristy.

The double entrance door was designed by Athos Bulcão, creator of more artworks for Brasília than any other artist and a member of Niemeyer's team at NOVACAP (Companhia Urbanizadora da Nova Capital do Brasil).[89] Made of black-coated aluminium so as not to compromise the clarity of the white curvilinear form, it is recessed and pierced with colourful square glass openings. Athos Bulcão also decorated the ceiling with a large cross at the centre, surrounded by symbolic motifs – sun, moon and fish – all in white, against a light grey background. The higher wall is punctuated by a square opening above roof level, but the bell housed here in the earlier scheme has been wisely omitted.

The Praça dos Três Poderes

I remember one day I was in a cinema at the Champs Elysées. The film was O homem do Rio, and when the plane flew over the Três Poderes Square, the audience, without knowing I was there, applauded enthusiastically. That was the most spontaneous appraisal I have received to this date.

Oscar Niemeyer, *Meu sósia e eu*

Approaching the city from the direction of the presidential residence, the visitor reaches the triangular terraced embankment of the Praça dos Três Poderes, paved in white *pedra portuguesa*, at the eastern tip of the Monumental Axis. In his 'Report', Costa argued that the 'modern application of this ancient oriental technique' – that is, raising the city's capitol complex on a high platform – 'ensures the cohesion of the project as a whole and gives it

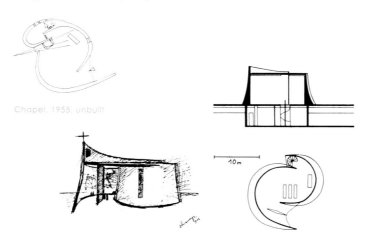

Chapel, 1955, unbuilt

Chapel of the Palácio da Alvorada, Brasília, 1956-58

85 Stirling, pp. 155–61.   **86** Oscar Niemeyer, interview in Salvaign, p. 7.
87 Niemeyer, 1998, p. 34.   **88** Beauvoir, p. 566.   **89** The collaboration between Athos Bulcão and Niemeyer began in 1942, when the two first met at the studio of Roberto Burle Marx. Niemeyer admired Bulcão's gouaches and invited him to work on a mural for the Theatre of Belo Horizonte (unexecuted). Bulcão's first mural was created for the Sul America Hospital in Rio de Janeiro in 1955. He first came to Brasília as a member of Niemeyer's team, employed by NOVACAP, and eventually took up permanent residence in the new capital. His murals and panels have been given national heritage status.

surprising monumental emphasis'.[90] The fifth Brazilian constitution of 1946 had carefully separated the three branches of government. By positioning the buildings for the three governmental powers at the corners of an equilateral triangle, Costa asserted their autonomy. Taking advantage of the topography of the site, he raised the monumental esplanade on a second, higher platform and positioned the National Congress on this higher level, giving it prominence over the houses for the executive and the judiciary. He also proposed low, rectilinear blocks for the Palácio do Planalto (Presidential Palace) and the Supremo Tribunal Federal (Supreme Court), but distinguished the Congress with a dome and a single, high-rise slab. A reflective pool and a grove of buriti palms from the cerrado were also included, the latter as a homage to Le

Palácio do Planalto seen through a grove of buriti palms from the cerrado, included in Costa's Plano Piloto as a homage to Le Corbusier

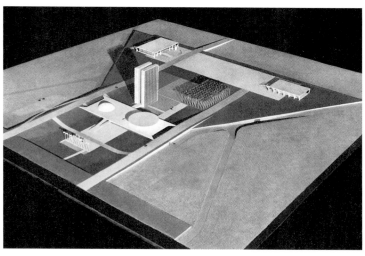

Model of the Praça dos Três Poderes with the Palácio do Planalto (Presidential Palace) and the Supremo Tribunal Federal (Supreme Court) at the base of the triangle, and the National Congress at the apex, 1958

Oscar Niemeyer, second from the left, Israël Pinheiro and Lúcio Costa, to his left, explaining the model of the Praça dos Três Poderes to Juscelino Kubitschek, seated, in the Laranjeiras Palace, Rio de Janeiro, 29 November 1958

Corbusier, who introduced palms into the vocabulary of modern Brazilian architecture, with his proposal for Rio's Cidade Universitária (1936). The 300 × 100-metres square between the low-lying Palácio do Planalto and the Supreme Court, at the two corners of the base of the triangle and approximately 8.5 metres lower than the ceremonial esplanade of the Monumental Axis, further highlights the elevated legislature.

Niemeyer respected Costa's scheme, but he also tried to link the government complex architecturally to the Palácio da Alvorada. The Palácio do Planalto and the Supremo Tribunal Federal, both designed in 1958 and completed in 1960, are also characterized by white-marble-clad monumental colonnades, their curves redeeming the austerity of rectilinear forms. Detached from the main body of the buildings, these graceful colonnades hold high the structures' floating platforms, while stepping lightly down on 'the Versailles of the people'.[91] Set at a right angle to the building's glass walls, and stretched away from the platforms, they suggest openness and accessibility, inviting the citizens to enter the houses of their government. As Niemeyer has explained, he designed these colonnades with a moving spectator in mind, who would be able to walk around them and view them from close and variable angles – something that is not possible at the Alvorada. In this way, he both related these buildings to the presidential residence and differentiated them, with a view to expressing their more public nature.

With the columns of the Alvorada, the Planalto and the Supremo Tribunal Federal, Niemeyer is said to have created the three Brazilian orders. Given traditional anthropomorphic readings of the columnar orders, he may have thought of his Brazilian orders as symbolic of the three 'races' of the Brazilian mixture. Associations with classical antiquity were drawn from an early day. Niemeyer appreciates these but also invokes the historic architecture of colonial Brazil, emphasizing originality and historical conti-

90 Lúcio Costa, 1966, p. 14.   91 Lúcio Costa, 'Saudação aos críticos de arte' (1959), in Lúcio Costa, 1997, p. 299.

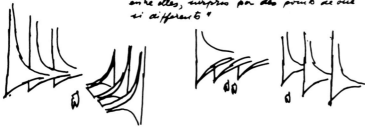

"Je les faites fines, très fines, et les palais comme s'ils touchaient seulement le sol"

"Je ne voulais pas les colonnes collées au palais, rectangulaires, toujours egales. je les ai eloigné du palais. je les ai fait avec des courbes et des droites en permettant au public de se promener entre elles, surpris par des points de vue si différents"

'I did not want columns stuck against the palace, rectangular, all the same,' explains Niemeyer, 'I positioned them at a distance from the palace and designed them with curves and straight lines, allowing the public to walk through them and be astonished by the variable points of view.'

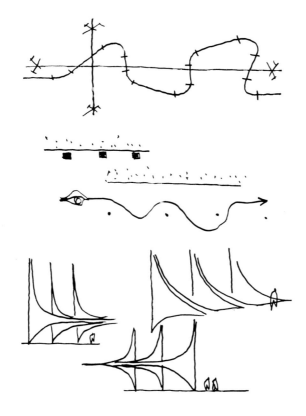

nuity, injecting the Apollonian image with the distinctly Brazilian Dionysian spirit of his beloved curves through a mechanism of hybridization. In 1960, in his 'Form and Function in Architecture', Niemeyer wrote:

> In the three Palaces . . . I have restricted my speculations to the form of the supports or columns strictly so called. I did not want to adopt the usual sections – cylindrical or rectangular columns – which would have been simpler and cheaper, but sought other forms that, even though they might run counter to certain functionalist precepts, would give the buildings character, lightening them and creating an appearance of unattachment, as though they were merely resting on the ground . . . This justifies the forms adopted, with the ends tapering to a point, forms that greet the visitor with new and unexpected aspects; spreading out in a series of harmonious curves or, when he stands in the middle of the [Square] of the Three Powers, surrounding him – as Jean-Paul Sartre puts it – in the fan, as it were, of their plastic interplay; or again changing and acquiring new and different aspects, as though they were not just things, inert and static . . . And it pleased me to feel that these forms imbued the Palaces with features, however modest, that were original on their own, and – which is till more important for me – forge a link with the old architecture of colonial Brazil, not by the obvious use of the elements common to those days, but by expressing the same plastic intention, the same love of curves and richly refined forms that is so telling a characteristic of the colonial style.[92]

On the north side of the Praça dos Três Poderes, the Palácio do Planalto faces the square, with its long side equalling the square's width, but it is also separated from the central public area by one of the two avenues bordering the Monumental Axis, which crosses the square and continues towards the Palácio da Alvorada. This arrangement allows the creation of a sort of civic antechamber or forecourt in front of the Planalto, from which a ceremonial ramp leads directly to the first-floor official reception area. The marble-clad speaker's rostrum is also positioned in the forecourt, framed by the tiptoeing colonnade and linked by an open bridge to the first-floor veranda. As at the Alvorada, the structural function of the external colonnades is limited; defying gravity and technocratic reason, they barely touch the ground, burdened only with the loads of the wide roof overhang and the veranda that surrounds the aluminium-and-glass body of the building roughly a quarter of the way up its height.

As columns of luxury, 'based entirely on poetry' and created for a 'magic effect', they may be compared to Frank Lloyd Wright's overscaled pillars in the hall of the Administration Building

92 Niemeyer, 1993b, pp. 309–11.

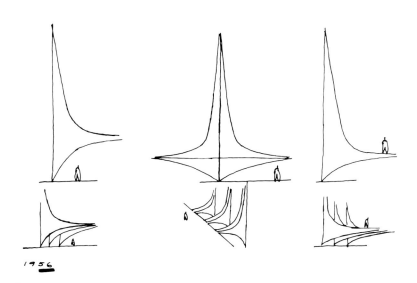

Mas foi em Brasília, nos palácios da nova Capital que a forma plástica mais me preocupou, desejoso de encontrar solução nova, estrutural, que o caracterizasse. São as colunas recurvadas, acabando em ponta, que as fazem leves e vazadas, como que apenas <u>tocando</u> <u>o solo</u>.

1956

(11)

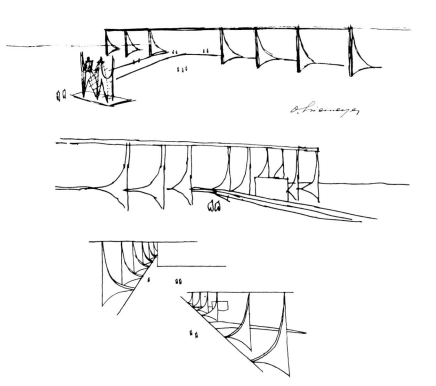

Palácio do Planalto, Praça dos Três Poderes, Brasília, 1958–60

for the Johnson Wax Company in Racine, Wisconsin, singled out by Giedion for their 'apparent pointlessness'.[93] Extending Niemeyer's repertoire of inverted forms, Underwood sees the flying columns of the Planalto and the Supreme Court as the inverted buttresses of a medieval cathedral.[94] They may have also been inspired by the *cerrado*'s 'dry and stunted trees', which to Niemeyer 'seemed to strain up from the ground as if resisting the soil's attempts to pull them back down into the earth'.[95] Bearing in mind the old analogy between the column and the human body, it is tempting to read the columnar chorus of the Planalto as an expression of the triumph of the collective values of the democratic polis, a representation of the collective chorus of the citizens, in whose rhythm the actions of the president are bound, and which, as in Athenian tragedy, always has the last word. The raised arms of Bruno Giorgi's *Os Candangos* or *Os Guerreiros* (*The Warriors*, 1960), on the Praça dos Três Poderes, recall the curves of the Alvorada colonnade.

Entry into the Planalto for daily operations is at ground level, via a passage across a shallow, reflective pool. This level is recessed, allowing the glass box above it to float high above the ground on its large platform and exposing on three sides a row of oval, aluminium-clad structural columns. The three upper floors are cantilevered beyond the supporting columns, wrapped in an unbroken glass-and-aluminium curtain wall. At first-floor level, the reception areas and banqueting hall look out towards the square and the landscaped garden to the rear of the building. The double-height Noble Hall or Hall of Mirrors, set on the side of the square, is enlivened by the free-flowing plate of the mezzanine, which seems suspended in mid-air, recalling a similar arrangement

Palácio do Planalto: view of the main (south) elevation

93 Giedion, 1939, p. 38.   **94** Underwood, 1994b, p. 117.   **95** Niemeyer, 2000b, p. 82.

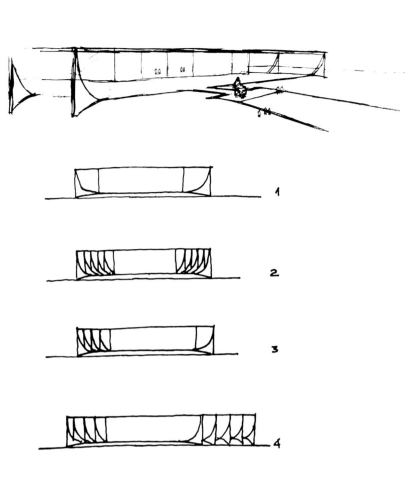

1

2

3

4

5

Supremo Tribunal Federal, Praça dos Três Poderes, Brasília, 1958–60; Bruno Giorgi's *Os Candangos* or *Os Guerreiros* (*The Warriors*, 1960) stand on the 'Versailles of the people'.

PP Palácio do Planalto
(Presidential Palace)
ST Supremo Tribunal Federal
(Supreme Court)
CN Congresso Nacional
(National Congress)
P Parking
AN Congressional annex
IT Palácio do Itamaraty
(Ministry of Foreign Affairs)
TC Treasury (replaced by the
Ministry of Justice)
EM Esplanada dos Ministérios
(Esplanade of the Ministries)
MI Ministries 1-11
CA Cathedral
SCS Cultural sector, south
SCN Cultural sector, north
TO National Theatre
ER Traffic intersection
and bus platform
SDS Entertainment sector, south
SDN Entertainment sector, north
SHS Hotel sector, south
SHN Hotel sector, north

Plan of the Monumental Axis

Palácio do Planalto: view of the main (south) elevation from the forecourt
with the speaker's rostrum

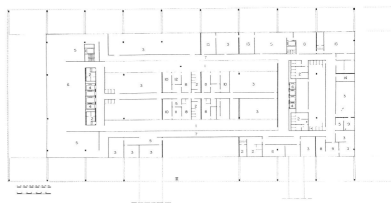

third floor plan

1	garden	7	corridor	12	assistant chief of the
2	toilets	8	audience room		president's civilian advisers
3	officials	9	chief of the cabinet	13	staff rooms
4	elevators	10	secretary	14	chief of the president's
5	waiting room	11	assistant chief of the		civilian advisers
6	public hall		president's military advisers	15	butler's pantry

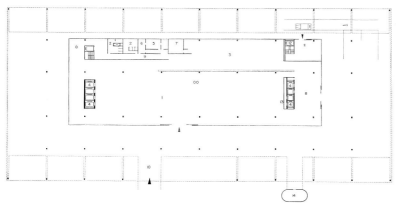

ground floor plan

1	lobby	6	first-aid room		
2	toilets	7	director	11	president's lounge
3	officials	8	officials' lounge	12	president's elevator
4	elevators	9	corridor	13	public elevator
5	closet	10	ramp	14	speaker's rostrum

N

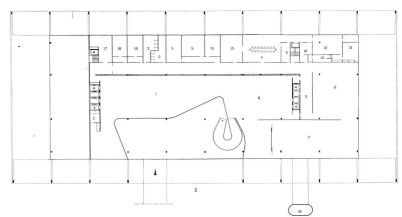

second (mezzanine) floor plan

1	gallery				
2	toilets	8	drawing room	14	president's bedroom
3	officials	9	assistants' room	15	audience room
4	elevators	10	secretary	16	audience room
5	waiting room	11	dispatch	17	butler's pantry
6	public hall	12	president's office	18	lavatories
7	reception room	13	president's room	19	speaker's rostrum

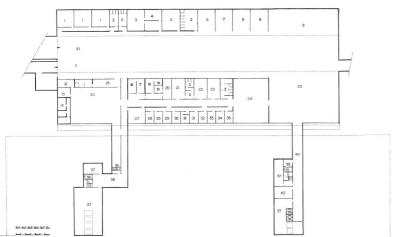

basement plan

1	bedrooms	12	cellar	23	armoury		
2	toilets	13	pantry	24	soldiers' quarters		
3	electric power plant	14	cold storage	25	garage	34	workshop
4	workshops	15	control	26	kitchen	35	office
5	cloakroom	16	guard officer	27	printing plant	36	elevators
6	illumination control	17	guard commander	28	post office	37	machine shops
7	paint room	18	officer's room	29	telegraph operators	38	entrance
8	mechanics workshop	19	toilets	30	lavatory	39	president's foyer
9	washing and greasing	20	commander's room	31	radio chief	40	president's entrance
10	truck ramp	21	dining room	32	radio operators	41	president's elevator
11	car ramp	22	recreation room	33	radio room	42	electric power plant

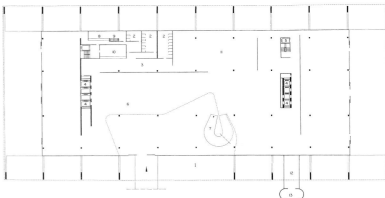

first floor plan

1	banqueting hall			
2	toilets	8	butler's pantry	
3	corridor	9	dumb-waiter	
4	elevators	10	cloakroom	
5	president's elevator	11	salon	
6	Noble Hall or Hall of Mirrors	12	passage to speaker's rostrum	
7	ramp	13	speaker's rostrum	

Palácio do Planalto, Brasília

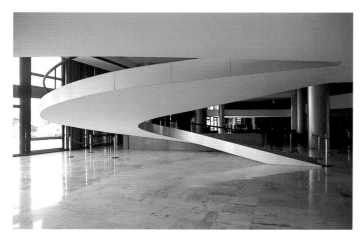

at the Brazilian Pavilion of the 1939 New York World's Fair. A broad, free-floating, helicoidal ramp provides ceremonial access to the mezzanine. A symphony of reflective materials adds sparkle, spectacle and ceremony to the interior: polished white marble for the floor, mirror panelling for the walls, anodized aluminium for the columns and ramp revetments. The offices of the president and the president's personal staff are on the mezzanine, while those of the executive staff – heads of military and civilian departments – are located on the top floor. This last floor is divided lengthways into three parts with winter gardens, which serve to illuminate and ventilate this cellular plan.

The Supreme Court hovers closer to the ground, its narrow north side facing the Praça dos Três Poderes and a statue of *Justice* by Alfredo Ceschiatti nearby. This façade addressing the square is free of the screening colonnade. The civic pavement

gently rises to lift the citizen onto the floating veranda. The flying columns of the Supreme Court, along its two long sides, are similar in design to those of the Planalto but of more graceful proportions. Niemeyer says that he conceived the columns of the two low buildings on the Square of the Three Powers as the 'structural element which acts as a common denominator for the two buildings', helping to achieve a desirable unity and that 'sense of sobriety of the great Squares in Europe within the scale of values demanded by Lucio Costa's magnificent project'.[96] The Supreme Court's columns embrace the glass box like a set of flight feathers, never fully obscuring one another, irrespective of the angle of view, like pleats fluidly unfolding and refolding, carrying the eye along. Their marble cladding touches the earth at one infinitely small point, concealing a slightly larger concrete base. To borrow a phrase used by the poet Paul Claudel to describe Vaslav Nijinsky's performance in Brazil, the effortless dance of Niemeyer's ethereal colonnades marks the 'victory of breath over weight'.[97] The fluid, fan-like effect is best appreciated when walking along the verandas: the great white marble leaves open and close languorously, in slow, perpetual motion, seemingly the source of the cool breeze under the large roof overhangs.

The square columns supporting the roof slab are exposed on the front and rear elevations yet effaced in their dark-grey, powder-coated aluminium sheathing. The mezzanine level is held at a slight distance from the glazing, borne up on white, circular, rendered-concrete columns. At the centre of the steel-and-glass box is positioned a double-height court chamber, surrounded by rooms for the public, judges and staff. It features a wall lined with a travertine bas-relief by Athos Bulcão (1969) and an arching wooden ceiling like an upside-down vessel hovering overhead, allowing daylight to enter from the side. On the top floor, a central library – above the court chamber – is surrounded by offices and study rooms. A smaller courtroom is also located on this floor.

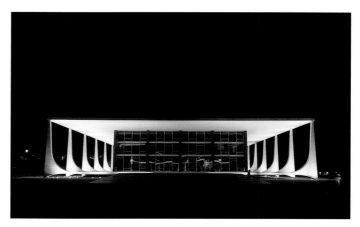

96 Niemeyer, 1958b, p. 6.   **97** Paul Claudel, quoted in Calil, p. 566.

Supremo Tribunal Federal: view of the marble colonnade

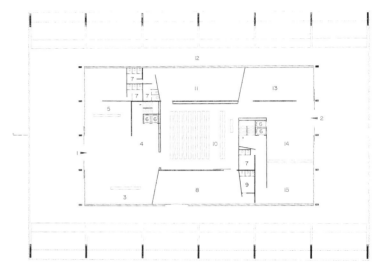

ground floor plan

1	public entrance	6	elevators	11	public waiting room
2	officials' entrance	7	toilets	12	gallery
3	information	8	judges' chambers	13	judges' cloakroom
4	public hall	9	judges' toilets	14	officials' waiting room
5	porter	10	high court chamber	15	supervisors

Supremo Tribunal Federal, Brasília

Supremo Tribunal Federal: view of the marble colonnade

Supremo Tribunal Federal: high court chamber with travertine bas-relief by Athos Bulcão (1969)

National Congress, Brasília, 1958–60: the main (west) elevation with the ceremonial ramp faces the mall; its raised, monumental esplanade offers open views towards the Praça dos Três Poderes and Lake Paranoá to the east

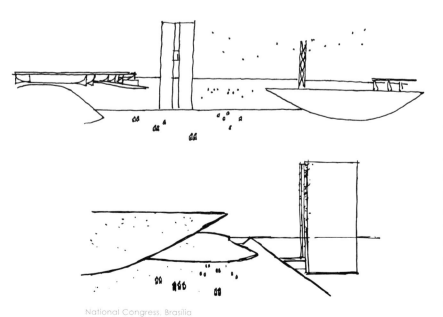

National Congress, Brasília

On the west side of the Praça dos Três Poderes, the privileged palace of the National Congress (1958–60) was designed by Niemeyer to provide the dominant focus of the Monumental Axis without compromising visual openness. The separation of the functions of the National Congress allowed him to configure the building as an artificial landscape, shaping the city's definitive 'skyline' and celebrating rather than merely serving its programme.[98] It is positioned between two embankments, prescribed by Costa to provide roof-level access from the two avenues passing on either side, integrating the space of democracy with the city's street space. With its primary elevation turned towards the 'broad sweeping lawns' of the ceremonial mall, this building addresses the city rather than the square. A long ramp, positioned off-centre, provides access to the white-marble-paved 'monumental esplanade' of the people, affording views towards the square.[99]

98 Lúcio Costa, ' "Ingredientes" da concepção urbanística de Brasília' (n.d.), in Lúcio Costa, 1997, p. 282; Niemeyer, 1998, p. 34.   99 Niemeyer, 1993b, p. 311.

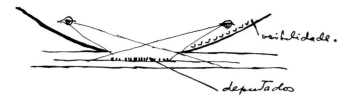

National Congress: the inverted dome of the Chamber of Deputies and the cupola of the Senate

Niemeyer recalls Le Corbusier's remark atop this ramp, during his last visit to Brazil in 1962: 'There is invention here!'[100]

Set in the shallow depression of the manipulated terrain, the orthogonal, uniform, glazed, lower part of the building almost disappears in the shaded area under the mighty, white marble line of its roof plate. On this firm, new horizon of the national legislature, the shallow dome of the Senate is elegantly partnered with the inverted, saucer-like, larger dome of the Chamber of Deputies, 'horizontally stretched to meet the requirements of internal visibility', like a spaceship that has reached the Brazilian earth.[101] The modern structure of the legislature is thus superimposed on the structure associated with Brazil's archaic politics: the patriarchal

casa grande. Norma Evenson also notes the schematic similarity between Brasília's National Congress and Matthew Nowicki's unbuilt project of 1950 for the provincial assembly of Punjab in Chandigarh.[102]

Opening towards the sky, the concave form of the Chamber of Deputies symbolizes the openness of the lower house towards the electorate, while the cupola of the upper house is turned inwards, towards its legislative task. The inversion of the cupola, the

100 Le Corbusier, quoted in Niemeyer, 2004, p. 150.   101 Niemeyer, 1998, p. 40.   102 In Nowicki's scheme are found both the flat, platform-like building with the assembly on its roof, and a long ramp leading to the roof; Evenson, 1973, p. 194, n. 13.

National Congress: the dome of the Senate under construction

'Baroque figure par excellence' suggests an infinite unfolding towards the sky.[103] Niemeyer refers to the strategy of revisiting 'an ancient form that belongs in the visual vocabulary of architecture' and inverting it 'to attain . . . [a] lighter visual effect', returning to the theme of a world upside down, where the last shall be first and the first last.[104] Assuming a form that is the inversion of the dominant one, the Chamber of Deputies proposes an alternative and autonomous architectural tradition for Brazil, if not a political one too, in dialogue with that of the Old World of Europe and that of North America. The strategy may be indebted to the proposals of Uruguayan artist and theorist Joaquím Torres-García (1874–1949), put forward in his Latin Americanist manifesto of 1935, *The School of the South*, and illustrated by his *South America's Inverted Map*, where the south looks toward the north from above.

In 1959, Pier Luigi Nervi examined the drawings for the Chamber of Deputies 'in a small exhibition on Brazilian architecture held at the new headquarters of Unesco in Paris', and noted another inversion, precisely the one that helped Niemeyer to achieve the desired 'lighter visual effect':

> The construction is to be in reinforced concrete, so it will have a stony image that reminds us of the natural ability of such materials (both natural and artificial) to resist compression, while on the contrary the 'keystone' of the system can only be provided by very powerful ring-shaped reinforcement . . .

What will be the sensation, for the spectator, of the looming, enormous mass, mysteriously launched and projected by a narrower ring at the base, in the total inversion of the more spontaneous arrangement, in which the base would be wider than, or at least equal to, that which rises from it?[105]

Through the puffy cumulus clouds racing across the blue skies of Brasília soar the twin twenty-seven-storey towers of the Secretariat, one for the senators and one for the deputies, positioned between the two cupolas, closer to the smaller one of the Senate. They float in the pool to the east of the main building with their narrow, opaque side towards the low block, to which they are connected by a passageway. The towers are connected to each other at the eleventh, twelfth and thirteenth floors. Local figurative imagination claims the H configuration of the Secretariat stands for humanity. Although dominant in height, these administrative office towers that serve and guard the democratic process do not compete with the sculpturally assertive legislative chambers; they balance the asymmetrical composition, underscoring its orientation towards the enormous sky. Niemeyer's aim was 'to create the play of forms and shapes which make architecture what it is, and which Le Corbusier so well defined'.[106] The epic ensemble dominating the 'Cidade-Ceu' ('Sky City'), as Brasília is sometimes called, is reflected in the water of the pools on either side, Niemeyer's ubiquitous instrument of narcissism that transforms his buildings into flowers conscious of their beauty.

Lúcio Costa held the Rio Ministry of Education building as the 'definitive symbol' of a new architecture, characterized by the conscious integration of architecture and structure.[107] In 1954, the English architect Peter Craymer remarked:

> Brazilians have a conception of architecture in which the structural skeleton plays a far more important and fundamental role in the appearance of the building than it does in Europe, and for this reason the engineer is bound to be enthusiastically involved in research into new structures and new formal solutions, and the barrier between the architectural and the engineering professions – unfortunately so common over here – is not to be found in Brazil, and this achievement is not least among the architectural triumphs of Niemeyer, Reidy, Bernardes and their compatriots.[108]

Niemeyer has repeatedly acknowledged his dependence on the dedicated support of his structural engineers for the realization of the forms that spring from his imagination. In Brasília, vital and effective collaboration with Joaquim Cardozo enabled him to take advantage of the achievements of twentieth-century engi-

103 Deleuze, p. 124. **104** Niemeyer, 1998, p. 40. **105** Nervi, 1959, p. 55. Nervi posed the question: 'Will this sensation be enjoyment of beauty, or a kind of frightened awe?' **106** Niemeyer, 1958b, p. 6. **107** Lúcio Costa, 'Muita construção, alguma arquitetura e um milagre' (1951), in Lúcio Costa, 1997, p. 167. **108** Craymer, p. 236.

neering – considered to be endowed with the quality of monumentality – to sustain his journey into unknown formal territories, realizing structures that expressed both collective aspirations and faith in modern science. After all, the so-called 'scientific myth' had been firmly positioned at the basis of republican Brazil's foundational ideology, exemplified by the positivist motto of 1889, 'Ordem e Progresso'.

The emphasis of Niemeyer's designs, however, is not on the time-bound scientific fact, but on the timeless aesthetic qualities engineering has been mobilized to help achieve. What is offered to posterity is not the engineering solution but the architectural expression; formal innovation takes priority over scientific rationalism. Brazilian contemporaries like Affonso Eduardo Reidy shared Niemeyer's approach to the integration of architecture's formal and structural coordinates. In *L'Architecture d'Aujourd'hui*'s special issue on 'Architects and Engineers' of 1961, Reidy argued that 'structure is not an end in itself but a means to realize an idea . . . [and] the basic structural idea is born together with the architectonic conception'.[109] Sharing Niemeyer's vision of structural solutions emancipated from a narrowly conceived rationality, in Brasília, Cardozo remained enthusiastically committed to the expansion of the structure's architectural potential.

Defending plastic freedom against accusations of formalism, in 1960 Niemeyer wrote:

Plastic freedom is bitterly opposed in certain sectors of contemporary architecture. This opposition comes from the timid, from those who feel that they are better off and more comfortable encompassed by rules and restrictions . . . they react defensively against plastic speculation in the elements of structure, which they want strictly functional, considering such speculation to be formalistic and contrary to technical reasoning . . .

They insist, for instance, on solutions based on simple and compact plans, aiming at pure geometrical volumes – a solution that I sometimes adopt, without, however, accepting it as dogmatic – and to this end, they cram into preestablished forms complex programs . . . which, if they are to meet precisely those functional requirements so zealously defended, stand in need of a different, more complex treatment . . . And so, in order to maintain the desired purism, apparent purism, they create true formalism . . . and monotony, stripping buildings of the indispensable character that should be suggested by what they are to be used for . . .

I endeavor to shape my projects, characterizing them whenever possible by the structure itself, which is never based on the radical imposition of functionalism, but – and always – on a search for new and varied solutions, logical if possible

within the static system . . . I accept any device, any compromise, convinced that architecture is not just a matter of engineering, but an exteriorization of mind, imagination, and poetry.

In the Palace of Congress, for instance, the composition was worked out according to this principle, taking into account the demands of architecture and urbanism, volumes, free spaces, visual depth and perspective, and especially the intention of endowing it with a character of great monumentality by means of the simplification of its elements and the adoption of pure, simple forms.[110]

The Chamber of Deputies rises 10 metres above the flat plane, has a diameter of 62 metres, and originally provided seating for 528 members and 120 guests (later modified to 399 plus 585). Roofing the bowl-shaped form was challenging for Joaquim Cardozo, who devised a traction ring to support a shallow cupola, incorporated within the concave external form. The ceiling is suspended from the internal cupola. Thanks to a concrete ring, externally, the roof appears flat. The Senate accommodates 115 members and 150 guests. Its parabolic dome, 39 metres in diameter, is visible internally. Both cupolas are externally rendered and painted white.

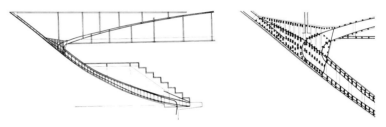

Joaquim Cardozo, structural engineer, detail of the structure of the inverted dome of the Senate

The two houses are accessed from the low, two-storey block. The official entrance is on the side of the Monumental Axis (west), via the scissor ramp perpendicular to the building, leading up to the marble esplanade, or straight ahead to the wide, black granite veranda in front of the double-height Salão Negro (Black Salon), also with a black granite floor finish. As so often, Niemeyer has no use for monumental doorways. The Salão Negro is the major reception area, serving both houses of the National Congress, the black soul of a white building, which turns the racist theory of the black person with a white soul on its head. On a daily basis, members of the Congress and other government officials enter the Black Salon from the garage in the basement. Inside, the rear, white marble wall is flanked by two staircases leading to the two chambers. The marble wall is inlaid with four polished, black granite vertical axes, of equal length but variable width and align-

109 Reidy, p. 3.   110 Niemeyer, 1993b, pp. 309–11.

ment, which pick up the syncopated tempo of the human body in motion. Niemeyer holds this wall panel by Athos Bulcão (1960) as a prime example of the ideal integration of art and architecture, resulting from close collaboration between architect and artist.[111] The adjacent Salão Nobre (Noble Salon), with Mies's Barcelona chairs and stools and a stained-glass, free-standing screen by Marianne Peretti, is reserved for state receptions.

On the upper floor of this building are found the two plenary assembly halls, with separate entrances for members, press and spectators. On the east of this level, the side of the larger pool, is the 200-metre-long Salão Verde (Green Salon), with green carpet and furniture designed by Niemeyer, originally intended to be a common foyer for senators and deputies but later divided by a

[111] Niemeyer explains that, following discussions with Bulcão, the two men decided that the best solution would be to create a mural using the material already selected for the interior finishes of the building; Niemeyer, 1963g, p. 13.

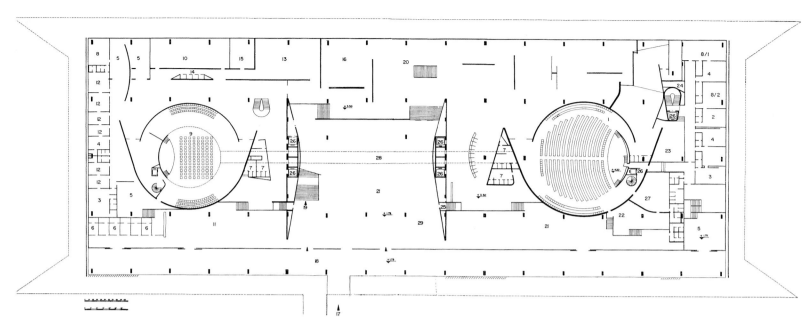

first floor plan

1   assembly hall (deputies) with seating for 528 members and 120 guests
2   committee rooms
3   president
4   secretariat
5   waiting room
6   conference room
7   deputies' and senators' toilets
8   vice-president
9   assembly hall (senate) with seating for 115 members and 150 guests
10   toilets
11   press room
12   assistants
13   salon
14   telephones
15   café
16   directory
17   public entrance
18   entrance to gallery
19   entrance to upper gallery
20   deputies' and senators' lounge
21   public lounge
22   mail and telegraph room
23   deputies' waiting room
24   ventilation shaft
25   passage to public toilets
26   elevators
27   typing pool
28   elevated passageway
29   sorting

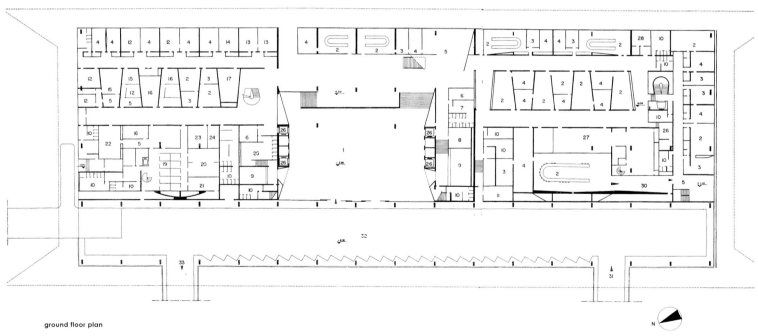

ground floor plan

1   deputies' and senators' hall
2   committee rooms
3   president
4   secretaries
5   waiting rooms
6   barbers
7   deputies' toilets
8   telephone operators
9   cloakroom
10   public toilets
11   telephone switchboard
12   assistants
13   halls
14   minority leader
15   majority leader
16   committee rooms
17   room in reserve
18   entrance
19   storage
20   lavatories
21   archives
22   printing shop
23   air-conditioning plant
24   electrician
25   senators' toilets
26   elevators
27   stenographers' room
28   physician
29   pantry
30   passageway
31   ramp
32   parking
33   exit

National Congress, Brasilia

west elevation

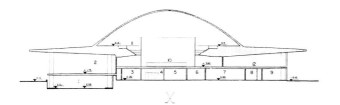

section through Senate

1	garage	5	director	9	assemblies
2	public passage	6	passageway	10	assembly hall
3	archives	7	meeting room	11	public
4	collectors	8	passageway	12	senators' lounge

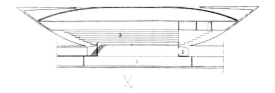

section through Chamber of Deputies

1	assembly hall
2	press box
3	public

National Congress, Brasília

glass wall. This hall contains the largest number of specially commissioned artworks: *Alegoria de Brasília*, a painting by Emiliano Di Cavalcanti; *Araguaia*, a stained-glass piece by Marianne Peretti; *Pedra sobre Pedra*, a sculpture by André Bloc symbolic of the building of a city, a gift of the French government; *O Anjo*, a gilded bronze statue by Alfredo Ceschiatti; a green, abstract, decorative sculptural piece by Athos Bulcão (1976); and internal tropical gardens by Roberto Burle Marx against an abstract, blue-and-white *azulejo* mural by Bulcão (1971). Rooms for the press and visitors are also located on this level. The lower floor contains eight committee rooms for senators and twelve for deputies, as well as offices and service rooms. The interiors are generally sober; the colours suggest the Brazilian flag, perhaps inspired by Mies's use of the colours of the German national emblem at the Barcelona Pavilion.

Over the years following the inauguration of Brasília in 1960, it became necessary to provide additional accommodation facilities for the National Congress. Four annexes have already been constructed on either side of the Monumental Axis, and a fifth one is currently under construction, linked to the main building by subterranean passages. All Brasília's government buildings required additional accommodation soon after their completion and have acquired series of annexes over the years. The decision to restrict the size of each building in the first place was a conscious one, of a symbolic and political nature, already embedded in Costa's Plano Piloto, to which Niemeyer fully adhered. Small size guaranteed grand presence by means of lofty proportions in the relationship of buildings and open spaces, rather than by means of large scale and mass. It enabled Niemeyer to prioritize symbolic repre-

sentation – designing forms that provided each government building with an easily recognizable sign – and to furnish the city with seemingly complete buildings within the limited time of three years; that is, by the set inauguration day. The construction of several annexes for each government building over the years following the city's inauguration has also allowed for expansion in manageable stages and according to need. These annexes generally house auxiliary functions and remain subordinate in form and size to the buildings they were constructed to serve, taking care not to contaminate the visual signature of the latter.

The Ministry of Justice and the Palácio do Itamaraty

Two solemn rows of identical steel-frame ministry slabs, as prescribed by Costa – initially eleven, eventually seventeen in total, ten to the north and seven to the south – house the state bureaucracy and guard the Monumental Axis between them. Following Le Corbusier's admonition, the buildings of Brasília are no longer 'lips pinching the edges of streets. They [are] isolated prisms far from each other.'[112] Initially, no air conditioning was provided and shading was deemed inadequate. It was reported that 'at least one Minister had two offices, one on each side of the building, and changed over at midday'.[113] Adjustable light-green plastic vertical louvres were added to offer protection against the sun on the long glazed northern façades of the ministries, introducing an element of variation that alleviates monotony without compromis-

112 Le Corbusier, 1991, p. 170.   **113** Crease, 1962, p. 258.

ing simplicity. The narrow, opaque concrete façades towards the Esplanada dos Ministérios are faced with grey ceramic tiles. The solemn phalanx of repetitive, ten-storey-high units (102 metres long, 18 metres wide, 40 metres high) underscores the symbolic importance of the major government buildings on the Praça dos Três Poderes. The arrangement brings to mind Henry-Russell Hitchcock's contribution to the 1948 debate 'In Search of a New Monumentality', when he anticipated the creation of 'communal structures whose monumentality will form the proper climax of the pattern of more or less repetitious units'.[114] Ministry annexes were also constructed later, to the north and south, farther away from the Monumental Axis.

Only two ministries were architecturally differentiated: the Ministry of Justice (1962–70, with Milton Ramos, modified in 1986), the first ministry established after Brazil's proclamation of independence in 1822; and the Palácio do Itamaraty (Ministry of Foreign Affairs, 1962–70, with Milton Ramos and Olavo Redig de Campos), which assumed the responsibility of representing the country and receiving her distinguished foreign guests. Situated

nearest the National Congress, colonnaded and finished in exposed concrete, which grants them a somewhat more earthly appearance, they negotiate the transition from the utilitarian office slabs of the other ministries to the ethereal, white marble palaces of the three governmental powers. Both were designed in 1962 and each consists of a square pavilion set within landscaped pools by Burle Marx, accompanied by an eight-storey office block accommodating administrative functions. Lush tropical gardens are also found inside the pavilions. Their material and aesthetic qualities are closely linked with those of Reidy's exquisite Museum of Modern Art in Rio de Janeiro.

The prominent water feature of the primary (south) elevation of the Ministry of Justice pavilion, to the north side of the Monumental Axis, evokes Moorish precedents, related to the Brazilian tradition via the Portuguese settlers. Niemeyer has also proposed a comparison with the Baroque Trevi Fountain in Rome, sustaining the dialogue with Europe. Exposing his fierce wish to sur-

114 Henry-Russell Hitchcock, in 'In Search of a New Monumentality', 1948, p. 125.

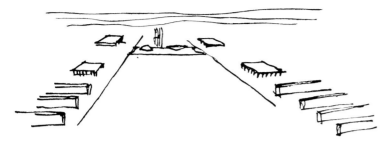

The eastern end of the Monumental Axis with the Ministry of Justice and the Palácio do Itamaraty (Ministry of Foreign Affairs) to the north and south side of the axis respectively, negotiating the transition from the repetitive office slabs of the other ministries to the marble palaces of the three governmental powers

South elevation of the Ministry of Justice pavilion, original version, prior to Niemeyer's modification of its arches in 1986

pass the monuments of the Old World, he boasts that he has achieved a more accomplished integration of building and fountain.[115] He has described this façade with the water cascades as 'architecture and nature hand in hand, invoking another favoured characteristic of Brazil's 'sacred heritage' and privileged *locus* of *brasilidade*.[116] From the early twentieth century, waterfalls and cascades had been most frequently explored in Brazilian film documentaries as images of extraordinary natural beauty, also containing a promise of industrialization. A journalist commenting on the film *A estrada de ferro Noroeste* (*The Noroeste Railway*, 1918) highlighted 'the beautiful waterfall of Itapura . . . which not even the celebrated Niagara Falls can outshine . . . A scene of beauty, for the time being, and an incalculable source of wealth in the future, when its 50,000 horsepower of energy is harnessed.'[117] Niemeyer's hybrid 'fountain façade' for one of the monuments of Brazil's 'city and park' portrayed nature and tech-

nology working 'hand in hand'. As already noted, the idea of a synthesis of industry and nature, such as that envisaged by Oswald de Andrade, had been firmly established at the centre of tropicalist Brazilian Modernism.[118]

The tall arches of the south elevation – originally semi-circular, like those of the loggia to the north – were modified in 1986 by Niemeyer himself to accompany the murmur of the water with a visual element of rippling movement. Movement is more forcefully suggested on the portico of the west elevation, where columns and *brises-soleil* merge into one architectural element, making the most of the region's potent sunlight to enhance visual impact. These giant, capricious *brises-soleil* set in concrete, irregularly spaced and of seemingly random widths, recall both Iannis Xenakis's *pans de verre ondulatoires* (undulating glazing) at Le Corbusier's Dominican monastery of La Tourette at Eveux-sur-l'Arbresle (1953–60) and the rows of concrete *brises-lumière* (light-breaks) of the chapel at Ronchamp. The dissonant concrete fins are reflected in the dark waters of the landscaped pool, from which they emerge like the buttressed roots of some huge trees on the banks of the Amazon. They dramatize effects of light and shadow, unlocking glimpses of the glass box behind the portico

Ministry of Justice, Brasília, 1962–70, modified 1986; view of the primary (south) elevation of the main pavilion set in a pool landscaped by Roberto Burle Marx

115 Niemeyer claims that his was the first 'fountain façade' as opposed to the Trevi's 'façade fountain'; Underwood, 1994b, p. 132.   116 Oscar Niemeyer, quoted in Katinsky, p. 32.   117 Bernadet, p. 554.   118 See Chapter One, pp. 25, 34 and Chapter Four, pp. 164–67.

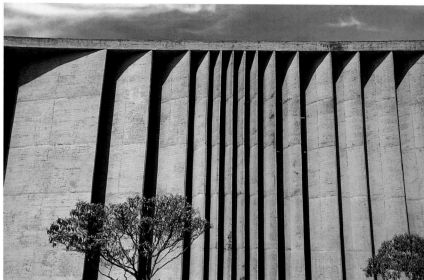

Ministry of Justice: close-up of west portico

Ministry of Justice: view of the main pavilion's west elevation with columns and *brises-soleil* merging into one architectural element

Le Corbusier, Dominican monastery of La Tourette, Eveux-sur-l'Arbresle, France, 1953–60: view of *pans de verre ondulatoires* designed by Iannis Xenakis

when viewed on the diagonal. Set at seemingly arbitrary angles, apparently pivoting but in fact static, they swing into rippling movement as the viewer walks by, magnifying, petrifying and thus granting monumentality to the effect produced by the familiar – and, by the time Brasília was built, ubiquitous – adjustable *brises-soleil*, an emblematic feature of Brazil's modern architecture. A zone of informal interaction is created in the cool, shaded area of the loggia near the entrance on this side, framed by luxuriant vegetation.

On the fourth (east) elevation, towards the Praça dos Três Poderes, the peristyle of the Ministry of Justice assumes its simplest configuration: six slender rectangular pillars rise at regular intervals, perpendicular to the façade. To negotiate the transition from one façade to the next, Niemeyer kept all corner intercolumnar spaces free of arches.

Similar effects have been conjured by Niemeyer, Burle Marx and Bulcão at the pavilion of the Palácio do Itamaraty on the south side of the Monumental Axis, which houses the ceremonial

Palácio do Itamaraty, originally named Palácio dos Arcos, Brasília 1962–70: view of the main pavilion set in a pool landscaped by Roberto Burle Marx

functions of the Ministry of Foreign Affairs, the General Secretariat and offices for the minister.[119] Originally named Palácio dos Arcos (Palace of the Arches) and recalling Le Corbusier's High Court at Chandigarh (1951–55), in March 1967 it adopted the popular designation of the seat of the Ministry of Foreign Affairs from 1899 to 1970 – a nineteenth-century Carioca mansion named after its first owner, Francisco José da Rocha, Count of Itamaraty. The arched openings of the Neoclassical mansion may have been intentionally echoed in the arched façades of Niemeyer's building. The second, nine-storey building of the Itamaraty complex is located to the rear of the iconic pavilion and has been nicknamed 'Yellow Submarine' because of the 8,649 yellow brises-soleil used to weave the canvas of its principal, north elevation. Library, archives, the Alexandre de Gusmão Foundation (FUNAG) and the Communications Sector have been accommodated in Annex II, a circular ziggurat built in the 1970s to Niemeyer's design, and nicknamed the 'Wedding Cake'.

With uncharacteristic modesty, Niemeyer refers to the main Itamaraty pavilion, a building of undeniable elegance and calm, as 'a correct, generous but commonplace solution . . . to please everybody'.[120] It appears to consist of a square glass box with minimal, uniform detailing, floating on a dark pool within a bare-concrete colonnaded structure that rises majestically from the reflective water surface, reaching one storey higher than the glazed cella. The top floor is deeply recessed and invisible from the viewpoint of the street so that the glass box appears independent of the concrete roof. The almost classical restraint is offset by sculptural refinement. Peristyle columns are the primary component of façade delineation here, reflecting the ideal of egalitarianism. They have a narrow wedge section, set perpendicular to the façades; the columns at the corners are set on the diagonal. They

119 This was the first time Roberto Burle Marx was invited to work in Brasília, by the minister of foreign affairs, Vladimir Murtinho.   120 Niemeyer, 1998, p. 22.

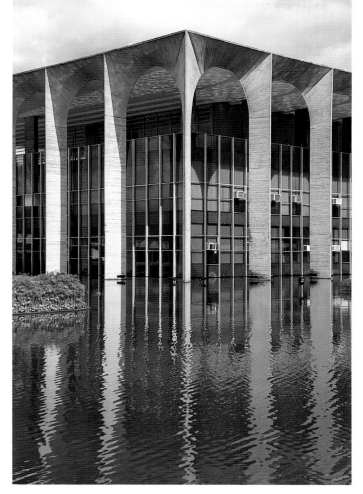

The ceremonial pavilion of the Palácio do Itamaraty consists of a glazed cella floating on a dark pool, surrounded by a bare-concrete peristyle.

are joined by shallow arches, also of a wedge section, integrated with the wedged edges of the roof overhangs. As a result, the roof appears paper thin; on the outermost planes of the pavilion, the concrete peristyle has been abstracted to a wire line diagram. The soffit appears to levitate at a tangent to the arches, and is painted white to reinforce the illusion. The corner arches are narrower and not perfectly arched, to correct optical distortion.

Palácio do Itamaraty; close-up of the exquisitely crafted concrete arcade

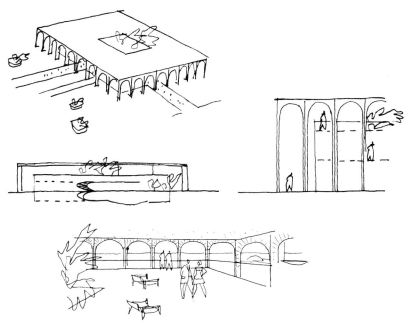

Palácio do Itamaraty, Brasília

Lightness is sustained as the central theme, achieved through inventive treatment of the raw concrete at a time when this material was primarily associated with Brutalist expression. In an imaginative inversion of expectations, the *béton brut* structure at the Palácio do Itamaraty, has been relieved of all weight and solidity and made to appear lighter than the glazed part of the building. The warm ochre-pigmented concrete has a striated surface that captures the light so as to enhance the desired effect. Once again undermining the reliable meaning of signs, Niemeyer's irreverent subversion of codes of material expression sought the kind of aesthetic sensation that results when the familiar relation between material and weight is rendered strange.

The visual and haptic qualities of the concrete surface have been achieved through skilful crafting of the timber shuttering in delicate strips, also conceived to conceal the casting seams. The strips were cut and numbered with extreme precision before a full-size mould was constructed. This treatment of bare concrete contrasts sharply with contemporaneous Brutalist applications, which treasured raw appearance and a surface scarred by crude formwork, harsh edges and even accidents and poor workmanship to connote authenticity, simplicity and stark purity. Niemeyer's approach to the naked surface of concrete is closer to Perret's: 'if we pay concrete the honour of cutting, hammering, chiselling and rusticating it,' the French architect argued, 'we obtain surfaces whose beauty is enough to alarm those whose business is to sell natural stone.'[121] All concrete was prepared by hand on site, using electric mixers and wheelbarrows.

121 Perret, p. 245.

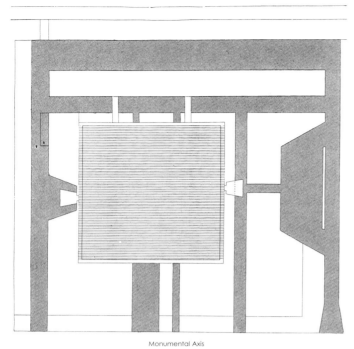

Monumental Axis

site plan

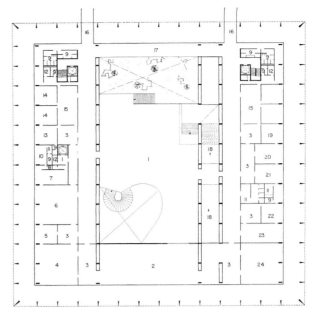

first floor plan

1 reception hall	9 toilets	17 corridor
2 treaty room	10 room	18 ramp
3 vestibule	11 cloakroom	19 vice chief of cabinet
4 ambassador	12 pantry	20 assembly room
5 chief of protocol	13 chief of cabinet	21 master of ceremonies
6 minister	14 officers	22 congress
7 minister's secretary	15 functionaries	23 general secretariat
8 telephone	16 administration corridor	24 salon

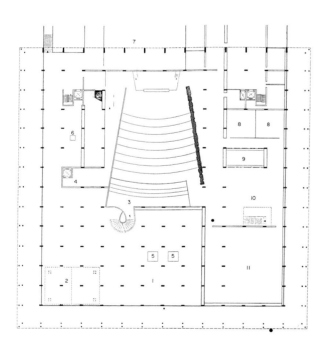

basement plan

1 plant room	
2 underground water tank	7 cloakroom
3 auditorium	8 assembly hall
4 minister's hall	9 secretariat
5 foundation for centrifuge	10 hall for members of congress
6 trapdoor to elevator machinery	11 reception room

Palácio do Itamaraty, Brasília

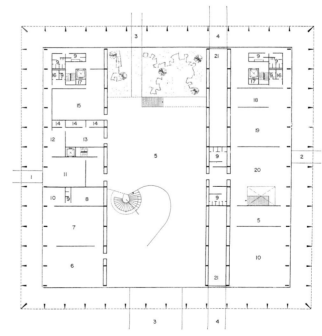

ground floor plan

1 minister's entrance	8 archives	15 cloakroom
2 entrance for congress members	9 toilets	16 pantry
3 public entrance	10 functionaries	17 waste disposal
4 ramp	11 minister's hall	18 bar
5 ceremonial lobby	12 administration	19 salon
6 exhibition	13 porter	20 hall for congress members
7 map storage	14 storage	21 ramp

The glass panes of the Palácio do Itamaraty's cella extend to form a parapet for the roof terrace. Behind them is concealed a row of load-bearing columns that appear on the roof terrace, sandwiched between two tropical-wood-veneered panels. Under the concrete pergola, at the centre of the roof, a garden by Burle Marx with sculptures by Maria Martins and Alfredo Ceschiatti appears to hover slightly above the white marble floor on a slim platform. The glass panes of the top-floor reception hall pivot vertically to unite inside and outside spaces. Burle Marx designed also the gardens on the small islands in the pool that surrounds the building, combining plants from the Amazon and the *cerrado*. Bruno Giorgi's *Meteor* sculpture (1967), also in the reflective pool, symbolizes the five continents.

On the ground floor a large, central, columnless, white marble hall is dominated by a wide, partially carpeted exposed-concrete stair that spirals sensually upwards, Niemeyer's affirmation of Auguste Perret's view of stairways as 'the mark of a civilization'.[122]

The curve of the stair is picked up by the overhanging slab of the first floor, which has an exposed-concrete rim, accentuating spatial fluidity. This staircase served as a cue for Bulcão's design (1966) for a white marble bas-relief covering the extensive blind walls of the ceremonial hall commissioned by Niemeyer with the explicit requirement to offset the vastness of the space. A series of vertical trapezoids of variable width and angles balance the horizontality of the space, introducing a human-scale element through an abstraction of the syncopated movement of the rotating and oscillating body moving gallantly up or down the blue carpet of Niemeyer's stair.[123] At the top of this stair, on gala nights, the foreign minister and the president of the republic receive foreign dignitaries. Niemeyer has stubbornly refused to add a rail-guard (the one installed in 1970 was soon removed); during state receptions, Itamaraty employees form a human rail-guard for the protection of Brazil's distinguished visitors. The design of the floor is also by Bulcão, with slabs of white marble in varying sizes from Minas Gerais. To the south, the hall overlooks an internal water garden by Burle Marx, with sculptures by Maria Martins and Zélia Salgado.

On the first floor, the wood-and-iron trellised parapet that Bulcão designed (1967) to divide the ceremonial hall and the treaty room consists of dense, irregularly spaced, vertical elements reminiscent of Xenakis's *pans de verre ondulatoires*. It offsets Niemeyer's long horizontal lines, introducing into the large space an intimate musical rhythm. Small white, black and red iron pieces playfully arranged between the vertical wooden slats break the continuity of the large screen, bringing together Brazil's celebrat-

122 Auguste Perret, quoted in Britton, p. 148.   123 Farias, p. 47.

Above and below: the vast marble lobby of the Palácio do Itamaraty is dominated by a ceremonial stairway, perhaps Niemeyer's most elegant and seductive. Its fluid helicoidal movement is picked up by the slab of the first floor, while its sculptural qualities and the delicacy of its exposed-concrete surface can be further appreciated by those descending to the auditorium in the basement.

ed 'three races'. The General Secretariat and the minister's office are also located on this floor. In the luxuriously finished ceremonial rooms the national colours have again been given prominence: blue and the green and yellow of the imperial flag, for the royal houses of Bragança and Habsburg, reinterpreted by the republic as symbolizing Brazilian forests and Brazilian gold. Music, more precisely the image of a 'wide singing space', guided the artist Fayga Ostrower in creating her masterpiece, *Itamaraty Polyptych* (1968), a monumental series of engravings commissioned for the building.[124] Throughout the building, antique furniture is combined with modern Brazilian designs, specially created for the Palácio do

Itamaraty, and a large number of artworks by Brazil's colonial and modern artists. The steel-and-leather furniture in the reception hall is by Oscar and Anna Maria Niemeyer. The dining suite in jacaranda is by Bernando de Figueiredo (1965). A white bas-relief by Rubem Valentim, a sculpture-altar with stylized elements inspired by the Candomblé religion, can be found in the auditorium lobby in the basement of the building.

The National Theatre and the Metropolitan Cathedral

In no other building is Athos Bulcão's sculptural intervention (1966) more prominent or better integrated with the architecture than at the National Theatre of Brasília (1958–81), built with Milton Ramos and technical adviser Aldo Calvo and positioned at the intersection of the Monumental and Highway-Residential axes, near the road platform, on the north side of the esplanade. The lateral (south), canted elevation of the building is entirely covered with rows of small concrete blocks of variable size, which take full advantage of Brasília's sharp light. The rhythmic play of white cubes and their shadows greets those passing by on foot or by car, inviting theatregoers up a concrete ramp that ascends to a hall, at ground-floor (foyer) level, from which two elevators lead directly to the terrace restaurant.

Niemeyer considered a number of alternative schemes for the two theatres required by the brief: a large one for opera and ballet performances, seating two thousand, and a smaller, five-hun-

124 Herkenhoff, 1993, pp. 53–54.

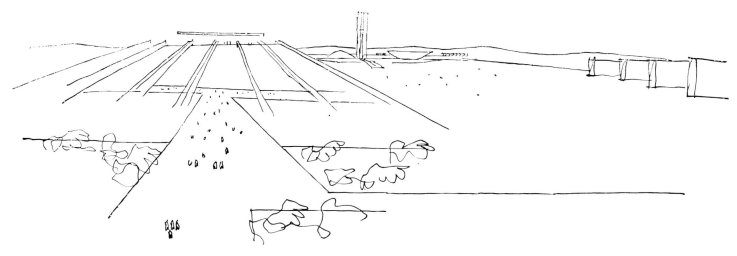

View of the west façade of the National Theatre with the National Congress in the distance. A bridge leads from the Highway-Residential Axis to the foyer of the larger of the two theatres housed in the building.

National Theatre, Brasília, 1958–81, at the intersection of the Monumental and Highway-Residential axes, set in Roberto Burle Marx's gardens, which pay homage to the flora of the *caatinga*: view of west and south façades

National Theatre: close-up of Athos Bulcão's concrete relief (1966) on the south elevation facing the Monumental Axis

dred-seat theatre. The final solution was inspired by Mies van der Rohe's 1953 project for the National Theatre of Mannheim. The two auditoria are set with their stages back to back in a single volume, a pyramidal frustum with a trapezoidal base, framed by gardens of cacti and other succulent plants – Burle Marx's homage to the flora of the *caatinga*, the arid region of the Northeast. Four levels have been sunk below ground to avoid creating a large built mass that would cause undesirable visual interference and alter the proportions of Costa's plan. The two theatres may be used separately or combined into a single space. Niemeyer was particularly concerned to devise a system that would make it possible

to vary the size of the stage, extending it around the audience 'so as to integrate [theatregoers] within the performance, thus avoiding the division that still persists between actor and spectator and furnishing actors and stage designers with a new field for professional speculation'.[125] Unfortunately, the theatres have disappointed in terms of their acoustic performance.

The main entrance for the large theatre is on the west façade, via a bridge leading from the Highway-Residential Axis to a spacious foyer, open on two levels, with lush tropical gardens under a

125 Oscar Niemeyer, quoted in Stäubli, p. 105.

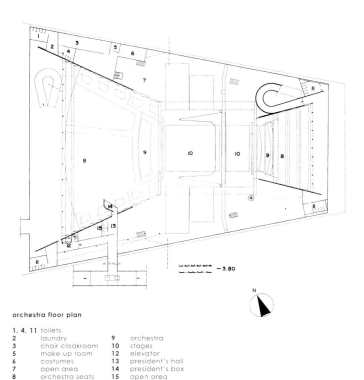

orchestra floor plan

1, 4, 11	toilets	9	orchestra
2	laundry	10	stages
3	choir cloakroom	12	elevator
5	make-up room	13	president's hall
6	costumes	14	president's box
7	open area	15	open area
8	orchestra seats		

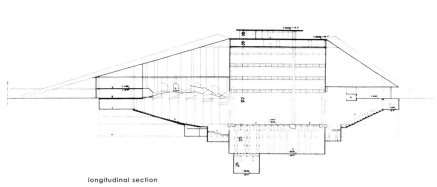

longitudinal section

A	exhibition gallery	G	light controls
B	foyer	H	stage elevators
C	foyer	I	kitchen
D	orchestra floor	J	restaurant
E	stages	K	artists' lounge
F	orchestra		

National Theatre, Brasília

National Theatre: foyer of the larger theatre, under a sloping glass roof, with tropical gardens by Roberto Burle Marx and staircase leading to the exhibition gallery on the mezzanine

sloping glass roof. Sculptural incident is provided in the shape of a wide, spiralling staircase – Niemeyer's ubiquitous catwalk, with its comfortable concrete treads, partly lined in carpet, unfolding into a three-dimensional fan around a circular column. The green carpet amplifies the fan-like visual effect of the stair and conceals a concrete beam, making the treads appear to float in mid-space. It also serves as Niemeyer's minimal means of protecting the users of his sculptural stairway by suggesting they keep a distance from the hazardous unbalustered edge. A similar arrangement on the east side of the pyramid serves the smaller theatre. The president's box in the large theatre is entered through an underground pas-

sage accessed by car on the south side of the building. Atop the truncated pyramid, Niemeyer positioned a symbolic citizens' box: a glass pavilion restaurant under an overhanging flat roof with an open terrace on three sides, surveying Brazil's monumental theatre of government.

Brasília's Metropolitan Cathedral of Nossa Senhora Aparecida (structural engineer Joaquim Cardozo, construction manager Carlos Magalhães da Silveira), on the south side of the esplanade, beyond the row of ministries, was designed in 1958, entered into the Conservation Registry in 1967, consecrated and inaugurated on 31 May 1970 and refurbished in 1987. As already indicated, the cathedral pays homage to the highly theatrical, 'essentially Brazilian', eighteenth-century ecclesiastical architecture of Minas Gerais – the Barroco Mineiro.[126] Yet, for no other Brasília monument do Niemeyer's words ring truer: 'The quest for an original solution obsessed me.' He confides that he took particular delight in making the centrally planned cathedral of Brazil's new federal capital 'different from all the cathedrals yet built'.

Niemeyer wrought his magic in weaving together the earth of Brasília with the programme of the Roman Catholic cathedral. Disregarding normative typologies, he submerged all internal spaces underground, blurring the contours of the building programme and incorporating the limitless, firm horizon of Brasília in the building of its most important church. Renouncing the need for a principal façade, he sought a solution 'which could be

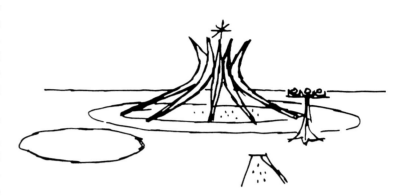

Metropolitan Cathedral of Nossa Senhora Aparecida, Brasília, 1958–71, refurbished 1987

Metropolitan Cathedral of Nossa Senhora Aparecida

approached from any angle with the same purity of vision'.[127] Brasília's cathedral absorbs the urban space around it and is, in turn, absorbed by the city Kubitschek likened to a cathedral.

Locating the earth-bound part of the programme underground also allowed for a manipulation of the building's apparent scale in such a way as to affirm the secondary role of religion in a secular modern state, without compromising the cathedral's magnitude and monumentality. The pilgrims who arrive at the large plaza prescribed by Costa's plan find themselves already atop the city's holiest building, surrounded by the distinctive silhouette of its central dome, the cupola of the baptistery, smaller structures that signal stair routes to the baptistery and the sacristy, and the sculptural belfry. The latter resembles a rake that ploughs the sky, Brasília's second earth to be cultivated, pregnant with the prom-

ise of fertility. There are, of course, historical precedents for promenade spaces on the roofs of cathedral buildings. Atop Brasília's cathedral, however, there are no gargoyles gleefully awakening the dormant conscience of sinners; for, in the old Portuguese saying, 'beneath the equator there is no sin'.

The art historian Leopoldo Castedo regards Niemeyer's 'revolt against functionalism' and ability to 'relentlessly attack the conventional' as characteristics of a Baroque sensibility.[128] Without resorting to historical motifs, Niemeyer used explicit references to historic precedents to enhance the legibility and effectiveness of his unorthodox tactics, increasing the potency of the cathedral's

126 Tarsila do Amaral, quoted in Schwartz, p. 541. 127 Niemeyer, 'Cathedral of Brasília', in *Oscar Niemeyer: Notebooks of the Architect*, n.p. 128 Castedo, p. 108.

dissonant elements. His iconoclastic denunciation of received typologies is based on in-depth understanding of historical models, clearly connoted and then ingeniously subverted. In a passage on centrally planned Baroque churches, Paul Frankl comments: 'All entrances are necessary evils. We are not supposed to enter such a church slowly and approach its centre step by step. We are supposed, as if by magic, to arrive with one bound at this central point.'[129] Alfredo Ceschiatti's four evangelists, three to the left and one to the right, mark the Via Crucis (Sacred Way) to the Metropolitan Cathedral, set perpendicular to the Monumental Axis. In Brasília, however, Niemeyer has audaciously inverted the penitent's arduous ascent along Aleijadinho's steep Via Crucis at the eighteenth-century Santuário do Bom Jesus de Matosinhos in Congonhas do Campo, venerated by modern Brazil's heritage builders: a gentle descent leads 3 metres below ground level into a dark narthex, from which the worshipper rapidly emerges into the brightest church nave ever conceived. And, in the Brazilian tradition of expressions of faith, which favours direct communication with the divine, believers are offered 'the unique possibility . . . to look through the transparent glass, watching the infinite space, where they believe the Lord to be'.[130]

Niemeyer contrasts the light-filled central space of Brasília's cathedral – a sort of hybrid of nave and cloister – to 'the old dark cathedrals reminding us of sin'.[131] Launching a second assault against an architectural – and theological – tradition that puts excessive emphasis on sin or the 'fall', exalting the soul while degrading the body, Niemeyer reaffirmed the Antropofagist 'refus[al] to conceive a spirit without a body', challenging the religious rhetoric that provided the ideology for the conquest of the New World and justification for the enslavement of Africans.[132] Brasília's cathedral of light and happiness denies a radical separation between the sacred and the profane, revalorizing that other, 'native, lyric, and festive Christianity' exalted by Gilberto Freyre, echoing the joyous atmosphere of those 'mulatto' religious festivals that horrified nineteenth-century European travellers like Prince Ferdinand Maximilian.[133] 'I did not want to repeat the traditional contrast (bright exterior and shadowy interior) of earlier cathedrals, which evokes an atmosphere of penitence and punishment,' Niemeyer asserts. 'On the contrary, I wanted visitors, entering the nave after passing through the dark gallery, to experience the contrast between light and colour, a feeling of peace and hope.'

In Brasília, hope and redemption are close at hand. While the city's secular monuments float free of their earthly moorings, the cathedral is earthborn, its heavenly dome lowered to the level of the approaching believers, rather than aspired to from far below,

Metropolitan Cathedral: Alfredo Ceschiatti's statues of the evangelists mark the Via Crucis to the ramp that descends into the underground narthex

The light-filled nave of the metropolitan cathedral: view towards the altar. The stained-glass panels between the concrete ribs are by Marianne Peretti and the suspended angels by Alfredo Ceschiatti.

129 Frankl, p. 28.   130 Niemeyer, 2000a, p. 43.   131 Niemeyer, 2000b, p. 173.   132 Oswald de Andrade, 2000, p. 591.   133 Freyre, 1956, p. 239; Schwarcz, 2004, pp. 198–211.

only at the last minute respectfully set apart, floating in purifying water. 'I had to build a cathedral which would not need crosses or saints to symbolize the "House of God",' says Niemeyer. 'I remembered cathedrals of the past, each reflecting the progress of the epoch in which they were built, conquering space with daring structures.'[134] Celebrating Brazil's technological progress, as does Brasília itself, the cathedral's concrete dome 'bloomed like a flower in the middle of the desert . . . dressed in the whimsical fashion of my architecture'.[135]

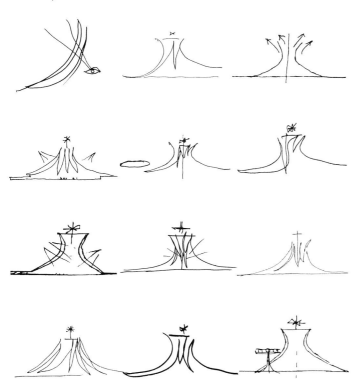

Metropolitan Cathedral, Brasília

Metropolitan Cathedral: view of the dome and the sculptural belfry

At once concise and exuberant, the cathedral is composed of sixteen elegantly tapered concrete legs (Niemeyer had initially proposed twenty-one), joined together by a concrete disc and extending above it, reaching for the sky. They are held in place by a concrete ring beam, 70 metres in diameter, concealed below the shallow pool. These pre-cast structural elements became the cathedral's primary carriers of function and meaning, redolent with multiple associations. In order to express 'a religious idea, a moment of prayer', Niemeyer says, they rise upwards 'in a gesture of calling and communication'.[136] For Niemeyer, as for Perret before him, 'It is the skeleton in reinforced concrete, designed so as to remain visible in the interior as on the exterior, that adorns the building.'[137] According to Paulo Mendes da Rocha, the dome of Brasília's cathedral is Brunelleschi's Florentine dome inverted.[138] It is also said to conjure images of hands clasped in prayer, Christ's crown of thorns, the Queen of Heaven, the Eucharistic chalice, or the arched ribs and flying buttresses of Gothic architecture.[139] To these might be added the symbolism of the centre of the world, where the three cosmic levels – earth, heaven and underworld – meet. Niemeyer's early sketches suggest the cosmological image of the sacred mountain, an *axis mundi* connecting heaven and earth.

The ribbed concrete-and-glass dome over the circular nave demonstrates with the greatest clarity Niemeyer's search for 'a clear and beautiful structural form that would define and distinguish [Brasília's] main buildings', exemplifying his favourite adage: 'after the . . . structures were finished, architecture was already present'.[140] The construction of the Metropolitan Cathedral was financed solely by contributions from the faithful. As these took a long time to reach the required level, the sun-drenched nave remained literally open to the sky and passing clouds, as in Niemeyer's early sketches, until 1971, when stained-glass panels designed by Marianne Peretti to span the distance between the concrete ribs were finally installed. The pool of water serves both symbolic and practical functions, protecting the glazed parts of the dome from activities such as children's play, which other, more rigid structures such as Niemeyer's theatre pyramid or his Paulista 'Oca' at the Ibirapuera Park consciously invite. The original 2,200 square metres of glass panel, a modern interpretation of the monumental painted ceilings of eighteenth-century Brazilian Baroque churches, were modified by the artist in 1987, when

134 Niemeyer, 'Cathedral of Brasília', in *Oscar Niemeyer: Notebooks of the Architect*, n.p.   **135** Niemeyer, 2000b, p. 123.   **136** Niemeyer, 1975b, p. 313.   **137** Auguste Perret, quoted in Britton, p. 150.   **138** Paulo Mendes da Rocha, 2006.   **139** Niemeyer denies he ever intended such literal associations, just as he denies he ever intended the suggestions aroused by the Alvorada colonnades. But, as Eero Saarinen said in relation to the images evoked by his TWA Terminal, 'that doesn't mean that one doesn't have the right to see it that way, or to explain it to laymen in those terms, especially because laymen are usually more literally than visually inclined'; quoted in Merkel, p. 210.   **140** Niemeyer, 1960; Niemeyer, 1992, p. 126.

Metropolitan Cathedral: the bundle of sixteen sickle-shaped concrete ribs rises from a concrete ring beam, 70 metres in diameter, resting on concrete piles. The white marble-lined walls and floor are united in a single element. The underground passageway leads to the sacristy.

Niemeyer directed restoration work at the cathedral, which included coating the concrete ribs with protective white paint. Although the problems of the original glass panels have been partially solved, the latest ones remain prone to breakage, as they do not adequately resist wind forces.

A minimal white iron cross marks the summit of Brasília's cosmic mountain. Inside the vast circular nave, holding four thousand people, the marble-paved floor curls upwards so that floor and walls are united in a single element, preserving the predominance of the 40-metre-high dome and thus symbolically assuring communication with the transcendental world. The conceptual elimination of the nave walls allows for direct passage from the initiatory darkness of the narthex into the space of the celestial dome, directly connecting the earthly with the heavenly realm. White marble enhances the luminosity of the nave, while also linking the cathedral architecturally to Brasília's other major buildings.

Secondary elements on the plaza clearly defer to the main architectural event of the translucent central dome. The egg-shaped opaque concrete cupola of the baptistery, also painted white, stands at a distance, to the east of the monumental, concrete-and-glass dome. The baptistery may be accessed via an external white marble spiral stair or from the circular nave via a subterranean passage. A symmetrical passage leads to the sacristy. Athos Bulcão's blue, green and white polished tiles (1977) animate the sober, relatively dark interior of the baptistery, clearly contrasting with the luminous space where the initiated congregate. A residence for Brasília's archbishop is currently under con-

struction in the vicinity of the cathedral, also submerged below ground, in accordance with the original plan and in collaboration with Carlos Magalhães and Fernando de Andrade.

Brasília's Residential Horizon and the Life of the Pilotis

Lilia Moritz Schwarcz argues that, from the eighteenth century in Brazil, '"civilization" led to a growing division between the public and private spheres'.[141] The 'civilizing' urban operations that transformed Rio de Janeiro during the first half of the twentieth century effected the spatialization of this division. In Brasília, such a division was planned from the beginning, in accordance with the principles of zoning defined in the Athens Charter by CIAM (the Congrès Internationaux d'Architecture Moderne). Lúcio Costa's 'Report' prescribed:

A continuous sequence of large [quadras][142] set in double or single lines along both sides of the residential highway axis, each surrounded by rows of large trees. For each [quadra] one particular type of tree would be chosen, the ground would be sown with grass and, on the inner approaches, an additional curtain of bushes and shrubbery, to make them seem to merge into the scenery, would be planted to protect the residential area on all sides from the view of passers-by (figure 13) . . .

Within these 'super-quadras' the residential buildings themselves could be designed in many ways provided that two general principles are always observed: a maximum uniform height (possibly six stories raised on pillars) and separation of vehicular and pedestrian traffic, particularly in the approaches to the primary school and the local shopping centers existing in each [quadra] (figure 8).

On the far side of the [quadras] runs the service highway for truck traffic and a strip along the other side of that highway is reserved for the installation of garages, repair shops, wholesale warehouses, etc. Beyond these utilities another strip of land is set aside, equivalent to a third row of [quadras], for flower and vegetable gardens and orchards. Churches, high schools, cinemas and retail stores have been placed on broad strips which join the service and residential axis highways at intervals and are served alternately by one or the other . . .

Social gradation can easily be regulated by giving a higher value to certain [quadras], as, for example, the single

141 Schwarcz, 2004, p. 147.   **142** Brasília's residential block complexes are known as 'superquadras', a term introduced by Costa's 'Report'. In it, however, he uses mostly the term 'quadra' to refer to these complexes. To avoid further confusion, in the above quotation, the translator's 'square' has been replaced with Costa's 'quadra'.

[*quadras*] bordering on the embassy sector . . . Along the residential highway axis, the [*quadras*] closer to the highway will naturally be valued more highly than the inner [*quadras*], which will permit gradations proper to the [*quadras*] in sets of four and will lead to a certain degree of social coexistence and thus avoid undue and undesirable class distinctions. Furthermore, big differences in standards between one [*quadra*] and another will be neutralized by the urbanization plan proposed and would not in any case prevent any of them from possessing the social comforts to which all are entitled. Such differences will be the result only of a greater or lesser population density, of more or less space attributed to each individual and each family and of the choice of materials and the degree and quality of finishing . . .

Isolated sectors have also been foreseen, surrounded by trees and open countryside, to be sold in lots for private homes. It is suggested that the layout here be of saw-toothed lots, so that the houses built on the corner lots will stand out in the landscape well separated from each other; this layout will not impede independent service access to all the lots (figure 15). Also foreseen is the eventual construction of individual houses with a high architectural standard – regardless of their size – but in such cases it will be obligatory to space the houses at least one kilometer . . . from each other to accentuate the exceptional nature of such concessions.[143]

Brasília's planner held the *superquadra*, Brasília's complex of residential slabs, as his most important achievement in the new federal capital.[144] They were conceived to be three times larger than the usual city block – each measuring 280 × 280 metres, with a buildable area of 240 × 240 metres, and three thousand inhabitants – in an attempt 'to reconcile [the] broad and generous scale [of the Monumental Axis] with the scale of daily life . . . that is far more intimate', thereby preventing the city from 'being divided in two'.[145]

According to Costa, the precursor of Brasília's apartment blocks is to be found in his Parque Guinle six-storey residential slabs on *pilotis* in Rio de Janeiro (1948–54) – a radically humanized version of Le Corbusier's Unité d'Habitation in Marseilles, 'reduced . . . to the scale of the individual, closer to the ground and more in agreement with our tradition'.[146] The Pessoa Commission's 1955 plan of Vera Cruz had also separated the functions of the city, in accordance with the principles of the Athens Charter, and had proposed to house the population of the 'future capital of Brazil'

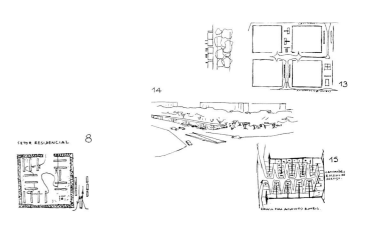

1   Square of the Three Powers
2   Esplanade of the ministries
3   Cultural sector
4   Public service centre
5   Banking sector
6   Bus platform
7   Amusement sector
8   Business sector
9   Hospitals
10 Hotels
11 Television tower
12 Conference centre
13 Sports sector
14 Buriti square
15 Cemetery
16 Airport
17 Residential sector
18 University
19 Embassies
20 Parks

A   Presidential Palace
B   Supreme Court
C   National Congress
D   Ministry of Justice
E   Ministry of Foreign Affairs
F   Pantheon of the Country Tancredo Neves
G   Cathedral
H   Presidential Residence

Brasília: Plano Piloto with residential areas along the shores of Lake Paranoá

143 Lúcio Costa, 1966, pp. 15–16.   **144** El-Dahdah, p. 11.   **145** Zapatel, p. 19.   **146** Lúcio Costa, 'Parque Guinle' (1940s), in Lúcio Costa, 1997, p. 205. His unrealized projects for a workers' town in Monlevade (1934) and the university campus in Rio de Janeiro have also been put forward by Costa as forerunners of the *superquadra*; see Nobre, pp. 33–39.

Lúcio Costa, sketches illustrating the 'Report' supporting his Plano Piloto: residential units or *superquadras* (figure 8) with uniform apartment slabs of six storeys on *pilotis* and separation of vehicular and pedestrian traffic (figure 13), surrounded by rows of large trees (figure 14). Every four *superquadras* form a 'neighbourhood unit' (figure 13). The Plano Piloto included isolated sectors of private single-family houses (figure 15).

in 'large *quadras*' of 1 square kilometre, each accommodating five thousand inhabitants. The document that accompanied the plan of Vera Cruz explained: 'following Le Corbusier, we must separate the pedestrian from the infernal traffic of motor cars, which circulate freely. The distances the pedestrian will have to travel within the *quadras* do not exceed 250 metres'. The planners of Vera Cruz envisaged the subdivision of the *quadras* in smaller units and the inclusion of 'free spaces for schools, gardens, leisure activities and small shops (neighbourhood unit)'.[147] Costa never acknowledged the Pessoa Commission's plan as a precursor of Brasília.

He clearly indicates that his Brasília apartments on *pilotis* were not meant to keep residents away from the evils Le Corbusier found on the ground – 'the noise, the dust, and the dog droppings' – but to free the ground, and lay a green carpet on it, 'in the English manner . . . on which people can lay [sic] down, set up their chairs, stretch out, hang out, exercise, and play at leisure'.[148] Maria Elisa Costa has computed that the *superquadras* offer an average green area of 85 square metres per apartment or 17 square metres per resident.[149] They have certainly become the most lively areas of the city, especially during lunch and dinner times, when Brasília's life buzzes around their seemingly endless array of eateries.

Lúcio Costa explicitly contrasted the *superquadras* with 'closed-off, gated, and privatized "enclaves"'.[150] Their unprogrammatic green areas were envisaged as spaces of 'total freedom', with no fences or doormen, forging a reconciliation between private and public domains, promoting new modes of collective living and interaction between the residents. Maria Elisa Costa suggests that 'Brasília's residential scale offers a compelling alternative to conventional cities'. Residents identify with their *superquadras* as they would identify with their street in a conventional city: they say '"my superquadra" just as they would say "my street."'[151] Already in 1962, David Crease reported that, in Brasília's *superquadras*,

> the ground, in fact, is the community centre; informal social life, the street-corner and front-window life so essential to the Latin tradition, is . . . transformed into the life of the *pilotis* . . .
>
> There is a sense of urban texture rather than of urban enclosure; the animation of the traditional street and square is there, but has gained in the second dimension, spreading loosely among the abstract geometry of the buildings.

He also observed that, at times of festival, the 'lucky minority' inhabiting the *superquadras*, who had arrived in Brasília from all parts of the country, came to celebrate together in these common spaces. And these lively festivals reflected a 'fusion [from which] a new and truly national culture [was] hesitantly emerging'.[152]

Costa was particularly concerned to create a 'sensation of total freedom' in the residential areas, avoiding rigid lines within and between the *superquadras*, employing rows of trees to demarcate their limits – a 20-metre-wide 'wall of foliage that . . . sways in the wind, that breathes, and that you can see through' – and planning adequate space for children's play so that they 'remain naturally under control'. According to the Plano Piloto, which the first constructed *superquadras* respected, each *superquadra* with 2,500 to 3,000 residents was equipped with a convenience store, a *jardim da infância* (nursery) and an *escola-classe* (primary school), accessible from all apartments without crossing a street – a powerful reference point for the community.

Lúcio Costa showing the model of a 'neighbourhood unit' to Mies van der Rohe, at the office of NOVACAP, in the Ministry of Education and Public Health, Rio de Janeiro, 1957

147 Comissão de Localização da Nova Capital Federal, 'Memorial do estudo preliminar para a cidade de Vera Cruz, futura capital do Brasil, apresentado pelos engenheiros Raul Penna Firme, Roberto Lacombe e José Oliveira Reis' (2 June 1955), quoted in Vidal, p. 192.   148 Le Corbusier, quoted in Peter, p. 143; Lúcio Costa, quoted in Zapatel, p. 21.   149 Maria Elisa Costa, 2005, p. 30.   150 Lúcio Costa, quoted in Gorovitz, p. 42.   151 Maria Elisa Costa, 2005, p. 31.   152 Crease, 1962, p. 261.

Aerial view of Brasília's *superquadras*

The Plano Piloto included 98 *superquadras*, later increased to 120, arranged along the two 6-kilometre wings of the arched Residential Axis in three parallel rows, one to the east (numbered in even hundreds) and two to the west (in odd hundreds). A fourth row provided low-income housing. Uniform in height, density (limited by law to 15 per cent) and architectural treatment, the *superquadras* were conceived to create a second, residential horizon in Brasília, at a human scale, with a rhythmic pattern of built volumes and trees – of the same height as buildings when mature – and in dialogue with the civic horizon of the Monumental Axis.

Every four *superquadras* were to form a 'neighbourhood unit', based on the model of the Athens Charter, with an adjacent zone termed *entrequadra* – an area of 'social coexistence' to help overcome 'undue and undesirable class distinctions'. The *entrequadras* were equipped with community amenities such as

churches, cinemas, health centres, sports clubs, community centres, post offices, police stations, car service stations and two-storey shop strips facing the *superquadras*. According to a visionary programme designed by pioneer educationalist Anísio Teixeira as an exemplary model for education throughout the country, full-day *escolas-parque*, one for each neighbourhood unit, complemented the *escolas-classe* with a programme of cultural, art and craft activities. In 1992, Costa admitted that 'services were very well planned, but then were set aside by city administrators'.[153] Only one *entrequadra* was developed as intended. By 1962, Brasília was already the Brazilian city with the highest proportion of vehicles. The residential highway was meant to provide Brasília's residents with easy access to work, free of the traffic jams that befell Rio de Janeiro.

153 Lúcio Costa, quoted in El-Dahdah, pp. 19–22.

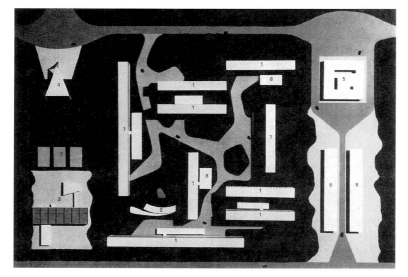

1 apartment block
2 escola-classe
3 escola-parque
4 church
5 cinema
6 shops
7 sports
8 nursery

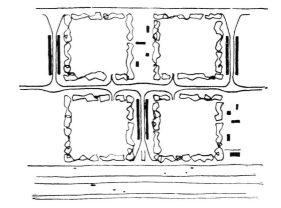

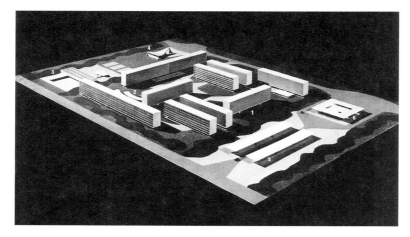

Model of superquadra with adjacent *entrequadra*

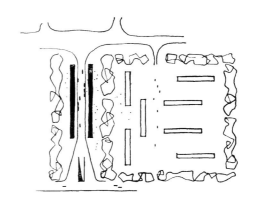

Brasília's *superquadras* under construction

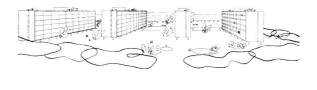

Niemeyer's sketches for a 'neighbourhood unit'

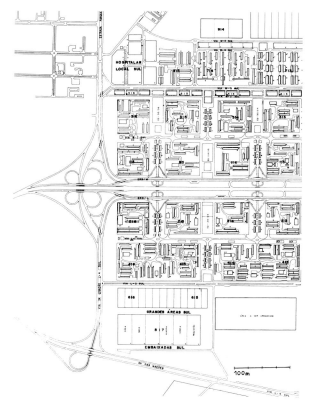

Plan of *superquadras* built at the end of Asa Sul (South Wing)

contravention of the Plano Piloto's stipulation that the lakeside area remain public property, reserved for sports and entertainment facilities, 'to preserve its natural beauty intact, landscaping it with woods and fields in a natural and rustic manner so that all the urban population can enjoy its simple pleasures'.[155]

Reporting on her 1960 visit to Brasília, guided by Niemeyer himself, Simone de Beauvoir expressed admiration for Niemeyer's public buildings, where 'one escapes – at last! – from the functional', but was not impressed by the city's residential sector:

> In any case, what possible interest could there be in wandering about these six- or eight-storey quadra and super quadra, raised on stilts and all, despite superficial variations, exuding the same air of elegant monotony? . . . the street, that meeting-ground of riverside dwellers and passers-by, of stores and houses, of vehicles and pedestrians – thanks to the capricious, always unexpectedly changing mixture – the street, as fascinating in Chicago as in Rome, in London as in Peking, in Bahia as in Rio, sometimes deserted and dreaming, but alive even in its silence, the street does not exist in Brasília and never will . . . While he was with us, Niemeyer sadly wondered out loud: 'Is it possible to create Socialist architecture in a non-Socialist country?'; he answered his own question: 'Obviously not.' Social segregation here is more radical than in any other city, since there are luxury blocks, middle-income blocks and low-income blocks. The people who live in them do not mix.[156]

The proposed maximum building height of six storeys on *pilotis* – 'the height of buildings prior to the advent of elevators', as Costa pointed out – was adhered to for the main housing blocks, eleven per *superquadra* on average, as in Costa's initial sketches. Designated by letters, these had a footprint of 12 × 80 metres with six to twelve apartments per floor. As well as rows of low-income, three-storey apartment houses, the *superquadras* were complemented by rows of family houses one, two or three storeys high. Niemeyer developed prototypes for this sort of housing for the Fundação de Casa Popular (Popular Housing Foundation) and the Caixa Econômica (National Savings Bank).

Despite Costa's egalitarian discourse, by 1962, it was reported that a clear spatial separation of classes was in place, 'with "laboring classes" in satellite towns, "middle and junior ranks of government and business" in the superblocks of the Plano Piloto, and an "elite" decamped to lakeside residential subdivisions'.[154] The latter inhabited individually designed detached houses in

De Beauvoir echoes James Holston's forty-four-page-long lament on 'The Death of the Street' – the term 'street' does not feature at all in Costa's 'Report', as Holston observes – and the disorientation this elimination produces in Brasília. The Modernist 'elimination of the figural street' and the privileging of open space result, according to Holston, in an inversion 'of the entire mode of perceiving architecture', breaking with 'the baroque planning convention of figure and ground'. Holston argues that Brasília's first settlers, inhabitants of the *superquadras* of Asa Sul (South Wing), adapted the plan to their needs, rejecting the garden entrances to commercial units and converting their service entrances into shop fronts, thus transforming prescribed service zones along vehicular roads into traditional shopping streets. 'As a result', he concludes, 'habit reproduced the street in practice where it had been architecturally denied.'[157]

According to Crease's 1962 report, however, the inversion analyzed by Holston was not the result of spontaneous rejection of

154 Vale, p. 121, quoting David Snyder. Alex Shoumatoff reported that José Aparecido de Oliveira, federal district governor from 1985 to 1988, 'determined to straighten things out. He invited the triumvirate who had created the city – Niemeyer, Costa, and Burle Marx – to come back and rectify the situation . . . Niemeyer set himself up in an office in the Buriti Palace [the seat of government of the federal district] and launched an attack on the privatization by the rich of the city's public land . . . Niemeyer planned to give the lakeshore back to the people by putting in a bicycle path all the way around the lake, even if it meant displacing

the *churrascarias*, or barbecue pits, in the backyards of the ambassadors' residences. An international furor erupted over the proposed bikeway, but in the end Niemeyer and Aparecido had their way. At the same time the governor clamped down on 170 illegal *loteamentos* that had invaded the capital's greenbelt. Many of the lots had ex-generals as their figureheads – the sort of *mordomia*, or cronyism, that has plagued the growth and development of Brasília'; Shoumatoff, pp. 210–11. **155** Lúcio Costa, 1966, p. 16. **156** Beauvoir, p. 565. **157** Holston, pp. 101–44.

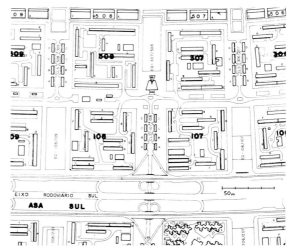

Neighbourhood unit of Superquadras Sul (SQS) 107, 108, 307 and 308, 1958–59, built according to the prescriptions of the Plano Piloto

Departamento de Arquitetura da NOVACAP, *Escola-Classe*, Superquadra Sul 308, Brasília, 1957–59, photograph of 1961. This was the first primary school constructed in Brasília.

the garden shop entrances but of the need for these shops to serve the row of houses built for the employees of NOVACAP along the west side of the South Wing. Avenue W3 (Sul), between these single-storey houses and the shops of the South Wing, became a busy commercial street in place of the minor service road originally to the rear of the shops.[158] Eventually, however, this inversion became the rule as residents naturally opted for greater choice and free movement between shops, cafés and restaurants beyond those of their own *superquadra*.

On 21 April 1960, 94 blocks, 500 single-storey and 222 two-storey houses had been completed within the *superquadras*, complemented with schools and shopping facilities.[159] The neighbourhood unit of Superquadras Sul (SQS) 107, 108, 307 and 308 was fully operative, and included the Chapel of Nossa Senhora de Fátima, more intimately known as 'Igrejinha' ('Little Church'), a nursery, an *escola-classe*, an *escola-parque* with theatre, a health centre, shops and the elegant, ox-blood-red Cine Brasília (1960) – Niemeyer's first cinema for Brasília.

Designed by Niemeyer, the SQS 107 and 108 (1958–59) defined the typology of the residential slabs constructed by NOVACAP, aiming to give a uniform appearance, and impart formal purity to the living quarters of the new capital (compromised by recent developments promoted by building speculators, especially in the North Wing). Their formal simplicity was conceived in contrast to the monumental architecture of Brasília's public build-

158 Crease, 1962, p. 262.   **159** Evenson, 1973, p. 163.

ings, with its highly figurative content. The SQS 308 (1959) was designed by Sérgio Rocha and Marcelo Graça Couto Campelo with José Ricardo Abreu and Luiz Acioli for the architects of the Banco Central do Brasil. Its façade is cut by continuous horizontal strips formed by opaque elements below the rows of glazing, accentuated by colour and directly linked to Costa's Nova Cintra apartment block in Parque Guinle, Rio de Janeiro. It benefits from landscaped gardens by Burle Marx and tile murals by Athos Bulcão and remains one of the city's favourite addresses.

Comparing the floor plan of the SQS 308 with that of Niemeyer's SQS 108, James Holston points out fundamental differences. While the first adopted the plan typical of twentieth-century middle- to upper-middle-income family apartments in residential blocks throughout other Brazilian cities, thus reproducing the status quo, Niemeyer attempted to effect a rupture with the past, introducing 'changes in residential planning as a means of changing residential organization' and destabilizing traditional patterns of Brazilian domestic life. Following the established model, the SQS 308 provided separate entrances and circulation systems for masters and servants. The 'public' zone of each flat is entered through a hall accessed by the 'social' elevator, while a service elevator leads to a service corridor with laundry facilities and doors to maids' chambers with shower room and kitchen. In accordance with the organization model of the casa grande, signifying higher social status (and increasing property value), in larger apartments, kitchens are well distanced from the social and intimate areas, with a copa – a space of informal gathering and interaction, similar to the back room of the English Victorian terrace house – mediating between the masters' and servants' quarters.

As at his own first house in Rio de Janeiro almost twenty years earlier, Niemeyer proposed a common entrance for each block and, although he included a separate service elevator, he eliminated service corridors and thus separate circulation systems for the two classes of inhabitant, providing each apartment with a single entrance. Niemeyer's maids' rooms are 'so small as to discourage habitation' – a device that may be partly responsible for many Brasília families replacing live-in maids with day maids. Significantly, Niemeyer also did away with the copa, encouraging full use of the public areas of the house, following free-planning principles. Holston postulates that Niemeyer sought 'to sabotage customary practices in the stratified divisions of domestic space and social relations . . . tr[ying] to make people recognize these devices through the experience of inconvenience and absurd juxtaposition'.[160] The elimination of balconies in the early superquadras is also consistent with Costa's objective of encouraging use of the neighbourhood facilities and common green areas, fostering collective living. Confirming Niemeyer's observation that the society of Brasília was 'still that of the past', however, his maids' rooms were still used to confine servants to 'little better

than prison cells', and the residents of his superquadras found it difficult to abandon customary social and living practices.[161]

What distinguishes Brasília's apartment blocks from those of other Brazilian cities is that the segregated service areas traditionally concealed within interior courts are fully exposed in Brasília to public view, located as they are along one of each block's two long elevations (the two narrow elevations are blind). The 'problem' was addressed through the shielding of the entire service façades behind combogó screens, yet these serve only to highlight the somewhat unintended inversion, drawing attention to, both concealing and revealing, that side of Brazilian domestic life that those who can afford it prefer to keep hidden. With notable exceptions, the heavily screened façades and arrangement of the blocks back to back compromised natural ventilation and lighting, giving preference to social and cultural needs over climatic ones, turning solar-shading systems to social-shading ones.

On the 'other' side of the residential slabs, extensive glazing proclaimed the presence of the apartments' main living areas. From an early stage, variations in apartment sizes and material finishes differentiated the superquadras in terms of the amount of luxury they afforded their occupants. The degree of contrast between the 'open' public façade and the 'closed' service side of a block also corresponded to the degree of luxury it promised its residents. At the SQS 308, for example, the glazed public façade contrasts sharply with the rear, entirely screened elevation. The contrast is less pronounced in Niemeyer's SQS 108, where a system of horizontal and vertical concrete blades creates a deep public façade, offering better protection against the sun, while also reflecting Niemeyer's attempt to bridge the distance between the two zones of domestic life and their protagonists.

Brasília's first primary school, Escola-Classe Júlia Kubitschek, named after Juscelino Kubitschek's mother, who was a schoolteacher, was located in the Núcleo NOVACAP or Candangolândia. It opened on 15 October 1957, teachers' day, to serve the needs of the children of those who built Brasília: NOVACAP employees, manual workers and Núcleo Bandeirante entrepreneurs.[162] It was built in twenty days to Niemeyer's design, a simple, temporary building made of wood, strikingly similar to the Catetinho, comprising a horizontal box on slender pilotis, with a low-pitch roof, faced with latticed panels, reached by a long, linear external ramp. It catered for three hundred pupils in two shifts.

Niemeyer's Escola-Parque at SQS 307/308, inaugurated on 12 September 1959 and refurbished in 1987, is a rather more sophisticated version of the wooden prototype: a simple orthogonal volume of pronounced horizontality, seemingly levitating on slim, tri-

160 Niemeyer, 1993c, p. 41; Holston, pp. 173–82. 161 Niemeyer, 1993c, p. 41; Gilberto Freyre, quoted in Evenson, 1973, p. 186. 162 For the Núcleo Bandeirante, see Chapter Six, p. 216, n. 42.

Escola-Classe Júlia Kubitschek, Núcleo NOVACAP or Candangolândia, Brasília, 1957, demolished

angular pillars set perpendicular to the main façade. This and the other schools and libraries included in the early *superquadras* featured custom-designed wall tiles, *combogó* sunscreens and internal landscaped gardens. Juscelino Kubitschek looked forward to 'creating [in Brasília] a new generation of Brazilians pervaded for the first time in history with a feeling of fraternity arising from a process of education and living together'.[163] Oscar Niemeyer sought to ensure that this generation would live and be educated in an environment that employed the revolutionary alphabet of Brazilian architecture's self-assured bid for a national modernity.

Escola-Parque, Superquadras Sul 307/308, Brasília, 1958–59, refurbished 1987

The Third Wing of Brasília

The University of Brasília (UnB) was founded in 1961 as a radically new and dynamic university with an international outlook, striving for innovation and aiming to serve as a model for educational reform throughout the country. In 1962, Niemeyer was appointed coordinator of the Faculty of Architecture. The university campus, named after the first UnB Rector (1961–62), Darcy Ribeiro, is located on the banks of the Paranoá Lake, to the west of the North Wing of the Residential Axis, beyond the north embassies' sector. In the first years after the inauguration of the new capital, it became the centre of Brasília's intellectual life. Responding to tight time and budget requirements, Niemeyer adopted industrial construction methods for the first buildings of the UnB, in collaboration with João da Gama Filgueiras Lima (Lelé), the architect who, over the next decades, would dedicate himself to the development of practicable industrialized building components and construction techniques, with outstanding results, especially in the health sector.

For the university, including its Praça Maior, monumentality was to be avoided, Niemeyer proclaimed. The primary goals of the design were simplicity and flexibility, creating a contrast between Brasília's monumental civic centre and the university's 'environment of speculation and research . . . unfortunately only for a small minority of privileged persons'.[164] The first completed UnB building was the Centre for Planning of the University of Brasília (CEPLAN, 1961), which included the small School of Architecture (today the School of Art), with Niemeyer its first director. The architects Ítalo Campofiorito, Glauco Campelo and João da Gama Filgueiras Lima (Lelé), all at the time between 28 and 30 years old, were its first lecturers. This single-storey orthogonal pavilion is composed of dense, modular, prefabricated, vertical concrete elements and horizontal beams that form a large concrete trellis, uniting enclosed spaces, internal patio gardens by Alda Rabello and covered, in-between areas of circulation, teaching or informal gathering. The tempered, cloister-like atmosphere inside this building is conducive to concentration and creativity. The play of light and shade and the luxuriant vegetation are the only means employed to alleviate the austerity of the interior. The walls of the auditorium feature sketches from Niemeyer's hand.[165]

Adroit material simplicity, total integration of architecture and structure, spatial clarity, emphatic introversion, technological invention and tectonic rigour are also the main characteristics of the Central Institute of Sciences (ICC, 1963–71), nicknamed by Darcy Ribeiro the 'Minhocão' ('Big Worm'), because of its 720-metre-long open curve. Accommodating all major faculties in one

163 Kubitschek, 1966, p. 7.   **164** Niemeyer, 1962d, pp. 8–11.   **165** See Niemeyer, 1963a, pp. 26–31.

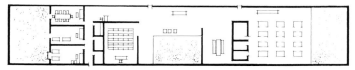

Centre for Planning of the University of Brasília (CEPLAN), including the School of Architecture (today the School of Art), University of Brasília (UnB), Brasília, 1961

structure was considered the most economical solution, allowing them to share use of spaces and to 'collaborate effectively'.[166] This low-budget, 120,000-square-metre, two-storey building is the university's unconventional *machine à émouvoir*, composed with only six prefabricated and pre-stressed concrete elements, laid out in the form of two long, parallel structures, separated by open 15-metre-wide gardens.[167] The wider (30-metre) west wing was intended to accommodate amphitheatres and special-use spaces, while the narrower (25-metre) east wing provided flexible space for laboratories and lecture rooms, protected by *brises-soleil* – the only element animating the building's austere exterior. For future expansion, Niemeyer proposed the construction of 'new units with absolute freedom of design' at the rear of the building. Their 'variations in forms and roofs, which the horizontal line of the

building [will] accentuate', Niemeyer suggested, 'will be the outstanding feature of the architecture: unforeseen and dynamic as science itself'.[168]

On either side of the open gardens, densely colonnaded, double-height loggias negotiate the transition between closed and open spaces. These areas of circulation and informal gathering are, in turn, divided lengthways into two zones: a covered promenade near the closed spaces and a zone of gardens flanking the open space and partially shaded by a lattice of dense concrete beams. Here, as elsewhere in Niemeyer's buildings, columns and beams serve a dual role as both structural elements and shading devices, effecting an almost cinematic articulation of light and shadow. With its gardens – by Miguel Alves Pereira and Nelson Saraiva – now mature, and the exposed concrete ageing gracefully and giving it an air of permanence, the unadorned and unobtrusively supportive architecture of the ICC creates an atmosphere of great intensity, evoking that of medieval monastic colleges. Its manifold qualities are most effectively communicated through direct experience.

Although one of the least known of Niemeyer's buildings, the ICC is a self-conscious, mature proposition, bringing together some of the key themes and strategies developed in his earlier work. Its most striking and pleasant spaces are the double-height, programmatically indeterminate, in-between spaces of the curvy loggias – spaces that allow for active, inventive interpretation beyond mere use. Obliquely viewed, the dense, bare-concrete colonnades produce a forceful, clear rhythm that may be infinitely performed, modified, layered, amplified or silenced by the moving body and the wind that shakes the air plants and their shadows. Of all Niemeyer's buildings in Brasília, this may be the most sensuously effective, seductive and dynamic, relying on a continuous, dialogical exchange between architecture and inhabitation that may be seen as a metaphor for the pedagogical interchange. The internal, long, semi-open spaces – hybrids of serene cloisters for resting, contemplation or poetic reverie and fluently unwinding streets to stroll along – are masterfully proportioned, responding to the light and mood of every hour of the day, interweaving spatial and temporal experience, cool like lush forests in the middle of the 'bare, hostile and silent' *cerrado*.[169] They offer a free voyage of discovery, where the visitor does not get lost as in a labyrinth, but neither hastens along as in a direct corridor route. Ithaca remains always somewhat elusive, somewhere around the curve – a promise that inspires and sustains a joyful journey of inquiry and creative exploration, a pretext for a dance along a long arc of fresh insights.

166 Niemeyer, 1968, pp. 26–27.   **167** 'something to arouse emotion'; Le Corbusier, 1989, p. 211 (in a caption to a photograph of a detail of the Parthenon, which in French reads: 'Voici la machine à émouvoir'). **168** Niemeyer, 1963d, p. 36.   **169** Niemeyer, 2000b, p. 122.

Central Institute of Sciences (ICC), nicknamed the 'Minhocão' ('Big Worm'), University of Brasília (UnB), Brasília, 1963–71: composed with six prefabricated and pre-stressed concrete elements, the austere exterior of this 720-metre-long structure contrasts with its intensely evocative interior. The gardens are designed by Miguel Alves Pereira and Nelson Saraiva.

Inviting free appropriation, the unhierarchical, unifying spaces of the ICC's loggias allude to the familiar icons of the Brazilian landscape. Amid luxuriant vegetation and at points overgrown by climbers, the grey pillars and canopy of beams evoke images of tropical rainforests, with shafts of light penetrating the exuberant vegetal growth at different angles, picking out details at random. During Brasília's days of heavy rains alternating with long spells of intense sunshine, such images become even more vivid. Strolling along the long, curvy garden fronts, the body is subjected to an

experience akin to that of a leisurely walk along the legendary Brazilian sweeping beach. The complete interiorization of the tropical gardens – symbolically the dominated Other of the 'school' associated with dominant European thought – inverts the commonplace arrangement of a building within landscaped grounds, impregnating Brazil's model new school with that legendary Dionysian *espirito de brasilidade*. This is also a building that acknowledges the passing of time and bears the marks of its maturity with wisdom.

A long block, 10 metres high and 16 metres wide, with undulating walls, composed of curved, prefabricated, 5-metre-wide wall sections, gave the university's Institute of Theology (1963) the desired effect of plasticity. Although much altered in subsequent years, it was originally organized as a seminary with convent facilities, connected by a narrow passage to a large church with a free-form plan at a small distance. The entire three-storey block is encased within an independent columnar structure. The columns stand 6 metres from the undulating walls at 10-metre intervals, with slightly arched beams spanning between them. Dense perpendicular beams shade the roof terrace, which functions as a cloister. Exposed concrete and 'toned down' finishes were meant to 'harmonize with the philosophy of poverty and humility' of the building's users, combined, however, with 'a different style of architecture – call it baroque if you will'.[170]

Notwithstanding their figurative element and cultural allusions, Brasília's polished white marble monument-ideograms show affinities with the 'concrete poems', aestheticism and emphasis on visual stimuli and invention of the 1950s' Concretist movement of the Rio–São Paulo axis. Based on the geometric abstraction of the early twentieth century and, ironically, influenced by Max Bill's sculpture *Tripartite Unity* and the work of Bauhaus master Josef Albers, this movement was also inspired by industrialization and Brasília's utopian promise of a technologically advanced civilization in tune with the future. For Mário Pedrosa, Concretism signalled a renewal in the language of the Brazilian visual arts in line with Brazilian architecture and the 'ultramodern, ultranew city that was in the process of being built'.[171]

Niemeyer's later works for Brasília, on the other hand, like the Ministry of Justice, the Palácio do Itamaraty and, most importantly, the ICC, resonate with the ideas of the Carioca Neo-Concretist artists, developed after 1959 as a critique of the dogmatism, rigid parameters and 'dangerous rationalist extreme' of Paulista Concretism.[172] The Neo-Concretist emphasis on the multi-sensory nature of perception is particularly evident. Attracted to the phenomenology of Maurice Merleau-Ponty and the philosophical sys-

170 Niemeyer, 1963e, p. 52.   **171** Mário Pedrosa, quoted in Milliet, p. 389.
172 Gullar et al., p. 496.

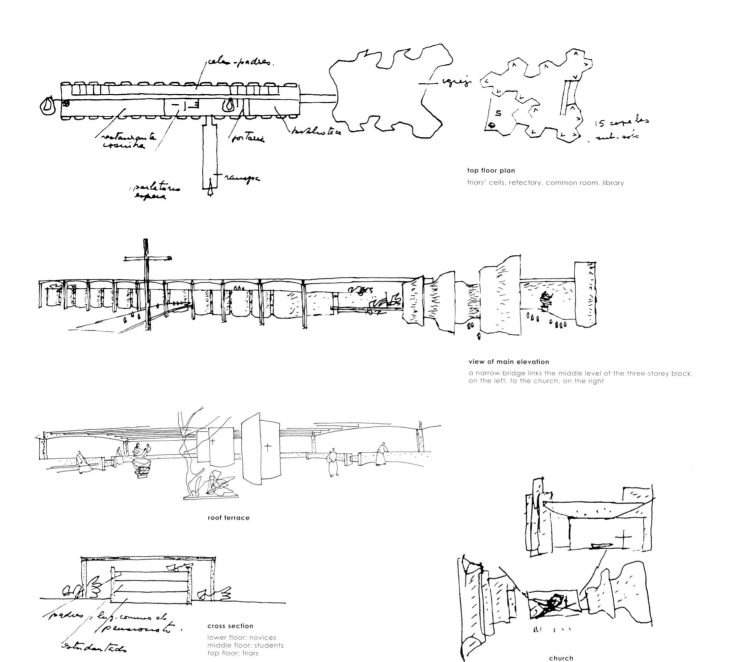

top floor plan
friars' cells, refectory, common room, library

view of main elevation
a narrow bridge links the middle level of the three-storey block, on the left, to the church, on the right

roof terrace

cross section
lower floor: novices
middle floor: students
top floor: friars

church

Institute of Theology, University of Brasília (UnB), Brasília, 1963

tems of Suzanne Langer and Ernst Cassirer, Neo-Concretist artists such as Hélio Oiticica, Aluísio Carvão, Lygia Clark, Amilcar de Castro, Lygia Pape and Franz Weissmann, along with the poets Theon Spanudis and Reynaldo Jardim and the critics Mário Pedrosa and Ferreira Gullar, rejected the idea of object-based art. Instead they invited the active physical engagement of the spectators in the artworks, favouring the concept of the haptic gaze, associating the visual with the tactile and promoting 'a synthesis of

sensory and mental experiences: a body that is transparent to phenomenological knowledge, perceptible in its totality'.[173]

The centralization of the extra-functionalist and intensively sensorial garden spaces of the ICC points to the centrality of the sensorial experience, inverting the strategy of building a defence

173 Herkenhoff, 2004, pp. 327–31.

against the dangers of the 'green hell', and enticing an immersion in the space of the Dionysian Other. 'Crelazer' ('Creasure': creation + leisure), the term Oiticica would invent in 1968, may be appropriately applied to the space of creativity, pleasure and leisure at the centre of the ICC. The theatrical element of this space, like that of Neo-Concretist artworks, lies in its call to the spectator to become a central, active performer rather than remain a passive observer or user. In fact, at the ICC, immersion and interaction are mandatory; without movement, circulation, procession or wandering, the full meaning of its open-ended spaces is lost.

In a short story by João Guimarães Rosa (1908–67), 'The Third Bank of the River' (*Primeiras Estórias*, 1962), the father leaves the family home in the *sertão*, yet he remains close to it, forever silent, eternally 'suspended in the mirror smoothness of the river', searching for the third bank of the river. The architecturally unobtrusive University of Brasília on the banks of Lake Paranoá did not remain a mere observer of events during the years following the military coup of 31 March 1964, which outlawed the National Union of Students (União Nacional de Estudantes, UNE) and forced into exile the minister of education, Darcy Ribeiro, and the second UnB rector, Anísio Teixeira. Students mobilized on a national scale, demanding reform of Brazil's anachronistic education system.

In 1965, *Módulo* – 'not a subversive journal' – was forced to close, and Niemeyer was one of a group of approximately two hundred UnB members of staff who resigned in protest of staff purges and oppression.[174] On 30 August 1968, student demonstrations led to police invasion and occupation of the campus and the arrest of five hundred students and members of academic staff. Congress denounced police violence and the Chamber of Deputies upheld democratic principles. On 13 December 1968, a Presidential Act suspended Congress indefinitely (it reopened in 1970). Over the following months, rigid media censorship steadily increased, along with police brutality including gruesome torture and killings and executive and military control over the government and its citizens. State legislatures and upcoming elections were suspended and the judiciary was attacked as repression mounted and Brazil descended deep into authoritarianism.[175]

Protecting the Unity of Brasília

Niemeyer was at the Victória hotel in Lisbon, on his way to Israel, where he had been invited to work on a series of major projects, when he heard on the radio the news about the military *coup d'état*. The police ransacked his office and the headquarters of *Módulo*. He spent the following six months working in Israel and, the day after his return to Brazil, was interrogated at the army headquarters.

My life went on without any major problems. I was the architect responsible for Brasília and – as everybody knew – I had worked there since the beginning, honestly, without a break, for next to nothing . . . It was during the [General Emílio Garrastazú] Médici government [1969–74], however, that the reactionaries decided to put an end to my work as an architect. Problems began when my design for the new airport terminal in Brasília [1965] was turned down because it was circular.[176]

Elsewhere, Niemeyer recalls:

[The] Air Force Minister declared to the press: 'The place for communist architects is in Moscow' . . .

But it was not only professionally that they tried to hit me. I remember my beloved house in Mendes, and the day when the construction of a new road nearby caused the overflow of a small river in the vicinity, destroying the house . . .

Another violence, not only against me but also against the former president JK, was the demolition of Julia Kubitschek School [in Brasília], which I had designed. Another road ostensibly built towards it.[177]

Niemeyer's prodigious outpouring of works for Brasília continued over the years immediately following the inauguration of the capital, when he designed the Federal District General Hospital (1960); the Metalworkers Institute (1960); the Amador Theatre and Choro Club (1962); the Yacht Club (1961), Tennis Club (1960) and Touring Club (1962); the Franco-Brazilian Cultural Centre (1962–64); and the Acoustic Shell (1963) for a large open-air theatre seating eight thousand. Pampulha's New Yacht Club (1962) is a version of Brasília's Touring Club, with the same massive umbrella roof consisting of 'suspension bridge'-profile concrete beams, threaded together by two longitudinal beams, supported by two rows of square tapering columns. At the time, this building was selected by the *Architectural Review* to illustrate 'the changing face of Brazilian architecture . . . slowly emerging from its cocoon of Corbusian *idées recues* [sic]'.[178] Niemeyer himself dates Brazilian architecture's break with Le Corbusier to his own early work at Pampulha in the 1940s.[179] Le Corbusier visited Brazil for the last time in 1962. Of Brasília, he spoke with admiration: 'I have seen the new city. It is magnificent in its invention, courage and optimism; it

174 Niemeyer, 1968, p. 50. *Módulo* resumed operation in 1975. Niemeyer's editorial in July 1979 openly declared its interests 'in the problems of art and culture, integrated with the struggle for democracy, for amnesty and for human rights, what unites and inspires our Brazilian brothers'; Niemeyer, 1979a, n.p. **175** See Skidmore, 1988, pp. 73 ff. **176** Niemeyer, 2000b, p. 85. See also Niemeyer, 1968, pp. 70–81. **177** Niemeyer, 2004, p. 194–96. **178** 'Pampulha Yacht Club: Structuralism in Recent Brazilian Architecture', 1962, p. 307. **179** Niemeyer, 1974, p. lxxxi. Niemeyer suggests that what distinguishes Le Corbusier's architecture from his own work is the former's 'use of limited spans with the structural elements very much in evidence . . . which draw attention to the celebrated robustness of his work', in contrast to Niemeyer's quest for lightness.

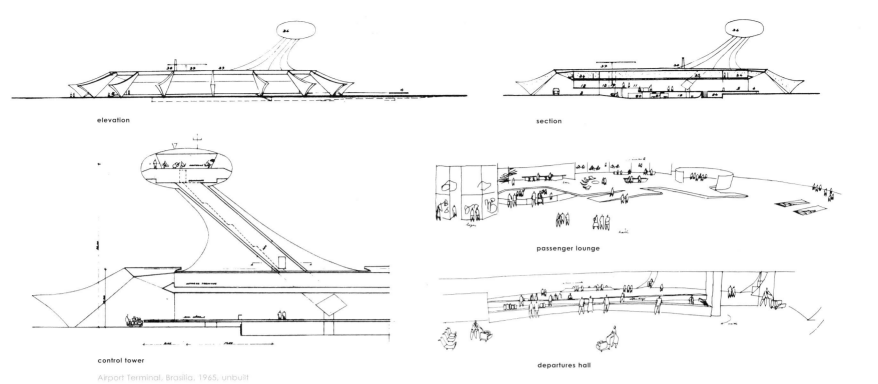

elevation

section

control tower

passenger lounge

departures hall

Le Corbusier congratulating Oscar Niemeyer, Brasília, 1962; between the two, the architect Ítalo Campofiorito

speaks from the heart . . . In the modern world Brasília is unique . . . My voice is that of a traveler in the world and in life. Permit me, friends in Brazil, to say thank you to you!'[180]

Following the 1964 coup, Niemeyer writes,

Brasília lost that aspect of an immense *chantier* (construction site) it had in Juscelino Kubitschek's days, work became scarce and our brother workers, who had given all of themselves for nothing, soon left the New Capital for good. Deadened by the reactionary forces, I left for the Old World taking with me my regrets and disappointments and my architecture.[181]

In 1967, Niemeyer was forced into exile. Nevertheless, he continued to contribute buildings for Brasília: the Palácio do Jaburu (1967), official residence of the vice-president enjoying extensive gardens by Roberto Burle Marx with plants from the *cerrado*; the Costa e Silva Bridge (1967–76, named after Brazil's second military president after the coup) beaming across the lake with three arches that echo Brasília's monumental architecture, and serving the needs of the lakeside residents; several Ministry Annexes; and a bus terminal (Estação Rodoferroviária, 1970). Most controversially, he designed a group of buildings for the Ministry of the Army (1968–73) with landscaping by Roberto Burle Marx, using pre-cast elements for the main office block and including an auditorium (Teatro Pedro Calmon, 1968–72) with seating for 1,180, a relief by Athos Bulcão and an undulating roof reminiscent of Niemeyer's 1948 proposal for an extension to the Ministry of Education in Rio de Janeiro. To the same complex belongs the monumental sword-guard-like, concrete, asymmetrical palanquin known as the Espada de Caxias Cupola (reviewing stand, 1965), which recycled Niemeyer's 1949 project for a monument to Rui Barbosa.[182]

180 Le Corbusier with Jeanneret, 1999, vol. 7, p. 8. **181** Niemeyer, 1985, p. 74. **182** The Duke of Caxias (1803–80) is a hero of Brazilian military history, who was made patron of Brazil's armed forces in 1961. He rose to prominence during the war against Paraguay (1865–70), and was rewarded by Emperor Pedro II with the title of duke in 1869. Since 1931, the cadets at the Brazilian military academy of Agulhas Negras have carried a copy of the Sword of Caxias – a relic at the Instituto Histórico e Geográfico Brasileiro. The Day of the Soldier is celebrated on Caxias's birthday, 25 August. In 1941, the Modernist sculptor Victor Brecheret won a public competition to create a statue of the duke in São Paulo. The statue, with the duke's sword in an upright position, was completed posthumously in 1960, and may have partly inspired Niemeyer's palanquin.

Costa e Silva Bridge, Brasília, 1967

Espada de Caxias Cupola, reviewing stand, Ministry of the Army, Brasília, 1965

Teatro Pedro Calmon, Ministry of the Army, Brasília, 1968–72

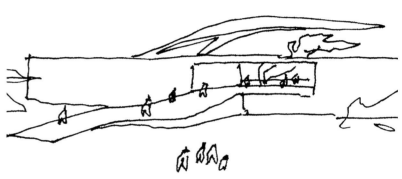

Memorial to the Indigenous People, Brasília, 1982

In 1970, Niemeyer lamented the poor quality of the architecture that appeared in Brasília post-1964, supported by 'reactionary forces'. At the same time, however, he noted that exactly the same authorities who rejected his airport project commissioned him to design the New Army Headquarters.[183] In the 1970s, Niemeyer also designed office buildings for Brasília, such as the Headquarters of Denasa (1972), the Headquarters of Telebras (1973) and the Headquarters of Manchete (1978). During the years following the Médici 'national security state', when the democratic *abertura* ('opening') began to move Brazil towards liberalization, Niemeyer completed in Brasília the Headquarters of the International Labour Organization (1983) and the Memorial to the Indigenous People (1982), inspired by the architecture of the Bororos Indians. In 1975 the ban on *Módulo* was lifted and in 1978 Niemeyer championed the re-establishment of democracy, becoming founding president of the Centro Brasil Democrático (CEBRADE, Centre for a Democratic Brazil) – an organization of intellectuals publicly against the military, including Sérgio Buarque de Holanda and publisher Ênio Silveira.

In 1984, Brasília was again alive with rumours of a military coup in the making. On 15 January 1985, however, the electoral college elected civilian Tancredo Neves to the presidency and, although he died before he could be sworn in, a civilian government took power on 15 March 1985. Tancredo Neves's coffin ascended the ramp of the Palácio do Planalto before thirty thousand grief-stricken onlookers, and José Sarney (Neves's vice-president) assumed the presidency,

> becom[ing] the holder of the largest foreign debt on the face of the earth, as well as the greatest internal debt. My inheritance included the deepest recession in [Brazil's] history, the highest rate of employment, an unprecedented climate of violence, potential political disintegration and the highest rate of inflation ever recorded in [Brazil's] history – 250 per cent a year, with the prospect of reaching 1,000 per cent.[184]

183 Niemeyer, 1982, pp. 55–57. 184 José Sarney, quoted in Skidmore, 1988, p. 261. In 1988 and 1989 the annual inflation rate was over 1,000 per cent.

The new republic's constitution, which went into effect on 5 October 1988, advanced social and political rights and 'eliminated the final formal vestiges of the authoritarian regime'.[185] In 1985, legislation gave illiterates the right to vote. In 1989, at the first direct presidential elections since 1960, with an 82 per cent turnout (100 million voters), Fernando Collor de Mello defeated Luiz Inácio da Silva (Lula) by a slim margin.[186] Taking office in March 1990, he was forced out by Congress in 1992 over accusations of government corruption. He was succeeded by his vice-president, Itamar Franco, and, at the next presidential election, Fernando Henrique Cardoso, a sociologist from the University of São Paulo who had entered politics in the 1970s, won an easy victory over Lula. Thanks to his neoliberal economic policies, Cardoso won a second easy victory over Lula in 1998. But on 27 October 2002, Lula, a former lathe operator and leader of the 1978 metalworkers' strikes, born to a poor, illiterate peasant family in the state of Pernambuco, became the first Brazilian president to come from the working classes. The founder of the Workers Party (Partito dos Trabalhadores, PT) was elected with the largest vote in the history of Brazil, both in absolute and percentage terms (61.7 per cent), to lead the world's fourth largest democracy.

Under the new democracy, Niemeyer continued to produce works for Brasília and its satellite towns: the House of the Singer in the satellite city of Ceilândia (1986); a building for the Oscar Niemeyer Foundation (1988), which began as an exhibition space for the architecture of Brasília; an elegant and smartly organized flower market stand (1989); the Banco do Brasil Training Centre (1990); and the centrally planned Greek Orthodox Church of Saint George (1986) – a rather unresolved translation of Byzantine precedents. The composition of cylinder and dome was revisited a few years later, when Niemeyer produced a much smaller and more successfully proportioned version for the Chapel of Santa Cecília (1989) in Miguel Pereira, Rio de Janeiro state, beside the eighteenth-century house at the *fazenda* of former federal district governor José Aparecido de Oliveira. Niemeyer completed Brasília's Federal Audit Court with Lelé in 1993, the Office of the Attorney General of the Republic in 1999, and the buildings of the Cultural Complex (Complexo Cultural da República João Herculino): to the south of the Monumental Axis the National Museum (Museu da República Honestino Guimarães, completed in 2006) and National Library (Biblioteca Nacional Leonel de Moura Brizola, completed in 2006), which lack the refinement of his earlier projects for Brasília, and to the north the Music Centre, Cinema Complex and Planetarium (under construction).

Niemeyer remains committed to the project of Brasília: 'when I visit Brasilia', he says, 'I feel that our effort was not in vain; that Brasilia marked a heroic period of labor and optimism.'[187] On the one hand, he maintains his conviction 'that the solution for [social] problems is beyond the reach of architects and architecture and

Chapel of Santa Cecília, *fazenda* of José Aparecido de Oliveira, Miguel Pereira, Rio de Janeiro state, 1989

185 Fausto, p. 317.   186 'The total vote for president in 1960 was 12.6 million. In 1989, it turned out to be 82 million'; Skidmore, 1999, p. 192. 187 Niemeyer, 2000b, p. 174.

Aerial view of the National Library and the National Museum, Brasília, completed 2006

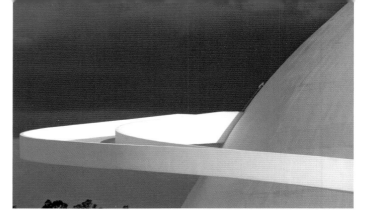

National Library

Oscar Niemeyer on the site of the National Museum, Brasília, 29 April 2005

National Museum: close-up of the external ramp that leads to the gallery on the mezzanine; views of the interior with serpentine ramp and free-flowing mezzanine

requires, in fact, a coherent attitude of backing up progressive movements to this end outside the professional field'.[188] On the other, his commitment to the architectural dimension of utopia is sustained by his belief in the utopian dimension of architecture. From the early days of Brasília, his overriding wish was 'that [his buildings] should become useful and permanent and capable of transmitting beauty and emotion'.[189] And beauty, for Niemeyer, has a redemptive power. 'It is strange how the power of beauty makes us forget so much injustice,' he exclaims.[190]

Configuring the visual identity of Brazil's 'Capital of Hope', he has striven to instil in his architecture the promise of a release, aiming 'above all to withdraw the visitor – be it for a few brief instants – from the difficult problems, at times overwhelming, that life poses for all of us'.[191] 'At the heart of every utopia, there is not only a dream but also a protest,' posited Oswald de Andrade.[192] In Brasília, at the heart of Niemeyer's architecture of protest against pre-established aesthetic categories, there appears to be also a dream of promoting new forms of dialogue with architecture and the city, a dream that the new Brazilian 'past' or heritage that this work proposes may encourage Brazilians to reimagine themselves and their future.

E espero que Brasília seja uma cidade de homens felizes; homens que sintam a vida em tôda a sua plenitude, em toda a sua fragilidade; homens que compreendam o valor das coisas simples e puras – um gesto, uma palavra de afeto e solidariedade.

Oscar Niemeyer

'And I hope that Brasília will be a city of happy people: people who will experience life in all its fullness, in all its fragility: people who will understand the value of simple and pure things – a gesture, a word of affection and solidarity.'

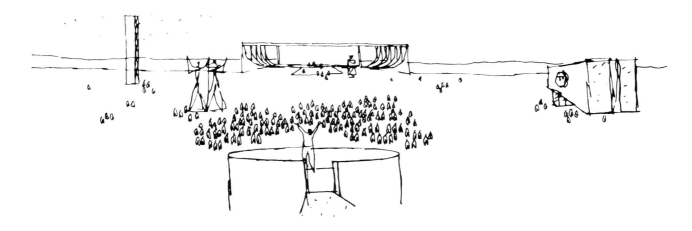

Um dia o povo ouvirá o que deseja e a liberdade e os direitos humanos serão conquistas irreversíveis.

Oscar Niemeyer 18.4.78

188 Niemeyer, 1966, p. 21.   **189** Niemeyer, 1958b, p. 6.   **190** Niemeyer, 1958a, n.p.   **191** Niemeyer, 1993b, p. 313.   **192** Oswald de Andrade, quoted in Stam, 1997, p. 239.

'One day the people will hear what they want and liberty and human rights will become irreversible conquests.'

One day I had to leave my country,
calm beach and palm tree . . .
Caetano Veloso, 'A Little More Blue' (1971)

In 1916, the young French composer Darius Milhaud (1892–1974) arrived in Rio de Janeiro as secretary to the deputy ambassador of the French legation to Rio, the poet Paul Claudel (1868–1955). 'Intrigued and fascinated' by Brazil's popular rhythms, Milhaud exhorted his friends, who included learned Brazilian musicians like Heitor Villa-Lobos, to understand and appreciate 'the melodic invention of a prodigious imagination' that he identified in the work of Brazil's popular composers, to whom his own work became indebted.[1] Following a brief North American sojourn in 1918, upon his return to Paris, Milhaud wrote a small orchestra piece called *Le boeuf sur le toit* (*The Ox on the Roof*, 1919), which met with tremendous success on the European scene. The title – Surrealist *avant la lettre* – was borrowed from a popular tango by the Brazilian Zé Boiadêro ('O boi no telhado', 1917). The following year, a symphonic ballet of the same name, with script by Jean Cocteau, scenography by Raoul Dufy and choreography by Leonide Massine, premiered at the Comédie des Champs-Élysées. A piano piece called 'Le Boeuf sur le toit' became a hit at the renowned Parisian Gaya Bar, where jazz was played, and when the owner moved to larger premises at 28 rue Boissy d'Anglas in December 1921 the legendary bar-restaurant Le Boeuf sur le Toit was born. It became the epicentre of the Parisian avant-garde in the 'Roaring Twenties', frequented by Igor Stravinsky, Jean Cocteau, Louis Aragon, André Breton, Blaise Cendrars, Constantin Brancusi, Francis Picabia, Pablo Picasso, Coco Chanel, Yvonne Printemps, Éric Satie, André Gide, Gaston Gallimard, Arthur Rubinstein, Paul Claudel and so on, as well as by wealthy Brazilians like Paulo Prado, who paid frequent visits to Paris. *Le Boeuf sur le*

toit, a lithograph by Dufy, and Francis Picabia's famous Dada painting *L'Oeil Cacodylate* (1921, Centre Pompidou, Paris) used to hang in the bar.

Blaise Cendrars's decisive role in the Brazilian Modernists' 'rediscovery' of Brazil, especially their appreciation of her popular culture and Baroque heritage, has already been noted.[2] Cendrars also acted as a link between early twentieth-century Brazilian artists spending long periods of time in Paris and European Modernists with a taste for the exotic. Cendrars presented Oswald de Andrade to Jean Cocteau, Tarsila do Amaral to Fernand Léger, Victor Brecheret to Brancusi, and Villa-Lobos to Les Six.[3] Villa-Lobos, in turn, was instrumental in Oswald de Andrade and Tarsila do Amaral's cultural appropriation of Afro-Brazilian values. In 1922, Gilberto Freyre met the Brazilian pioneer of abstract painting, Vicente do Rêgo Monteiro, in Paris. In 1923, one year after the official birth of Brazilian Modernism at the São Paulo Semana de Arte Moderna, Anita Malfatti, Tarsila do Amaral, Oswald de Andrade, Victor Brecheret, Vicente do Rêgo Monteiro and Emiliano Di Cavalcanti were all in the French capital.

In the 1920s, Paris was full of well-heeled Brazilians doing their 'military service' in Modernism, buying artworks by the likes of Robert Delaunay, André Lhote and Léger, and delighting their Parisian acquaintances with their exotic wit and irreverent attitudes.[4] Tongue-in-cheek, Villa-Lobos told the Parisian press that 'his genuinely indigenous melodies had been jotted down by him in the middle of the Amazon jungle, when he was on the point of being devoured by singing, dancing cannibals'.[5] Tarsila do Amaral's *A negra* was painted in Paris in 1923, and Oswald de Andrade's poetry collection *Pau Brasil* was also published in Paris in 1925.[6]

The great Brazilian novelist of the nineteenth century Joaquim Maria Machado de Assis (1839–1908) had one of his characters

1 Darius Milhaud, quoted in Calil, p. 566.   2 See Chapter One, pp. 26–27.   3 Sevcenko, pp. 96–97. Darius Milhaud was one of Les Six. The others were Georges Auric, Louis Durey, Arthur Honegger, Francis Poulenc and Germaine Tailleferre.   4 Tarsila do Amaral, quoted in Cattani, p. 382. As indicated by a letter to Fernand Léger from his gallerist, Léonce Rosenberg (1923), Brazil was regarded at the time as a potential new art market, following the collapse of the German and Russian ones, and Tarsila

do Amaral was a precious link to this potentially lucrative market: Herkenhoff, 2005, pp. 16–19.   5 José Miguel Wisnik, pp. 557–58.   6 See Chapter One, pp. 23–24. In the prologue to *Pau Brasil*, Paulo Prado wrote: 'from the top of an atelier in Place Clichy - the navel of the world - [Oswald de Andrade] discovered in bewilderment his own land. The return to his fatherland confirmed, in the delight of *Manuelino* discoveries, the amazing fact that Brazil actually existed': Paulo Prado, quoted in Bonet, p. 521.

speak of death as 'going to the other Europe, the eternal one'.[7] A European or, more precisely, a Parisian 'death' seems often to have been the necessary condition for the rebirth of Brazil's twentieth-century artists – from Emiliano Di Cavalcanti to Lygia Clark (1920–88) and Sérgio Camargo (1930–90) – as Brazilian artists producing a 'Pau-Brasil [art], for export'.[8] Art criticism and historical narratives tend to assume that currents in the world of art flow unidirectionally, from the hegemonic core countries to those on the periphery of power. They habitually map cultural exchanges as unequal, pointing to the formative apprenticeship of artists from marginal countries in the high art of European and North American cultural centres, and to the 'discoveries' of popular and tribal cultures by artists from the elite centres of art production. When the artists from the periphery visit, say, Paris, they learn from the dominant culture; when the representatives of the latter sojourn in Brazil, they enlighten the locals or, like Le Corbusier, risk reverting to uncivilized irrationality.

Cultural Antropofagia, or what Brazil's great musician and minister of culture since 2002, Gilberto Passos Gil Moreira (1942–, known as Gilberto Gil), has referred to as 'hacker ethics' – 'the uninterrupted re-making that produces culture, life, and the world' – is, as Gil pointed out, 'not a new thing. That's civilization as usual.'[9] Indeed, virtually all art is Antropofagist. Distortions, however, arise when colonialist thinking interprets cultural exchanges as asymmetrical, assumes that hegemonic Eurocentric centres have a monopoly on art and culture and a 'civilizing' mission, as well as exclusive access to the 'meal' of the 'captured warrior'.[10]

In modern Brazil, the desire to create a distinctly Brazilian identity was born out of a nationalist desire to challenge the hegemony of imposed foreign fashions and assault the devalorizations, voyeuristic distortions and stereotypes established by foreign predators hunting the primitive and exotic Other. In the words of art historian Edward J. Sullivan, 'Resistance and acceptance, and the urge to appropriate combined with flexibility and resilience shape the individuality of Brazilian cultural patterns'.[11] One of the greatest achievements of the Brazilian Movimento Antropofágico is that it rejected what Gil calls the 'fascism of the hegemony of one culture', shifting the centre of power, of art production and art export, in the minds of Brazilian artists, from the Old World of Europe to the New World of Brazil. Exalting the Brazilian Other and granting predatory rights to Brazilian intellectuals and artists, it effected a radical inversion of power-laden cultural relations and the direction of appropriation, turning the violence of colonization and colonialist discourse against the colonizers.[12] Oswald de Andrade's Antropofagist work was resuscitated by

the Concretist poets of the 1950s and the directors of Cinema Novo in the 1960s. In the early 1960s, Haroldo de Campos reiterated the Antropofagist principle:

> critical devouring of the universal cultural heritage . . . does not involve a submission (an indoctrination), but a transculturation, or, better, a 'transvalorization': a critical view of History as a negative function (in Nietzsche's sense of the term), capable of appropriation and of expropriation, de-hierachization [sic], deconstruction.[13]

In 1963, Niemeyer was awarded the International Lenin Prize in the Soviet Union and became an honorary member of the American Institute of Architects. On the occasion of the hundredth anniversary of the Mexican revolution in 1964, he received the Premio Benito Juárez. In 1965, he was honoured with the Médaille Joliot Curie of the city of Paris and the French Grand Prix International d'Architecture et d'Art. The same year, the Parisian Musée des Arts Décoratifs mounted the exhibition *Oscar Niemeyer: l'architecte de Brasilia*, curated by Jean Petit and Guy Dupuis. At the height of his career, Niemeyer started receiving commissions outside Brazil. From 1967, he was living in exile in Paris; at the request of Minister of Culture André Malraux, General Charles de Gaulle issued him with a licence to practise as an architect in France and, following a series of French commissions, he opened an office at 90 of the avenue des Champs-Élysées in 1972, managed by engineer Jacques Tricot. 'Fortunately, those who thought they would stop me, without knowing it granted me the best opportunity in my life as an architect', Niemeyer wrote. 'To go to the Old World, to show and make people understand my architecture, and later to see it accomplished and applauded.'[14] He has also often stressed that his intention was to bring to Europe 'not only the plastic freedom of [his] architecture but also the advancements in engineering in Brazil'.[15] Underlining its technologically progressive aspect, Niemeyer pointed to the export quality of his architecture in the sense promoted by Oswald de Andrade.

Niemeyer was not the only Brazilian at the time to emphasize the importance of resisting the neocolonialist marginalization of Brazil, which the nationalist policies of the military regime seemed to exacerbate. In 1967, the poet Augusto de Campos denounced the promotion of exports like ' "voodoo for tourists," as Oswald [de Andrade] would say', and applauded those innovators in music who resisted nationalist calls for the preservation of purity and promotion of the 'authentic' national tradition. Nationalist proposals, he argued, would

7 Assis, p. 235.   8 Oswald de Andrade, 1989, p. 311.   9 Gil; Gilberto Gil, quoted in 'Minister of Counterculture', 2005.   10 Le Corbusier, 1991, p. 16.   11 Sullivan, 2001, p. 7.   12 It should be noted, however, that, within Brazil, it was still the European and Europeanized elite that culturally appropriated, while denying equal rights to, dominated Brazilian black, mestizo and indigenous peoples.   13 Haroldo de Campos, quoted in Vieira, p. 103.   14 Niemeyer, 1992, p. 138. In 1971, Niemeyer was a member of the jury, chaired by Jean Prouvé, which awarded the commission for the Centre Pompidou to Richard Rogers, Renzo Piano and Gianfranco Franchini.   15 Niemeyer, 2000b, p. 174.

only permit [Brazilians] to provide musical raw material (exotic rhythms) for foreign countries. Bossa nova put an end to this state of things, transforming Brazil into an exporter, for the first time, of finished products from its creative industry and having composers like Jobim and interpreters like João Gilberto respected as true masters.[16]

One year later, the Neo-Concretist artist Hélio Oiticica defended against nationalist repression from the Right and from the Left

> those who attempt to create, in the words of Haroldo de Campos, a 'culture of exportation' – the only way to ingest and digest that which bombards us from outside and throw it back as a valid creation and as our own thing, thereby neutralizing the cultural colonialism to which they wish to permanently subject us.[17]

In the same vein, Tropicalismo cannibalized the music of the Beatles and rock music in order to 'demystify that fascist insistence on cultural isolation and on the national meaning of Brazilianness'.[18]

Niemeyer did not view his travels in Europe as a reverent return to the source, neither did he have any intention of showcasing an exotic trophy architecture. Sharing the desire to help shed 'this defeatist mentality, which claims that an underdeveloped country can only produce underdeveloped art', he highlighted that his work was not only fearlessly aesthetically challenging but structurally daring too.[19] He was keen both to export advanced Brazilian engineering and to masticate voraciously the technology and skilled labour force Europe had to offer in order to speculate freely at the cutting edge of his art. 'In Europe, my political concern was to show that we are not noble savages,' Niemeyer declares.[20] He has often repeated that he is particularly pleased by the high-quality construction of his European buildings. He valued equally the opportunity to build in Africa and the East, 'the cradle of civilization', where the architecture of the past bore evidence that 'functionalism is superseded and decadent'.[21]

New Political and Cultural Horizons for Lebanon, Israel and Algeria

In 1962, the Brazilian ambassador Bolivar de Freitas invited Niemeyer, on behalf of the Lebanese government, to design a Permanent International Fair complex for the city of Tripoli (partially realized). Niemeyer criticized the process that led to the selection of the site, arguing that it should have been preceded by in-

depth study of the urbanization of the region in order to guarantee the organic integration of the fair with the future expansion of the city. He would have also preferred a coastal site. His proposal put forward an entire new city quarter, with the fair as its focal point, accommodating a culture and leisure programme. Between the fair and the sea coast he proposed zones for hous-

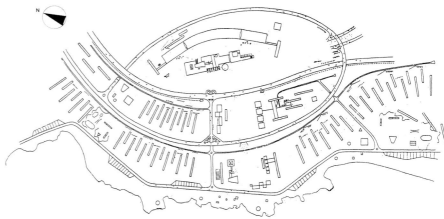

New city quarter with Permanent International Fair complex, Tripoli, Lebanon, 1962, partially realized

ing, commerce, sports, entertainment and tourism – the latter forming a link between the fair and the sea – paying particular attention to the problem of housing, which he saw as being debased and subjected to commercial interests.[22]

For the fair itself, Niemeyer 'rejected the common typology, repeated all over the world, with isolated pavilions', and 'returned to the ideas of nineteenth-century expositions'. His team proposed a 750 × 70 metres flat canopy – curved in plan – that would guarantee 'plastic discipline and unity'.[23] The pavilions of the various countries would be arranged under this 'single roof . . . economic and speedily built' and in the 'spirit of a pavilion . . . a mere shell to encase the exhibits'. This canopy of 'grandeur and simplicity' was offset by an ensemble of various forms, arranged parallel to its concave side, for the Pavilion of Lebanon, the Space Museum, an experimental theatre, an open-air theatre, a series of recreation spaces, a water tower and a restaurant at the highest point with a view of the whole fair. The entrance portico and the Housing Section were positioned at the two extremes of the 'great pavilion'. Administration services were accommodated in two separate blocks, parallel to the convex side of the long canopy. For the entrance portico Niemeyer conceived a hybrid structure in the vein of Brazil's Antropofagist tradition, which would 'express, by

16 Campos, p. 260.　**17** Oiticica, 2005a, p. 245.　**18** Gilberto Gil, quoted in Vianna, p. 96.　**19** Campos, p. 260.　**20** Oscar Niemeyer, in Wajnberg. In an interview of 2007, Niemeyer made a similar statement in relation to the Ministry of Education building: 'We wanted to do some-

thing very special . . . perhaps to show that we were something more than primitive Indians dancing colourfully for visiting Europeans and Northern Americans': in Glancey.　**21** Niemeyer, 1977b, pp. 32–34. **22** Niemeyer, 1963c, pp. 96–101.　**23** Niemeyer, 1968, p. 20.

the proportions and width of its spans, the architecture of today, enhanced in its details by the Arab tradition of [Lebanon].' The Housing Section included a hotel and the Museum of Dwelling, closing off the composition. A 'little train' would run 'all day long' between this point and the entrance portico. The Museum of Dwelling focused on a comparison between collective housing and the individual detached house, for which Niemeyer provided examples. The primary difference between the two, he postulat-

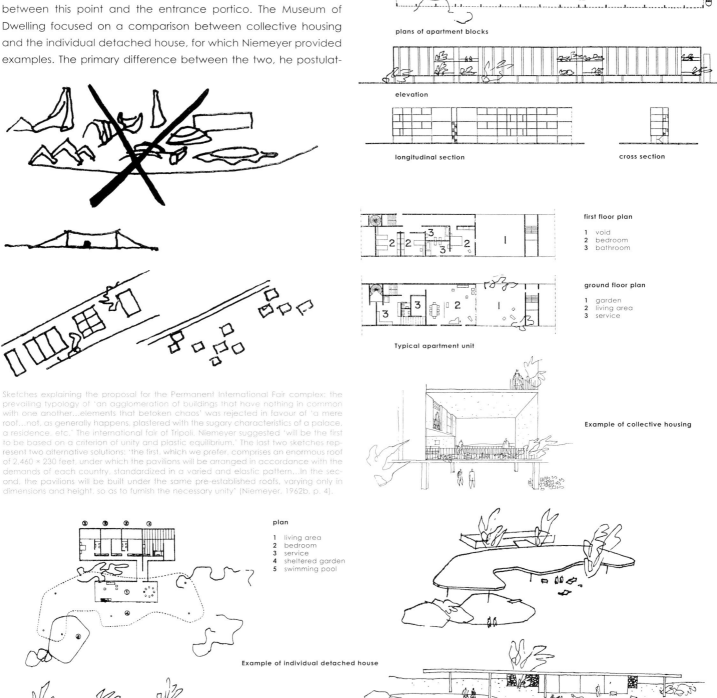

plans of apartment blocks

elevation

longitudinal section

cross section

first floor plan

1 void
2 bedroom
3 bathroom

ground floor plan

1 garden
2 living area
3 service

Typical apartment unit

Example of collective housing

Sketches explaining the proposal for the Permanent International Fair complex; the prevailing typology of 'an agglomeration of buildings that have nothing in common with one another...elements that betoken chaos' was rejected in favour of 'a mere roof...not, as generally happens, plastered with the sugary characteristics of a palace, a residence, etc.' The international fair of Tripoli, Niemeyer suggested 'will be the first to be based on a criterion of unity and plastic equilibrium.' The last two sketches represent two alternative solutions: 'the first, which we prefer, comprises an enormous roof of 2,460 × 230 feet, under which the pavilions will be arranged in accordance with the demands of each country, standardized in a varied and elastic pattern...In the second, the pavilions will be built under the same pre-established roofs, varying only in dimensions and height, so as to furnish the necessary unity' (Niemeyer, 1962b, p. 4).

plan

1 living area
2 bedroom
3 service
4 sheltered garden
5 swimming pool

Example of individual detached house

section

elevation

Permanent International Fair at Tripoli: Museum of Dwelling with examples for collective housing and for an individual detached house

ed, is that the former, 'upon which contemporary town-planning is founded [is] simple and built to a module', whereas the latter is characterized by 'plastic unrestraint . . . justified by the variety and individualization of the programmes'.[24]

Modern Brazilian architecture, especially its internationally acclaimed devices of solar control, had been a major influence on Israeli architecture during the decade preceding Niemeyer's arrival in Tel Aviv in April 1964 as a guest of the businessman Yekutiel Federmann. As in Brazil, where brises-soleil were related to the Moorish shading devices of colonial Portuguese architecture, in Israel the sunbreaks were legitimated on the basis of their origin in the 'Near East'. Their use was interpreted as a homecoming, 'from Brazil to [Israel]'.[25] Israel's efforts to use architecture combined with modern technology as a means to overcome underdevelopment are also comparable to similar efforts in Brazil. In June 1955, at the opening of the Brazilian Architecture exhibition at the Tel Aviv Museum, Mayor Haim Lebanon encouraged Israeli architects to travel to Brazil 'to study the contemporary modes of construction there and dare to adapt new forms'.[26] Niemeyer's invitation to Israel may be seen in the same light as that of Le Corbusier's to Brazil in the 1930s. The foreign star architect could act as a catalyst for the acceptance of new forms and audacious structures by the general public and help raise building rights and the value of the land for the benefit of ambitious real-estate entrepreneurs, like his host, who was also the backer of Niemeyer's Nordia and Panorama mixed-use developments for Tel Aviv (1964, unbuilt).

The municipal plan prohibited high-rise construction in Tel Aviv, limiting the height of buildings to twelve storeys. But Niemeyer argued that 'Tel Aviv's low horizon lacks landmark structures' and proposed for Kihar Hamedinah (1964, in collaboration with A. El-Hanani and I. Lotan, unrealized) three forty-storey office towers surrounded by a ring of ten-storey apartment blocks, which would guarantee 'open spaces, breathing spaces for a suffocating city.' His new forms for Israel, however, 'aroused heated public debate, perhaps one of the most bitter and prolonged struggles Israeli planning has known'. Zvi Elhyani argues that the Brazilian architect's ill-fated, vertical, high-density proposals for Tel Aviv, Haifa and Negev 'offered a dramatically different sense of place than the small scaled, horizontal and low densed [sic] Genius Loci the Zionist Movement wished to produce'. They implicitly critiqued,

Elhyani maintains, the Zionist conception of space, which, 'for ideological and strategic reasons . . . was premised on sprawl and dispersal and the avoidance of dominant urban centers and monumental objects'. Elhyani points out that Niemeyer was not aware of 'the ideological, economic, social and political underpinnings of the Sharon Plan' – the first national masterplan for the state of Israel, prepared in the early 1950s, just weeks after the establishment of the state, by the government planning division, headed by Aryeh Sharon. According to Elhyani, the Sharon Plan 'gave physical expression to the government's policy of dispersing the population . . . [and] served a clear policy of fixing borders and seizing land'.[27] But Niemeyer shunned accepted doctrine and criticized Israel's horizontal development as short-sighted, warning that available territory would soon be exhausted and open spaces endangered.

His masterplan for the desert city of Negev (1964, unrealized), with Hans-Georg Müller, Samuel Rawett and Guy Dimanche, for a population of eighty thousand, sought 'to integrate man on the scale of the ancient medieval cities'.[28] This nostalgia for the high-density pedestrian city of the past was in conflict with Israel's ideology of planning for its 'brethren, children of the diaspora . . . sons of the inner city . . . who grew up in the dark and narrow urban back streets . . . who too shall enjoy the live scent of the earth'.[29]

Niemeyer presented his ideal city 'like a kibbutz that grows, expands and keeps up to date without losing its human aspects of enthusiasm, solidarity and idealism'. Arguing that his solution 'anticipated the problems of the future' such as traffic congestion, shortage of land and overburdened services, he conceived Negev as 'a small, multipliable city . . . an oasis'.[30] It took the form of a vertical garden city with thirty-five-storey housing blocks containing apartments entered through private gardens open on two sides, which he thought 'everyone longs for'. This solution would combine 'genuine park' with 'genuine dwellings', allowing for the elimination of the motor car from areas of housing as well as from commercial and entertainment areas. Additionally, it would offer 'its inhabitants complete and optimum use of the surface area', protection from dust, sandstorms and so on, as well as 'the magnificent view over the Negev'.[31] Finally, it would help safeguard the limited resource of the earth for generations to come. Niemeyer proposed housing towers with no 'definitive' apartments but what he called 'building areas' with a few fixed elements such

24 Niemeyer, 1962b, pp. 4–5. **25** Dov Carmi, quoted in Elhyani, p. 95. **26** Haim Lebanon, quoted in Elhyani, pp. 95–96. **27** Oscar Niemeyer, quoted in Elhyani, p. 101; Elhyani, pp. 103 and 89–92. In his travel diary, published in 1968, Niemeyer appears also to have been unaware of the problems that beset his proposals following his departure; Niemeyer, 1968. At the time of his proposal, he had pleaded 'those who are going to examine our work, to compare it with what has already been done here – the Beersheeba and Eliat Plans, for instance – weighing the pros and cons with an open mind, so as to grasp the reasons for the vertical design of the city . . . if the comparison fails to convince them, if the evidence of so many advantages is not strong enough to overcome deep-rooted prejudice, it is to be hoped that they will not reject our project definitive-

ly, but only shelve it for a while, with the intention of reconsidering it anew in 3 or 4 years time'; Niemeyer, 1965b, pp. 4–5. **28** Niemeyer, 1965b, p. 5. **29** Text describing the Nordia neighbourhood, established in 1919 as a Jewish settlement on the outskirts of Jaffa, cited in Elhyani, p. 100. **30** Niemeyer, 1965b, p. 4; Niemeyer, 1993c, p. 135. **31** Niemeyer, 'Plan of the Town of Negev', in Oscar Niemeyer: Notebooks of the Architect, n.p. The site for the city was chosen by Niemeyer: 'a clear idea of the difficulties that lie ahead in the way of taboos, doubts, misunderstandings and inevitable short-sightedness, induced us to ask for the site first chosen (Bessor) to be changed, coming out in favor of a location in the heart of the Negev, for we are aware that actual construction would be postponed for several years': Niemeyer, 1965b, p. 5.

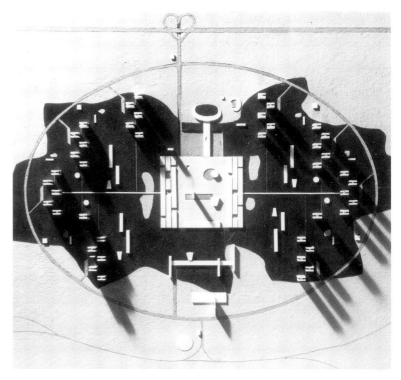

Masterplan for the new desert city of Negev, Israel, 1964, unrealized: model

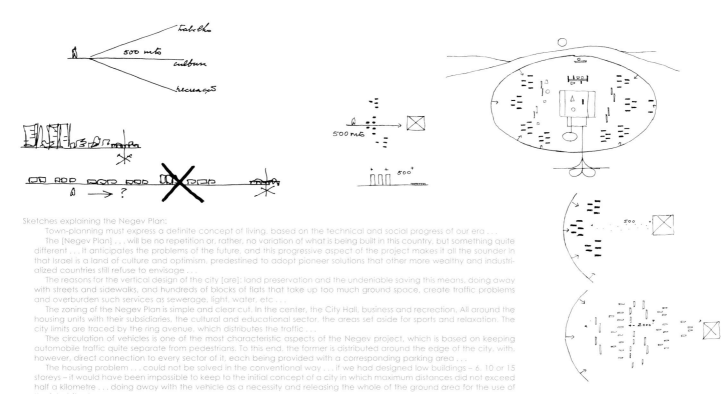

Sketches explaining the Negev Plan:

Town-planning must express a definite concept of living, based on the technical and social progress of our era . . .

The [Negev Plan] . . . will be no repetition or, rather, no variation of what is being built in this country, but something quite different . . . It anticipates the problems of the future, and this progressive aspect of the project makes it all the sounder in that Israel is a land of culture and optimism, predestined to adopt pioneer solutions that other more wealthy and industrialized countries still refuse to envisage . . .

The reasons for the vertical design of the city [are]: land preservation and the undeniable saving this means, doing away with streets and sidewalks, and hundreds of blocks of flats that take up too much ground space, create traffic problems and overburden such services as sewerage, light, water, etc . . .

The zoning of the Negev Plan is simple and clear cut. In the center, the City Hall, business and recreation. All around the housing units with their subsidiaries, the cultural and educational sector, the areas set aside for sports and relaxation. The city limits are traced by the ring avenue, which distributes the traffic . . .

The circulation of vehicles is one of the most characteristic aspects of the Negev project, which is based on keeping automobile traffic quite separate from pedestrians. To this end, the former is distributed around the edge of the city, with, however, direct connection to every sector of it, each being provided with a corresponding parking area . . .

The housing problem . . . could not be solved in the conventional way . . . if we had designed low buildings – 6, 10 or 15 storeys – it would have been impossible to keep to the initial concept of a city in which maximum distances did not exceed half a kilometre . . . doing away with the vehicle as a necessity and releasing the whole of the ground area for the use of the inhabitants . . .

[The last drawings] show how the distances would be lengthened if lower buildings were used . . .

The Negev Plan . . . might be reproduced indefinitely along the great ways of communication, etching out zones of agriculture, industry and recreation, and bringing, in an organic and orderly form, life and progress to the hinterland.
(Niemeyer, 1965b, pp. 3–11)

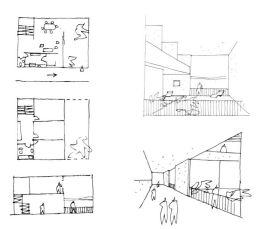

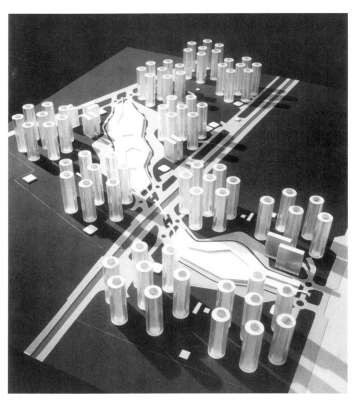

Apartment units with private gardens for the 'vertical collective housing' proposed for Negev: 'The design of the housing unit we are suggesting . . . giv[es] the apartment the true character of a home', argued Niemeyer (Niemeyer, 1965b, p. 8).

as garden, entrance and sanitary provisions, encouraging owners to plan their homes according to their individual needs and means.[32] He would advocate similar principles of compact living and programmatic integration in his masterplan for Grasse, France (1967, in collaboration with the Bureau d'Études et Recherches Urbanistiques and Claude Marlaut, Marc Emery and Hans-Georg Müller, unrealized), and in his thirty-storey residential towers for Barra da Tijuca (1969), along the Rio de Janeiro coastline, with a 'river' of low, commercial spaces running through them (sixty-one towers were planned but only three were completed, in 1972).

Niemeyer's proposal for the University of Haifa atop Mount Carmel (1964), with Hans-Georg Müller, Samuel Rawett and Guy Dimanche, sprang from the typologies he had developed in Brasília and Lebanon, also adopted in his project for the University of Ghana, Accra (1964, unbuilt). It put forward a 'monoblock' aimed at an economical integration and cross-fertilization of programmatic spaces and academic disciplines. It was also justified as appropriate to the natural beauty and symbolism of the site, 'which clearly suggest[ed] a compact solution, simple and monumental in aspect'.[33] The local press published Niemeyer's first assessment of the site, apparently made aboard the ship entering the port of Haifa:

> Mount Carmel is very exposed . . . I began to imagine [it] adorned with impressive urban structures. Not with low buildings that negate its horizons and cover it in a mess where one can no longer make out its vistas, its past and its struggles, but with tall edifices and turrets whose height and magnificence would give it the mark of distinction. Such buildings will leave many open spaces.[34]

To allow for construction in stages while guaranteeing the unity of the composition, Niemeyer proposed a monumental, 500-

Residential quarter with sixty-one thirty-storey towers for Barra da Tijuca, Rio de Janeiro, 1969, three towers completed in 1972: model

metre-long 'esplanade' in reinforced concrete (completed in 1971), a four-storey space to be progressively 'colonized'.[35] Eight large auditoria were incorporated under the esplanade, while a number of structures were envisaged projecting above the new, high ground of the modern acropolis, articulating the university's skyline: a twenty-eight-storey administration tower (the only one of these buildings to be constructed, and with thirty-one storeys); two long classroom wings; a library and communications centre in the form of an inverted pyramid; an egg-shaped synagogue; and a shell-shaped auditorium, terminating the esplanade at one end. At the other end of the esplanade, a series of terraces stepped down the mountainside, containing classrooms, dormitories and services. A grand, signature ramp provided for ceremonial ascent onto the city's new, concrete horizon of higher learning. The monumental scheme recalls the National Congress of Brasília.

Niemeyer's vision for this site, which had been designated a National Park and monument to the founder of Zionism, Theodore Herzel, was for an acropolis befitting a country 'being organized on the basis of science and work'.[36] At the ceremony for the laying of the foundation stone, Israel's prime minister justified the

32 Niemeyer, 1965b, pp. 7–9.   **33** Niemeyer, 1965a, p. 28.   **34** Oscar Niemeyer, quoted in Elhyani, p. 92.   **35** Niemeyer, 1968, pp. 44–45.
36 Niemeyer, 1968, p. 45.

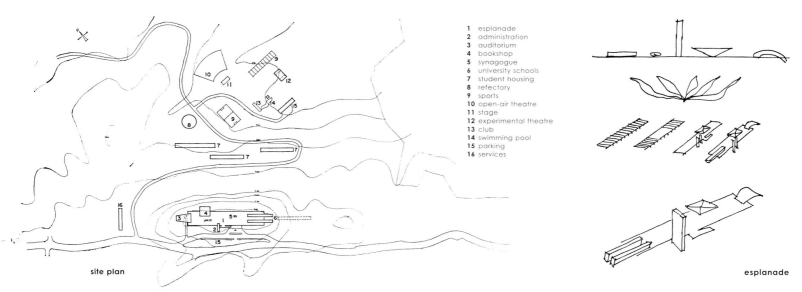

1 esplanade
2 administration
3 auditorium
4 bookshop
5 synagogue
6 university schools
7 student housing
8 refectory
9 sports
10 open-air theatre
11 stage
12 experimental theatre
13 club
14 swimming pool
15 parking
16 services

site plan   esplanade

University of Haifa on Mount Carmel, Haifa, Israel, 1964, partially realized

decision to build a new university campus on the basis of established Zionist ideology: 'population dispersal necessitates the dispersal of higher learning', he asserted. 'Thus', Elhyani infers, 'even Niemeyer's compact design, which like all his Israeli proposals criticized Israel's diffusion practices, was enlisted in the service of the Zionist ethos of population dispersal.'[37] Niemeyer has disavowed the project as implemented. Later constructions sought to 'correct' Niemeyer's reading of the site in the manner Karl Friedrich Schinkel had hoped in 1834 to correct the embarrassing 'disorder' of the Athenian Acropolis.

In the early 1930s, Anísio Teixeira, the director general of the Department of Education of the federal district of Rio de Janeiro, had vigorously promoted rationalist architecture as an appropriate expression and receptacle for a new, modern educational system. Teixeira viewed educational reform as a means to social reform. At the University of Brasília, conceived as a forward-looking institution of higher education, Niemeyer's innovative system of spatial organization sought to translate into built form, and facilitate the implementation of, the progressive ideas developed by Teixeira and Darcy Ribeiro. His proposal for the University of Cuiabá, Brazil (1968, unbuilt), was based on the new university model put forward in Brasília, as were his schemes for the universities of Haifa and Ghana, and those for the University of Algiers at Bab-Ezzouar, Algiers (1968–76, realized with significant alterations, renamed University of Sciences and Technology Houari Boumédiène), and, most importantly, his University of Constantine at Ain el Bey, Constantine (1969–72, with José Lopez, Luis Marçal, Jorge Moreira, Edgard Graef, Fernando Lopes Burmeister, Jorge Vale, Fernando Andrade, Arakawa and Pablo Ortuzar, renamed Mentouri University). Following independence from the French in 1962 educational modernization and democratization in Algeria

were regarded as means to modernize and democratize society as a whole. Niemeyer's architecture for the University of Constantine, the first university founded after independence, consciously embodied these goals.

Following the bloody Algerian War (1954–61), Algeria chose a path of state-controlled, socialist–nationalist development, which adopted the strategies of agrarian revolution, industrial revolution and cultural revolution. The aim of the latter was 'the affirmation and conso-lidation [sic] of Algerian independence, elevation of the level of education and technical competence, and the adoption of a style of life which is in harmony with the principles of the Socialist Revolution'.[38] Niemeyer was invited to give form to these aspirations by Houari Boumédiène, the socialist–authoritarian president from 1965 to 1978 of Algeria's ruling revolutionary council. He was inspired by feelings of solidarity for 'a new country [that] was taking shape in that Third World which fathered the African strain in my own nation. A country that had won its way to freedom and was growing in an upsurge of progress and socialism.' Arriving in Algeria in June 1968, he felt immediately 'attracted to this generous country, warmed by an ardent sun and fringed with beaches and mountains', reminding him of Brazil, and was filled with optimism, 'at a moment when the Arab world [was] being transformed into a pole of attraction'.[39] Niemeyer harnessed his energies to the twofold task of bringing about a rupture with Algeria's colonial architectural past and inaugurating an architecture able to express the major targets of the Algerian 'democratic revolution': industrialization and education.[40] His revolutionary ideas were received with sympathy by Boumédiène,

37 Elhyani, p. 105.   38 Slimane Madhar, quoted in Bourouh.
39 Niemeyer, 1976, pp. 18–21.   40 Niemeyer, 1993c, p. 131.

who maintained for Algeria an image of an avant-garde, revolutionary Third World state.

Niemeyer rejected the commissioning brief for the University of Constantine as 'reactionary and outmoded', and conveyed instead his vision of 'the university of the future' or 'the integrated university', embodied in a scheme for fifteen thousand students, which he presented in line with the post-colonial state's objectives.

> My idea of the university was based on centralization and flexibility, and for this reason, I rejected the traditional university with its dozens of buildings, one for each faculty, which occupied too much land ... requiring expensive structures ... Not to mention the multiplication of classrooms, lecture theatres and laboratories scattered among the faculties, adversely affecting scientific unity and standards.

> The university I propose is on a human scale, logical and compact. Suitable for the modifications which the future will require. My project requires only two buildings for teaching purposes: a classroom block and a science block. The first will contain all the classrooms and lecture theatres, and the second will contain the laboratories and research facilities. These will be complemented by the administration block, the library, the restaurant, the 'village', and the sporting complex ...

> Here are the practical advantages of my project compared with the architectural programme supplied: 11 buildings instead of 22 (2 teaching blocks instead of the 9 buildings envisaged for the faculties), and, in addition, 800 metres between the buildings instead of 5 kilometres of roads including electrical and gas installations, etc. I should also point out that the proposed solution allows the number of courses to be increased, bearing in mind that the University of Constantine is not only meant to train high-flying scientists but also the engi-

neers and teachers which Algerian education and industry require. The current deficiencies are the inevitable legacy of colonialism. The university of the future will unquestionably be more flexible; it will be closer to the students, eliminating separate faculties, in a continuous dialogue through the exchange of knowledge. I quote Clark Kerr, rector of the University of California: 'A major transformation is required. It will consist of establishing unity in the intellectual world. It is necessary to bring about the meeting of two, three or even more cultures, to open up new channels for intelligent dialogue within the various disciplines and their subdivision'. That is our idea of the university, a university which takes into account the socialist world in education.[41]

Niemeyer invited to Algeria a number of Brazilian academics and scientists, including Darcy Ribeiro, Heron de Alencar, Luiz Hildebrando Pereira da Silva, Euvaldo Matos and Ubirajara Brito, to support his project. He also relied on a Brazilian team of engineers, including Bruno Contarini, to help realize his structurally daring proposals, achieving 'an architecture so grandiose that the problems caused by the unskilled local manpower virtually disappeared'.[42] Except for the proposed underground passageways and the halls of residence, Niemeyer's scheme was faithfully executed and the modern kasbah of higher education soon came to take a place in the old, historic city of Constantine.

Ambitious to move Algeria swiftly to the forefront of engineering technology, Niemeyer designed the two-storey, 300-metre-long, reinforced-concrete classes and sciences buildings with 50-metre spans and 25-metre cantilevers, lifting them off the ground on two rows of pyramidal columns. A vertical slab accommodates the administration. Its long elevations are made to appear as separate planes with giant mullions in bare concrete, gently curling outwards at the bottom, as if they were about to slide off the tower and melt into the ground. The most spectacular of the complex's structures – one of the most striking examples of Niemeyer's ideal fusion of architecture and engineering – houses the university's aula magna. Its immense curved roof brings to mind the bird-like form of Eero Saarinen's TWA Terminal at Kennedy Airport, New York. But Niemeyer's giant bird rests with its white open wings reaching down to the ground, shading the deeply recessed glazed walls. A central beam spanning 80 metres forms a spine between the two huge, low-sweeping vaults. Niemeyer considers the University of Constantine 'one of my best projects ... beginning to show the Old World that there wasn't much they could teach us Latin Americans'.[43]

Niemeyer worked on Algerian projects for almost ten years, 'all the time ... feel[ing] that I was working for a different, fairer

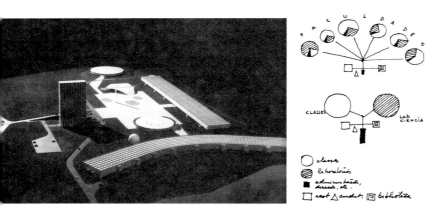

University of Constantine, renamed Mentouri University, Ain el Bey, Constantine, Algeria, 1969–72: model; diagram presenting the proposed solution as opposed to the traditional typology

41 Niemeyer, 'University of Constantine', in *Oscar Niemeyer: Notebooks of the Architect*, n.p. See also Niemeyer, 1976, p. 20.   42 Niemeyer, 1998, p. 25.   43 Niemeyer, 2000b, p. 95.

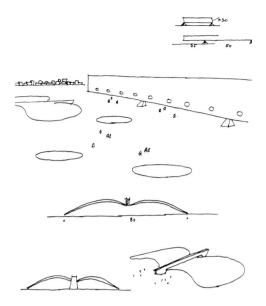

University of Constantine: sketches of main buildings

University of Constantine: views of the aula magna and administration tower

world that we would all like to see materialize'.[44] In contrast to his 'vertical city' proposals for Negev and Grasse, for the New City of Algiers (1968), with Marc Emery, he proposed a 'horizontal city', at a distance from the old capital, following the pattern of the city's spontaneous development already in progress. But his masterplan remained on paper. The low density of the proposed residential zone sharply contrasted with the high density of the ancient kasbah on the hill – a UNESCO World Heritage Site since 1992 – with its winding narrow streets. But its spatial organization and architectural forms were also clearly differentiated from the 'civilizing' forms of the nineteenth-century colonial city – the leading city of France's southern Mediterranean *départements*, with wide boulevards and power-laden architectural landmarks. Where French planning and housing policies, to which Le Corbusier had subscribed, had segregated the city's Muslim population, confining it in cramped living quarters, Niemeyer's groups of residential blocks, spreading along the coastline towards Cap Matifou, were set in an extensive landscaped area, 'because nature merits a place of particular prominence as humanity's indispensable companion in its suffering and dreams'.[45]

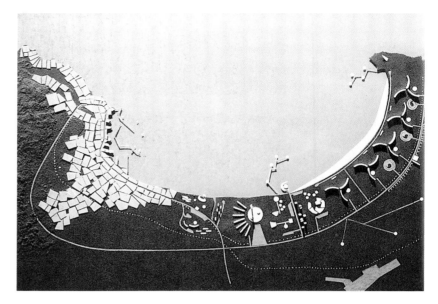

Mediating between the old and the new city, Niemeyer designed civic, administration and cultural centres for the liberated Algerian capital. Algeria's new 'palaces' radiated from a 200-metre-radius circular plaza with an imposing, 150-metre-long, concrete 'lance, pointing west', commemorating the Algerian Revolution, and a Museum.[46] On one side of the monumental sundial, Niemeyer laid twelve identical low, prefabricated ministry blocks and, on the opposite side, a version of Brasília's Praça dos Três Poderes, dominated by a large area of water. Here, he placed the Presidential Palace, the Assembly and the Ministry of Foreign Affairs. The arcades of the Assembly (and those of a 1974 scheme for the Ministry of Foreign Affairs), the most prominent of the three structures, suggest concessions to the Islamic architectural tradition. The tent-like forms of the other two monumental buildings revalorized the country's living Berber tradition.[47] In the post-colonial civic centre of the capital, Niemeyer claimed equal participation for the two ethnic groups or rather cultures of Algeria's population – Arab and Berber – implicitly opposing the government's culturally exclusive Arab-oriented policies and the hegemonic Arab–Muslim version of Algerian national identity.[48] Not surprisingly, Niemeyer's sympathies leant towards a

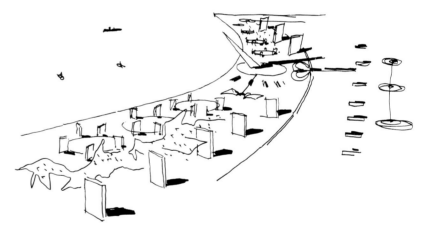

44 Niemeyer, 1976, p. 21.   **45** Oscar Niemeyer, quoted in Botey, p. 202.
46 Niemeyer, 2004, p. 214.   **47** According to architect Cláudio Queiroz, who worked at Niemeyer's office in Algeria for over ten years, Niemeyer's tent-like forms echo the profile of the Jebel Chenoua mountain range on the coast, just west of Algiers; personal communication, 9 November 2006.
48 It should be noted that Algerian Berbers do not constitute a homogeneous group. They do, however, share a collective cultural identity and struggle to win its recognition as one of the foundations of national Algerian identity. The majority of Algerian Berbers are Kabyles, and it is from this group that historical manifestations of cultural activism have issued. Affirmations of a Chaouian identity have also increased in recent years. See Maddy-Weitzman.

Masterplan for the New City of Algiers, Algeria, 1968, unrealized

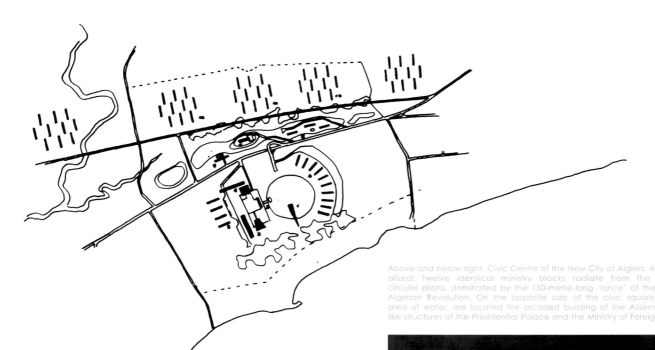

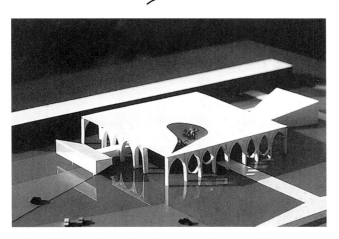

Ministry of Foreign Affairs, Algiers, Algeria, second scheme, 1974, unbuilt: model

culturally plural democratic unity and his masterplan for Algiers embodied this vision.

Less directly but powerfully evocative of local tradition, the new mosque (1968, unbuilt) Niemeyer designed for Algiers is an inspired example of modern religious architecture. A white mono-coque structure, like a fig-shaped bubble or a nomad tent, it was set afloat on the purifying waters of the Mediterranean opposite Algeria's new secular centre of power – a gesture drenched in reli-gious and political symbolism. It was to be made of concrete, which in the models looks more like fragile eggshell, fine Japanese porcelain or delicate hand-blown glass. Six elegant, sail-like columns form a circle at a distance from the main volume, stretch-ing their limbs centripetally to lift the precious pearl slightly above the surface of the water. Further out, a semicircular pier embraces

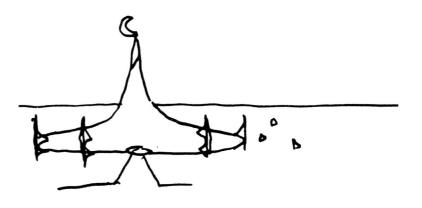

Mosque, Algiers, Algeria, 1968, unbuilt

Mosque, Algiers: model

the weightless structure from a respectful distance, then branches out to lead believers to the circular prayer hall, entered through an elliptical opening. Light comes in from above, through the only other opening allowed to break the continuity of the white membrane – a teardrop-shaped aperture near the pointed apex of the dome, crowned with a crescent. Niemeyer relays Boumédiène's reaction when he first saw the scheme for the mosque: 'your mosque is beautiful, but it is quite revolutionary'. Upon which the architect replied: 'yes president, it is a revolutionary mosque. The revolution cannot be stopped half-way.' This striking project appears today as fresh as it did when it sprang from Niemeyer's pen. 'But everything changed when Boumedienne died' in 1978.[49] Nevertheless, Niemeyer 'hop[es] that one day [the mosque] may be realized. It is one of my dreams.'[50]

Rethinking the Relation between Building and Urban Space

In the summer of 1965, Niemeyer visited the exhibition on Brasília at the Musée des Arts Décoratifs (Palais du Louvre, Paris), which received thirty thousand visitors in fifteen days, among them Juscelino Kubitschek and André Malraux. While in Paris, he worked

49 Niemeyer, 2000b, p. 106.   **50** Niemeyer, 1993c, p. 133.

on a masterplan for a tourist resort on the beach of Caesarea in Israel (1965, unrealized), commissioned by Edmond de Rothschild; a masterplan for Pena Furada, Algarve, Portugal (1965, unrealized), with Viana de Lima; and the masterplan for Grasse. The architect Jean Nicolas, a member of the French Communist Party's Commission of Architecture and Urbanism, played a decisive role in the party's decision to entrust to Niemeyer the project for the new Party Headquarters in Paris (1967–80, with Paul Chemetov, Jean Deroche, Hans Müller, José Luis Pinho, A. Gattos and Jean-Maur Lyonnet; curtain wall by Jean Prouvé; structural engineer Jean Tricot). The two architects, together with ex-minister and member of parliament Georges Gosnat, worked out the programme for the building, which was on a triangular corner site opening onto the place du Colonel Fabien (*nom de guerre* of Communist resistance hero Pierre Georges), in Paris's nineteenth *arrondissement*. The editor of the *Architectural Review* of March 1972 speculated that, 'Although the decision to build was taken before the 1968 elections (at which the party lost 40 seats) the new headquarters may also be seen as an act of consolidation, a bold and imaginative gesture which the leadership believed to be necessary at a time when the party's political fortunes stood at a low ebb.' The same article hailed Niemeyer's French Communist Party (PCF) Headquarters as 'probably the best building in Paris since Le Corbusier's Cité de Refuge for the Salvation Army' (1929–33).[51]

The maintenance of a 'balance between volumes and open spaces' was, according to Niemeyer, the guiding design principle. Consistent with the maximization of open, green spaces in his urban planning proposals over the previous years, Niemeyer's expressed objective was to reimagine and open up the urban ground, 'avoiding excessive occupation of the site', thus improving the quality of life in the densely built city. To create 'the example which the city needed', he offered back to Paris 'the green space which the municipal authorities, ecology and architecture all demanded'.[52] The idea of returning the site to the city also continued the tradition initiated by the site's previous owner, a trade union: they had allowed Constantin Melnikov's Russian Pavilion from the 1925 *Exposition des Arts Décoratifs et Industriels Modernes* in Paris to be re-erected there and used as a 'workers' university' (it was demolished during World War II).

Niemeyer's cardinal achievement lies in his skilful exploitation of the irregular site and the plastic manipulation and reinvigoration of the ground, which is freed but not abandoned, integrated into the building programme and reintroduced into the life of the city. Adopting 'the well-tried formula, first introduced in 1930 by Le Corbusier's Pavillon Suisse, of a tall slab contrasted with a low-lying and freer form', and turning the irregularity of the site to advantage, Niemeyer positioned an undulating slab for the secretariat at the highest point, preserving the natural slope of the terrain towards the square.[53] The vertical circulation tower and basement

French Communist Party Headquarters, Paris, 1967–80: view from the place du Colonel Fabien

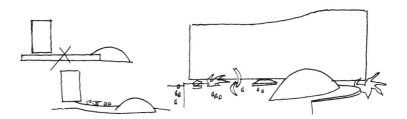

French Communist Party Headquarters, Paris, 1967–80: sketches exploring the relation between the building elements and the site

service and car-parking access are located between the slab and the neighbouring site behind it, with access from avenue Mathurin Moreau. The six-storey secretariat block is supported on ten pairs of columns carrying balanced cantilevered floors (and incorporating service ducts), and gathered at ground level onto five piers tied together by a beam.

The large open space is contiguous with the street (although a fence eventually introduced on the pavement line did compromise the design) and is organized around the Central Committee auditorium dome, which bulges out of the ground – an opaque, white mount against the dark tinted glass of the secretariat's undulating curtain wall. To prevent the 450-seat auditorium from dominating the public plaza, Niemeyer buried this volume underground, allowing only part of the dome to become visible. The dome is irregularly shaped, only its top segment being a section of a sphere. As the paved area slopes and wraps around it, its asym-

51 'Within Party Walls', 1972, pp. 133–34. **52** Niemeyer, 'Head Office of the French Communist Party', in *Oscar Niemeyer: Notebooks of the Architect*, n.p. **53** 'Within Party Walls', 1972, p. 134.

metry is accentuated and it acquires an endearing gentleness, becoming an ordinary, even humorous, object, seeking attention, keen to participate in the everyday life of the city – not a perfectly shaped Platonic volume suggesting a long pedigree the PCF might not have wanted to invoke. The street pavement flows into the site in the form of a sinuous ramp snaking through green ground, both ceremonial and promenade-like, then developing into an esplanade near the main block. When viewed from the roof, the dome with the ramp coiling around it forms the shape of a dove – an association cherished by the building's occupants. The concrete esplanade spills into avenue Mathurin Moreau. From this side, the dome looks like it is about to slide down and drift out into the street.

The plaza pavement peels off the ground and curls up where it slots under the main block, veiling the sturdy columns of the *pilotis* along the central longitudinal axis and allowing the undulating volume to appear to levitate weightlessly above the ground, pushing the Corbusian '*clean line of the underside of a building*' to new limits.[54] The lifted ground is mirrored by the lowest slab of the block, tapering towards a slim edge, intensifying the effect of lightness. Ground and slab come very close to each other but never meet. The lines created by the precisely crafted timber shuttering on the underside of the bare-concrete slab, perpendicular to the undulating walls, direct the eye towards the shadow margin, which suggests a new, seemingly infinite horizon where previously there was none. The curved ground prevents the viewer from getting close to the edge, safeguarding the illusion.

A jutting, white undulating canopy, invisibly attached to the underside of the administration block, signals the point of entry to approaching visitors. It is set in dialogue with another plastic intervention by Niemeyer, an abstract white sculpture to the left of the entrance. Preserving the building envelope and its underside intact and pointing to the main public spaces that lie underground, the entrance to the building is through an opening in the ground. A shallow stair narrows as it descends to a glass door. The undulating curtain wall was designed by Jean Prouvé. It was reported at the time that the all-glass façade was substituted, at Niemeyer's insistence, for one clad in *brises-soleil*, which the client had originally demanded for security reasons.[55] Prouvé's persistent quest for maximum clarity in form and tectonics, his unorthodox structures and penchant for constructional innovation made him an ideal collaborator for Niemeyer. He devised for the secretariat block a bespoke stainless-steel-and-glass façade 'of great finesse, deriving its rhythm primarily from its vertical stiffeners', avoiding horizontal lines so as to enhance Niemeyer's undulating curve.[56] To avoid the need for an air-conditioning system, he also incorpo-

French Communist Party Headquarters: view of the Central Committee auditorium dome and the esplanade from the roof terrace

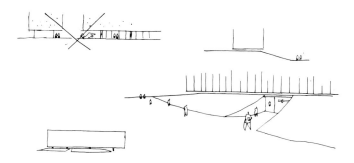

French Communist Party Headquarters: main entrance leading to the sunken 'foyer of the working classes'

Sketch of the 'foyer of the working classes' with the lower part of the auditorium dome visible *in the background*

54 Le Corbusier, 1991, p. 58, emphasis in the original. **55** Cantacuzino, p. 144. **56** Allégret, pp. 168–72.

rated glass panes that open outwards, the mechanism remaining invisible from the outside.

The reception hall or 'foyer of the working classes', as well as exhibition spaces and the auditorium, are all located underground – an area Niemeyer conceived as a 'prolongation of the site', spatially organized by means of built-in concrete furniture and raked ceilings and floors.[57] Deprived of natural light, these cavernous spaces are rather grim, overpowered by the bare reinforced concrete. 'Like the catacombs of the early Christians, they recall the secret origins of the party', Sherban Cantacuzino has suggested.[58] The only source of natural light, a glazed strip around the opaque auditorium dome, draws the visitor towards the skewed, dramatically lit, white walls of what looks like a spaceship that has pierced the ground and landed on the green carpet. The spacecraft theme continues in the airlock-like doors and other futuristic details of the auditorium. The foyer floor slopes towards the auditorium's entrance, and, upon crossing the threshold, the

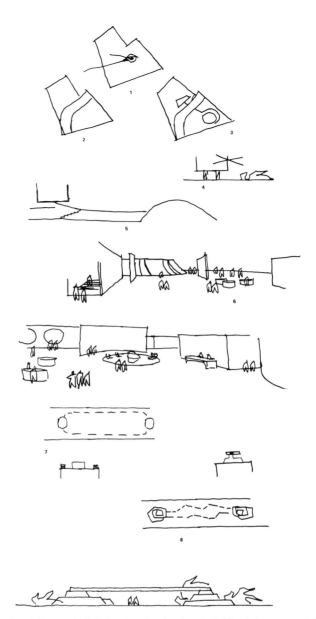

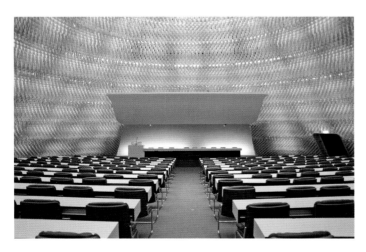

visitor is greeted by the sparkling spectacle of the dramatically illuminated cupola, intricately filigreed with thousands of light-diffusing anodized aluminium blades (lamelles).

Contrasting with the dark spaces underground, the top-floor refectory is filled with light – its glazing system also designed by Jean Prouvé – and enjoys views over Paris. Here and throughout the building – except in office corridors – ceiling, column and wall surfaces are left unplastered as bare or painted concrete, resulting in uncomfortably high levels of noise in the dining area. The refectory benefits from a terrace with a free-form opening to the sky behind the glazed façade. The entrance and serving areas feature blue-and-white glazed ceramic tiles by Athos Bulcão. A whole new landscape in bare reinforced concrete unfolds at

57 Niemeyer, 1968, p. 90.   58 Cantacuzino, p. 144.

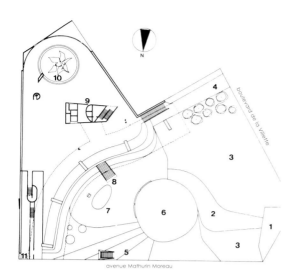

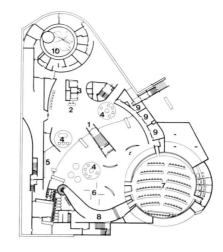

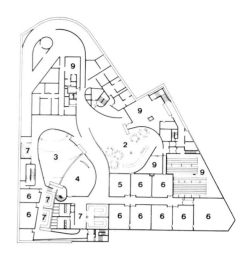

esplanade plan

1 entrance
   (place du Colonel Fabien)
2 ramp
3 lawn
4 service entrance
   (boulevard de la Villette)
5 entrance
   (avenue Mathurin Moreau)

6 auditorium dome
7 esplanade
8 main entrance
9 circulation tower
10 atrium
11 parking access

lower ground floor plan

1 main entrance
2 reception
3 elevators
4 lounge
5 bookshop
6 exhibition area

7 Central Committee
   auditorium
8 passage to basement
   meeting rooms
9 office
10 atrium

first basement plan

1 elevators
2 foyer
3 conference room
4 delegations room

5 TV studio
6 meeting room
7 lounge
8 services

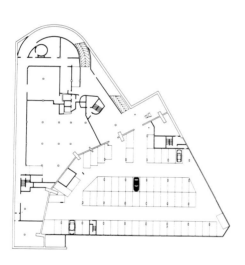

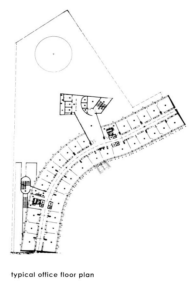

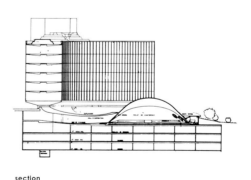

parking plan

typical office floor plan

section

French Communist Party Headquarters, Paris

rooftop level, replacing the roof garden Niemeyer had originally proposed. A series of sculptural events – free-form, ziggurat-like, *in-situ*-cast concrete formations – conceal services, and are offered for appropriation according to need and fancy. The curtain wall rises up to form a parapet at roof level so that this mountainous landscape is seldom revealed to viewers on the ground, poking above the curved block only when seen from a distance and belonging primarily to the polymorphous Parisian roofscape.

It was thanks to his links with the PCF and Jean Nicolas that Niemeyer received a number of other commissions in France. Jean Nicolas had already introduced a number of young architects, like Paul Chemetov and Jacques Kalisz, to the Communist-led municipalities of the new *département* of Seine-Saint-Denis, created in 1964 and known as the Parisian 'banlieue rouge'. In 1972, the General Council of Seine-Saint-Denis commissioned Niemeyer to design for its capital of Bobigny a building that would combine two programmes: that of the local Bourse du Travail (Labour Exchange) – practically an office building – and that of an eight-hundred-seat auditorium (later reduced to six hundred), primarily for the General Council, but also shared by the Bourse du Travail.

Niemeyer's *parti* for the Bourse du Travail (1972–78, with Luis Pinho, Jean-Maur Lyonnet, Jaques Tricot and Jacques Bardet), on a trapezoidal site bordered by avenue Jean Jaurès, rue de la République, rue des Bons Enfants and rue des Marais, reflects the twofold programme. A static, 'simple and economical' four-storey

horizontal office block with pronounced vertical mullions against dark reflective glazing is held aloft on six pairs of *pilotis*, 7.5 metres apart. Against this is set the dynamic, conch-like concrete structure of the auditorium, 'free and lyrical'.[59] The two structures operate independently but share a semi-submerged space – a public foyer that can also remain open outside working hours when the auditorium alone is in use. The latter has a trumpet-like section for acoustic purposes. Its radiating structural beams are expressed externally as nerves on the concrete surface and internally through fluorescent strip lighting.

Bourse du Travail, Bobigny, France, 1972–78: view from avenue Jean Jaurès

Bourse du Travail: the sunken part of the public plaza serves as a forecourt for the submerged foyer of the auditorium

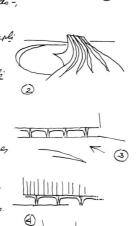

Bourse du Travail: 'explanation' of the design process

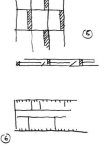

59 'L'œuvre d'Oscar Niemeyer en Seine-Saint-Denis', 2005.

Bourse du Travail: the radiating structural beams of the auditorium volume
are expressed internally through fluorescent strip lighting

At Bobigny, as in Paris, Niemeyer's most striking contribution lies in his sculptural integration of programme, form, structure and topography in order to satisfy the requirements of the building's primary users, while at the same time configuring a much-needed public space with no exchange value, which is seamlessly united with the streetscape and open to appropriation by residents. To this end, he sculpted the ground to create a new, artificially contoured and varied terrain, fertilizing parts of it with elements of the given programme while dynamizing others and diverting them towards the city. The 'whale', 'seagull' or 'albatross', as the sculptural volume of the auditorium has been dubbed, is a new object that consciously contrasts with the banality of its drab suburban surroundings – mainly ghetto housing estates. It is playfully toy-like so as not to intimidate and alienate its hosts, yet strange enough to intrigue them into active encounter. Its bright-yellow wall greets

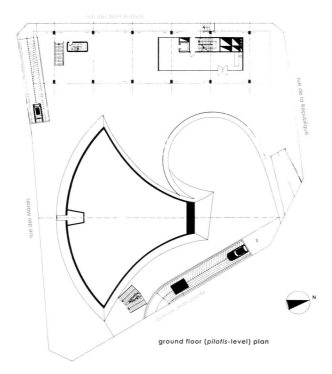

ground floor (*pilotis*-level) plan

basement (foyer level) plan

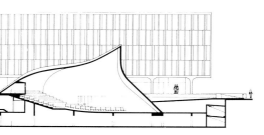
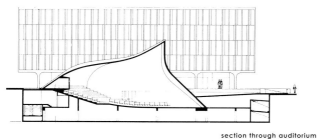

section through auditorium

Bourse du Travail, Bobigny

passers-by, and the sloping ground draws them round the overhanging concrete prow. Here a partly sunken open piazza with a concave boundary is hollowed out of the site, sheltered from northerly winds, also acting as a forecourt for the large foyer incised into the ground. Strata-like formations appear on the ceiling of the cavernous foyer, concealed lighting drawing out the dramatic character of their contour lines.

At the corner of the site, where avenue Jean Jaurès and the rue de la République meet, the ground rises towards the office block, coiling around the lower piazza to create a terrace serving primarily the Bourse du Travail. Without compromising the given programme, Niemeyer's concern at Bobigny was to invent, or rather to generate opportunities for the invention of, new dimensions of inhabitation over and above specified requirements and productivist working hours. His valorization and radicalization of the extra-functionalist spaces of the architectural programme stem from his ability to interrogate the relation of the preconceived programme to its specific location in the city, questioning its dominant role and exclusive rights to the site. What is achieved is a subtle shift of the centre of the architectural experience from the private to the public sphere, from the prescribed programme of functional space to a continuously reinvented programme of

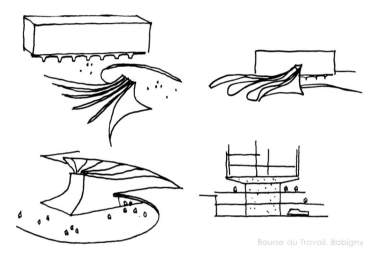

Bourse du Travail, Bobigny

Bourse du Travail: view from the corner of avenue Jean Jaurès with the rue de la République

60 Maria Stella Dutra, quoted in 'L'œuvre d'Oscar Niemeyer en Seine-Saint-Denis', 2005. 61 'L'œuvre d'Oscar Niemeyer en Seine-Saint-Denis', 2005. The first scheme was criticized for its resemblance to the Centros Integrados de Educação Pública (Integrated Centres of Public Education, CIEPs), a series of low-cost school buildings designed by Niemeyer for the state of Rio de Janeiro, using a modular construction system with prefabricated elements (1984–87).

spontaneous appropriation, from the individual building to the city, which the building interprets and thus reshapes.

Through his persistent search for new ways to address the relation between the individual building and the city, Niemeyer effectively redefined his concept of architectural 'spectacle'. He gradually moved beyond the idea of an architecture that is merely beautiful towards an architecture that is more consciously democratic in the sense of being open to those who cannot afford to commission it, and have no influence over or even access to it. Local skateboarders soon responded to the challenging contours and smooth surfaces of Bobigny's newcomer, effectively transforming the site of the Bourse du Travail into a site of leisure, at least outside office hours.

Following the completion of the Bourse du Travail at Bobigny, Niemeyer was invited by Jean Nicolas to contribute to the annual autumn festival organized by *L'Humanité*, the newspaper of the French Communist Party. From 1971, Nicolas encouraged young architects to design innovative temporary structures for this popular 'fête de l'Huma' at the new parc de La Courneuve in Seine-Saint-Denis. In 1978, he entrusted Niemeyer with the task of designing a large structure for the 'Grande Scène' (Great Stage), hosting concerts, debates and so on. Niemeyer's solution, with architect–engineer Hans Walter Müller, consisted of four construction-site cranes carrying a light steel-and-timber canopy with a red fabric cover, and was greatly appreciated for its lightness, practicality and technical exactitude, as well as for its symbolic power. It was praised for successfully dissociating the Communist annual gathering from events of the Woodstock variety, distinguished by its massive red canopy held up by 'the workers' tools'.[60]

A few years later, the director of *L'Humanité*, Roland Leroy, commissioned Niemeyer to design the newspaper's Headquarters (1987–89, with Jean-Maur Lyonnet), at the centre of Saint-Denis on a site to the north-east of the basilica – the first Gothic church. *L'Humanité*'s stone-clad, pseudo-classical elevation towards its historic neighbour, on place Pierre de Montreuil, was imposed by the planning authorities. It was designed by Jacques Bardet, one of the architects responsible for the 1980s revitalization programme for the centre of Saint-Denis, as a fit companion to the medieval church. The preservation of clear views towards the rose window of the basilica from rue Jean Jaurès was also a planning requirement. Niemeyer's curvilinear, Y-shaped plan makes the best of the tight site (which he never visited), and his initial proposal for a latticed concrete envelope indicated acknowledgement of the Gothic monument nearby. Under pressure from his client and the Mayor of Saint-Denis, Marcellin Berthelot, however, he revised his scheme and covered the building with a curtain wall of reflective laminated glass, adopting a technology employed by Peter Rice one year earlier for the great glass walls of the Cité des Sciences at La Villette.[61] *L'Humanité*'s office building was wel-

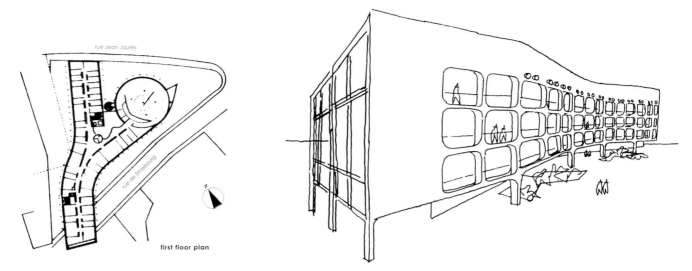

L'*Humanité* Headquarters: view of entrance (north-east) façade along rue Jean Jaurès

comed for its 'fusion of technologies . . . [at] a level of precision and perfection of performance that would have been impossible in the conditions of Brasilia in the late 1950s', demonstrating an ability 'to encompass the enhanced capabilities of the modern curtain-walling industry within an established canon of broad, curvilinear concrete structures from a much earlier time'. Contextual justification was considered superfluous for what was viewed as a 'self-referential' and 'authentic' architecture, as confident as that of its historic neighbour.[62]

By contrast, at Le Havre, Seine Maritime – one of the Norman ports from which French voyages sailed to Brazil in the sixteenth and early seventeenth centuries – Niemeyer's municipal Maison de la Culture (1972–82, with Jean-Maur Lyonnet, Georges Rosevègue, Charles Mourier, Albert Giry for acoustics, and scenographer Raymond Linotte, renamed Espace Oscar Niemeyer) is both a direct response to its context and a highly orig-

inal urban intervention. The centre of the Channel port city was virtually destroyed by Allied aerial bombing during the Second World War. A reconstruction project (1945–55) was undertaken by the Atelier de Reconstruction Auguste Perret (later Atelier de Reconstruction du Havre) – a group of twenty-four architects dedicated to the architectural principles of its *maître* and under his direction. Perret's 'adherence to a strict elementarist functionalism' resulted in a rigorously disciplined architecture governed by modularity, geometrical organization, symmetry and repetition, 'a monolithic unity in which both the major and minor buildings are held in contiguous relationship within the urban fabric'.

As already noted, Niemeyer has often paid tribute to Perret, endorsing his goal of forging an architectural language out of the structure of reinforced concrete and echoing his search for clarity through a deliberate reduction of expressive means. It may be that Niemeyer also feels a sense of solidarity with an architect whose work has been judged as formalist, indulgent, decorative and decadently monumental. With his bold intervention in the centre of Perret's reconstructed Le Havre, however, Niemeyer brought back to the city the architecture of 'grand gestures', 'astonishment and excitement' that Perret had unequivocally exiled. Karla Britton, author of a 2001 monograph on Perret, sees in Niemeyer's Maison de la Culture in place Gambetta (now place du Général de Gaulle) 'the flagrant antithesis of the whole idea of "structural classicism" . . . The juxtaposition of Niemeyer's white assemblage of cinema, theatre and gallery spaces next to the austerity of Perret's unrelenting orthogonality is striking, if not an overt conflict,' she adds.[63]

The concept of Maisons de la Culture was formulated in 1959 by André Malraux at the helm of the newly established French

62 'Oscar Niemeyer and the Bird of Paradise', 1993, p. 51.   63 Britton, pp. 198–201.

Maison de la Culture, Le Havre, France, 1972–82, bracketed by Perret's disciplined buildings; when read from the water, Niemeyer's white curvilinear cones resemble ocean liners afloat

Ministry of Culture, in the context of an ambitious post-war vision of decentralization and national unification. They were to be instituted in each *département* of the country with the mission of promoting the democratization or rather diffusion of (French high) culture as a 'common good', in all its manifestations but with a clear emphasis on theatre. The Musée des Beaux-Arts André Malraux (née Musée des Beaux-Arts du Havre), opened in 1961, was France's first Maison de la Culture, incarnating the concept of the art museum–cultural centre as developed by Georges Salles, director of the French National Museums, and the painter Reynold Arnould, first director of the new institution.[64] The remarkable all-glass building was hailed as the first museum of importance to have been built in France since the 1930s, and it was the first Le Havre building to break with the idiom adopted by Perret's team, reflecting an institution that 'eschew[ed] the idea of the monu-

mental "shrine museum", becoming, in Arnould's words, a "living organism", a "working tool" for "continuous creative activity"'.[65]

In 1967, it lost its dual function. The Maison de la Culture was separated from the museum and was provisionally installed in the Théâtre de l'Hôtel de Ville, adjoining the museum to the east. Following the student riots in Paris in May 1968, the cultural policy that had fostered the Maisons de la Culture was criticized as being imposed by the privileged few, exclusionary and bourgeois. In 1972, the Communist Le Havre municipality, led by André Duroméa, chose Niemeyer as the architect of its definitive Maison de la Culture, on a square measuring 120 × 120 metres on the site

64 It was designed by Guy Lagneau, Michel Weill and Jean Dimitrijevic (LWD), in collaboration with Jean Prouvé, Bernard Laffaille, René Sarger, André Salomon and Raymond Audigier.   **65** Abram, p. 278.

Perret himself had envisaged as 'the centre of Le Havre's intellectual and artistic life'.[66] The choice of Niemeyer as the architect of Le Havre's 'social condenser' may also be related to Malraux's interest in 'other' cultures. Georges Rosevègue, the Maison's director, welcomed the design for 'its confrontation of received ideas and established patterns of thought', hailing it as a 'synthesis of the art of spectacle and architecture'.[67] David Underwood assesses it in the context of Niemeyer's oeuvre as 'the most outspoken statement of the Brazilian architect's conquest of Europe'.[68]

Niemeyer blasted out Le Havre's flat earth to a depth of 3.7 metres and built in its place a fertile landscape of white volcanoes, plateaus and canyons, water cascades, wells, bridges, spiralling pathways and viewing terraces, in which a new culture could grow. The composition is oriented along the diagonal axis of the square, where a central valley functions as a large open foyer. A concrete cantilevered slab unites the various elements of the composition, dominated by two volcano-shaped volumes, stretching the ground of the city to form sinuous *marquises* that shelter various spaces accessed from the lower-level foyer-cum-promenade. Instead of housing the various cultural functions in a new building to be 'viewed from a single angle', Niemeyer opted for a vibrant cultural city within the city, making his architecture part of the continuously unfolding spectacle of culture and providing a new focal point for Le Havre.[69] Under the marine light indelibly associated with the birth of Impressionism through the landscapes of Eugène Boudin and Claude Monet, he rolled out a new, artificial, dynamic landscape fostering an osmotic relationship between city and culture, inviting all citizens to play an active role in the shaping of cultural activity, to 'facilitate the exchange of ideas, to organise encounters, to promote contact', thus returning to the ideas put forward by Arnould.[70]

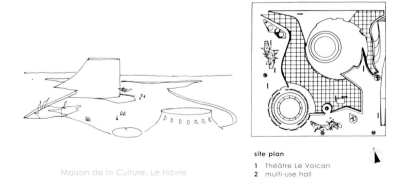

Maison de la Culture, Le Havre

site plan
1 Théâtre Le Volcan
2 multi-use hall

Rather than 'hiding every trace of structure', Niemeyer followed Perret's example and searched for available building technologies to give innovative form to a new conception of culture.[71] 'HERCULE', a computer programme derived from a NASA module for spatial calculation (EGI Office), was used for the construction of the largest of the two concrete shells. Although he did not think it appropriate to continue Perret's modular urban fabric, Niemeyer's intention was not to enter into conflict with the economical city, which had been an effective response to the post-war housing crisis. Rather he sought to complement it with the 'free and lyrical' cultural city that responded to a higher need, beyond utility and economy.[72]

The formal complexity and dynamism of the result are even more striking against Perret's austere, grey modular elevations, but the aim was a new symbiotic relationship. 'When I developed this project', Niemeyer explains,

> my main concern was to integrate it correctly in the architecture of the city. I did not plan, of course, to follow the same type of architecture, which represents a distant epoch, the impositions of the time, and its economics. I wanted my architecture to reveal a new stage in the field of reinforced concrete and to be so simple and abstract that, without being competitive, it accentuates the architectural impact that I imagined.[73]

The centre of Le Havre was inscribed in the UNESCO World Heritage list on 15 July 2005 for 'the innovative exploitation of the potential of reinforced concrete' by Perret and Niemeyer. The different forms adopted by the two architects reflect common principles. In Niemeyer's words, with which Perret would surely have agreed, 'new materials' and 'new techniques' imply that 'beauty will take different forms'.[74]

Sinking his cultural city below ground level, Niemeyer protected it from the port's blustery winds, reduced its visual impact on the existing cityscape and 'allow[ed] people to see it from a higher level', symbolically positioning the democratic city above the city of culture in response to contemporaneous criticism of outdated concepts of cultural institutions.[75] At the same time, this ingenious gesture allowed him to open up a series of public spaces, 'a grand open-air salon' for 'the meeting of [Le Havre's] inhabitants' around the monolithic concrete cones, intersecting with the latter at different levels and providing a forum for organized or spontaneous events, or simply for leisure and pleasure. Of all his projects outside Brazil, Niemeyer considers this as the one with the 'most dominant social content'.[76]

66 'Le Havre: Maison de la culture "le Volcan"'. 67 Georges Rosevegue, quoted in *La maison de la culture du Havre et le nouvel espace culturel Oscar Niemeyer*, 1981, n.p. 68 Underwood, 1994b, p. 181. 69 Oscar Niemeyer, quoted in *La maison de la culture du Havre et le nouvel espace culturel Oscar Niemeyer*, 1981, n.p. 70 Reynold Arnould, quoted in Abram, p. 278. 71 Britton, p. 198. 72 Oscar Niemeyer, quoted in *La maison de la culture du Havre et le nouvel espace culturel Oscar Niemeyer*, 1981, n.p. 73 Oscar Niemeyer, quoted in Underwood, 1994b, p. 181. 74 Niemeyer, 1993c, p. 194. 75 Niemeyer, 2004, p. 200. 76 Niemeyer, 1983, p. 44.

Maison de la Culture, Le Havre

The fluidly contoured, potent urban landscape is enriched with spectacular yet unimposing structures: zigzagging catwalk platforms that shred into broad spiralling ramps, sloping planes that draw pedestrians from the surrounding street pavements to the lower plaza, stairways, skylights, ventilation shafts, snaking fissures that open up to funnel light to the lower levels, shady loggias, an urban pond and patches of garden. The hyperbolic monolith of the theatre, named Le Volcan in 1990, dominates the composition, reflecting the privileging of theatre in the movement of cultural decentralization. Its asymmetrical shape and double-curvature geometry are reminiscent of the tower atop Le Corbusier's Assembly Palace at Chandigarh. But Niemeyer's pronounced asymmetry lends his white, whimsical tower a dynamic quality befitting its programme and role. Gilbert Luigi suggests that its form is also a reference to the local climate, since it echoes the silhouette of sails filled by the wind.[77]

Le Volcan's shell, which varies in thickness, contains a 1,200-seat amphitheatre and a 350-seat cinema. Malraux's idea was that the Maisons de la Culture would bring artists closer to the public. Niemeyer proposed an articulated and mobile stage to allow multiple arrangements, integrating the spectators with the spectacle.[78] His system was rejected, however, in favour of a classical theatre plan. The lower of the two volcano-shaped volumes, a minimally punctured circular hyperboloid, houses a multi-use hall, half-hemicycle, half-trapezoid, seating between two and five hundred; an eighty-seat auditorium; and meeting and rehearsal rooms. Through a row of narrow vertical perforations light is admitted into the upper-level office spaces, clinging onto the perimeter of the crater. Cafés, a restaurant, shops and administration offices are also accommodated in the spaces on the periphery of the low plaza, in accordance with the client's demands for combining cultural with commercial activities to foster greater cultural diffusion.

Viewed from the water and bracketed by Perret's orthogonal buildings to the south, north and west, the truncated, white curvilinear cones of the Maison de la Culture resemble ocean liners afloat.[79] Obviously delighted, Niemeyer reports that his Le Havre

Spiralling ramp calling for a leisurely walk between the two levels of he city, offering changing views of the Maison de la Culture

Maison de la Culture: Le Havre's 'grand open salon' 3.7 metres below street level, between the two volcano-shaped structures, the theatre, *on the left*, and the multi-use hall, *on the right*

77 Luigi, p. 28.   **78** Puppi, 1996, p. 123.   **79** Originally the white colour of the cones was less pronounced, as it was merely a pigment added to the concrete. Later, it became necessary to coat the structures with protective white paint.

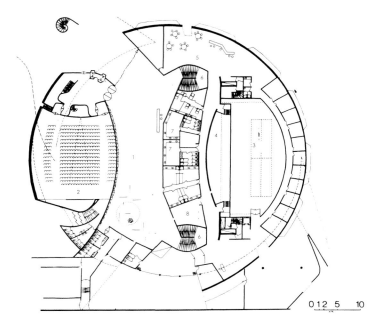

lower level plan

1 foyer and exhibition area
2 350-seat cinema or conference hall
3 stage elevator
4 orchestra pit
5 artists' lounge
6 stair to amphitheatre
7 dressing room
8 rehearsal room

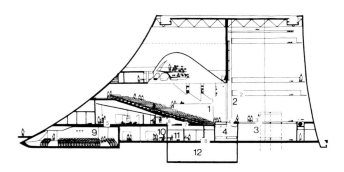

section

1 1,200-seat amphitheatre
2 stage
3 stage elevator
4 orchestra pit
5 350-seat cinema or conference hall
6 foyer and exhibition area
7 dressing room
8 air-conditioning plant room

Maison de la Culture: Théâtre Le Volcan

complex 'received an unexpected compliment from [Bruno] Zevi . . . : "I consider the Le Havre Square to be one of the ten best designs of contemporary architecture." '[80] The planning authorities of Vicenza, on the other hand, remained unconvinced by his proposal for a new Cultural Centre (1978–79, with Federico Motterle, unrealized) – a large open space dominated by 'two sculptures in white marble' for a theatre and a conference centre.[81]

80 Niemeyer, 1998, p. 25. **81** Oscar Niemeyer, quoted in Puppi, 1987, p. 148. **82** Norman Foster's new Wembley Stadium in London (2006), with its iconic arch, also bears a striking similarity to Niemeyer's 1941 design for a stadium in Rio de Janeiro, part of a competition project for a National Athletic Centre, with structural engineer Emilio Henrique Baumgart. Niemeyer's asymmetrical stadium for 130,000 spectators was also dominated by an arch, from which a marquee was suspended via cables, pro-

A New Monastic Landscape for La Sainte-Baume

Niemeyer received a number of other commissions in France, including the Headquarters of Renault at Boulogne-Billancourt, Hauts-de-Seine (1969, unbuilt); the office building Jullia for Société Générale in Fontenay-sous-Bois, Val-de-Marne (inaugurated in 2003, with Emile Schecroun and XAU Architects); and a commercial office tower, PB 17, at La Défense, Paris (1973, unbuilt), vertically divided into four sections separated by 'hanging gardens' – an idea taken up twenty years later by Norman Foster at his Commerzbank Headquarters in Frankfurt (1991–97).[82]

Office tower PB 17, La Défense, Paris, France, 1973, unbuilt: model

tecting the seating area. Niemeyer in turn has claimed inspiration for his arch from Le Corbusier's 1931 competition project for the Palace of the Soviets. According to William Curtis, the latter may be indebted to Eugène Freyssinet's designs for aircraft hangars; Curtis, 1986, p. 92. Niemeyer's Niterói Museum of Contemporary Art (1991–96) appears to be the source of the large structure that crowns Foster's Singapore Supreme Court (2000–05).

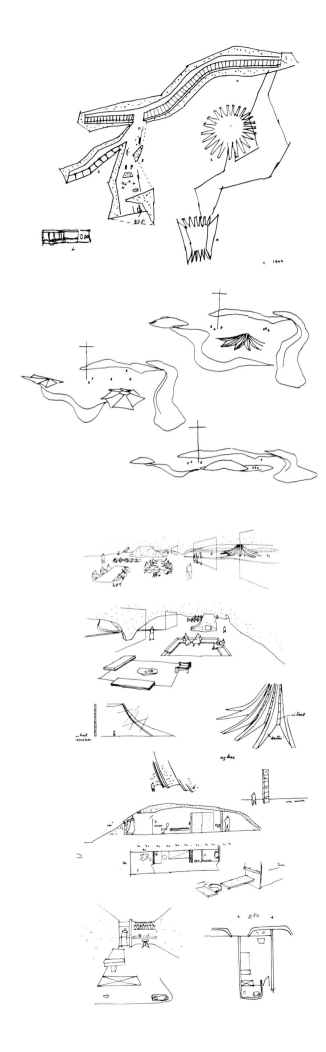

The most innovative of Niemeyer's unrealized French projects was his design for a Dominican monastery at La Sainte-Baume near Marseilles (1967). Its programme was defined in consultation with Père Morelli: 'a cultural and spiritual centre with 100 cells, a common-room, a refectory, a meeting room, a chapel and a conference room.' While this programme is very similar to that of Le Corbusier's Dominican monastery of La Tourette at Eveux-sur-l'Arbresle, the architectural composition is entirely different. Niemeyer's monastery was designed as an integral part of the arid and rocky landscape, pushing the ground-manipulation strategies he was developing at the time to their architectural extreme. At the centre, there is a centrally planned chapel, reminiscent of the dome of Brasília's Metropolitan Cathédral, its glazed truncated curvilinear cone held up by formidable concrete buttresses. It is surrounded by a daring, undulating and branching, smooth land formation that rhymes with a sinuous area of water, blurring the distinction between landscape and building, creating a fluid, artificial topography in reinforced concrete, 'in harmony with the tradition and the imposing beauty of Sainte-Baume'.

In the cave that opens up below the meandering wings are inserted communal living spaces and monastic cells, the latter turned towards the landscape and with a plan based on those of La Tourette but somewhat more spacious and with private shower rooms. Each cell is also provided with a small, private, sheltered terrace. The shallow dome of the semi-submerged conference room also suggests a natural landform, its low-key cupola anchoring the serpentine line of the watercourse and acting as a counterpoint to the exuberant formation of the chapel. Niemeyer related the cave-like wings of the monastery to the places of worship of early Christianity, 'devoid of all the refinements of civilization', and contrasted them to the 'sophisticated, almost Baroque shape' of the chapel. What he proposed was a clear distinction between the cavernous forms that shelter the earthbound, secluded, meditative life of the Dominican friars and the upward-surging, light-filled chapel, where they congregate for the Eucharistic liturgy.

The subterranean spaces of Niemeyer's monastery were also inspired by local tradition, which holds that Mary Magdalene, who came to Marseille and converted the people of Provence, retired to a cave in the Sainte-Baume mountains, her final resting place ('baumo' means 'holy cave' in Provençal). A Dominican monastery has marked the site since the thirteenth century. Le Corbusier had designed the church of St Mary Magdalene nearby, sculpted inside the rock (1947, unbuilt). Aware of the radically innovative nature of his project and probably also of the opposition to Le Corbusier's earlier subterranean scheme, Niemeyer consulted Père Morelli. He relays that the latter respond-

Dominican monastery, La Sainte-Baume, France, 1967, unrealized ed enthusiastically to the 'project and its integration into the religious tradition'.[83] The opportunity to design a monastery at an important pilgrimage site dedicated to the holiest of sinners must have pleased Niemeyer enormously. A resolute atheist, reader of Teilhard de Chardin, he recounts that there was an excellent rapport between him and the Dominican friars, with whom he enjoyed long conversations while designing the monastery at La Sainte-Baume.

In 1967, Niemeyer wrote:

> I am not a Catholic, but I feel an attraction towards religious matters, and especially towards religious speculation over matters I would deeply like to believe in. Now, with the Church integrated in the problems of our times, this attraction has increased. It was with great satisfaction that I heard [the Dominican friars] commenting on the attitude of Cardinal Spellman that 'it shames the cloth'.[84]

Niemeyer's wish to strip the forms of his monastery of 'the refinements of civilization' may also have been politically motivated, symbolizing his denouncement, and that of the Dominicans, of a civilization in the name of which Spellman promoted the Vietnam War. In 1970, Niemeyer withdrew from the American Academy of Arts and Sciences in protest against the war.

Niemeyer's attraction to the church may also have been fostered by the Brazilian Catholic Church's 'twofold radicalization' under the Médici dictatorship: its identification with the cry for social justice and its opposition to the military government through the adoption of 'a defiant stand on human rights'. Under military rule, Catholic activists were arrested and tortured. In 1985, the Catholic Church's leading publishing house, Editora Vozes, produced a report by the research team – comprising both clergy and laymen – of the São Paulo archdiocese *Brasil: Nunca Mais* (*Brazil: Never Again*) which, on the basis of official Military Justice records, documented human rights violations from 1964 to 1979.[85] This extraordinary documentary sold more than 100,000 copies in ten weeks. One year later, Niemeyer was invited to create *Tortura Nunca Mais* (*Torture Never Again*, unrealized) – a monumental sculpture dedicated to those tortured or 'disappeared' during the years of military rule. His 'human figure pierced by evil forces rep-

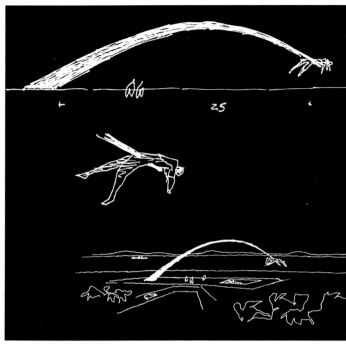

Monument *Tortura Nunca Mais* (*Torture Never Again*), 1986, unrealized

resented by an eighty-two-foot-long curved spear' was to be located in Rio's Parque do Flamengo – the large park at the centre of the city, created by Roberto Burle Marx with Affonso Eduardo Reidy between 1961 and 1965 (renamed Parque Brigadeiro Eduardo Gomes).[86]

In 1979, the Centre Georges Pompidou held a Niemeyer retrospective, planned to coincide with his election to the ordre national de la Légion d'honneur. The same year, he was awarded an honorary doctorate by the Université de Paris–Sorbonne. He closed his office on the Champs-Élysées in 1981. Three days before his hundredth birthday, Niemeyer became commandeur de la Légion d'honneur.

New Topographies of Leisure and Industry

At a meeting in Lisbon in 1966, Niemeyer received a commission from the brothers José and Erico Barreto to design the Park Hotel and Casino on a forested clifftop in Funchal, the capital of the Atlantic island of Madeira (1966–79, with architect Viana de Lima, engineer João Manuel Madeira e Costa, project manager José Lampreia and interior designer Daciano Monteiro da Costa). Located at the highest point of the site, the hotel is accommodated in a long, six-storey-high, curved block on *pilotis*, with two rows of rooms on each floor (Niemeyer had originally proposed only one row, along the concave side, with open views to the ocean). According to the account of Carlos Oliveira Santos, its wide spans,

83 Niemeyer, 'Dominican Convent', in *Oscar Niemeyer: Notebooks of the Architect*, n.p. **84** Niemeyer, 1968, p. 99. Francis Joseph Cardinal Spellman was one of the most powerful American cardinals of the time, archbishop of New York, a key figure behind the Cold War, intimate friend and personal advisor to Pope Pius XII, and active promoter of anti-Soviet policies and US involvement in the Vietnam War. **85** Skidmore, 1988, pp. 181–85, 268. The 1979 amnesty law initially intended for 'political' offenders effectively put tortures beyond the reach of justice. The amnesty was not challenged even by *Brasil: Nunca Mais*, which declared, 'It is not the intention of our Project to assemble a body of evidence to be presented at some Brazilian Nuremberg. We are not motivated by any sense of revenge.' Skidmore argues that 'Acceptance of the amnesty had another source: the "conciliatory" strain in Brazilian political culture . . . Brazilian elites over the last century have believed their people have a unique ability to resolve social crises peacefully.' Skidmore, 1988, pp. 268–69. **86** Niemeyer, 2000b, p. 132.

large columnless spaces – for example, a 3,500-square-metre restaurant – and daring cantilevers stretched engineers and available technology to the limit.[87] A separate circular building housing the casino is held up by thirty-one hyperboloid pillars, like buttresses or 'elegant paws', to use Viana de Lima's simile.[88] The cinema is found in the basement of a third, trapezoidal structure (originally a shell-like form) with foyer and exhibition space on the ground floor.

As in so many of Niemeyer's projects, the most sophisticated structures here are those that hyphenate the buildings, dash forth into the surrounding landscape or unfold languidly in shifting layers that generate a new, complex topography, integrating the buildings with their natural environment. Taking advantage of the slope of the site, Niemeyer inserted a large curvilinear terrace at the corner of the hotel block, jutting out over the swimming pool towards the beach and turning also sideways to look at the panorama of Funchal to the rear. The double-height hotel lobby and restaurant – at a lower level accessed via a ramp – are found under this deck, behind a large transparent façade energized by unevenly spaced mullions. An elaborate promenade, a broad leisurely catwalk between the main block and the casino, branches out halfway into a large spiral ramp reaching down into the lush garden. Similar topographical events occur inside the large spaces of the hotel and casino. Daciano da Costa speaks of a 'wilful geography' that blends into the tectonic plates of the island, and a number of motifs he devised for the interiors rhyme with Niemeyer's topographical design. In 1975, Portugal awarded Niemeyer the Order of Infante D. Henrique.[89]

With an increase in workforce from 335 in 1950 to more than 1,300 fifteen years later, the Mondadori Publishing Group had far outgrown its headquarters in via Bianca di Savoia in the centre of Milan when Arnoldo Mondadori decided to move the company to a purpose-built building in the green zone outside the city. A large site of 200,000 square metres was found 12 kilometres away in Segrate, where a new industrial zone was emerging close to Forlanini Airport and the road to Verona, where the company's printing division was located. The project for the new Mondadori Headquarters (1968–75) was entrusted to Niemeyer (with architects Luciano Pozzo and Glauco Campello, structural engineers Antonio Nicola and Giuseppe Voi, construction manager Giorgio Calanca, and landscape architect Pietro Porcinari).

The vision of the new president of Italy's largest publishing house, Arnoldo's son Giorgio Mondadori, coincided with Niemeyer's: as a tribute to the company's founder, Arnoldo, and all his collaborators (at the time more than 1,300), the new building would resist 'simplistic solutions of a false economy, so common for buildings of this type . . . to become a true expression of contemporary advances in technology and art'. Niemeyer argued that this approach would do justice to the creative activ-

ity of the Mondadori Group and, most importantly, would express a change of values. 'Today', he contended, 'what counts is human industry. It is appropriate to valorize anonymous labour', by housing it in the 'monumental' structures that result from the 'spectacular solutions' made possible by contemporary technology. His architecture, he firmly believed, would express the valorization of Mondadori's workforce by moving beyond mere functionality to encompass characteristics such as monumentality, beauty and even ornamentation, previously exclusive to the 'buildings where the high bourgeoisie lived or entertained itself'. He also pointed out that the available construction methods, especially casting, were far superior to those employed in Brasília a few years earlier, thus ensuring a high-quality finish.[90] As captivating today as when it was designed, the Mondadori Headquarters ranks among Niemeyer's greatest achievements. Hinting at its timeless appeal, he refers to it as 'a modern version of the Greek temple'.[91]

Mondadori Headquarters, Segrate, Italy, 1968–75

The strategy of breaking up the programme into various components allowed for their accommodation in forms suitable to, and expressive of, their function, woven into the landscape to maximize the integration of the vast site into the programme. At the centre of the site, a horizontal orthogonal structure (in a first scheme two undulating blocks) accommodates most of the office space. The editorial and creative teams are housed in a two-storey concrete building, stemming from the base of the main structure and spreading out to the rear in the shape of an enormous undulating willow leaf. Behind its sinuous, 190-metre-long, glazed north façade, open-plan office spaces face out towards

87 Carlos Oliveira Santos, pp. 103–17.   88 Viana de Lima, quoted in Carlos Oliveira Santos, p. 147.   89 Daciano da Costa, quoted in Carlos Oliveira Santos, p. 131.   90 Niemeyer, 1975c, pp. 12–13. 91 Niemeyer, 2007, http://www.lexpress.fr/mag/arts/dossier/architecture/dossier.asp?ida=461868&p=3.

expansive lawns. Its opaque curve to the south, along which services are paraded, is partly submerged in the lake. The lake-side terracing of the concrete volume suggests a landform rather than a building. Another low, terraced, concrete formation also sprouts out of the principal structure, then grows to form what looks like a large island, floating in the lake in front of the office building. Partly submerged, it receives its light primarily through a central, open, polygonal *piazzetta*, around which are arranged a simple Italian trattoria, a coffee bar, shops and so on for the Mondadori employees. Archives, a library and services are located in the basement. A sports complex, also for the Mondadori employees, is found at the rear of the site, next to the staff parking.

Blurring the distinction between building and site, Niemeyer generated a new, artificial landscape to accommodate various parts of the programme in its mounts, folds and crevices, allowing the 250-metre-long office building to carry the burden of representation. From the visitors' parking area, between the lake and the street, below the level of the water surface and concealed from the building complex by dense vegetation, steps lead up to a long bridge over the 20,000-square-metre artificial lake. To the right, a sculpture by Arnaldo Pomodoro rises from the lake to greet the visitor. Concrete benches along the way invite a pause for contemplation of the building vainly peering into the water mirror.[92] Its beauty lies in its two parallel, continuous, open colon-

Aerial view of the Mondadori Headquarters, photograph of 1975

92 The water from the lake is utilized for cooling and irrigation purposes. The air-conditioning plant is located beneath the lake.

Le projet du nouveau siège AME comprend des bureaux, salle de conférence, service généraux, restaurant, etc. Sa localisation et sa finalité suggèrent une architecture différente capable de caractériser l'importance de l'organisation. Dans ce cas, la beauté et l'invention architecturale constituent en soi-même une fonction considérable que d'autres raisons fonctionnelles doivent compléter et définir. Ce sont des caractéristiques qui s'intègrent entre elles, certaines touchant à la logique, au bon fonctionnement de l'ensemble, aux prévisions futures, d'autres aux nouveautés dues aux techniques actuelles et à l'aspect innovateur que l'architecture réclame.

caractéristiques du projet:

1. Les blocs principaux dont les formes libres mais logiques ont les services généraux centralisés. ①

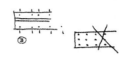

2. Les blocs séparés. Nous avons préféré cette solution pour deux motifs; d'abord pour leur donner une meilleure proportion, ensuite (la principale raison) pour ne pas créer au cours de la deuxième étape une confusion inutile et éviter l'aspect d'une œuvre inachevée qui subsisterait pendant trop longtemps. ②

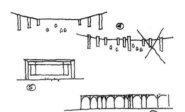

3. La flexibilité intérieure. La solution structurale que nous avons adoptée répond à l'esprit du projet, permettant les divisions mobiles indispensables. Dans ce but nous avons évité de nombreuses colonnes, garantissant ainsi la légèreté du bâtiment et la liberté de l'espace au rez-de-chaussée. ④ Cette idée nous a poussé à suspendre les étages dans une structure extérieure, au moyen de tirants verticaux, solution qui ne contrarie pas les exigences techniques ou économiques. ⑤

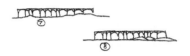

4. Les arcs en rythme varié, solution qui n'interfère pratiquement pas dans le problème structurale. ⑥

5. Pour les corps bas qui comprend les services généraux, nous proposons deux solutions: la première qui définit plastiquement ses éléments; l'auditorium, le restaurant, la bibliothèque, etc. ⑦ l'autre, celle que nous préférons, sans doute la plus belle et originale, met en valeur le bloc principale et crée à l'intérieur les ambiances inattendues qui constituent pour nous la véritable architecture. ⑧

Mondadori Headquarters, first scheme, 1968: 'explanation' of the design process

6. Les accès pourront être étudiés ultérieurement, soit par l'avenue Circonvallazione (solution qui nous paraît la meilleure) soit par le av. Provinciale ⑤ Les deux solutions maintiennent la façade principale du côté de l'av. Circonvallazione, comme il se doit. Les stationnements sont prévus pour 1000 véhicules.

Les différents arcs, le pan de verre des façades, les formes quasi abstraites des arcs généraux et le miroir d'eau qui enrichit le tout, sont les compléments plastiques de l'ensemble qui garantiront, nous l'espérons, à l'AME, l'importance désirée et à ses visiteurs l'effet que seules la surprise et la beauté peuvent provoquer.

oscar niemeyer.

Paris, 8/9/68

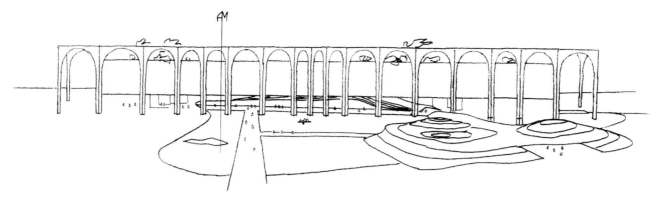

Mondadori Headquarters, first scheme, 1968

Oscar Niemeyer in front of the model of the first scheme
for the Mondadori Headquarters, photograph of 1969

Giorgio Calanca, Luciano Pozzo, Giorgio Mondadori and Oscar Niemeyer
looking at the model of the first scheme for the Mondadori Headquarters,
photograph of 1969

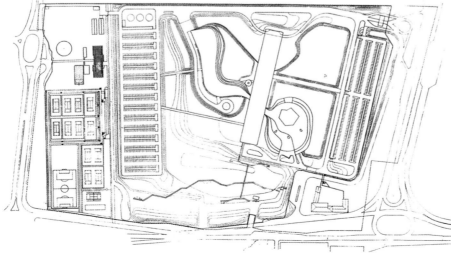

site plan

Mondadori Headquarters, Segrate,
final scheme, 1973

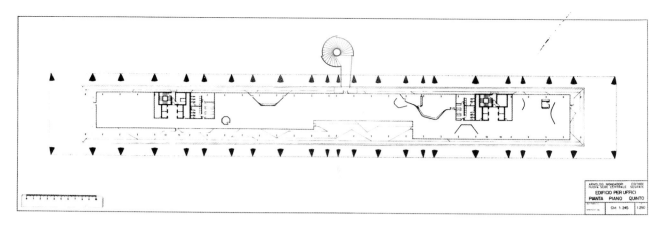

fifth floor plan

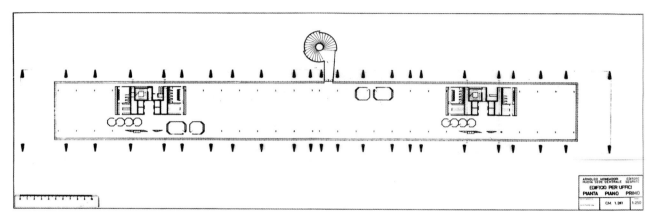

first floor plan

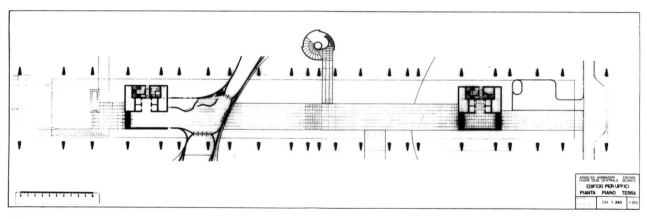

ground floor plan

Mondadori Headquarters, final scheme: office building

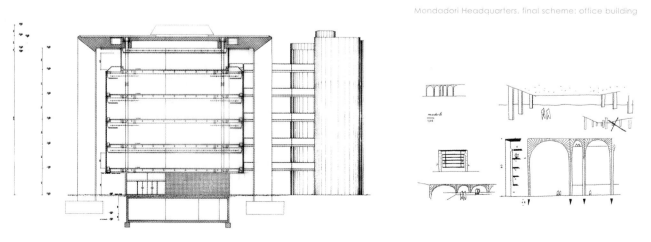

section   working sketches

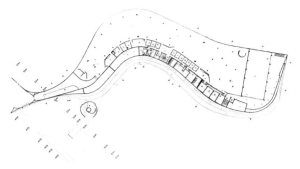

mezzanine plan

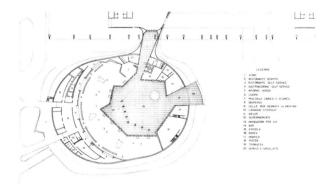

ground floor plan

LEGENDA

1 ATRIO
2 RISTORANTE SERVITO
3 RISTORANTE SELF-SERVICE
4 DISTRIBUZIONE SELF-SERVICE
5 RITORNO VASSOI
6 CUCINA
7 PIAZZALE CARICO E SCARICO
8 DISPENSA
9 CELLE PER DERRATE ALIMENTARI
10 LAVAGGIO STOVIGLIE
11 RIFIUTI
12 SUPERMERCATO
13 MONDADORI PER VOI
14 BAR
15 EDICOLA
16 BANCA
17 PORTICO
18 PIAZZA
19 TERRAZZA
20 SERVIZI E SPOGLIATOI

nades with a 30-metre span between them, each comprising twenty-three 25-metre-high columns. Giorgio Mondadori had visited Brasília and asked Niemeyer for a building along the lines of the Palácio do Itamaraty. The imposing, hand-crafted, fair-faced, *in-situ*-cast concrete arcades of the Mondadori Headquarters resemble those of Itamaraty but at Segrate Niemeyer incorporated a random aspect into the design, deploying the principle of irregular intervals applied by Iannis Xenakis in the *pans de verre ondulatoires* at La Tourette. Niemeyer speaks of a 'distinctive

Mondadori Headquarters: view of main façade

Mondadori Headquarters, final scheme: *top left,* editorial quarters; *bottom left and above,* island with restaurant, café and shops

rhythm' or, invoking Perret, of a 'symphony of posts' that conveys the idea of a perfect integration of architecture and structure.[93]

As in Brasília, here too monumentality lies in accentuated horizontality, ethereality and musicality. The structural engineers' ingenuity subordinated the individuality of the constituent parts to the unity of the composition: on each elevation, the twenty-two parabolic arches of variable width – from 3.5 to 15 metres – and variable curvature are united by a single parametric equation.[94] This solution helped overcome the formidable challenges of construction. Visual continuity was achieved through the casting of the triangular-section columns in a single pouring. A dedicated team of highly skilled carpenters patiently constructed the complex timber shuttering, adding visual and tactile texture to the musical colonnades. The precisely patterned surface of the concrete is virtually flawless. On a typical cold and foggy day it appears warm, soft and comforting. It has aged beautifully. The seemingly whimsical intercolumniation, creating an image at once serene and dynamic, is echoed by the unevenly spaced rows of poplars on the other side of the lake. Niemeyer claims inspiration from Rainer Maria Rilke: 'These trees are magnificent, but even more magnificent is the sublime and moving space between them.'[95]

93 Niemeyer, 2004, p. 204; Niemeyer, 1975c, p. 13.   94 Calanca, p. 21.
95 Niemeyer, 2004, p. 206.

Niemeyer attributed the source of the Mondadori Headquarters' colonnade to the image evoked by Rainer Maria Rilke: 'These trees are magnificent, but even more magnificent is the sublime and moving space between them.' A row of unevenly spaced poplars, on the other side of the lake, composes precisely such an image.

Unlike those at the Palácio do Itamaraty, the Mondadori Headquarters' graceful columns bear also a formidable structural load. Abolishing the traditional *pilotis*, Niemeyer suspended a five-storey prism of steel and glass from the roof beams between the two colonnades, concealed behind the elegantly shaped arches. The top floor of this cella is deeply recessed and enveloped in clear, mullionless glass, so that it disappears in the shade behind the arches, making the four lower storeys of the dark glass cella appear to levitate in mid-air, 3.4 metres off the ground. Two internal circulation towers provide contact with the ground, their walls at this level dissolving behind Athos Bulcão's playful cladding of black-and-white tiles, which prevent the eye from resting on their surface. To the rear of the building, an opaque circular stair tower is the only vertical element of the composition.

Mondadori Headquarters: *above*, open-plan office space; *below*, fifth-floor terrace

Niemeyer convinced Mondadori to move to working spaces radically different from those they were used to inhabiting. Office space that was totally open-plan, even for senior management, was considered highly innovative at the time and was criticized and ridiculed in the local press. It was adopted for the first time in Italy by this publishing house, which celebrated efficiency gains and the elimination of 'symbols of hierarchy'.[96] Fittings and furnishings were selected with an eye to their noise-absorption properties. Services were concealed behind false ceilings composed of light-diffusing anodized aluminium blades. At fifth-floor level, internal gardens and viewing terraces enhance the office landscape.

Following the completion of the Mondadori Headquarters, one of Niemeyer's most accomplished and enchanting projects, he was requested to design a building of 'expressive and symbolic power' to accommodate the FATA Engineering European Group Headquarters in Pianezza, near Turin (1975–80), with architect Massimo Gennari and structural engineer Riccardo Morandi. The client envisaged 'a healthy provocation in the anonymous and destroyed landscape of the industrial outskirts [of Turin], and at the same time . . . a fitting image of the growing economic and technological prestige of [the FATA Engineering Group]'. According to Niemeyer's collaborator in the project, Massimo Gennari, its 'greatest expressive power is inherent in the spectacular nature of the structural language'.[97]

Indeed, what it lacks in elegance, the FATA building makes up for in structural complexity, which demanded highly sophisticated construction methods. Pre-stressing and a combination of pre-cast and *in-situ*-cast reinforced-concrete elements were used. A large glazed volume is held 5 metres off the ground, seemingly effortlessly, by six powerful, 15-metre-high pylons, three along each of the long sides of the orthogonal volume. These pillars, measuring 3.6 × 1.5 metres, are hollow, made of concrete 40 centimetres thick. They support two longitudinal hollow, pre-stressed concrete trusses 107 metres in length (1.5 × 3.7 metres and 30 centimetres thick), from which the three-storey volume is suspended by means of fourteen cables. At each end, the suspended volume is cantilevered by 19.35 metres. Service networks are hidden in the hollow structural members.

A restaurant and service areas are located below ground level. The terrain is manipulated to slope down towards a glazed wall, allowing natural light into the restaurant and at the same time concealing the street and FATA's industrial neighbours behind a green meadow. Skylights and a courtyard with a relief by the Italian artist Nerone (Giovanni Ceccarelli) admit more natural light into the subterranean spaces. The top floor, behind the con-

96 *Espansione*, 1975, p. 38. In an interview with Noemi Lucarelli, Niemeyer declared: 'I don't consider open-plan the only solution, but the most democratic one'; 'L'Oscar dello spazio aperto', interview with Noemi Lucarelli, 1980, p. 92.   **97** Gennari, pp. 79–81.

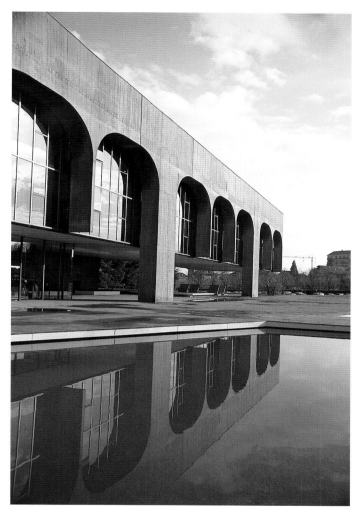

FATA Engineering European Group Headquarters, Pianezza, Italy, 1975–80: view of main façade

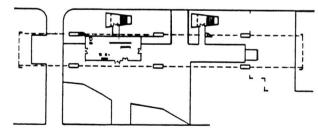

ground floor plan

elevation

FATA Engineering European Group Headquarters, San Mauro Torinese

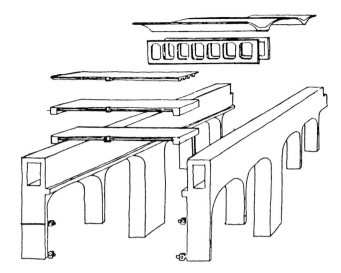

FATA Engineering European Group Headquarters: structural elements

crete beams, receives natural light through a centrally located terrace garden, open to the sky. Vertical circulation is through two concrete trapezoidal towers linked to the rear of the building by transparent volumes. The entrance lobby is also a bright, transparent pavilion under the hand-crafted, striped concrete soffit.

The large body of the building looming overhead relies on technological achievement to make an impact. Niemeyer thought it apposite to house an engineering-based company in a building that beats its chest in the name of engineering. Although a triumph of technical competence, technology is employed in a rather too literal fashion. The result demonstrates that, when the full-blown muscle of technology is celebrated for its own sake, architecture, sadly, remains poorly served, just as dance is not simply a matter of jumping high.

Shifting the emphasis from engineering to integrated site, programme and form manipulation for the Cartiere Burgo Headquarters in San Mauro Torinese, near Turin (1978–81, with Federico Motterle), Niemeyer designed a circular island building – 'a cathedral in the middle of the desert' – embraced by undulating lawns and composed of three principal spaces. At first sight, from the point of entry to the property, the striped black and white drum that defines the building appears to be suspended in the sky.[98] The illusion is amplified by the still waters of the artificial lake, a strip of grass between the two creating a horizontal axis of symmetry. Initially perceived as a single-storey volume with four attached circulation towers, the headquarters actually comprises three concentric levels. General services and a restaurant are arranged on the periphery of the lowest, semi-submerged level; at its centre is located a large vestibule with oval stained-glass windows by Marianne Peretti. The external ground dips towards the

98 The detailing of the external surface of the drum strongly resembles that of the façade of the Ministry of the Army in Brasília.

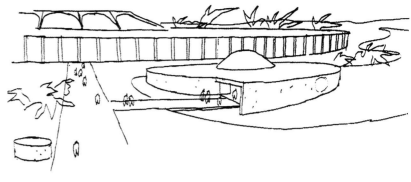

recessed glazed surfaces of this lower level to let in natural light, at the same time defining four radial access routes and creating the floating effect. The elongated drum contains the *piano nobile*: a large ring of open-plan office space for administrative staff, turned towards a cloistered garden. From the centre of the void, rises an arcaded dome, which accommodates a circular office space for the company's management (originally open-plan but eventually subdivided). Radiating bridges link its loggia to the roof of the larger ring. The steeply canted arches frame spectacular views to the snow-covered mountains.

While working on private commissions, Niemeyer was also invited to design a number of public buildings in Italy – including a slick scheme for the new Ponte dell'Accademia in Venice (1985), and one for a stadium in Turin (1987) – none of which was built. More recently, he designed an auditorium for Ravello (2000–, in planning), on a site overlooking the Amalfi Coast that has been hosting open-air concerts every summer since the 1930s. Niemeyer's design for a student hall of residence at St Anthony's College, Oxford, United Kingdom (1973), which proposed extensive use of prefabricated elements, also remained unrealized. The same fate befell his design for a leisure and swimming pool complex in Potsdam, Germany (2005). His latest offering to the city of Paris, a 6-metre-high red, steel wire line sculpture of an open hand holding out a flower as a sign of 'peace and friendship' between Brazil and France, was installed in January 2007 in front of Frank O. Gehry's American Centre (1994, today the Cinématèque Française), at place Léon Bernstein, parc de Bercy.[99] The Cultural

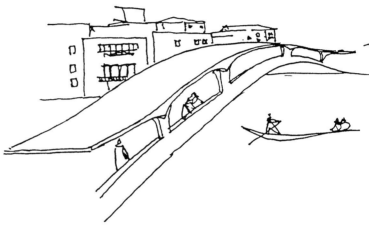

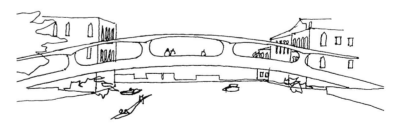

99 The model of Niemeyer's sculpture was officially presented to the mayor of Paris in 2005 by the president of Brazil, Luiz Inácio da Silva, in the context of a programme of events celebrating Brazilian culture, entitled '2005, Year of Brazil in France'. Gehry's building was also originally intended to strengthen cultural bonds – between France and the USA.

Centre Oscar Niemeyer (2006, in planning), named after its designer, who in 1989 received Spain's Prince of Asturias Prize, is expected to play a central role in the urban revitalization of Avilés – a former industrial port in the principality of Asturias, on Spain's north coast. His monumental sculpture of an open-mouthed beast confronted by a man brandishing the Cuban flag was offered to Fidel Castro on his eightieth birthday (13 August 2006) and erected in a large reflective pool of water, in a 20,000-square-metre plaza at the University of Information Science in Havana. The unveiling ceremony, on 28 January 2008, 'began with the reading of a message sent by Niemeyer in which he dedicated the monument to the struggle of the Cuban people in defense of their sovereignty against the imperialist monster'.[100]

From the mid-1970s, Niemeyer travelled back and forth between Brazil and Europe, but increasingly his collaborators took responsibility for the execution of his projects on the eastern side of the Atlantic. Although he treasured the opportunity to work abroad and export his Pau-Brasil architecture, during his years of

exile Niemeyer was increasingly burdened by nostalgia for Brazil, 'Where the sky is more blue'.[101] In 1982, he returned to 'the city of Brazilians' – João Gilberto's appellation for Rio de Janeiro – where he would spend the rest of his life.

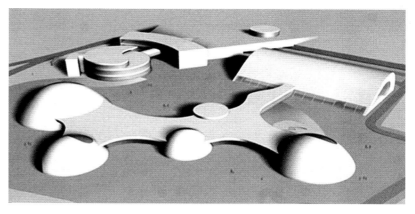

Leisure and swimming pool complex, Potsdam, Germany, 2005, unbuilt

Sculpture, place Léon Bernstein, Parc de Bercy, Paris, France, installed January 2007

100 http://embacuba.cubaminrex.cu/Default.aspx?tabid=7120.
101 'Onde o céu azul é mais azul' is a song by Francisco (de Moraes) Alves (1941) belonging to the *samba exaltação* genre, which emerged during the Vargas period, praising the virtues of the nation. It assumed some significance for Caetano Veloso, when the latter was imprisoned by the military regime, in early 1969. Veloso, pp. 247–8.

Chapter Nine

Reclaiming the Right to the Beach

*Sous l'*asfalto, *la plage!*

Rail surfing is an incredibly dangerous sport in which youths from Rio's *zona norte favelas* balance atop commuter trains travelling at over 80 kilometres per hour, dodging the high-voltage cables passing rapidly overhead.[1] In 1989 alone, 150 rail *surfistas* lost their lives in gruesome accidents and another 170 were injured. Attempts to stop the reckless sport have proven ineffective. Daniel Touro Linger ventures the suggestion that 'rail surfing is an icon for the fluid psychological equilibrium required to negotiate the dangers of lower-class life in these Brazilian slums, where fighting and police terror are rampant'.[2] The poor youths' free ride that shocks fare-paying fellow train travellers re-enacts, outside the invisible spaces of the poverty-stricken communities in which these youths live, the tragic reality of crossing streets where stray bullets from the police and drug-trafficking gangs are flying. The youths' disrespect for life is related to the perception that life in an environment where 'bullets talk' is worthless.[3] A flamboyant display of involuntarily acquired survival skills, the absurd sport reflects the absurd and adverse circumstances of the *surfistas*' everyday lives.

Linked by its transgressiveness to skateboarding, rail surfing seems, Linger suggests, 'symbolically counterposed to the wave surfing of the middle-class youths' – those of Rio's *zona sul*. Rail and wave surfing are thus portrayed as another manifestation of Rio de Janeiro's social and spatial segregation between the *morro* and the *asfalto*, literally meaning asphalt, but figuratively the spaces of the planned city with paved streets – that is, infrastructure – distinguishing them from the unplanned hillside 'invasions' on the *morros*.

The social and spatial segregation of Rio de Janeiro and Latin American cities in general is not a recent phenomenon. At the beginning of the twentieth century, Mayor Pereira Passos's urban renewal projects radically altered the geographic distribution of Rio's social classes. Under his 'civilizing' axe had fallen the downtown nightlife establishments 'where the popular classes occasionally rubbed shoulders with the elite', together with the *corticos* of the poor – '"nests" of yellow fever, of all infectious diseases, of

vice and crime', located in close proximity to the houses of Rio's late nineteenth-century bourgeoisie (and the government).[4]

However, representations of a 'divided city' – for example, Zuenir Ventura's book, *A cidade partida*, 1994 – ignore the continuous and complex cultural and economic interactions and (unequal) exchanges between the segregated parts of Latin American cities like Rio. While Brasília failed to fulfil the dream of a 'perfect social coexistence', Rio de Janeiro recovered its status as 'a symbol of [Brazilian] nationality'.[5] Rio's beaches – the largest, cheapest and most popular urban spaces of leisure and pleasure – were reasserted, somewhat romantically, as privileged repositories of the Brazilian multi-racial, egalitarian utopia – sites of freedom and fraternization for the entire spectrum of Brazilian society. In 1957, Billy Blanco sang:

> I'm not an Indian or anything . . .
> And if my skin is brown
> It's from the sun of the beach where I was born and happily
>   raised.
> I won't, I won't go to Brasília,
> Even if it's to make a pile.
> There's no comparing the life,
> Even hard, expensive –
> I want to be poor without leaving Copacabana.[6]

The epigraph to this chapter is a paraphrase of a slogan dating from the student riots in Paris in May 1968: 'Sous les pavés, la plage!' ('Under the cobblestones, the beach!')   1 The low-income neighbourhoods in Rio de Janeiro's *zona norte*, extending well beyond the municipal boundaries, are usually referred to as 'subúrbios', literally translated as 'suburbs', but with very different connotations from those this word carries in English. *Morro, favela* and *subúrbio* all refer to stigmatized low-income communities, mostly squatter settlements but sometimes, in the *zona norte*, also including *subúrbios* of social housing. In 2000, 19 per cent of the population of Rio de Janeiro lived in more than six hundred such communities. Since the 1980s, Rio de Janeiro has experienced an exodus of the population from the city centre and higher population growth rates in *favelas* than in the rest of the city.   2 Linger, p. 244, n. 7. The sport is now practised in many countries outside Brazil, including the USA, South Africa, Bangladesh and the UK.   3 Borrowed from a phrase in Paulo Lins's 1997 novel *Cidade de Deus*: 'Words fail. Bullets talk.'   4 Meade, pp. 43, 69. The second quotation is from the Brazilian Academy of Medicine (1884). 5 Journal of Companhia Urbanizadora da Nova Capital do Brasil, quoted in Holston, p. 20; Caetano Veloso.   6 A famous samba by Billy Blanco, recorded in 1957, cited in Epstein, p. 74.

Incidents such as the *arrastões* (dragnets or beach sweeps) of October 1992, however, when young *suburbanos* from the *zona norte* moved through the beaches of the *zona sul*, allegedly harassing bathers, appear, along with the ensuing media hysteria, to have dealt a fatal blow to the long-cherished utopia of the Rio beach.[7] 'What was unprecedented about the *arrastões*', argues Lorraine Leu, 'was the rupture to the social contract of cordiality that has traditionally helped to defuse class and racial conflicts in [Brazilian] public spaces.'[8] In a 1999 film, *O primeiro dia* by Walter Salles and Daniela Thomas (literally translated as 'The First Day', but released as *Midnight*), the first day of the millennium finds the main characters – the privileged middle-class Maria (Fernanda Torres), at a moment of personal crisis, and the fugitive police-commissioned assassin from the *favela* João (Luis Carlos Vasconcelos) – on the beach of Copacabana, committed to reclaiming hope and starting a new life. João meets his death on the beach; his utopia is denied. Maria emerges from the legendary sea baptized, reborn to a new awareness of the tragedies of death and the underclass in the 'marvellous city'.[9] With the exhaustion of the ideology of racial democracy and the erosion of the dream of social integration, Brazil's legendary optimism appears to have given way to pessimism and disillusion; the beach seems to have lost its credibility as a utopian, open, mixed and democratic space.

In his 1965 manifesto 'An Aesthetic of Hunger', subsequently published as 'L'esthétique de la violence' ('The Aesthetic of Violence'), Cinema Novo director Glauber Rocha declared: 'Cinema Novo shows that the normal behavior of the starving is violence; and the violence of the starving is not primitive . . . An esthetic of violence . . . is revolutionary.'[10] During the repressive years of Brazil's military dictatorship, from 1964 to 1985, social marginality was politicized and allegorized as a form of resistance and opposition. In 1966, Hélio Oiticica created in Rio de Janeiro the installation *Bólide caixa 18 (homenagem a Cara do Cavalo)* (*Flaming Meteorite Box No 18 [Homage to Horseface]*), a box that contained four newspaper-like photographs of the dead body of Cara do Cavalo – an urban outlaw executed by the police in 1964 – with open arms alluding to the Crucifixion. The artist's expressed intention was

> to honour what I think is the social revolt of the individual: that of the so-called *marginais* (social outcasts). Such an idea is very dangerous but something necessary for me. There is a contrast, an ambivalent aspect in the behaviour of the marginalised man. Next to a great sensibility there is violent behaviour and often, crime is a desperate search for happiness.[11]

Oiticica's message became more explicit in a 1968 banner: under the image of the same corpse appeared the slogan 'Seja marginal, Seja herói' ('Be an Outcast, Be a Hero'). Udigrudi (Underground) or Cinema Marginal (Marginal Cinema) films like Ozualdo Candeias's *A margem* (*In the Margin*, 1967) or Rogério Sganzerla's *O bandido da luz vermelha* (*Red Light Bandit*, 1968) portrayed marginal characters and locations without sentimentality. Their violent anti-heroes and sites of 'garbage' retained lyrical overtones, while also embodying a critique of the society that produced them. The metaphorization of the bandit and polemicization of violence in a climate of censorship and political repression gave way, in the 1970s, 1980s and 1990s, to neo-realist and 'brutalist' literary and film representations of outlaws devoid of heroism or any political intent, increasingly taking the form of armed cocaine-trafficking 'soldiers' performing cold-blooded acts of violence.

Since the 1980s, there has been an increase in crime and violence in Brazilian cities – symptoms of social unrest resulting from the exacerbation of chronic deprivation, social exclusion and inequality, exploited by transnational cocaine-trafficking networks.[12] Magnified, sensationalized and ultimately commodified by the media, this situation has brought with it a fear of urban public spaces among the inhabitants of Brazilian metropolitan areas. In July 1993, eight children and one young adult were murdered by military police while sleeping outside the Candelária Church in the centre of Rio de Janeiro. One month later, twenty-one innocent residents of the Rio *favela* Vigário Geral were assassinated by police forces seeking revenge. The massacre was closely followed by two *arrastões* on the beaches of Copacabana and Ipanema. In October 1994, 110 civil police officers raided private houses in Rio's Nova Brasília *favela*, abused residents and summarily executed fourteen suspected drug traffickers. Another raid with thirteen victims followed in May 1995.[13]

The emergence of what have been dubbed 'citizenships of fear' is reflected in media coverage of the *arrastões* as invasions

7 It has also been suggested that the *arrastões* had a political dimension: 'Benedita da Silva, a black woman running for mayor of the city at the time, was targeted as being connected to these youths, and some attribute her political defeat to the fear among members of the middle class that if she were elected, they could expect more of the same'; Goldstein. 8 Leu, p. 345. In December 1996, Mayor César Maia responded with an '*arrastão* of order', primarily targeting illegal street vendors. 9 See Nagib, 2003. 10 Glauber Rocha, p. 70. 11 Hélio Oiticica, quoted in Schøllhammer, p. 38. 12 'Both absolute and relative poverty got worse in Brazil during the 1980s as a result of the economic recession and the state's unsuccessful attempts to tackle inflation . . . By 1989, Rio had the most unequal distribution of income of any metropolitan area in Brazil . . . in 1991, some 3.5 million people were living below the poverty line . . . [and] more than one million people in Rio [12.4 per cent of households, were] living in *favelas* . . . In 1988, the metropolitan area of Rio contained over two million people living in dwellings lacking piped water'; Tolosa, pp. 210–13. 13 'By 1992 – the record year for military police killings in São Paulo – the number of civilians that these police killed reached 1,470, one-third of the total number of homicides in the state of São Paulo that year. By way of comparison with another notoriously violent city, the São Paulo figure represents more than sixty-one times the number of civilians – twenty-four – that the New York City police killed in 1992, and more than fifteen times the number of police killings per capita when compared with New York'; Cavallaro, 1997.

and in regular use of the trope of war.[14] The spilling over of violence by drug-trafficking gangs into the *asfalto* in Rio (2003) and São Paulo (2006) has been represented as an attack on the city; that is, 'as a dispute over city space'.[15] Discussing the phenomenon in its greater Latin American context, Susana Rotker has observed that this fear 'has been gradually changing the way in which people relate to urban space, their fellow citizens, the State and with the very concept of citizenship'.[16] Brazil is one of the most socially unjust societies in the world, where violence is the third most common cause of death and murder ranks first as the cause of death among people aged fifteen to twenty-four.[17] In her ground-breaking study of *Crime, Segregation, and Citizenship in São Paulo*, Teresa Caldeira demonstrates that 'The fear and the talk of crime . . . organize the urban landscape and public space, shaping the scenario for social interactions . . . [They] organize everyday strategies of protection and reaction that restrict people's movements and shrink their universe of interactions.'[18] Public space is increasingly identified with danger and violence.

In his 1995 installation *Fantasma* (*Phantom*, collection of the artist), Antonio Manuel placed a photograph of a hooded witness of the Candelária massacre in the middle of a threatening environment of floating pieces of carbon. Fear and violence affect all members of contemporary Latin American society, but especially the weakest and most vulnerable, whose lives are dominated by insecurity in terms of basic social rights. To quote Lúcio Kowarick, for these people, 'the sensation of living at risk is something rooted in [their] daily lives'.[19] They suffer most from organized crime relating to cocaine and firearm trafficking, as well as from what Caldeira calls 'the failure of the rule of law' – police corruption and brutal abuse and legal injustice.[20] Yet insecurity and anxiety are customarily presented by the media as predominantly affecting 'innocent' wealthy victims, terrorized and displaced from urban public spaces. Brutal violence and crime are strategically used in symbolic representations, with a fair amount of exoticism, to update the image of the marginal Other of Latin American society and justify injustice against them.[21]

In 1980, Kenneth Frampton wrote that Niemeyer's 'work at Brasilia . . . together with Costa's grid, evoked the aura of the *genre terrible*, the assertion of implacable form against remorseless nature; for beyond the order of Brasilia's Capitol . . . there lay the infinite extent of the jungle'.[22] The exotic jungle, both innocent and dangerous, persists as a synonym for Brazil, still perceived as a land 'on the periphery of culture'.[23] Brazil's extolled tropical exuberance has also been a violent exuberance, for both Brazilians like Alberto Rangel and Tarsila do Amaral and for foreign visitors like Theodore Roosevelt and Le Corbusier.

With the novelty of the spectacle of nature worn out, the Brazilian jungle is increasingly portrayed through glamorized and sensationalized images of urban violence. Fernando Meirelles and Kátia Lund's film of 2002, *Cidade de Deus* (*City of God*), nominated for four Academy Awards in 2004, and the television drama *Cidade dos homens* (*City of Men*, 2003–05) cast *favela* inhabitants as exotic primitives: drug traffickers as 'bruyt bestis' or blameless children, and prostitutes as comic shanty-town girls.[24] The infantilization, bestialization and eroticization of the exotic savages of colonial discourse is rearticulated in the outlandish behaviour of Brazil's contemporary primitives. This new exoticism disguises symptoms of social unrest as social and moral failings, pathologies of a part of the social body – the disenfranchised and destitute majority – that is being negatively stereotyped, vilified and criminalized. The severely disadvantaged and repressed victims – at times also criminals – of Brazil's unjust society, exposed to direct and indirect violence on a daily basis, are presented as the sole perpetrators of the violence assailing Brazilian society.

The stigmatization of the socially excluded as dangerous is not a new phenomenon. In 1929, Brazilian officials warned Le Corbusier of the 'extremely dangerous . . . savages' inhabiting Rio's *favelas*. The production and voyeuristic consumption of spectacularized *favela* violence, however, has reached unprecedented levels, satisfying the desire to affirm the morally and socially higher position of dominant *asfalto* audiences, and to recruit their support for police repression and harsh order laws. The the-

14 According to the United Nations special advisor Jean Ziegler, Brazil is living in a situation of war, a social war. Newspapers report on 'War in Rio'. João Moreira Salles's documentary of 1999 about urban violence in Rio de Janeiro was entitled *Notícias de uma guerra particular* (*News from a Private War*, with Kátia Lund). 'In an interview with *O Globo* in July 2006, the imprisoned boss of the Primeiro Comando da Capital (First Capital Command/PCC) gang in São Paulo, Marcola, described his "soldiers" as "strange anomalies of [Brazil's] crooked development"'; Cramer, 2006. **15** Leu, pp. 348–49. Again, this is not an entirely new phenomenon. As noted by Gilberto Freyre in the early twentieth century, in 'Rio de Janeiro, Valongo, the section set aside for the Negroes, who were not always passive or submissive, grew so large that frightened whites began to speak of the city as "besieged" by its African subcity'; Freyre, 1986, p. 171, n. 4. **16** Susana Rotker, quoted in Sánchez-Prado, p. 39. **17** Around 48 per cent of the national income goes to the richest 10 per cent of Brazil's population. According to the World Bank (2000), 'The poorest one-fifth of Brazil's 173 million people account for only a 2.2 per cent share of the national income. Brazil is second only to South Africa in a world ranking of income inequality. More than one-quarter of the population live on less than $2 a day and 13 per cent live on less than $1 a day'; 'Brazil Country Brief' (2003). A 2003 World Bank report notes: 'Income differences among the Brazilian population by gender and skin color account for an important part of overall income inequality, and this is due to disadvantages in wages, schooling, or both. Some 12 per cent of income inequality in Brazil is accounted for by income differences by skin color. The same figure for the United States is 2.4 per cent. Educational attainment is also widely unequal'; Instituto de Pesquisa Econômica Aplicada and Brazil Country Management Unit. **18** Caldeira, pp. 19–20. The large increase in homicide rates in the 1980s and especially in the 1990s in Rio de Janeiro and São Paulo affected mainly the poor periphery and shanty towns of the metropolitan regions. **19** Kowarick, p. 46. **20** Caldeira, p. 138. **21** As João Cezar de Castro Rocha points out, 'In recent years, with the increasing violence imposed by the ruthless logic of the drug dealers, the employment of the notion of the marginal should emphasize over and over the ambiguity of the term: the marginal can equally be the excluded or the criminal, and can even be both at once'; João Cezar de Castro Rocha, 2005, p. 31. **22** Frampton, 1992, p. 256. **23** Giedion, 1982, p. 94. **24** João Cezar de Castro Rocha, 2005, pp. 24–26. 'Bruyt bestis' is how a 1501 English chronicler described the first American natives brought to London by Bristol merchants; Honour, p. 8.

atrical and depoliticized presentation of violent criminals in films and even documentaries is also exploited by the tourist industry: visitors are carried up the hillsides of Rio in safari-style jeeps to catch a glimpse (and a shot) of the wild beasts of the Rocinha *favela* engaging in tribal warfare – a modern-day equivalent of Rouen's sixteenth-century 'Brazilian festivals'.[25]

In the 1950s, Lúcio Costa designed for Brasília's *superquadras* 'a green wall that breathed, not a green wall that defended against the enemy'.[26] In contemporary Brazil, including the federal district, the privileged elite's response to urban fear verging on paranoia is to resort to ever greater spatial segregation by constructing 'a city of walls, the opposite of the boundless public space of the modern ideal of city life'.[27] The middle and upper classes increasingly inhabit heavily guarded condominiums or closed-off communities with inaccessible internal streets, dashing through the city streets in bullet-proof cars.[28] For the streets and public spaces are dangerous; they are the new negative sites of Brazil.

In São Paulo, the world's fourth largest metropolis, members of the financial elite have altogether abandoned the streets and public spaces; that is, the very spaces that define the modern city. They live in gated communities, protected by electrified fences and patrolled by private armies, and work in fortified office buildings, commuting between the two in privately owned or chartered airborne limousines: 'civilian helicopter traffic here has become what industry executives describe as the busiest on Earth. Helicopter companies estimate that liftoffs average 100 per hour.' In 2002, São Paulo had '240 helipads, compared with 10 in New York City, allowing the rich to whisk to and from their well-guarded homes to work, business meetings, afternoons of shopping [in walled and patrolled exclusive malls], even church'.[29] Flora Süssekind contends that 'an imaginary representation of fear and violence is [also] what fundamentally organizes the dominant urban landscape of Brazilian contemporary literature'.[30]

Reimagining the Empty Continent

Introducing a special issue on Brazil in 1947, a journalist for the *Architectural Forum* spoke of Brazil's ' "colorful" history (one of the principal colors being blood)'.[31] Almost half a century later, Niemeyer's Memorial da América Latina (Monument to Latin America, 1986–92, structural engineer José Carlos Süssekind), opened in São Paulo. A monumental cultural complex conceived by Darcy Ribeiro and São Paulo governor Orestes Quércia, its centrepiece assumed the form of a 7-metre-high concrete open hand, 'represent[ing] an exploited and oppressed Latin America'. Niemeyer's monolithic *Mão* (Hand) summed up 'the political nature of the cultural center, which was more important to me

than its architecture'. It has 'its fingers slightly bent to convey despair', and, recalling Eduardo Galeano's book *Open Veins of Latin America* (1971), a wound in the shape of Latin America, with 'a trickle of blood running down to its wrist'. Perhaps alluding to Quércia's insistence that he lower the polemical tone of the

Mão (Hand), Memorial da América Latina, Barra Funda, São Paulo, 1986–92

inscription on its pedestal, Niemeyer wrote that his sculpture 'represented a critique and a forewarning rather than a provocation'. He continued:

> It brings to mind a shadowed past and a future full of hope and doubt. Our hope turned into bloodshed and revolt in 1989 as the United States invaded the small, unprotected country of Panama. This sort of criminal act should have roused the protest of all other countries that claim to be democratic nations – of all people who advocate democratic rule and the principle of equal rights, opportunity, justice, and freedom. The U.S. justification for the invasion – the defense of a democratic regime – is certainly preposterous, given that the U.S. government overtly supported Latin American dictatorships during many years.
>
> At such times we must react. We must protest. We must not accept this criminal intervention into the affairs of our

25 Le Corbusier, 1991, p. 9. On Rouen's sixteenth-century 'Brazilian festivals', see Chapter Six, p. 212.　　**26** Lúcio Costa, quoted in Maria Elisa Costa, 2002, p. 276.　　**27** Caldeira, p. 314.　　**28** Walls with guarded gates have also appeared around settlements in the poor urban periphery of São Paulo, as well as in Brasília's satellite cities; Kowarick, p. 20.　　**29** Faiola, p. A01.　　**30** Flora Süssekind, 2002, p. 9.　　**31** *Architectural Forum*, p. 66.

exploited and offended Latin America. This large concrete hand, an expression of my anticipated protest, thus acquires another significance. It is no longer a simple sculpture, but a plea that all visitors to the Memorial da América Latina become aware of the drama experienced by our brothers throughout this continent. Although still poor and underdeveloped, Latin America is fully aware of its rights, sorrows, and hopes.

Niemeyer's 'protest sculpture', the only raw-concrete structure among a group of white buildings, annotates the memorial complex's vast open spaces. Deliberately left barren and unprotected, they were intended to function primarily as places expressing protest rather than as sociable places, voids to be contemplated as such. In these large, empty spaces lie the memorial's great strength and perhaps also its weakness. Strength because this relentlessly negative landscape is a powerful spatial expression of *Five Centuries of the Pillage of a Continent* – Galeano's subtitle: a plundered landscape, scarred by a history of exploitation and violence, which has taken the place of Latin America's legendary tropical garden. An abstract, bright red, steel sculpture of a tropical flower by Neo-Concretist Franz Weissmann (1911–2005) greets the visitor who emerges into the vast open space from the underground station, perhaps chosen by Niemeyer as a symbol of that lost Eden. But the cultural complex's most public, open spaces fail to integrate with its monolithic programmatic spaces and, most importantly, with the fabric of the city's daily life. This makes their designer sound hopelessly optimistic in his wish that the Memorial da América Latina would 'convey an appeal, a message of faith and solidarity for all Latin American people . . . [and] invite them to come together, share experiences, and fight more effectively on behalf of this highly neglected and endangered continent'.[32] Bruno Giorgi's abstract marble sculpture *Integração* (*Integration*) stands in a pool of water, unapproachable, dwarfed by Niemeyer's bleeding *Hand*.

At a time when Tropicalist parrots and banana trees had become *à la mode*, Niemeyer resisted the commodification and consumption of Tropicália imagery. Despite persistent criticism, he refused to prettify the 'cold and unwelcoming' space between the white buildings of São Paulo's new cultural complex, denying its users the comfort of a shady garden and confronting them instead with a dystopic, sterile landscape, dried up, bereft of its most valuable energies, hostile to any form of growth, intended to provoke a process of critical engagement with the harsh realities of the city and the continent. The complex is located in Barra Funda, a north-western industrial district of central São Paulo, on a busy traffic intersection, where train, underground and multiple bus lines converge. A railway line runs along one side of the site,

while an expressway divides the complex into two parts, connected by a curving pedestrian ramp that heightens rather than repairs the fragmentation of the city and the complex. Niemeyer eventually conceded to pressure and filled the open space in the northern part of the complex with 160 Jerivá palms, earning it the designation 'Praça da Sombra' ('Square of the Shade').

The principal open space of the memorial, the Praça Cívica or Praça do Sol (Square of the Sun), lies in its southern part. With

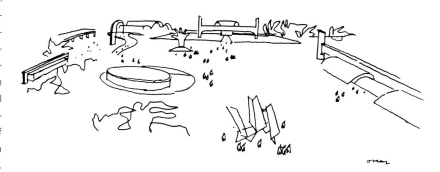

Aerial view of the Memorial da América Latina: to the south (right) of Avenida Auro Soares de Moura Andrade, the Salão de Atos Tiradentes (Tiradentes Ceremonial Assembly Hall), the Victor Civita Library and the circular Marta Traba Gallery (originally a restaurant) are ranged around Praça Cívica or Praça do Sol (Square of the Sun); to the north (left) of the expressway lies Praça da Sombra (Square of the Shade) with the Latin American Parliament, at the centre, the monumental Simón Bolívar Auditorium, the long Pavilhão da Criatividade (Pavilion of Creativity) and the Centro Brasileiro de Estudos Latino-americanos (Brazilian Centre of Latin American Studies); the Passarela do Amor (Footbridge of Love) links the two parts of the complex

32 Niemeyer, 2000b, pp. 133–36.

capacity for 40,000 people, the sun-baked Praça Civica is afforded little opportunity to participate in urban politics or intervene in the spatial articulation of the city. Before Niemeyer, Lina Bo Bardi had also 'invented' a large empty space and returned it to the inhabitants of São Paulo; Niemeyer's Praça Civica, however, does not enjoy the highly privileged location of Bo Bardi's São Paulo Art Museum (MASP, 1957–68) on Avenida Paulista, the city's most important avenue, at the heart of its densely built central business district. For that reason, his gesture does not resonate as powerfully. Offering no relief from the dizzying summer heat, Niemeyer's alienating Praça Civica exposes the experience of vulnerability, unveiling the cruel reality of the abandonment of urban public space at a time when violence and the fear of violence increasingly dominate Latin America's urban landscape, restricting encounters and thus threatening urban society. 'Sweat, blood, and poverty have marked our disjointed and oppressed Latin America', Niemeyer wrote 'to explain' his open hand. Recalling Le Corbusier's *Main Ouverte* (*Open Hand*, 1952) for Chandigarh – 'a symbol of peace and reconciliation . . . open to receive the wealth created, to distribute to the peoples of the world' – Niemeyer also attached a message of hope to his sculpture: 'Now it is crucial that we adjust this continent, unite it, and transform it into an untouchable monolith capable of insuring its independence and happiness.'[33]

Fenced in, cut off from the city, the Memorial da América Latina is an island of cultural activity that comes alive during art or film festivals, weekly free concerts or the *festas típicas* of the various regions of Latin America, often organized by São Paulo's Latin American communities. It is only when filled with this kind of '*Fête* (a celebration which consumes unproductively, without other advantage but pleasure . . .)', to borrow Henri Lefebvre's term, that the Praça Civica gives a chance to the dream of an urban society that stems from 'the coming-together of people from different classes, with different occupations and patterns of existence', enabling 'the elimination of antagonisms that find their expression in segregation'.[34] On these collective occasions, a constant flow of people allows the Passarela do Amor (Footbridge of Love) to challenge the hegemony of the car race on the expressway, and the leisurely rhythms of the colourful human coil overshadow the linear multi-lane avenue abandoned to the incessant march of cars. For Niemeyer, artworks, public spaces for congregation and festival, and cultural festivals themselves – even though institutionally organized rather than spontaneous and spatially contained rather than integrated with urban daily life – are still capable of nourishing utopian visions: in the case of the Memorial da América Latina, a search for a politically united,

Lina Bo Bardi, *Museu de Arte de São Paulo (MASP)*, São Paulo, 1957–68

strong and happy Latin America. His Praça Civica, in Latin America's largest city, awaits the advent of a utopian moment. And, to remember Oswald de Andrade, 'at the heart of every utopia there is not only a dream but also a protest'.[35]

The Praça Civica is defined by the monumental Salão de Atos Tiradentes (Tiradentes Ceremonial Assembly Hall), the Victor Civita Library, devoted exclusively to Latin America, and the Marta Traba Gallery (originally a restaurant) – a low circular building floating on water. The first two buildings are formally linked, being

Passarela do Amor, Memorial da América Latina

33 Niemeyer, 2000b, p. 136; Le Corbusier, 1997, p. 97; Niemeyer, 2000b, p. 136. **34** Lefebvre, 1996, p. 66; Lefebvre, 1984, p. 190. **35** Oswald de Andrade, quoted in Stam, 1997, p. 239.

composed of a few pre-cast elements – enormous concrete vaults, sweeping down to the ground on one side and supported by immense concrete beams on the other. The beams – 60 metres long for the assembly hall and 90 metres for the library – project beyond the sides of the vaults, anchored by vertical pillars, which David Underwood sees as rising 'majestically like the bell towers of a great baroque church'.[36] This religious association is echoed by official descriptions of the assembly hall as a 'secular cathedral' dedicated to ceremonial functions.[37] In the soaring 30-metre-high space under its wedged vault, Cândido Portinari's 18 × 3-metre mural *Tiradentes*, created in 1948 to honour Brazil's sacrificed saviour, is displayed as a secular altarpiece. Bas-reliefs by the Argentine-born artist Hector Julio Páride Bernabó (1911–97, known as Carybé), who found inspiration in the Afro-Brazilian culture of Bahia, and by Napoleon Potyguara Lazzaroto (1927–98), from Curitiba, celebrate Latin America's ethnically and culturally diverse society. As in the complex's library and auditorium buildings, light filters through large black-tinted glass curtain walls, carried by vertical steel space trusses, the latter serving both structural and solar-control purposes – a new contribution to the large repertoire of modern Brazilian sunbreaking devices. The two pillars that frame the assembly hall stand in two symmetrical square reflecting pools either side of the walkway to the entrance, which is located under the imposing beam. In the pool to the right of the entrance, a concrete pyramidal rostrum stands altar-like, addressing large gatherings in São Paulo's Latin American forum.

Formally defined by its massive central beam, supporting two smaller vaults on the side of the square and a larger vault to the rear, the Victor Civita Library is a reference centre, aiming to promote awareness and debate about issues concerning Latin America. It is institutionally linked to the Centro Brasileiro de Estudos Latino-americanos (CBEAL, Brazilian Centre of Latin American Studies) in the northern part of the memorial. The external form of the library reflects the internal organization of its open space: the reading room occupies the area under the higher vault to the rear, while an auditorium (slightly submerged) and audio-visual section are accommodated under the two lower concrete vaults, the narrower and the wider, respectively. An even lower glass vault is slotted between these two last vaults to define the entrance area – the only brightly lit space in the building. An internal circulation spine is located under the central beam. Specially designed artworks – a stained-glass panel by Marianne Peretti and a ceramic panel by Mario Gruber – separate the different areas of the library. Its long bays are lit through the glass side walls and through circular openings in the internally fair-faced concrete vaults.

At the centre of the Praça da Sombra stands the Latin American Parliament, a building added three years after the inau-

Victor Civita Library, Memorial da América Latina: principal elevation

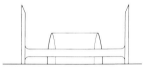

Salão de Atos Tiradentes, Memorial da América Latina: principal elevation

Victor Civita Library, Memorial da América Latina: entrance area under the glass vault

site plan

1 Salão de Atos Tiradentes
2 Victor Civita Library
3 main entrance
4 information centre
5 Marta Traba Gallery
6 Passarela do Amor
7 Centro Brasileiro de Estudos Latino-americanos
8 Pavilhão da Criatividade
9 Simón Bolívar Auditorium
10 toilets

Memorial da América Latina, São Paulo

36 Underwood, 1994b, p. 198.   **37** http://www.memorial.sp.gov.br/memorial/ContentBuilder.do?open=subespacoCulturais&ma=me&pagina=salaAtos.

guration of the complex. It is the permanent seat of the unicameral organism the Parlatino, created on 10 December 1964 and institutionalized on 16 November 1987, bringing together representatives from the national parliaments of Latin America, who meet here biannually. The circular assembly chamber, with 414 seats for delegates, 70 for press, and 65 for the general public, is positioned on the first floor, at the centre of the five-storey cylindrical concrete structure. A cupola is suspended from six radiating large beams, which protrude above the building's flat roof. Entirely covered with light-diffusing anodized aluminium blades, it recalls the auditorium cupola of the French Communist Party Headquarters in Paris. The parliament's foyer, at the centre of the ground floor, is embraced by service areas. Offices for administration, committee rooms and so on are arranged on the periphery of the second, third and fourth floors. The entire building is covered with a black glass skin, alleviated by the addition of a white ramp that leads from the ground floor to the press area of the parliament chamber and by a white sculptural canopy that marks the entrance. It is somewhat surprising that Niemeyer did not produce a more elaborate scheme for the Latin American Parliament. The diagrammatic design is formally well integrated in the memorial complex but rather disappointing considering its political nature. Niemeyer's low-key, relatively mundane house for the Latin American Parliament, however, is consistent with the complex's emphasis on the utopia of a united Latin America.

The largest building of the complex, the Simón Bolívar Auditorium, used for performances and congresses as well as the reception of heads of state, is undeniably more impressive than the parliament building. It is a third variation on the theme of structural vaults and beams, or what Niemeyer called 'architecture reduced to two or three elements: clear, simple and different . . . No filigree work.'[38] In the context of the socio-political aims of the memorial, this building holds a more central position, since it stimulates 'the coming-together of people from different classes, with different occupations and patterns of existence', or what Alvar Aalto considered 'the ideal form of human association, "an open and voluntary encounter of independent individuals"'.[39]

Its three spaces fit into an asymmetrical butterfly plan perpendicular to the square: a monumental foyer and the larger of two wedge-shaped auditoria are in the larger wing, towards the square, and the smaller auditorium is in the rear wing. The building's section also reflects its internal spatial articulation. The two auditoria, under the two larger vaults of three set in parallel, can be united to seat 1,600 spectators in the stalls on either side of the 300-square-metre orthogonal stage. The full effect of the sweeping lines of Tomie Ohtake's sculpture on the flank wall is best

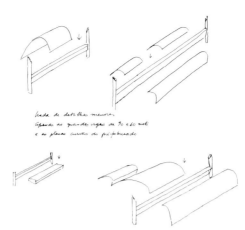

Enormous pre-cast concrete vaults and beams are the component elements of the principal buildings of the Memorial da América Latina; *top left*, the assembly hall; *top right*, the library; *below left*, the Brazilian Centre of Latin American Studies; *below right*, the auditorium.

appreciated on these occasions. The spacious entrance foyer, under the lowest of the vaults, on the Praça da Sombra, is furnished with a T-plan balcony – a concrete vessel floating in midspace and granting the best views of the gathering crowd, two slowly unfolding spiral staircases and a central ceremonial ramp, enticing spectators to ascend to the auditorium or simply to move along leisurely. Alfredo Ceschiatti's bronze dove surveys the space from its high pedestal. A dark-mirror-clad wall intensifies the effect of the artist's and the architect's sculptures.

The Centro Brasileiro de Estudos Latino-americanos – 'the motor of the Memorial, faithful to the ideals of Bolívar', according

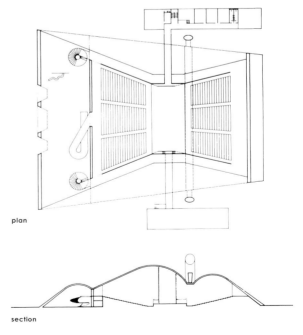

plan

section

Simón Bolívar Auditorium, Memorial da América Latina.

38 Niemeyer, 'Latin America Memorial', in *Oscar Niemeyer: Notebooks of the Architect*, n.p.   **39** Lefebvre, 1984, p. 190; Weston, 1995, p. 214, quoting Alvar Aalto.

to Ribeiro – and the Pavilhão da Criatividade (Pavilion of Creativity) are also located in the northern part of the memorial complex. The former formally references Lina Bo Bardi's suspended São Paulo Art Museum, while the latter is a long, one-storey-high, gently curving structure reminiscent of Niemeyer's 'great pavilion' for the Permanent International Fair at Tripoli, concealing views of the railway line. Housing a collection of Latin American craftwork commissioned by Darcy Ribeiro, the Pavilion of Creativity is justly criticized by Underwood for proposing an elitist distinction between 'the high modernism of the Brazilians, which unifies (i.e., controls) the complex, and the craft art of the rest of Latin America, which is put on display and thus effectively commodified'. Underwood also highlights the political nature of the project in relation to the ambitions of Orestes Quércia who, aspiring to Brazil's presidency, commissioned Niemeyer in an attempt to portray himself as the worthy heir of Juscelino Kubitschek. Supporting Quércia's ambitions, Ribeiro suggested that, with the Memorial da América Latina, the governor of São Paulo followed in the footsteps of the former president who 'revolutionized Brazilian architecture in the 1940s, when he chose Oscar [Niemeyer] to build Pampulha'.[40]

For all its civic qualities, in terms of its role in promoting what Lefebvre defined as the 'right to the city' – that is, returning part of the city's wealth and space to its occupants – Niemeyer's complex did not revolutionize Brazilian architecture. At the level of public urban investment, it represents a significant improvement in comparison to Pampulha, benefiting all residents rather than the privileged few and providing opportunities for interaction between different social groups. Its large, open, event-seeking spaces invite all citizens to lay claim to urban territory through their participation in public, cultural, non-commercial spectacles that strengthen a feeling of belonging to an urban community and a continental one. Niemeyer concentrated his efforts on 'plastic unity' and structural 'audacity', but relied on past achievements and a severely restricted formal and material palette, which lacked the density of consideration at the basis of his earlier work and suggested, if only temporarily, a tired master.[41] When compared with earlier applications of similar parabolic forms, those of the ageing Niemeyer – at the time in his eighties – clearly lack the light-handedness and refinement of the adventurous designer of the Pampulha Church of São Francisco de Assis or the Diamantina Youth Club. Such qualities, however, would not have been entirely appropriate in the harsh environment of Barra Funda.

Niemeyer's contribution to the architectural landscape of São Paulo acknowledges local working methodologies with which, pace Guilherme Wisnik, he had long been experimenting, even though he invested them with a different political message. In so-called Paulista Brutalism, as exemplified by the work of João Batista Vilanova Artigas and later Paulo Mendes da Rocha from the 1960s onwards, the idea of 'treat[ing] any building as if it was a piece of infrastructure' had found in long cantilevers, muscular supports, enormous box slabs and pre-stressed reinforced-concrete members that spanned great lengths the means to fuse aesthetic expression with the mechanics of construction. Wisnik argues that the aim of this approach was 'the affirmation of national sovereignty based upon the use of one's own technology and ability to express the local conditions of production and labour'. He also draws a parallel with Arte Povera and Glauber Rocha's 'aesthetic of hunger'. Niemeyer's (and Affonso Eduardo Reidy's) economy of means resulted from a rigorous pursuit of the total integration of form and structure, which, as noted, Artigas welcomed in 1958. Niemeyer's overt display of technical expertise – at times so literal that it risks betraying anxiety rather than witnessing achievement – shared Artigas's and the Brazilian Communist Party's aim of 'constructing [and showcasing] a country through the development of its productive forces', as well as that Paulista 'vanity' criticized by Sérgio Ferro in 1986, which increasingly isolated Brazilian architecture from international debate.[42]

But in contrast to Artigas, Niemeyer invested his assemblies of megastructural elements with a positive rather than a negative message, more Pop Art than Arte Povera, touting the country's modernity rather than radicalizing its Third World backwardness. Recalling Oswald de Andrade's barbaro tecnizado ('technicized barbarian'), Artigas, in projects like his oxymoronic Faculty of Architecture and Urbanism (1961–69) at the University of São Paulo, embraced modern technology for its expressive potential but rejected polished bourgeois finishes on ethical grounds, using conspicuously crude Brutalist surfaces to expose and allegorize the brutality of Brazil's social, political and economic reality, teasing beauty and poetry out of deliberately unpolished surfaces. Like Cinema Novo's 'Imperfect Cinema', to use Julio García Espinosa's designation, the poverty of Artigas's finishes is a symbolic (and moralizing) poverty, but it is not primitive or folkloric; his alternative aesthetics should not be mistaken for indicators of underdevelopment.

In a similar vein, Lina Bo Bardi's 'poor architecture', explored through a series of projects with a social content in the 1970s

40 Underwood, 1994b, pp. 207, 202. Ribeiro's reference to Simón Bolívar gestures towards the latter's more inclusive vision of Latin America. Richard Gott notes that the term 'Latin America' was coined in the middle of the nineteenth century under the influence of French conceptions of Latinité or Latinidad. It 'gave prominence to the population of European or Latin American descent while effectively rubbing-out the Indians and the Blacks'. It 'firmly located Latin America in the white world of the West . . . [and] successfully replaced the visionary and more inclusive projects of Simón Bolívar and José Martí'; Gott, p. 270. In the catalogue of the 1955 Museum of Modern Art exhibition Latin American Architecture Since 1945, Henry-Russell Hitchcock noted: 'At first thought Latin America, by the name we apply to it, might be assumed to be more of a piece ethnically, and hence psychologically, than is in fact the case'; Hitchcock, 1955, p. 26.
41 Niemeyer, 'Latin America Memorial', in Oscar Niemeyer: Notebooks of the Architect, n.p.   42 Guilherme Wisnik, 2004, pp. 48–50. As Niemeyer wrote in relation to his Algerian projects, his structurally daring structures also aim to create 'an architecture so grandiose that the problems caused by the unskilled . . . manpower virtually disappear'; Niemeyer, 1998, p. 25.

João Batista Vilanova Artigas, Faculty of Architecture and Urbanism, University of São Paulo, São Paulo, 1961–69

Lina Bo Bardi, SESC Pompéia Factory, sports, leisure and education complex, São Paulo, 1977–86

and 1980s, was an attempt to acknowledge the reality of those excluded from consumer society's luxurious finishes, offering 'pre-craftsmanship' as a non-Eurocentric alternative, 'inciting Brazilians to adapt [cannibalize] the industrial revolution to their own needs and to reinvent [carnivalize] consumer culture to fit their desires'.[43] With reference to her 'cultural citadel', the SESC Pompéia Factory (Serviço Social do Comércio, 1977–86), a sports, leisure and education complex in São Paulo, Bo Bardi spoke of ugliness, mixing the 'primitive' of the popular with the 'civilized' of the erudite. Her radicalization of ugliness for the 'citadel of freedom', as the complex was nicknamed, subverts both the industrial ideals embodied in the old factory on the site – which was preserved at her instigation – and 'bourgeois ideals of pleasure' and leisure.[44] Wary of producing 'noble savage' architecture for exoticist consumption, Niemeyer, on the other hand, insisted on 'export quality', finely handcrafted concrete surfaces, relying on the abundance of low-cost labour. The resources put at his disposal, however, would never again be as generous as those available for the construction of Brasília's palaces, which partly explains his latter-day white-washing of concrete surfaces.

At São Paulo's Latin American agora, Niemeyer employed megastructural elements as space-defining building blocks. But he did not explore the potential of his imposing megalithic structures sufficiently to articulate a new, inspiring urban landscape that imaginatively blended programme, form, structure and topography, as he had so masterfully in Paris, Bobigny or Le Havre. This is the shortcoming of the Memorial da América Latina – a discontinuous public arena sowed with self-centred architectural fragments. Lina Bo Bardi's São Paulo Art Museum and Paulo Mendes da Rocha's Brazilian Museum of Sculpture (1985–95) – one of Brazil's most strikingly beautiful architectural works of these decades – represent much more eloquent and bolder seizures of Paulista urban territory, critical of land-occupation value systems and the erosion of urban life and stimulating a democratic use and pleasurable experience of the city.

In July 1968, in the Parque do Flamengo of Rio de Janeiro, Hélio Oiticica had experimented with an environmental installation that Rogério Duarte baptized *Apocalipopótese* to

> designate a certain type of experience related to the concept, also of his invention, of the 'probject' in which the 'finished work' doesn't exist as such but rather as open structures or purely 'germinating structures,' in which individual participation is the very creation, whether it is immediate or takes place in the imagination which creates and modifies it.[45]

It is perhaps as an architectural *Apocalipopótese* that the Memorial da América Latina may function best; that is, as an

43 Lima and Vivanco, p. 57.   **44** Olivia de Oliveira, p. 113.
45 Oiticica, 2005a, p. 252.

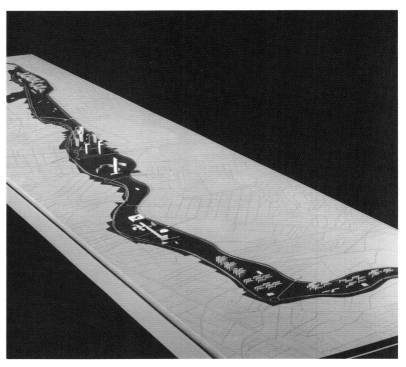

experimental, open-ended field, interrupting the production cycles of the city with participatory events that begin with Niemeyer's 'germinating structures' to reimagine and modify the urban experience and what Eduardo Subirats calls *El Continente Vacío* (*The Empty Continent*, 1994). The germinating shadows cast by the buildings on the Praça Cívica suggest an incomplete, open-ended tapestry, inviting active participation in the creative weaving.

The Memorial da América Latina belongs to a group of large-scale public projects that Niemeyer became involved with after his return to Brazil, and that reflect a renewed concern for the city, for popular culture, and for some form of engagement with the masses or rather the *povo* (people). The most ambitious of these aimed to address the problem of the deterioration of the quality of public urban space in São Paulo – a result of the lack of an over-all urban strategy and aggressive, largely uncontrolled, land spec-ulation. Commissioned by Mayor Jânio Quadros in 1986, Niemeyer produced a plan for the reurbanization of the Tietê River, notori-ously polluted and 'walled in by two big avenues . . . which cut off the river from the city as if it were something forbidden'. Along the south bank of the section of the Tietê that defines São Paulo's northern limit, Niemeyer proposed an 18-kilometre-long green park to give the city 'the green lung it lacks' and effect a 'recon-ciliation between the river and the city'. Within this green zone – an area of 10 million square metres from 500–1,000 metres wide – he proposed a civic centre, a cultural centre, two large areas of housing, offices and sports and recreation facilities.

Niemeyer boldly professed that this radical 'urbanistic surgery . . . would mean for São Paulo much more than the construction of

Rio Branco Avenue [Avenida Central] meant to Rio de Janeiro – a feat which Le Corbusier considered to be of the greatest impor-tance'. And he added: 'Of course, it is a full scale enterprise which would . . . require demolitions, expropriations and so forth. Problems that we consider of minor importance in comparison with the profound and irrefutable transformation it will represent for this hermetic, compact and polluted city.' Echoing Keynesian theory, which dominated post-war mainstream economic

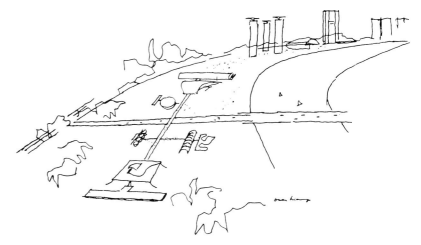

thought and policy, Niemeyer also justified the economic feasibility of such a large project, requiring significant public expenditure (fiscal stimulus or deficit spending), on the basis of the 'volume of construction', which presumably would stimulate economic growth.[46]

For Niemeyer, the Tietê River urbanization project represented a 'great opportunity to give São Paulo a new leisure district . . . a beachlike environment that the city lacked'. He 'imagined São Paulo dwellers strolling along the banks of the Tietê and, as in Copacabana, pretty women in bikinis, children playing on the shore of a clean and refreshing river'.[47] But Niemeyer and Quadros's Tietê dream remained on paper for a number of reasons: the 1980s economic recession; post-Brasília disenchantment with developmentalism and grandiose state-led projects; the success of grass-roots housing movements in raising awareness of extreme social segregation and the need to address the city's acute housing problem; and political changes in the preceding two decades, which led to fundamental policy shifts. For all its utopian visions of a democratic and pleasurable urban life and its potential to redress the fragmentation of São Paulo by carving through it a green thoroughfare, it was frankly out of touch with the scale and magnitude of the city's mounting problems and urgent needs.

Gradually, public funds have been directed towards urban operations in an attempt to reverse the process of inner-city degradation and exodus, especially among low-income groups. The housing emergency has been targeted and efforts have been made to improve the life of what Pedro Fiore Arantes calls São Paulo's 'hidden city' – the enormous sprawling urban periphery, home to almost 8 million low-income residents.[48] For example, the Guarapiranga River Basin Environmental Sanitation Project (1993–2000), supported by the World Bank, benefited fifty-two favela communities in terms of basic infrastructure, recreation areas and housing.

Since 1950, Brazil has witnessed the world's fastest urban growth. In 2000, 81.2 per cent of Brazilians (138 million) lived in urban areas in comparison to 26.3 per cent of the population in 1940. In April 2005, Ermínia Maricato, former secretary for housing and urban development for the city of São Paulo (1989–92) and deputy minister of cities responsible for urban development policy, spoke at the World Bank Urban Research Symposium of an 'urban crisis', reporting that Brazil's eleven metropolitan areas, with 55 million inhabitants, contained 80 per cent of the country's favelas.[49]

São Paulo has 40 per cent of Brazil's favelas, which from the 1980s grew faster than other areas of the city, partly through migration within São Paulo itself.[50]

Brazil's 1988 constitution included a chapter on urban policy, 'aimed at ordaining the full development of the social functions of the city and ensuring the well-being of its inhabitants'. On 14 February 2000, the 26th Amendment recognized access to housing as a social right and, with the enactment of Federal Law No. 10.257 of 10 July 2001, 'City Statute' ('Estatuto da Cidade'), Brazil embedded the notion of the 'right to the city' in its constitution. This ground-breaking new law, which regulates the constitution's chapter on urban policy, gives priority to the social functions of urban property and the city and promises to support municipal initiatives to solve mounting urban, social and environmental problems, improve the quality of urban life, ensure the democratic management of cities, and 'democratize the conditions of access to urban land and housing'.[51] In 2003, the Ministry of Cities was founded, to spearhead and coordinate programmes for the elaboration and implementation of an inclusive and sustainable urban development policy, predominantly targeting the low-income population.

Despite financial constraints, in São Paulo and other Brazilian cities tangible outcomes have already been achieved by the adoption of new, democratic housing and planning policies; the expansion of resources for land tenure regularization; comprehensive upgrading and urban integration of low-income settlements; the introduction of incentives for the production of low-income housing; and the facilitation of community initiatives for new, government-financed housing. These results have inspired new hope that it is possible to tackle effectively social and economic exclusion, spatial segregation, environmental vulnerability and urban violence through urban reform that guarantees rights of citizenship for all São Paulo dwellers.[52]

Back to Utopia

In 1980, Lina Bo Bardi restored the Oficina Theatre in São Paulo, running a street through the building from its entrance on Rua Jaceguai to its exit on Rua Japurá so that the theatre would set its 'foot on the road'. She claimed inspiration from Le Corbusier's letter to Brazil's minister of education, Gustavo Capanema: 'Mr Minister, don't order theaters with stages and seating, leave the Squares, the Streets, the Green, free; just order the construction of wooden Tréteaux [boards or stages] open to the People and the Brazilian People will occupy them, 'improvising' with its natural elegance and intelligence.'[53] Three years later, Rio de Janeiro state's first directly elected governor, Leonel de Moura Brizola, and vice-governor and secretary of culture Darcy Ribeiro commissioned

46 Niemeyer and Team, 1986, n.p.   47 Niemeyer, 2000b, p. 134.
48 See Arantes, pp. 190–99. The centre of São Paulo experienced a negative growth rate during the 1980–91 and 1991–2000 periods.
49 Maricato, 2005.   50 See Recamán, pp. 131–38.   51 Edésio Fernandes, 2003.   52 See Integrating the Poor, 2004, Chapter One, pp. 8–24.   53 Le Corbusier, quoted in Olivia de Oliveira, p. 186, emphasis in the original.

Niemeyer to bring the street to the theatre. Constructed in four months, Rio's Passarela do Samba (Sambódromo or Samba Stadium, structural engineer José Carlos Süssekind) was inaugurated on 2 March 1984, just in time for Brazil's most popular spectacle, the samba schools parade, which has become largely synonymous with carnival. Effectively, a whole street was set aside for 'the greatest show on earth', furnished with permanent pre-cast concrete structures to replace the temporary steel bleachers of the past. Avenida Marques de Sapucaí, where the samba parade had been held since 1978, lies near Praça Onze, the birthplace of the most famous Brazilian beat, destroyed with the opening of Avenida Presidente Vargas in the early 1940s, and mourned in numerous popular songs.

In slave-owning Brazil 'with its fixed hierarchy', writes Lilia Moritz Schwarcz, 'the "white people's" festivals mostly took place inside palaces and theatres . . . while the "black people's" festivals happened in the city streets and the plantations' slave quarters'. The parade of the samba schools, argues Richard Parker, is situated between the colonial 'white people's' carnaval do salão (salon carnival) and the 'black people's' carnaval da rua (street carnival):

> Ordered and controlled by the state, it has . . . replaced the frightening chaos of carnivalesque play with what is, in its own way, a highly disciplined alternative . . . Focusing on the world of samba, with all of its connotations of savagery, poverty, and marginality, yet re-creating this world as a fantastic spectacle of color and movement, the parade creates a kind of utopian illusion. Nowhere is the world created by the festival more completely and absolutely opposed to the world of normal daily life, of work, suffering, and sadness, than in the parade of the samba schools.[54]

The Sambódromo – a state-sponsored street-cum-theatre with expensive boxes and grandstands suspended above standing areas, and an ordered and controlled parade ground – hosts the spectacle that originated in the city's marginalized spaces. Retaining strong links with these origins, the stadium reflects exactly the in-between situation of the Rio carnival. Monumentalizing Brazil's twentieth-century revalorization of her black culture, it embodies the national ideology of mestiçagem, which retains its hold on the Brazilian imagination. As Robert Stam points out, carnival 'dramatizes certain utopian aspirations of Brazilian culture – freedom, equality, the mingling of races. In its symbolic thrust, at least, carnival translates a profoundly democratic and egalitarian impulse.'[55] Niemeyer's Sambódromo granted a permanent stage and thus legitimacy to these utopian aspirations annually incarnated in carnival.

When first imported from Portugal, carnival was a private, elite affair, celebrated in halls and theatres. In this Eurocentric form

'Carnival's zenith, according to Mello Moraes, was between 1854 and 1871, which is when the merrymakers went into the streets and made it a national festival'. It was still a high-society event, however, until the 1880s when, 'to the distress of the carioca elite' it began to share the streets with entrudo – an older, more popular, playfully violent Portuguese import, repressed in 1853 – and its allegorical floats satirized the emperor as Pedro Banana or Pedro Cashew.[56] In the 1920s, a new form of carnival emerged in the hills and swamps behind Rio's dockyards – a neighbourhood known as Little Africa because it was inhabited by African immigrants from Bahia, who made their way to Rio de Janeiro after the abolition of slavery. The Baiana tias presided over the terreiros – large, open indoor or outdoor spaces or 'houses' where Candomblé religious rites were celebrated – and became central figures in the formation of the samba schools of Rio's carnival.

The first recorded samba, 'Pelo Telefone' (1917), by Joaquim Maria dos Santos, known as Donga, was composed at the house of tia Ciata, also known as 'Little Mother of Terreiro de João Alaba'. Venetian-style carnival marchas (parades) were held on Avenida Central, but in Little Africa's Praça Onze Little Carnival attracted revellers from the nearby morros like Deixa Falar ('Let Them Talk') from Estácio Hill – the first group to call itself an Escola de Samba (samba school), because it practised in a nearby school. The first carnival desfile (parade) was held in Praça Onze in 1930, and the first contest in 1932. Under President Getúlio Vargas, samba schools, previously repressed, achieved legitimacy and received official support and public funding in exchange for serving in the processes of nation and national history building. In 1935, the Afro-Dionysian parade, with samba music and dance, baterias (percussion bands), enredos (plots or themes) and fantasias (sumptuous costumes), graced Avenida Presidente Vargas. Introduced in 1943, Baiana costumes, honouring the matriarchs of Little Africa, became mandatory for one unit of each samba school.[57]

By the 1960s, the samba schools had been invaded by the middle and upper classes. From 1963, temporary bleachers were constructed and tickets sold. And in 1965 Rio's carnival was accurately described as 'the largest popular spectacle in the world'.[58] The samba parade became increasingly professionalized, bureaucratized and commercialized, somewhat along the lines of football. The Sambódromo did not change this reality. According to Niemeyer, it attempted only to reverse some of the spatial characteristics of the parade, 'which had lately been entirely corrupted'. Evoking its African roots, the festival was given a

54 Schwarcz, 2004, p. 196; Parker, p. 159.   **55** Stam, 1989, p. 130.
56 Schwarcz, 2004, pp. 219–20.   **57** The last carnival in Praça Onze took place in 1942. In 1941, Herivelto Martins and Grande Otelo composed 'Praça Onze', a samba that became a hit of the 1942 carnival and the enduring hymn to Praça Onze.   **58** Parker, p. 158.

permanent home at its place of origin, away from the usual tourist haunts of Rio and in a setting where it is overlooked by the surrounding *favelas*, from which the oldest samba schools descend. Its enormous *terreiro* 'corrected' another 'error', Niemeyer explains, as the temporary bleachers had walled in and reduced the parade width to 7 metres, 'blocking the people's view of their favorite spectacle'. Raising the bleachers 5 metres above the ground allowed for spectator space at the level of the esplanade. Apotheosis Square, at the climax of the 700-metre-long runway, was intended to 'offer a new aspect to the parade' and a high note to the architectural composition.[59] It is crowned by a 25-metre-high, slender, double parabolic arch, supporting a thin concrete slab, dramatically cantilevered over the stepped stage. A small museum nests behind Apotheosis Square.

Eerily empty during most of the year, the Sambódromo is entirely transformed during the four-day-and-night spectacle for which thousands of people work extremely hard throughout the year. This event recovers and re-enacts for its 100,000 spectators, year after year, Brazil's mythical spatio-temporal landscape, 'incorporating contradictory interpretations within a single whole . . . [and] offer[ing] a fundamentally popular counterpart to the myths of origin of elite writers such as Paulo Prado and Gilberto Freyre'. Niemeyer and Ribeiro harboured the ambition of creating a new symbol for the city of Rio. But this is in some ways the most utilitarian of Niemeyer's structures, almost disappearing from the city for most of the year, only periodically reintegrated by means of the samba schools' tropical rites. During carnival it overshadows all other Rio icons, not with its architecture but by emerging from its mundane and ordinary existence to embrace a collective representation of Brazilian reality that focuses 'on the sensual nature of Brazilian life, on the chaotic mixture of races and cultures that has given rise to a new world in the tropics'. Niemeyer's architecture shares with Rio's carnival the creative celebration of uncompromising freedom, exuberant play, rebellious sensuality and tropical pleasure, the abolition of established norms and overturning of imposed values. To paraphrase the 'Manifesto Antropófago', Niemeyer's architecture was 'never catechized. What [it] really made was Carnival.' Like carnival, it continuously reinvents its contours, grasping 'the opportunity to manipulate the webs of meaning and the systems of power', remaining 'open to many divergent interpretations'.[60] But Niemeyer is no fool; at the Sambódromo he would not compete with the samba schools. The only two artworks – Marianne Peretti's mural and an *azulejo*-clad wall by Athos Bulcão – are found behind Apotheosis Square, decorating the museum rather than the stadium.

The Sambódromo stages the annual collective dream of a utopian tropical world, retreating into the background during the time of festival. *Pace* Underwood, it does not have the power to effect the '"domestication" of the carnival ritual'.[61] More than

Passarela do Samba or Sambódromo, samba stadium, Rio de Janeiro, 1984

twenty years after its construction, carnival goes on unabated in all its unbridled exuberance, with more than two hundred groups parading through the streets and squares of Rio de Janeiro. Following the successful revitalization, after decades of deterioration, of some of the city's central areas through the progressive urban reform policy of the 1990s, it is not only the festivities that have regained their rights to the inner city of Rio but also some low-income residents – for example, those in the restored historic *cortiço* on Rua Senador Pompeu (1996) –. The city's music scene has returned to the rehabilitated Lapa area, between the centre and the *zona sul*, where Rio's bohemian nightlife flourished in the 1920s and 1930s, and about which Niemeyer frequently reminisces.

Darcy Ribeiro justified the building of the Sambódromo on the basis of savings from the annual construction of bleachers, which could now be invested in social reform projects. Niemeyer enthusiastically welcomed his proposition to house 200 classrooms for 15,000 underprivileged pupils in the space beneath the bleachers that serve as administration offices during carnival. The samba groups have thus returned to the school. Accommodating the world's largest Afro-Dionysian festival and 'the biggest school ever built in Brazil',[62] the Sambódromo satisfies the demands of Oswald de Andrade's 'Carib Revolution'.

59 Niemeyer, 2000b, p. 21. Niemeyer notes that Apotheosis Square was Ribeiro's idea; quoted in Underwood, 1994c, pp. 151–52.   **60** Oswald de Andrade, 2000, p. 591; Parker, p. 163.   **61** Underwood, 1994c, p. 140.   **62** Oscar Niemeyer, quoted in Underwood, 1994c, p. 150.

Supporting the Right to the School, the Museum and the Beach

The social programme of the Sambódromo should be viewed in the context of Governor Brizola's policy of social and educational inclusion, influenced by the innovative ideas of Brazilian educationalist Paulo Freire (1921–97) who, like Darcy Ribeiro and Brizola himself, had been exiled by the 1964 military coup. The Centros Integrados de Educação Pública (Integrated Centres of Public Education, CIEPs, 1984–87, structural engineer José Carlos Süssekind) are popularly known as Brizolões, after Brizola. Created during Brizola's first government (1983–87; the second was 1991–94), under the direction of Darcy Ribeiro, their objective was to offer free, comprehensive elementary education primarily to economically disadvantaged children in the state of Rio de Janeiro, with integrated services and programmes for healthcare, nutrition, sports and culture. Niemeyer asserts that what was revolutionary about the CIEPs was their educational aspect: 'These two projects [the Sambódromo and the CIEPs]', he writes, 'have triumphed against all odds after a whole bunch of lies were invented in an attempt to snuff them out.'[63]

Although Brazil's illiteracy rates had been gradually declining as a result of the expansion of public education, chronic underinvestment in public education during the military dictatorship had meant that by 1980 the national illiteracy rate stood at an alarming 25.9 per cent (45.4 for the poor Northeast), and youth illiteracy at 16.5 per cent for the fifteen–twenty-four age group, compared with 2.8 per cent for Argentina and 1.7 per cent for Cuba.[64] According to Ribeiro, full-time integrated education would help address the needs of children from low-income families, providing them with an education as well as a meaningful childhood at school – as opposed to the streets – for forty hours a week (including time for supervised study), the equivalent of their parents' working time. The new educational infrastructure was conceived as an instrument to fight inequality and social exclusion and to promote the exercise of citizenship. The aim was to build five hundred school complexes for six hundred children each – one-fifth of all pupils in the state of Rio de Janeiro – giving priority to low-income areas on the metropolitan periphery.

Niemeyer's early sketches indicate that he had entertained more ambitious plans for the CIEPs, with forms that recall favourite

CIEP Tancredo Neves on Rua do Catete, Rio de Janeiro; the first of Niemeyer's 506 constructed prefabricated Centros Integrados de Educação Pública (Integrated Centres of Public Education), inaugurated 8 May 1985

63 Niemeyer, 2000b, p. 20.   64 According to the 2000 Demographic Census, Brazil's illiteracy rate was at 13.6 per cent, while more than half of the population over fifteen years of age had not completed eight years of primary education. Again, these numbers do not reflect large regional disparities and racial inequalities.

themes like the volcano of Le Havre, and amenities such as churches and swimming pools. He finally settled for a relatively modest yet adequately equipped model. Most schools were constructed on generously proportioned sites and include: a central, long, orthogonal building; a multi-purpose covered hall for sports and cultural events with changing rooms and shower facilities, which many pupils did not enjoy in their family houses; and a book-and-video library, surmounted by a smaller structure containing emergency accommodation for twelve pupils. The principal building develops around a central ramp linking its three levels and becoming the building's circulatory and social heart. On the ground floor, the ramp overlooks a large, covered recreation area, flanked by medical and dental services and a refectory seating two hundred children, with kitchens for the preparation of free meals. On the other two floors are located the classrooms, directed study areas, an auditorium and administration offices. Water towers and leisure facilities are situated on the roof. A CIEP *compacto* version was employed on smaller sites.

To benefit from economies of scale, Niemeyer proposed a modular system of construction using prefabricated, easily multipliable, reinforced-concrete elements. The scale and strong colours of the CIEPs' principal building turn them into a focal point for peripheral neighbourhoods that possess no other landmarks. Oblivious to critics who defamed the CIEPs as 'sumptuous', complaining that their cost per pupil is three times that of conventional schools and building and maintenance costs twice as high, Niemeyer attests that he consciously designed them so as 'to stand out from the surrounding buildings', functioning as community centres and giving economically disadvantaged children 'access to what only the rich enjoy today'.[65]

With amenities inspired by those of old religious schools for the privileged, like the one Niemeyer attended as a child, the CIEPs were intended to herald a new era in Brazilian education, which was suffering the effects of a dualist and inegalitarian educational system that over the twenty-one-year dictatorship had favoured private schooling and seriously neglected children from poor and lower-middle-class families. A 1983 constitutional amendment established that 'the Union will allocate, annually, never less than 13 per cent, and the States, the Federal District and the Municipalities a minimum of 25 per cent of tax revenues to the maintenance and development of schooling'. With his generously designed schools, Niemeyer defended the right to education and the social function of schools, supporting Brazilian educators who viewed free public schooling as 'an instrument in the struggle against discrimination and poverty'.[66]

In 1993, 54.9 per cent of the budget of the state of Rio de Janeiro was absorbed by the construction of the CIEPs. Of the 506 constructed school complexes, 343 currently function as CIEPs. Denouncing critics of the ambitious project who favoured a 'sim-

CIEP Tancredo Neves: view of street elevation

pler [architecture], closer to the people', Niemeyer retorted that 'the idea of architectural simplicity is sheer demagogy, unacceptable discrimination'.[67] He would certainly agree with Theodor Adorno that this kind of 'vainly praised simplification' risks enmeshing architecture 'in false consciousness'.[68] Brazil's 1988 constitution declared access to compulsory and free education 'a subjective public right' and increased the resources allocated to education. Although a number of school buildings have suffered from lack of maintenance and their programmes have been severely curtailed by lack of funding, the CIEPs remain popular with local communities, while they represent a rare initiative to provide much-needed social and educational resources to the most disadvantaged communities of Rio de Janeiro.

Brizola's first CIEP, however, was not designed by Niemeyer. The CIEP Presidente João Goulart, named after Brizola's brother-in-law, the president overthrown by the 1964 military coup, was installed in 1983 in a converted building at the foot of Morro do Cantagalo, at the exact point where the elite neighbourhood of Ipanema meets the Cantagalo *favela*. The building was initially constructed to house the luxury Panorama Palace Hotel – a project strongly associated with the policies of Carlos Lacerda, governor from 1960 to 1965 of Guanabara state (as the federal district of Rio de Janeiro became known),[69] who initiated a partially successful campaign for the removal of *favelas* that obstructed the development of valuable real estate in Rio de Janeiro's prestigious *zona sul*. In 1961, with the expectation that Cantagalo would be

65 Niemeyer, 2000b, pp. 21, 176. **66** Gadotti, 1992. **67** Niemeyer, 2000b, pp. 21, 176. **68** Adorno, 2004, p. 298. **69** The federal district of Rio de Janeiro took this name after the national capital was moved to Brasília in 1960. In 1975, the city of Rio de Janeiro became a municipality.

cleared, investors keen to capitalize on the site's spectacular views began construction of the high-rise Panorama Palace, but building came to a halt in 1964. A succession of institutions occupied the unfinished building, which by 1981 was in ruins.

Following a series of unpopular and at times violent *favela* clearances during the military dictatorship, Brizola's transformation of the Ipanema hotel into a school and community centre for the *favelas* of Cantagalo, Pavão and Pavãozinho symbolized a new policy towards the *favelas* that was radically different from those of his predecessor. Niemeyer invokes Friedrich Engels to express his own opposition to *favela* clearance and relocation of their residents to

> workers housing and popular housing . . . terms that indicate capitalist discrimination. They represent demagogic and paternalistic objectives that don't attend to the scale of the misery. In fact . . . they hamper the nascent revolution, to remove the *favelados* from the most valuable areas, to bury them in these horrible ghettos called *conjuntos proletários* [proletarian complexes], or under pretext of security and ecology, to turn the *favelas* to real estate profit.[70]

The new Estrada de Cantagalo provided the hillside residents with access to the hotel building, so that they could ride its two elevators from street level twenty-one storeys up to their school.[71] The act of commissioning the architect of the monuments of Brasília to design school complexes for Rio's *favela* communities resonated with similar significance. Having persistently refused over the previous decades to contribute to state-led social housing projects and thus 'conspire with the demagogic and paternalistic objectives such projects represented', Niemeyer's enthusiastic acceptance of the invitation to design the CIEPs indicates that he genuinely believed in the good intentions of the new democratic administration in bringing some of the citizenship rights of the *asfalto* to the *morros*.[72] The aim of his architecture, he insists, was 'to rectify a pervasive fallacy in [Brazil], which was to have the buildings in [the *favelas*] feature a substandard architecture, as if siding with the poverty that characterizes the neighborhood'. For the children from the *favelas*, he suggests, entering the schools 'constituted the beginning of a better life'.[73] Again, Niemeyer echoes Adorno's line: 'Art respects the masses by presenting itself to them as what they could be rather than by adapting itself to them in their degraded condition.'[74]

Another controversial project of Brizola's first term in office was the inauguration of a new bus route that established a fast connection between the main suburban station of *zona norte* and Ipanema. For the first time, this bus service eased access to the beaches of the *zona sul* for the residents of some of the poorest and most remote communities of the city. By the end of the 1990s, the underground network reached Copacabana, further improv-

ing access to Rio's most prized public space, 'the place from which all distances seem to be measured'.[75] Elite residents of the *zona sul* claim a direct link between the influx of newcomers and the *arrastões* and invasions of the sand, pavements and streets of Rio's affluent southern neighbourhoods.

Although access to Rio's fabled beach has never been restricted, it has been shown to be 'highly segregated through habit, prejudice, and personal ties'.[76] And it has always been more accessible to the residents of the *zona sul*, which includes a number of large *favelas*, and those who can afford leisure time. For those living close to the ocean, the urban beach functions as an extension of their living rooms – a space in between the private and the public sphere, city and nature. But, as already noted, it also represents the eminent spatialization of the utopian aspirations of Brazilian society – freedom, equality, the mingling of classes and races. In 1973, Evenson went as far as to apply to the Copacabana neighbourhood Patrick Geddes's definition of a 'superslum'; 'that is, an area which, although fashionable and expensive, exhibits building congestion equivalent to that of many poor districts . . . an amiable, well-heeled slum whose inhabitants live there by choice'. In Copacabana, she found 'all the characteristic slum pleasures', like children playing in the streets, and nothing of 'the antiseptic air of many middle-class districts', although she did point out that its 'social mixture' results from 'the presence of a large service class'.[77]

When public transport made the population mix on the beach, at least on sunny Sundays and public holidays, more truly representative of that of the city as a whole, Rio's wealthy, primarily white minority became visible as such and were overwhelmed by racist fear and hatred. Although low-income Cariocas have always been part of beach life – for example, as vendors – the new sunbathers from the *zona norte* claimed their place on the beach without engaging in any economic activity or relationship of exchange, thus challenging the Carioca elite's domination of the prime public space of the city, claiming equal rights with their fellow *zona sul* citizens. Their presence prompted calls for, and acts of, repression, leading in turn to the *arrastões*, which turned the beach into a stage of urban social protest. The most important and symbolic public space in Carioca, and by extension Brazilian, life became an object of contestation, the site of confrontations between the various groups that claimed it as their stake. In this sense, its central role in urban public life and its vocation of social integration have, in fact, been reasserted and reinforced by facts on the ground.

70 Niemeyer, 1980b, p. 26.   **71** Freeman, p. 209.   **72** Niemeyer, 2000b, p. 175.   **73** Niemeyer, 2004, p. 226.   **74** Adorno, 2004, p. 313.   **75** Evenson, 1973, p. 14.   **76** Freeman, p. 332. See also Freeman, pp. 299 ff.   **77** Evenson, 1973, p. 15.

It is precisely as the site of class and racial tensions and antagonisms, as the site where power is contested, that the urban beach is now turning from an idealized space of democracy without true democratic participation into Rio's central urban public space, where citizens' rights are enacted and continually renegotiated. Through the *arrastões*, the residents of the *zona sul* were reminded of the disquieting fact that the beach and the city belong to all citizens. The groups that now share, and fight over, Rio's beach are, to paraphrase Lefebvre, 'rivals in their love of the [beach]': the ultimate urban space for the consumption of pure pleasure, positing use value over exchange value, best representing the unproductive value of the city. 'As for the rich and powerful, they will always feel threatened,' Lefebvre contends. And they will 'justify their privilege in the community by sumptuously spending their fortune: buildings, foundations, palaces, embellishments, festivities'.[78]

In this spirit, in 1991, Jorge Roberto Silveira, mayor of Niterói, just across Guanabara Bay from Rio de Janeiro, and his secretary of culture, architect Ítalo Campofiorito, commissioned Niemeyer to design the Museu de Arte Contemporânea (Museum of

Contemporary Art, 1991–96, structural engineer Bruno Contarini), primarily for the artworks owned by João Leão Sattamini – one of Brazil's foremost collectors of modern art. Undiplomatically, Niemeyer refused to consider the preselected sites. He was determined to install the museum on a rocky promontory overlooking the beach at Boa Viagem, designing Niterói's first civic landmark primarily for the city's most valuable collection of all: the spectacular display of Rio's seductively contoured rocks, hills and mountain ranges, islands, bays and forests, surrounding the deep blue sea of Guanabara Bay – the stuff of nineteenth-century Brazilian paintings, as Silveira noted.[79] A few years later, with the museum in place, on Niemeyer's ninetieth birthday, Eduardo Galeano would write that the mountains of Rio were 'designed by God, on the day when God thought he was Niemeyer'.[80]

Unintimidated by the breathtaking scenery, Niemeyer fully implicated it in his composition while preserving the two – nature and artwork – as clearly distinct, refusing to let his building blend in with its surroundings, masterfully escaping the trap of infantile mimicry as well as the pitfall of delusory, hubristic competition. 'Man intervenes in Nature', Niemeyer maintains, 'turning it into the the-

Rio de Janeiro across Guanabara Bay, steel engraving, drawn by E. Duncan, engraved by T. A. Prior, published by Blackie & Son, *circa* 1840

78 Lefebvre, 1996, p. 67.   **79** Jorge Roberto Silveira, in Niemeyer, 1997b, p. 24.   **80** Eduardo Galeano, quoted in Niemeyer, 2002, n.p.

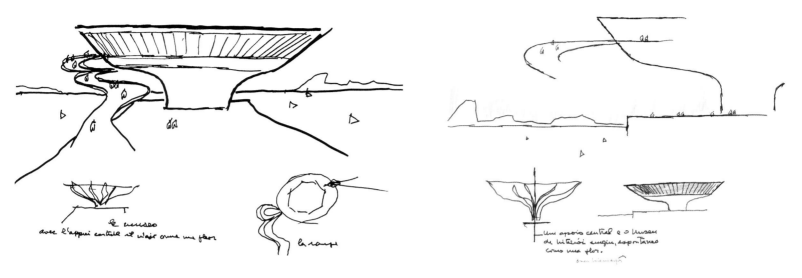

Museu de Arte Contemporânea, Niterói, Rio de Janeiro state. 1991–96

Museu de Arte Contemporânea: Niterói's first civic landmark enjoys a significant presence in the fabled landscape and a splendid panorama of Guanabara Bay.

The saucer-like volume of the Niterói Museum of Contemporary Art spreads out imperiously from a central stalk, like 'a flower growing over the fantastic landscape'.

ater of his illusions.'[81] As ultimate proof of maturity, which may, after all, be the reward of old age, at Niterói he had the audacity to introduce into the marvellous landscape an element of controlled dissonance, which is resolved the moment the visitor steps into the viewing gallery at the museum's perimeter. Gleaming white against the sky like a paper cut-out by Henri Matisse, the curvaceous museum is clearly visible from aeroplanes approaching Rio's Santos Dumont Airport across the bay, from the street along the shore, and from the beaches astride the Boa Viagem outcrop. It beckons visitors from afar, touting the successful reinvention of 'Rio's mistreated stepsister' as a tourist destination.[82] Enticing a regular stream of visitors, Niterói's new landmark has been much more successful in establishing links with Rio de Janeiro than have the regular ferry crossings and the 14-kilometre-long highway bridge that opened in 1974.

Endorsing the oft-observed resemblance of his museum to a flying saucer or spaceship, Niemeyer appeared dressed as its pilot at the beginning of Marc-Henri Wajnberg's documentary film of 2000, and proceeded to land it imperiously on the edge of the rocky promontory. The saucer-like volume is cantilevered out from a stout central stalk, 9 metres in diameter, like 'a flower growing over the fantastic landscape', recalling Niemeyer's 1950s project for the Museum of Modern Art in Caracas.[83] But, while the straight lines of the inverted pyramid for Caracas responded to the lines of the densely built city it overlooked, at Niterói, Niemeyer responded to a landscape Gilles Deleuze could have used to illustrate his

description of the baroque 'fold [that] unfurls all the way to infinity'.[84] He drew a 'line which springs from the ground, and without interruption grows and unfolds, sensually, up to the roof'.[85] Then he surrounded the museum's sturdy stem with a circular reflecting pool that echoes the bay below, dispensing with the need for a railing and prolonging the continuous concrete spiralling ribbon. At the breath of a breeze, the rippling water reflects up onto the white underside of the seemingly weightless concrete flower and brings it alive. A similar shimmering effect is created at night, with the help of thirty-six lights in the pool. Thus freed of a solid base, the spacecraft relies on a long serpentine ramp to counterbalance its laconic image and link its three circular floor plates – with radii of 18 to 20 metres – to the large plaza-cum-beach on the sunny, northern side of the museum.

In sharp contrast to Le Corbusier in 1929, who 'improved' Rio's spectacular *corniche* with 'the only line that can harmonize with the vehement caprice of the mountains: the horizontal', Niemeyer found in the landscape 'the main guidelines' for his design.[86] Atop the ramp, the oblique line of the museum directs the eye to the parallel, sloping side of the Pão de Açúcar; the slight indentation of Rio's emblematic rock is echoed by the broad strip of dark glazing that syncopates the surface of Niterói's concrete chalice. The ramp coils up languorously, then shreds into two. The first ribbon

81 Niemeyer, 2000b, p. 123.   82 Beauvoir, p. 541.   83 Oscar Niemeyer, in Wajnberg.   84 Deleuze, p. 3.   85 Niemeyer, 1997b, pp. 24, 12.   86 Le Corbusier, 1991, p. 245; Niemeyer, 1998, p. 39.

The sturdy stem of the Museu de Arte Contemporânea rises from a reflective pool that echoes the bay below the rocky promontory.

stretches out and docks on the white saucer, giving access to the first level, which is divided by six radiating reinforced-concrete walls and accommodates reception facilities and administration areas. The second ribbon folds back and spirals upwards, delivering the visitor to the lower of the two gallery levels. The inner, double-height hexagonal core of this intermediate level is partitioned off and dedicated to the museum's permanent collection. Narrow, oblique openings between the walls that define the central hexagon capture seductive glimpses of the landscape beyond the darker, perimeter viewing gallery.

The viewing gallery is given over to the captivating panorama, admitted through the building's continuous visor, furnished with a built-in carpeted bench running along the window sill. The radially canted external wall ensures that no direct sunlight enters this space, inducing concentration on the sun-drenched spectacle across the bay to the south. From the viewing gallery, a sculptural spiral stair with a pleated, white-painted concrete underside leads to the top floor, where another perimeter gallery houses temporary displays, overlooking the permanent exhibition space

on the lower level. In this top-level gallery, the carpeted floor curls up at a distance from the white wall, keeping the visitor within the confines of the space and concealing the source of crushing light that dissolves the solidity of the outer wall, creating the impression of an infinite space beyond, 'a kind of daydream space' like those by James Turrell – an entirely appropriate extension to a physical space where artworks are displayed.[87]

A seventy-seat auditorium, a bar and restaurant accessed via an external staircase, archives, technical facilities and storage spaces have been delegated to a lower level, partly sunk below the public square and partly, for the bar and restaurant area, open towards the bay. The storage space in the central pier, linked to the galleries by lift, has proven to be rather limited. Sadly, because of financial constraints, the quality of the museum's finish has also been compromised. Despite its minor shortcomings, however, the Museum of Contemporary Art remains one of Niemeyer's

87 James Turrell, quoted in King.

The oblique line of the Museu de Arte Contemporânea directs the eye to the parallel, sloping side of the Pão de Açúcar on the Rio de Janeiro side of Guanabara Bay.

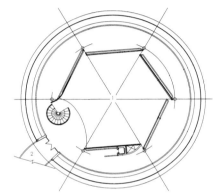

upper level gallery plan

intermediate level gallery plan

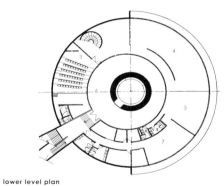

lower level plan

1 gallery
2 ramp
3 auditorium
4 restaurant
5 bar
6 archives
7 kitchen
8 reception
9 administration

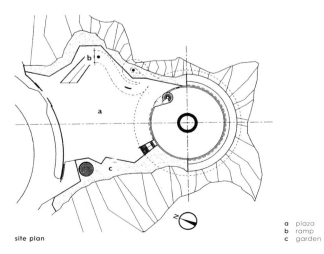

site plan

a plaza
b ramp
c garden

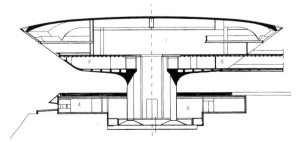

cross section

Museu de Arte Contemporânea, Niterói

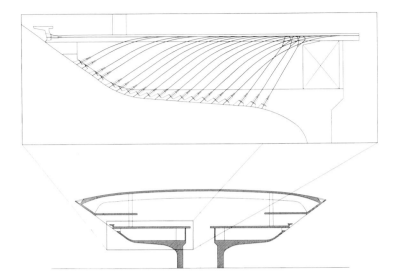

Museu de Arte Contemporânea: structure

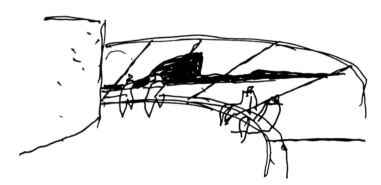

Museu de Arte Contemporânea: the awe-inspiring panorama is admitted into the perimeter gallery through the building's continuous visor.

major achievements. For Niterói, it has become a source of civic pride and the definitive symbol of the city.

By lifting the building off the ground, 'the panorama became even more magnificent', says Niemeyer – and an integral part of the spatial experience. In a classic Niemeyer inversion – carnivalization – of conventional hierarchies of space and use, he turned the democratic royal box at the perimeter of Niterói's theatrical museum into the centrepiece of its interior space, where visitors can savour the sensation of floating in the midst of the fabled landscape. Consistent with the Anthropofagist strategy, what dominates the building from the outside, underlining the public nature of the museum, is its great seductive ramp, with its broad, folding and twisting ribbons set ablaze by a fiery red, all the more powerful against the white square, 'emphasis[ing] access . . . in the form of a promenade around the architecture'.[88]

The idea of a dynamic ramp attached to, or rather drawn out of, a prominent landmark, acting as a powerful magnet that attracts pedestrians up to an elevated public space, first appeared in Niemeyer's unexecuted project for the Ribeirão das Lages Water Tower in the state of Rio de Janeiro (1941, structural engineer Emílio Baumgart). Commissioned to design a more satisfactory solution than that proposed by the Ministry of Education and Public Health's Water Service, Niemeyer recognized the landmark status that the 50-metre-high utilitarian structure would assume. He redesigned it, making it more slender, taller and lotus-shaped, and superimposing on the circular ground-floor volume housing the pumps a public square borne up on slender columns. A wide, folding ramp was appended for the sole purpose of sweeping pedestrians up to the public observation terrace.

Similar ramps, transgressing functional requirements and inviting the public to appropriate them as promenades, have been unfurled in many of Niemeyer's projects, from the Brazilian Pavilion at the 1939 New York's World Fair to the National Congress in Brasília and the Maison de la Culture in Le Havre. The more public the nature of the building, the longer the ramps seem to be and the more elaborate the journey they propose as they strive to abolish, or at least suppress, the borderline between open public space that includes all citizens and enclosed public space that introduces modes of exclusion. Mediating between the street and the building on which they dock and allowing space to flow between the two, Niemeyer's ramps ease, by significantly prolonging, the transition between the space that belongs to the city and the space of the building, provoking dialogue with the user and inventive interpretation. Their plan and gradient are commensurate with the frame of mind they intend to induce in the user, imposing a slow, axial, ceremonial movement that gradually

88 Oscar Niemeyer, 'Museum of Contemporary Art', in *Oscar Niemeyer: Notebooks of the Architect*, n.p.

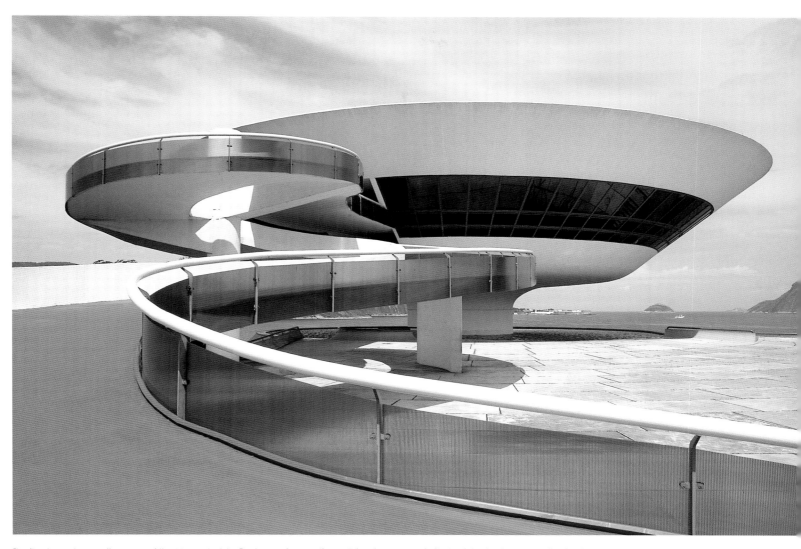

The flamboyant serpentine ramp of the Museu de Arte Contemporânea entices a leisurely promenade that celebrates the surrounding landscape and connects the public plaza on the northern side of the museum to the first-floor reception area and to the lower of the two gallery levels.

elevates body and mind; or proposing an initiatory descent, dramatizing the passage through a dark space into a space filled with light; or calling for a careless stroll along a broad walkway that encourages social interaction; or stimulating a dynamic, spiralling movement that elicits feelings of anticipation; or prompting a spirited, dance-like walk along the capricious space folds of an aerial garden path; or enticing a leisurely, gently swinging and swaying movement along a beach-like strip of flying ground that carries bodies uselessly back and forth for the unadulterated pleasure of the promenade, the delight of the chance encounter and the sheer joy of changing vistas.

At Niterói, there is a clear hierarchy between open public space and the space of the museum, which, positioned as it is on the edge of the peninsula with only the smallest possible footprint, rescues urban public space on the landside street – a space typi-

cally prioritized in Niemeyer's public buildings as fundamental for the enactment of the rights of citizenship. Notably, the new public plaza of the Museum of Contemporary Art and its flamboyant ramp have proven more popular than the galleries, especially on days with good weather, offering a variety of spatial opportunities for promenading, and balconies for observation or reverie. Where doorways to houses of high culture are often forbidding or intimidating, Niemeyer's bright red ramp becomes a sort of aerial root for the museum, inviting people on the square below to take a casual walk up and explore. Its two ribbons do not end on a wall – another familiar Niemeyer gesture – but flow into the building through glass doors that are recessed out of view and easily penetrable.

Circulation devices are often painfully incarcerated, but the Niterói ramp, emancipated from the building's plan and transcending all built contours and constraints, has been granted an autonomy that allows it to roam freely in space, drape and fold in the air, exceeding the requirements of its utility. Released to the world beyond the building, it challenges the hegemony of the programmatic space of the museum, identified with the *asfalto* of the segregated city. Rather than serving the white museum's formal spaces, Niemeyer's playful, colourful ramp subordinates the museum's function to the whims of urban players, inverting – carnivalizing – the familiar relationship between primary and ancillary or served and servant spaces – in this case, between exhibition gallery and circulation – thereby sabotaging the commodification of the space of the museum. Sadly, the subsequent installation of railing between the street pavement and the square seriously compromises the intentions of Niemeyer's project.

Reinforcing the links between Rio de Janeiro and Niterói, Niemeyer also designed a new passenger ferry station for the Charitas company (1999–2006). The success of the Museum of Contemporary Art also led to a series of other commissions, including the Museum of Brazilian Cinema (2001–) and a group of buildings on a large civic square on the coast, near the passenger ferry terminal and bus station, collectively baptized Caminho Niemeyer (Niemeyer Promenade). As the ferry from Rio approaches Niterói, visitors are greeted by the People's Theatre (1999–2006), with its sensually undulating, white concrete canopy echoing the curves of the mountains in the background. The Memorial Roberto Silveira, an information centre (1999–2006) has also been completed. The new premises for the Oscar Niemeyer Foundation (1999–), which Niemeyer intends to develop into a centre for art education, are currently under construction. A Roman Catholic cathe-

The ramp of the People's Theatre sweeps spectators up a spiral promenade granting views across the bay to Rio de Janeiro and leading to the elevated semi-open foyer.

Oscar Niemeyer Foundation, Caminho Niemeyer, Niterói, Rio de Janeiro state, 1999–: the dome under construction, 2003

dral (1999–) – a typologically innovative, centrally planned semi-open ecclesiastical building with a suspended 40-metre-diameter cupola and capacity for 3,800 worshippers – and a larger Baptist cathedral (1999–) for 5,000 people are awaiting funding.

In recent years the city of Niterói has been experiencing rapid urban and economic growth. By investing part of its new wealth in public and civic projects, it attests and publicizes its commitment to promoting a gratifying and dignified urban experience for its citizens. It is hoped that Niterói's new civic square will not be fenced off, for, in the words of the nineteenth-century Bahian poet Castro Alves, 'the square [and the beach] belongs to the people as the sky belongs to the condor!' (from the poem 'A praça', 1864).

People's Theatre, Caminho Niemeyer, Niterói, Rio de Janeiro state, 1999–2006: east elevation facing the large civic square

While the Niterói museum was under construction, Niemeyer explored ways of establishing a relation between a private building and the street in a very different environment: the densely built neighbourhood of Copacabana. Although the unavoidable gate and guard were eventually installed, Niemeyer left the ground-floor area of the Hotel SESC Copacabana (Serviço Social do Comércio, 1995) largely open, contiguous with the street pavement, inviting passers-by to walk under the hotel block into the sunny courtyard to the rear. The entire building is set back from the street line, creating a wide, semi-public forecourt. The dark glass façade of the street elevation is covered with dazzling rippling yellow aluminium ribbons that both acknowledge and camouflage air-conditioning units behind their folds. Turning a typical unsightly feature of Rio's buildings into an opportunity to introduce an element of Baroque exuberance and movement onto the street, Niemeyer revalorized and dynamized the urban façade in its role as the point of contact between the public space of the city and the private interests it accommodates.

Hotel SESC Copacabana, Rio de Janeiro, 1995: close-up of street elevation with rippling aluminium ribbons concealing the air-conditioning units

Hotel SESC Copacabana, Rio de Janeiro, 1995: street elevation

In 2002 Niemeyer completed another urban building with civic aspirations, in the southern city of Curitiba, capital of the state of Paraná, with a population of 1.8 million (3.2 million in the greater metropolitan area). The NovoMuseu – Arte, Arquitetura e Cidade (New Museum – Art, Architecture and City, 2001–02), renamed Oscar Niemeyer Museum soon after its inauguration, consists of two parts. The first is a low, 200 × 30-metre, orthogonal, top-lit school building on *pilotis*, designed by Niemeyer himself in 1967 as the Edifício Castelo Branco, for the Paraná Institute of Education (constructed 1974–76), and now extensively remodelled by Brasil Arquitetura. The second is a new, independent structure, dubbed 'the eye' and intended as the museum's highlight (with Jair Valera and Ana Elisa Niemeyer, structural engineer José Carlos Süssekind). The two buildings are linked by Niemeyer's sinuous split ramps and a subterranean passage. Located on a large, prestigious urban site, the NovoMuseu borders Curitiba's civic centre to the south, across from Rua Deputado Mário de Barros, where the

state's three powers are represented by the Governor's Palace, the State Assembly and the Court of Justice, with other state institutions also bordering the large civic square. To the north and east is a relatively low-density residential area, and to the west is the large Papa João Paulo II Park, designed by Roberto Burle Marx with vegetation typical of the Paraná plateau. The City Hall is located to the south of the civic centre.

Curitiba's NovoMuseu was commissioned by the governor of Paraná, Jaime Lerner (1937–), at a time when Curitiba was a candidate, with Rio de Janeiro, Salvador and Recife, for the first Latin American affiliate of the Solomon R. Guggenheim Foundation. Rio de Janeiro was eventually selected as the site of the first Guggenheim Museum south of the equator, but Jean Nouvel's exoticist design of 2002, mostly underwater, with its sunken 'savage unfathomable garden', set apart from the city on an island behind a gigantic, free-standing white wall, for the exclusive use of the few, was fiercely and successfully opposed by Rio's inhabi-

NovoMuseu – Arte, Arquitetura e Cidade, renamed Oscar Niemeyer Museum, Curitiba, Paraná, 2001–02: the long sinuous ramps hyphenate the museum's two structures, the monumental 'eye', *in the foreground*, and the former Edifício Castelo Branco, *in the background*, designed by Niemeyer in 1967 and converted by Brasil Arquitetura

tants.[89] Niemeyer and Brasil Arquitetura's NovoMuseu contrasts sharply with Nouvel's design, not only in having a much lower budget, but also, and most importantly, in terms of its relationship with the city, extending a beach-like ramp towards Curitibanos in welcome to their new civic space.

Marcelo Ferraz of Brasil Arquitetura emphasizes the public urban nature of the museum, manifested in the open ground-floor space within its *pilotis*, addressing the 'city, the community and the visitor'. In this area, the fully glazed spaces of the reception, tourist information centre and restaurant admit views of the city, the new 'eye' and the park – a space of great symbolic importance in a city that prides itself on its pioneer environmental protection policy and extensive urban parkland.[90] Niemeyer's 'eye' became a popular city landmark before its official opening. Curitiba's Sunday strollers came to be photographed or simply to walk aimlessly up and down the ramps of this new attraction – the legacy of Lerner, the architect–urbanist and state governor who rose to fame as mayor of the celebrated capital of sustainability.

The 'eye' of the NovoMuseu proved immediately successful with Curitiba's citizens and visitors.

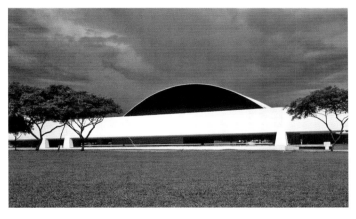

View from the adjacent Papa João Paulo II Park to the west of the NovoMuseu

89 Nouvel p. 46.   **90** Marcelo Ferraz, quoted in Figueroia, p. 44. Curitiba's twenty-six urban parks cover nearly one-fifth of the city, providing 52 square metres of green space per inhabitant. They serve both flood control and recreation purposes and are highly prized by Curitibanos. In 1977, Curitiba hosted Brazil's first national conference on urban parks and gardens.   **91** UNICEF awarded Jaime Lerner the Child and Peace Prize in 1990. The same year, Lerner received the United Nations Environmental Award.

The NovoMuseu should be considered in the context of the internationally acclaimed comprehensive strategy guiding Curitiba's urban development since the approval of its Plano Director, designed by Jorge Wilheim, in 1966. Jaime Lerner's innovative and integrative social, economic, environmental and urban reform programmes during the three terms of his administration (1971–75, 1979–84 and 1989–92), followed and advanced even by his adversaries, catapulted the city into the international limelight in the 1990s. Successfully engaging Curitiba's citizens, they included creative programmes for waste management and recycling, revitalization of central city areas – initiated at a time when such areas were abandoned to decline in other Brazilian cities – mechanisms for social inclusion focusing on the city's youth, strict anti-pollution regulations, low-income housing programmes, and improvement of services for the city's extensive *favelas*.[91] The benefits these programmes have brought to all, especially the most disadvantaged of Curitiba's citizens, have led to her recognition as 'the most innovative city in the world', in the words of the chairman of the Second United Nations Conference on Human Settlements (Habitat II) in Istanbul in June 1996.

Lerner's success story started with a revolutionary plan to oppose the destruction of much of the city's historic architecture and downtown urban life, threatened by the construction of an overpass in the place of Rua Quinze de Novembro. Instead, in 1972, Lerner turned Curitiba's main shopping street into Brazil's first pedestrian street. At a time when the focus of urban policy in the rest of Brazil was on facilitating vehicular traffic, with public urban interventions reduced to the construction of highways, overpasses, tunnels and parking areas that corroded urban public spaces, Curitiba adopted a vision of a human-scale city with a mix of uses and incomes.

The NovoMuseu, with more than 30,000 square metres of exhibition space and a variety of internal and external public spaces, complements the city's revitalized and extensively pedestrianized commercial centre with a new urban magnet dedicated to art, architecture and urbanism, right next to its civic centre, recycling an old building and adding a monumental structure to the city's skyline to enhance civic pride and this area's image. Contrasting with the introverted gallery space of the museum's low building, conceived by Marcelo Ferraz as an 'exhibition factory', Niemeyer's 'eye' is the citizens' grand salon or Curitiba's civic cathedral, with an unmistakeable iconic presence. Balanced on a high, vibrant yellow pedestal, its structure consists of a large concrete vault, 30 × 70 metres in plan, supported by two longitudinal, bow-shaped, pre-stressed, T-section concrete beams rising 5.5 metres at their highest point. These, in turn, rest on two enormous pillars, measuring 9.1 × 1.2 metres each, forming the two sides of the pedestal, with the beams cantilevered by 30 metres on either side.

Brasil Arquitetura: first-floor exhibition area of the remodelled former Edifício Castelo Branco, part of the NovoMuseu

Subterranean passage linking the two structures of the NovoMuseu

Large gallery space under the vault of the 'eye' surveying the city to the east of the NovoMuseu

Services and ancillary spaces are accommodated in the lower area of the 'eye', between the two gigantic beams. The 2,100-square-metre gallery space above, 10.9 metres high at its apex, is dramatically lit through large glazed walls that grant open views towards the city and the park. At night the large vault becomes a spectacular chandelier composed of thousands of light-diffusing, anodized aluminium blades. The full-height glazing incorporates a shading device – a black aluminium beehive mesh, filling the voids of the diagonally-gridded steel structure, and sandwiched between the tinted-glass panes. Successful in terms of solar control, this device has a catastrophic effect during the daytime, when its intricate shadow patterns are cast on the artworks. Despite their technical failure, these large openings point to the city as a stimulus and an integral part of the museum's public space, subtly undermining the primacy of the aesthetic experience.

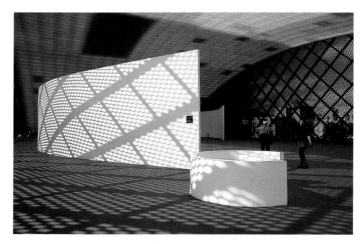

NovoMuseu: the diagonally-gridded, full-height glazing of the 'eye' incorporates a black aluminium beehive mesh that acts as a shading device but proves problematic for the display of artworks.

From the surrounding streets, the 'eye' is perceived as an enormous, site-specific sculpture, at once strange and amiable, announcing the presence of the museum. Its pedestal stands in a large pool of water surrounded by lawns. One of Curitiba's iconic, highly efficient and fully accessible glass 'tube stations' – emblematic of the city's model public transportation system, used by 75 per cent of Curitibanos – has been installed in front of the 'eye' on Rua Marechal Hermes. Further along, a broad ramp with a grey surface like that of the pavement invites walkers to deviate from their linear path and stroll leisurely through Curitiba's new recreation area. Like a permanently lowered drawbridge, it diverts the flow of pedestrian traffic towards the citizens' new cultural castle. Only a few metres away from the street and already hovering above the water, the ramp turns to allow walkers to re-establish contact with the city before they decide to continue down to the low, familiar old school building, now open to a larger public, or up towards the newcomer. The upper ramp turns to dock high up on the pedestal, where the entrance to the 'eye' is located.

As if to reinforce the association between his ramps and the beach, Niemeyer's sketches of female nudes appear on the ceramic tiles of the yellow stalk. For Niemeyer always imagines the beach as an eminently feminine space and a space of useless pleasure, in contrast to the masculine, business-oriented space of the linear street. Curitiba, too, now has a long curvy beach – the ramp, serving as an architectural metaphor for a space onto which Niemeyer projects his ideal of a good life, a public urban space where achievements may be savoured and new beginnings contemplated.

In a city with one of Brazil's fastest urban growth rates and a higher economic growth than the national average, social disparities and soaring crime rates continue to breed conflict and mutual resentment between the *morro* and the *asfalto*. Here, too, violence and the fear of violence continue to affect Curitibanos' relations to urban space and their fellow citizens. Streets are perceived as dangerous and a wealthy minority retreats into gated communities. For Niemeyer, the streets and squares of the city are the places where architecture, the most public of the arts, has the power to contribute to the construction of a society of equal rights – the society Brazil looks forward to as it regains faith in its ability to foster progressive change, if not the kind of rapid total transformation the builders of Brasília had dared envisage.

While he continues to invest his public buildings with the power to 'touch and enthuse', Niemeyer also strives to provide new ways in which city dwellers may relate to them, inventing spatial strategies to shift the location of spectacle from the private, commercial interior to the public exterior. Emphasizing the public nature and urban function of the museum or theatre as opposed to their pedagogical role, Niemeyer questions the dominant mode of experiencing and relating to a building for the display or perform-

View of the NovoMuseu's east elevation facing the city: split ramps propose a gentle stroll from Rua Marechal Hermes over the water to the entrance in the stalk of the 'eye' or to the open ground-floor space in the *pilotis* of the former Edifício Castelo Branco.

NovoMuseu: a recurring motif of Niemeyer's architecture, the flying beach-like urban ramp underscores the public nature of the building from which it sprouts, weaves its programme into the fabric of the city, celebrates a public space of useless pleasure and affirms its significance in the democratic city.

ance of art. To the same end, he prioritizes the openness and accessibility of spatial devices emancipated from the building programme and released into the public space of the city. What Niemeyer aims to achieve is the democratization of the architecture commissioned by the wealthy and politically powerful elite, which he turns towards the anonymous crowd of the city, urging them to claim their right to 'the theater of his illusions'.[92]

The extent to which this architecture of joy, spectacle and pleasurable promenading provides a firm ground for political optimism remains debatable. Yet, it is important to stress that Niemeyer's civic landmarks address and value the streets of the city and seek creative ways to extend the streets, privileging those who still inhabit these new 'negative' sites of Brazil over those overcome by fear of the street. In a symbolic revalorization of the democratic spaces of the city that have become increasingly marginalized, Niemeyer unfolds into the streets and squares over-scaled, beach-like ramps that have no closing hours and no guards. They represent the kind of democratic space that has become the most persistently elusive goal of his architecture and of Brazil's politics. As a space that keeps alive the dream of an egalitarian society and demands its fulfilment, the flying urban ramp, dynamized with the irreverent curves of the beach, exemplifies the element of 'protest' that Niemeyer sees as permeating all his work.[93] Niemeyer knows all too well that architecture cannot evade the realities of power and does not have the capacity to resolve social tensions. But it can function as a critique, it can produce and energize real sites of positive struggle between the *morro* and the *asfalto*, and it can create spatial possibilities for the transcendence of tensions.[94]

'A postcard of Brazil in the middle of Hyde Park'

Artworks, Adorno argues, 'are usually critical in the era in which they appear; later they are neutralized, not least because of changed social relations'. A number of Niemeyer's early works have reached the stage when they are 'entombed in the pantheon of cultural commodities', which endangers 'their truth content'.[95] Niemeyer is increasingly aware of this unavoidable condition. Without disavowing his early revolutionary production, he knows that, to a large extent, 'the thorn is removed' from works like those at Pampulha or the house at Canoas, and accepts the belated recognition of his achievements outside Brazil.

In 2003, recognition came in the form of an unexpected commission to design the Serpentine Gallery Summer Pavilion in Hyde Park, London (structural engineer José Carlos Süssekind), touted by the gallery's director, Julia Peyton-Jones, as a commission that intends to 'expose people to the finest contemporary architecture'.[96] As Niemeyer's earlier schemes for a student hall of residence at St Anthony's College, Oxford, and a hotel in Brighton (1998) had not been realized, he was eligible for the annual commission of the temporary pavilion, which is offered at short notice only to architects of worldwide acclaim who have not completed a structure in the United Kingdom at the time of the invitation. With this commission, the ninety-five-year-old Niemeyer was grouped together with Zaha Hadid (designer of the 2000 pavilion), Daniel Libeskind (2001, with Arup), Toyo Ito (2002, with Arup), MVRDV (2004, unrealized), Álvaro Siza and Eduardo Souto de Moura (2005, with Arup), Rem Koolhaas and Cecil Balmond (2006, with Arup), Olafur Eliasson and Kjetil Thorsen (2007), and Frank Gehry (2008) as one of the architects who 'consistently extend the boundaries of architectural practice'.[97]

As a Serpentine Gallery trustee and advisor on the annual architecture commission, Zaha Hadid was instrumental in the selection of Niemeyer as the architect of the fourth summer pavilion. Aptly, she described the image he created on the gallery's lawn, near the Serpentine Lake, as 'a postcard of Brazil in the middle of Hyde Park'.[98] Niemeyer reports that he was asked for 'everything that expresses my architecture', in the form of a 300-square-metre pavilion, to function as a 'café by day and a forum for learning, debate and entertainment at night', for three months, from 20 June to 14 September.[99]

To facilitate the dismantling and reassembly of the pavilion, he responded with a steel-frame structure, resulting in a configuration that was more rigid than his other tent-like structures in reinforced concrete, such as the Chapel of Nossa Senhora de Fátima, the Military Cathedral of Nossa Senhora da Paz, or the Teatro Pedro Calmon for the Ministry of the Army, all in Brasília. His first sketch of the pavilion's profile repeated the diagram Niemeyer used in his explanation of his 1962 proposal for the Permanent International Fair at Tripoli, to illustrate his idea of the structure that 'truly express[es] the spirit of a pavilion . . . reduced to a mere roof, a mere shell'.[100] To reassure his patrons, however, he subsequently accentuated the ultimate Niemeyer gesture: a sweeping curve with an upward thrust, defining the principal space of the pavilion. The oblique lines of the aluminium-clad white canopy, its strongly tapered section, and the long dashing lines of the ramp – curved in early sketches, but straightened out later – lent the pavilion an air of dynamism, speed and movement, streamlining the structure that had only temporarily touched down in London's royal park. To suggest a structure that defies gravity and to take in the park more fully, Niemeyer floated the main floor 1.5 metres off the ground – a rather awkward dimension, yet one that endeared the pavilion to

92 Niemeyer, 2000b, pp. 163, 123.   **93** Niemeyer, 2000b, p. 169.   **94** A number of instances in which Niemeyer deployed Antropofagist strategies of carnival have already been discussed. His overscaled, playful ramps may be interpreted as a further instance of carnival tactics, betraying that 'consciousness of carnival' as 'the site of struggle' between conflicting tendencies, with all its political ambiguities, that Robert Stam sees permeating 'all Brazilian life and art'; see Stam, 1989, pp. 128 ff.   **95** Adorno, 2004, p. 299.   **96** Peyton-Jones, 2005.   **97** Peyton-Jones, 2003, pp. 11–20.   **98** Zaha Hadid, quoted in Kimmelman.   **99** Niemeyer, 2004, p. 204; Peyton-Jones, 2003, pp. 11–20.   **100** Niemeyer, 1962b, p. 4. See Chapter Eight, p. 317. The pavilions are erected every summer on the lawn of the Serpentine Gallery and then sold and may be reinstalled on new locations.

children, who appreciated the intimate hiding places beneath the raised platform. Most importantly, the raising of the pavilion enabled him to stretch out on the Serpentine lawn his long, folded, signature Pau-Brasil ramp, reaching up from the paved path and seducing walkers onto a new kind of pleasurable promenade in the park.

The pavilion's elevated floor was supported by four recessed concrete columns, two of which continued up to the roof. The dynamic, asymmetrical profile of the Brazilian vessel, clearly outlined in white, was set against the symmetrical pavilion of the gallery itself, was built in 1934. The transparent façade of Niemeyer's pleasure pavilion addressed the park, claiming priority over the enclosed gallery space, itself originally a tea pavilion in Kensington Gardens. Niemeyer must have sensed that, in London, the spatial and symbolic value of the park as the ultimate urban space for the consumption of pure pleasure, representing the unproductive value of the city, is comparable to that of the beach in Rio de Janeiro. Towards the gallery, he turned a fiery red wall, enlivened by the shifting afternoon shadow of the classical building's roof lantern. A perpendicular staircase provided less glamorous access to the pavilion from this side. Semi-submerged, 1 metre below ground level, what was called an auditorium but was really a more intimate lounging space, in excess of program-

Serpentine Gallery Summer Pavilion, Hyde Park, London, United Kingdom, 2003

Serpentine Gallery Summer Pavilion under construction

Serpentine Gallery Summer Pavilion: the principal (south-east), transparent façade addressed the park; Niemeyer's signature Pau-Brasil ramp seduced walkers up to the elevated space of the pavilion

matic requirements, included a screen projecting Marc-Henri Wajnberg's documentary. Linked by an internal staircase to the main floor, this space offered views to the lawn through clerestory windows. Deeply recessed, the glass walls of the lower space underscored the lightness of the floating vessel.

Lightness, a dynamic profile, the play of curves and straight lines, simplicity, colour, and unity are the characteristics Niemeyer listed in his 'Necessary Explanation' of the 2003 Serpentine Gallery Pavilion – the kind of text with which he habitually accompanies

his sketches to justify a design proposal to a client.[101] His structural engineer, José Carlos Süssekind, added that Niemeyer's was 'a project that performs the miracle of "monumentality" on a very small scale'.[102] From the opening night, the London audience started whispering about the scandalous sketches of reclining female nudes, larger than life, printed on the reverse of the vertical red wall – a eulogy to all girls from Ipanema, which rhymes with Iracema – triumphing over the old tea pavilion in the background.[103]

Niemeyer's irreverent, 'provocative' gesture, his 'sexual references' and 'flagrant' embracing of colour and curves were at the centre of Mark Wigley's talk at the Serpentine Pavilion in July 2003. Wigley began by saying that the ninety-five-year-old Niemeyer 'is finally being celebrated, we are even able to talk about him, because he actually doesn't hurt us anymore . . . we think we can look at curves, even sex in a non-sexual way'. Despite the fact that colour and curves are not exclusive to Niemeyer's work, Wigley went on to say, 'long before he talks about sex, his architecture

101 Niemeyer, 2003c, p. 7. Niemeyer writes that, from the early days of his career, his unusual forms 'obliged' him to write 'explanatory texts to go along with each project', always seeking to provide practical justifications. This developed into 'a very particular working process', as he discovered that these texts helped him to 'test' his architectural solutions: 'When I come to a solution, I describe it in an explanatory text. If after reading it [it] satisfies me, I start the definitive drawings. If, otherwise, the arguments do not sound reasonable, I return to my drawing board'; Niemeyer, 2000b, pp. 19–21. Models also play a vital role in Niemeyer's design process, which begins with drawings at a scale of 1 : 500.   **102** 'Oscar Niemeyer (Architect), José Carlos Süssekind (Structural Engineer) and Julia Peyton-Jones (Director, Serpentine Gallery) in Conversation', in Niemeyer, 2003c, p. 57.   **103** 'Garota de Ipanema' ('The Girl from Ipanema') is a well-known bossa nova song composed in 1962 by Antônio Carlos Jobim with lyrics by Vinicius de Moraes. On Iracema (an anagram of America), one of the symbolic parents of Brazil, see Chapter Four, pp. 165–67.

is immediately interpreted as sexual, and therefore not to be trusted'. To a large extent, Wigley implied, this is because Niemeyer is Brazilian.[104] The Eurocentric, essentialist image of Brazil remains erotic and the Brazilian utopia persistently carnal. As Wigley has argued elsewhere, ever since Leon Battista Alberti, sexual desire, associated with 'the degenerate realm of erotic play', and 'pleasure understood as excess' have been condemned as 'dangerous'. Architecture's role has been established as that of cleansing social order of the body and guaranteeing the purity of space, especially public space, through the veiling of sexuality – 'understood as feminine' – which subordinates and controls the feminine and 'marks a spatial and moral limit to the architecture of reason' – understood as masculine.[105]

Niemeyer's aesthetics of excess and his repertoire of exuberant curves and tropical colour are still today associated with sensuality, eroticism and irrationality. The modern-day 'inventor of filth' is deemed untrustworthy, intoxicated by what Alberti called the 'noxious influence of Venus'.[106] His overt references to sexuality imply a defiant resistance to one of the principal edicts of the 'civilizing' colonization project: the domestication and privatization of sexuality; that is, its expulsion from the public domain. Even though current architectural discourse may have neutralized irrationality to a large extent, in Niemeyer's recuperation of the forbidden and his rebellious call to hedonism, a Dionysian subversive current threatens to override good manners and upset the otherwise becalmed Apollonian respectability of his architecture in the

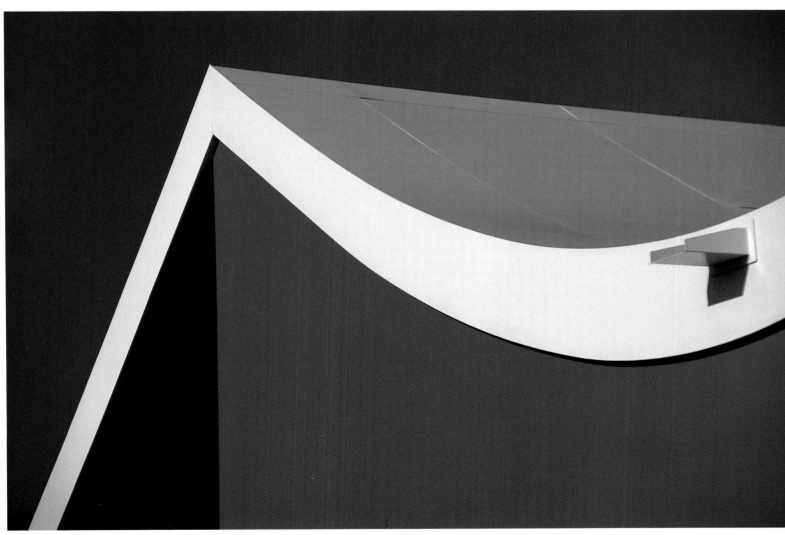

Serpentine Gallery Pavilion: detail of the north-west façade

104 Wigley, 2003.   **105** Wigley, 1992, pp. 343 ff. 'As always', writes Wigley, 'reason is threatened by the fantasized sexual mobility of the feminine'; Wigley, 1992, p. 355.   **106** A Florentine critic denounced Michelangelo in 1549 as an 'inventor of filth'; Leon Battista Alberti, quoted in Wigley, 1992, p. 349.

name of that irreverent spirit of Oswald de Andrade's 'Carib Revolution . . . The Golden Age heralded by America. The Golden Age. And all the *girls*.'[107]

In London or the United States, Wigley summed up, 'if you declare the primary imagery of your building to be sexual, that remains a threat'. Niemeyer's emphatic positing of pleasure as 'the primary principle', both in the sense that he takes 'pleasure in the design' and that he proposes an experience of pleasure to the visitors of his buildings, continues to distance him from 'his colleagues', for whom 'the primary rejection of pleasure [is] the first move'.[108]

Niemeyer's pleasure principle and his unfailing architectural defence of the right to pleasure epitomize the transgressive thrust of his work, his persistent deviation from prevailing norms, and wilful violation of conservative, prudish decorum. His architectural protest against the puritanical denunciation of pleasure as wasted energy consistently deploys the powerful Antropofagist strategy of 'transformation of the Tabu into a totem' to exorcize the taboos of bourgeois work ethics.[109] The sustained radicalization of the eroticized tropical Other represents the dreaded thorn that has not yet been removed from the work of the centenarian radical architect Oscar Niemeyer.

107 Oswald de Andrade, 2000, p. 591, emphasis in the original.
108 Wigley, 2003.   **109** Oswald de Andrade, 2000, p. 591.

Bibliography

Abram, Joseph, 2006, 'Musée des beaux-arts du Havre: Jean Prouvé and LWD'. In *Jean Prouvé: The Poetics of the Technical Object*, ed. Alexander von Vegesack (Weil am Rhein: Vitra Design Museum, exhibition catalogue), pp. 278–79.

Adorno, Theodor W., 1979, 'Functionalism Today', trans. June O. Newman and John H. Smith, *Oppositions* 17 (summer), pp. 31–41.

—— 1984, 'Veblen's Attack on Culture'. In Theodor W. Adorno, *Prisms*, trans. Samuel and Shierry Weber (Cambridge, Massachusetts: MIT Press), pp. 73–94.

—— 2004, *Aesthetic Theory*, ed. Gretel Adorno and Rolf Tiedemann, trans. Robert Hullot-Kentor (London: Continuum).

Agrest, Diana, Patricia Conway and Leslie Kanes Weisman (eds), 1996, *The Sex of Architecture* (New York: Harry N. Abrams).

'Aleijadinho e seu tempo: Fé, engenho e arte', 2006 (Rio de Janeiro: Centro Cultural Banco do Brasil, exhibition leaflet).

Allégret, Laurence, 2006, 'Prouvé as an Engineering Consultant and the Blanc-Manteax Workshop'. In *Jean Prouvé: The Poetics of the Technical Object*, ed. Alexander von Vegesack (Weil am Rhein: Vitra Design Museum, exhibition catalogue), pp. 168–73.

Alves Pereira, Miguel, 1997, *Arquitetura, texto e contexto: o discurso de Oscar Niemeyer*. Arquitetura e Urbanismo Series (Brasília: Universidade de Brasília).

Amaral, Aracy A., 1998, *Artes Plásticas na Semana de 22* (São Paulo: Editôra 34).

Amaral, Aracy A., and Paulo Herkenhoff, 1993, *Ultramodern: The Art of Contemporary Brazil* (Washington, D.C.: National Museum of Women in the Arts, exhibition catalogue).

Amaral, Tarsila do, 2000, 'Pau-Brasil Painting and Antropofagia' (1939). In *Brasil 1920–1950: De la Antropofagia a Brasília*, ed. Jorge Schwartz (Valencia: IVAM, VEGAP, exhibition catalogue, bilingual edition), pp. 587–89.

Anderson, Benedict, 1991, *Imagined Communities: Reflections on the Origin and Spread of Nationalism*, 2nd ed. (London and New York: Verso).

Anderson, Stanford, 1987, 'The Fiction of Function', *Assemblage* 2, pp. 19–31.

Andrade, Mário de, 1996, 'Brazil Builds' (1944). In Mauricio Lissovsky and Paulo Sergio Moraes de Sá, *Colunas da Educação: A construção do Ministério da Educação e Saúde (1935–1945)* (Rio de Janeiro: Ministério da Cultura, Instituto do Patrimônio Hisórico e Artístico Nacional, and Fundação Getúlio Vargas, Centro de Pesquisa e Documentação da História Contemporânea do Brasil), pp. 187–91.

—— 2000, 'Modernist Movement' (1942). In *Brasil 1920–1950: De la Antropofagia a Brasília*, ed. Jorge Schwartz (Valencia: IVAM, VEGAP, exhibition catalogue, bilingual edition), pp. 593–601.

Andrade, Oswald de, 1989, 'Pau-Brasil Poetry Manifesto' (1924). In *Art in Latin America: The Modern Era, 1820–1980*, ed. Dawn Ades (New Haven and London: Yale University Press), pp. 310–11.

—— 1990, *A Utopia Antropofágica* (São Paulo: Secretaria de Estado da Cultura and Globo).

—— 2000, 'Cannibalist Manifesto' (1928). In *Brasil 1920–1950: De la Antropofagia a Brasília*, ed. Jorge Schwartz (Valencia: IVAM, VEGAP, exhibition catalogue, bilingual edition), pp. 591–92.

Andreas, Paul, and Ingeborg Flagge (eds), 2003, *Oscar Niemeyer: A Legend of Modernism* (Basle: Birkhäuser, Frankfurt: Deutsches Architektur Museum, exhibition catalogue, bilingual edition).

Andreoli, Elisabetta, and Adrian Forty (eds), 2004, *Brazil's Modern Architecture* (London: Phaidon).

Anelli, Renato, 2003, 'Mediterraneo ai tropici: Patii e giardini. Transformazioni del patio mediterraneo nell'architettura brasiliana', *Casabella* 7081, year 67 (February), pp. 86–95.

Ante-Projeto da Exposição do IV Centenário de São Paulo, 1952 (São Paulo: Edições de Arte e Arquitetura).

Arantes, Pedro Fiori, 2004, 'Reinventing the Building Site'. In *Brazil's Modern Architecture*, ed. Elisabetta Andreoli and Adrian Forty (London: Phaidon), pp. 170–201.

Architectural Forum, 1947, vol. 87, no. 5 (November), special issue on Brazil.

Architectural Review, 1944a, vol. 95, no. 567 (March), special issue on Brazil.

Architectural Review, 1944b, vol. 95, no. 569 (May), special issue on Oscar Niemeyer.

Architecture d'Aujourd'hui, 1947, year 18, nos 13–14 (September), special issue on Brazil.

Architecture d'Aujourd'hui, 1952, year 23, nos 42–43 (August), special issue on Brazil.

Architecture d'Aujourd'hui, 1960, year 31, no. 90 (June–July), special issue on Brazil.

Architecture d'Aujourd'hui, 1974, year 45, no. 171 (January–February), special issue on Oscar Niemeyer.

Architecture d'Aujourd'hui, 1987, no. 251 (June), special issue on Brazil.

Architecture d'Aujourd'hui, 2005, no. 359 (July–August), special issue on Brazil.

'Architettura Moderna al Brasile', 1993, *Casabella* 11, no. 64 (April), p. 177.

Arens, W., 1979, *The Man-Eating Myth: Anthropology and Anthropophagy* (Oxford and New York: Oxford University Press).

Arnau, Frank, 1960, *Brasilia: Phantasie und Wirklichkeit* (Munich: Prestel).

Art and Architecture in Brazil: From Aleijadinho to Niemeyer, 1984, ed. José Renato Santos Pereira (Ministry of Industry and Commerce, Brazilian Tourism Authority, exhibition catalogue).

Artigas, João Batista Vilanova, 1999, *Caminhos da arquitetura* (São Paulo: Cosac & Naify and Fundação Vilanova Artigas).

—— 2003a, 'A Arquitetura Moderna Brasileira' ('Os caminhos da arquitetura', 1952). In *Depoimento de uma geração*, 2nd ed. revised and enlarged, ed. Alberto Xavier (São Paulo: Cosac & Naify), pp. 195–97.

—— 2003b, 'Revisão crítica de Niemeyer' (1958). In *Depoimento de uma geração*, 2nd ed. revised and enlarged, ed. Alberto Xavier (São Paulo: Cosac & Naify), p. 240.

Asbury, Michael, 2005, 'Changing Perceptions of National Identity in Brazilian Art and Modern Architecture'. In *Transculturation: Cities, Spaces and Architectures in Latin America*, ed. Felipe Hernández, Mark Millington and Iain Borden. Critical Studies Series, vol. 27 (Amsterdam and New York: Rodopi), pp. 59–75.

Assis, Joaquim Maria Machado de, 1998, *Dom Casmurro*, trans. John Gledson (New York and Oxford: Oxford University Press).

Assunção, Matthias Röhrig, 2005, 'Brazilian Popular Culture or the Curse and Blessings of Cultural Hybridism', *Bulletin of Latin American Research* 24, no. 2 (April), special issue: 'Brazilian Popular Culture in Historical Perspective', pp. 157–66.

Athos Bulcão, 2001 (Brasília: Fundação Athos Bulcão, bilingual edition).

Augusto, Sérgio, 1988, 'Hollywood Looks at Brazil: From Carmen Miranda to Moonraker'. In *Brazilian Cinema*, ed. Randal Johnson and Robert Stam (Austin: University of Texas), pp. 352–61.

Azevedo, Fernando de, 1950, *Brazilian Culture: An Introduction to the Study of Culture in Brazil* (New York: Macmillan Company).

Bachelard, Gaston, 1983, *Water and Dreams: An Essay on The Imagination of Matter*, trans. Edith R. Farrell (Dallas: Pegasus Foundation).

Bald, Sunil, 2002, 'In Aleijadinho's Shadow: Writing National Origins in Brazilian Architec-

ture', *Thresholds* 23, http://architecture.mit
.edu/thresholds/issue-contents/23/bald23/
bald23.htm.

Banco Boavista, 1991, 'Annual Report' (Rio de Janeiro).

Banham, Reyner, 1975, *Age of the Masters: A Personal View of Modern Architecture* (London: Architectural Press [1962 as *Guide to Modern Architecture*]).

Bardi, P.M., 1964, *The Tropical Gardens of Burle Marx* (Amsterdam and Rio de Janeiro: Colibris Editore).

—— 1984, *Lembrança de Le Corbusier: Atenas, Itália, Brasil* (São Paulo: Nobel).

Barthes, Roland, 1997, *The Eiffel Tower and Other Mythologies*, trans. Richard Howard (Berkeley, Los Angeles and London: University of California Press).

Bastide, Roger, 1978, *Images du nordeste mystique en noir et blanc* (Pandora).

Bastos, Maria Alice Junqueira, 2003, *Pós-Brasília: Rumos da Arquitetura Brasileira* (São Paulo: Perspectiva).

Basualdo, Carlos, 2005, 'Tropicália: Avant-Garde, Popular Culture, and the Culture Industry in Brazil'. In *Tropicália: A Revolution in Brazilian Culture*, ed. Carlos Basualdo (São Paulo: Cosac & Naify and Gabinete Cultura, Chicago: Museum of Contemporary Art, exhibition catalogue), pp. 11–28.

Basualdo, Carlos (ed.), 2005, *Tropicália: A Revolution in Brazilian Culture* (São Paulo: Cosac & Naify and Gabinete Cultura, Chicago: Museum of Contemporary Art, exhibition catalogue).

Batista, Geraldo Nogueira, Sylvia Ficher, Francisco Leitão and Dionísio Alves de França, 2006, 'Brasilia: A Capital in the Hinterland'. In David L.A. Gordon, *Planning Twentieth Century Capital Cities* (New York and London: Routledge), pp. 164–81.

Beauvoir, Simone de, 1968, *Force of Circumstance*, trans. Richard Howard (Harmondsworth: Penguin [1963 in French]).

Bengio, Ofra, and Gabriel Ben-Dor (eds), 1999, *Minorities and the State in the Arab World* (Colorado: Lynne Rienner Publishers).

Benjamin, Andrew, 2001, 'Allowing Function Complexity: Notes on Adorno's "Functionalism Today" ', *AA Files*, no. 41, pp. 40–45.

Bentes, Ivana, 2003, 'The Sertão and the Favela in Contemporary Brazilian Film', trans. Vladimir Freire. In *The New Brazilian Cinema*, ed. Lúcia Nagib (London and New York: I.B. Tauris, Oxford: Centre for Brazilian Studies, University of Oxford), pp. 121–37.

Berman, Marshall, 1988, *All that Is Solid Melts into Air: The Experience of Modernity*, 2nd ed. (London: Penguin).

Bernadet, Jean-Claude, 2000, 'Precarious Balance between Avant-Garde and Culture Industry'. In *Brasil 1920–1950: De la Antropofagia a Brasília*, ed. Jorge Schwartz (Valencia: IVAM, VEGAP, exhibition catalogue, bilingual edition), pp. 551–57.

Bill, Max, 1954. In 'Report on Brazil', *Architectural Review* 116, no. 694 (October), pp. 238–39.

—— 2003, 'Architect, Architecture and Society' (1953). In *Oscar Niemeyer: A Legend of Modernism*, ed. Paul Andreas and Ingeborg Flagge (Basle: Birkhäuser, Frankfurt:

Deutsches Architektur Museum, exhibition catalogue, bilingual edition), pp. 115–22.

Bingaman, Amy, Lise Sanders and Rebecca Zorach (eds), 2002, *Embodied Utopias: Gender, Social Change and the Modern Metropolis* (London: Routledge).

Blaser, Werner, 1996, *West Meets East: Mies van der Rohe* (Basle, Boston, Berlin: Birkhäuser).

Bloc, André, 1952, 'Ayons confiance dans l'architecture contemporaine', *Architecture d'Aujourd'hui* 23, nos 42–43 (August), p. 2.

Bloch, Ernst, 1979, 'Formative Education, Engineering Form, Ornament', *Oppositions* 17 (summer), pp. 45–51.

Bloomer, Jennifer, 1992, ' "D'OR" '. In *Sexuality & Space*, ed. Beatriz Colomina. Princeton Papers on Architecture Series (New York: Princeton Architectural Press), pp. 163–83.

Bonduki, Nabil, 2000, 'Affonso Eduardo Reidy: The Architect of Public Spaces'. In *Affonso Eduardo Reidy*, ed. Nabil Bonduki (Lisbon: Editorial Blau), pp. 11–29.

—— (ed.), 2000, *Affonso Eduardo Reidy* (Lisbon: Editorial Blau).

Bonet, Juan Manuel, 2000, 'Brazilian Enlightenment'. In *Brasil 1920–1950: De la Antropofagia a Brasília*, ed. Jorge Schwartz (Valencia: IVAM, VEGAP, exhibition catalogue, bilingual edition), pp. 519–23.

Botey, Josep Ma., 1996, *Oscar Niemeyer* (Barcelona: Gustavo Gili).

Bourouh, Chaoura, 1997, 'The State, Development, and Civil Society: The Case of Algeria'. In *Civil Society and Social Reconstruction*, ed. George F. McLean. Cultural Heritage and Contemporary Change, Series I: Culture and Values, vol. 16, http://www.crvp.org/book/Series01/I-16/chapter_iv.htm. Last accessed October 2006.

Bracco, Sergio, 1967, *L'Architettura Moderna in Brasile*. L'Architettura Contemporânea Series (Bologna: Cappelli).

Brandão, Zeca, 2006, 'Urban Planning in Rio de Janeiro: A Critical Review of the Urban Design Practice in the Twentieth Century', *City & Time* 2 (2): 4, http://www.ct.ceci-br.org. Last accessed December 2006.

Brasilia, 1960 (London: Brazilian Government Trade Bureau).

Brasília, n.d. (Rio de Janeiro: Divisão Cultural, Ministério das Relações Exteriores).

Brasilia: History, City Planning, Architecture, Building, 1960 (São Paulo: Acropole, bilingual edition).

Brazil, 1986 (Amsterdam: Time-Life Books). 'Brazil Country Brief', 2003, http://wbln0018.worldbank.org/LAC/LAC.nsf/ECADocByUni/A220784F5BC3A1FB85256DB40070253B?Opendocument. Last accessed December 2006.

'Brazilian Preview', 1953, *Architectural Review* 114, no. 679 (July), pp. 228–34.

Britton, Karla, 2001, *Auguste Perret* (London: Phaidon).

Browning, Barbara, 1995, *Samba: Resistance in Motion* (Bloomington and Indianapolis: Indiana University Press).

Bruand, Yves, 2003, *Arquitetura Contemporânea no Brasil* (São Paulo: Perspective).

Bullrich, Francisco, 1969, *New Directions in Latin American Architecture* (New York: George Braziller).

Burgess, Helen J., 2004, 'Futurama, Autogeddon: Imagining the Superhighway from Bel Geddes to Ballard', *Rhizomes* 8 (spring), 'Retro-Futures', http://www.rhizomes.net/issue8/futurama/ index.html. Last accessed December 2006.

Burle Marx, Roberto, 2003, 'Depoimento' (1977). In *Depoimento de uma geração*, 2nd ed. revised and enlarged, ed. Alberto Xavier (São Paulo: Cosac & Naify), pp. 297–304.

Burns, E. Bradford, 1968, *Nationalism in Brazil: A Historical Survey* (New York: Frederick A. Phaeger).

—— 1970, *A History of Brazil* (New York and London: Columbia University Press).

Bury, John, 1991, *Arquitetura e Arte no Brasil Colonial*, ed. Myriam Andrade Ribeiro de Oliveira, trans. Isa Mara Lando (São Paulo: Nobel).

Calanca, Giorgio, 1975, 'I problemi da risolvere', *Espansione*, no. 70 (August–September), supplement, pp. 20–21.

Caldas, Miguel P., and Rafael Alcadipani, 2003, 'Post-Colonialism in Latin American Management: The Genesis and Trail of North American Reference in Brazilian Culture and Management', CMS Conference, http://www.mngt.waikato.ac.nz/research/ejrot/cmsconference/2003/proceedings/postcolonial/Caldas.pdf. Last accessed March 2005.

Caldeira, Teresa P.R., 2000, *City of Walls: Crime, Segregation, and Citizenship in São Paulo* (Berkeley and Los Angeles: University of California Press).

Calil, Carlos Augusto Machado, 2000, 'Translators of Brazil'. In *Brasil 1920–1950: De la Antropofagia a Brasília*, ed. Jorge Schwartz (Valencia: IVAM, VEGAP, exhibition catalogue, bilingual edition), pp. 563–78.

Calsat, J.H., 1945, 'Le brise-soleil', *Architecture d'Aujourd'hui* 16, no. 3 (September–October), pp. 22–23.

Calvino, Italo, 1974, *Invisible Cities* (Orlando, Florida: Harcourt Brace and Company).

Campos, Augusto de, 2005, 'The Explosion of "Alegria, Alegria" ' (1967). In *Tropicália: A Revolution in Brazilian Culture*, ed. Carlos Basualdo (São Paulo: Cosac & Naify and Gabinete Cultura, Chicago: Museum of Contemporary Art, exhibition catalogue), pp. 257–60.

Cantacuzino, Sherban, 1972, 'Headquarters for the French Communist Party, Paris', *Architectural Review* 151, no. 901 (March), pp. 143–44.

Capanema, Gustavo, 2003, 'Depoimento sobre o edifício do Ministério da Educação', interview with Alberto Xavier, José Carlos Coutinho and Luiz Fisberg (1968). In *Depoimento de uma geração*, 2nd ed. revised and enlarged, ed. Alberto Xavier (São Paulo: Cosac & Naify), pp. 121–31.

Caporali, Renato, 1989, ' "Conjunto JK" trajectoires d'une utopie urbaine', *Cahiers du Brésil Contemporain*, no. 8, http://www.revues.msh-paris.fr/vernumpub/04-Renato

%20Caporali.pdf. Last accessed February 2007.

Cardozo, Joaquim, 1946, 'Rebirth of the Azulejo', *Architectural Review* 100, no. 600 (December), pp. 178–82.

—— 1955, 'Arquitetura Brasileira: características mais recentes', *Módulo* 1, no. 1 (March), pp. 6–9.

Carvalho, Martha de Ulhôa, 1995, 'Tupi or not Tupi MPB: Popular Music'. In *The Brazilian Puzzle: Culture on the Borderlands of the Western World*, ed. David J. Hess and Roberto A. DaMatta (New York: Columbia University Press), pp. 159–79.

Casali, Valerio, 2004, 'La nature comme paysage'. In Maria Bonaiti et al., *Le Corbusier et la nature* (Paris: Fondation Le Corbusier, Éditions de la Villette), pp. 63–73.

Casciani, Stefano, 2003, 'Niemeyer Revisited', *Domus* 863 (October), pp. 84–93.

—— 2005, 'The Depth Behind a Surface', *Domus* 887 (December), supplement: 'Design and Matter' 2, pp. 38–45.

Castedo, Leopoldo, 1964, *The Baroque Prevalence in Brazilian Art* (New York: Charles Frank).

Castro, Ruy, 2000, *Bossa Nova: The Story of the Brazilian Music that Seduced the World* (Chicago: A Cappella).

—— 2004, *Rio de Janeiro: Carnival under Fire* (London: Bloomsbury).

Cattani, Icleia Maria Borsa, 2001, 'Places of Modernism in Brazil'. In *Brazil: Body and Soul*, ed. Edward J. Sullivan (New York: Guggenheim Museum, exhibition catalogue), pp. 380–87.

Cavalcanti, Lauro, 1995, *As preocupações do belo* (Rio de Janeiro: Taurus).

—— 2003, *When Brazil Was Modern: Guide to Architecture 1928–1960*, trans. Jon Tolman (New York: Princeton Architectural Press).

—— 2004, 'Architecture, Urbanism and the Good Neighbor Policy: Brazil and the United States'. In *Latin American Architecture 1929–1960*, ed. Carlos Brillembourg (New York: Monacelli Press), pp. 50–59.

—— (ed.), 2000, *Modernistas na repartição* (Rio de Janeiro: Universidade Federal do Rio de Janeiro, Ministro da Cultura and IPHAN).

Cavallaro James, 1997, 'Police Brutality in Urban Brazil', ed. Anne Manuel, Human Rights Watch/Americas, http://www.hrw.org/reports/1997/brazil/. Last accessed January 2007.

Çelik, Zeynep, 1996, 'Gendered Spaces of Colonial Algiers'. In *The Sex of Architecture*, ed. Diana Agrest, Patricia Conway and Leslie Kanes Weisman (New York: Harry N. Abrams), pp. 127–40.

Cendrars, Blaise, 2000, 'São Paulo' (1924). In *Brasil 1920–1950: De la Antropofagia a Brasília*, ed. Jorge Schwartz (Valencia: IVAM, VEGAP, exhibition catalogue, bilingual edition), p. 613.

Choay, Françoise, 1990, 'Souvenirs d'ailleurs'. In *Jean Prouvé 'constructeur'*, ed. Raymond Guidot and Alain Guiheux (Paris: Centre Pompidou), pp. 215–17.

'Cités nouvelles', 1961, *Architecture d'Aujourd'hui* 31, no. 93 (December 1960–January 1961), pp. 4–37.

Claeys, Gregory, and Lyman Tower Sargent (eds), 1999, *The Utopia Reader* (New York and London: New York University Press).

Coelho Frota, Lélia, 2000, 'A Painter and Visual Artist in the Brazilian Modernist Movement'. In *Roberto Burle Marx: Landscapes Reflected*, ed. Rossana Vaccarino (New York: Princeton Architectural Press), pp. 25–40.

Cohen, Jean-Louis, 2006, 'Hands that See: The CNAM Lectures (1958–71)'. In *Jean Prouvé: The Poetics of the Technical Object*, ed. Alexander von Vegesack (Weil am Rhein: Vitra Design Museum, exhibition catalogue), pp. 48–55.

Coleman, Debra, Elizabeth Danze and Carol Henderson (eds), 1996, *Architecture and Feminism* (New York: Princeton Architectural Press).

Collins, Christiane C., and George R. Collins, 1984, 'Monumentality: A Critical Matter in Modern Architecture', *Harvard Architectural Review* 4 (spring), pp. 15–35.

Colomina, Beatriz, 1996a, 'Battle Lines: E.1027'. In *The Sex of Architecture*, ed. Diana Agrest, Patricia Conway and Leslie Kanes Weisman (New York: Harry N. Abrams), pp. 167–82.

—— 1996b, *Privacy and Publicity: Modern Architecture as Mass Media* (Cambridge, Massachusetts: MIT Press).

—— 1999, 'The Private Site of Public Memory', *Journal of Architecture* 4, no. 4 (winter), pp. 337–60.

—— 2002, 'Where Are We?'. In *Architecture and Cubism*, ed. Eve Blau and Nancy J. Troy (Montréal: Canadian Centre for Architecture, with Cambridge, Massachusetts and London: MIT Press), pp. 141–66.

—— (ed.), 1992, *Sexuality & Space*. Princeton Papers on Architecture Series (New York: Princeton Architectural Press).

Comas, Carlos Eduardo Dias, 1998a, 'Latin American Memorandum: The Architecturally Exemplary Nature of the Marginal', *2G International Architecture Review*, no. 8 'Latin American Architecture: A New Generation' 4, pp. 129–32.

—— 1998b, 'Modern Architecture, Brazilian Corollary', *AA Files*, no. 36 (summer), pp. 3–13.

—— 1998c, 'Niemeyer's Oasis: A Brazilian Villa of the Fifties', *Arquine*, Revista internacional da arquitectura (spring), pp. 46–57.

—— 2002a, 'Modern (1930 to 1960)'. In *Architecture Brazil 500 Years: A Reciprocal Invention*, ed. Roberto Montezuma (Recife: Federal University of Pernambuco, bilingual edition), pp. 183–238.

—— 2002b, 'Niemeyer's Casino and the Misdeeds of Brazilian Architecture', *Journal of Romance Studies* 2, no. 3, pp. 73–87.

Conduru, Roberto, 2004, 'Tropical Tectonics'. In *Brazil's Modern Architecture*, ed. Elisabetta Andreoli and Adrian Forty (London: Phaidon), pp. 56–105.

'Conversation in Brasilia Between Robert Harbinson and George Balcombe', 1961, *Journal of the Royal Institute of British Architects*, 3rd ser., 68, no. 13 (November), pp. 490–94.

Corrêa, Elyane Lins, 1999, 'Oscar Niemeyer: Reflexiones sobre la Arquitectura (Una Lectura de Sus Escritos 1936–1998)' (Ph.D. diss., Escuela Tecnica Superior de Arquitectura de Barcelona, Departament de Composició Arquitectónica).

Corrêa, Marcos Sá, 2005, *Oscar Niemeyer: Ribeiro de Almeida Soares* (Rio de Janeiro: Relume).

Costa, Lúcio, 1950, 'Foreword'. In Stamo Papadaki, *The Work of Oscar Niemeyer* (New York: Reinhold), pp. 1–3.

—— 1952, 'Imprévu et importance de la contribution des architectes Brésiliens au développement actuel de l'architecture contemporaine', *Architecture d'Aujourd'hui* 23, nos 42–43 (August), pp. 4–7.

—— 1966, 'Report by Lúcio Costa'. In Willy Stäubli, *Brasilia* (Stuttgart: Alexander Koch), pp. 12–16.

—— 1997, *Lucio Costa: Registro de uma vivência*, 2nd ed. (São Paulo: Empresa das Artes).

—— 2000, 'Reasons of the New Architecture' (1936). In *Brasil 1920–1950: De la Antropofagia a Brasília*, ed. Jorge Schwartz (Valencia: IVAM, VEGAP, exhibition catalogue, bilingual edition), pp. 622–29.

—— 2001a, *Com a palavra*, ed. Maria Elisa Costa (Rio de Janeiro: Aeroplano).

—— 2001b, *Lucio Costa XXe siècle brésilien: témoin et acteur*, ed. Jean-Loup Herbert, trans. Maryvonne Lapouge-Pettorelli (Saint-Étienne: Publications de l'Université de Saint-Étienne).

—— 2002, *Arquitetura* (Rio de Janeiro: José Olympio).

—— 2003, 'Oportunidade perdida' (1953). In *Depoimento de uma geração*, 2nd ed. revised and enlarged, ed. Alberto Xavier (São Paulo: Cosac & Naify), pp. 181–84.

Costa, Maria Elisa, 2001, 'Être: maître mot'. In Lúcio Costa, *Lucio Costa XXe siècle brésilien: Témoin et acteur*, ed. Jean-Loup Herbert, trans. Maryvonne Lapouge-Pettorelli (Saint-Étienne: Publications de l'Université de Saint-Étienne), pp. 21–22.

—— 2002, 'Brasília'. In *Architecture Brazil 500 Years: A Reciprocal Invention*, ed. Roberto Montezuma (Recife: Federal University of Pernambuco, bilingual edition), pp. 241–99.

—— 2005, 'The Superquadras in Number and Context'. In *Lucio Costa: Brasilia's Superquadra*, ed. Farès El-Dahdah (Munich, London and New York: Prestel, with Harvard Design School), pp. 25–31.

Couto, Thiago Segall, 2004, 'Patrimônio modernista em Cataguases: razões de reconhecimento e o véu da crítica', *Vitruvius*, Texto Especial 264 (November), http://www.vitruvius.com.br/arquitextos/arq000/esp264.asp. Last accessed March 2006.

Cramer, Christopher, 2006, 'The Sense that War Makes', *Open Democracy* (5 October), http://www.opendemocracy.net/globalization-vision_reflections/war_sense_3970.jsp. Last accessed December 2006.

Craymer, Peter, 1954. In 'Report on Brazil', *Architectural Review* 116, no. 694 (October), pp. 235–36.

Crease, David, 1962, 'Progress in Brasilia', *Architectural Review* 131, no. 782 (April), pp. 257–62.

—— 1964, *Brasilia 1964: An Englishman's Report on Life in the New Capital of Brazil* (London:

Commercial and Information Service of the Brazilian Embassy).

Cunha, Euclides da, 1944, *Rebellion in the Backlands* (*Os Sertões*), trans. Samuel Putman (Chicago and London: University of Chicago Press [1902 in Portuguese]).

Curtis, William J.R., 1986, *Le Corbusier: Ideas and Forms*, 2nd ed. (London: Phaidon).

—— 1987, *Modern Architecture Since 1900* (Oxford: Phaidon).

Cury, Carlos Roberto, 2000, 'Anísio Teixeira (1900–71)', *Prospects: Quarterly Review of Comparative Education* 30, no. 4, pp. 509–20.

Dal Co, Francesco, 2005, ' "La princesse est modeste" '. In Arata Isozaki et al., *Katsura Imperial Villa*, ed. Virginia Ponciroli (Milan: Electa), pp. 387–89.

Damaz, Paul F., 1963, *Art in Latin American Architecture* (New York: Reinhold).

Deckker, Zilah Quezado, 2001, *Brazil Built: The Architecture of the Modern Movement in Brazil* (New York: Spon Press).

Deleuze, Gilles, 1993, *The Fold: Leibniz and the Baroque*, trans. Tom Conley (London: Continuum).

Dos Passos, John, 1963, *Brazil on the Move* (Garden City, New York: Doubleday & Co).

Drexler, Arthur, 1955, 'Preface and Acknowledgments'. In Henry-Russell Hitchcock, *Latin American Architecture Since 1945* (New York: Museum of Modern Art), pp. 8–9.

Dudley, George A. 1994, *A Workshop for Peace: Designing the United Nations Headquarters* (New York: Architectural History Foundation, Cambridge, Massachusetts: MIT Press).

Dulio, Roberto, 2007, *Oscar Niemeyer: il palazzo mondatori* (Milan: Electa).

Dunn, Christopher, 1999, 'Tropicalism and Brazilian Popular Music under Military Rule'. In *The Brazilian Reader: History, Culture, Politics*, ed. Robert M. Levine and John J. Crocitti (Durham, North Carolina: Duke University Press), pp. 241–47.

Eastwick-Field, John, and John Stillman, 1959, 'Out of the Form', *Architectural Review* 125, no. 749 (June), pp. 386–97.

Eggener, Keith L., 2002, 'Placing Resistance: A Critique of Critical Regionalism', *Journal of Architectural Education (JAE)* 55, no. 4 (May), pp. 228–37.

—— 2006, 'Nationalism, Internationalism and the "Naturalisation" of Modern Architecture in the United States, 1925–1940', *National Identities* 8, no. 3 (September), pp. 243–58.

El-Dahdah, Farès (ed.), 2005, *Lucio Costa: Brasilia's Superquadra* (Munich, London and New York: Prestel, with Harvard Design School).

Elhyani, Zvi, 2004, 'Horizontal Ideology, Vertical Vision: Oscar Niemeyer and Israel's Height Dilemma'. In *Constructing a Sense of Place: Architecture and the Zionist Discourse*, ed. Haim Yacobi (Burlington, Vermont: Ashgate), pp. 89–115.

Eliovson, Sima, 1991, *The Gardens of Roberto Burle Marx* (Portland, Oregon: Timber Press).

Epstein, David G., 1973, *Brasília, Plan and Reality: A Study of Planned and Spontaneous Urban Settlement* (Berkeley, Los Angeles and London: University of California Press).

Ermakoff, George, 2003, *Rio de Janeiro 1900–1930: Uma crônica fotográfica* (Rio de Janeiro: George Ermakoff, bilingual edition).

Espansione, 1975, no. 70 (August–September), supplement.

Espejo, L. Arturo, 1984, *Rationalité et formes d'occupation de l'espace: le projet de Brasilia* (Paris: Anthropos).

Eulalio, Alexandre, 2001, *A Aventura Brasileira de Blaise Cendrars*, 2nd ed., revised and enlarged by Carlos Augusto Calil (São Paulo: Editôra da Universidade de São Paulo and Fapesp).

Evenson, Norma, 1969, 'The Symbolism of Brasília', *Landscape* 18, no. 1 (winter), pp. 19–28.

—— 1973, *Two Brazilian Capitals: Architecture and Urbanism in Rio de Janeiro and Brasília* (New Haven and London: Yale University Press).

—— 1975, 'Brasília: "Yesterday's City of Tomorrow" '. In *World Capitals: Toward Guided Urbanization*, ed. H. Wentworth Eldredge (Garden City, New York: Doubleday & Co), pp. 470–506.

Fabris, Andreas, 2000, 'Forms of (Possible) Modernity'. In *Brasil 1920–1950: De la Antropofagia a Brasília*, ed. Jorge Schwartz (Valencia: IVAM, VEGAP, exhibition catalogue, bilingual edition), pp. 533–39.

Faiola, Anthony, 2002, 'Brazil's Elites Fly Above Their Fears: Rich Try to Wall Off Urban Violence', *Washington Post Foreign Service*, Saturday 1 June, p. A01. http://www.washingtonpost.com/ac2/wp-dyn/A42332-2002May31. Last accessed December 2006.

Farias, Agnaldo, 2001, 'A Builder of Space'. In *Athos Bulcão* (Brasília: Fundação Athos Bulcão, bilingual edition), pp. 34–47.

Farret, Ricardo L., 1983, 'The Justification of Brasilia: A Political-Economic Approach', *Third World Planning Review* 5, no. 2 (May), pp. 137–48.

Fausch, Deborah, 1996, 'The Knowledge of the Body and the Presence of History – Toward a Feminist Architecture'. In *Architecture and Feminism*, ed. Debra Coleman, Elizabeth Danze and Carol Henderson (New York: Princeton Architectural Press), pp. 38–59.

Fausto, Boris, 1999, *A Concise History of Brazil*, trans. Arthur Brakel. Cambridge Concise Histories Series (Cambridge: Cambridge University Press).

Featherstone, Mike, Scott Lash and Roland Robertson (eds), 1995, *Global Modernities* (London, Thousand Oaks and New Delhi: SAGE).

Fernandes, Edésio, 2003, 'A New Statute for Brazilian Cities', http://portal.unesco.org/shs/en/file_download.php/10f9607afa47161a457fedb4c22b08e4city_statute.pdf. Last accessed November 2006.

Fernandes, Inês Palma, 2003, 'Building Brasília: Modern Architecture and National Identity in Brazil' (Ph.D. diss., Princeton University).

Figuerola, Valentina, 2003, 'Concreto, Poesia e Niemeyer', *AU: Arquitetura & Urbanismo* 18, no. 106 (January), pp. 38–45.

Fils, Alexander, 1988, *Brasília: Moderne Architektur in Brasilien* (Düsseldorf: Beton-Verlag).

—— (ed.), 1982, *Oscar Niemeyer: Selbstdarstellung, Kritiken, Oeuvre* (Münsterschwarzach: Benedict Press, Frölich & Kaufmann).

Fiori Arantes, Pedro, 2004, 'Reinventing the Site'. In *Brazil's Modern Architecture*, ed. Elisabetta Andreoli and Adrian Forty (London: Phaidon), pp. 170–201.

Fishman, Robert, 1987, *Bourgeois Utopias* (New York: Basic Books).

Frampton, Kenneth, 1992, *Modern Architecture: A Critical History*, 3rd ed. revised and enlarged (London: Thames and Hudson).

—— 2000, 'Preface'. In *Latin American Architecture: Six Voices*, ed. Malcolm Quantrill (in collaboration with Kenneth Frampton, Michael L. Tribe, Diana Barco, Pablo J. Rodríguez P., and Galia Solomonoff). Studies in Latin American Architecture Series (Texas A&M University Press), pp. ix–xii.

—— 2002, *Le Corbusier: Architect of the Twentieth Century* (New York: Harry N. Abrams).

—— 2004, 'Le Corbusier and Oscar Niemeyer: Influence and Counter-influence, 1929–1965'. In *Latin American Architecture 1929–1960*, ed. Carlos Brillembourg (New York: Monacelli Press), pp. 34–49.

Franco, Jean, 1970, *The Modern Culture of Latin America: Society and the Artist* (Harmondsworth: Penguin).

Frank, Patrick (ed.), 2004, *Readings in Latin American Modern Art* (New Haven and London: Yale University Press).

Frankl, Paul, 1968, *Principles of Architectural History: The Four Phases of Architectural Style, 1420–1900*, ed. and trans. James F. O'Gorman (Cambridge, Massachusetts: MIT Press).

Fraser, Valerie, 2000a, *Building the New World: Studies in the Modern Architecture of Latin America 1930–1960* (London and New York: Verso).

—— 2000b, 'Cannibalizing Le Corbusier: The MES Gardens of Roberto Burle Marx', *Journal of the Society of Architectural Historians* 59, no. 2 (June), pp. 180–93.

Freeman, James Patrick, 2002, 'Face to Face but Worlds Apart: The Geography of Class in the Public Space of Rio de Janeiro' (Ph.D. diss., University of California, Berkeley).

Freyre, Gilberto, 1943, 'Casas de residência no Brasil', *Revista do Serviço do Patrimônio Histórico e Artístico Nacional*, Ministério da Educação e Saúde, Rio de Janeiro, 7, pp. 99–127.

—— 1956, *The Masters and the Slaves (Casa Grande e Senzala): A Study in the Development of Brazilian Civilization*, trans. Samuel Putman (New York: Alfred A. Knopf, Borzoi Books on Latin America [1946 in English, 1933 in Portuguese]).

—— 1963, *New World in the Tropics: The Culture of Modern Brazil* (New York: Alfred A. Knopf [1945 as Brazil: An Interpretation]).

—— 1964, 'Foreword'. In Leopoldo Castedo, *The Baroque Prevalence in Brazilian Art* (New York: Charles Frank), pp. 10–13.

—— 1968, *Brasis, Brasil e Brasília* (Rio de Janeiro: Gráfica Record).

—— 1970, *Order and Progress: Brazil from Monarchy to Republic*, ed. and trans. Rod W. Horton (New York: Alfred A. Knopf [1959 in Portuguese]).

—— 1974, *The Gilberto Freyre Reader*, trans. Barbara Shelby (New York: Alfred A. Knopf).

—— 1986, *The Mansions and the Shanties (Sobrados e Mucambos): The Making of Modern Brazil*, trans. E. Bradford Burns (Berkeley and Los Angeles: University of California Press [1963 in English, 1936 in Portuguese]).

Friedman, Jonathan, 1995, 'Global System, Globalization and the Parameters of Modernity'. In *Global Modernities*, ed. Mike Featherstone, Scott Lash and Roland Robertson (London, Thousand Oaks and New Delhi: SAGE), pp. 69–90.

Gadotti, Moacir, 1992, 'Conflicts between Public and Private Schooling and the Brazilian Constitutions', http://www.paulofreire.org/ Moacir_Gadotti/Artigos/Ingles/On _Education/Conflicts_between_public_and _private_schooling_in_Brazil_1992.pdf. Last accessed November 2006.

Garcia, Eugenio Vargas, 2000, 'Anglo-American Rivalry in Brazil: The Case of the 1920s', working paper series CBS-14-2000 (Oxford: Centre for Brazilian Studies, University of Oxford), http://www.brazil.ox.ac.uk/ workingpapers/Eugenio14A.pdf. Last accessed March 2006.

Garfield, Seth, 2004, 'Mario Juruna: Brazil's First Indigenous Congressman'. In *The Human Tradition in Brazil*, ed. Peter M. Beattie (Wilmington, Delaware: Scholarly Resources), pp. 287–304.

Gautherot, Marcel, 1966, *Brasilia*, introduction by Wladimir Murtinho, text and description of the plates John and France Knox (Munich: Wilhelm Andermann).

Gennari, Massimo, 1982, 'A Project of Oscar Niemeyer in Turin: The New Offices for the FATA Co.', *L'Industria del Cemento* 2, pp. 78–100.

Giedion, Sigfried, 1939, 'The Dangers and Advantages of Luxury', *Focus*, no. 3 (spring), pp. 34–39.

—— 1949, *Space, Time and Architecture: The Growth of a New Tradition* (Cambridge, Massachusetts: Harvard University Press).

—— 1950, 'Alvar Aalto', *Architectural Review* 107, no. 638 (February), pp. 77–84.

—— 1952, 'Le Brésil et l'architecture contemporaine', *Architecture d'Aujourd'hui* 23, nos 42–43 (August), p. 3.

—— 1956, 'Brazil and Contemporary Architecture'. In Henrique E. Mindlin, *Modern Architecture in Brazil* (New York: Reinhold), pp. ix–x.

—— 1982, 'Brasilien und die heutige Architektur' (1953). In *Oscar Niemeyer: Selbstdarstellung, Kritiken, Oeuvre*, ed. Alexander Fils (Münsterschwarzach: Benedict Press, Frölich & Kaufmann), pp. 94–96.

—— 1984, 'The Need for a New Monumentality' (1944), *Harvard Architectural Review* 4 (spring), pp. 53–61.

—— (ed.), 1951, *A Decade of New Architecture* (Zurich: Girsberger).

Gil, Gilberto, 2004, Speech delivered at New York University, 20 September. Voices of Latin American Leaders Series, http://www.nyu .edu/voices/rsvp?action=4&projectid=7. Last accessed July 2006.

Gilbert, Alan (ed.), 1996, *The Mega-City in Latin America* (Tokyo: United Nations University Press).

Glaeser, Ludwig, 1977, *Ludwig Mies van der Rohe: Furniture and Furniture Drawings from the Design Collection and the Mies van der Rohe Archive* (New York: The Museum of Modern Art).

Glancey, Jonathan, 2007, ' "I pick up my pen. A building appears" ', *Guardian*, 1 August, http://arts.guardian.co.uk/art/architecture/ story/0,,2139073,00.html. Last accessed September 2007.

Goldstein, Donna M., 2003, *Laughter Out of Place: Race, Class, Violence, and Sexuality in a Rio Shantytown*. California Series in Public Anthropology, 9 (Berkeley: University of California Press).

Gomes, Paulo Emílio Salles, 2000, 'Cinema: Tracing a Path in Underdevelopment'. In *Brasil 1920–1950: De la Antropofagia a Brasília*, ed. Jorge Schwartz (Valencia: IVAM, VEGAP, exhibition catalogue, bilingual edition), pp. 603–8.

Goodwin, Philip L., 1943, *Brazil Builds: Architecture New and Old 1652–1942* (New York: Museum of Modern Art, exhibition catalogue, bilingual edition).

Gordon, David L.A., 2006, *Planning Twentieth Century Capital Cities* (New York and London: Routledge).

Gorelik, Adrián, 2007, 'Brasilia: museo della modernità', *Casabella* 753, year 71, no. 3 (March), pp. 13–21.

Gorovitz, Matheus, 2005, 'Unidade de Vizinhança: Brasilia's "Neighbourhood Unit" '. In *Lucio Costa: Brasilia's Superquadra*, ed. Farès El-Dahdah (Munich, London and New York: Prestel, with Harvard Design School), pp. 41–47.

Gott, Richard, 2007, 'The 2006 SLAS Lecture: Latin America as a White Settler Society', *Bulletin of Latin American Research* 26, no. 2 (April), pp. 269–89.

Graham, Richard, 1999, 'Free African Brazilians and the State in Slavery Times'. In *Racial Politics in Contemporary Brazil*, ed. Michael Hanchard (Durham, North Carolina, and London: Duke University Press), pp. 30–58.

Gropius, W., 1965, 'L'architetto e la società', *Casabella* 297 (October), pp. 18–21.

Gropius, Walter, and Mrs Gropius, 1954. In 'Report on Brazil', *Architectural Review* 116, no. 694 (October), pp. 236–37.

Guegen, Pierre, 1946, 'Chapelle à Pampulha (Brésil). Oscar Niemeyer, architecte. Peintures de Portinari', *Architecture d'Aujourd'hui* 17, no. 9 (December), pp. 54–56.

Guimaraens, Cêça de, 1996, *Lucio Costa: um certo arquiteto em incerto e secular roteiro* (Rio de Janeiro: Relume Dumará).

Gullar, Ferreira, Lygia Clark, Lygia Pape et al., 2004, 'Neo-Concrete Manifesto' (1959). In *Inverted Utopias: Avant-Garde Art in Latin America*, ed. Mari Carmen Ramírez and Héctor Olea (New Haven and London: Yale University Press, with Houston: Museum of Fine Arts, exhibition catalogue), pp. 496–97.

Guzmán, Tracy L. Devine, 2005, ' "Diacuí Killed Iracema": Indigenism, Nationalism and the Struggle for Brazilianness', *Bulletin of Latin American Research* 24, no. 1 (January), pp. 92–122.

Hamerman, Conrad, 1995, 'Roberto Burle Marx: The Last Interview', *Journal of Decorative and Propaganda Arts* 21, Brazil Theme issue, pp. 156–79.

Hanchard, Michael, 1999, 'Black Cinderella? Race and the Public Sphere in Brazil'. In *Racial Politics in Contemporary Brazil*, ed. Michael Hanchard (Durham, North Carolina, and London: Duke University Press), pp. 59–81.

—— (ed.), 1999, *Racial Politics in Contemporary Brazil* (Durham and London: Duke University Press).

Haney, Lynn, 2002, *Naked at the Feast: The Biography of Josephine Baker* (London: Robson).

Harris, Elizabeth D., 1987, *Le Corbusier: Riscos Brasileiros* (São Paulo: Nobel).

Hartman, Hattie, 1998, 'Big Mac and Prize to Go', *Building Design* (16 October), pp. 12–19.

Haw, Alex, 2005, 'Beleaguered Nations', *Blueprint*, no. 234 (September), pp. 48–51.

Heathcote, Edwin, 2004, 'A Carnival in Concrete', *Financial Times*, 31 January, p. W18.

Henket, Hubert-Jan, 2002, 'Architecture is Invention', interview with Oscar Niemeyer. In *Back from Utopia: The Challenge of the Modern Movement*, ed. Hubert-Jan Henket and Hilde Heynen (Rotterdam: 010 Publishers), pp. 146–49.

Henket, Hubert-Jan, and Hilde Heynen (eds), 2002, *Back from Utopia: The Challenge of the Modern Movement* (Rotterdam: 010 Publishers).

Herkenhoff, Paulo, 1993, 'The Contemporary Art of Brazil: Theoretical Constructs'. In Aracy A. Amaral and Paulo Herkenhoff, *Ultramodern: The Art of Contemporary Brazil* (Washington, D.C.: National Museum of Women in the Arts, exhibition catalogue), pp. 34–109.

—— 1995, 'The Jungle in Brazilian Modern Design', trans. Kim Mrazek Hastings, *Journal of Decorative and Propaganda Arts* 21, Brazil Theme issue, pp. 239–59.

—— 2004, 'The Hand and the Glove'. In *Inverted Utopias: Avant-Garde Art in Latin America*, ed. Mari Carmen Ramírez and Héctor Olea (New Haven and London: Yale University Press, with Houston: Museum of Fine Arts, exhibition catalogue), pp. 326–37.

—— 2005, 'Tarsila: deux et unique'. In *Tarsila do Amaral: peintre Brésilienne à Paris 1923–1929* (Paris: Maison de l'Amérique latine, exhibition catalogue), pp. 12–51.

Hess, Alan, and Alan Weintraub, 2006, *Oscar Niemeyer Houses* (New York: Rizzoli).

Hess, David. J., and Roberto A. DaMatta (eds), 1995, *The Brazilian Puzzle: Culture on the Borderlands of the Western World* (New York: Columbia University Press).

Heynen, Hilde, 1999, *Architecture and Modernity: A Critique* (Cambridge, Massachusetts, and London: MIT Press).

Hilpert, Thilo, 2005, ' "Do You Know Erlenbach?": Le Corbusier in the Context of Summer 1965', *Fondation Le Corbusier Bulletin* 27 (March), pp. 3–6.

Hitchcock, Henry-Russell, 1955, *Latin American Architecture Since 1945* (New York: Museum of Modern Art, exhibition catalogue).

—— 1993, 'The International Style Twenty Years After' (1951). In *Architecture Culture 1943–1968: A Documentary Anthology*, ed. Joan Ockman (with the collaboration of Edward Eigen) (New York: Rizzoli), pp. 138–48.

Hobsbawm, Eric, and Terence Ranger (eds), 1983, *The Invention of Tradition* (Cambridge: Cambridge University Press).

Holanda, Frederico de, 1989, 'Brasília: The Daily Invention of the City', *Ekistics* 56, no. 334 (January–February), no. 335 (March–April), pp. 75–83.

Holanda, Frederico de, Ana Maria Passos Mota, Antônio Alexandre Cavalcante Leite, Laura Regina Simões de Bello Soares and Patrícia Melasso Garcia, 2002, 'Eccentric Brasília', *Urban Design International* 7, no. 1 (March), pp. 19–28.

Holanda, Sérgio Buarque de, 1996, *Visão do Paraíso: os motivos edênicos no descobrimento e colonização do Brasil*, 6th ed. (São Paulo: Editôra Brasiliense [1959]).

—— 2002, *Raízes do Brasil*, 26th ed. (São Paulo: Companhia das Letras [1936]).

Holford, William, 1957, 'Brasília: A New Capital City for Brazil', *Architectural Review* 122, no. 731 (December), pp. 395–402.

—— 1960a, 'Brasília' (lecture delivered at the RIBA, on 8 December 1959), *Journal of the Royal Institute of British Architects*, 3rd ser., 67, no. 5 (March), pp. 154–59.

—— 1960b, 'The Pilot Plan: Its Qualities and Objectives'. In *Brasília* (London: Brazilian Government Trade Bureau), pp. 8–17.

—— 1962, 'Brasília: The Federal Capital of Brazil', *The Geographical Journal* 128, no. 1 (March), pp. 15–17.

Holston, James, 1989, *The Modernist City: An Anthropological Critique of Brasília* (Chicago and London: Chicago University Press).

Honour, Hugh, 1975, *The New Golden Land: European Images of America from the Discoveries to the Present Time* (New York: Random House).

Hooper, Barbara, 2002, 'Urban Space, Modernity, and Masculinist Desire: The Utopian Longings of Le Corbusier'. In *Embodied Utopias: Gender, Social Change and the Modern Metropolis*, ed. Amy Bingaman, Lise Sanders and Rebecca Zorach (London: Routledge), pp. 55–78.

Hornig, Christian, 1981, *Oscar Niemeyer: Bauten und Projekte* (Munich: Heinz Moos).

Huret, Marcel, 1959, 'Radio Cinéma Télévision', 26.6, http://www.filmfestival.gr/tributes/2003-2004/cinemythology/uk/film28.html. Last accessed September 2004.

Huxley, Aldous, 1999, 'Brave New World Revisited' (1958). In *The Utopia Reader*, ed. Gregory Claeys and Lyman Tower Sargent (New York and London: New York University Press), pp. 362–63.

Huxtable, Ada Louise, 1988, 'On Awarding the Prize', http://www.pritzkerprize.com/bunnei.htm#On%20Awarding%20the%20Prize. Last accessed December 2006.

'In Search of a New Monumentality', 1948, symposium by Gregor Paulsson, Henry-Russell

Hitchcock, William Holford, Sigfried Giedion, Walter Gropius, Lúcio Costa and Alfred Roth, *Architectural Review* 104, no. 621 (September), pp. 117–28.

Instituto de Pesquisa Econômica Aplicada and Brazil Country Management Unit, Poverty Reduction and Economic Management Sector Unit, Latin America and the Caribbean Region, 2003, 'Brazil: Inequality and Economic Development', Report No. 24487-BR, vol. 1: Policy Report, October, http://wbln0018.worldbank.org/LAC/LACInfoClient.nsf/d29684951174975c85256735007fef12/6bdf1e43f715655785256df2005afa04/$FILE/Brazil%20Inequality%20Report_Main_doc.pdf. Last accessed March 2006.

Integrating the Poor: Urban Upgrading and Land Tenure Regularisation in the City of São Paulo, 2004 (São Paulo: Cities Alliance).

Interbau Berlin 1957, 1957 (Berlin: Internationale Bauausstellung im Berliner Hansaviertel, exhibition catalogue).

Irigoyen, Adriana, 2000, 'Frank Lloyd Wright in Brazil', *Journal of Architecture* 5 (summer), pp. 137–57.

Jackson, K. David, 1994, 'Three Glad Races: Primitivism and Ethnicity in Brazilian Modernist Literature', *Modernism/Modernity* 1, no. 2 (April), pp. 89–112.

Jaguaribe, Beatriz, 2004, 'Favelas and the Aesthetics of Realism: Representations in Film and Literature', *Journal of Latin American Cultural Studies* 13, no. 3 (December), pp. 327–42.

Johnson, Randal, and Robert Stam (eds), 1988, *Brazilian Cinema* (Austin: University of Texas).

Katinsky, Julio, 1991, *Brasília em três tempos: A arquitetura de Oscar Niemeyer na Capital* (Rio de Janeiro: Revan, bilingual edition).

Kidder Smith, G.E., 1944, 'The Architects and the Modern Scene', *Architectural Review* 95, no. 567 (March), special issue on Brazil, pp. 78–84.

Kimmelman, Michael, 2005, 'The Last of the Moderns', *New York Times*, 15 May, http://www.nytimes.com/2005/05/15/magazine/15NIEMEYER.html?pagewanted=1&ei=5088&en=a3ec479b1ddf6805&ex=1273896000&partner=rssnyt&emc=rss. Last accessed July 2006.

King, Elaine A., 2002, 'A Conversation with James Turrell', *Sculpture* 21, no. 9 (November), http://www.sculpture.org/documents/scmag02/nov02/turrell/turrell.shtml. Last accessed December 2006.

Klotz, Heinrich, 1982, 'Die röhrenden Hirsche der Architektur, Kitsch in der modernen Baukunst' (1977). In *Oscar Niemeyer: Selbstdarstellung, Kritiken, Oeuvre*, ed. Alexander Fils (Münsterschwarzach: Benedict Press, Frölich & Kaufmann), p. 107.

Kowarick, Lúcio, 2004, 'Housing and Living Conditions in the Periphery of São Paulo: An Ethnographic and Sociological Study', working paper no. CBS-58-2004 (Oxford: Centre for Brazilian Studies, University of Oxford), http://www.brazil.ox.ac.uk/workingpapers/Lucio%20Kowarick%2058.pdf. Last accessed November 2006.

Krohn, Carsten, 2003, 'Order and Progress: Oscar Niemeyer, Urbanist'. In *Oscar Niemeyer: A Legend of Modernism*, ed. Paul Andreas and Ingeborg Flagge (Basle: Birkhäuser, Frankfurt: Deutsches Architektur Museum, exhibition catalogue, bilingual edition), pp. 37–44.

Kubitschek, Juscelino, 1960, 'Brasilia: interview de Juscelino Kubitschek, président des États-Unis du Brésil', *Architecture d'Aujourd'hui* 31, no. 90 (June–July), pp. 2–3.

—— 1966, 'Foreword'. In Willy Stäubli, *Brasilia* (Stuttgart: Alexander Koch), p. 7.

Labrusse, Rémi, 2002, 'Decoration Beyond Decoration'. In *Henri Matisse: Drawing with Scissors – Masterpieces from the Late Years*, ed. Olivier Berggruen and Max Hollein (Munich: Prestel, exhibition catalogue), pp. 67–85.

La maison de la culture du Havre et le nouvel espace culturel Oscar Niemeyer, 1981 (Le Havre: M.C.H.).

Lara, Fernando Luiz Camargos, 2001, 'Popular Modernism: An Analysis of the Acceptance of Modern Architecture in 1950s Brazil' (Ph.D. diss., University of Michigan).

—— 2002, 'One Step Back, Two Steps Forward: The Maneuvering of Brazilian Avant-Garde', *Journal of Architectural Education (JAE)* 55, no. 4 (May), pp. 211–19.

Le Corbusier, 1946, 'Urbanisme 1946: les travaux ont commencé [sic]!', *Architecture d'Aujourd'hui* 17, no. 9 (December), pp. 3–4.

—— 1947a, 'La Cidade dos Motores', *Architecture d'Aujourd'hui* 18, nos 13–14 (September), p. 97.

—— 1947b, *UN Headquarters* (New York: Reinhold).

—— 1947c, *When the Cathedrals Were White: A Journey to the Country of Timid People* (New York: Reynal & Hitchcock).

—— 1948, *Concerning Town Planning* (New Haven: Yale University Press).

—— 1963, *Módulo* 8, no. 32 (March), p. 22.

—— 1987a, *Aircraft* (London: Trefoil [1935]).

—— 1987b, *The City of Tomorrow and Its Planning* (New York: Dover [1925 in French as *Urbanisme*, 1929 in English]).

—— 1987c, *The Decorative Art of Today*, trans. James I. Dunnett (Cambridge, Massachusetts: MIT Press [1925 in French]).

—— 1989, *Towards a New Architecture*, trans. Frederick Etchells (London: Butterworth Architecture [1923 in French]).

—— 1991, *Precisions: On the Present State of Architecture and City Planning* (Cambridge, Massachusetts, and London: MIT Press).

—— 1997, *The Final Testament of Père Corbu: A Translation and Interpretation of Mise au point by Ivan žaknić*, ed. Ivan žaknić. Henry McBride Series in Modernism and Modernity (New Haven and London: Yale University Press).

—— 2006, *Conférences de Rio*, ed. Yannis Tsiomis (Paris: Flammarion).

Le Corbusier with Pierre Jeanneret, 1999, *Œuvre complète*, 7 vols (Basle, Boston and Berlin: Birkhäuser [1929–1965]).

Le Corbusier: Rio de Janeiro 1929–1936, 1998 (Rio de Janeiro: Secretaria Municipal de Urbanismo, Centro de Arquitetura e Urbanismo do Rio de Janeiro, exhibition catalogue).

Leenhardt, Jacques, 2003, 'Roberto Burle Marx: la ville comme paysage'. In *Cruauté et utopie: villes et paysages d'Amérique latine*, ed. Jean-François Lejeune (Brussels: CIVA, Centre International pour la Ville, l'Architecture et le Paysage, exhibition catalogue), pp. 183–95.

Lefebvre, Henri, 1984, *Everyday Life in the Modern World* (New Brunswick, New Jersey: Transaction).

—— 1996, *Writings on Cities* (Oxford: Blackwell).

'Le Havre: Maison de la culture "le Volcan"', n.d., Fiche DOCOMOMO, http://www.archi.fr/DOCOMOMO-FR/fiche-havre-volcan-va.htm. Last accessed December 2006.

Leite, Rui Moreira, 2004, 'Flávio de Carvalho: Media Artist Avant la Lettre', *Leonardo* (online), http://mitpress2.mit.edu/e-journals/Leonardo/isast/spec.projects/MoreiraLeite/moreiraleite.html, print version in *Leonardo* 37, no. 2. Last accessed June 2006.

Lejeune, Jean-François (ed.), 2003, *Cruauté et utopie: villes et paysages d'Amérique latine* (Brussels: CIVA, Centre International pour la Ville, l'Architecture et le Paysage, exhibition catalogue).

Lemos, Celina Borges, 1995, 'The Modernization of Brazilian Urban Space as a Symbol of the Republic', *Journal of Decorative and Propaganda Arts* 21, Brazil Theme issue, pp. 219–31.

'Les courbes vitales d'Oscar Niemeyer', 2005, *Architecture à vivre*, no. 27 (November–December), pp. 48–53.

Leu, Lorraine, 2004, 'The Press and the Spectacle of Violence in Contemporary Rio de Janeiro', *Journal of Latin American Studies* 13, no. 3 (December), pp. 343–55.

Levi, Rino, 2000, 'The Architecture and Aesthetics of the City' (1925). In *Brasil 1920–1950: De la Antropofagia a Brasília*, ed. Jorge Schwartz (Valencia: IVAM, VEGAP, exhibition catalogue, bilingual edition), pp. 619–20.

Levine, Robert M., and John J. Crocitti (eds), 1999, *The Brazilian Reader: History, Culture, Politics* (Durham, North Carolina: Duke University Press).

Lévi-Strauss, Claude, 1965, *Tristes Tropiques: An Anthropological Study of Primitive Societies in Brazil*, trans. John Russell (New York: Atheneum [1955 in French, 1961 in English]).

—— 2000, 'Preface [to Saudades de São Paulo]' (1996). In *Brasil 1920–1950: De la Antropofagia a Brasília*, ed. Jorge Schwartz (Valencia: IVAM, VEGAP, exhibition catalogue, bilingual edition), pp. 614–16.

Lima, Zeuler, and Sandra Vivanco, 2002, 'Culture Translated and Devoured: Two Brazilian Museums by Lina Bo Bardi', *Journal of Romance Studies* 2, no. 3 (winter), pp. 45–60.

Linger, Daniel Touro, 1992, *Dangerous Encounters: Meaning of Violence in a Brazilian City* (Stanford, California: Stanford University Press).

Lispector, Clarice, 1972, 'The Chicken' (1960). In Clarice Lispector, *Family Ties*, trans. Giovanni Pontiero (Austin: University of Texas Press).

—— 2000, 'Brasília' (1962). In *Brasil 1920–1950: De la Antropofagia a Brasília*, ed. Jorge Schwartz (Valencia: IVAM, VEGAP, exhibition catalogue, bilingual edition), pp. 629–30.

Lissovsky, Mauricio, and Paulo Sergio Moraes de Sá, 1996, *Colunas da Educação: A construção do Ministério da Educação e Saúde (1935–1945)* (Rio de Janeiro: Ministério da Cultura, Instituto do Patrimônio Histórico e Artístico Nacional, and Fundação Getúlio Vargas, Centro de Pesquisa e Documentação da História Contemporânea do Brasil).

'L'œuvre d'Oscar Niemeyer en Seine-Saint-Denis', 2005, *Les points de repères du 93*, no. 44 (September), http://www.archi.fr/CAUE93/ressources/pdf/pdr-44.pdf. Last accessed December 2006.

'L'Oscar dello spazio aperto', interview with Noemi Lucarelli, 1980, *Trasparenze* (2nd quarter), pp. 85–94.

Loos, Adolf, 1962, 'Ornament und Verbrechen' (1908). In Adolf Loos, *Sämtliche Schriften* (Vienna: Verlag Herold), pp. 276–88.

Lovell, Peggy A., 1999, 'Women and Racial Equality at Work in Brazil'. In *Racial Politics in Contemporary Brazil*, ed. Michael Hanchard (Durham, North Carolina, and London: Duke University Press), pp. 138–53.

Lucio Costa 1902–2002, 2002 (Brasília: Centro Cultural Banco do Brasil, exhibition catalogue, bilingual edition).

Luigi, Gilbert, 1987, *Oscar Niemeyer: une esthétique de la fluidité* (Marseilles: Parenthèses).

Maak, Niklas, 2003, 'Back to the Future: Oscar Niemeyer and Retro-Futurism'. In *Oscar Niemeyer: A Legend of Modernism*, ed. Paul Andreas and Ingeborg Flagge (Basle: Birkhäuser, Frankfurt: Deutsches Architektur Museum, exhibition catalogue, bilingual edition), pp. 69–76.

Macedo, Danilo Matoso, 2005, 'As obras de Oscar Niemeyer em Belo Horizonte', *Desdobramentos Recentes da Arquitetura Moderna*, http://www.mdc.arq.br/mdc/txt/mdc02-txt05.pdf. Last accessed December 2006.

Machado, Lia Zanotta, and Themis Quezado de Magalhães, 1987, 'Brasilia: Space, Utopia and Way of Life', *Architecture d'Aujourd'hui*, no. 251 (June), p. 39.

Maddy-Weitzman, Bruce, 1999, 'The Berber Question in Algeria: Nationalism in the Making?'. In *Minorities and the State in the Arab World*, ed. Ofra Bengio and Gabriel Ben-Dor (Colorado: Lynne Rienner), http://www.ciaonet.org/book/bengio/bengio02.html. Last accessed August 2006.

Maricato, Ermínia, 2005, 'Política Nacional de Desenvolvimento Urbano'. In World Bank, 'Land Development, Urban Policy and Poverty Reduction', Urban Research Symposium, April, http://worldbank.org/urban/symposium2005/presentations/Erminia1.pdf. Last accessed December 2006.

Martins, Carlos, 2000, 'Building Architecture, Building a Country'. In *Brasil 1920–1950: De la Antropofagia a Brasília*, ed. Jorge Schwartz (Valencia: IVAM, VEGAP, exhibition catalogue, bilingual edition), pp. 578–85.

—— 2003, 'Ville et paysage dans la construction du Brésil'. In *Cruauté et utopie: villes et paysages d'Amérique latine*, ed. Jean-François Lejeune (Brussels: CIVA, Centre International pour la Ville, l'Architecture et le Paysage, exhibition catalogue), pp. 64–73.

—— 2006, 'Gregori Warchavchik: combates pelo futuro'. In Gregori Warchavchik, *Arquitetura do século XX e outros escritos*, ed. Carlos A. Ferreira Martins (São Paulo: Cosac & Naify), pp. 11–29.

Maurício, Lúcia Velloso, 2004, 'Literature and Representations Concerning Full-time Public Schooling', *Revista Brasileira de Educação* 27 (September–December), pp. 40–56, http://www.scielo.br/scielo.php?script=sci_arttext&pid=S1413-24782004000300004&lng=en&nrm=iso. Last accessed December 2006.

McCann, Bryan, 1999, 'The Invention of Tradition on Brazilian Radio'. In *The Brazilian Reader: History, Culture, Politics*, ed. Robert M. Levine and John J. Crocitti (Durham, North Carolina: Duke University Press), pp. 474–82.

McLeod, Mary, 2002, 'Undressing Architecture: Fashion, Gender and Modernity'. In *Back from Utopia: The Challenge of the Modern Movement*, ed. Hubert-Jan Henket and Hilde Heynen (Rotterdam: 010 Publishers), pp. 312–25.

Meade, Teresa A., 1997, *'Civilizing' Rio: Reform and Resistance in a Brazilian City, 1889–1930* (University Park, Pennsylvania: The Pennsylvania State University Press).

Mehrtens, Cristina, 1999, 'The "Gold for São Paulo" Building, 1932 [sic]'. In *The Brazilian Reader: History, Culture, Politics*, ed. Robert M. Levine and John J. Crocitti (Durham, North Carolina: Duke University Press), pp. 162–65.

Melendez, Adilson, 2003, 'Em dois edifícios, museum combina o passado e o presente, de olho no futuro', *Projeto/Design* 275 (January), pp. 40–55.

Mello, Eduardo Kneese de, 1960, 'Why Brasilia'. In *Brasília: History, City Planning, Architecture, Building* (São Paulo: Acropole, bilingual edition), pp. 5–17.

Mello, Neli Aparecida de, François-Michel Le Tourneau, Hervé Théry and Laurent Vidal, 2004, *Brasilia, quarante ans après* (Paris: Institut des hautes études de l'Amérique latine, IHEAL).

Merkel, Jayne, 2005, *Eero Saarinen* (London: Phaidon).

Mesquita, Ivo, 2000, 'Brazil'. In *Latin American Art in the Twentieth Century*, 2nd rev. ed., ed. Edward J. Sullivan (London: Phaidon), pp. 201–31.

Metz, Tracy, 1997, ' "Form Follows Feminine": Niemeyer, 90, Is Still Going Strong', *Architectural Record* 185, no. 12 (December), p. 35.

Meurs, Paul, and Esther Agricola, 1988, *Brazilië: Laboratorium van Architectuur en Stedenbouw* (Rotterdam: Nai Uitgevers).

'Mies in America: An Interview with James Ingo Freed Conducted by Franz Schulze', 1989, in *Mies van der Rohe: Critical Essays*, ed. Franz Schulze (New York: Museum of Modern Art), pp. 172–99.

Milhaud, Darius, 2000, 'Brazil' (1949). In *Brasil 1920–1950: De la Antropofagia a Brasília*, ed. Jorge Schwartz (Valencia: IVAM, VEGAP, exhibition catalogue, bilingual edition), pp. 609–11.

Milliet, Maria Alice, 2001, 'From Concretist Paradox to Experimental Exercises of Freedom'. In *Brazil: Body and Soul*, ed. Edward J. Sullivan (New York: Guggenheim Museum, exhibition catalogue), pp. 388–96.

Mindlin, Henrique E., 1956, *Modern Architecture in Brazil* (New York: Reinhold).

'Minister of Counterculture', 2005, *Guardian*, 14 October, http://technology.guardian.co.uk/news/story/0,16559,1592359,00.html. Last accessed December 2006.

The Modern City Facing the Future, 2000, conference proceedings, Sixth International DOCOMOMO Conference, Brasilia, 19–22 September.

Módulo Especial, 1997, 'Oscar Niemeyer: 50 anos de aquitetura', special issue on Oscar Niemeyer.

Moholy-Nagy, Sibyl, 1959, 'Brasília: Majestic Concept or Autocratic Monument?', *Progressive Architecture*, no. 40 (October), pp. 88–89.

Montaigne, Michel de, 1999, 'Of the Cannibals' (1580 in French). In *The Utopia Reader*, ed. Gregory Claeys and Lyman Tower Sargent (New York and London: New York University Press), pp. 99–103.

Monteiro, Marta Iris, 2001, *Burle Marx: The Lyrical Landscape*, trans. Ann Wright (London: Thames and Hudson).

Montezuma, Roberto (ed.), 2002, *Architecture Brazil 500 Years: A Reciprocal Invention* (Recife: Federal University of Pernambuco, bilingual edition).

Moraes, Vinícius de, 1960, 'Prefácio'. In *Orfeu da Conceição: tragédia carioca* (Rio de Janeiro: Livraria São José), http://www.jobim.com.br/publics/orfeu/prefacio_vin.html. Last accessed March 2004.

——1961, 'Sinfonia da Alvorada', http://www.jobim.com.br/dischist/sinfalv/alvorada_vintext.html. Last accessed July 2004.

More, Thomas, 2005, *Utopia* (The Project Gutenberg eBook), http://www.guteberg.org/files/2130/2130-h/2130-h.htm [1516 in Latin].

Mostafavi, Mohsen, 2001, 'Landscape as Plan: A Conversation with Zaha Hadid (December, January 2001)', *El Croquis* 103, 'Zaha Hadid 1996–2001'.

Motta, Lia, 1987, 'A SPHAN em Ouro Prêto: uma história de conceitos e critérios', *Revista do Patrimônio Histórico e Artístico Nacional*, no. 22, pp. 108–22.

Mumford, Eric, 2002, *The CIAM Discourse on Urbanism, 1928–1960* (Cambridge, Massachusetts, and London: MIT Press).

Mumford, Lewis, 1949, 'Monumentalism, Symbolism and Style', *Architectural Review* 105, no. 628 (April), pp. 173–80.

——1956, 'The Sky Line: The Drab and the Daring', *The New Yorker* 31, 4 February, pp. 82–88.

——1958, *The Culture of Cities* (London: Secker & Warburg [1938]).

Nagib, Lúcia, 2003, 'Death on the Beach – The Recycled Utopia of *Midnight*'. In *The New Brazilian Cinema*, ed. Lúcia Nagib (London: I.B. Tauris, with Oxford: Centre for Brazilian Studies, University of Oxford), pp. 157–72.

——2004, 'Talking Bullets: The Language of Violence in *City of God*', *Third Text* 18, issue 3, pp. 239–50.

——(ed.), 2003, *The New Brazilian Cinema* (London: I.B. Tauris, with Oxford: Centre for Brazilian Studies, University of Oxford).

Nervi, Pier Luigi, 1959, 'Critica delle strutture', *Casabella-Continuità* 223 (January), pp. 55–56.

——1962, 'Relations entre architectes, ingénieurs et constructeurs', *Architecture d'Aujourd'hui* 32, no. 99 (December 1961–January 1962), pp. 4–5.

Neto, Torquato, 2005, 'Torquatália III' (1968). In *Tropicália: A Revolution in Brazilian Culture*, ed. Carlos Basualdo (São Paulo: Cosac & Naify and Gabinete Cultura, Chicago: Museum of Contemporary Art, exhibition catalogue), p. 238.

Neutra, Richard, 1982, 'Planung – ein menschliches Problem auf individueller Basis' (1959). In *Oscar Niemeyer: Selbstdarstellung, Kritiken, Oeuvre*, ed. Alexander Fils (Münsterschwarzach: Benedict Press, Frölich & Kaufmann), pp. 102–4.

Niemeyer, Oscar, 1947a, 'Ce qui manque à notre architecture', *Architecture d'Aujourd'hui* 18, nos 13–14 (September), p. 12.

——1947b, 'Pampulha: l'architecture', *Architecture d'Aujourd'hui* 18, nos 13–14 (September), p. 22.

——1955a, 'Fala Niemeyer', *Módulo* 1, no. 1 (March), p. 47.

——1955b, 'Le Corbusier', *Módulo* 1, no. 1 (March), p. 3.

——1955c, 'Problemas atuais da arquitetura brasileira', *Módulo* 1, no. 3 (December), pp. 19–20.

——1956a, 'Museu de Arte Moderna de Caracas' (lecture delivered to the National Faculty of Architecture, Rio de Janeiro), *Módulo* 2, no. 4 (March), pp. 39–45.

——1956b, 'Notes on Brazilian Architecture'. In Stamo Papadaki, *Oscar Niemeyer: Works in Progress* (New York: Reinhold), pp. 11–14.

——1957, 'Considerações sôbre a arquitetura brasileira', *Módulo* 2, no. 7 (February), n.p.

——1958a, 'A cidade contemporânea', *Módulo* 2, no. 11 (December), pp. 5–10.

——1958b, 'Depoimento', *Módulo* 2, no. 9 (February), pp. 3–6.

——1959a, 'A imaginação na arquitetura', *Módulo* 3, no. 15 (October), pp. 6–11.

——1959b, 'Unidade urbana', *Módulo* 2, no. 12 (February), n.p.

——1960, 'Minha experiência em Brasília', *Módulo* 3, no. 18 (June), pp. 11–16.

——1961, 'Joaquim Cardozo', *Módulo* 6, no. 26 (December), pp. 4–7.

——1962a, 'Contradição na arquitetura', *Módulo* 7, no. 31 (December), pp. 17–20.

——1962b, 'Feira Internationale e Permanente do Líbano em Trípoli', *Módulo* 7, no. 30 (October), pp. 1–23.

——1962c, 'Habitação pré-fabricata em Brasília', *Módulo* 6, no. 27 (March), pp. 27–37.

——1962d, 'Praça Maior da Universidade de Brasília', *Módulo* 7, no. 28 (June), pp. 7–15.

——1963a, 'Escritório do Ceplan', *Módulo* 8, no. 32 (March), pp. 26–31.

——1963b, 'Exposição de Brasília, em Paris', *Módulo* 8, no. 33 (June), pp. 8–11.

——1963c, 'Foire Internationale et Permanente du Liban à Tripoli', *Architecture d'Aujourd'hui* 33, no. 105 (December 1962–January 1963), pp. 96–101.

——1963d, 'Instituto de Ciências', *Módulo* 8, no. 32 (March), pp. 34–38.

——1963e, 'Instituto de Teologia', *Módulo* 8, no. 32 (March), pp. 51–56.

——1963f, 'Le Corbusier', *Módulo* 8, no. 32 (March), p. 23.

——1963g, 'Preface'. In Paul F. Damaz, *Art in Latin American Architecture* (New York: Reinhold, 1963), p. 13.

——1965a, 'Conjunto Nordia', *Módulo* 10, 39 (March–April), pp. 17–24.

——1965b, 'Plano Neguev', *Módulo* 10, no. 39 (March–April), pp. 1–12.

——1965c, *Textes et dessins pour Brasilia* (Paris: Forces Vives).

——1965d, 'Universidade de Haifa', *Módulo* 10, no. 39 (March–April), pp. 27–35.

——1966, 'Thoughts on Brasilia'. In Willy Stäubli, *Brasilia* (Stuttgart: Alexander Koch), pp. 21–23.

——1968, *Quase memórias, viagens: tempos de entusiasmo e revolta, 1961–1966* (Rio de Janeiro: Civilização Brasileira).

——1974, 'A Selection of Extracts from Interviews with Oscar Niemeyer Recently Published in Brazil', *Architecture d'Aujourd'hui* 45, no. 171 (January–February), pp. lxxxi–lxxxiii.

——1975a, 'Depoimento', *Módulo* 10, no. 40 (September), pp. 32–33.

——1975b, *Oscar Niemeyer* (Milan: Mondadori).

——1975c, 'Valorizzare il lavoro dell'uomo', *Espansione*, no. 70 (August–September), supplement, pp. 12–13.

——1976, 'Arquitetura brasileira na Argélia', *Módulo* 11, no. 43 (June–July–August), pp. 16–25.

——1977a, 'Considerações sobre a arquitetura brasileira', *Módulo* 11, no. 44 (December 1976–January 1977), pp. 34–41.

——1977b, 'Viagens, origens e influências na arquitetura', *Módulo*, no. 46 (July–August–September), pp. 31–34.

——1978a, *A forma na arquitetura* (Rio de Janeiro: Avenir, Coleção Depoimentos).

——1978b, 'Dois projetos para a Barra da Tijuca', *Módulo*, no. 50 (August–September), pp. 72–83.

——1978c, 'Problemas da arquitetura, 1: o espaço arquitetural', *Módulo*, no. 50 (August–September), pp. 54–61.

——1978d, 'Problemas da arquitetura, 2: as fachadas de vidro', *Módulo*, no. 51 (October–November), pp. 44–50.

——1979a, 'Ao leitor', *Módulo*, no. 54 (July), n.p.

——1979b, 'Problemas da arquitetura, 3: arquitetura e técnica estrutural', *Módulo*, no. 52 (December 1978–January 1979), pp. 34–39.

——1979c, 'Problemas da arquitetura, 4: o pré-fabricado e a arquitetura', *Módulo*, no. 53 (March–April), pp. 56–59.

——1979d, 'Problemas da arquitetura, 5: o mercado de trabalho', *Módulo*, no. 54 (July), pp. 94–95.

——1979e, 'Uma cidade para o Amanhã', *Módulo*, no. 56 (November–December), pp. 77–84.

——1980a, 'Entrevista Oscar Niemeyer', *Módulo*, no. 58 (April–May), pp. 26–27.

——1980b, 'Metamorphose', *Módulo*, no. 58 (April–May), pp. 22–25.

——1980c, 'Problemas da arquitetura, 6: o problema estrutural e a arquitetura contemporânea', *Módulo*, no. 57 (February), pp. 94–97.

——1980d, 'Problemas da arquitetura, 7: método de trabalho', *Módulo*, no. 58 (April–May), pp. 86–89.

——1980e, *Rio: De província a metrópole* (Rio de Janeiro: Avenir).

——1982, 'Die Entwicklung von Brasília bis 1970' (1970). In *Oscar Niemeyer: Selbstdarstellung, Kritiken, Oeuvre*, ed. Alexander Fils (Münsterschwarzach: Benedict Press and Frölich und Kaufmann), pp. 55–57.

——1983, 'Centro Cultural – Le Havre, França', *Módulo*, no. 74 (February), pp. 42–47.

——1985, *Oscar Niemeyer*, ed. Hélio Penteado (São Paulo: Almed, bilingual edition).

——1987a, 'Bilancio confidenziale'. In Lionello Puppi, *Guida a Niemeyer* (Milan: Arnoldo Mondadori), pp. 162–63.

——1987b, 'Fare architettura oggi' (1947). In Lionello Puppi, *Guida a Niemeyer* (Milan: Arnoldo Mondadori), p. 159.

——1988a, 'Acceptance Speech', Pritzker Architecture Prize, http://www.pritzkerprize.com/bunnei.htm. Last accessed May 2006.

——1988b, 'Interview'. In Luis Carlos Prestes, Hélio Silva, Antonio Houaiss et al., *Perfil do Pensamento Brasileiro* (Rio de Janeiro: Bolsa do Rio and Sindicato dos Escritores do Rio de Janeiro), pp. 179–96.

——1988c, 'Monument to the People', interview with Patrick Garnett, *Building Design*, 24 June, pp. 22–26.

——1992, *Meu sósia e eu* (Rio de Janeiro: Revan, bilingual edition).

——1993a, *Conversa de arquiteto* (Rio de Janeiro: Revan, 1993).

——1993b, 'Form and Function in Architecture' (1960). In *Architecture Culture 1943–1968: A Documentary Anthology*, ed. Joan Ockman (with the collaboration of Edward Eigen) (New York: Rizzoli), pp. 309–13 (originally in *Módulo* 5, no. 21 (December 1960), pp. 2–7).

——1993c, *Niemeyer par lui-même: L'architecte de Brasília parle à Edouard Bailby* (Paris: Ballard).

——1994a, 'All I Ever Saw and Loved in My Life', interview with Ítalo Campofiorito, *World Architecture*, no. 26, pp. 28–29.

——1994b, *Projects for the Veneto* (Toronto: Italian Cultural Institute, bilingual edition).

——1997a, 'Coming Soon: Hanoi'. In *Oscar Niemeyer 1937–1997* (Tokyo: TOTO Shuppan, Gallery MA Books, bilingual edition), pp. 10–11.

——1997b, *Museu de Arte Contemporânea de Niterói* (Rio de Janeiro: Revan, bilingual edition).

——1998, *Oscar Niemeyer* (Rio de Janeiro: Prefeitura da Cidade do Rio de Janeiro, exhibition catalogue, bilingual edition).

——1999, 'Le Corbusier by Oscar Niemeyer' (1963). In Le Corbusier with Pierre Jeanneret, *Œuvre complète 1957–1965*, vol. 7, pp. 9–10.

——2000a, *My Architecture* (Rio de Janeiro: Revan).

——2000b, *The Curves of Time: The Memoirs of Oscar Niemeyer* (London: Phaidon).

——2002, *Minha Arquitetura – 2002* (Rio de Janeiro: Revan).

——2003a, 'Current Problems with Brazilian Architecture' (1955). In *Oscar Niemeyer: A Legend of Modernism*, ed. Paul Andreas and Ingeborg Flagge (Basle: Birkhäuser, Frankfurt: Deutsches Architektur Museum, exhibition catalogue, bilingual edition), pp. 123–27.

——2003b, 'O problema social na arquitetura' (1955). In *Depoimento de uma geração*, 2nd ed. revised and enlarged, ed. Alberto Xavier (São Paulo: Cosac & Naify), pp. 184–88.

——2003c, *Serpentine Gallery Pavilion 2003* (London: Serpentine Gallery and Trolley).

——2004, *My Architecture 1937–2004* (Rio de Janeiro: Revan).

——2005, *Casas onde morei* (Rio de Janeiro: Revan).

——2006, *A marquise e o projeto original do parque ibirapuera* (São Paulo: Imprensa Oficial).

——2007, ' "Je cherche toujours à inventer" ', interview with Axel Gyldén, *LEXPRESS.fr*, 21 November, http://www.lexpress.fr/mag/arts/dossier/architecture/dossier.asp?ida=461868&p=1. Last accessed November 2007.

——n.d., *Oscar Niemeyer: Notebooks of the Architect* (Brussels: CIVA, International Centre for Urbanism, Architecture and Landscape, folio).

Niemeyer, Oscar, and Team, 1986, *Parque do Tietê: plano de reurbanização da margem do Rio Tietê* (São Paulo: Almed).

Niesewand, Nonie, 1998, 'Future Father', interview with Oscar Niemeyer, *Wallpaper** (January–February), pp. 39–40.

Nietzsche, Friedrich, 2001, *The Gay Science*, ed. Bernand Williams, trans. Josefine Nauckhoff, poems trans. Adrian del Caro (Cambridge: Cambridge University Press).

Nobre, Ana Luiza, 2005, 'Guinle Park: A Proto-Superquadra'. In *Lucio Costa: Brasilia's Superquadra*, ed. Farès El-Dahdah (Munich, London and New York: Prestel, with Harvard Design School), pp. 33–39.

Nouvel, Jean, 2003, 'Guggenheim Museum in Rio de Janeiro, Rio de Janeiro, Brazil 2002', *a+u: Architecture and Urbanism* 395 (August), pp. 44–51.

Nowicki, Matthew, 1993, 'Origins and Trends in Modern Architecture' (1951). In *Architecture Culture 1943–1968: A Documentary Anthology*, ed. Joan Ockman (with the collaboration of Edward Eigen) (New York: Rizzoli), pp. 150–56.

Nunes, Benedito, 2004, 'Anthropophagic Utopia: Barbarian Metaphysics'. In *Inverted Utopias: Avant-Garde Art in Latin America*, ed. Mari Carmen Ramírez and Héctor Olea (New Haven and London: Yale University Press, with Houston: Museum of Fine Arts, exhibition catalogue), pp. 57–61.

'O arquiteto da paz', n.d., *Correio Caros Amigos*, http://carosamigos.terra.com.br/da_revista/edicoes/ed74/niemeyer.asp. Last accessed February 2006.

Ockman, Joan, 1996, 'Mirror Images: Technology, Consumption, and the Representation of Gender in American Architecture Since World War II'. In *The Sex of Architecture*, ed. Diana Agrest, Patricia Conway and Leslie Kanes Weisman (New York: Harry N. Abrams), pp. 191–210.

Ockman, Joan (ed. with the collaboration of Edward Eigen), 1993, *Architecture Culture 1943–1968: A Documentary Anthology* (New York: Rizzoli).

Ohye, Hiroshi, 1954. In 'Report on Brazil', *Architectural Review* 116, no. 694 (October), p. 237.

Oiticica, Hélio, 2004, 'Tropicália: March 4, 1968'. In *Readings in Latin American Modern Art*, ed. Patrick Frank (New Haven and London: Yale University Press), pp. 177–79.

——2005a, 'The Plot of the Earth That Trembles: The Avant-Garde Meaning of the Bahian Group' (1968). In *Tropicália: A Revolution in Brazilian Culture*, ed. Carlos Basualdo (São Paulo: Cosac & Naify and Gabinete Cultura, Chicago: Museum of Contemporary Art, exhibition catalogue), pp. 245–54.

——2005b, 'Tropicália: The Image Problem Surpassed by that of Synthesis' (1969). In *Tropicália: A Revolution in Brazilian Culture*, ed. Carlos Basualdo (São Paulo: Cosac & Naify and Gabinete Cultura, Chicago: Museum of Contemporary Art, exhibition catalogue), p. 309.

Oliveira, Luis, 1999, 'Planet Niemeyer', *Architectural Review* 205, no. 1226 (April), pp. 72–75.

Oliveira, Olivia de, 2002, 'Lina Bo Bardi: Built Work', *2G International Architecture Review*, nos 23–24, 3–4, bilingual edition.

Oliven, Ruben George, 2000, 'Brazil: The Modern in the Tropics'. In *Through the Kaleidoscope*, ed. Vivian Schelling, trans. Lorraine Leu (London and New York: Verso), pp. 53–71.

Ortiz, Renato, 2000, 'Popular Culture, Modernity and Nation'. In *Through the Kaleidoscope*, ed. Vivian Schelling, trans. Lorraine Leu (London and New York: Verso), pp. 127–47.

Oscar Niemeyer 1937–1997, 1997 (Tokyo: TOTO Shuppan, Gallery MA Books, bilingual edition).

'Oscar Niemeyer and the Bird of Paradise', 1993, *World Architecture*, no. 26, pp. 30–51.

'Oscar Niemeyer: La ville radieuse', 2002, *Connaissance des arts*, no. 591 (February), pp. 48–55.

'Oscar Niemeyer: Project for a House in Santa Monica, California', 1964, *Arts + Architecture* (September), pp. 20-28.

Outtes, Joel, 2003, 'Disciplining Society through the City: The Genesis of City Planning in Brazil and Argentina (1894–1945)', paper presented at a research seminar on Latin America, Helsinki, 22 May, http://www.helsinki.fi/hum/ibero/xaman/articulos/2003_01/outtes.html. Last accessed September 2005.

Pádua, José Augusto, 2004, 'Nature Conservation and Nation Building in the Thought of a Brazilian Founding Father: José Bonifácio

(1763–1838)', working paper CBS-53-2004 (Oxford: Centre for Brazilian Studies, University of Oxford), http://www.brazil.ox.ac.uk/workingpapers/Jose%20Augusto%20Padua%2053.pdf. Last accessed May 2006.

Palácio da Alvorada, n.d. (Brasília: Casa Civil, Secretaria de Administração, Coordenação de Relações Públicas, bilingual edition).

'Pampulha Yacht Club: Structuralism in Recent Brazilian Architecture', 1962, *Architectural Review* 132, no. 789 (November), p. 307.

Panofsky, Erwin, 1995, 'The Ideological Antecedents of the Rolls-Royce Radiator'. In Erwin Panofsky, *Three Essays on Style*, ed. Irving Lavin (Cambridge, Massachusetts: MIT Press), pp. 127–65.

Papadaki, Stamo, 1950, *The Work of Oscar Niemeyer* (New York: Reinhold).

—— 1956, *Oscar Niemeyer: Works in Progress* (New York: Reinhold).

—— 1960, *Oscar Niemeyer* (New York: George Braziller).

—— Stamo Papadaki Papers (C0845), Manuscripts Division, Department of Rare Books and Special Collections, Princeton University Library.

Palácio Itamaraty: Brasília, Rio de Janeiro, 2002 (Brazil: Banco Safra).

Parker, Richard G., 1991, *Bodies, Pleasures, and Passions: Sexual Culture in Contemporary Brazil* (Boston: Beacon Press).

Passarela do Samba, n.d. (Rio de Janeiro: Governo do Estado do Rio de Janeiro, Prefeitura do Rio de Janeiro, Secretaria de Ciência e Cultura, Riotur, and Avenir).

Pastore, José, 1969, *Brasília: a cidade e o homem. Uma investigação sociológica sôbre os processos de migração, adaptação e planejamento urbano* (São Paulo: Companhia Editôra Nacional and Editôra da Universidade de São Paulo).

'Pavillon pour une source thermale', 1947, *Architecture d'Aujourd'hui* 18, nos 13–14 (September), pp. 76–77.

Pazos Alonso, Cláudia, and Claire Williams (eds), 2002, *Closer to the Wild Heart: Essays on Clarice Lispector* (Oxford: Legenda, European Humanities Research Centre, University of Oxford).

PCR Services Corporation for City of Santa Monica Planning Division, 2003, 'Strick House, 1911, La Mesa Drive, Santa Monica, California: City Landmark Assessment Report' (Santa Monica, California), http://pen.ci.santa-monica.ca.us/planning/landmark/agendas/2003/1911%20La%20Mesa%20PCR%20rpt%20w%20pics.pdf. Last accessed February 2005.

Pedrosa, Mário, 2003a, 'A arquitetura moderna do Brasil' (1953). In *Depoimento de uma geração*, 2nd ed. revised and enlarged, ed. Alberto Xavier (São Paulo: Cosac & Naify), pp. 98–105.

—— 2003b, 'O depoimento de Oscar Niemeyer' (1958). In *Depoimento de uma geração*, 2nd ed. revised and enlarged, ed. Alberto Xavier (São Paulo: Cosac & Naify), pp. 241–44.

Peña, Richard, 1988, 'How Tasty Was My Little Frenchman'. In *Brazilian Cinema*, ed. Randal Johnson and Robert Stam (Austin: University of Texas), pp. 191–99.

Penna, J.O. de Meira, 1960, 'Brasilia: urbanisme politique', *Architecture d'Aujourd'hui* 31, no. 90 (June–July), pp. 4–7.

—— n.d., 'Brazil Builds a New Capital'. In *Brasília* (Rio de Janeiro: Divisão Cultural, Ministério das Relações Exteriores), n.p. (Originally in *Landscape* 5, no. 21 (Spring 1956), pp. 17–22).

Peralva, Osvaldo, 1991, 'Brasília Redeemed'. In Julio Katinsky, *Brasília em três tempos: A arquitetura de Oscar Niemeyer na Capital* (Rio de Janeiro: Revan), p. 61.

Perret, Auguste, 2001, 'Concrete' (undated). In Karla Britton, *Auguste Perret* (London: Phaidon), pp. 244–45.

Pessôa, José, 2005, 'Protected by Law: The Superquadra's "Historic" Modernity'. In *Lucio Costa: Brasilia's Superquadra*, ed. Farès El-Dahdah (Munich, London and New York: Prestel, with Harvard Design School), pp. 79–89.

—— (ed.), 1999, *Lucio Costa: Documentos de Trabalho* (Rio de Janeiro: IPHAN).

Peter, John, 2000, *The Oral History of Modern Architecture: Interviews with the Greatest Architects of the Twentieth Century*, ed. Diana Murphy (New York: Harry N. Abrams).

'Petit historique du brise-soleil: extrait de l'œuvre de Le Corbusier', 1947, *Architecture d'Aujourd'hui* 18, nos 13–14 (September), p. 10.

Petit, Jean, 1995, *Niemeyer: Architetto e Poeta* (Milan: Ulrico Hoepli).

—— 1997, 'Oscar Niemeyer: Sculptor of Space'. In *Oscar Niemeyer 1937–1997* (Tokyo: TOTO Shuppan, Gallery MA Books, bilingual edition), pp. 90–92.

Pevsner, Nikolaus, 1961, 'Modern Architecture and the Historian or the Return of Historicism', *Journal of the Royal Institute of British Architects*, 3rd ser., 68, no. 6 (April), pp. 230–40.

—— 1972, *An Outline of European Architecture*, 7th ed. reprinted with revised bibliography (London: Penguin [1943]).

—— 2002, *Pevsner on Art and Architecture: The Radio Talks*, ed. Stephen Games (London: Methuen).

Peyton-Jones, Julia, 2003, 'Director's Foreword'. In Oscar Niemeyer, *Serpentine Gallery Pavilion 2003* (London: Serpentine Gallery and Trolley), pp. 11–20.

—— 2005, 'Fast-Forward Architecture', RIBA Trust Annual Lecture 2005, 21 April, RIBA, London, http://www.architecture.com/go/Architecture/Events_4504.html. Last accessed December 2006.

Philippou, Styliane, 2003, 'From Rio de Janeiro to Brasília: Ideology, National Identity and Public Buildings in Brazil, 1920–1960', *I Architektoniki os Techni*, no. 8 (June), pp. 2–5.

—— 2004, 'The Primitive as an Instrument of Subversion in Twentieth-Century Brazilian Cultural Practice', *arq: Architectural Research Quarterly* 8, nos 3–4, pp. 285–98.

—— 2005, 'Modernism and National Identity in Brazil or How to Brew a Brazilian Stew', *National Identities* 7, no. 3, pp. 245–64.

—— 2006, 'Utopian Modernism in the Land of the Future: Brasília, the "Capital of Hope" '. In *Nowhere Somewhere: Writing, Space and the Construction of Utopia*, ed. José Eduardo Reis and Jorge Bastos da Silva (Oporto: Universidade do Porto), pp. 181–99.

Prestes, Luis Carlos, Hélio Silva, Antonio Houaiss et al., 1988, *Perfil do Pensamento Brasileiro* (Rio de Janeiro: Bolsa do Rio and Sindicato dos Escritores do Rio de Janeiro).

Puppi, Lionello, 1987, *Guida a Niemeyer* (Milan: Arnoldo Mondadori).

—— 1996, *Oscar Niemeyer 1907* (Rome: Officina).

Quantrill, Malcolm (ed. in collaboration with Kenneth Frampton, Michael L. Tribe, Diana Barco, Pablo J. Rodríguez P., and Galia Solomonoff), 2000, *Latin American Architecture: Six Voices*. Studies in Latin American Architecture Series (Texas A&M University Press).

Ragot, Gilles, 2003a, 'Construction d'un récit sur la modernité'. In Gilles Ragot, Thierry Jeanmonod, Nicolas Nogue and Chantal Callais, *L'invention d'une ville: Royan années 50* (Paris: Centre des monuments nationaux Monum, Éditions du patrimoine, Cahiers du Patrimoine 65), pp. 11–21.

—— 2003b, 'La ville "la plus cinquante" de France'. In Gilles Ragot, Thierry Jeanmonod, Nicolas Nogue and Chantal Callais, *L'invention d'une ville: Royan années 50* (Paris: Centre des monuments nationaux Monum, Éditions du patrimoine, Cahiers du Patrimoine 65), pp. 109–211.

Ragot, Gilles, Thierry Jeanmonod, Nicolas Nogue and Chantal Callais, 2003, *L'invention d'une ville: Royan années 50* (Paris: Centre des monuments nationaux Monum, Éditions du patrimoine, Cahiers du Patrimoine 65).

Rama, Angel, 1996, *The Lettered City*, ed. and trans. John Charles Chasteen (Durham, North Carolina, and London: Duke University Press).

Ramírez, Mari Carmen, and Héctor Olea (eds), 2004, *Inverted Utopias: Avant-Garde Art in Latin America* (New Haven and London: Yale University Press, with Houston: Museum of Fine Arts, exhibition catalogue).

Real, Patricio del, 2007, 'Building a Continent: MOMA's Latin American Architecture Since 1945 Exhibition', *Journal of Latin American Cultural Studies* 16, no. 1 (March), pp. 95–110.

Recamán, Luiz, 2004, 'High-Speed Urbanisation'. In *Brazil's Modern Architecture*, ed. Elisabetta Andreoli and Adrian Forty (London: Phaidon), pp. 106–39.

Rego, Jose Lins do, 1952, 'L'homme et le paysage', *Architecture d'Aujourd'hui* 23, nos 42–43 (August), pp. 8–14.

Reidy, A. E., 1962. In 'Positions perspectives de l'architecte et de l'ingénieur de structure', *Architecture d'Aujourd'hui* 32, no. 99 (December 1961–January 1962), p. 3.

'Report on Brazil', 1954, *Architectural Review* 116, no. 694 (October), pp. 235–50.

Resende, Beatriz, 2000, 'Brazilian Modernism: The Canonised Revolution'. In *Through the Kaleidoscope*, ed. Vivian Schelling, trans.

Lorraine Leu (London and New York: Verso), pp. 199–216.

Rezende, Cláudia Barcellos, and Márcia Lima, 2004, 'Linking Gender, Class and Race in Brazil', *Social Identities* 10, no. 6, pp. 757–73.

Rhodes, Colin, 2000, 'Through the Looking-Glass Darkly: Gendering the Primitive and the Significance of Constructed Space in the Practice of the Brücke'. In *Gender and Architecture*, ed. Louise Durning and Richard Wrigley (Chichester, West Sussex: John Wiley & Sons), pp. 189–207.

Ribeiro, Darcy, 1992, 'Oscar'. In Oscar Niemeyer, *Meu sósia e eu* (Rio de Janeiro: Revan), pp. 123–25.

—— 2000, *The Brazilian People: The Formation and Meaning of Brazil*, trans. Gregory Rabassa (Gainesville: University Press of Florida [1995 in Portuguese]).

Richards, J.M., 1949, 'Reassessment 2: The Great Pyramid', *Architectural Review* 105, no. 629 (May), pp. 245–47.

—— 1950, 'The Next Step', *Architectural Review* 107, no. 639 (March), pp. 165–81.

—— 1959, 'Brasilia', *Architectural Review* 125, no. 745 (February), pp. 95–104.

—— 1960, 'The Architectural Revolution in Brazil'. In *Brasilia* (London: Brazilian Government Trade Bureau), pp. 18–30.

Roberto, Milton, 1952, 'Dix années d'architecture', *Architecture d'Aujourd'hui* 23, nos 42–43 (August), pp. 27–28.

Rocha, Glauber, 1988, 'An Esthetic of Hunger' (1965). In *Brazilian Cinema*, ed. Randal Johnson and Robert Stam (Austin: University of Texas), pp. 69–71.

Rocha, João Cezar de Castro, 2002, 'Brazil as Exposition', lecture delivered at the 'Grand Expositions' conference, Yale University, October 2001, http://www.lehman.cuny.edu/ciberletras/v08/rocha.html. Last accessed December 2006.

—— 2005, 'The "Dialectic of Marginality": Preliminary Notes on Contemporary Brazilian Culture', working paper no. CBS-62-05 (Oxford: Centre for Brazilian Studies, University of Oxford), www.brazil.ox.ac.uk/workingpapers/Joao%20Cezar%20Castro%20Rocha%2062.pdf. Last accessed December 2006.

Rocha, Paulo Mendes da, 2006, 'Rocha and Concrete', interview, *Pesquisa*, no. 123 (May), http://www.revistapesquisa.fapesp.br/?art=1695&bd=1&pg=2&lg=en. Last accessed December 2006.

Rogers, Ernesto, 1954. In 'Report on Brazil', *Architectural Review* 116, no. 694 (October), pp. 239–40.

Rovira, Josep M., 2003, *José Luis Sert 1901–1983* (Milan: Electa).

Rubin, W. (ed.), 1984, *'Primitivism' in Twentieth Century Art* (New York: Museum of Modern Art).

Rudofski, Ber., 1939, 'Cantieri di Rio de Janeiro', *Casabella* 11, no. 136 (April), pp. 12–17.

Sagar, Jagdish, 2002, 'Revisiting Chandigarh'. In *Back from Utopia: The Challenge of the Modern Movement*, ed. Hubert-Jan Henket and Hilde Heynen (Rotterdam: 010 Publishers), pp. 368–75.

Saint-Amour, Paul K., 2003, 'Modernist Reconnaissance', *Modernism/Modernity* 10, no. 2 (April), p. 349–80.

Salvaign, Matthieu, 2001, *Oscar Niemeyer* (Paris: Assouline, 2001).

Sampaio, Suzanna, 2003, 'Sao Paulo – the Impact of Change and the Recovery of Intangible Heritage', www.international.icomos.org/victoriafalls2003/papers/B1-1%20-%20Sampaio.pdf. Last accessed July 2004.

Sánchez-Prado, Ignacio M., 2006, '*Amores Perros*: Exotic Violence and Neoliberal Fear', *Journal of Latin American Cultural Studies* 15, no. 1 (March), pp. 39–57.

Sansone, Livio, 2003, *Blackness Without Ethnicity: Constructing Race in Brazil* (New York and Basingstoke: Palgrave Macmillan).

Sant'Anna, Affonso Romano de, 1998, *Baroque, the Soul of Brazil*, trans. Diane Grosklaus (Rio de Janeiro: Comunicação Maxima).

Santos, Carlos Oliveira, 2001, *O Nosso Niemeyer* (Campo das Letras, bilingual edition).

Santos, Cecília Rodrigues dos, Margareth Campos da Silva Pereira, Romão Veriano da Silva Pereira and Vasco Caldeira da Silva, 1987, *Le Corbusier e o Brasil* (São Paulo: Tessela, Projeto).

Santos, Milton, 1996, 'São Paulo: A Growth Process Full of Contradictions'. In *The Mega-City in Latin America*, ed. Alan Gilbert (Tokyo: United Nations University Press), pp. 224–40.

Sartoris, Alberto, 1996, 'Oscar Niemeyer or a Concentrated and Emblematic Architecture'. In Josep Ma. Botey, *Oscar Niemeyer* (Barcelona: Gustavo Gili), pp. 9–13.

Sbriglio, Jacques, 1996, *Apartment Block 24 N.C. and Le Corbusier's Home* (Paris: Fondation Le Corbusier, Basle: Birkhäuser, bilingual edition).

Schelling, Vivian (ed.), 2000, *Through the Kaleidoscope*, trans. Lorraine Leu (London and New York: Verso).

Schøllhammer, Karl Erik, 2001, 'From the Malandro (Rogue) to the Traficante (Drug Trafficker): Two Constellations of Violence in Brazilian Culture', *Diálogos Latinoamericanos*, no. 4, pp. 37–46.

Schorske, Carl E., 1998, *Thinking with History: Explorations in the Passage to Modernism* (Princeton: Princeton University Press).

Schwarcz, Lilia Moritz, 1999, *The Spectacle of the Races: Scientists, Institutions, and the Race Question in Brazil, 1870–1930*, trans. Legand Guyer (New York: Hill and Wang).

—— 2003, 'Not Black, not White: Just the Opposite. Culture, Race and National Identity in Brazil', working paper no. CBS-47-2003 (Oxford: Centre for Brazilian Studies, University of Oxford), http://www.brazil.ox.ac.uk/workingpapers/Schwarcz47.pdf. Last accessed April 2005.

—— 2004, *The Emperor's Beard: Dom Pedro II and the Tropical Monarchy of Brazil*, trans. John Gledson (New York: Hill and Wang).

Schwartz, Jorge, 2000, 'Tupí or not Tupí: The War Cry of Literature in Modern Brazil'. In *Brasil 1920–1950: De la Antropofagia a Brasília*, ed. Jorge Schwartz (Valencia: IVAM, VEGAP, exhibition catalogue, bilingual edition), pp. 539–48.

—— (ed.), 2000, *Brasil 1920–1950: De la Antropofagia a Brasília* (Valencia: IVAM, VEGAP, exhibition catalogue, bilingual edition).

Scott, Felicity, 1999, 'Underneath Aesthetics and Utility: The Untransposable Fetish of Bernard Rudofsky', *Assemblage* 38 (April), pp. 59–89.

Scully, Vincent, 1977, 'Introduction'. In Robert Venturi, *Complexity and Contradiction in Architecture*, 2nd ed. (London: The Architectural Press), pp. 9–11.

Segawa, Hugo, 1997, 'Oscar Niemeyer: A Misbehaved Pupil of Rationalism', *Journal of Architecture* 2, no. 4 (winter), pp. 291–311.

—— 2001, 'After the Miracle: Brazilian Architecture 1960–2000'. In *Brazil: Body and Soul*, ed. Edward J. Sullivan (New York: Guggenheim Museum, exhibition catalogue), pp. 558–69.

—— 2002, *Arquiteturas no Brasil 1900–1990*, 2nd ed. (São Paulo: Editôra da Universidade de São Paulo [1998]).

Segre, Roberto, and Rafael Lopez Rangel, 1982, *Architettura e territorio nell'America Latina* (Milan: Electa).

Séron-Pierre, Catherine, 2002, 'Oscar Niemeyer: Complex Residential Copan, Sao Paulo, 1951–57', *Moniteur Architecture AMC*, no. 123 (March), pp. 76–79.

Sert, J.L., F. Léger, and S. Giedion, 1993, 'Nine Points on Monumentality'. In *Architecture Culture 1943–1968: A Documentary Anthology*, ed. Joan Ockman (with the collaboration of Edward Eigen) (New York: Rizzoli), pp. 29–30.

Sevcenko, Nicolau, 2000, 'Peregrinations, Visions and the City: From Canudos to Brasília, the Backlands Become the City and the City Becomes the Backlands'. In *Through the Kaleidoscope*, ed. Vivian Schelling, trans. Lorraine Leu (London and New York: Verso), pp. 75–107.

Shohat, Ella, and Robert Stam, 1994, *Unthinking Eurocentrism: Multiculturalism and the Media* (London: Routledge).

Shoumatoff, Alex, 1990, *The Capital of Hope: Brasília and Its People* (New York: Vintage Books).

Silva, Ernesto, 1997, *História de Brasília: um sonho, uma esperança, uma realidade*, 3rd ed. (Brasília: Linha Gráfica Editôra).

Skidmore, Thomas E., 1967, *Politics in Brazil 1930–1964: An Experiment in Democracy* (Oxford and New York: Oxford University Press).

—— 1988, *The Politics of Military Rule in Brazil, 1964–1985* (Oxford and New York: Oxford University Press).

—— 1993, *Black into White: Race and Nationality in Brazilian Thought*, 2nd ed. (Durham, North Carolina, and London: Duke University Press).

—— 1999, *Brazil: Five Centuries of Change* (Oxford and New York: Oxford University Press).

Sodré, Nelson Werneck, 1978, *Oscar Niemeyer*, Coleção 'Eu', vol. 3 (Rio de Janeiro: Graal).

Sousa-Leão, J. de, 1944, 'Brazil: The Background', *Architectural Review* 95, no. 567 (March), special issue on Brazil, pp. 59–63.

Souza, Renato César José de, 1998, 'A arquitetura em Belo Horizonte nas décadas de 40 e 50: utopia e transgressão'. In *Arquitetura da modernidade*, ed. Leonardo Barci Castriota (Belo Horizonte: UFMG and Instituto de

Arquitetos do Brasil – Departamento MG), pp. 185–207.

Spade, Rupert, 1971, *Oscar Niemeyer* (New York: Simon and Schuster).

Spiro, Annette, 2002, *Paulo Mendes da Rocha: Bauten und Projekte – Works and Projects* (Sulgen: Niggli, bilingual edition).

Staden, Hans, 1928, *Hans Staden: The True History of His Captivity 1557*, trans. Malcolm Letts (London: George Routledge [1557 in German]).

Stam, Robert, 1997, *Tropical Multiculturalism: A Comparative History of Race in Brazilian Cinema and Culture* (Durham, North Carolina, and London: Duke University Press).

—— 2003, 'Cabral and the Indians: Filmic Representations of Brazil's 500 Years'. In *The New Brazilian Cinema*, ed. Lúcia Nagib (London: I.B. Tauris, with Oxford: Centre for Brazilian Studies, University of Oxford), pp. 205–28.

Stäubli, Willy, 1966, *Brasilia* (Stuttgart: Alexander Koch).

Stephenson, Glenn V., 1970, 'Two Newly-Created Capitals: Islamabad and Brasilia', *Town Planning Review* 41, pp. 317–32.

Stirling, James, 1956, 'Ronchamp: Le Corbusier's Chapel and the Crisis of Rationalism', *Architectural Review* 119, no. 711 (March), pp. 155–61.

Subirats, Eduardo, 2000, 'From Surrealism to Cannibalism'. In *Brasil 1920–1950: De la Antropofagia a Brasília*, ed. Jorge Schwartz (Valencia: IVAM, VEGAP, exhibition catalogue, bilingual edition), pp. 523–27.

Sullivan, Edward J., 2001, 'Brazil: Body and Soul'. In *Brazil: Body and Soul*, ed. Edward J. Sullivan (New York: Guggenheim Museum, exhibition catalogue), pp. 2–33.

—— (ed.), 2000, *Latin American Art in the Twentieth Century*, 2nd rev. ed. (London: Phaidon).

—— (ed.), 2001, *Brazil: Body and Soul* (New York: Guggenheim Museum, exhibition catalogue).

Summerson, John, 1943, 'The Brazilian Contribution', review of *Brazil Builds: Architecture New and Old 1652–1942*, by Philip L. Goodwin, *Architectural Review* 93, no. 557 (May), p. 135.

Süssekind, Flora, 2002, 'Deterritorialization and Literary Form: Brazilian Contemporary Literature and Urban Experience', working paper CBS-34-2002 (Oxford: Centre for Brazilian Studies, University of Oxford), http://www.brazil.ox.ac.uk/workingpapers/Sussekind34.pdf. Last accessed January 2004.

—— 2005, 'Chorus, Contraries, Masses: The Tropicalist Experience and Brazil in the Sixties'. In *Tropicália: A Revolution in Brazilian Culture*, ed. Carlos Basualdo (São Paulo: Cosac & Naify and Gabinete Cultura, Chicago: Museum of Contemporary Art, exhibition catalogue), pp. 31–56.

Süssekind, José Carlos, 2003, 'The Integration between Architecture and Structure in Oscar Niemeyer's Work'. In *Oscar Niemeyer: A Legend of Modernism*, ed. Paul Andreas and Ingeborg Flagge (Basle: Birkhäuser, Frankfurt: Deutsches Architektur Museum, exhibition catalogue, bilingual edition), pp. 45–53.

Tabacow, José (ed.), 2004, *Roberto Burle Marx: Arte & Paisagem* (São Paulo: Studio Nobel).

Tafuri, Manfredo, 1976, *Design and Utopia: Design and Capitalist Development* (Cambridge, Massachusetts, and London: MIT Press).

Tafuri, Manfredo, and Francesco Dal Co, 1976, *Modern Architecture* (Milan: Electa, London: Faber and Faber), 2 vols.

Tarsila do Amaral: peintre brésilienne à Paris 1923–1929, 2005 (Paris: Maison de l'Amérique latine, exhibition catalogue).

Telles, Edward E., 2002, 'Racial Ambiguity Among the Brazilian Population', *Ethnic and Racial Studies* 25, no. 3 (May), pp. 415–41.

Tinem, Nelci, and Lúcia Borges, 2000, 'Brazil in Modern Architectural Handbooks'. In *The Modern City Facing the Future*, conference proceedings, Sixth International DOCOMOMO Conference, Brasilia, 19–22 September, pp. 113–23.

Tolosa, Hamilton, 1996, 'Rio de Janeiro: Urban Expansion and Structural Change'. In *The Mega-City in Latin America*, ed. Alan Gilbert (Tokyo: United Nations University Press), pp. 203–23.

Torre, Susana, 2002, 'The Esthetics of Reconciliation: Cultural Identity and Modern Architecture in Latin America'. In *Back from Utopia: The Challenge of the Modern Movement*, ed. Hubert-Jan Henket and Hilde Heynen (Rotterdam: 010 Publishers), pp. 138–45.

Tota, Antônio Pedro, 2000, *O imperialismo sedutor: a americanização do Brasil na época da Segunda Guerra* (São Paulo: Companhia das Letras).

Tournikiotis, Panayotis, 2002, *Adolf Loos* (New York: Princeton Architectural Press).

Treib, Marc, 1993, 'Axioms for a Modern Landscape Architecture'. In *Modern Landscape Architecture: A Critical Review*, ed. Marc Treib (Cambridge, Massachusetts, and London: MIT Press), pp. 36–67.

—— (ed.), 1993, *Modern Landscape Architecture: A Critical Review* (Cambridge, Massachusetts, and London: MIT Press).

—— (ed.), 2002, *The Architecture of Landscape, 1940–1960* (Philadelphia: University of Pennsylvania Press).

Trigo, Beningo (ed.), 2002, *Foucault and Latin America: Appropriations and Deployments of Discursive Analysis* (New York and London: Routledge).

Tschumi, Bernard, 1996, *Architecture and Disjunction* (Cambridge, Massachusetts, and London: MIT Press).

Tsiomis, Yannis, 1997, 'Brasilia', *Architecture d'Aujourd'hui*, no. 313 (October), pp. 78–79.

—— 1998, '1936, Le Corbusier parle, dessine, projette'. In *Le Corbusier: Rio de Janeiro 1929–1936* (Rio de Janeiro: Secretaria Municipal de Urbanismo, Centro de Arquitetura e Urbanismo do Rio de Janeiro, exhibition catalogue), pp. 142–45.

—— 2006, 'Le Corbusier au Brésil – 1936'. In Le Corbusier, *Conférences de Rio*, ed. Yannis Tsiomis (Paris: Flammarion), pp. 7–49.

Underwood, David, 1992, ' "Civilizing" Rio de Janeiro: Four Centuries of Conquest through Architecture', *Art Journal* 51, no. 4 (winter), pp. 48–56.

—— 1994a, *Oscar Niemeyer and Brazilian Free-form Modernism* (New York: George Braziller).

—— 1994b, *Oscar Niemeyer and the Architecture of Brazil* (New York: Rizzoli).

—— 1994c, 'Popular Culture and High Art in the Work of Oscar Niemeyer', *Anales del Instituto de Investigaciones Estéticas* 65, pp. 139–55.

—— 1994d, 'Women, Clouds and Oscar Niemeyer', *Progressive Architecture* (December), pp. 67–73.

Vaccarino, Rossana, 2000a, 'Introduction'. In *Roberto Burle Marx: Landscapes Reflected*, ed. Rossana Vaccarino (New York: Princeton Architectural Press), pp. 7–12.

—— 2000b, 'The Correspondence of Time and Instability'. In *Roberto Burle Marx: Landscapes Reflected*, ed. Rossana Vaccarino (New York: Princeton Architectural Press), pp. 41–60.

—— 2002, 'The Inclusion of *Modernism*: Brasilidade and the Garden'. In *The Architecture of Landscape, 1940–1960*, ed. Marc Treib (Philadelphia: University of Pennsylvania Press), pp. 206–37.

—— (ed.), 2000, *Roberto Burle Marx: Landscapes Reflected* (New York: Princeton Architectural Press).

Vale, Lawrence J., 1992, *Architecture, Power, and National Identity* (New Haven and London: Yale University Press).

Valladares, Licia, 2000, 'A gênese da favela carioca: a produção anterior às ciências sociais', *Revista Brasileira de Ciências Sociais* 15, no. 44 (October), pp. 5–34.

Vegesack, Alexander von (ed.), 2006, *Jean Prouvé: The Poetics of the Technical Object* (Weil am Rhein: Vitra Design Museum, exhibition catalogue).

Veloso, Caetano, 2003, *Tropical Truth: A Story of Music and Revolution in Brazil*, trans. Isabel de Sena, ed. Barbara Einzig (London: Bloomsbury).

Venturi, Robert, 1977, *Complexity and Contradiction in Architecture*, 2nd ed. (London: The Architectural Press [1966]).

Vianna, Hermano, 1999, *The Mystery of Samba: Popular Music and National Identity in Brazil* (Chapel Hill, North Carolina, and London: University of North Carolina Press).

Vidal, Laurent, 2002, *De Nova Lisboa à Brasília: l'invention d'une capitale (XIXe–XXe siècles)* (Paris: IHEAL, Institut des hautes études de l'Amérique latine).

Vieira, Else Ribeiro Pires, 1999, 'Liberating Calibans: Readings of *Antropofagia* and Haroldo de Campos' Poetics of Transcreation'. In *Post-Colonial Translation: Theory and Practice*, ed. Susan Bassnett and Harish Trivedi (London and New York: Routledge), pp. 95–113.

Vincent, Claude, 1947, 'The Modern Garden in Brazil', *Architectural Review* 101, no. 605 (May), pp. 165–72.

—— 1948, 'The Background and the Sculpture', *Architectural Review* 103, no. 617 (May), pp. 203–09.

Vivanco, Sandra Isabella, 2005, 'Trope of the Tropics: The Baroque in Modern Brazilian Architecture, 1940–1950'. In *Transculturation:*

Cities, Spaces and Architectures in Latin America, ed. Felipe Hernández, Mark Millington and Iain Borden. Critical Studies Series, vol. 27 (Amsterdam and New York: Rodopi), pp. 189–201.

Vollers, Karel, 1990, 'Oscar Niemeyer', *Wiederhall* 12, pp. 12–20.

Warchavchik, Gregori, 2000, 'On Modern Architecture' (1925). In *Brasil 1920–1950: De la Antropofagia a Brasília*, ed. Jorge Schwartz (Valencia: IVAM, VEGAP, exhibition catalogue, bilingual edition), pp. 620–21.

—— 2006, *Arquitetura do século XX e outros escritos*, ed. Carlos A. Ferreira Martins (São Paulo: Cosac & Naify).

Weisman, Marina, 2000, 'Introduction'. In *Latin American Architecture: Six Voices*, ed. Malcolm Quantrill (in collaboration with Kenneth Frampton, Michael L. Tribe, Diana Barco, Pablo J. Rodríguez P., and Galia Solomonoff). Studies in Latin American Architecture Series (Texas A&M University Press), pp. 3–19.

Weston, Richard, 1995, *Alvar Aalto* (London: Phaidon).

—— 1996, *Modernism* (London: Phaidon).

—— 2002, *Twentieth-Century Residential Architecture* (London: Laurence King).

Wigley, Mark, 1992, 'Untitled: The Housing of Gender'. In *Sexuality & Space*, ed. Beatriz Colomina. Princeton Papers on Architecture Series (New York: Princeton Architectural Press), pp. 327–89.

—— 2003, 'Oscar Niemeyer: Architecture and Fashion', talk presented at the Serpentine Gallery Summer Pavilion, London, 4 July.

Williams, Daryle, 2001, *Culture Wars in Brazil: The First Vargas Regime, 1930–1945* (Durham, North Carolina, and London: Duke University Press).

Wirth, John D., 1970, *The Politics of Brazilian Development 1930–1954* (Stanford, California: Stanford University Press).

Wisnik, Guilherme, 2001, *Lucio Costa* (São Paulo: Cosac & Naify).

—— 2004, 'Doomed to Modernity'. In *Brazil's Modern Architecture*, ed. Elisabetta Andreoli and Adrian Forty (London: Phaidon), pp. 20–55.

Wisnik, José Miguel, 2000, 'Antropofagia and Music'. In *Brasil 1920–1950: De la Antropofagia a Brasília*, ed. Jorge Schwartz (Valencia: IVAM, VEGAP, exhibition catalogue, biligual edition), pp. 557–63.

'Within Party Walls', 1972, *Architectural Review* 151, no. 901 (March), pp. 133–34.

Xavier, Alberto (ed.), 2003, *Depoimento de uma geração*, 2nd ed. revised and enlarged (São Paulo: Cosac & Naify).

Young, Theodore Robert, 1998, 'Anthropophagy, Tropicalismo, and *Como era gostoso meu francês*', paper prepared for delivery at the 1998 meeting of the Latin American Studies Association, Chicago, September, http://168.96.200.17/ar/libros/lasa98/Young.pdf. Last accessed May 2004.

Zapatel, Juan Antonio, 2005, 'Regarding the Superquadra: An Interview with Lucio Costa' (1992). In *Lucio Costa: Brasilia's Superquadra*, ed. Farès El-Dahdah (Munich, London and New York: Prestel, with Harvard Design School), pp. 19–23.

Zevi, Bruno, 1950, *Towards an Organic Architecture* (London: Faber & Faber).

—— 1999, *Erich Mendelsohn: The Complete Works* (Basle: Birkhäuser).

—— 2003, 'A moda lecorbusiana no Brasil' (1971). In *Depoimento de uma geração*, 2nd ed. revised and enlarged, ed. Alberto Xavier (São Paulo: Cosac & Naify), pp. 163–66.

Zweig, Stefan, 1942 [1941], *Brazil: Land of the Future*, trans. Andrew St. James (London: James, Cassell).

Documentary Films

Andrade, Joaquim Pedro de, 1967, *Brasília: contradições de uma cidade nova* (Filmes do Serro).

Bernacchi, Adriana, n.d., *Oscar Niemeyer: Una sede per un editore*.

Brayne, William, 1968, *Oscar Niemeyer: Architect of Brasilia*. CBC Television Series (Canadian Broadcasting Corporation, British Broadcasting Corporation, National Educational Television, USA, and Bayerischer Rundfunk, West Germany).

Clairval, Cécile, and Olivier Ricard (producers), 1974, *Une architecture lyrique, Oscar Niemeyer* (Paris: Channel 2, French Television).

Leftel, Tamara, 1994, *Eu, Roberto Burle Marx* (Soraia Cals).

Maciel, Fabiano, 2005, *Oscar Niemeyer: a vida é um sopro* (Rio de Janeiro: Sérgio Alexandre Martins Celeste and Santa Clara Comunicação).

Motta Filho, Geraldo, *The Line: Lucio Costa and the Modern Utopia*, 2003 (Rio de Janeiro: Grupo Novo de Cinema e TV).

Oscar Niemeyer: Child from the Stars, 2001 (São Paulo: Vídeo Filmes).

Tamarski, G., 1960, *Brasília* (London: The Brazilian Government Trade Bureau).

Tendler, Silvio, 1980, *Os anos JK* (São Paulo: Hélio Paulo Ferraz, Versátil).

Wajnberg, Marc-Henri, 2000, *Oscar Niemeyer: un architecte engagé dans le siècle* (Paris: ARTE France and Panic Productions; Brussels: RTBF, Télévision Belge Francophone, and Wajnbrosse Productions, São Paulo: Polo de Imagem).

Index

A page number followed by *n* refers to information in a footnote. Page numbers in italics refer to illustrations or information in a caption. Portuguese names are entered under the last element; any exceptions will have a cross-reference. Buildings are indexed under place, usually a city, and/or under their architect's name. Niemeyer's works are also listed by name at the end of his index entry.

Palácio da Alvorada 236–39, 237–38, 245, 246, 252, 255, 256–68, 257–63, 265–68, 269
Palácio do Itamaraty 283, 285–90, 286–90, 346
Palácio do Jaburu 309
Palácio do Planalto 269, 269, 270–74, 271–74
Pantheon of the Country Tancredo Neves 241, 246
Paris exhibition on (1965) 157, 178, 190, 261, 262, 271, 315, 326
Pevsner's defence of architecture 14
Plano Piloto 217n, 218, 219, 220, 223–24, 223, 225–26, 225, 229–34, 251–52, 282, 296–99, 297, 301
Pombal 240–41, 240, 241, 246, 246
population 217
Praça dos Trés Poderes 232–33, 232, 233, 240–41, 241, 245, 245, 246, 246, 247, 268–82, 269–82
precursors of 73, 298
residential areas and social stratification 227–28, 241, 296–97, 301
residential blocks and zoning 296–304
road and transportation networks 223–24, 223, 225–26, 227–28, 227, 240, 296, 299
satellite towns 216n, 227–28, 228, 241, 301, 311
schools and educational facilities 298, 299, 302, 303–4, 304
size and finite form 234, 282
social problems and planning of 227–28, 241, 247, 301
superquadras 217n, 223, 227, 296–304, 299–302
Supreme Court 246, 246, 269, 269, 271, 272, 274, 274–75
Teahouse 246
Teatro Pedro Calmon 309, 310
Television Tower (Costa) 224–25, 225
and Tropicalismo 248
University buildings 304–8, 304–7, 321
water features 283–87, 284, 289
as World Heritage Site 234
Brasília (journal) 213n
brasilidade 22, 27, 34, 164, 181, 248, 284
espirito de brasilidade 12, 82, 85, 306
myths and symbols of 30–33
and tropical nature 33–36
Brazil, Vital 88
Brazil
and 'air age' 223–35
Church and state in 218, 220, 220
and Cold War 229
construction of national past 41, 42, 82, 90–91, 238, 245
dictatorship 33, 179, 248, 263, 308, 340, 353, 367, 368
eroticization and feminization of 102, 200, 385
Estado Nôvo (1937-1945) 33, 179, 212
export of art and culture 23, 25, 314–16
foundation myths 165–67
as Garden of Eden 34, 35, 212
illiteracy rates 366
income inequalities 354n
independence 22n
interior as authentic Brazil 214
as land of the future 35, 41–42, 215
military coup and return to democracy 308–11, 340
Ministry of Cities 363
national identity 18–42
new architecture for 35–42, 90–91, 255
Orphée Noir representation of 212

as patriarchal society 148, 235, 238, 245
planned cities 89, 241
political hierarchy 245
political isolation 229, 315
political upheavals 308–11
post-war industrialization 123–24, 140–41, 175–76, 229
redefinition of colonial heritage 28–30, 33–34, 41–42, 54, 218
road and transportation networks 213, 223–24, 240, 296, 299
social stratification 124–25, 227, 352–54
symbolic parents of 165–67
urban growth 124, 145, 352n, 363
as world power 240
and World War II 87, 141n
see also Brazilian Modernism
Brazil Builds exhibition (MoMA) 9, 57n, 72, 87–88, 183, 224
Brazilian Modernism 8–17, 220
architecture and tropicalism 35–42, 60, 72, 164, 284
and the arts 24–26, 34
and Baroque 13–15, 27–30, 41, 158, 179
birth of architectural Modernism 36–38, 43–88
and gardens 36, 39–41, 166, 284 see also gardens
Eurocentric criticism of 13–17, 101, 177–80, 204–5
'exuberance' of 8, 13, 14, 178, 180
and industrial modernization 175–76
as 'national style' 9, 15, 17, 255
international recognition for architecture 9, 16–17, 87–88, 140
synthesis of industry and nature 25, 34, 166–69, 284
Brazilian Pavilion, 1889 Exposition Universelle, Paris 39, 83
Brazilian Pavilion, 1939 New York World's Fair 77, 82–87, 83–85, 92, 169, 189, 374
Brazilianism 23, 55
Brazilianization 20–24, 31–35, 40, 43, 50, 60, 212
brazilwood/pau-brasil 25
Brecheret, Victor 314
Monumento às Bandeiras 167
Breton, André 314
brises-soleil 9, 10, 178n
in ABI Headquarters (Roberto) 77
and colonial rotulas 72, 78
in Costa's Parque Guinle apartment blocks 72–73, 73
as emblematic feature of Brazilian Modernism 72, 73, 132–33, 285
international diffusion of 72
and Israeli architecture 318
mass produced in São Paulo 72
in Ministry of Education 61, 62–63, 63
in Ministry of Justice 285, 285
Niemeyer's variations of 76, 77, 105, 129–30, 130–31, 133–35, 133–35, 145, 146, 149–50, 167, 168, 285, 285
as response to local conditions 72–73
Brito, Fernando 90n
Brito, Ubirajara 322
Britton, Karla 334
Brizola, Leonel de Moura 364, 366, 367, 368
Browning, Barbara 205
Bruand, Yves 93–94, 149, 157
Brunelleschi, Filippo 104
Brunhs, Angelo 74

Brutalist architecture 287
Paulista Brutalism 360
Buenos Aires 18, 20n
Bulcão, Athos 160, 206, 303, 309
and Burle Marx 268n
Chapel of Nossa Senhora de Fátima 221, 221
Edifício Liberdade 150, 151
French Communist Party Headquarters 329
Mondadori Headquarters 348
National Congress 280, 282
National Theatre 290, 291
Palácio da Alvorada 266, 267
Palácio da Alvorada chapel 268
Palácio do Itamaraty 289–90
Sambódromo 365
Sul America Hospital 268n
Supreme Court 274, 275
Bunshaft, Gordon 146n
Lever House building, New York 146, 147
Burle Marx, Roberto 11, 15, 38, 39–40, 41, 88, 163, 179, 218n, 340
Araxá Thermal Baths Pavilion 103, 103
Brasília gardens and landscape 234–35, 282, 283, 283, 286, 289, 291, 291, 292, 303, 309
Copacabana mosaic pavements 49–50, 50
gardens and architecture 108–9, 112, 181–82, 210
gardens to Niemeyer's houses 185, 185, 186, 186, 191, 191–92, 193, 203, 206, 207, 208, 209, 209
Ibirapuera Park project (unrealized) 164, 165
Ministry of Education gardens 11, 52, 62, 63–64, 64, 67–68, 68
Museum of Modern Art gardens, Rio de Janeiro 50, 50
Pampulha gardens 91, 91, 92, 96, 105, 108, 112
Recife public gardens 39, 39–40, 52
Schwartz House garden 38, 52
Sul America Hospital gardens 160
use of curves 67–68, 68, 112
Burle Marx, Walter 83
Burlington, Lord 181, 182
Burmeister; Fernando Lopes 321
Burns, E. Bradford 24
Burton Tremaine House, Santa Monica, California (unbuilt) 193–94, 194–95

C
Cabral, Pedro Álvares 34, 218, 220
cacti 36, 36, 39, 39
Caesarea
Rothschild, Edmond de: House (unbuilt) 206, 206
tourist resort (unrealized) 327
'café-com-leite', 'República do' 123
Cahiers d'Art (journal) 36
Calanca, Giorgio 341, 344
Calatrava, Santiago 16
Caldeira, Teresa 354
California
Burton Tremaine House, Santa Barbara (unbuilt) 193–94, 194–95
Strick, Joseph and Anne: House, Santa Monica 140, 140
Calvino, Italo: Invisibile Cities 17, 266
Calvo, Aldo 290
Camargo, Sérgio 315
Camillo, Sitte 20n
Caminha, Pêro Vaz de 34
Campello, Glauco 304, 341

'Brasília Revisited' 227, 234n, 250
and *Brazil Builds* exhibition 87
on Brazilian Modernism 177–78, 179, 253, 255n
Brazilian Pavilion, 1939 New York World's Fair 77, 82–87, 83–85
Brazilian Pavilion, 1964 Milan Triennale 177, 177
brises-soleil in work 72, 73
and Burle Marx 52
Cidade Universitária plan, Rio de Janeiro (unrealized) 73, 74, 231
Diamantina and colonial heritage 28, 29, 62, 63
director of Escola Nacional de Belas Artes 52
Edifícios Nova Cintra, Bristol and Caledônia, Parque Guinle 38–39, 72, 73, 297, 303
on end of 'Brazilian Style' 253–54
Fontes, Ernesto G.: House at Tijuca, Rio de Janeiro 19, 19, 267
on housing and residential areas 296–301
on influence on Niemeyer 16
and Le Corbusier 19, 43, 46, 57
Ministry of Education and Public Health 9, 11, 52, 53, 55–61, 64–72, 278
and monumentality 250, 251–52, 268–69
Museu das Missões, São Miguel das Missões 78
Niemeyer at practice of 51, 82, 183
on Niemeyer's work 73, 129, 255n
on 'plastic intention' 11, 129
'Reasons of the New Architecture' 41, 55–56, 86, 110
on Rio de Janeiro 218n
Schwartz House, Rio de Janeiro 38, 39, 52
social purpose of modern architecture 227
and SPHAN 78, 82, 91
Television Tower, Brasília 224–25, 225
Warchavchik collaboration 38, 39
on Warchavchik's house 36
workers' houses in Gamboa, Rio de Janeiro 38
Costa, Maria Elisa 217n, 233n, 298
Côte d'Azur: Nara Mondadori Holiday House 206
Craymer, Peter 278
Crease, David 234n, 252, 298, 301–2
crime and violence in Brazil 353–55, 381
exoticization and spectacularization of 354–55
Cruls (Luiz) Commission 214
Cuiabá: university (unrealized) 321
cultural nationalism
and industrial and economic growth 124, 229
and Modernism 33–34
Pau-Brazil culture for export 23, 25, 314–16
and Tropicalismo 248, 316
cultural syncretism 47n
Cunha, Ayres Câmara 167
Cunha, Euclides da 54, 239, 245n
Os Sertões 32, 39, 213, 214
Curitiba
NovoMuseu (Oscar Niemeyer Museum) 378–81, *378–81*
social and urban policy 379
Curtis, William 16, 338n
curves
Affonso Eduardo Reidy's serpentine slabs 147n
'A[f]rodisiac curves' 12, 152
Alvar Aalto's use of 147, 147n
Burle Marx's use of 67–68, 68, 112
eroticization and feminization of 98, 100, 102, 147–49, 152, 200, 385
and gendered city 145–49
Le Corbusier on 102n, 147–48

and nature 147
Niemeyer on 97, 98, 100, 101, 121
in Niemeyer's architecture 97–98, 99–101, 121–22, *121–22*, 145–49, 150–52, 384–86
polymetric rhythms of Casa das Canoas 204–6, *204–5*

D
dadaism 22, 176n
Dal Co, Francesco 16, 205
de Beauvoir, Simone 268, 301
Debret, Jean-Baptiste 61, *61*, 76
Debussy, Claude 224
Deckker, Zilah Quezado 56, 146n
Deixa Falar (samba school) 364
Delaunay, Sonia 36
Deleuze, Gilles 8, 71, 371
democracy and monumentality 250–51, 252, 266, 271, 333, 381–82
Deroche, Jean 327
developmentalism 229, 242
Di Cavalcanti (Emiliano Augusto Cavalcanti de Albuquerque) 21, 24, 98, 162, 267, 315
Brasília works 282
Edifício Triângulo mosaic 135–36
and Le Corbusier in Rio 19, 103
in Paris 314
Diacuí Canualo Aiute 167
Diamantina, Minas Gerais 28, 29, 62, *62*
airport terminal 156, *157*
Hotel Tijuco 162, *162*, 163
influence on Brasília architecture 235, 255, 256, 264, 264
Júlia Kubitschek School 162–63, *163*
market hall 264, *264*
Youth Club 157–58, *158*, *159*
Dias, Antônio Gonçalves: 'I-Juca-Pirama' 26
Dimanche, Guy 318, 320
Diniz, Countess Sylvia 22
Dionyzisation 35, 64, 85, 101, 152, 182, 385–86
Disney, Walt
Saludos Amigos 127n
The Three Caballeros 88n, 128
Dodsworth, Henrique 82
Donga (Joaquim Maria dos Santos) 27
'Pelo Telefone' 364
Donne, John 244
Dorfles, Gillo 41
Drexter, Arthur 140
drug-trafficking and violence 353, 354
Duarte, Rogério 361
Duchartre, Pierre-Louis 22
Dudley, George A. 137, 138, 139
Dufy, Raoul 314
Dumont, Mineiro Alberto Santos 224
Duprat, Goldino 47n
Duprat, Raimundo da Silva 20n
Dupuis, Guy 315
Duroméa, André 335

E
Eames, Charles and Ray 267
Eckard, Wolf von 247n
El-Hanani, A. 318
Elhyani, Zvi 318, 321
Eliasson, Olafur 382
Emendabili, Galileo: *Obelisco dos Heróis de 32* 167
Emery, Marc 117, 320, 324

Engels, Friedrich 368
engineering and architecture 158–59, 278–79
entrance sequences
Casa das Canoas 197–98
Church of São Francisco de Assis, Pampulha 113–14, *115*
Palácio da Alvorada 265, *265*, 266
use of ramps 374–75, 383, *383*
entrequadra 299, *300*
entrudo 364
Epstein, David 227
eroticization of Brazil 102, 200, 385
Escobar, Ildefonso 214
Escolas de Samba 364
Espinosa, Julio García 360
espirito de brasilidade 12, 82, 85, 306
Estado Nôvo (1937-1945) 33, 179, 212
Estelita, Gauss 164
A estrada de ferro Noroeste (film) 284
ethnography and racism 31n
Eurocentrism 13n, 14, 17, 102, 181, 189, 315
European critics and Brazilian Modernism 177–80
Europe: Niemeyer's work in *see* France; Germany; Italy; Norway; Portugal; Spain; United Kingdom
European cultural influences 20, 22, 26, 314
in Brasília 229, 231, 235, 283–84
Evenson, Norma 9, 35n, 252, 265, 277, 368
Exposition des Arts Décoratifs et Industriels Modernes, Paris (1925) 79, 226, 327
exuberance
of Brazilian Modernism 178, 180
of Niemeyer's work 13–14, 15

F
fado 23
Fascism and architecture 55
favela samba 31
favelados 24, 27, 354–55
in *Orphée Noir* 211–12
favelas 20n, 24, 24, 124, 125, *125*, 352n
alternative social housing 147n, 368
Brasília as escape from 216
Brasília's *favelas* 216, 241
clearance for development 367–68
exoticization in film 354–55
Le Corbusier on architecture and inhabitants of 19
Niemeyer's valorization of architecture 128, 129, 197–98
origins of 216
São Paulo 363
social exclusion and social problems 352–53
fazenda 186, 236, *237*, 238, 239
Federmann, Yekutiel: House, Herzlija, Israel (unbuilt) 206, 318
Fernandes, Florestan 72
Ferraz, Marcelo 379
Ferrera, Carlos Frederico 88
Ferret, Claude 16
Ferriss, Hugh 139
Ferro, Sérgio 360
Figueiredo, Bernando de 290
Figueiredo Júnior, Afonso Celso de Assis 35
Filho, André 43n
Filho, José Mariano 55
film *see* cinema
Firme, Raul Pena 218n

Ministry of Education and Public Health, Rio de Janeiro 9–11, *10–11*, 14, 52–72, *52–53*, 56–59, *61*, *63–71*, 82, 88, 110, 255
    azulejos 60, 61, *62*, *62*, 64*n*, 66, 69, 70, 178–79
    'camouflage architectural' 62
    and monumentality 66, *66*, 231
    Niemeyer's extension proposal 119, 121–22, *121–22*
    in *Orphée Noir* 212
Miranda, Carmen (Maria do Carmo Miranda da Cunha) 31, 83
Miranda, Léonel: House, Rio de Janeiro 191–93, *191–93*
miscegenation *see mestiçagem*/race mixing/miscegenation
Modern Architecture: International Exhibition exhibition (MoMA) 87, 90
Módulo (journal) 109, 158, 178, 180*n*, 241, 247
    forced closure 308, 310
    Niemeyer's self-critical review 252–53, 254
Moholy-Nagy, Sibyl 250
Mondadori, Arnoldo 341
Mondadori, Giorgio 341, *344*, 346
Mondadori Headquarters, Segrate, Italy 341–48, *341–48*
Montaigne, Michel de 23, 25, 176, 212, 236
Monteiro, Vicente do Rêgo 314
    Antropófago 22
Montigny, Auguste-Henri-Victor Grandjean de 54, 60
monumentality
    anti-monumentality and Modernism 250, 251, 266
    Architectural Review symposium 231, 234*n*, 251
    and Brasília 231, 250–313
    and immortality 252, 263
    and Niemeyer's architecture 66–67, 251, 252, 263, 264, 357–58, 384
    political associations 250, 251, 252, 266
Moorish heritage 38–39, 40, 61–62, 283, 318
Moraes, Mello 364
Moraes, Vinícius de 167, 384*n*
    'Garota de Ipanema' 384*n*
    Orfeu da Conceição 211–12, *211*
    Sinfonia da Alvorada (*Sinfonia de Brasília*) 244
Morand, Paul 18*n*
Morandi, Riccardo 348
More, Sir Thomas: *Utopia* 196
Moreira, Gilberto Passos Gil *see* Gil, Gilberto
Moreira, Jorge *11*, 52, 53, *55*, 59, 64–72, 74, 218*n*, 321
    Rio Grande do Sul Railway Central Administration Headquarters, Porto Alegre (competition winning entry) 157
Morelli, Père 339–40
morros 20, 129, 200, 352*n*
    and *asfalto* 352–54, 381–82
mosaics 135–36, *136*
    Banco Boavista 132, *133*
    pastilha mosaics in São Francisco de Assis, Pampulha 113, *113*
    pavements/*pedra portuguesa* 47, *48*, 49–50, *49*, *50*, 68, 98*n*, 113, 182, 207–8, 268
Mota e Silva, Djanira da 267
Motta, Nelson 248*n*
Motterle, Federico 338, 349
Mount Favella 216
Moura, Eduardo Souto de 382
Mourier, Charles 334
mulata/mulatto 12, 31, 32, 47, 98, 102*n*, 103, 200

Müller, Hans 327
Müller, Hans Walther 333
Müller, Hans-Georg 318, 320
Müller, Werner 133, 156, 162
Mumford, Lewis 93, 178, 205, 251
Murgel, Ângelo 89
Museum of Modern Art (MoMA), New York: exhibitions
    Brazil Builds 9, 57*n*, 72, 87–88, 183, 224
    From Le Corbusier to Niemeyer: 1929–49 194
    Latin American Architecture Since 1945 140, 205
    Modern Architecture: International Exhibition 87, 90
music
    and architecture 206–7, 256
    as Brazilian export 314, 315–16
    see also bossa nova; samba
Mussolini, Benito 53, 55
muxarabi (lattice-work) 62, *62*, 63, 72
MVRDV 382

N
Nabuco, Joaquim 240
national developmentalism 229, 242
National Factory of Motors 226
national symbols 31
    architecture of Brasília 251, 252, 255
nationalism
    Brasília as embodiment of nation 229–34, 245, 251, 252, 254, 255
    and export of art and culture 25, 315–16
    mestiço nationalism 31, 31–32, 47, 72, 167
    and Modernism 24
    and post-war growth 124
nature
    Brasília and natural landscape 233, 234, 284, 306
    and Brazilian architecture 15, 35, 36, 64, 67–69, 72–73, 112, 164, 176
    and curves in architecture 147, 148–49
    European scientific expeditions 34
    and idleness 175–76
    as ingredient of *brasilidade* 33–36
    and Niemeyer's architecture 181–210, 233, 234, 284, 306, 369, *370–75*, *371–72*, 374
    as 'sacred heritage' 33–34
    and industry 25, 34, 166–69, 284
    see also gardens; landscape; tropicalism
Negev city masterplan, Israel 228, 318–20, *319–20*
Neoclassical architecture 54, 60–61, 242, 243, 262
neocolonial architecture 19, 78–79
    rejection of 'neocolonialismo' 28, 54, 78
Neo-Concretism 306–7, 308, 316, 356
Nerone (Giovanni Ceccarelli) 348
Nervi, Pier Luigi 158*n*, *221*, 264*n*, 278
Neto, Prudente de Morais: House in Gávea, Rio de Janeiro 188–89, *188–89*
Neto, Torquato 248
Neutra, Richard 41, 194, 252
Neves, José Maria da Silva: School Complex Viscount de Congonhas do Campo, São Paulo 54
Neves, Tancredo 149, 246, 310
New York
    Lever House building 146, *147*
    United Nations Headquarters 83, 137–40, *137–39*, 261–62
    see also Museum of Modern Art (MoMA)
New York World's Fair (1939) 150

Brazilian Pavilion 77, 82–87, *83–85*, 92, 169, 189, 374
Nicola, Antonio 341
Nicolas, Jean 327, 330, 333
Niemeyer, Ana Elisa 378
Niemeyer, Anna Maria 238, 290
    Rio chaise longue *203*
Niemeyer, Oscar 46, *250*, *255*, *269*, *309*, *312*, *344*
    African element in work 9, 12, 101–2, 152
    Antropofagist architecture 129, 148, 152, 200, 245, 386
    on architecture as invention 90
    on artworks and decoration 69, 71, 101–2, 280
    awards and prizes 15, 139–40, 146*n*, 315, 340, 341, 351
    Baroque allusions 12, 13–14, 97, 101, 109, 112, 114, 179, 236*n*, 242, 262, 268, 293–95
    on Bauhaus 103–4
    beauty and monumentality 252, 263, 264
    birth and family house 46–47, *47*
    as Brasília competition judge 231*n*
    on Brasília as national architecture *261*
    on Brasília and social aspect of design for 228, 247, 301
    on Brazilian architecture 90–91, 100, 178, 180, 253
    on Brazilian society 180, 227, 240
    on *brises-soleil* 62*n*
    on Burle Marx 64*n*
    Casas onde morei 183
    'City of Tomorrow' article 228
    as civil servant 254
    on columns for palaces of Brasília 262, 270
    Communist Party membership 89, 140
    The Curves of Time (memoirs) 46
    drawing technique 263
    early career at Costa's practice 51
    early works and projects 72–82
    Edifício Ypiranga and studio in, Rio de Janeiro 46, *46*
    emancipation from Costa and Le Corbusier 17, 82
    engineering and architecture of 158–59, 278–79
    and European architecture 33, 104, 231, 252, 283–84
    favela valorization 128, 129
    on *favela* clearances 368
    'Form and Function in Architecture' 270
    on functionalism 97
    gardens and architecture of 181–210
    on harmony in Brasília architecture and planning 255–56
    on imperial palms 68
    on improvisation in early work 152–53
    international commissions 314–51
    international reputation and criticism 15–16, 88, 251
    justification of formal solutions 119, 121, 132, 161, 384
    on Le Corbusier 57*n*, 90, 104, 147*n*, 197
    and Le Corbusier and Ministry of Education 57*n*, 67
    and Le Corbusier and UN Headquarters design 137–39
    Le Corbusier's influence on architecture of 75, 76, 92, 100, 125, 267
    lightness as quality of work 66–67, 156, *231*, 265, 328, 384
    on *Mão* sculpture as political protest 355–56